Microsoft® Access® 2010 VBA Programming Inside Out

Andrew Couch

ISBN: 978-0-7356-5987-2

Fourth Printing: August 2014

Printed and bound in the United States of America.

Microsoft Press books are available through booksellers and distributors worldwide. If you need support related to this book, email Microsoft Press Book Support at *mspinput@microsoft.com*. Please tell us what you think of this book at *http://www.microsoft.com/learning/booksurvey*.

Acquisitions and Developmental Editor: Kenyon Brown
Production Editor: Teresa Elsey
Editorial Production: Octal Publishing, Inc.
Technical Reviewer: Alan Cossey
Indexer: Denise Getz
Cover Design: Twist Creative • Seattle
Cover Composition: Karen Montgomery
Illustrator: Robert Romano

pour Pamela, ma raison d'être

Contents at a Glance

**Part 1: VBA Environment
and Language**

Chapter 1
Using the VBA Editor and Debugging Code... 3

Chapter 2
Understanding the VBA Language Structure 39

Chapter 3
Understanding the VBA Language Features.. 89

**Part 2: Access Object Model
and Data Access Objects (DAO)**

Chapter 4
Applying the Access Object Model......... 127

Chapter 5
Understanding the Data Access
Object Model 161

**Part 3: Working with Forms
and Reports**

Chapter 6
Using Forms and Events 231

Chapter 7
Using Form Controls and Events.......... 273

Chapter 8
Creating Reports and Events 323

**Part 4: Advanced
Programming with VBA Classes**

Chapter 9
Adding Functionality with Classes 339

Chapter 10
Using Classes and Events 359

Chapter 11
Using Classes and Forms................. 381

**Part 5: External Data and
Office Integration**

Chapter 12
Linking Access Tables 395

Chapter 13
Integrating Microsoft Office 437

Part 6: SQL Server and SQL Azure

Chapter 14
Using SQL Server 483

Chapter 15
Upsizing Access to SQL Server............ 543

Chapter 16
Using SQL Azure........................ 589

Part 7: Application Design

Chapter 17
Building Applications 631

Chapter 18
Using ADO and ADOX................... 659

Table of Contents

Introduction xix

Part 1: VBA Environment and Language

Chapter 1: **Using the VBA Editor and Debugging Code** 3

Debugging Code on a Form 4
    Entering the VBA Editor 5
    The Application and VBA Code Windows 6
Creating Modules and Procedures 8
    Creating a Module 10
    Creating a Procedure 11
    Executing a Subroutine 13
    Executing a Function 15
    Viewing and Searching Code 16
    Split Window 17
    Searching Code 19
Debugging Code in a Module 20
    Debug Commands 23
Breakpointing Code 23
    Set Next Command 25
    Breakpoint Step and Run Commands 26
    Displaying Variables in the Locals Window 29
    Tracing Procedures with the Call Stack 30
    Watching Variables and Expressions 31
    Adding Conditional Watch Expressions 32
    Working with the Immediate Window 33
    Changing Code On-the-Fly 34
Using the Object Browser and Help System 35
    Configuring the Help System 35
    Working with the Object Browser 36
Summary 37

What do you think of this book? We want to hear from you!

Microsoft is interested in hearing your feedback so we can continually improve our books and learning resources for you. To participate in a brief online survey, please visit:

microsoft.com/learning/booksurvey

Chapter 2:   **Understanding the VBA Language Structure.** **39**

VBA Language Settings 40

  Comments 40

  Setting *Option Explicit* 41

  Selecting *Option Compare*. 43

  Compiling Code. 44

  Conditional Compilation 45

  References 46

Working with Constants and Variables 49

  Improving Code Quality with Constants. 49

  The *Enum* Keyword. 51

  Variables and Database Field Types. 52

  Handling *NULL* Values, *IsNull* and *Nz* 53

  Using Static Variables 55

  Using Global Variables. 56

  Variable Scope and Lifetime 57

  Working with Arrays. 59

  Type Structures 65

Functions and Procedures 66

  Managing Code with Subroutines 67

  Defining *ByRef* and *ByValue* Parameters 70

  Private and Public Procedures 72

  Optional and Named Parameters 73

  The *ParamArray* Qualifier 75

  Organizing Code in Modules and Class Modules 76

Control Statements and Program Flow 77

  IF... Then... Else... Statements. 77

  IIF Statements 78

  Choose Statements 79

  Select Case Statements. 80

  TypeOf Statements 80

  For and *For Each* Loops 81

  Do While and *Do Until* Loops 82

  Exit Statements 84

  The *With* Statement 85

  GoTo and *GoSub* 86

  Line Continuation 86

  Splitting SQL Over Multiple Lines 86

Summary 87

Chapter 3:   **Understanding the VBA Language Features** **89**

Using Built-In Functions 90

  Date and Time Functions. 90

  String Functions. 92

Domain Functions 95

  Constructing *Where* Clauses. 97

SQL and Embedded Quotes. 98

Using VBA Functions in Queries... 101
The *Eval* Function 102
Shell and *Sendkeys* 102
The *DoEvents* Command 103
Objects and Collections 103
Object Variables 105
Is Nothing, IsEmpty, IsObject 106
Creating Maintainable Code 108
Naming Access Document Objects 108
Naming Database Fields 109
Naming Unbound Controls.. 110
Naming Variables in Code.. 110
Indenting Code 113
Other Variable Naming Conventions..................................... 113
VBA and Macros.. 114
Access Basic 114
Converting Macros to VBA 115
Error Handling 115
On Error Resume Next 116
Err Object.. 117
On Error GoTo... 118
Developing a General Purpose Error Handler 118
OpenArgs and Dialog Forms.. 121
Err.Raise... 122
Summary 123

Part 2: Access Object Model and Data Access Objects (DAO)

Chapter 4:   **Applying the Access Object Model**......................... **127**
The *Application* Object Methods and Properties................................ 128
The *Run* Method 128
The *RunCommand* Method.. 129
Simplifying Filtering by Using *BuildCriteria* 130
The *ColumnHistory* and *Append Only* Memo Fields..................... 130
Examining *TempVars*... 132
Invoking the Expression Builder....................................... 133
The *CurrentProject* and *CurrentData* Objects................................ 134
Retrieving Version Information... 135
Changing Form Datasheet View Properties.............................. 136
Object Dependencies... 137
The *DoCmd* Object 138
Controlling the Environment... 138
Controlling Size and Position 139
Application Navigation 140
Data Exchange... 142
Manipulating the *Forms* and *Reports* Collections 143
Using the Expression Builder.. 144

Referencing Controls on a Subform. 145
Creating Access Objects in Code 149
Using the *Screen* Object 150
Changing the Mouse Pointer Shape 150
Working with the *ActiveForm* and *ActiveControl*. 151
Enhancing the User Interface. 152
Setting and Getting Options. 152
Locking Down Access. 154
Monitoring Progress with *SysCmd*. 155
Custom Progress Bars. 156
Selecting Files with the Office *FileDialog* 157
Summary 160

Chapter 5:   **Understanding the Data Access Object Model** **161**
The DAO Model 162
DAO, ADO, and References. 163
Working with Databases. 164
The *DBEngine* Object 165
The *Workspace* Object 165
Transactions 166
The *Errors* Collection 171
The *Database* Object 173
CurrentDB, *DBEngine*, and *CodeDB* 175
The *TableDefs* Collection and Indexes. 179
Managing Datasheet Properties 184
Relationships 186
Manipulating Data with *Recordset*s 188
Searching 188
Bookmarks. 191
Field Syntax 191
Filter and *Sort* Properties. 193
Adding, Editing, and Updating Records 193
Multiple-Values Lookup Fields 194
Attachment Fields 197
The *OLE Object* Data Type. 206
Calculated Fields 210
Cloning and Copying *Recordset*s 212
Reading Records into an Array. 215
Working with Queries in Code 215
Temporary *QueryDefs* 216
QueryDefs and *Recordset*s. 218
Creating *QueryDefs*. 218
QueryDef Parameters. 220
Investigating and Documenting Objects. 222
Containers and Documents. 222
Object Properties 224
Sample Applications 224

Documenting a Database by Using the DAO 224
Finding Objects in a Database by Using the DAO 225
Summary 227

Part 3: Working with Forms and Reports

Chapter 6:   **Using Forms and Events** **231**

Displaying Records 233
Bound and Unbound Forms 233
Modal and Pop-Up Forms 234
Open and *Load* Events 235
Filtering by Using Controls 236
Filtering by Using the *Filter* Property 243
Filtering by Using Another Form 245
The ApplyFilter Event 247
Unload and *Close* Events 248
Working with the *RecordsetClone* 248
Refresh, Repaint, Recalc, and *Requery* Commands 250
Calling Procedures Across Forms 251
Interacting with Records on a Form 253
The *Current* Event 253
Deactivate and *Activate* Events 255
Setting the Timer Interval Property of the *Timer* Event 255
The *Mouse* Events 260
Editing and Undo on a Record 262
BeforeUpdate and *AfterUpdate* Events 262
Locking and Unlocking Controls 264
BeforeInsert and *AfterInsert* Events 265
The *Delete* Event 267
KeyPreview and Key Events 268
The *Error* Event 269
Saving Records 270
Summary 271

Chapter 7:   **Using Form Controls and Events** **273**

Control Events 274
The *Click* and *DblClick* Events 275
The *BeforeUpdate* Event 276
The *AfterUpdate* Event 276
The *GotFocus* and *LostFocus* Events 277
Combo Boxes 278
Synchronizing Data in Controls 278
Combo Box *RowSource* Type 280
Combo Box Columns 282
Value List Editing 284
Table/Query Editing 285

List Boxes. 286
        Multiple Selections 286
        Multiple Selections with Two List Boxes 290
        Using the List Box as a *Subform* 292
The *TreeView* Control 295
        Adding the *TreeView* Control 296
        Populating the Tree 298
        Adding Graphics 301
        Expanding and Collapsing Nodes 303
        Drag-and-Drop 303
        Deleting a Node with Recursion. 307
        Adding Nodes 309
The *Tab* Control 311
        Refreshing Between Tabs and Controls. 311
        The *OnChange* Event 314
        Dynamically Loading Tabs. 314
Summary 321

Chapter 8:   **Creating Reports and Events** **323**
Report Event Sequences. 324
        Creating Drill-Down Reports and Current Event. 326
        Creating a Boxed Grid with the *Print* Event 327
        Layout Control and the *Format* Event. 330
Report Layout Control 331
        Driving Reports from a Form 331
        Reducing Joins with a Combo Box. 333
        Programming a Report Grouping 333
        Packing Address Information with a *ParamArray* 334
        Control of Printers. 335

Part 4: **Advanced Programming with VBA Classes**

Chapter 9:   **Adding Functionality with Classes.** **339**
Improving the Dynamic *Tab* Control 340
        Creating a Class Module 341
        The *Let* and *Get* Object Properties. 342
        Creating an Object with *New* and *Set* 343
        Collection of Objects 345
        Creating Collection Classes 346
        Using Classes with the Dynamic Tab 351
        Simplifying the Application with Classes 352
Creating a Hierarchy of Classes 354
        Creating a Base Class 354
        Derived Classes 355
Summary. 357

Chapter 10:   **Using Classes and Events** **359**

WithEvents Processing. 360
    Handling Form Events 360
    Handling Control Events 362
    Asynchronous Event Processing and *RaiseEvent* 363
Abstract and Implementation Classes 370
    Abstract Classes. 370
    Implementation Classes. 372
    Implementing an Abstract Class. 373
    Hybrid Abstract and Non-Abstract Classes 376
Friend Methods 378
Summary 379

Chapter 11:   **Using Classes and Forms.** **381**

Opening Multiple Instances of a Form. 381
Classes and Binding Forms. 383
    Binding a Form to a Data Access Object *Recordset*. 383
    Binding a Form to an Active Data Object *Recordset*. 384
ActiveX Controls and Events 386
    Adding a *Slider* Control 386
    The *UpDown* or *Spin* Control 388
Summary 391

Part 5: External Data and Office Integration

Chapter 12:   **Linking Access Tables.** **395**

Linking Access to Access. 396
    Using the Database Splitter. 397
    Linked Table Manager 398
    Automating Relinking 398
Linking to Excel and Text Files 406
    Linking to Excel 406
    Linking to Text Files 407
Linking to SQL Server 407
    Setting up the Sample Database 407
    Creating a DSN 410
    Connecting to SQL Server Tables. 416
    Refreshing SQL Server Linked Tables. 417
    Connecting to a View in SQL Server 418
    Refreshing SQL Server Views 419
Linking to SQL Azure. 420
    SQL Azure DSN 420
    Connecting to SQL Azure 424
Linking to SharePoint Lists. 426
    Relinking SharePoint Lists 428
Linking Access Web Databases 430
    Relinking to an Access Web Database. 432
Summary 435

Chapter 13: **Integrating Microsoft Office** **437**

Working with Objects and Object Models 438
  Early vs. Late Binding and *CreateObject* vs. *New* 438
  The *GetObject* Keyword 440
  Opening Existing Files 442
Connecting Access to Word 443
  Generating Documents from a Placeholder Document 444
  Opening a Placeholder Document 446
  Merging Data with Bookmarks 447
Connecting Access to Excel 451
  Writing Data to a Spreadsheet 452
  Reading Data from a Spreadsheet 459
  Reporting with Excel Linked to Access 460
  Using MS Query and Data Sources 468
Connecting Access to Outlook 471
  Extracting Information from Outlook 472
  Creating Objects in Outlook 475
  Writing to Access from Outlook 477
Summary 480

Part 6: SQL Server and SQL Azure

Chapter 14: **Using SQL Server** **483**

Introducing SQL Server 484
  Programs vs. Services 484
  Client-Server Performance 485
  SQL Server Versions 486
  SQL Express and SQL Server Products 487
  Database File Locations 489
  Log Files and Recovery Models 490
  Instances 491
  Windows Services 492
  System Databases 493
  System Tables 494
Getting Started with the SQL Server Management Studio 495
  Running the Demo Database Script 495
  Creating a New Database 496
Creating Tables and Relationships 496
  Database Diagrams 496
  Tables, Relationships, and Script Files 499
  Changing the Design of a Table 500
  Using the *Identity* Property 504
Working with Views 505
  Graphical Interface 505
  Views and Script Files 506
  CROSSTAB Queries 509

Working with Stored Procedures 511
Introducing T-SQL 517
    Defining Variables.. 517
    Using *CAST* and *CONVERT* 518
    Built-In Functions 519
    System Variables 520
    Controlling Program Flow 521
    Error Handling... 523
Working with Triggers.. 526
Working with Transactions... 530
    Transaction Isolation Levels.. 532
    Nesting Transactions 533
User-Defined Functions 534
Getting Started with SQL Server Security 536
    Surface Area Configuration.. 536
    SQL Server Authentication 538
    Windows Authentication 541
Summary 542

Chapter 15:   Upsizing Access to SQL Server................................ 543

Planning for Upsizing 543
    Text Data Types and UNICODE.. 544
    Date and Time Data 544
    Boolean Data 546
    Integer Numbers... 547
    Real Numbers, Decimals, and Floating-Point Numbers....................... 547
    Hyperlinks.. 547
    IMAGE, VARBINARY(Max), and *OLE Data* 547
    Memo Data 547
    Currency 548
    Attachments and Multi-Value Data....................................... 548
    Required Fields 549
    Cycles and Multiple Cascade Paths 549
    Mismatched Fields in Relationships....................................... 550
    Replicated Databases and Random Autonumbers 551
    Unique Index and Ignore Nulls... 553
    Timestamps and Row Versioning.. 554
    Schemas and Synonyms... 556
The Upsizing Wizard and the SQL Server Migration Assistant 558
    The Upsizing Wizard.. 558
    Upsizing to Use an Access Data Project 561
    SSMA... 564
Developing with Access and SQL Server 574
    The *dbSeeChanges* Constant... 574
    Pass-Through Queries 575
    Stored Procedures and Temporary Tables 578

            Handling Complex Queries 579
            Performance and Execution Plans 582
            SQL Server Profiler 586
        Summary 588

Chapter 16:   **Using SQL Azure** **589**
        Introducing SQL Azure 590
            Creating Databases 590
            Firewall Settings 591
            Using Management Studio 592
            Developing with the Browser Interface 595
        Migrating SQL Databases 596
            Creating a Set of Tables 597
            Transferring Data with the SQL Server Import and Export Wizard 599
            Backing up and Copying a Database 603
        The Data Sync Feature 604
            The Data Sync Agent 605
            Sync Groups and Sync Logs 610
            Changing Data and Database Structure 612
            Conflict Resolution in Data 613
            Changes to Table Structure 613
        Planning and Managing Security 615
        Building Multi-Tenanted Applications 617
            User Tables and Views 617
            Application Tables and Views 619
            Managing Security 623
        SQL Server Migration Assistant and Access to Azure 624
        Summary 628

Part 7: Application Design

Chapter 17:   **Building Applications** **631**
        Developing Applications 631
            Application Navigation 632
            Ribbon Design 639
            32-Bit and 64-Bit Environments 649
            Working with the Windows Registry 650
            Using the Windows API 651
        Completing an Application 653
            Splash Screens 653
            Progress Bars 653
            Error Handling 654
            Locking Down an Application 654
        Deploying Applications 655
            Protecting Your Design with ACCDE Files 655
            Runtime Deployment 655
            Single and Multiple Application Files 655

DSNs and Relinking Applications. 656
Depending on References. 656
Updating Applications 656
Summary 657

Chapter 18:   **Using ADO and ADOX** **659**
ActiveX Data Objects. 660
Cursors 661
Asynchronous Operations. 662
Forms and ADO *Recordsets* 662
Working with SQL Server 663
Connection Strings 663
Connecting to SQL Server 664
Command Object 666
Stored Procedures. 666
Multiple Active Result Sets and Performance 668
MARS and Connections 669
ADOX 672
Summary 673

Index **675**

Introduction

Microsoft Visual Basic for Applications (VBA) is an exceptional programming language and environment. The language has grown out of a need to have a programming language that would allow more business-focused individuals to write programs, but equally support the programming features that developers look for in a product. The environment is as important as the language because of its unique features, allowing code to be quickly modified while being debugged.

The Access Basic language in early product versions evolved into the VBA language, which provided a cross-product language for the Microsoft Office products. This all coincided with the revolution of an event-driven approach to programming, which was very important, because the emphasis on being a programmer shifted from writing thousands of lines of code to writing snippets of code in response to events. This also led to a change of emphasis from writing large libraries of code to understanding how to manipulate the object models in the environment—a focus which has progressed with .NET, albeit using namespaces instead of object models.

Even with the introduction of object-oriented programming, VBA has kept pace with the expectations of modern programming. The two products that have shaped VBA the most are Microsoft Excel and Microsoft Access; Excel introduced VBA and originally gained VBA programming features in advance of these becoming available within Access.

A significant strength of VBA is that it is universal to the Microsoft Office suite of programs; all the techniques we describe in this book can be applied to varying degrees within the other Office products. A major turning point for these products was the ability through OLE Automation to be able to drive one product from another, and to cut and paste code between the different environments with a minimum amount of change to the code. This was a revolutionary feature introduced with the programming language of Access Basic, conforming to the new VBA standard established in Excel. VBA suddenly provided the long-awaited platform for the simple integration of the Office products and building solutions that could easily exploit the strengths of each component product in the Office suite. The combination of Access and VBA offers an extremely productive environment within which to construct applications.

VBA has often been criticized for its simplicity as a language when compared to languages such as C++ and C#. Quite to the contrary, the big advantage of VBA is that this simplicity leads to more easily maintainable and reliable code, particularly when developed by people with a more business-focused orientation to programming. Looking toward the future, the emphasis in modern programming has moved from the language syntax to the intricacies of understanding the objects that the language manipulates, so the emphasis on the specific syntax of languages is starting to blur.

In the .NET world, the conflict between using VB.NET, which originates from VBA, and C# continues, because even though the objects being manipulated are now common, there are subtle differences between the languages, which means that developers moving from VBA to C# can often feel that they are being led out of their comfort zone, especially when they need to continue to use VBA for other applications.

Access has often been criticized for creating poor performance applications where a proto-type turns into a business critical system, propagating a support nightmare for information technology departments, and leading to applications that eat up network bandwidth. It has also been stated that the product is never used for mission-critical applications. The truth is that both Access and Excel are pivotal to many organizations, but the people answering that mission-critical question are often not willing to admit to this because it is perceived as vulnerability. The problem with using Access and Excel is that Rapid Application Develop-ment (RAD) can often come to mean final application without recourse to a more struc-tured oversight of what is being developed, and as data volumes and user communities grow, so too the inevitable flaws in not having designed a scalable solution are exposed.

This book details how Access and VBA are not a problem, although their success is often their downfall in the hands of those lacking some direction on how to effectively develop applications. The big problem with Access is that the underlying database engine is extremely efficient and can compensate for a design that normally would not scale. So if you convert your Access database data to be located in Microsoft SQL Server, Microsoft SQL Azure, or Microsoft SharePoint, you might find that the existing application design techniques for searching and displaying data need to be revised. Our advice is to take into account the mantra of Client-Server design, which is to minimize the amount of data being transferred in any operation.

In this book, we would like to make our contribution toward creating a better informed community of developers, and show how to better develop applications with VBA.

Who This Book Is For

This book is aimed at two types of reader. First, we want to enable the reader who has worked with Access and developed applications to move to the next level of development. We want to help that reader to more fully develop applications with a deeper understand-ing of what it means to program with VBA.

Our second target audience is the more experienced VBA programmer, who needs the assistance of a good instructional text to move up a gear and explore the more advanced aspects of VBA programming. As well, we have devoted a significant number of our pages to supporting you in developing with both SQL Server and cloud computing.

Assumptions About You

We make a basic assumption in this book that you are experienced either in working with Access or that you have a strong programming background, which means that you can learn VBA programming in Access very quickly. We will spend no time explaining how to create a table, form, or report, and if you cannot do this, you need to first learn these actions in more detail. We recommend our companion text *Microsoft® Access® 2010 Inside Out* by Jeff Conrad and John Viescas.

If you have some VBA Programming experience, you can skim over Chapters 1–3. If your experience level is not such that you are comfortable skipping chapters, Chapters 1–3 will, we hope, give you a key appreciation of the power of the VBA development environment.

How This Book Is Organized

This book allows you to either start at the beginning and work through each chapter or to dip into specific chapters or topics to investigate a particular feature of VBA. To enable dipping into the book, each part is designed to be self-contained.

Part 1, "VBA Environment and Language"

In Chapters 1, 2, and 3, we provide a foundation that demonstrates how to program with VBA. We start by showing you how to debug, write, and modify code (gaining confidence with the VBA environment is the first step to efficiently developing applications within it). Then we move on to an in-depth exposition of the VBA language, which can act both as a reference for coding syntax and a solid introduction to the language.

Part 2, "Access Object Model and Data Access Objects (DAO)"

Chapters 4 and 5 dig deep into programming with the objects that make up Access, including the DAO programming language, which is the bread and butter programming technique for any Access VBA developer.

Part 3, "Working with Forms and Reports"

Chapters 6, 7, and 8 illustrate how to apply VBA when working with forms, controls, and reports. This develops your core techniques in understanding how to apply VBA for building the key interface components in applications.

Part 4, "Advanced Programming with VBA Classes"

Chapters 9, 10, and 11 are for some developers more esoteric than the rest of this book, but they illustrate how you can exploit VBA to embrace the most advanced concepts of modern computing by using object-oriented programming. There are a lot of cunning tricks and techniques in these chapters that are worth reading about, and many of the ideas in these chapters will take you forward in also handling development with .NET.

Part 5, "External Data and Office Integration"

In Chapters 12 and 13, we address the issue of how to link Access to external data and write VBA to communicate both with other Office applications and external data sources such as SQL Server and SharePoint.

Part 6, "SQL Server and SQL Azure"

Chapters 14, 15, and 16 provide a comprehensive description of how to extend the reach of Access applications by moving the back-end data into SQL Server, and then onto SQL Azure. Chapter 14 is dedicated to equipping developers with a solid understanding of how to develop code with SQL Server, during which we explain both how to use the SQL Server Management Studio and write programs using Transact SQL (T-SQL).

Chapter 15 moves on to look at converting Access Databases to SQL Server by using both the Upsizing Wizard and the SQL Server Migration Assistant (SSMA). Chapter 16 discusses how to move your databases into the cloud either by using the SQL Server Import and Export Wizard feature in the SQL Server Management Studio from a local SQL Server, or SSMA from an Access Database. We discuss how you can exploit the unique features of Office in directly constructing links to Azure, building multi-tenanted solutions and using the soon to be released new Data Sync features in SQL Azure.

Part 7, "Application Design"

The last part of this book, Chapters 17 and 18, shows you a number of ideas for helping you to create applications, including a discussion of how to design the user interface, building ribbons, utilizing the Windows API, and working with ADO and ADOX. In Chapter 17, we will step through the process of building applications. This chapter ties together all the lessons you learn throughout the book, making references back to other sections.

Features and Conventions Used in This Book

This book uses special text and design conventions to make it easier for you to find the information you need.

Text Conventions

Convention	Meaning
Boldface type	This indicates user input that you are instructed to type; for example, "Click the Save As command, name the file **NewFile_01**, and then click OK."
Ctrl+F	Keystroke combinations are presented as Ctrl+G, which means to hold down the Ctrl key and press the letter G on the keyboard, at the same time.
Object names	When we need to draw your attention to a specific technical term, program elements, or an object in the sample database, it will be presented in italic; for example, "Open the form *frmSample* and right-click the *ListBox* control."

Design Conventions

INSIDE OUT   This statement illustrates an example of an "Inside Out" heading

These are the book's signature tips. In these tips, you get the straight scoop on what's going on with the software—inside information about why a feature works the way it does. You'll also find handy workarounds to deal with software problems.

Note
Notes offer additional information related to the task being discussed.

About the Companion Content

You'll see references to the sample files and bonus content throughout the book. A complete list of the key database files follows (we have not listed all the smaller support files for each chapter).

We have also included in the bonus content (which is located within the file sets for Chapters 5, 7, and 18) additional application files that contain more code examples and provide useful utilities to add to your program libraries.

To access and download the companion content, visit: *http://go.microsoft.com/FWLink/?Linkid=223727*.

Chapter or topic	Content
Chapter 1	● VBAEnvironment.accdb
Chapter 2	● VBAExamples.accdb
Chapter 3	● VBAFeaturesExamples.accdb
Chapter 4	● AccessObjectModel.accdb
Chapter 5	● DAOExamples.accdb
	● CountryLibrary.accdb
	● Find_IT.accdb
	● DocDAO.accdb
Chapter 6	● FormExamples.accdb
Chapter 7	● Controls.accdb
	● TreeBuilder.accdb
Chapter 8	● Reports.accdb
Chapter 9	● BuildingClasses.accdb
	● BuildingClassesAfterExportImport.accdb
Chapter 10	● ClassesAndEvents.accdb
Chapter 11	● ClassesAndForms.accdb
Chapter 12	● Employees_be.accdb
	● Sample_fe.accdb
	● WebDatabase.accdb

Chapter or topic	Content
Chapter 13	• ExcelAnalysis.accdb
	• OfficeApplications.accdb
	• OutlookContacts.accdb
	• WordQuote.accdb
Chapter 14	• SQLServerExamples.accdb
	• SQL Server Script files
Chapter 15	• Northwind_ProblemsAndFixes.accdb
	• SQLServerCodeExamples.accdb
	• SQL Server Script files
Chapter 16	• Northwind_ForAzure.accdb
	• SQLAzureCodeExamples.accdb
	• SQL Azure Script files
Chapter 17	• ApplicationDevelopment.accdb
	• ApplicationDevelopment64Bit.accdb
	• ApplicationDevelopment_2007.accdb
Chapter 18	• ADOExamples.accdb
	• DocADOX.accdb
	• SQL Server Script files
Bonus Content	• Chapter 5: Find_IT.accdb, DocDAO.accdb
	• Chapter 7: TreeBuilder.accdb
	• Chapter 18: DocADOX.accdb

Your Companion eBook

The eBook edition of this book allows you to:

- Search the full text

- Print

- Copy and paste

To download your eBook, please see the instruction page at the back of this book.

Access Versions

All of the examples in the book are designed to run with Access 2010 32-bit.

If you are using Access 2010 64-bit, you should also be able to use the examples with the following revisions: in Chapter 17, use ApplicationDevelopment64Bit.accdb. The Bonus material databases have versions called Find_IT64Bit.accdb, DocADOX64Bit.accdb, and DocDAO64bit.accdb. The file TreeView.accdb has no equivalent 64-bit version, as this control is not supported in the 64-bit environment.

The majority of the code examples in this book will work on older versions of Access, and we have provided a set of .mdb files for this in Access 2002–2003 file format. However, the older the version that you use, the less likely will be the compatibility. There are several topics in Chapters 4, 5, 13, and 17 which were either not present in earlier versions of Access or have undergone a significant amount of change.

In some chapters, we have inevitably had to construct examples that rely on a hardwired path; in these situations you might find it easier either to construct your own example, as described in a chapter, or move the files to a path that matches the completed example. Where possible, we have provided assistance and advice in the sample databases to overcome any path problems.

Acknowledgments

A good technical book needs an author who is well informed and passionate, and I hope I can live up to that expectation. But it also needs contributions from a team of people to turn the idea into a reality.

First, my thanks to Kenyon Brown at O'Reilly Media; without his asking me to propose to write this book, it would have never have been started. Your diligence throughout the entire process has been splendid.

Next, I offer immense gratitude to Alan Cossey, who acted as technical reviewer on this book; having acted as a technical reviewer myself, I can greatly appreciate all of his time and recommendations made during the review process.

I would also like to thank Bob Russell at Octal Publishing, Inc., for acting as my copy editor; Bob has not only ensured that the flow of the book has a professional polish, but also caused me to reflect on the meaning of many parts of the text.

I would like to thank my good friend Jeff Conrad at Microsoft. Jeff is a great advocate for Access and helped wonderfully in answering and passing along many of my comments and questions to the Microsoft teams.

Numerous thanks also to those members of UK Access User Group for helping in testing my solutions to difficult technical issues. You can't beat a good community of developers!

My thanks also to Dianne Russell at Octal Publishing, Inc., for managing the copy editing and composition, and Betsy Waliszewski, senior marketing manager, for promotional activities.

Finally, I would like to thank my wife, Pamela, for her patience, and my son, Michael, for his assistance at various stages in helping with chapter layouts.

Andrew Couch
July 2011

Support and Feedback

The following sections provide information on errata, book support, feedback, and contact information.

Errata & Support

We've made every effort to ensure the accuracy of this book and its companion content. Any errors that have been reported since this book was published are listed on our Microsoft Press site:

http://go.microsoft.com/FWLink/?Linkid=268715

If you find an error that is not already listed, you can report it to us through the same page.

If you need additional support, email Microsoft Press Book Support at *mspinput@microsoft.com*.

Please note that product support for Microsoft software is not offered through the addresses above.

We Want to Hear from You

At Microsoft Press, your satisfaction is our top priority, and your feedback our most valuable asset. Please tell us what you think of this book at

http://www.microsoft.com/learning/booksurvey

The survey is short, and we read every one of your comments and ideas. Thanks in advance for your input!

Stay in Touch

Let's keep the conversation going! We're on Twitter: *http://twitter.com/MicrosoftPress*.

PART 1

VBA Environment and Language

CHAPTER 1
Using the VBA Editor and Debugging Code . . .3

CHAPTER 2
Understanding the VBA Language Structure 39

CHAPTER 3
Understanding the VBA Language Features . .89

Using the VBA Editor and Debugging Code

Debugging Code on a Form. 4

Creating Modules and Procedures. 8

Debugging Code in a Module 20

Breakpointing Code. 23

Using the Object Browser and Help System. 35

The Microsoft Visual Basic for Applications (VBA) Editor is more than a simple editing tool for writing program code. It is an environment in which you can test, debug, and develop your programs. Understanding the unique way in which the editor allows you to make modifications to application code while the execution of the code is paused will help you to learn how to quickly develop your applications and master the techniques for debugging code.

In addition to changing code on-the-fly as it executes, you can switch across to the Microsoft Access 2010 application window while your code is paused, create a query, run the query, copy the SQL to the clipboard, and then swap back to the programming environment to paste the SQL into your code. It is this impressive flexibility during the development cycle that makes developing applications with VBA a productive and exhilarating experience.

In this chapter, you will work with examples of program code written in the VBA language. The VBA language itself is systematically explained in Chapter 2, "Understanding the VBA Language Structure," and in Chapter 3, "Understanding the VBA language Features." So, before reading this chapter (or while you're reading it) you might want to either skim read those chapters or simply refer to specific topics as they arise in this chapter. We have also included some examples of Data Access Object (DAO) programming code. In this chapter, we will be providing only limited explanations of the DAO development environment, just to place it into the context of building real applications. For more detailed information about it, see Chapter 5, "Understanding the Data Access Object Model."

To successfully work with VBA, you need an understanding of the language, the programming environment, and the objects that are manipulated by the code. Getting started means dipping into different topics as you begin to build sufficient knowledge to effectively use VBA.

By the end of this chapter, you will understand:

- The different ways that you can run and debug sections of program code.

- How to modify program code while it is paused and then resume execution.

- How to work with the different windows in the programming environment.

- Where code is stored in a VBA application.

- How procedures are created.

> **Note**
>
> As you read through this chapter, we encourage you to also use the companion content sample database, **VBAEnvironment.accdb**, which can be downloaded from the book's catalog page.

Debugging Code on a Form

To begin, open the sample database, VBAEnvironment.accdb, which opens the startup form, *frmVBAStartsHere*, shown in Figure 1-1.

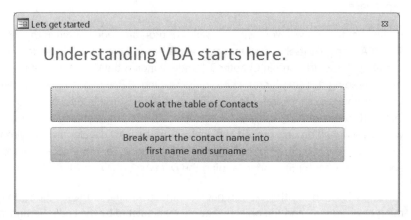

Figure 1-1 The startup form, *frmVBAStartsHere*.

The sample database contains program code with errors intentionally integrated into it. The *frmVBAStartsHere* form is designed to show how the code will break into Debug mode when it encounters an error. As you work through this chapter, you will fix these errors.

Click the button labeled Look At The Table Of Contacts. A pop-up window appears, as shown in Figure 1-2.

Figure 1-2 In this Access pop-up window, you can either end the code execution or click Debug to investigate the error.

If you click the End button, the program code stops executing. But as you want to debug the code, click the Debug button.

Entering the VBA Editor

When entering debugging mode, the program stops in the VBA editor and highlights the line of code at which it failed in yellow, as shown in Figure 1-3.

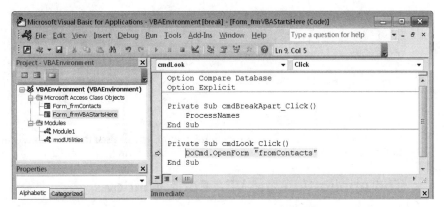

Figure 1-3 Choosing Debug opens the VBA Editor and highlights the program code line that generated the error.

In this example, the problem is a simple spelling error. The database contains a form called *frmContacts*, not *fromContacts*. Access displays an error message that fully describes the problem. It also provides you with the opportunity to edit the text to correct the misspelling, as shown in Figure 1-4.

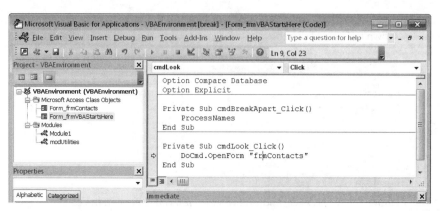

Figure 1-4 Code stopped at the error line. Notice in the Project Explorer pane on the left that the entry form *_frmVBAStartsHere* is highlighted. This tells you that you are viewing the form's code module.

DoCmd.OpenForm is a command that allows the program code to open the specified form. *DoCmd* is a shorthand way of saying, "do the macro command." After correcting the misspelling, you can either press the F5 key or click the Continue button on the toolbar to allow the program to continue execution. Figure 1-5 demonstrates the results after continuing to execute the code, which now opens the *frmContacts* form.

Figure 1-5 After correcting the programming error, you can see the result of executing *DoCmd.OpenForm*, which opens the requested Access form.

The Application and VBA Code Windows

Notice that in your Windows task bar there are two windows open: one window containing your Access application interface, and in the second window, the VBA Editor. When working with application code you can normally switch between the Editor and the application windows, as shown in Figure 1-6.

Figure 1-6 With the VBA editor open, you have two windows for Access, and you can switch between the application window and the VBA Editor window.

If you choose to close the forms you will be prompted to save the changes that you have made to the code on the form, as shown in Figure 1-7.

Figure 1-7 The prompt to save changes to the *frmVBAStartsHere* form.

CAUTION

It is very easy to click the wrong button and lose your design changes. Ensuring that you click the Save button after making any changes to code means that you always know that your changes have been saved. If your program code closes objects as part of its execution, separate dialog boxes for saving changes can pop up, and you can easily forget to save a change. In the unlikely event that the Access application crashes and you have not been saving your design changes, any unsaved changes will be lost.

INSIDE OUT   Code behind a form or report is located in the class module of a form or report

The last example illustrates how program code can be located in a form's class module. Code is written behind a form ("Code Behind a Form" or CBF) to respond to events when the user interacts with the form and the form's controls, Figure 1-8 shows the relationship between controls on a form and the procedures in the form's class module.

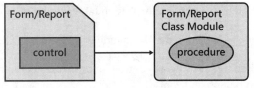

Figure 1-8 Code written in a form or report class module is normally related to events on the form or report, and not normally shared in any other part of the application.

The term *class module* relates to VBA classes discussed later in the book, the form's module is called a class module because it can handle events from the controls and form sections; this is a feature that you can construct within your own module classes.

When code is written behind a form's event, it is a subroutine, but it is also possible to have functions and subroutines on a form that are not directly associated with any single control. This normally occurs when you have a need for an operation to be performed by several controls. In this case, the code will be marked in the General section of the form's class module.

You have now learned that:

- When a code problem occurs, you can click Debug to display the code and fix the problem.

- VBA programs can be edited when the code is paused and then instructed to continue execution after you have fixed any errors.

- Regularly saving your changes after altering code is good practice.

- Program code can be stored in the class module of a form or report.

Creating Modules and Procedures

In the last section, you saw that when the program code goes into Debug mode, the Editor window is displayed. However, you can access the editing environment by using several different methods, as described in the following list:

- Press Alt+F11 (this applies to all Microsoft Office products).

- Press Ctrl+G. This displays the Immediate window in the Editor and automatically opens the Editor window, if it is not already open.

- On the ribbon, on the Create tab, click Module. This creates a new module and enters the Editor.

- In a form or report, on the ribbon, on the Design tab, click the View Code icon.

- Click any of the modules shown in the Navigation window.

- Right-click a Form/Report's sections or controls, and then select Build Event, where there is code written behind an event.

If you are not already in the Editor, then open the sample database and press Alt+F11 to go there.

The VBA Editor comprises a number of windows. If you accidently close one, or need to show a window that is not already displayed, click View on the menubar to open the window, as shown in Figure 1-9.

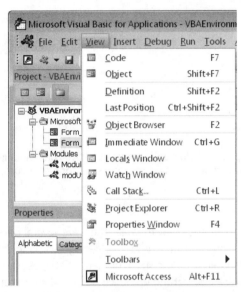

Figure 1-9 From the View menu, you can open different types of Editor windows. Note the Project window in the background with its expandable folders. This is a map of all the code modules in the application. Double-click any form or report to open the document's code module.

The Project pane normally contains two folders. The first folder, Microsoft Access Class Objects, contains your forms and reports (only objects with an associated code module are shown). Clicking one of these objects displays the existing code module. The term Class refers to the special nature of a Form/Report module; it handles the events for the object. These are sometimes simply called Form/Report modules. The separate Modules folder below the Form/Report modules contains general purpose program code that can be used in various parts of your application; these are sometimes called general or global modules (this folder is only shown after you have created a module).

Below the Project pane is the Properties pane for the project. You can use this window to change the name of the project or of a module (see Figure 1-10). The VBA project name property should be changed if you use the operating system to copy a database to create a new file, as the file copy operation does not change the VBA project name inside the database.

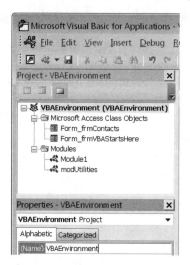

Figure 1-10 The Project pane displays all forms and reports that have code modules. You can use the Modules tab for writing code that is not tied to a particular form or report.

Creating a Module

You can use the Project window to create a new module. There are several different ways to add a new module; the method shown in Figure 1-11 involves right-clicking the Modules tab, and then selecting Insert | Module from the shortcut menu that appears. This method is used when you want to concentrate on setting up new modules when you are in the middle of writing and debugging code.

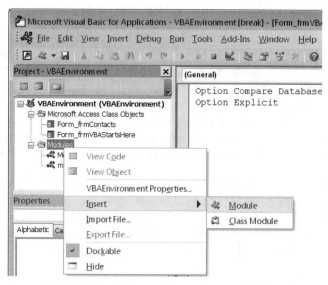

Figure 1-11 Creating a new module or class module from the Project pane.

When you create a new module, it is automatically assigned a default name (for example Module1). When you click the save button, you will be prompted to give the module a permanent, more meaningful name. Figure 1-12 shows the new module before it has been saved with an alternative name. You might also notice that when you save the new module, it contains two special *Option* keyword lines of text. This is explained in detail in Chapter 2, but for the moment, you can ignore this.

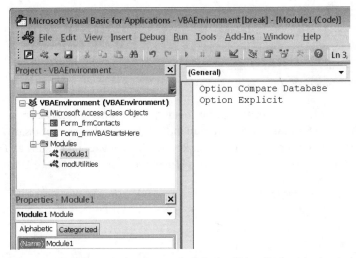

Figure 1-12 After creating a new module, it will be displayed using a default name such as Module1, Module2, Module3, and so on.

When you click the save option on the toolbar or close the database, you are prompted to replace the default module name with something more meaningful.

Creating a Procedure

Modules contain *procedures*, and the procedures contain program code. Use the Insert menu to open the Add Procedure dialog box (see Figure 1-13), in which you can add a new Sub (subroutine), Function, or Property (class modules only). There is also an option to prefix the procedure with the keyword *Static*, which makes variables hold their value when repeatedly executing the procedure (static variables are described in Chapter 2).

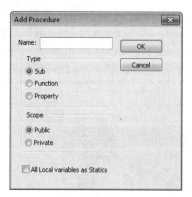

Figure 1-13 The Add Procedure dialog box.

There is another, quicker mechanism for creating a new procedure: click any empty area, type the keyword **Sub** {name} or **Function** {name} (be sure you are not inside an existing sub or function), and then press the Enter key. The VBA environment adds an *End Sub* keyword automatically to complete the procedure block, as shown in Figure 1-14).

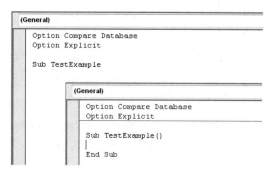

Figure 1-14 Creating a new procedure by using the *Sub* keyword. The window in the background shows the keyword and the procedure name typed in; the foreground window shows the result after pressing return.

Type the word **MsgBox**, enter a space, and then type a double quotation mark. As you do this, IntelliSense assists you as you type in each part of the syntax for the *MsgBox* procedure, as shown in Figure 1-15.

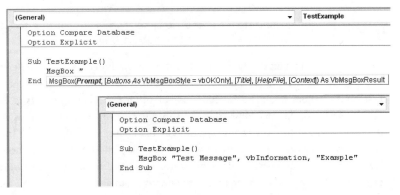

Figure 1-15 The built-in pop-up *MsgBox* procedure has three parts: the text to display; a constant that is used to indicate what buttons and images to display; and finally, the title for the window.

Executing a Subroutine

The *subroutine* code you created can be executed two ways. The first way is to click the green Continue button on the toolbar menu or press the F5 key (you need to have the cursor positioned inside the procedure on any part of the code). This should then display the message box.

The second way is to type the name of the subroutine into the Immediate window, and then press Return, as demonstrated in Figure 1-16.

Figure 1-16 You can type a subroutine name into the Immediate window, and then press the Return key to execute it.

The second type of procedure in VBA is called a *function*. The key difference between a function and a subroutine is that functions are always expected to return a value. Functions are fully explained in Chapter 2.

To create a function, you can type **Function {*name*}**, similar to the way you entered your subroutine (you should try this).

INSIDE OUT   Changing a procedure type from a subroutine to a function or from a function to a subroutine.

VBA allows you to quickly change a subroutine into a function, and vice versa. After you change the first line of the procedure, the VBA Editor automatically changes the *End Sub* statement to an *End Function* (and all other *Exit Sub* statements to *Exit Function* statements), thereby converting the subroutine into a function. This is very useful if you have larger blocks of code (spotting all the changes to make would be difficult) and leads to improved productivity when developing code. Figure 1-17 shows the original subroutine in the first window (background). In the second (middle) window, you can see the word Sub has been edited to Function. Finally, as shown in the foreground window, when you click off the line of code, the VBA Editor automatically changes the code *End Sub* to *End Function*.

Figure 1-17   As soon as you click off where you replaced the keyword *Sub* with *Function*, VBA changes the *End Sub* to *End Function*.

Because a function returns information, you are going to modify the program code to match Figure 1-18 so that it returns a value.

The *MsgBox* statement can be written in two different ways: the first is to write it when you want to display a message with an OK button (where it looks like a Sub [see Figure 1-17]); the second way is illustrated in Figure 1-18, where you want to gather input from a user (it behaves like a function).

```
(General)                                                    ▼    TestExample

  Option Compare Database
  Option Explicit

  Function TestExample()
      If MsgBox("Test Message", vbYesNo, "Example") = vbYes Then
          TestExample = "Yes button was pressed"
      Else
          TestExample = "No button was pressed"
      End If
  End Function
```

Figure 1-18 The *MsgBox* function prompts the user with two buttons (Yes and No), and then tests to see which button the user pressed.

After you have typed in a call to either a built-in procedure or your own procedure, you can right-click the shortcut menu to display information on the parameters for the procedure or get assistance with selecting constant values (see Figure 1-19). The *MsgBox* function has alternative constants for the second parameter (*vbYesNo*) shown in Figure 1-18, which control the buttons and graphics displayed in a message box. To change a constant value in the *MsgBox* routine, hover the mouse over the existing value, right-click to display the shortcut menu, and then select List Constants. This simplifies entering a new constant value.

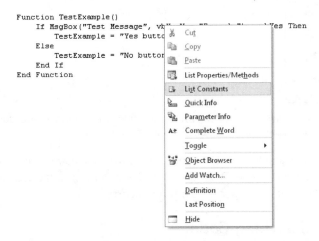

Figure 1-19 Accessing the shortcut menu to display information about the parameters for the procedure. Other options on this menu include providing quick information on the function.

Executing a Function

To run a function, you can press the F5 key, but this will not display the returned value. (In Chapter 2, you will see that functions can be used to assign a returned value to a variable.) You can also call the function from the Immediate window by using the "?" (question mark) symbol adjacent to the function name to display the returned value, as shown in Figure 1-20. Notice that when you execute a function you need to add parentheses "( )" after the function name; a function needs to show that it accepts parameters even when it has no parameters.

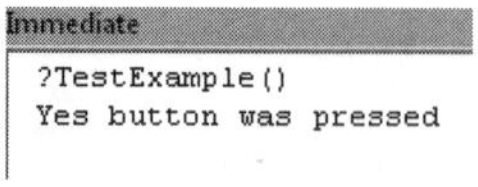

```
Immediate
?TestExample()
Yes button was pressed
```

Figure 1-20 Executing a function from the Immediate window. Use the ? (question mark) character to return a value from the function.

In this section, you have seen how program code can be written in a module that is not connected to a form or report. These code units are called *standard modules,* or sometimes general modules or global modules. Figure 1-21 illustrates how a standard module is an object that is independent of any form or report. Compare this to Figure 1-8, which showed a class module of a form or report that is attached to the Form/Report. Code written in these procedures can link to other procedures in the same or different modules. The code will normally not be specific to a single form. Form-specific code is better written inside a form's class module

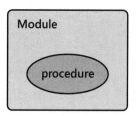

Figure 1-21 A schematic view of a module, which can contain one or more procedures. The procedures can be a combination of functions and subroutines.

You should now understand that program code can be written either in the class module of a form or report (when the code is specific to the Form/Report), or it can be written in a standard module (when it is not specific to a Form/Report).

Viewing and Searching Code

Module code can be viewed either showing the code for a single procedure (Procedure view) or the entire module (Full Module view), using the scrollbars to browse through its contents, as shown in Figure 1-22.

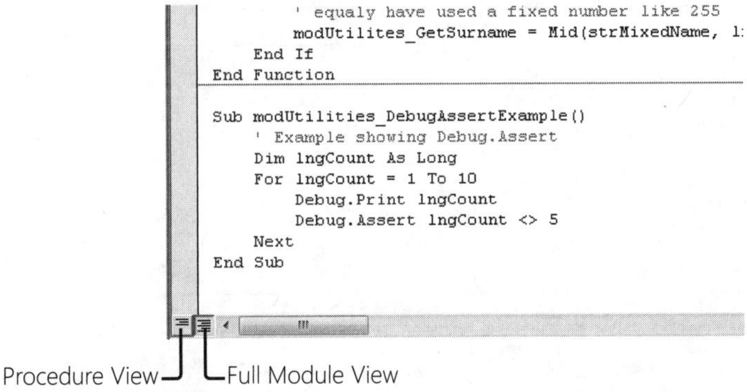

' equaly have used a fixed number like 255
modUtilites_GetSurname = Mid(strMixedName, 1:
End If
End Function
Sub modUtilities_DebugAssertExample()
' Example showing Debug.Assert
Dim lngCount As Long
For lngCount = 1 To 10
Debug.Print lngCount
Debug.Assert lngCount <> 5
Next
End Sub
Procedure View
Full Module View

Figure 1-22 Using the buttons in the lower-left corner of the code window, you can display either a single procedure or a scrollable list of all the procedures in the module.

Split Window

The module code window can also be switched to a Split view (see Figure 1-23). This gives you the ability to compare code in two different procedures, one above the other.

Tools
Add-Ins
Window
Help
Split
Tile Horizontally
Tile Vertically
Cascade
Arrange Icons
(General)

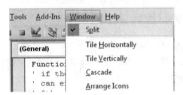

Figure 1-23 Use the Window menu to enable the Split view option.

Drag the splitter bar in the center of the screen up or down to change the proportion of the screen that is used to display each procedure. The scrollbars and the PgUp/PgDown buttons can be used independently in each window to browse through the procedures in the module. Figure 1-24 illustrates the split window view.

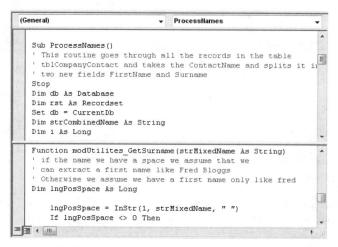

Figure 1-24 Viewing two procedures at the same time in Split view mode.

Dragging the splitter bar to the very top of the screen and releasing it will remove the split view. Similarly, by moving the mouse to the top right, just above the vertical scroll bars, the mouse pointer will change shape and you can drag down the splitter bar (this can be a little tricky to do and you will find the Window menu easier to use for this).

Use the drop-down menu located on the upper-right portion of the window to select any procedure within a module (see Figure 1-25). This applies to each of the windows when using the split view, as well.

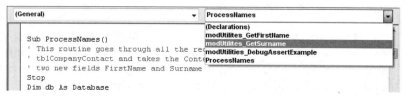

Figure 1-25 Use the drop-down menu to quickly display any function or subroutine in a module. For standard modules the drop-down on the top left only has one available choice called General; for class modules there will be other values shown in the drop-down.

> **Note**
> If you click the drop-down menu in the upper-left portion of the window, you will see only the General option. However, if you are displaying a form or report class module, as shown in Figure 1-26, you will see a list of the form sections and controls, and the drop-down menu at the upper-right will now display the events for the object selected in the lefthand list.

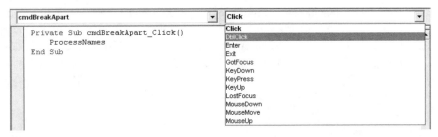

Figure 1-26 In a Form/Report class module, the drop-down menu on the left lists the controls and sections in the document. The drop-down menu on the right shows all possible events for the selected section or control. Events that have code associated with them are displayed in a bold font.

If you have multiple code windows open, you can use the Windows menu to change between the open windows. You also have the option to tile (horizontally or vertically) or cascade the open windows, as shown in Figure 1-27.

Figure 1-27 The Window menu in the Editor allows multiple, open module windows to be viewed in Tile mode or Cascade mode.

Searching Code

If you need to find a procedure or a piece of code, press Ctrl+F to open the Find dialog box and locate the code in the current procedure, module, project, or block of selected text (use the mouse to select and highlight the text before pressing Ctrl+F), as demonstrated in Figure 1-28.

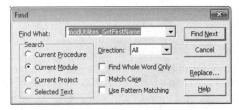

Figure 1-28 Use the Find dialog box to search and replace code fragments within a procedure, module, project, or selected text.

To view the definition of a variable or procedure (see Figure 1-29), position your cursor on it, right-click to open the shortcut menu, and then click Definition. Alternatively, again with your cursor on the procedure or variable, press Shift+F2 to go to the definition. If the code is in a different module, the appropriate module will be opened automatically.

```
Do While Not rst.EOF
    strCombinedName = rst!ContactName
    rst.Edit
    rst!FirstName = modUtilites_GetFirstName(rst!ContactName)
```

Figure 1-29 Viewing the definition of a procedure or variable.

Additionally, referring still to Figure 1-29, if you click the text *modUtilites_GetFirstName* in the subroutine *ProcessNames*, and then press Shift+F2, the body of the code for the procedure is displayed.

Debugging Code in a Module

To demonstrate how code is debugged, we will use a routine that splits a person's name from a combined field in the *frmContacts* form into separate first name and surname. Figure 1-30 shows the Contact Name in the first record split into the FirstName and Surname fields.

Figure 1-30 Using VBA code, the contact's full name, which is contained in the Contact Name field, is split into corresponding FirstName and Surname fields.

Return now to the opening *frmVBAStartsHere* form, and then press the button labeled Break Apart The Contact Name Into First Name And Surname, as shown in Figure 1-31.

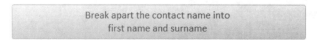

Figure 1-31 Click the Break Apart The Contact Name Into First Name And Surname button on the *frmVBAStartsHere* form to trace through and debug the application code for splitting apart the Contact Name field.

The code will pause at a *Stop* statement, as depicted in Figure 1-32.

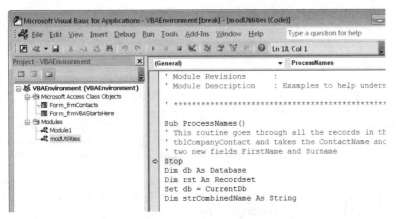

Figure 1-32 Hardcoded (permanent) breakpoints using the *Stop* keyword are a useful reminder when developing code that it is incomplete, but they should not be included in any final application.

Notice in Figure 1-32 that the code has stopped in the *modUtilities* module, and not in the form's class module.

Figure 1-33 presents the code behind the button. This code calls the procedure *Process-Names* in the module *modUtilities*.

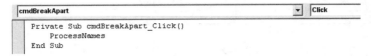

```
Private Sub cmdBreakApart_Click()
    ProcessNames
End Sub
```

Figure 1-33 The code behind the button is written in the *Click()* event. This code calls the *ProcessNames* routine, which is has been written in a module.

In Chapter 2, you will learn about naming conventions. The convention adopted in this book is to add a prefix to procedures in modules so that we can easily see in which module a procedure is defined. In the preceding example, if you had called the *modUtilities_ ProcessNames* procedure rather than *ProcessNames*, it would be easier to see how the code on the form linked to the code in the module (in this case, we have not followed the convention to illustrate the point).

There is another feature in the VBA Editor that can help display how the modules have been linked together. Selecting the Call Stack from the View menu displays the path from the forms class module to the procedure in the utilities module. Figure 1-34 illustrates that this procedure was called from a form (indicated by the "Form_" prefix) with the name *frm-VBAStartsHere*, from the control called *cmdBreakApart* on the *Click* event for the control.

Figure 1-34 The Call Stack is a visual aid that helps to establish where you are in the code. In this example, reading from top to bottom, you are in the code unit *modUtilites_ProcessNames*, which was called from the code unit *cmdBreakApart_Click*, which is in the form *frmVBAStartsHere*.

INSIDE OUT
Creating code in a module and linking the code to the form or report

In earlier sections, you looked at how program code can be written in a form's class module, and then you saw how more general purpose code can be written in a stand-alone module that is not connected to a form or report. The code on the form or report can be linked to the code in a standalone module. This is shown diagrammatically in Figure 1-35.

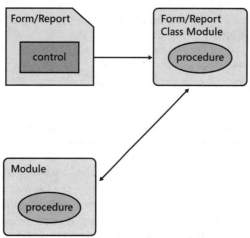

Figure 1-35 Code in a form or report class module can call code in a module. The module can contain code that is used in several parts of the application.

As an alternative to placing the code *ProcessNames* in a module, you can instead either write the code behind the *OnClick* event in the form or add the code as a subroutine to the form's class module. Which of these alternatives you choose depends on whether the code can be used in different parts of the form or in more than one form or report in the application. Because the *ProcessNames* routine can be called from a maintenance form or as part of a process for importing data, we have placed the code in a general purpose utilities module.

Debug Commands

Debugging code involves several operations. These operations are:

- Stopping or breakpointing the code so that it pauses at the correct point for investigation.

- Examining and monitoring variables.

- Modifying and repeating the code execution.

Debug.Print is a command that displays values of program variables or expressions in the Immediate window when developing code:

```
Debug.Print strCombinedName, rst!FirstName, rst!Surname
```

There is another debug command called *Debug.Assert*, which can be used to halt the execution of program code when a specific condition is *False*. For example, the following code halts execution when *lngCount* = 5 (note that the *Debug.Assert* stops when the condition is false):

```
Sub modUtilities_DebugAssertExample()
    ' Example showing Debug.Assert
    Dim lngCount As Long
    For lngCount = 1 To 10
        Debug.Print lngCount
        Debug.Assert lngCount <> 5
    Next
End Sub
```

Breakpointing Code

The *Stop* and *Debug.Assert* statements are hardcoded breakpoints, but you can also have soft breakpoints that you can use when you interact with a block of code and need to find out why the code is failing or behaving in a particular way.

There are three ways to enter a breakpoint. First, you need to locate the line in which you want to insert the breakpoint, and then do one the following:

- Press the F9 Key.

- On the Debug tab, click Toggle Breakpoint.

- Click in the margin next to the line of code (this is the easiest method).

Figure 1-36 shows the code paused at the *Stop* statement and a soft breakpoint highlighted farther down the page.

Figure 1-36 The code discontinues execution at the *Stop* statement. Note the highlighted break-point farther down the page

Unlike *Stop* statements, which need eventually to be removed from the code, breakpoints are not remembered after you close the database. You can use the Debug menu to clear all breakpoints in the application, or you can press Ctrl+Shift+F9.

With the breakpoint set, you want the code to execute until it reaches it. Use the Continue button (see Figure 1-37) or press F5 to instruct the code to continue execution until it either completes, or reaches a breakpoint.

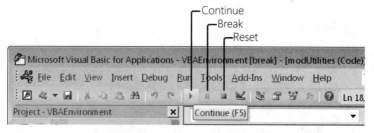

Figure 1-37 Three of the buttons on the Run menu are also displayed on the menu bar—Continue (F5), Break (Ctrl+Break), and Reset (which halts code execution).

Press F5 to continue the code execution to reach the breakpoint shown in Figure 1-38.

```
Set rst = db.OpenRecordset("tblCompanyContact", dbOpenDynaset)
Do While Not rst.EOF
    strCombinedName = rst!ContactName
    rst.Edit
    rst!FirstName = modUtilites_GetFirstName(rst!ContactName)
    rst!Surname = modUtilites_GetSurname(rst!ContactName)

    Debug.Print strCombinedName, rst!FirstName, rst!Surname

    rst.Update
    rst.MoveNext
Loop
```

Figure 1-38 Code continues to execute until it either reaches the next breakpoint or completes execution.

The *ProcessNames* routine is an example of programming with a *RecordSet* object, which is discussed in Chapter 5, "Understanding the Data Access Object Model." The program code loops through each record in the table and changes the *Firstname* and *Surname* fields.

If you switch to the Access application window and open the table *tblCompanyContact*, you can investigate whether your code has worked. And as it turns out, it has not worked as desired; Figure 1-39 shows that the entire contact name has been copied into the *FirstName* field. The name was not split apart, as intended.

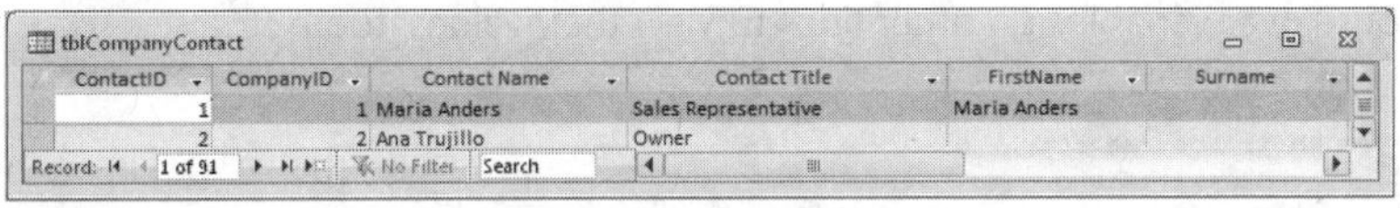

tblCompanyContact

ContactID	CompanyID	Contact Name	Contact Title	FirstName	Surname
1	1	Maria Anders	Sales Representative	Maria Anders	
2	2	Ana Trujillo	Owner		

Record: 1 of 91 No Filter Search

Figure 1-39 With the code paused at a breakpoint, you can switch to the application window and open other Access objects (in this case a table) to see the changes made to the data. Here, you can see that the code has not split apart the Contact Name.

Set Next Command

If you move the cursor over the first line in the loop and then right-click, you can use the *Set Next* statement to make the code go back and repeat the operation. This is typical of how code is debugged. After identifying an error, you can move back to an earlier point in the code to investigate it.

To change the current execution point to a different line of program code, place the cursor on the line that begins with `strCombinedName =`, right-click to display the shortcut menu, and then click Set Next Statement, as shown in Figure 1-40.

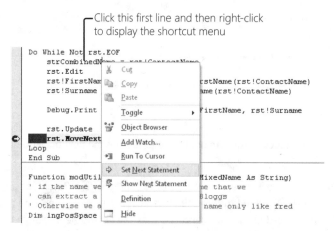

Figure 1-40 Changing the current execution point to a different line by using Set Next Statement.

After you click Set Next Statement, the yellow highlighted line changes, as shown in Figure 1-41. Notice also that you can display the values of the variable by hovering the mouse over it. (This is not restricted to variables in the highlighted line of code; you can hover the mouse over variables on other lines to view their values, too.)

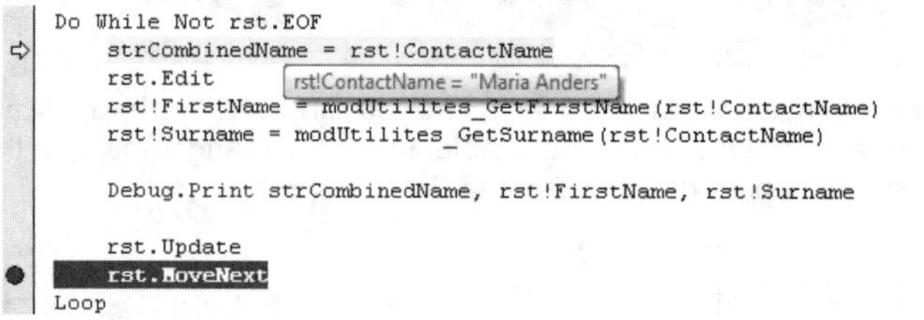

```
Do While Not rst.EOF
    strCombinedName = rst!ContactName
    rst.Edit         rst!ContactName = "Maria Anders"
    rst!FirstName = modUtilites_GetFirstName(rst!ContactName)
    rst!Surname = modUtilites_GetSurname(rst!ContactName)

    Debug.Print strCombinedName, rst!FirstName, rst!Surname

    rst.Update
    rst.MoveNext
Loop
```

Figure 1-41 Hovering the mouse over any variables in the program code will display the variable values.

As an alternative to using Set Next Statement to change the execution point, you can also grab the yellow arrow on the side margin and drag it to a different line of code.

Breakpoint Step and Run Commands

You now know that this code has a fault, but rather than using the Continue (F5) execution method that you just saw in the previous section, you can single step through the code to locate the problem by using the Debug menu or hotkeys, as shown in Figure 1-42.

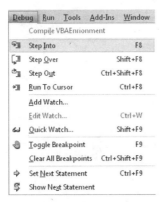

Figure 1-42 Using the Step commands on the Debug menu, you can trace through the execution of your code.

You can do this in several ways. One way is to keep clicking the Debug menu options, but it is much faster to use the following function key combinations to step through the code:

- **F8**   Follows the code execution to the next step.

- **Shift+F8**   Moves over a procedure call and executes everything in the procedure, but does not show you the detailed execution steps.

- **Ctrl+Shift+F8**   Indicates that you have examined the procedure in enough detail and want to complete the execution of this current procedure, but stops once you have returned to the calling code.

- **Ctrl+F8 or right-clicking and selecting Run To Cursor**   Process all the lines until you reach the current position of the cursor.

- **Locate a line, right click, and then select Set Next Statement.**

It is important to remember that when you press either Shift+F8 or Ctrl+Shift+F8, both operations cause any code to execute. If you do not want the code to execute, then locate the next line that you do want to execute, and then use Set Next Statement to change the execution point.

For the purposes of this example, keep pressing the F8 key until you arrive at the point shown in Figure 1-43.

Figure 1-43 shows the unmodified code and the mouse hovering over the variable. The displayed value for the variable leads you to spot the logical error.

```
Function modUtilites_GetFirstName(strMixedName As String)
' if the name we have a space we assume that we
' can extract a first name like Fred Bloggs
' Otherwise we assume we have a first name only like fred
Dim lngPosSpace As Long

    lngPosSpace = InStr(1, strMixedName, " ")
    If lngPosSpace <> strMixedName = "Maria Anders"
        ' so no space found and we assume the entire name
        ' is the first name
        modUtilites_GetFirstName = strMixedName
    Else
        ' So what we need is all the characters up to the space
        modUtilites_GetFirstName = Left(strMixedName, lngPosSpace - 1)
    End If

End Function
```

Figure 1-43 Pressing F8 repeatedly brings you to this point in the code. Notice the displayed value for the variable.

The bug in this code occurs because of a space in a name. The position of the space could be represented by a value of lngPosSpace 6, yet the code states that when lngPosSpace <> 0, we have found the entire name. So the logical test is the wrong way around. The following line needs to be changed from:

If lngPosSpace <> **0** Then

to:

If lngPosSpace = 0 Then

The problem with the code in Figure 1-43 is that it has branched into the wrong part of the processing. You would have expected the code to branch into the statements after the *Else* keyword. The mistake here is in testing for <> when you should be testing for =. You need to now fix the code.

To fix the code, edit the <> to an = sign, as shown in Figure 1-44. Then right-click the line containing the *IF* statement and select Set Next Statement (this means that we can repeat the last action). Figure 1-44 shows the modified code and the result of selecting Set Next Statement to change the execution point back to the line containing the coding error.

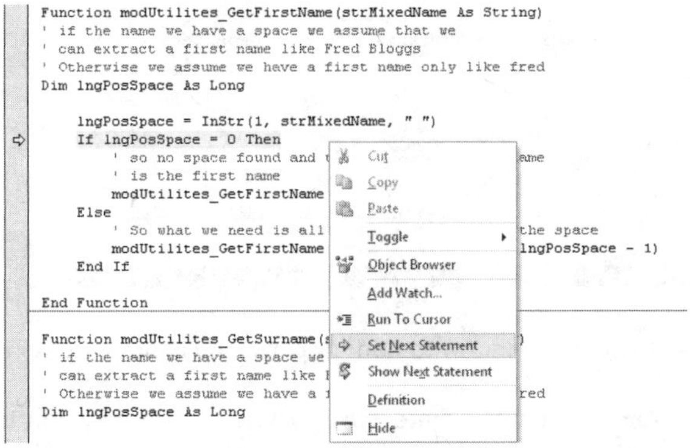

```
Function modUtilites_GetFirstName(strMixedName As String)
' if the name we have a space we assume that we
' can extract a first name like Fred Bloggs
' Otherwise we assume we have a first name only like fred
Dim lngPosSpace As Long

    lngPosSpace = InStr(1, strMixedName, " ")
    If lngPosSpace = 0 Then
        ' so no space found and (         )ame
        ' is the first name
        modUtilites_GetFirstName
    Else
        ' So what we need is all            the space
        modUtilites_GetFirstName          lngPosSpace - 1)
    End If

End Function

Function modUtilites_GetSurname(s               )
' if the name we have a space we
' can extract a first name like f
' Otherwise we assume we have a          red
Dim lngPosSpace As Long
```

Context menu items:
- Cut
- Copy
- Paste
- Toggle ▶
- Object Browser
- Add Watch...
- Run To Cursor
- Set Next Statement
- Show Next Statement
- Definition
- Hide

Figure 1-44 After changing the <> operator to =, right-click the mouse over the line where you changed the code and select Set Next Statement to go back and repeat executing the step from the code line that has now been corrected.

As before, press F8 to follow the code execution (you will also need to fix a similar coding error in the procedure *modUtilites_GetSurname*). Figure 1-45 shows how the code execution point has branched to the correct point to extract the first name.

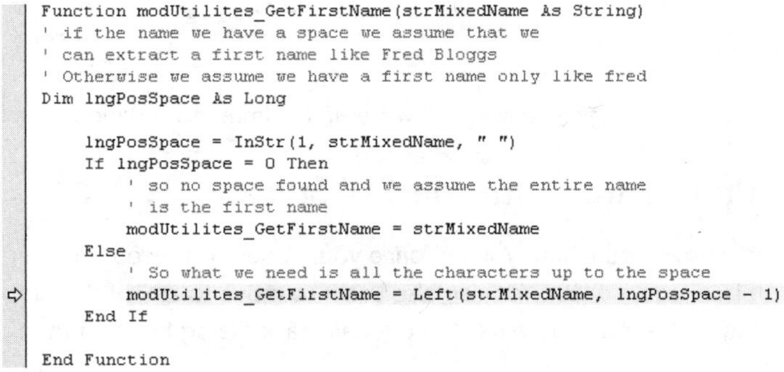

```
Function modUtilites_GetFirstName(strMixedName As String)
' if the name we have a space we assume that we
' can extract a first name like Fred Bloggs
' Otherwise we assume we have a first name only like fred
Dim lngPosSpace As Long

    lngPosSpace = InStr(1, strMixedName, " ")
    If lngPosSpace = 0 Then
        ' so no space found and we assume the entire name
        ' is the first name
        modUtilites_GetFirstName = strMixedName
    Else
        ' So what we need is all the characters up to the space
        modUtilites_GetFirstName = Left(strMixedName, lngPosSpace - 1)
    End If

End Function
```

Figure 1-45 This time, pressing F8 to step through the code takes the program to the correct processing statements.

There are a number of ways to see the result of evaluating an expression. The easiest method is to hover the mouse pointer over the expression, but you can also paste a code fragment into the Immediate window and see the result before executing the line of code (this is useful when you want to see the values for different parts of a complex expression).

Displaying Variables in the Locals Window

The Locals window gives you an instant view of the values in your program variables. This is particularly useful for complex variables that have many components, such as a *Recordset*. Figure 1-46 displays the local variables in your procedure.

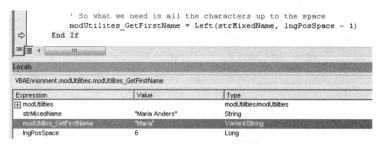

Figure 1-46 You can use the Locals window to both display and change values in variables.

In either the Locals window or the Immediate window, you can directly edit the values in variables, as shown by the highlighted value in Figure 1-47.

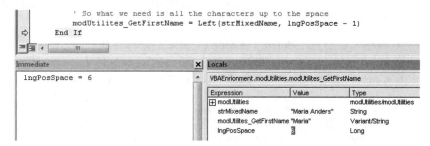

Figure 1-47 Variables can also be assigned values in the Immediate Window.

Tracing Procedures with the Call Stack

The Call Stack shows you where you are once your code has moved through several layers of execution (see Figure 1-48). You can also use it to move to any of the procedures shown by just clicking on the procedure itself in the Call Stack dialog box and then pressing the Show button.

Figure 1-48 You can use the Call Stack to help find where you are in your code, or you can use it to move directly to a procedure.

In Figure 1-48, the top line in the Call Stack dialog box shows the current routine that is executing. Below that is the succession of routines that were called to take the execution to its current point. Double-click any routine in the call stack to display that routine's code (note that the execution point remains unchanged if you do this).

Watching Variables and Expressions

The Watches window is particularly useful for monitoring values as you iterate in a loop. With the Watches window displayed, you can right-click and add an expression or variable to be monitored. Figure 1-49 shows the shortcut menu to add a *Watch* variable.

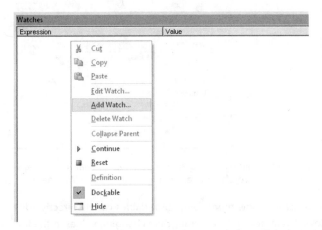

Figure 1-49 The Watches window is particularly useful when debugging repeating loops in code.

INSIDE OUT   Investigating values in variables with complex structures

Normally, *Watch* variables are simple values, but if you add a more complex type of object (in this case a field from a *Recordset*), you get a lot more information. Figure 1-50 shows the result of adding a *Recordset*'s field value to the Watches window. This kind of variable is discussed in Chapter 5, and at this point, we only want to illustrate how more complex objects can be examined by using the Watches window.

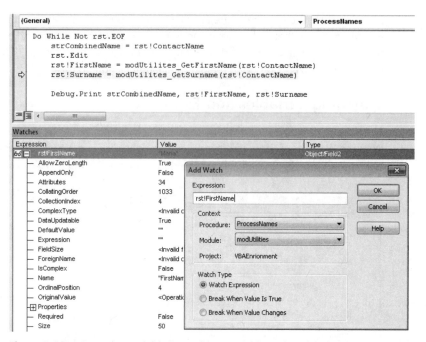

Figure 1-50 A *Recordset* variable is an object variable; rather than holding a single value, it has a more complex structure, shown here being added to the Watches window.

Figure 1-51 demonstrates how more complex variables can be directly edited in the Watches window. You might find this easier than changing values in the Immediate window.

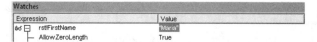

Figure 1-51 The values for watched variables can be directly edited.

The ability to drill up and down into more complex structures is also a feature shared by the Locals window.

Adding Conditional Watch Expressions

Rather than use *Debug.Assert* or modify your code with a *Stop* statement, you can add expressions to conditionally pause the execution of your code when an expression is *True* or when a value changes. Figure 1-52 shows the inclusion of a *Watch* variable that will cause the code to break execution when a specific condition holds.

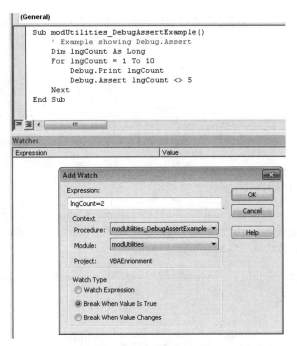

Figure 1-52 Adding a *Watch* expression to break the execution of the code.

One last word regarding the Watches window: be aware that the settings are not permanent. They are cleared once you exit the application.

Working with the Immediate Window

The Immediate window is a scratch pad for performing calculations as well as a powerful tool to display and modify properties of tables, queries, and forms as they are executing. Figure 1-53 presents some examples that you should try typing into the Immediate window. Type a question mark beside the item that you want to calculate, and then press Enter.

The Immediate window will continuously scroll as more information is displayed and there is no option to clear the window (to clear the window, you highlight all text in the window and press the Delete key).

```
Immediate
?forms.Count
 1
?forms(0).Name
frmVBAStartsHere
?forms(0).Caption
Lets get started
?currentdb.TableDefs.Count
 17
?currentdb.TableDefs("tblCompanyContact").RecordCount
 91
```

Figure 1-53 The Immediate window is a combination scratch pad and a tool to display and modify properties of tables, queries, and forms.

Changing Code On-the-Fly

Throughout this chapter, you have seen how to change your program code while it is executing, and you might wonder if there are limitations on doing this? The answer is yes, but it doesn't often get in the way of your development.

In the example shown in Figure 1-54, we have defined a new variable while the code is executing.

```
Sub ProcessNames()
' This routine goes through all the records in the table
' tblCompanyContact and takes the ContactName and splits it into
' two new fields FirstName and Surname
Stop
Dim db As Database
Dim rst As Recordset
Set db = CurrentDb
Dim strCombinedName As String
Dim i As Long
```

Figure 1-54 The new variable 'i' has been added while code is executing.

If you try deleting (or changing) variables while the code is executing, you will be presented with a warning that this will cause the code to stop executing (you might decide to add a comment after the variable to remind yourself to delete it later when the code is no longer executing).

For example, if we now decide that we have made a mistake and want to change the name of our new variable in Figure 1-54 from 'i' to something different, then you will see the warning shown in Figure 1-55. This means that you either must ignore your change (select Cancel and fix it later) or stop code execution.

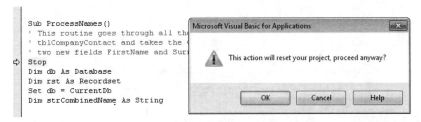

```
Sub ProcessNames()
' This routine goes through all th
' tblCompanyContact and takes the
' two new fields FirstName and Sur
⇨ Stop
  Dim db As Database
  Dim rst As Recordset
  Set db = CurrentDb
  Dim strCombinedName As String
```

Figure 1-55 A warning appears if you attempt to delete variables while the code is executing.

Using the Object Browser and Help System

In this section, you will look at how you can configure the behavior of the Help system and the use of the Object Browser as an alternative method for locating help on objects.

Configuring the Help System

VBA has an excellent Help system. To use it, simply click a word that you do not understand, and then press F1. However, it's best to have the Help system set to work with Show Content Only From This Computer; otherwise, many of the help topics might not easily locate help for a particular keyword, function, or method. Figure 1-56 shows this setting being changed at the bottom of the figure.

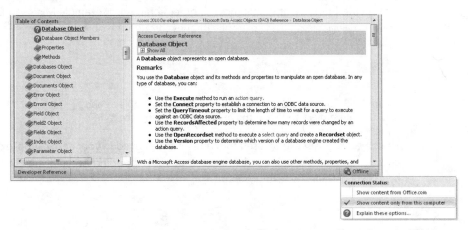

Figure 1-56 With the Help screen open, setting the Help system to Show Content Only From This Computer can offer better identification of keywords.

Access comes with an extensive Help system, and by highlighting a keyword in code (for example *CurrentDb*) and pressing F1, you can display help on the statement or object, as shown in Figure 1-57.

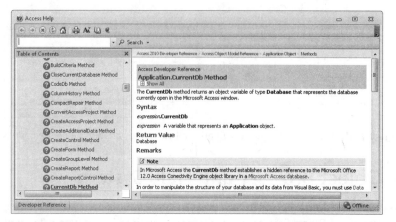

Figure 1-57 Press F1 when you have the cursor on a VBA keyword to locate the keyword in the VBA Help system.

Working with the Object Browser

As you move into more advanced programming (as well as progress through this book), you will see that when you work with objects outside of the Office suite, getting help by pressing F1 will not always display the help information for the object. In this case, you can use the Object Browser (Figure 1-58) either by using the toolbar or pressing the F2 key. Later in this book, we add references to other libraries (for example Microsoft Excel). Help is then also available on these external libraries through the object browser.

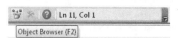

Figure 1-58 You can use the object browser to locate objects and help on your project code and the built-in features in Access.

The object browser can be used for code units designed in your application, external referenced programming units, and Office components including Access (Figure 1-59) where we have searched for the text *Currentdb*.

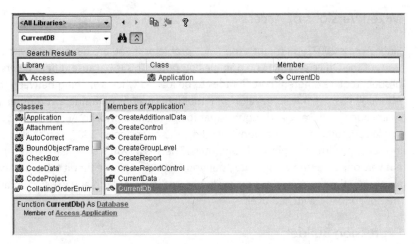

Figure 1-59 When you have located an item in the object browser, press F1 to display the help file that describes the object.

Summary

The VBA Editor and debugging environment in Access offers many useful features to assist you and enhance your productivity in developing applications. Among these features are:

- VBA allows you to significantly modify program code while it is executing. The features for stepping backwards and forwards through the code while it is paused permits you to very quickly isolate logic errors in your code and rectify them. There are minor restrictions on the changes that you can make to the code without the need to restart the code.

- The ability to have both code executing and being able to redesign associated objects such as queries and forms (other than the form that is currently executing the code) is another useful productivity feature.

- The Immediate window is one of the most productive features of the VBA environment. With it, you can test and modify properties of the executing form while the form is executing code.

- The search features that allow you to locate code either by pressing Shift+F2 on an executing procedure or Ctrl+F for general searching. Again, these tools offer unique productivity.

We end this chapter with some general comments on developing within the VBA environment.

Mixed Versions of Access

Since Access 2007, you might experience problems if you are developing with multiple versions of the Office products on a single computer. This is because different versions of the product require different core libraries to be loaded when switching between the versions. Although it is possible to develop with multiple versions on a single computer, it is not recommended, and we would suggest that for all versions prior to Access 2007, you can use a single computer, but for versions including and after Access 2007, you should consider having separate virtual or physical computers. There is a switch over feature to support different versions on a single computer, but you might find that either it takes an unacceptable amount of time to switch or you easily become vulnerable to any issues if library references are not correctly switched over.

Expression Builder

The Expression Builder is an indispensible tool when building applications to find the correct syntax when referring to controls on a form. Unfortunately, the VBA environment does not have an Expression Builder option. The easiest way to get around this problem is to go into the Query design tool, create a dummy query, and then go to the Criteria and right-click, selecting Build, which will bring up the Expression Builder (Chapter 4, "Applying the Access Object Model," discusses this in more detail).

Object Browser

When using 32-bit Microsoft ActiveX controls in a 64-bit operating system, the controls might appear to work well, but there appear to be problems that cause Access to crash when using the Object Browser to display the associated help information.

Debugging Modal Forms

When a user is interacting with a modal form, he or she cannot interact with other objects on the desktop. Debugging code on modal forms is more challenging because you cannot easily interact with other Access objects, such as checking data values in a table or query. The best advice here is to remove the modal property when debugging the form and then set it back to modal once you have resolved any problems in your code.

Understanding the VBA Language Structure

VBA Language Settings. 40

Working with Constants and Variables 49

Functions and Procedures. 66

Control Statements and Program Flow 77

The popularity of Microsoft VBA as a programming language comes from the simplicity and productivity that the language offers. You will easily pick up the general principles and syntax of VBA; the more complex part of programming is in understanding the use of the language to control how your code interacts with other objects, such as tables, queries, forms, and reports that make up your application.

With Microsoft Access/VBA, you can often solve a problem by using several different techniques. It is this flexibility that is so valuable when you have a difficult problem that you cannot easily solve by using one method; you can often take an alternative approach to solving the problem. Deciding on the best approach to solving a problem can be challenging, and as you gain experience with the language, you will find your own preferred methods for solving different types of problems.

Chapter 1, "Using the VBA Editor and Debugging Code," focused on familiarizing you with the programming environment. In this chapter, you're going to look at a large number of VBA code examples that take you through the structure of the language. If you are new to VBA, you should review this chapter in conjunction with Chapter 1 to strengthen your understanding of both the language and environment.

After reading this chapter, you will:

- Have an overview of all the key language features and know where to refer back to when you need help with syntax.

- Understand how application code is structured and how you should plan to organize and develop your own code.

- Feel confident in writing program code and following the code written by other programmers.

> **Note**
>
> As you read through this chapter, we encourage you to also use the companion content sample database, VBAExamples.accdb, which can be downloaded from the book's catalog page.

VBA Language Settings

In this section, we discuss the different settings in the VBA environment that affect how the language operates. You can customize how the VBA Editor behaves as you write code by making adjustments in the Options dialog box. There are also some options that have a more subtle impact on your development. To access the Options dialog box, click Tools | Options, as shown in Figure 2-1.

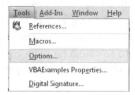

Figure 2-1 VBA Editor Options are available from the Tools menu.

From the perspective of writing code, one option that some developers choose to switch off is Auto Syntax Check. With this option enabled, the VBA Editor monitors the syntax of your code as you type. When it detects an error, it displays a warning message box. Some developers find that this slows them down, thus they switch off the option. But even when this option is disabled, syntax errors are still highlighted in colored code; only the message boxes are not shown. We would recommend that when starting out you leave this option active and later evaluate whether it helps or hinders your entering code.

Comments

Comments that you add either at the beginning of a line or after a code statement are indicated by a single quotation mark before the comment. The line will then appear colored green. To remove the comment, remove the single quote. Comments are used extensively in this book to document operations, but you can also use a comment quotation mark to disable a line of code.

VBA also has a feature for defining blocks of code as comments without the need to repeatedly enter the single quotation mark on each line. To do this, first highlight the lines of code that you want to mark as a comment, right-click the Editor menu bar, and then select the Edit menu bar option. The new menu bar has two buttons: one for commenting, and the other for uncommenting blocks of code.

Setting *Option Explicit*

You can use the VBA Editor Options dialog box shown in Figure 2-2 to alter the behavior of the environment.

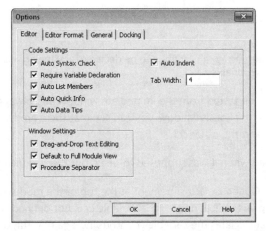

Figure 2-2 Selecting the Require Variable Declaration option will reduce programming errors.

When Require Variable Declaration is selected and a new module is created, the *Option Explicit* directive is added at the top of a module (*Option Compare Database* is explained in the next section):

```
Option Compare Database
Option Explicit
```

Looking in the *modUtils* module, the *Option Explicit* keyword at the top of the module is commented out (this simulates what happens when you do not have the Require Variable Declaration option selected when creating a module) to demonstrate how difficult it can be to spot errors when this option is not selected, as shown in Figure 2-3.

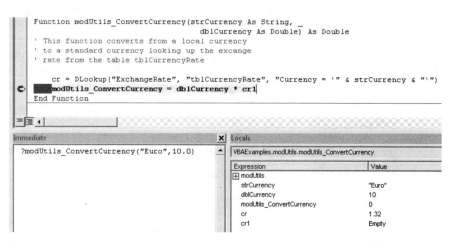

```
Function modUtils_ConvertCurrency(strCurrency As String, _
                            dblCurrency As Double) As Double
' This function converts from a local currency
' to a standard currency looking up the excange
' rate from the table tblCurrencyRate

    cr = DLookup("ExchangeRate", "tblCurrencyRate", "Currency = '" & strCurrency & "'")
    modUtils_ConvertCurrency = dblCurrency * cr1
End Function
```

Immediate

`?modUtils_ConvertCurrency("Euro",10.0)`

Locals

VBAExamples.modUtils.modUtils_ConvertCurrency

Expression	Value
⊞ modUtils	
strCurrency	"Euro"
dblCurrency	10
modUtils_ConvertCurrency	0
cr	1.32
cr1	Empty

Figure 2-3 Because you are not forcing all variables to be declared, any typing mistakes are assumed to be referencing new variables.

Notice how the function can be tested from the Immediate window and always returns the incorrect value, 0. Looking at the Locals window, you can see that there are two currency rate variables, one called cr and the other cr1.

This is an error: *cr1* was typed when it was supposed to be *cr*, but this is difficult to spot.

If you now uncomment the *Option Explicit* statement at the top of the module and try to run the code, a warning appears indicating that the variable *cr* is not defined. Then, after adding a *Dim* statement that declares the variable *cr* and trying again to run or compile the code, another warning displays, this time indicating that the variable *cr1* has not been declared, as shown in Figure 2-4; this would allow the programming error to be spotted and corrected.

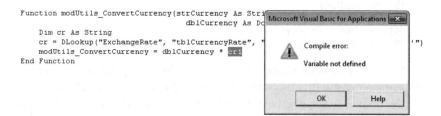

Figure 2-4 Uncommenting *Option Explicit* forces the declaration of the variable *cr*, which renders the *cr1* typing error easily detected.

Once you have added *Option Explicit* to the module, rather than running the code to see the problem, you only need to select Debug | Compile from the menus to find any undefined variables.

The combination of forcing variables to be declared and regularly compiling your code (which is explained in the next section) during development will help you avoid many programming errors.

Selecting *Option Compare*

In the previous section, you saw that the first line in any module is *Option Compare Database*. This line determines how VBA performs string comparisons, which are carried out character by character, reading from the left, as shown in the following:

```
Option Compare {Binary | Text | Database}
```

The following gives a brief description of each of the properties for the *Option Compare* declaration:

- **Binary**   Specifies that "AAA" is less than "aaa", the letter 'A' comes before 'a' (case sensitive A...Z, then a...z).

- **Text**   Specifies that "AAA" = "aaa" when comparing a string (case insensitive).

- **Database**   This is unique to Access. It means use local settings for comparisons (behaves similar to the Text option for most systems).

Comparing "a" with "ab" will give the answer that "a" is less than "ab" (when all characters match, the shorter string is less than a longer string), and "abc" is less than "ac" (because b comes before c).

In *modOption*, we have provided a function called *modOption_OrderWords*. To test this procedure, comment out the appropriate *Option Compare* statement at the top of the module, and then type the examples shown in Figure 2-5 into the Immediate window (the first result is shown with *Option Compare Binary*, the second with *Option Compare Text*).

```
Immediate
?modOption_OrderWords("AB,a,ab,B,c,C")
AB,B,C,a,ab,c
?modOption_OrderWords("AB,a,ab,B,c,C")
a,ab,AB,B,C,c
```

Figure 2-5 The *modOption_OrderWords* function uses the *Split string* function to split apart a string into an array of words.

There is also a string function called *StrComp* that can be used to perform string comparisons without needing to change the *Option Compare* for the entire module, if you need to use different comparison techniques.

Chapter 2

Compiling Code

VBA is an interpreted computer language; this means that the program code is not pre-converted into machine-dependent executable code. The code is written in a text form and then prepared in a tokenized form called *p-code* (once compiled) the p-code is processed for execution at runtime. This has the advantage of allowing great flexibility in debugging and altering code as it executes.

Compiling the code prepares the p-code prior to runtime, which means that the code will execute a little bit faster. But the biggest bonus is that it allows you to detect and correct errors at an early point during development.

One keyword, *Option Explicit*, performs a valuable task when you compile the code in your application. If you have *Option Explicit* in all your modules and you compile the code, it will stop at every instance where you have used a variable but have not declared the variable; this action is available on the Debug menu, as shown in Figure 2-6. If the option is grayed out, this means that all the code in the your database is compiled.

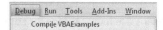

Figure 2-6 Regularly compiling your code ensures that errors are quickly identified.

Another option that you might consider is *Compile On Demand* (click Tools | Options (General)). If you leave this option selected, when you run a procedure in a module (the default is on), only that procedure is checked; other procedures will be checked as they are demand loaded (required to be used). If you had another procedure in the same module with an undeclared variable, this would not be detected. Clearing the option means that all the procedures in the current module are checked when you attempt to run any procedure in that module. Some developers prefer to not to use this option; however, if you regularly use the Debug | Compile option, then all code in the application is compiled anyhow, which renders the decision to enable or disable the *Compile On Demand* option as not important.

The following application property can be used to check whether an application is in a compiled state:

```
application.IsCompiled
```

INSIDE OUT   The /*Decompile* command line switch

Over a period of time, Access databases can bloat (which means the database size increases more than expected). Regularly compacting and repairing a database reduces the database bloat. There is an additional bloat that can occur in the VBA code, and one method for reducing this bloat is to decompile and then recompile the database. Advice as to when and whether you should regularly decompile a database varies, but a good rule-of-thumb is to only decompile if you believe you have significant bloat, or if the application is behaving in an unexpected way. This can assist in resolving an obscure problem.

To decompile a database, you need to open the database by using a link for Access that includes the /*Decompile* command line switch, as shown in the following:

```
"C:\Program Files (x86)\Microsoft Office\Office14\MSACCESS.EXE" /Decompile
```

You can create a shortcut on the desktop to do this by browsing to the installed directory of Microsoft Office and right-clicking and dragging the MSACCESS.EXE program into an appropriate folder (selecting to create a shortcut). Next, right-click this new shortcut, select Properties, and then edit the Target property to include the /*Decompile* switch. Launching Access by using the shortcut then means that the first database that you open will automatically be decompiled. You can then compile, and then compact and repair the database.

Conditional Compilation

Keywords prefixed with a # symbol (*#Const*, *#If*, *#Else*, *#End If*) are called compiler directives. These special keywords allow you to include or exclude blocks of code based on a flag.

One use for these directives is if you are building an application that needs to run in different versions of Access and you want a simple method for setting a flag to ensure that code that is only available in a particular product version is compiled. This saves you from having to manually comment out code that might not be available in that particular product version.

An example of this is the *RecordSet2* object, which handles attachment data and is not available in versions prior to Access 2007. In these earlier versions, you would need to use the older *RecordSet* object.

Another use for compiler directives is to switch on debugging statements to help when resolving code problems, as demonstrated in the following:

```
#Const Pre2007Version = False
#Const Debugging = True

Sub modCompiler_OpenRecordSet()
    Dim db As Database

    #If Pre2007Version Then
        Dim rst As DAO.Recordset
    #Else
        Dim rst As DAO.Recordset2
    #End If

    Set db = CurrentDb
    Set rst = db.OpenRecordset("Customers")
    #If Debugging Then
        Debug.Print "Recordset opened : "; rst.Name
    #End If

    rst.Close
    Set rst = Nothing
    db.Close
    Set db = Nothing
End Sub
```

In this example you would manualy set the constant Pre2007Version to True or False.

References

References inform Access about the core libraries of objects that will be used in the VBA project. With different versions of Access, you get different default references. This is because different versions of Access need different versions of the libraries (and also in part because Microsoft has changed default recommendations concerning which libraries you should be using; notably Data Access Objects (DAO), which is the default in older versions and newer versions after Access 2003, and ActiveX Data Objects (ADO), which is the default in Access 2000/2002, when the default was changed).

Later in this book, we will be adding new entries to the references when we work with external libraries, such as ADO, ActiveX, and the other Office products.

In the VBA Code Editor, click Tools | References to see your current references. They should appear as shown in Figure 2-7.

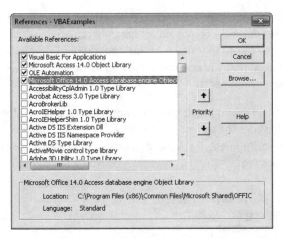

Figure 2-7 The standard references that are added when you create a new database with Access 2010.

References can be changed and alternative libraries can be loaded. You need to take care when doing this, but if you do make a mistake, then references can be added back in.

If you save your .accdb file in an .mdb format (assuming you have no new product features that prevent you from doing this), then the references will be changed as older libraries are loaded, as is shown in Figure 2-8.

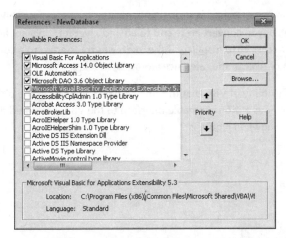

Figure 2-8 References when converting an .accdb to .mdb format or creating an .mdb file with Access 2010.

Chapter 2

The references shown in Figure 2-7 are now replaced with those shown in Figure 2-8, which means that the new Access database engine object library is replaced with the older DAO library, and an additional reference to Visual Basic for Applications Extensibility is added (which we would recommend that you consider removing by clearing the reference if moving the database to older environments)

If you move a database to an environment that does not have a required reference library, the library is tagged as missing. The easiest way to detect a missing library is to try to compile the code in the new environment. If you need to programmatically check references, the following code can be used:

```
Sub mod_ForEach()
    ' for each looping is used with collections of objects
    Dim ref As Access.Reference
    For Each ref In Access.References
        Debug.Print ref.Name, ref.FullPath, ref.IsBroken
    Next
End Sub
```

In this example, the *IsBroken* property is used to detect a broken or missing reference. Missing or broken references can be a serious problem that you need to resolve.

INSIDE OUT   Visual Basic for Applications Extensibility

Oddly, as of this writing, a reference to Visual Basic for Applications Extensibility is only added to a project when you convert an .accdb to an .mdb, yet it is only applicable on a computer that has Access 2010 installed; if the .mdb was transferred to a computer with an older version of Access, the reference would be missing.

It is a tribute to the flexibility of VBA that this library, which appears in the object browser as VBIDE, provides a programmable interface to the VBA integrated developer environment (IDE), as shown in Figure 2-9.

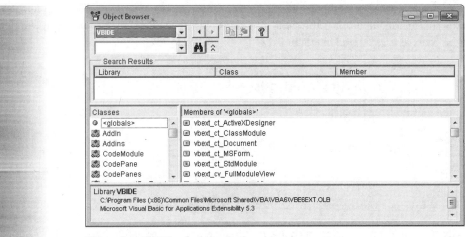

Figure 2-9 VBIDE references in the object browser.

Working with Constants and Variables

In this section, you will be looking at the use of constants and variables in your application.

Improving Code Quality with Constants

Access contains built-in constants, and when you start typing a function such as *strComp* (string comparison function), IntelliSense assists you with its completion, as shown in Figure 2-10.

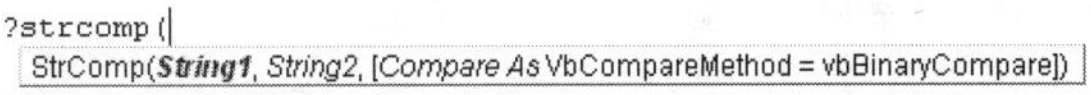

```
?strcomp (|
     StrComp(String1, String2, [Compare As VbCompareMethod = vbBinaryCompare])
```

Figure 2-10 IntelliSense provides assistance for built-in procedures as well as your own procedures.

As you continue to type (often you need to type a space, comma, or bracket), Access presents a drop-down list of constants. In this example, once you reach the third parameter position, you see the constant values shown in Figure 2-11.

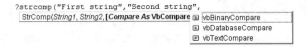

Figure 2-11 After you've completed typing a procedure, right-click it and select Quick Info to view the IntelliSense displayed for the procedure call.

When you right-click while the mouse pointer is over different parts of an existing function, the shortcut menu displays the same IntelliSense assistance that you receive when you type the code, as is illustrated in Figure 2-12.

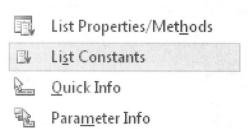

List Properties/Methods

List Constants

Quick Info

Parameter Info

Figure 2-12 You can use the shortcut menu to display IntelliSense assistance.

Constants make your program code easier to read and subsequently maintain. For example, if you want to test a string to ensure that there are fewer than the 40 characters for a known database text field, you can use an expression such as the following:

```
Function modUtils_CheckCompanyName(strInputString As String) As Boolean
    If Len(strInputString) > 40 Then
        modUtils_CheckCompanyName = False
    Else
        modUtils_CheckCompanyName = True
    End If
End Function
```

But if at some later point you want to extend the allowable length to 50 characters, then you would need to search and replace this in the program code. Not only is this a tedious job, but you risk changing other occurrences of the number 40 in your code that might be used for a different purpose. So, instead of having the number 40 in the program code, we could use a *constant*, as shown here:

```
Const lngMaxCompanyName = 40

Function modUtils_CheckCompanyName(strInputString As String) As Boolean
    If Len(strInputString) > lngMaxCompanyName Then
        modUtils_CheckCompanyName = False
    Else
        modUtils_CheckCompanyName = True
    End If
End Function
```

Constants need to be declared either at the top of a module before any procedures or inside a procedure. If you define the constant inside a procedure, then it cannot be used outside of that procedure.

If you want a constant that can be referenced outside of the module in any part of your system, then add the *Global* keyword:

```
Option Compare Database
Option Explicit
Global Const lngMaxCompanyName = 40 ' Available in any part of the application
```

Or you can use the *Public* keyword rather than *Global*, which are interchangeable terms in this context (*Global* is an older VBA syntax, but it is still very popular):

```
Public Const lngMaxCompanyName = 40 ' Available in any part of the application
```

In the previous examples, you have not been completely rigorous when defining your constants (but this is commonly what VBA developers do); with the constant *lngMaxCompanyName*, you imply that this is a long number by using the *lng* prefix. However, if you want to be accurate in how you make this definition, you should also explicitly include the variable type:

```
Public Const lngMaxCompanyName as long = 40
```

Whether a constant is available only inside a procedure (defined at the top of the procedure), at any place in the module (defined at the top of the module), or in any module in the application (defined at the top of the module with the *Global* or *Public* keyword) is called the *scope* of the constant. Some developers choose to prefix a global constant with the letter g to indicate global scope, for example *glngMaxCompanyName*.

A general principle that is regarded as good software engineering practice is to give your definitions a minimum scope. This would suggest that you restrict a constant to being defined in a procedure if that is the only place where it is used. However, many developers will define all their constants at the top of a module so that they are all in one place.

Sometimes, developers prefer to keep all of their constants in a special module and declare them as global/public. This way, they can easily see them all in one place. This is a good idea, but in some circumstances, you might prefer to keep the constants in the same module as the code that uses them, because then if you import the module into another application, it has all its constants defined within the module. This comes back to the general idea of scope—designing self-contained modules has a lot of advantages because they can be more easily tested and moved between applications.

Scope is not unique to constants, though; variables and procedures also work within the construct of scope.

The *Enum* Keyword

You have seen that for built-in functions, IntelliSense can provide a list of available constant names. You can add this feature to your own applications by using the *Enum* keyword (enumerate), and it will automatically integrate with the IntelliSense, as shown in both the following sample and Figures 2-13 and 2-14.

```
Enum enumCustomerStatus
    ucActive = 1
    ucInactive = 2
    ucPending = 3
End Enum
```

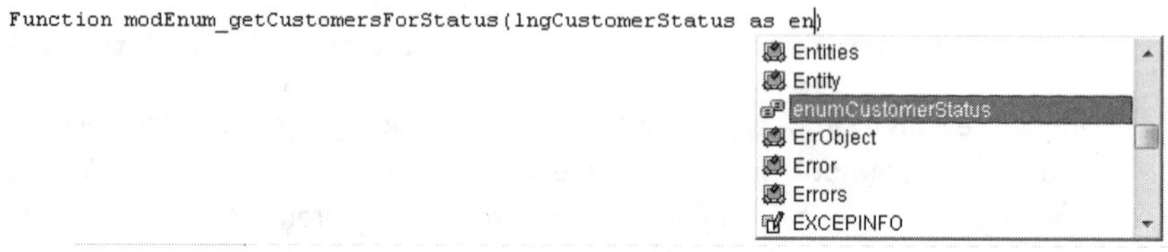

Figure 2-13 IntelliSense displaying the *Enum* structure when creating a procedure.

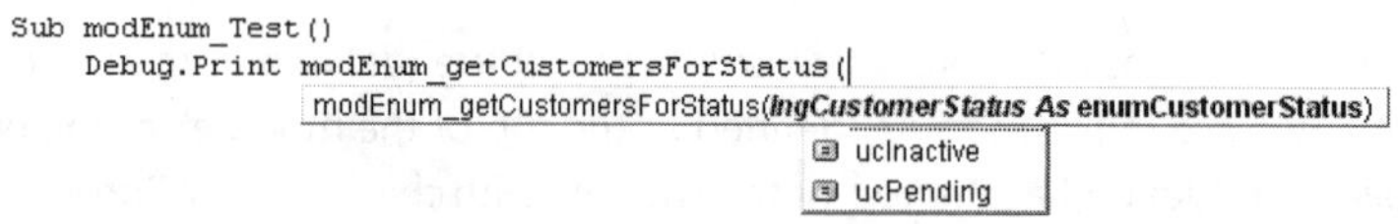

Figure 2-14 IntelliSense displaying values defined for your *Enum* structure.

Variables and Database Field Types

Variables are placeholders that can either contain or refer to information. If you are using the *Option Explicit* keyword, then each variable must be defined before it can be used.

Variables are defined by using the *Dim* (Dimension) keyword, followed by an appropriate data type. If no type is specified, the variable will be of a special type called the *variant data type*.

A large amount of programming in databases relates to manipulating the data held in the database fields. In many situations, choosing a data type for a variable involves specifying a data type that is compatible with the field's data type, as described in the following table:

Database field type	Variable type
Text	*String*
Memo	*String*
Number (*Byte, Integer, Long Integer, Single, Double, Replication Id, Decimal*)	(*Byte, Integer, Long, Single, Double, String*)
Date/Time	*Date*
Currency	*Currency*

Database field type	Variable type
Yes/No	Boolean
OLE Object	Object
Hyperlink	String
Attachment	Attachment Object
Calculated	To match calculated result type

Declaring one variable per line makes the code easier to read and helps to highlight problems if you have inadvertently omitted the data type, as is demonstrated in the line that contains *strCompany* in the code that follows:

```
Sub modUtils_VariableDefinitions()
    Dim strCompanyName As String     ' string
    Dim lngCompanyNo As Long         ' long
    Dim varCompanyCode As Variant    ' variant
    Dim unknown                      ' variant is the default
    ' the following is dangerous because strCompany
    ' will be a variant data type
    Dim strCompany, strAddress As String
End Sub
```

Variant variables are not bad, but they can hide errors that would otherwise be spotted.

Handling *NULL* Values, *IsNull* and *Nz*

When you read a data value from a field into a variable, you need to take care in how you handle the value *NULL*, which indicates that the field does not contain a value. The only type of variable that can hold the value of *NULL* is a variant variable. You could make all your variables variant, but this can mean that without very careful programming, you can miss errors when the variants end up holding values other than what was intended. For example, a variant variable that holds a date will automatically change to holding a string if you add some text to the variable value. It can be very difficult to keep track of what kind of data is held in your variant variable and debug subsequent problems. To help sort it all out, you can use the *VarType* function, which returns an integer indicating the current type of data held in a variant variable:

```
Sub modUtils_Variants()
    Dim varChanging As Variant
    varChanging = 1
    Debug.Print "Numeric value : " & VarType(varChanging)
    varChanging = #1/1/2010#
    Debug.Print "Date value : " & VarType(varChanging)
    varChanging = varChanging & " is a date"
    Debug.Print "String value : " & VarType(varChanging)
End Sub
```

We would suggest that you restrict the use of variant variables to special circumstances.

This still leaves the problem of what to do when you have a *NULL* value in a database field when you attempt to read the value into a variable.

There are two possible actions: either test the field and only assign the value to the variable when it is *NOT NULL*, or use the *Nz* function to convert a *NULL* to a safe value for the variable. When working with the *Nz* function, you can either accept the functions default choice for replacing a null value, or you can specify what default should be used. The following examples can be found in the procedure called *modNULLsReadingData* (protecting the *Boolean* is not essential as this is never *NULL*; Access treats this as false when a value has not been explicitly assigned):

```
' Protecting with the Nz function accepting a default
strTextField = Nz(rst!NullText)
lngNumberField = Nz(rst!NullNumber)
boolYesNoField = Nz(rst!NullYesNo)
dtDateTimeField = Nz(rst!NullDateTime)

Debug.Print strTextField, lngNumberField, boolYesNoField, dtDateTimeField

' Protecting with the Nz function and specifying the default
strTextField = Nz(rst!NullText, "")
lngNumberField = Nz(rst!NullNumber, 0)
boolYesNoField = Nz(rst!NullYesNo, False)
dtDateTimeField = Nz(rst!NullDateTime, #12:00:00 AM#)

Debug.Print strTextField, lngNumberField, boolYesNoField, dtDateTimeField

' Protecting by not setting a value
If Not IsNull(rst!NullText) Then strTextField = rst!NullText
If Not IsNull(rst!NullNumber) Then lngNumberField = rst!NullNumber
' A Yes/No field when null always appears false
If Not IsNull(rst!NullYesNo) Then boolYesNoField = rst!NullYesNo
If Not IsNull(rst!NullDateTime) Then dtDateTimeField = rst!NullDateTime

Debug.Print strTextField, lngNumberField, boolYesNoField, dtDateTimeField
```

NULL means no value, and this is different from an empty string or 0. For example, suppose that you have a field that holds a customer's business value to an organization for which a value of *Zero* means you have not engaged in any business with the customer, and *NULL* means you don't yet have a figure for the business value. For circumstances such as this, when performing calculations, you might need to carefully consider how *NULL* and *Zero* values are treated.

When calculating the average value of sales for your customers, if you have 5 customers with sales values of (100, 200, 0, NULL, NULL), to calculate the average, first sum all the sales for customers and then divide by the number of customers. The question is how do you treat a customer with *NULL* or *Zero* business value?

You could calculate an answer using three different calculations, as follows:

```
(100 + 200 +0) / 5
```

or

```
(100 + 200 + 0) / 3 or (100+200) / 2.
```

The SQL aggregate function (*AVG*) and Domain function (*DAVG*) ignore *NULL* values, and would use the calculation (100 + 200 + 0) / 3.

If you wanted to include the *NULL* values and treat these as 0, then you can use *AVG(Nz([Turnover],0))*, where the *Nz* function converts *NULL* to 0 and gives the answer (100+200+0+0+0)/5.

If you wanted to exclude both *Zero* and *NULL* values, then you can use an *IIF* function to convert 0 to *NULL* by using *AVG(IIF([Turnover] = 0,NULL,[Turnover]))*, which gives the answer (100+200)/2.

Using Static Variables

In the previous examples in which variables are defined inside a procedure, the values held in the variables only exist as long as the procedure is executing. Once the procedure completes execution, the internal variables lose their values.

However, there will be circumstances for which you want to persist these values after the procedure has finished execution. For these situations, you can use the *Static* keyword, as shown in the following:

```
Sub modNULLs_ExampleOfAStaticVariable()
    Static lngCallCount As Long
    lngCallCount = lngCallCount + 1
    Debug.Print lngCallCount
End Sub
```

If you execute this code several times from the Immediate window, you can see how the variable maintains its previous value on each subsequent execution of the procedure, as shown in Figure 2-15.

```
Sub modNULLs_ExampleOfAStaticVariable()
    Static lngCallCount As Long
    lngCallCount = lngCallCount + 1
    Debug.Print lngCallCount
End Sub

Static Sub modNULLs_ExampleOfAStaticVariable2()
    Dim lngCallCount As Long
    lngCallCount = lngCallCount + 1
    Debug.Print lngCallCount
End Sub
```

```
Immediate
modNULLs_ExampleOfAStaticVariable
 1
modNULLs_ExampleOfAStaticVariable
 2
modNULLs_ExampleOfAStaticVariable
 3
```

Figure 2-15 Each time you call the procedure with the *Static* variable it remembers its previous value; the *Static* keyword preservers the contents of variable.

The *Static* keyword can also be used before declaring the procedure name: *Static Sub...*, in which case all of the variables in the procedure will be *Static*. (This is not an often-used feature in VBA.)

Although this variable exists for as long as the application is running (it has an application lifetime) it has local scope and is only visible inside the procedure.

Using Global Variables

Global variables are variables to which you want to assign application scope and lifetime (you can equally use the term public rather than global when defining this variable type). As with constants, developers often gather up all the global variables into a single module for ease of maintenance, as illustrated here:

```
Global userName As String

Sub modGlobal_SetUsername()
    userName = "Andrew"
End Sub

Sub modGlobal_GetUsername()
    Debug.Print userName
End Sub

Sub modGlobal_GenerateError()
' generates a divide by 0 error, this causes the
' global variable to lose its value
    Dim lngCount As Long
    lngCount = 5 / 0
End Sub
```

This example demonstrates one drawback of global variables: if the program generates an error condition (that is not handled by an error handler), then the global variables lose their values. Figure 2-16 shows how the last call to *modGlobal_GetUsername* does not return a value, as would be expected.

```
Immediate
 modGlobal_SetUsername

 modGlobal_GetUsername
 Andrew

 modGlobal_GenerateError

 modGlobal_GetUsername
```

Figure 2-16 Global variables lose their value if an error occurs. Here, there is no value shown when calling *modGlobal_GetUserName* because a program error was generated by the *modGlobal_GenerateError* procedure.

To prevent this from causing a problem, you can consider not working directly with the global variable, but instead using a function to retrieve the value from the global variable. You can also have the function test to verify that the global variable has a valid value; if it does not, then reload the global variable, as shown in the following:

```
Sub modGlobal_GetUsername2()
    If userName = "" Then
        modGlobal_SetUsername
    End If
    Debug.Print userName
End Sub
```

Variable Scope and Lifetime

You have seen that variables and constants can be defined inside a procedure, and when they are, by default, their scope is limited to within the procedure, and their lifetime can be regarded as the duration of the procedure execution.

These constraints, however, are not set in stone. A variable defined in a procedure can have its lifetime extended to that of the application by using the keyword *Static* when defining the variable.

You can extend the scope and lifetime of both variables and constants by defining them at the top of a module. The scope is then opened up to all procedures defined within the module, and these procedures can now refer to the module-level definitions. The lifetime for module-level definitions depends upon the type of module within which they are defined. In a Form/Report class module, they exist for as long as the Form/Report is open. For other modules, the lifetime is that of the application, because these modules are demand loaded into memory.

Using the *Public* or *Global* keywords when making a definition at the top of a module gives the variable an application lifetime and application scope. In a Form/Report class module you cannot use the keyword *Global*, but you can use the keyword *Public* for a variable (this allows the variable on the form to be referenced like a property of the Form); constants on a Form/Report class module cannot be made either *Public* or *Global*.

INSIDE OUT   A summary of scope rules

There are two concepts that you need to understand about these rules. First, a Form/Report class module is *not* the same as a module (this is described in the following sections).

Second, the terms Public/Global and Private/Dim are to some extent interchangeable (but this is not always the case). Global and Dim are best used when you want to explicitly control the scope of a variable, whereas Public/Private are more appropriately used when defining the scope of procedures (except in a Form/Report when you want to expose a variable as a property of the Form/Report). This is described in the table that follows.

	Dim/Private	Static	Global/Public
Procedure	Procedure Scope and Procedure lifetime	Procedure Scope and Application lifetime when defined in a Module or Form/Report lifetime when defined in a Form/Report class module	These definitions are allowed but it would be considered as unconventional to define global variables inside a Procedure when contained in a Module (see below for rules in a Form/Report Class Module).
Module level	Module Scope and Application lifetime	Not Allowed	Application Scope and lifetime
Form/Report class module level	Module Scope and Form/Report lifetime	Procedure Scope and Form/Report lifetime	Only allowed a Public variable with Application scope and Form/Report lifetime.

Variables that have the same names and same level of scope are not allowed, but variables with different levels of scope can have the same name. VBA understands that you mean to refer to the variable with local scope. The results of running these tests are shown in Figure 2-17.

```
    Dim strCompanyName As String

    Sub modScope2_TestingVariableScope()
        ' this sets the global variable strCompanyName
        modScope_SetGlobalVariable
        strCompanyName = "Module Scope"
        Debug.Print "Module Level : " & strCompanyName
        modScope2_LocalProcedure
    End Sub

    Sub modScope2_LocalProcedure()
        Dim strCompanyName As String
        strCompanyName = "Procedure Scope"
        Debug.Print "Procedure Level :" & strCompanyName
    End Sub
```

Immediate
```
modScope2_TestingVariableScope
Module Level : Module Scope
Procedure Level :Procedure Scope
?strCompanyName
Global Scope
```

Figure 2-17 The same variable defined in three different places illustrates the scope rules.

In this example, we have defined a global variable called *strCompanyName* in another module (*mod_Scope*), and the call *modScope_SetGlobalVariable* assigns a value to the global variable.

Code in the local procedure sees the local scope variable; other procedures in the module see the module-level variable; and procedures outside this module see the global variable value.

You might find it useful to use the convention of adding the prefix letter "m" for module scope variables and "g" for global scope variables.

Working with Arrays

Arrays can be used when you need to have a set of similar variables; for example, if you need to hold a list of all states in memory, you could define a set of variables called *strStateCA*, *strStateCO*, and so on, or *strState1*, *strState2*, and so forth. But this would be very difficult to work with, so VBA gives you the option to define an array, which acts like a list of values.

First, you create a query that displays a unique list of [State/Province] field values in the *Customers* table by using the following SQL, with the results shown in Figure 2-18:

```
SELECT DISTINCT Customers.[State/Province]
FROM Customers
WHERE ((Not (Customers.[State/Province]) Is Null));
```

Chapter 2

Figure 2-18 A query or table with one column is like a simple array of single values.

Next, the following code shows how you can load this list of states into an array in memory:

```vba
Sub modArray_StatesInAnArray()
    ' loads a list of states into an array of fixed size
    Const lngArraySize = 20
    Dim lngCounter As Long
    Dim varAState As Variant ' needs to be a variant for
    ' use in the ForEach loop
    Dim strState(lngArraySize) As String
    Dim db As Database
    Set db = CurrentDb
    lngCounter = 0
    Dim rst As Recordset
    Set rst = db.OpenRecordset("SELECT DISTINCT [State/Province] " & _
                " FROM Customers WHERE [State/Province] IS NOT NULL", _
                              dbOpenDynaset)
    Do While Not rst.EOF
        If lngCounter > lngArraySize Then
            'this would cause a problem
            Stop
        End If
        strState(lngCounter) = rst![State/Province]
        lngCounter = lngCounter + 1
        rst.MoveNext
    Loop

    For Each varAState In strState
        If varAState <> "" Then
            Debug.Print varAState
        End If
    Next
    Debug.Print "Lower bound : " & LBound(strState)
    Debug.Print "Upper Bound : " & UBound(strState)
    rst.Close
    Set rst = Nothing
    db.Close
    Set db = Nothing
End Sub
```

Near the top of this procedure, you define the array as having a fixed size of 20 items
(0, 1, 2 ... 19).

> **Note**
>
> All arrays in Access are 0-based, which means that they start counting at 0.

Dynamic Arrays

It is also possible to have arrays that can change size and the number of dimensions by
using the *ReDim* statement. These arrays can also maintain existing data when they change
size by using the *Preserve* keyword. The following code starts with an estimate of there
being eight states in the dataset and then changes the array size, adding more items as
required:

```
Sub modArray_StatesInADynamicArray()
    ' loads a list of states into an array of dynamic size
    Dim lngArraySize As Long
    Dim lngCounter As Long
    Dim strAState As Variant ' needs to be a variant for
    ' use in the ForEach loop
    Dim strState() As String
    lngArraySize = 8
    ReDim strState(lngArraySize)

    Dim db As Database
    Set db = CurrentDb

    lngCounter = 0
    Dim rst As Recordset
    Set rst = db.OpenRecordset("SELECT DISTINCT [State/Province] " & _
                        " FROM Customers WHERE [State/Province] IS NOT NULL", _
                                dbOpenDynaset)
    Do While Not rst.EOF
        If lngCounter > lngArraySize Then
            'this would cause a problem
            ' allocatate 5 more values and save existing values
            lngArraySize = lngArraySize + 5
            ReDim Preserve strState(lngArraySize)
        End If
        strState(lngCounter) = rst![State/Province]
        lngCounter = lngCounter + 1
        rst.MoveNext
    Loop
```

Arrays that are going to be dynamically changed in size *cannot* be defined with a fixed size; you either need to define the array initially with no size and then *ReDim* the array when you come to use it:

```
Dim strState() As String
```

Or, you can use the *ReDim* statement when you first define the array dynamically with a variable:

```
lngArraySize = 8
ReDim strState(lngArraySize) As String
```

VBA allows you to define arrays with up to 60 dimensions.

Multi-Dimensional Arrays

Arrays can have more than one dimension. A two-dimensional array, for example, is like a spreadsheet; the columns are one dimension, the rows are a second dimension, and each cell holds a single value.

In the next example, you construct a one-dimensional array of states, and a second one-dimensional array of cities. The procedure then defines a two-dimensional array indexed by the State and then the City. This is a sparsely populated array (most array elements have no value), but it is relatively easy to index when constructed in this manner. To find an item, you look up the state in the *States* array (and retrieve an index), then to find a City, you look it up in the *Cities* array (and retrieve a second index). Then you can index the element in the main array by using the values obtained from the lookup, as demonstrated in the following code:

```
Sub modArray_TwoDimensionalArray()
    ' First we create our array of states
    ' Then we create an array of city names
    ' Then we have a two dimensional array which counts the
    ' Customers in each city for each state

    Const lngStates = 30
    Const lngCities = 100

    Dim lngCounter As Long
    Dim strState(lngStates) As String
    Dim strCity(lngCities) As String
    Dim lngStateIndex As Long
    Dim lngCityIndex As Long

    ' The following will be a very sparsely populated array
    Dim lngCustomers(lngStates, lngCities) As Long

    Dim db As Database
    Set db = CurrentDb
    lngCounter = 0
```

```
Dim rst As Recordset
Set rst = db.OpenRecordset("SELECT DISTINCT [State/Province] " & _
            " FROM Customers WHERE [State/Province] IS NOT NULL", _
                        dbOpenDynaset)
Do While Not rst.EOF
    strState(lngCounter) = rst![State/Province]
    lngCounter = lngCounter + 1
    rst.MoveNext
Loop

rst.Close
lngCounter = 0
Set rst = db.OpenRecordset("SELECT DISTINCT [City] " & _
                " FROM Customers WHERE [City] IS NOT NULL", _
                        dbOpenDynaset)
Do While Not rst.EOF
    strCity(lngCounter) = rst![City]
    lngCounter = lngCounter + 1
    rst.MoveNext
Loop
rst.Close
lngCounter = 0
' Now we index our multi-dimensional array using
' the other two arrays
Set rst = db.OpenRecordset("SELECT [ID], [City],[State/Province] " & _
                " FROM Customers WHERE [State/Province] IS NOT NULL" & _
                        " AND [City] IS NOT NULL", _
                        dbOpenDynaset)
Do While Not rst.EOF
    ' For each customer, lookup the state index
    For lngStateIndex = 0 To lngStates - 1
        If strState(lngStateIndex) = rst![State/Province] Then
            Exit For
        End If
    Next
    ' Next lookup the city index
    For lngCityIndex = 0 To lngCities - 1
        If strCity(lngCityIndex) = rst![City] Then
            Exit For
        End If
    Next
    lngCustomers(lngStateIndex, lngCityIndex) = _
lngCustomers(lngStateIndex, lngCityIndex) + 1
    rst.MoveNext
Loop .

' Now summariese the results
For lngStateIndex = 0 To lngStates - 1
    For lngCityIndex = 0 To lngCities - 1
        If lngCustomers(lngStateIndex, lngCityIndex) > 0 Then
            Debug.Print strState(lngStateIndex), strCity(lngCityIndex), _
                lngCustomers(lngStateIndex, lngCityIndex)
        End If
    Next
```

Chapter 2

```
        Next
        rst.Close
        Set rst = Nothing
        db.Close
        Set db = Nothing
End Sub
```

The preceding example illustrates a rather subtle point about arrays; although an array can actually hold a complex structure of data at each array point (for example, you can have a multi-dimensional array of type structures), the indexing into the array is always through a simple numerical value.

INSIDE OUT   Determining the dimensions of an array

There is no feature in the VBA language for determining dynamically the number of dimensions in an array, but you can establish this by using an error handler in a routine that returns the array dimension, as follows:

```
Function modArray_Dimensions(ar() As Variant) As Long
    ' determine the dimensions of an array using an error trap
    ' set the constant at least 1 more than maximum dimensions
    ' to be checked
    Const lngMaxDimensions As Long = 20
    Dim lngDimensions As Long
    Dim lngDim As Long
    On Error GoTo Err_Handler
    For lngDimensions = 1 To lngMaxDimensions
        lngDim = UBound(ar, lngDimensions)
    Next
    ' code will never get here
    Stop
    Exit Function
Err_Handler:
    modArray_Dimensions = lngDimensions - 1
End Function

Sub modArray_TestDimensions()
    Dim lngDimensions As Long
    Dim ar() As Variant
    ReDim ar(5, 5)
    lngDimensions = modArray_Dimensions(ar)
    Debug.Print "Array dimension is " & lngDimensions
    ReDim ar(5, 5, 5)
    lngDimensions = modArray_Dimensions(ar)
    Debug.Print "Array dimension is " & lngDimensions
End Sub
```

Option Base

All arrays and collections in Access are 0-based, but if you are working with Microsft Excel, you will find that all the collections are 1-based. It is possible to change in a module the base that Access uses. We don't recommend doing this without a very good reason, but you will find this referenced in the documentation. The following code example demonstrates how the base can be changed. The line that attempts to print the value of *strState(0)* will generate an error because you are now working with a 1-based array:

```
Option Compare Database
Option Explicit
Option Base 1

Sub modArray2_ChangedBase()
    Dim strState(2) As String
    strState(1) = "MA"
    strState(2) = "MN"
    Debug.Print strState(0)
End Sub
```

Type Structures

A type structure allows you to construct a record-like structure in memory. These are often used when working with the Windows API where external procedure calls require you to define a structure. Another use is when you need to hold multiple data values for an array; here you can define an array of types:

```
Type PageInfo
    strPageName As String
    strPageSubForm As String
    strRelatedPage As String
    blCanBeLoaded As Boolean
End Type


Sub modArray_Types()
    Dim AvailablePages(2) As PageInfo
    Dim lngPage As Long
    AvailablePages(0).strPageName = "List Products"
    AvailablePages(0).blCanBeLoaded = True
    For lngPage = 0 To UBound(AvailablePages)
        Debug.Print AvailablePages(lngPage).strPageName
    Next
End Sub
```

If you define a type in a form's class module, you need to explicitly state *Private Type* when making the definition (but most types would not be defined in a form or report class module).

Functions and Procedures

VBA code is written in terms of procedures that are stored in modules. There are two kinds of procedures: the subroutine and the function.

Functions are different from subroutines with respect to where they can be used; a function can be called from the query grid and a macro command (you can't do any of this with a subroutine). Functions return a value (even if you don't explicitly state what the return type is); subroutines do not. As a result, the syntax for calling a function is slightly different from that for calling a subroutine. The following code example demonstrates a function and subroutine that perform the same operation:

```
Sub modProcParam_Sub(strName As String)
    strName = UCase(strName)
End Sub

Function modProcParam_Funct(strName As String) As String
    modProcParam_Funct = UCase(strName)
End Function
```

The function returns a value, so you use the following syntax:

```
Dim strName As String
strName = "andrew"
strName = modProcParam_Funct(strName)
```

There are two possible forms for the syntax to call a subroutine (*Call* is the less used and older form of the syntax):

```
strName = "andrew"
modProcParam_Sub strName
Call modProcParam_Sub(strName)
```

If you are using the *Call* syntax, then the parameters are enclosed in brackets; if you do not use the *Call* syntax, then the parameters are not enclosed in brackets.

Subroutines are automatically created when you choose to build code in response to a built-in event on a form or report.

INSIDE OUT **Variations on standard rules for calling functions and procedures**

There are two unusual variations of the calling syntax for functions and subroutines (although we wouldn't recommend using them).

It is possible to use the *Call* syntax with a function (although for a function returning a value, you would not capture the return value, as follows:

```
Call modProcParam_Funct(strName)
```

If a subroutine has only one parameter, then you are allowed to have parentheses surrounding the single parameter, as shown here:

```
modProcParam_Sub (strName)
```

Managing Code with Subroutines

Traditionally, subroutines allow complex and large processing blocks of code to be broken down into smaller steps. Breaking down one large block of code into several smaller blocks of code (subroutines) offers a number of advantages. One advantage is that you can often then identify similar blocks of code that can be generalized by using parameters to reduce the total amount of code that you need to produce. A second advantage is that it makes the code look simpler and more structured, which eases maintenance.

In the *modSub_ProcessSQL* procedure, we have an example of a program that breaks apart simple SQL statements:

```
Sub modSub_ProcessSQL(strSQL As String)
    ' Break apart an SQL string into component parts
    ' Extracts SELECT and WHERE clauses
    ' SQL order of keywords is
    ' SELECT..FROM...WHERE..GROUP BY.. HAVING
    ' Does not handle UNION or nested SELECT statements

    ' Extract the SELECT part of the SQL
    Dim strSelect As String
    Dim strWhere As String

    Dim lngPosSelect As Long
    Dim lngPosWhere As Long
    Dim lngPosEnd As Long

    lngPosSelect = InStr(1, strSQL, " FROM ")
    If lngPosSelect = 0 Then
        Exit Sub
    Else
        strSelect = Trim$(Mid(strSQL, 1, lngPosSelect))
    End If

    Debug.Print strSelect
    lngPosWhere = InStr(lngPosSelect + 6, strSQL, " WHERE ")
    If lngPosWhere = 0 Then
        Exit Sub
    End If
```

```
        lngPosEnd = InStr(lngPosWhere + 6, strSQL, " GROUP BY ")
        If lngPosEnd = 0 Then lngPosEnd = 255
        strWhere = Trim$(Mid(strSQL, lngPosWhere, lngPosEnd))
        Debug.Print strWhere
End Sub
```

Looking at this procedure, you can see that the idea of searching for a pattern is repeated twice. If you extend this routine to look for other patterns, you would be repeating more similar code units. Breaking this into two subroutines allows a more structured approach to developing the code, as demonstrated in the following:

```
Sub modSub_SliceOutString(strSQL As String, _
                          strFromPattern As String, _
                          strToPattern As String, _
                          strSlice As String)
    ' look for a substring strPattern searching
    ' after lngStartPos and return the substring
    Dim lngEndPos As Long
    Dim lngStartPos As Long
    lngStartPos = InStr(1, strSQL, strFromPattern)
    If lngStartPos = 0 Then
        strSlice = ""
        Exit Sub
    End If
    If strToPattern = "" Then
        lngEndPos = Len(strSQL)
    Else
        lngEndPos = InStr(lngStartPos, strSQL, strToPattern)
    End If
    If lngEndPos <> 0 Then
        strSlice = Trim$(Mid(strSQL, lngStartPos, _
                     lngEndPos - lngStartPos + 1))
    End If
End Sub


Sub modSub_ProcessSQL2(strSQL As String)
    ' Break apart an SQL string into component parts
    ' Extracts SELECT and WHERE clauses
    ' SQL order of keywords is
    ' SELECT..FROM...WHERE..GROUP BY.. HAVING
    ' Does not handle UNION or nested SELECT statements

    ' Extract the SELECT part of the SQL
    Dim strSelect As String
    Dim strWhere As String
    modSub_SliceOutString strSQL, "SELECT ", " FROM ", strSelect
    If strSelect = "" Then
        Exit Sub
    End If
    Debug.Print strSelect
    modSub_SliceOutString strSQL, " WHERE ", "", strWhere
```

```
    If strWhere = "" Then
        Exit Sub
    End If
    Debug.Print strWhere
End Sub
```

The initial cost in terms of lines of code is slightly higher than the original code, but as we added more different kinds of searching, we would see a dramatic reduction in the total amount of code. In addition, the main processing code is now easier to read.

The second type of procedure is the function, which is traditionally used to perform an operation and then return a result.

Apart from the restrictions described earlier regarding where a function or subroutine may be called, you can make subroutines and functions perform similar jobs, so deciding on which to use might cause some confusion.

Looking back at our previous example (*modSub_SliceOutString*), you can see that the subroutine returns a single result in the variable *strSlice*. This would be a good candidate for using a function; instead, and we could rewrite this as follows:

```
Function modSub_SliceOutStringFn(strSQL As String, _
                            strFromPattern As String, _
                            strToPattern As String) As String
    ' look for a substring strPattern searching
    ' after lngStartPos and return the substring
    Dim lngEndPos As Long
    Dim lngStartPos As Long
    lngStartPos = InStr(1, strSQL, strFromPattern)
    If lngStartPos = 0 Then
        modSub_SliceOutStringFn = ""
        Exit Function
    End If
    If strToPattern = "" Then
        lngEndPos = Len(strSQL)
    Else
        lngEndPos = InStr(lngStartPos, strSQL, strToPattern)
    End If
    If lngEndPos <> 0 Then
        modSub_SliceOutStringFn = Trim$(Mid(strSQL, lngStartPos, _
                    lngEndPos - lngStartPos + 1))
    End If
End Function
```

If you look at *modSub_ProcessSQL3*, which calls the function, you will see the following syntax is used:

```
strWhere = modSub_SliceOutStringFn(strSQL, " WHERE ", "")
```

Another advantage of a function is that you can use the value it returns to indicate whether it encountered a problem. This then allows the calling code to more easily handle errors. Using a function in this way means that the function can also be used to perform the traditional approach performed by subroutines of breaking down a program into more manageable chunks, as shown in the following:

```
Function modProcParam_Funct2(strName As String) As Boolean
    On Error Resume Next
    strName = UCase(strName)
    If Err <> 0 Then
        modProcParam_Funct2 = False
        Exit Function
    End If
    modProcParam_Funct2 = True
End Function

Sub modProcParam_Calling2()
    Dim strName As String
    strName = "andrew"
    If Not modProcParam_Funct2(strName) Then
        ' we have a problem and need some kind of action
    End If
End Sub
```

In the previous function, you could have structured the *IF* statement to read as follows:

```
IF modProcParam_Funct2(strName) = False
    Then
```

But because the function returns a *Boolean* result, you can avoid the need to explicitly test this against *True* or *False*.

Sometimes, the decision as to whether to use a function or a subroutine can be a difficult. If a procedure only returns a single result of its processing and is in some way calculative in its operation, then a function is often a better choice.

Defining *ByRef* and *ByValue* Parameters

Both functions and subroutines can be passed values called *parameters* (or *arguments*) the procedure then uses these parameters to assist with the processing. By using parameters, you can use procedures flexibly in different parts of the application.

Depending on how the parameters have been defined, a procedure can alter the values of parameters; this is a way of passing back changes to several parameters to the calling program.

INSIDE OUT

Default referencing of parameters in subroutines and functions

VBA uses the call-by-reference convention, which means that if your procedure alters a parameter value, then after control returns to the calling program, the calling program will see the altered value. One reason for using call-by-reference is that it improves efficiency because it passes a reference and not a copy of the data.

You can also use call-by-value (unless you are passing an object as a parameter, which always uses *ByRef*). This means that the procedure receives a copy of the parameter values, and any changes the procedure makes to these values will *not* be seen by the calling program because the copies are discarded when the procedure is finished. Although it is not as efficient as call-by-reference, you can consider call-by-value to be safer, because it is not possible for you to overlook a subtle side-effect where the procedure alters the parameters used by the calling program.

VBA does not force you to explicitly state *ByVal* or *ByRef* when defining parameters; the default is *ByRef*. Most VBA developers tend to disregard making this choice when declaring parameters.

If at some later point in time you intend to copy your VBA code into VB.NET, then you will find that VB.NET demands that you have used *ByVal* or *ByRef* for all parameters on functions and subroutines. You will also need to remove the *Call* keyword when calling any procedures.

In *modProc*, you see three different methods for defining a function, with Figure 2-19 showing the results:

```
Function modProc_VerySimple(lngFirst As Long, _
                                    lngSecond As Long) As Long
    ' Not specifying a parameter ByVal or ByRef
    ' means let access decide on what to do
    lngFirst = lngFirst + 3
    modProc_VerySimple = lngFirst + lngSecond
End Function
Function modProc_VerySimpleByVal(ByVal lngFirst As Long, _
                                    ByVal lngSecond As Long) As Long
    ' the ByVal, says pass a copy of the parameter
    ' so any changes to the copies are lost once the procedure ends
    lngFirst = lngFirst + 3
    modProc_VerySimpleByVal = lngFirst + lngSecond
End Function
Function modProc_VerySimpleByRef(ByRef lngFirst As Long, _
                                    ByRef lngSecond As Long) As Long
```

Chapter 2

```
        ' the ByRef, says pass a reference to the parameter
        ' so any changes to the copies effect the parameter
        lngFirst = lngFirst + 3
        modProc_VerySimpleByRef = lngFirst + lngSecond
End Function
```

```
Immediate
TestingAverySimpleFunction
Function modProc_VerySimple(10,50)
Local variables after call :              13              50
Function modProc_VerySimpleByRef(10,50)
Local variables after call :              13              50
Function modProc_VerySimpleByValue(10,50)
Local variables after call :              10              50
Function modProc_NoTypes(10,50)
Local variables after call  :             13              50
```

Figure 2-19 Use the ByVal keyword to prevent the calling program's Local variable from being changed by the function call.

Figure 2-19 shows that if you do not specify any setting or use *ByRef*, the subroutine or function is able to change your parameter values (the variable in the outer program has a value of 10, which then is changed to 13).

If you are not going to explicitly state *ByVal* or *ByRef*, then it can be useful to copy any parameter that you do not intend to change into a local variable so that any changes you make to the values will not affect the original parameters, as demonstrated in the following:

```
Function modProc_VerySimpleProtected(lngFirst As Long, _
                                     lngSecond As Long) As Long
        ' Not specifying a parameter ByVal or ByRef
        ' means let access decide on what to do
        Dim lngLocalValue As Long
        lngLocalValue = lngFirst
        lngLocalValue = lngLocalValue + 3
        modProc_VerySimpleProtected = lngLocalValue + lngSecond
End Function
```

Isolating a problem caused by a function or subroutine that changes a parameter value by mistake can prove to be very difficult.

Private and Public Procedures

It could be argued that VBA encourages a sloppy programming style; it is possible to let yourself be a little lazy and not be precise about defining variables, variable data types, and the use of *ByVal* and *ByRef* settings on parameters. But because VBA is so forgiving, developers who would otherwise find a more formal programming languages difficult to work with can be more productive (although the more liberal your programming style, the more likely you are to suffer from unexpected side effects.) Another important point regarding VBA is that it has evolved over time, and preferences, standards, and programming styles have also evolved. But it is important that VBA allows older program code to run in newer environments. VBA might not be perfect, but it is extremely productive and intuitive to use.

With variables, you saw that the concept of scope allowed for local and global/public variable definitions. Functions and subroutines also have similar scope rules; these are specified by using the keywords *Public* or *Private*.

By default, when you create a procedure in a VBA module, that procedure is given a global scope (application-wide scope), which is the same as using the *Public* keyword. And if you define a procedure in the class module of a form or report, its scope is local, and thus visible only to other procedures in the same module, which is equivalent to using the *Private* keyword.

The best practice is to always define procedures with local scope or *Private*, and only change this to *Public* when you explicitly want to open up the procedure to be referenced by other modules in the application.

You are allowed to have a procedure with the same name in two different modules, as long as the procedure name is declared as *Private*. This means that if you are developing a module that will be imported into other applications, marking most of your procedures as *Private* will avoid conflicts with any similarly named procedures in the application into which you import the module.

Optional and Named Parameters

The *modProcParam* module contains examples of using both *named parameters* and *optional parameters*.

Using named parameters is not part of how the function or subroutine is defined, but it is related to how you call the procedure. Named parameters mean that you can pass the parameters in any order. When passing each parameter you must specify which parameter you mean for each value by using a := in the syntax, as illustrated in the following:

```
Sub modProcParam_Test()
    Debug.Print modProcParam_NamedParameters _
            ("Andrew", "Couch")
    Debug.Print modProcParam_NamedParameters _
            (strFirstName:="Andrew", strSurname:="Couch")
    Debug.Print modProcParam_NamedParameters _
            (strSurname:="Couch", strFirstName:="Andrew")
End Sub
```

It is only when you begin to use optional parameters that using named parameters starts to offer a benefit in terms of the flexibility you have when calling procedures.

Optional parameters are part of the procedure definition; when declaring a parameter as optional you have the choice to provide a default value, which is used when the optional parameter is not supplied.

```
Function modProcParam_OptionalParameters _
    (strFirstName As String, _
    strSurname As String, _
    Optional boolAddSpace As Boolean = False, _
    Optional boolCapitalLetters As Boolean = False) As String

    Dim strResult As String
    If boolAddSpace Then
        strResult = Trim(strFirstName & " " & strSurname)
    Else
        strResult = Trim(strFirstName & strSurname)
    End If
    If boolCapitalLetters Then
        strResult = UCase(strResult)
    End If
    modProcParam_OptionalParameters = strResult
End Function
Sub modProcParam_TestOptional()
    Debug.Print modProcParam_OptionalParameters _
        ("Andrew", "Couch", True)
    Debug.Print modProcParam_OptionalParameters _
        (strSurname:="Couch", _
         strFirstName:="Andrew", boolAddSpace:=True)
    Debug.Print modProcParam_OptionalParameters _
        ("Andrew", "Couch", , True)
End Sub
```

When you are not using named parameters, insert a space for any optional parameters that you are not going to provide. You also omit any optional parameters declared at the end of the procedure call.

For example, you are *not* able to write the following:

```
Debug.Print modProcParam_OptionalParameters("Andrew", "Couch", ,)
```

Instead, you write this without any of the optional parameters being specified, as follows:

```
Debug.Print modProcParam_OptionalParameters("Andrew", "Couch")
```

But if you only want to specify the last optional parameter, you write:

```
Debug.Print modProcParam_OptionalParameters("Andrew", "Couch", , True)
```

INSIDE OUT   Specifying default values for optional parameters

If you intend to copy your VBA code into VB.NET, you will find that VB.NET demands that you provide a default value for any optional parameter. VBA, conversely, does not demand that you give optional parameters a default value. Therefore, you might find it useful to follow the convention of placing all optional parameters at the end of your list of parameters and giving every optional parameter a default value.

The *ParamArray* Qualifier

ParamArray is a qualifier that can be applied to the last parameter defined in the list of parameters for a procedure. This indicates that what follows will be a list of variant values of undefined length (this is why it needs to be defined after any fixed parameters):

```
Sub modProcParam_ParamArray(ParamArray varParameterArray())
    ' ParamArray must be the last defined parameter
    Dim lngCount As Long
    For lngCount = 0 To UBound(varParameterArray)
        Debug.Print lngCount, varParameterArray(lngCount) _
                ; VarType(varParameterArray(lngCount))
    Next
End Sub

Sub modProcParam_ParamArray_Test()
    modProcParam_ParamArray Date, 100, "A Text String"
End Sub
```

If you are planning to pass an array as one of these parameters, you need to be quite careful about the syntax; the array will be passed as a single variant parameter array, as shown in the following:

```
Sub modProcParam_ParamArray2(ParamArray varParameterArray())
    ' ParamArray must be the last defined parameter
    ' Because we are passing an array we have an array
    Dim lngCount As Long
    For lngCount = 0 To UBound(varParameterArray)
        Debug.Print lngCount, varParameterArray(lngCount) _
                ; VarType(varParameterArray(lngCount))
    Next
End Sub

Sub modProcParam_ParamArray_Test2()
    modProcParam_ParamArray2 Date, 100, "A text string"
End Sub
```

Chapter 2

Organizing Code in Modules and Class Modules

Program code can be placed in any of the three different kinds of modules, and then linked together, as shown in Figure 2-20.

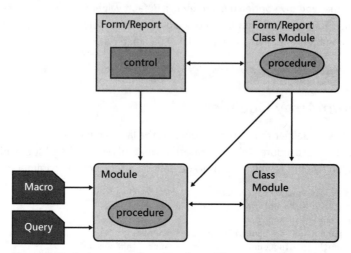

Figure 2-20 Code can be placed in three different types of modules.

The following describes the type of code that is typically contained by each of the modules:

- **Form/Report Class Module** Each Form/Report can have an optional code module that contains code specific to that Form/Report.

- **Module** Code that is either not specific to a form or that will be used in many parts of an application can be placed in a module.

- **Class Module** Object-oriented code (this is discussed later).

Code can be activated from several parts of Access.

- **Macros** The *RunCode* macro command can call a *Public* VBA function held in a module. An example would be during startup, where an *AutoExec* macro calls startup code.

- **Queries** An expression can call a *Public* VBA function.

- **Form/Reports** Controls and events on forms and reports can directly link to *Public* VBA procedures.

- A Form/Report class module can call Public code in either a module, class module, or in another Form/Report module (if the other Form/Report is open).

> **Note**
>
> Normally, forms do not call code on other forms. However, there are certain circumstances when a form opens another form for which it is desirable to call code on the target form. To see an example of this, read Chapter 5, "Understanding the Data Access Object Model."

Control Statements and Program Flow

The examples in this section illustrate the use of conditional statements in your program code to control the program flow.

IF... Then... Else... Statements

The simplest form of an *IF* statement involves testing a condition and then executing a single action based on the result of that test, as illustrated here:

```
Sub modIF_IF_Simple(Rating As Long)
    If Rating = 1 Then Debug.Print "Approved, first class company to deal with"
    If Rating = 2 Then Debug.Print "Approved, good company to deal with"
End Sub
```

When an *IF* statement requires more than one resulting action, you use the *End If* statement to indicate the end of a set of actions. You are at liberty to use *End If* even when you have only one action:

```
Function modIF_IF(Rating As Long) As String
    ' Use of IF statement
    ' Return appropriate text for a rating
    If Rating = 1 Then
        modIF_IF = "Approved, first class company to deal with"
        Exit Function
    End If
    If Rating = 2 Then
        modIF_IF = "Approved,good company to deal with"
        Exit Function
    End If
    If Rating = 3 Then
        modIF_IF = "Approval required before signing contract"
        Exit Function
    End If
    modIF_IF = "Company rating is not specified"
End Function
```

The advantage of the code above is that it is very easy to read; the disadvantage is that it does not communicate how the different branches are related to each other.

A more structured approach is to nest the logical path by using the *Else* statement, as shown in the following:

```
Function modIF_IF1(Rating As Long) As String
    ' Use of IF statement
    ' Return appropriate text for a rating
    If Rating = 1 Then
        modIF_IF1 = "Approved, first class company to deal with"
    Else
        If Rating = 2 Then
            modIF_IF1 = "Approved,good company to deal with"
        Else
            If Rating = 3 Then
                modIF_IF1 = "Approval required before signing contract"
            Else
                modIF_IF1 = "Company rating is not specified"
            End If
        End If
    End If
End Function
```

The preceding code uses a simple *Else* keyword to show the reader where the logic flows when the condition is not *True*. An alternative to *Else* is the *ElseIf* statement, which cascades the logic with fewer statements; the final *Else* statement is reached only if all preceding tests fail:

```
Function modIF_IF2(Rating As Long) As String
    ' Use of IF statement nested
    ' Return appropriate text for a rating
    If Rating = 1 Then
        modIF_IF2 = "Approved, first class company to deal with"
    ElseIf Rating = 2 Then
        modIF_IF2 = "Approved,good company to deal with"
    ElseIf Rating = 3 Then
        modIF_IF2 = "Approval required before signing contract"
    Else
        modIF_IF2 = "Company rating is not specified"
    End If
End Function
```

IIF Statements

The last example of the *IF* structure involves using the *IIF* statement, which can be nested. You might have seen this technique used in calculations on queries:

```
Function modIF_IIF(Rating As Long) As String
    ' Use of IIF statement
    ' Return appropriate text for a rating
    modIF_IIF = _
        IIf(Rating = 1, "Approved, first class company to deal with", _
        IIf(Rating = 2, "Approved,good company to deal with", _
```

```
IIf(Rating = 3, "Approval required before signing contract", _
                "Company rating is not specified")))

End Function
```

INSIDE OUT   Evaluating all parts in an *IIF* statement

Using an *IIF* statement in VBA code produces an interesting side effect: all parts of the *IIF* statement are evaluated during execution. Thus, the code that follows will generate a divide by zero error, even when the expression should not appear to need the result:

```
Sub modIF_IIF_Gotcha()
    ' All parts of the IIF get evaluated, so this
    ' code will generate a divide by zero error
    Dim lngTotal As Long
    Dim lngDivisor As Long
    Dim dblResult As Double

    lngTotal = 10
    lngDivisor = 0
    dblResult = IIf(lngDivisor = 0, 0, lngTotal / lngDivisor)
    Debug.Print dblResult
End Sub
```

You might be surprised to learn that if you had used this on a Query grid, you would not have the same problem (if converting an existing *IIF* expression in the Query grid to use a custom VBA function, care needs to be taken with this statement, a solution using an *IF* statement would not have this problem).

Choose Statements

As the number of ways that your code can branch increases, *IF* structures begin to become more difficult to read, so you might choose other equivalent structures. The *Choose* structure is an alternative to the *IIF* for use directly in queries, and is demonstrated in the following code example:

```
Function modIF_Choose(Rating As Long) As String
    ' Use of Choose statement
    ' Return appropriate text for a rating
    modIF_Choose = _
        Nz(Choose(Rating, "Approved, first class company to deal with", _
                          "Approved,good company to deal with", _
                          "Approval required before signing contract"))
    ' Choose returns null if index not in list
```

```
        If modIF_Choose = "" Then
            modIF_Choose = "Company rating is not specified"
        End If
End Function
```

Select Case Statements

The *Select Case* structure is an excellent choice when you have a larger number of choices. It is always a good idea to add a *Case Else* statement at the end of this structure to accomodate the possibility that none of the conditions hold; otherwise, your code will generate an error:

```
Function modIF_Select(Rating As Long) As String
    ' Use of SELECT CASE statements
    ' Return appropriate text for a rating
    Select Case Rating
        Case 1: modIF_Select = "Approved, first class company to deal with"
        Case 2: modIF_Select = "Approved,good company to deal with"
        Case 3: modIF_Select = "Approval required before signing contract"
        Case Else: modIF_Select = "Company rating is not specified"
    End Select
End Function

Function modIF_Select2(Rating As Long) As String
    ' Use of SELECT CASE statements
    ' Return appropriate text for a rating
    Select Case Rating
        Case 1: modIF_Select2 = "Approved, first class company to deal with"
        Case 2: modIF_Select2 = "Approved,good company to deal with"
        Case 3: modIF_Select2 = "Approval required before signing contract"
        Case Is > 3: modIF_Select2 = "Company rating is not specified"
    End Select
End Function
```

TypeOf Statements

The last example of conditional logic shows you how to use the *TypeOf* keyword, which can be used with controls on a form to take different actions, based upon the type of the control. This can be important because the different controls can have some different properties:

```
Sub modIf_TypeOf()
    ' This is a very special variation on the IF statement
    ' used to determine the type of a control on a form
    Dim ctrl As Control
    ' open the form
    DoCmd.OpenForm "frmCustomers"
    ' set a variable to point at a control on the form
    Set ctrl = Forms!frmCustomers.Controls!Company
```

```
    If TypeOf ctrl Is TextBox Then Debug.Print "Textbox"
    If TypeOf ctrl Is ListBox Then Debug.Print "ListBox"
    If TypeOf ctrl Is CommandButton Then Debug.Print "CommandButton"

    DoCmd.SelectObject acForm, "frmCustomers"
    DoCmd.Close
End Sub
```

For and *For Each* Loops

The second part of program control flow involves repeating an operation multiple times. The *modLoop* module contains examples of the code that you use to do this. These examples demonstrate working with a *Recordset* object. The *Recordset* allows you to scan through a set of records and perform an operation. In the example that follows, you use the *RecordCount* property to determine how many times you need to repeat the operation.

> **Note**
> Using *Recordset*s and the *RecordCount* property are explained in detail in Chapter 5.

```
Sub mod_Loop_FOR()
    Const lngMaxRecords = 100
    Dim lngCount As Long
    Dim rc As Long
    Dim db As Database
    Dim rst As Recordset
    Set db = CurrentDb
    Set rst = db.OpenRecordset("SELECT * FROM Customers", dbOpenDynaset)
    If Not rst.EOF Then
        ' process the data
        ' make sure we know how many records we have
        rst.MoveLast
        rc = rst.RecordCount
        rst.MoveFirst
        For lngCount = 1 To rc
            If Not IsNull(rst!Rating) Then
                Debug.Print rst!Company & " has a rating " & rst!Rating
            End If
            If lngCount > lngMaxRecords Then
                Exit For
            End If
            rst.MoveNext
        Next
    End If
    rst.Close
    Set rst = Nothing
    db.Close
    Set db = Nothing
End Sub
```

The preceding code also includes a test to limit the number of times that you move around the loop by using an *Exit For* statement.

When you are repeating an operation for each object in a collection, you can use a *For Each* Loop, as shown in the following:

```
Sub modLoop_ForEach()
    ' for each looping is used with collections of objects
    Dim ref As Access.Reference
    For Each ref In Access.References
        Debug.Print ref.Name, ref.FullPath, ref.IsBroken
    Next
End Sub
```

Do While and *Do Until* Loops

Often, you don't know exactly how many times you need to perform an operation, but you do know conditions under which you want to perform the processing. In this situation, you can use a *Do While* loop, as presented in the following example:

```
Sub mod_Loop_DO()
    ' example using a DO loop
    Dim db As Database
    Dim rst As Recordset
    Set db = CurrentDb
    Set rst = db.OpenRecordset("SELECT * FROM Customers", dbOpenDynaset)

    Do While Not rst.EOF
        ' process the data
        If Not IsNull(rst!Rating) Then
            Debug.Print rst!Company & " has a rating " & rst!Rating
    '        If rst!Rating = 1 Then Exit Do
        End If
        rst.MoveNext
    Loop

    rst.Close
    Set rst = Nothing
    db.Close
    Set db = Nothing
End Sub
```

The *Do While* loop can either test for the exit condition at the top of the loop, or as shown in the following code, at the bottom of the loop:

```
Sub mod_Loop_DOa()
    ' example using a DO loop
    Dim db As Database
    Dim rst As Recordset
    Set db = CurrentDb
```

```
Set rst = db.OpenRecordset("SELECT * FROM Customers " & _
    "WHERE ID IS NULL", dbOpenDynaset)

' This is a dangerous processing loop in this case
' because if the recordset had no records it would fail
' because a loop like this always executes at least once
Do
    ' process the data
    If Not IsNull(rst!Rating) Then
        Debug.Print rst!Company & " has a rating " & rst!Rating
'           If rst!Rating = 1 Then Exit Do
    End If
    rst.MoveNext
Loop While Not rst.EOF

rst.Close
Set rst = Nothing
db.Close
Set db = Nothing
End Sub
```

When testing at the bottom of a loop, the loop always executes once. In the preceding example, we added *WHERE ID IS NULL* to the SQL being used to open the *Recordset* to better illustrate a potential problem with always executing the loop at least once: in a situation in which there is no data to process, an error is generated, as shown in Figure 2-21.

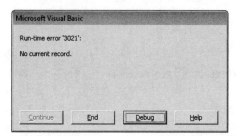

Figure 2-21 An error message appears because the code attempts to refer to data in a *Recordset* when the *Recordset* is empty.

You can also use the keyword *Until*, which means to continue the loop until a specific condition holds and then stop the loop. The preceding example included the following loop condition:

```
Do While NOT rst.EOF
```

You could equally use the following:

```
Do Until rst.EOF
```

The ability to prefix the test with the keyword *NOT* means that these statements are interchangeable.

It is also possible to use a *While … Wend* structure (in the sample *mod_Loop_While*) instead of a *Do* loop, as shown here:

```
While Not rst.EOF
    ' process the data
    If Not IsNull(rst!Rating) Then
        Debug.Print rst!Company & " has a rating " & rst!Rating
' below we see an example of the syntax for existing a loop
'        If rst!Rating = 1 Then Exit Do
    End If
    rst.MoveNext
Wend
```

Exit Statements

Both the *For* loop and the *Do While* Loop have corresponding *Exit* statements (*Exit For* and *Exit Do*) that you use to discontinue the loop. These statements are useful for preventing an infinite loop (a loop that never ends). The following code shows an example of the *Exit Do* statement:

```
Sub mod_Loop_DO2()
    ' example using a DO loop protecting against
    ' an infinite loop
    Const lngMaxCount = 100
    Dim db As Database
    Dim rst As Recordset
    Set db = CurrentDb
    Set rst = db.OpenRecordset("SELECT * FROM Customers", dbOpenDynaset)
    Dim lngCount As Long
    lngCount = 0
    Do Until rst.EOF
        ' process the data
        If Not IsNull(rst!Rating) Then
            Debug.Print rst!Company & " has a rating " & rst!Rating
'            If rst!Rating = 1 Then Exit Do
        End If
        lngCount = lngCount + 1
        If lngCount > lngMaxCount Then
            MsgBox "infinite loop detected"
            Exit Do
        End If
'        rst.MoveNext
    Loop
    rst.Close
    Set rst = Nothing
    db.Close
    Set db = Nothing
End Sub
```

In the preceding example, the *rst.MoveNext* statement is commented out; this means that loop will never reach the end of file *EOF*. By adding a counter and setting a maximum number of times the loop can be executed, you can prevent an infinite loop.

For functions, you can use the *Exit Function* statement to exit a procedure without executing any remaining code; for subroutines, use the *Exit Sub* statement.

The *With* Statement

The *With ... End With* statement helps to improve the readability of your code. Within the statement, you can use the . (period) or ! (exclamation) characters to refer to the object's properties and methods without fully stating the object's name. The following example shows how to manipulate a *Recordset* object by using the *With* statement:

```
Sub modWith_RecordsetExample()
    Dim db As Database
    Dim rst As Recordset
    Set db = CurrentDb
    Set rst = db.OpenRecordset("Customers", dbOpenDynaset)

    rst.MoveLast
    Debug.Print rst.RecordCount
    rst.MoveFirst
    Do While Not rst.EOF
        Debug.Print rst!Company
        rst.MoveNext
    Loop

    ' using a with statement
    With rst
        .MoveLast
        Debug.Print .RecordCount
        .MoveFirst
        Do While Not .EOF
            Debug.Print !Company
            .MoveNext
        Loop
    End With

    rst.Close
    Set rst = Nothing
    db.Close
    Set db = Nothing
End Sub
```

GoTo and *GoSub*

You can use the *GoTo* and *GoSub* statements to set an unconditional branch to another part of your code, as demonstrated here:

```
Sub modGoTo_GoTo(strName As String)
    If Len(strName) = 0 Then
        ' Executing a simple GoTo
        GoTo ExitPointLabel
    End If
    If Len(strName) > 255 Then
        ' Executing a simple GoTo
        GoTo ExitPointLabel
    End If
Exit Sub
ExitPointLabel:
    MsgBox "String value not acceptable"
End Sub
```

VBA also supports *On ... GoSub* or *On ... GoTo* keywords, which were needed in early versions of the BASIC programming language; these statements are now rarely used, with the exception of *On ... GoTo* for error handling purposes.

Line Continuation

Long lines of VBA code can be difficult to read. The "_" (underbar) character is the line continuation character that allows you to break an unwieldy line of code into several shorter lines to make it easier to read. In the following example, we have placed each parameter of the function on a separate line, using the line continuation character to make the procedure easier to read.

```
Function modProcParam_OptionalParameters _
    (strFirstName As String, _
    strSurname As String, _
    Optional boolAddSpace As Boolean = False, _
    Optional boolCapitalLetters As Boolean = False) As String
End Function
```

Splitting SQL Over Multiple Lines

This second example shows how to format a block of SQL that has been pasted into the VBA code. Note the "&" (ampersand) and "_" (underbar) characters are used together to split the SQL over several lines:

```
Sub modstr_LineContinuation()
    ' example showing line continuation character
    ' used with a SQL string
    Dim strSQL As String
    strSQL = "SELECT Customers.Company, " & _
            "Customers.[Last Name], " & _
            "Customers.[First Name] " & _
            "FROM Customers " & _
            "WHERE (((Customers.[Job Title])='owner'))"
End Sub
```

In the preceding example, the tab character aligns each line of code to the same start-ing point (if you try to do this on the first line, Access will autocorrect your indentation, as shown in the code).

Summary

In this chapter, you were introduced to the VBA programming language structure. The fol-lowing points summarize key areas with which you should now be familiar:

- The importance of forcing all variables to be declared before use, and how the refer-ences manage the libraries that are used when writing program code.

- The different types of variables and constants that can be used in your code and the concepts of scope and lifetime of variables.

- How functions and subroutines are defined and organized into modules, and how scope and lifetime also apply to these procedures.

- The language statements for controlling the flow of program logic.

Understanding the VBA Language Features

Using Built-In Functions 90

Domain Functions 95

SQL and Embedded Quotes 98

Objects and Collections. 103

Creating Maintainable Code. 108

VBA and Macros 114

Error Handling 115

I n Chapter 2, "Understanding the VBA Language Structure," we focused on the core Microsoft VBA language structures that deal with constants, variables, procedures, and controlling the flow of program logic. In this chapter, you look at specific language features, including the use of built-in functions and working with SQL in code.

You will also see how to build upon our structural understanding of the VBA language by incorporating error handling and planning to develop code to improve the maintainability of your applications.

After reading this chapter, you will:

- Be able to use the built-in functions to enhance your application.

- Understand the differences between working with ordinary variables and object variables.

- Understand the benefits of using appropriate naming conventions to make your application development easier to maintain.

- Be able to write effective error handling routines.

Note

As you read through this chapter, we encourage you to also use the companion content sample database, VBAFeaturesExamples.accdb, which can be downloaded from the book's catalog page.

Using Built-In Functions

VBA has more than 120 built-in functions. You will look at some of the more popular of these, which we have split into logical groups.

Date and Time Functions

The family of date and time functions allow you to retrieve values for dates and times, extract the values, and add or subtract values (see the *modDates* module for examples), as demonstrated in the following code, with the results of executing these statements shown in Figure 3-1:

```
Sub modDates_Examples()
    Debug.Print "Date function : " & Date
    Debug.Print "Time function : " & Time
    Debug.Print "Now function : " & Now

    Debug.Print "DateAdd function : " & DateAdd("d", 5, Now)
    Debug.Print "DateDiff function : " & DateDiff("d", Now _
                        , DateAdd("d", 5, Now))
    Debug.Print "DatePart function : " & DatePart("w", Date)
    Debug.Print "DateSerial function : " & DateSerial(2015, 6, 3)
    Debug.Print "DateValue function : " & DateValue("1 january 2015")

    Debug.Print "Weekday function : " & Weekday(Date)
    Debug.Print "WeekdayName function : " & WeekdayName(5)

    Debug.Print "Day function : " & Day(Date)
    Debug.Print "Month function : " & Month(Date)
    Debug.Print "MonthName function : " & MonthName(2)
    Debug.Print "Year function : " & Year(Date)

    Debug.Print "Hour function : " & Hour(Now)
    Debug.Print "Minute function : " & Minute(Now)
    Debug.Print "Second function : " & Second(Now)
End Sub
```

```
Immediate
Date function : 1/26/2011
Time function : 9:26:21 AM
Now function : 1/26/2011 9:26:21 AM
DateAdd function : 1/31/2011 9:26:21 AM
DateDiff function : 5
DatePart function : 4
DateSerial function : 6/3/2015
DateValue function : 1/1/2015
Weekday function : 4
WeekdayName function : Thursday
Day function : 26
Month function : 1
MonthName function : February
Year function : 2011
Hour function : 9
Minute function : 26
Second function : 21
```

Figure 3-1 Examples of the various date and time functions.

Time values also have a default date value; the 30th December, 1899 is used to indicate that time-only information is being stored in a *Date* variable or database field type, which is shown in Figure 3-2. When viewing data in tables and queries, Microsoft Access hides this value and only shows the time component. There is no Time data type.

```
Immediate
?format(#15:30#,"hh:mm:ss dd mmmm yyyy")
15:30:00 30 December 1899
```

Figure 3-2 Time-only data has the default date 30 December 1899 assigned.

INSIDE OUT Default dates representing time-only data and moving data between database systems

Care must be taken when moving time-only data from Access into other data storage systems. For example, the earliest date in Microsoft SharePoint is 1 January 1900, which means that before moving the time data from Access to SharePoint, you need to change the date, 30 December 1899, to 1 January 1900 (you also need to check that you have no date data before this date). For SQL Server, the earliest date that can be held in a *DateTime* data type is 1 January 1753, so when entering time-only data, SQL Server will take 1 January 1900 to represent time-only data.

You can perform direct arithmetic operations on date data, as illustrated in Figure 3-3.

Chapter 3

```
Immediate
?date
1/26/2011
?date+30
2/25/2011
?DateAdd("d",30,date)
2/25/2011
?date-1
1/25/2011
?DateAdd("d",-1,date)
1/25/2011
```

Figure 3-3 VBA supports direct date arithmetic and also provides functions for these operations.

Although VBA understands that when you add or subtract one from a date, you are adding or subtracting one day, you might prefer to use built-in functions, such as *DateAdd*, *Date-Diff*, and *DateSerial* for directly manipulating dates. For example, the first parameter of the *DateAdd* function is the interval, which can take a value in seconds, hours, quarters, days, and other increments, and then add the value to a date.

String Functions

VBA supports a rich variety of string functions. The simplest string operation is adding, or concatenating, strings together, as demonstrated in the following, with the results shown in Figure 3-4:

```
Sub modStr_ConcatenateStrings()
    Dim varFirstName As Variant
    Dim varSurname As Variant
    ' above represent field values from a table
    varFirstName = "Andrew"
    varSurname = Null

    ' note using + can be dangerous as "a string" + null = null
    Debug.Print "Using the &", varFirstName & varSurname
    Debug.Print "Using a plus", varFirstName + varSurname

    Debug.Print "Safer Checking ", Trim(Nz(varFirstName) & _
                " " & Nz(varSurname))
End Sub
```

```
Immediate
modStr_ConcatenateStrings
Using the &    Andrew
Using a plus   Null
Safer Checking             Andrew
```

Figure 3-4 The results of string concatenation.

Note that when you concatenate strings, you are more likely to use the "&" (ampersand) character rather than the "+" (plus) character because this prevents *NULL* values from propagating through string expressions, making the overall result *NULL* (unless, of course, you want to have *NULLs* propagate through the calculation; adding *NULL* to a string sets the result to NULL and also requires the use of a variant variable to hold the result).

The *Nz* function will convert *NULL* values to a safe value (in this case an empty string), and this is often combined with the *Trim* function to remove any leading or trailing spaces.

The following is a summary of important string functions:

- **Left**, **Right**, **Mid**   String extraction.

- **Len**   Sets the length of a string.

- **Trim**, **LTrim**, and **RTrim**   Removes spaces.

- **Space** and **String**   Adds space characters (Space) or a number of repeating characters (String).

- **Upper**, **Lower**, and **StrConv** (supports proper case)   Changes case.

- **InStr**, **InStrReverse**   Searches for a string inside another string.

- **Replace**   Replaces a substring with another string.

- **Split**   Breaks a string into words.

- **Join**   Reassembles words that were broken up by *Split* back into strings.

- **ASC** and **Chr**   Get the ASCII code for a character (ASC), or make the character from the ASCII code (Chr).

- **Format**   Formats a string.

- **StrComp**   Compares strings.

- **vbCR**, **vbCRLF**, **vbLF**, **vbTab**   Constants for formatting.

INSIDE OUT   Functions that return variant or string data

You might notice that many of the string functions (and some other VBA functions such as the *Format* function) have two forms; for example, *UCase* and *UCase$*. This is to large extent historical (beginning on page 113, we discuss the use of a $ symbol at the end of a variable name to indicate the data type); the *UCase* function has an advantage over the *UCase$* function in that it can return *NULL* values. The current Help system does not mention the older forms such as *UCase$* (but if you search in the object browser you will find these functions). The result from using *UCase$* with *NULL* is shown in Figure 3-5.

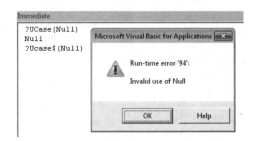

Figure 3-5 An error message appears because the older *UCase$* function cannot handle *NULL* values.

The *Format* Function

You use the *Format* function to display numeric, date/time, and string data, by using built-in and custom formatting (there is an extensive description of this function in the Help system). For numeric data, the *Format* function supports separate formatting options when values are positive, negative, zero, or null; for formatting dates there are options for the *FirstDayOfWeek* and *FirstWeekOfYear*.

The *ASC* Function

The *ASC* function returns an integer representing a character code. In the following example, the ASC function removes all characters in a string, except letters and digits:

```
Function modStr_ProcessCharacters()
    ' removing characters from a string
    Dim strInput As String
    Dim strOutput As String
    Dim lngStrLength As Long
    Dim lngCount As Long
    Dim strChar As String
    Dim lngChar As Long
    strInput = "An 'example' of #(a string."
    lngStrLength = Len(strInput)
    strOutput = ""
    For lngCount = 1 To lngStrLength
        strChar = Mid(strInput, lngCount, 1)
        lngChar = Asc(strChar)
        ' space is 32
        ' 0 to 9 is character codes 48 to 57
        ' A to Z is character codes 65 to 90
        ' a to z is character codes 97 to 122
```

```
        If (lngChar = 32) _
          Or (lngChar >= 48 And lngChar <= 57) _
          Or (lngChar >= 65 And lngChar <= 90) _
          Or (lngChar >= 97 And lngChar <= 122) Then
            strOutput = strOutput & strChar
        End If
    Next
    Debug.Print strOutput
End Function
```

The *Mid* Function

The *Mid* string function is one of the string extractors (*Mid, Left, Right*). It has a unique property that is not shared by the *Left* and *Right* string functions; you can use the *Mid* string function to directly replace values inside a string, as demonstrated in the following:

```
Function modStr_Mid()
    ' Example showing the use of the Mid function
    ' to change parts of a string
    Dim strInput As String
    strInput = "vba PROGRAMMING language"

    Mid(strInput, 1, 3) = UCase(Mid(strInput, 1, 3))
    Debug.Print strInput
    Mid(strInput, 6, 12) = LCase(Mid(strInput, 6, 12))
    Debug.Print strInput
    Mid(strInput, 17, 8) = "xxxxxxxx"
    Debug.Print strInput
    ' Changes the string to the following
    ' VBA Programming xxxxxxxx
End Function
```

Domain Functions

Domain functions allow you to quickly get information without expending a lot of effort on writing program code, but be warned: if you abuse these functions, it can result in a performance hit. The following code presents examples of the *DLOOKUP* and *DCOUNT* functions, with the result shown in Figure 3-6:

```
Sub modDom_Basic()
    ' Find the name of company with ID =1
    Debug.Print DLookup("Company", "Customers", "[ID] = 1")

    ' How many companies contain the letter A in their name
    Debug.Print DCount("*", "Customers", "[Company] like '*A*'")
    ' The following also works but is more complex as it uses a double quote
    ' as the string delimiter
    Debug.Print DCount("*", "Customers", "[Company] like ""*A*""")
End Sub
```

```
Immediate
modDom_Basic
Company
  29
```

Figure 3-6 A procedure calling a Domain function.

Each domain function consists of three parts:

- **Expr**   What you want back

- **Domain**   Which table or query to look in

- **Criteria**   What criteria to use to locate the record

Domain functions are not restricted to use in code; they can also be used to display data on a control on a form, as shown in Figure 3-7, or used in part of an expression in a query, as shown in Figure 3-8.

Figure 3-7 Using a Domain function on an unbound control on a form.

Exercise care when using Domain functions to calculate a column on the Query grid or in a continuous form because the function will be called repeatedly as each record is displayed, which can lead to performance issues, as demonstrated in Figure 3-8.

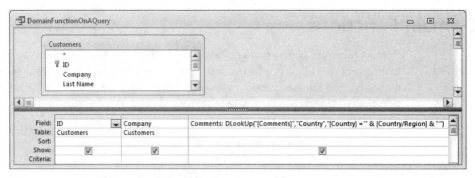

Figure 3-8 An inefficient use of a Domain function on a query.

Constructing *Where* Clauses

Specifying the criteria for a domain function involves observing a set of rules. These rules apply equally to any *Where* clause or SQL that you generate in program code, as described in the following list:

- All date values need to be enclosed within # symbols and must be formatted to the date format used in the United States (mm/dd/yyyy)—even for international users of VBA.

- All strings need to be enclosed within single quotation marks (you can use double quotes, but double quotes need to be doubled up embedding in strings).

- Numbers do not need to be enclosed within any extra characters.

The following code presents examples of working with dates (see the *modDom_Dcount* module for full details in this example):

```
' example showing syntax when searching on a date value
' note US date format is required in the where clause
Dim dtStartDate As Date
Dim dtEndDate As Date
dtStartDate = "1 January 2010"
dtEndDate = "20 january 2010"

' using an explicit date
intRc = DCount("*", "[Customers]", _
        "[LastContactedDate] BETWEEN #1/1/2010# AND #1/20/2010#")

' using variables to load the dates
intRc = DCount("*", "[Customers]", _
            "[LastContactedDate] BETWEEN #" & _
             Format(dtStartDate, "mm/dd/yyyy") & "#" & _
            " AND #" & Format(dtEndDate, "mm/dd/yyyy") & "#")

' building a where clause for the citeria

strWhere = "[LastContactedDate] BETWEEN #" & _
            Format(dtStartDate, "mm/dd/yyyy") & "#" & _
            " AND #" & Format(dtEndDate, "mm/dd/yyyy") & "#"

intRc = DCount("*", "[Customers]", strWhere)
```

The use of the "*" characters in the *DCount("*")* operates like the SQL aggregate, *Count("*")*. Use "*" to count by the primary key. If you use *Count("[ID]")* rather than "*" (and *[ID]* was the primary key), it would give the same answer. If you choose another field such as *[E-mail Address]*, it would not necessarily give the same answer, because a *Count* or *DCount* ignores *NULL* values.

The following code presents examples of using a string in the criteria, surrounded by single quotation marks:

```
intRc = DCount("*", "[Customers]", _
          "[Company] like '* A*'")


' using a variable
intRc = DCount("*", "[Customers]", _
          "[Company] like '*" & strCompany & "*'")


' using a where clause
strWhere = "[Company] like '*" & strCompany & "*'"
intRc = DCount("*", "[Customers]", strWhere)
```

When searching on a numeric, you do not need to add any delimiters:

```
' example showing syntax when searching on a numeric value
Dim intRating As Long
intRating = 1
    intRc = DCount("*", "[Customers]", _
          "[Rating] = 1")
' using a variable
intRc = DCount("*", "[Customers]", _
          "[Rating] = " & intRating)


strWhere = "[Rating = " & intRating
```

The preceding examples introduced the *DCount* and *DLookup* functions. You have also seen the *DMin, DMax, DAvg, DSum, DFirst, DLast, DStDev, DStDevP, DVar*, and *DVarP* functions.

SQL and Embedded Quotes

Embedded single quotes occur in proper names, such as O'Reilly, and in other parts of text, and it is only once you start to manipulate SQL in code that these names prove to be a serious problem and can cause code to fail.

The problem is rooted in the *WHERE* clause, and how this clause is constructed to handle a text string comparison in which you need to have embedded single quotes surrounding the text value. When you have an additional embedded quote in the criteria, the quotation marks then become unbalanced (for every open quote, there should be a close quote).

There are two ways to solve this problem. Either you need to replace a single embedded quote with two embedded quotes, or you need to use double quotes as delimiters, as shown in the following code (the results are presented in Figure 3-9):

```
Sub modQuotes_Embedded()
    ' this simulates what happens when a user
    ' types the value into a control
```

```
     Dim strMatch As String
     Dim strCriteria As String
     Dim lngID As Long

     strMatch = "O'Reilly"
     strCriteria = "[Last Name] = '" & strMatch & "'"
     Debug.Print strCriteria
     On Error Resume Next ' skip the error that the next line generates
     lngID = Nz(DLookup("[ID]", "Customers", strCriteria))
     If Err <> 0 Then
         Debug.Print Err.Description
     End If
     Debug.Print lngID

     strMatch = "O'Reilly"
     ' replace an embedded single quote with two single quotes
     strMatch = Replace(strMatch, "'", "''")
     strCriteria = "[Last Name] = '" & strMatch & "'"
     Debug.Print strCriteria
     lngID = Nz(DLookup("[ID]", "Customers", strCriteria))
     Debug.Print lngID

     ' use double quotes as delimiters
     strMatch = "O'Reilly"
     strCriteria = "[Last Name] = """ & strMatch & """"
     Debug.Print strCriteria
     lngID = Nz(DLookup("[ID]", "Customers", strCriteria))
     Debug.Print lngID
End Sub
```

```
Immediate
modQuotes_Embedded
[Last Name] = 'O'Reilly'
Syntax error (missing operator) in query expression '[Last Name] = 'O'Reilly''.
 0
[Last Name] = 'O''Reilly'
 4
[Last Name] = "O'Reilly"
 4
```

Figure 3-9 Searching for embedded quotes in strings.

In the preceding example, the first attempt to handle the embedded quote causes the program to fail. (For the purposes of demonstration, we have added an *On Error Resume Next*, to prevent this from stopping the code execution) The second part of the code, which uses a replace function to replace a single quote with two single quotes, is a solution to this problem.

The third solution—using outer double quotes—works, but it will fail if it encounters text containing an embedded double quote. In this case, you need to replace an embedded double quote with two double quotes.

Therefore, the rule is that if you delimit with single quotes, double up any embedded single quotes, and if you delimit with double quotes, then double up any embedded double quotes.

INSIDE OUT
DFirst and DLast functions can give inconsistent results after compacting a database

DFirst and *DLast* can in certain circumstances have an unusual side effect; after you compact and repair a database, you can get a different answer when using these functions (*DMin* and *DMax* do not have this problem). Figure 3-10 shows a new date value entered in the table.

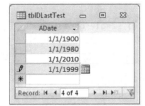

Figure 3-10 Entering a new date value record to the end of the table.

The table in Figure 3-10 defines the *ADate* field as the primary key. After typing in a new record *DLast*, it will give the last entered record. Figure 3-11 shows the value returned in the Immediate window.

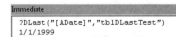

Figure 3-11 *DLast* returning the last record.

If you close and re-open the table, you see the records re-ordered, as shown shown in Figure 3-12, but the value given by *DLast* is unchanged (because it represents the last record added).

Figure 3-12 Records are now re-ordered as the date field is part of the primary key.

However, after we compact and repair the database, the value for *DLast* will then be changed (because a side effect of compaction is to re-order the physical rows by primary key), the result of which is shown in Figure 3-13, where *DLast* now returns a different value.

```
Immediate
?DLast("[ADate]","tblDLastTest")
1/1/2010
```

Figure 3-13 Following compaction, the value that *DLast* returns will now be different.

A database function that can return different results depending on whether the database has been compacted could cause problems in your program code.

Using VBA Functions in Queries

One advantage that functions have over subroutines is that they can be incorporated directly into the Query grid. This means that you can directly call both custom and built-in functions from the Query grid in expressions to create columns, and in *Where* clauses to filter data.

As demonstrated in the code example that follows, when using a function in an expression on the Query grid, it will be called for every record returned in the grid; as long as the function is not too complicated, acceptable performance should be achieved:

```
Function modStr_ConcatenateName(varFirstName As Variant, _
                                varLastName As Variant) As String
' Function used on queries to add together first and last names
    modStr_ConcatenateName = Trim(Nz(varFirstName, "") & _
                                " " & Nz(varLastName, ""))
End Function
```

When designing this function, we chose to define the parameters to be of a *Variant* data type to allow for the possibility of null values in the fields (this is often a very important point to consider). The function is shown in Figure 3-14, used as an expression on the Query grid. Suitable VBA functions can also be used in criteria on the grid.

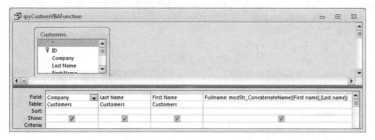

Figure 3-14 Adding a call to a custom VBA function on the Query grid.

Chapter 3

Another circumstance for which this approach can be effective is when you have very complex expressions using nested *IIF* functions; if the logic of the nested *IIF* functions is difficult to follow, the functions can be simplified by using VBA conditional logic.

The *Eval* Function

The *Eval* function allows you to build VBA expressions dynamically at runtime and then execute the expression, which can return a string or numeric (*Eval* can also return a date data type):

```
Sub modEval_Arithmetic()
    Dim strExpression As String
    strExpression = "20 / 1.2"
    Debug.Print "Numeric calculation gives :" & Eval(strExpression)

    strExpression = "Format(DateAdd('d', 5, Date()),'dd mmmm yyyy')"
    Debug.Print "Date calculation gives " & Eval(strExpression)

    strExpression = "Forms.Count"
    Debug.Print "Number of open forms is " & Eval(strExpression)
End Sub
```

Shell and *Sendkeys*

Use the *Shell* command to start an external program asynchronously (control might return to your program before the program you start has finished execution).

With the *SendKeys* action, you can send a series of keystrokes to the active window. *SendKeys* can be used in conjunction with the *Shell* command to send keystrokes to an external application, as shown in the following example:

```
Sub modShellSendkeys_RunCalculator()
    ' Shift +, Ctrl is ^ and Alt is %
    Shell "notepad.exe", vbNormalFocus
    SendKeys "This is being written in notepad" & vbCrLf, True
    ' display the file menu
    SendKeys "%F", True
End Sub
```

This second example starts a copy of Access, which opens a database with the *Decompile* command switch:

```
Sub modShellSendkeys_DecompileAccess()
    ' shell a copy of access with the decompile switch
    Dim strCommand As String
    strCommand = "msaccess.exe " & _
                 Application.CurrentProject.Path & _
                 "\NewDatabase.accdb /Decompile"
    Shell strCommand, vbNormalFocus
End Sub
```

The *DoEvents* Command

The *DoEvents* command instructs the operating system to process other events and process any keystrokes generated by the *SendKeys* action before then returning execution to your program. This command is useful when you want to ensure that time is being allowed for repainting and updating information being displayed to the user, and to allow other applications time to undertake processing operations.

To see how this works, open the *frmDoEvents* form, which displays a status message text box and has a button to update the status messages. If you click the button, you will see the status message "Phase 1 completed" displayed. Now if you comment out the *DoEvents* statements, when you click the button, you only see the last message displayed; with the *DoEvents* command enabled, you see the status message change as the processing progresses:

```
Private Sub cmdDoEvents_Click()
    Const lngLoopMax = 1000
    Dim lngCounter As Long
    Dim lngRecordCount As Long
    Me.txtStatus = "Starting Processing"
    DoEvents
    For lngCounter = 1 To lngLoopMax
        lngRecordCount = DCount("*", "Customers")
    Next
    Me.txtStatus = "Phase 1 completed"
    DoEvents
    For lngCounter = 1 To lngLoopMax
        lngRecordCount = DCount("*", "Customers")
    Next
    Me.txtStatus = "Completed Processing"
End Sub
```

Objects and Collections

As you read through this book you will learn about many different objects and how to manipulate them. You will also find that objects are sometimes gathered together and held inside other objects called *collections*; a collection object holds a set of objects which are of a similar type. For example a *Recordset* contains a *Fields* collection and the *Fields* collection contains the set of *Field* objects in the *Recordset*.

Objects can have a number of properties and methods. A property is a characteristic that can be read or written; a method is something that you can call to manipulate the object.

> **Note**
> A quick way to determine that you are working with an object is to enable IntelliSense and then type in the name and press the "." (period) key. If it is an object, IntelliSense displays a list of methods and properties associated with it.

Collections, by contrast, only have a few properties and methods.

Key Collection Properties:

- **Count**   Counts how many objects are in the set.

  Collections in Access are 0-based: *Collection(0), Collection(1)...Collection(Count-1)*. But in products like Microsoft Excel, collections are 1-based: *Sheet(1), Sheet(2).. Sheet(Count)*.

Key Collection Methods:

- **Add**   Adds an object.

- **Delete** or **Remove**   Removes an object.

As an example, the *TableDefs* collection is the collection that contain all the tables in the database (both real tables and linked tables). Figure 3-15 shows some of the *TableDef* properties.

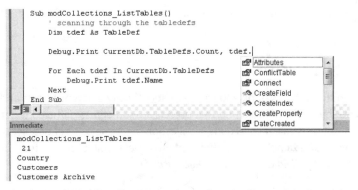

Figure 3-15 A *TableDef* has properties such as *Attributes*, *DateCreated* and *Connect*. It also has methods such as *CreateField*, *CreateIndex* and *CreateProperty*.

Objects are normally given singular names such as a *TableDef*, and the collections have plural names such as the *TableDefs* collection.

Object Variables

To refer to objects, we use object variables. In the preceding section, we defined a *TableDef* object, and we used the *For ... Each* loop to run through the *TableDefs* collection getting a reference to each object in the collection.

Unlike a normal variable, which acts like a slot in memory in which values are held, an object variable is a reference in memory to an object (it is not a copy of the object); in many computer languages, this is called a pointer (because it points to an object).

If you need to create an object variable which points to a single object or collection, use the *SET* command. The code below uses two object variables, the *db* object variable references the current database and the *tdef* object variable is set to point at a specific table:

```
Sub modObject_SingleObjectReference()
    ' getting a reference to a TableDef object
    Dim tdef As TableDef
    Dim db As Database
    Set db = CurrentDb
    Set tdef = db.TableDefs("Customers")
    Debug.Print tdef.Name
    Set tdef = Nothing
    db.Close
    Set db = Nothing
End Sub
```

INSIDE OUT   Tidying up object variables after use

Once the program code has finished execution, it is considered good practice to set any object variables to *Nothing*, which clears the reference in memory, some objects also have a *Close* method, and again it is considered good practice in this case to close the object variable.

Using the *Close* method and setting the variable to *Nothing* are not normally essential operations because once the code completes execution and the variables go out of scope, any tidy-up operations should be automatically taken care of; you might find that programmers omit these final tidy-up operations.

The *New* keyword which can be used to create a new object in memory, in the example below the *New* keyword is used to create a new table with a single field. Creating objects can be more complicated as there can be other rules to be observed, in this example once you have created objects, you need to save them (append) into collections:

```
Sub modObject_CreatingAnObject()
    ' create a table with a single field
    ' if re-running this code you will
    ' need to check that the table does not already exist
    Dim tdef As TableDef
    Dim fld As Field
    Dim db As Database
    Set db = CurrentDb
    Set tdef = New TableDef
    tdef.Name = "NewTable"
    Set fld = New Field
    fld.Name = "CustomerID"
    fld.Type = dbLong
    fld.Attributes = dbAutoIncrField
    tdef.Fields.Append fld
    db.TableDefs.Append tdef
    Set fld = Nothing
    Set tdef = Nothing
    db.Close
    Set db = Nothing
    Application.RefreshDatabaseWindow
End Sub
```

Is Nothing, IsEmpty, IsObject

Object variables that have not been assigned to a valid object have a value of *Nothing*. You can use *Is Nothing* to determine whether the variable has been assigned a value, or an assignment failed. *IsObject* can be used to determine if a variable is an object variable, or if a variant variable has a *vbObject* type (error trapping is often required with this test). Examples of these functions are shown in the following code, with the results shown in Figure 3-16:

```
Sub modNothingIsNothing()
    Dim db As Database
    Dim strName As String
    If db Is Nothing Then
        Debug.Print "Is Nothing Test is True"
    Else
        Debug.Print "Is Nothing Test is False"
    End If
    If IsObject(strName) Then
        Debug.Print "IsObject Test is True"
    Else
        Debug.Print "IsObject Test is False"
    End If
    Set db = CurrentDb
```

```
        If db Is Nothing Then
            Debug.Print "Is Nothing Test is True"
        Else
             Debug.Print "Is Nothing Test is False"
        End If
        Set db = Nothing
    End Sub
```

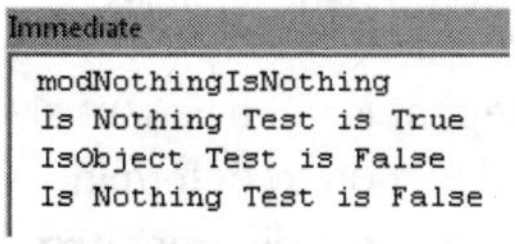

```
Immediate
modNothingIsNothing
Is Nothing Test is True
IsObject Test is False
Is Nothing Test is False
```

Figure 3-16 *Is Nothing* can be used to detect when an object variable
has not been assigned a value.

The previous example demonstrates how when you have finished using an object variable,
you explicity set the variable to *Nothing*. This is considered to be good practice rather than
assuming that the variable will be set to *Nothing* once it goes out of scope when the procedure ends.

Variant variables can be tested with the *IsEmpty* function to establish whether they have
been assigned a value, the results of the following code are shown in Figure 3-17:

```
Sub modNothing_IsEmpty()
    Dim strCustomer As String
    Debug.Print "Variable declared but not initialized, " & _
        "IsEmpty() : " & IsEmpty(strCustomer)
    strCustomer = "Test Customer"
    Debug.Print "Variable assigned a value, IsEmpty() : " & _
        "IsEmpty(strCustomer)"
    Dim varCustomer As Variant
    Debug.Print "Variant declared but not initialized, " & _
        "IsEmpty() : " & IsEmpty(varCustomer)
    varCustomer = "Test Customer"
    Debug.Print "Variant assigned a value, IsEmpty() : " & _
        IsEmpty(varCustomer)
    Debug.Print "Variant contains data : " & VarType(varCustomer)

    If VarType(varCustomer) = vbString Then
        Debug.Print "Variant variable contains a string"
    End If
    varCustomer = 1
    Debug.Print "Variant contains data : " & VarType(varCustomer)
End Sub
```

Chapter 3

```
Immediate
 modNothing_IsEmpty
 Variable declared but not initialized, IsEmpty() : False
 Variable assigned a value, IsEmpty() : IsEmpty(strCustomer)
 Variant declared but not initialized, IsEmpty() : True
 Variant assigned a value, IsEmpty() : False
 Variant contains data : 8
 Variant variable contains a string
 Variant contains data : 2
```

Figure 3-17 The results from using *IsEmpty* and *VarType* on variant variables.

The preceding shows that using *IsEmpty* on a variable that is not a variant always returns false. The example also shows the use of the *VarType* function to determine what kind of data is contained in the variant variable. Note that assigning a different item of data to a variant variable can change the variant type.

Creating Maintainable Code

The topic of how you should name objects and variables in VBA is one that always attracts controversy amongst developers. There is no enforced rule on how best to do this. In this section, we want to give you some suggestions and reasoned arguments as to why people adopt different naming conventions. The best advice we can give is to find a convention that suits your development style and try to stick to the convention so that your code is consistent.

Naming Access Document Objects

In an Access application, the first objects that need to be named are *Form*, *Report*, *Table*, and *Query*. Developers tend to name objects by functional area; for example, in the order processing part of a system, you could have forms named such as *OrderList*, *OrderDetails*, *OrderList_ForExport*, and so on, where the Order prefix indicates the order processing function in the system.

The advantage of this naming convention is that the Order forms are all naturally sorted alphabetically together. Other useful conventions with forms are to group them by behavior. For example, some forms are used for data maintenance, and others are pop-ups (the forms used for making selections prior to generating a report). With this convention you could have *frmOrders*, and *dlgOrders*, and *rptOrders*. This is a two-level classification for which the prefix *rpt*, *frm*, and *dlg* indicates the behavior of the form, and then you use the functional area (in this case Orders) for a sub-classification. Another popular convention is to name a form's subform as *frmOrdersSubOrderDetails*, using the word *Sub* or *SubForm* as part of the name.

Tables and queries are sometimes displayed in a single combined list in Access; typically when specifying a *RecordSource* for a form. This has led to a convention of using *tbl* or *qry* as a prefix to distinguish between the two types of objects.

Modules can be prefixed with *mod*. This is useful when you start prefixing the procedures with the module name. This then draws the distinction between code on a form (without a module prefix) and code in a general module (with a prefix).

Many developers adopt *camel* notation. This is when you capitalize the first letter of each word in the name, such as *OrderDetails*. Spaces are often avoided, and using the _ (under-bar) character is used to break words apart. The table that follows presents some common naming strategies.

Object type	Prefix	Examples
Form	frm, dlg, rpt	frmOrders, dlgOrders, rptOrders
SubForm	frm{}Sub{}	frmOrdersSubDetails
Report	rpt	rptOrderList
SubReport	rpt{}SubRep	rptOrderListSubOrderDetails
Table	tbl{}	tblOrders, tblOrderDetails
Query	qry{}	qryOrdersUK
Macro	mcr{}_Name	mcrOrders_SaveOrder
Module	mod	mod_Utilities
Procedure in a Module	mod_procname	mod_Utilities_ReplaceString

Events for controls on a form and the form itself have underbars added by Access; for example, *CompanyName_OnClick()*.

Naming Database Fields

Most developers name database fields with a simple functional name such as ProductDescription and ProductCode, or Product_Description and Product_Code. Here again, the camel notation is very popular.

You should avoid using spaces and special characters such as %, and &; names such as R&D Budget or Sales% might look meaningful, but they can be very painful to fix at some later date when you try to publish a database to SharePoint, for example.

Where names have spaces (which is not recommended because it inevitably makes things difficult with some other technologies), you often need to use square brackets to refer to the names in program code; for example, a field called Company Name could be referenced in a *Recordset as rst![Company name]*.

Naming Unbound Controls

When a field is added to a form, unless the field already exists on the form, Access assigns the control a name to match the field name. When naming unbound controls, such as command buttons or calculated expressions, using a standard prefix is important, because once you add code behind the control, if you have not named the control, then it is very difficult to figure out what a control does—say for example, one named *Text0*. The table that follows lists some common controls and the prefixes that are typically used when naming them.

Control	Prefix
Command Button	cmd
Text	txt
Combo Box	cbo
List Box	lst
Check Box	chk
Group Control	grp

Other problems that you need to be aware of can occur after you have named a control and attached code. If you change the control name, then existing code becomes orphaned and no longer executes. This is because Access concatenates the control name and an "_" (underbar) character with the event name, such as *CompanyName_OnClick()*.

When you copy and paste controls between Access objects, any associated code is not copied. One very attractive feature of embedded macros and controls is that when you copy and paste them between forms the embedded macro code is copied along with the control (except when working with web forms, where paste operations are not supported).

Naming Variables in Code

Some developers prefer to use a convention when naming variables. For example, a string variable for *CompanyName* might be called *strCompanyName*, and for a numeric long integer ID, the name might be *lngID*.

One argument against using this convention is that you might find the code more difficult to read. Another argument is the loss of meaning as the number of different types of objects that you work with increases. In .NET, where you have hundreds of objects, the prefix can become either meaningless or difficult to consistently assign. However, the bulk of VBA Access code manipulates a small number of different types of objects, and much of the naming prefix convention has grown up historically with the product.

The first argument for using a prefix on variable types is that you are less likely to make an error in program code by passing a string variable on a function call that expects a long value parameter. This argument spurs the question, is your development environment clever enough to spot this mistake at runtime?

Fortunately, a modern environment such as VBA can spot this mistake at an early stage when compiling the code (even if the error message is sometimes difficult to fully understand), as shown in Figure 3-18.

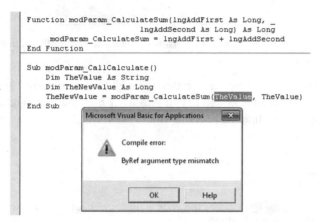

Figure 3-18 VBA recognizes an attempt to pass the wrong kind of parameter on a function call.

However, the following code, which does not specify a variable type for the function parameters, would pass compilation and not be detected as a potential conflict because the parameter types are not specified in the function definition; they are assumed to be variants, and a string value is a valid variant value:

```
Function modParam_CalculateSum(lngAddFirst, _
                              lngAddSecond) As Long
     modParam_CalculateSum = lngAddFirst + lngAddSecond
End Function

Sub modParam_CallCalculate()
    Dim TheValue As String
    Dim TheNewValue As Long
    TheNewValue = modParam_CalculateSum(TheValue, TheValue)
End Sub
```

The preceding code will fail with a type mismatch inside the function when it attempts to add the string and numeric data types together.

The second argument for using prefixes is that if, for example, you have a form with a bound control called *Company*, using a variable called *Company* will cause confusion, as illustrated in Figure 3-19, whereas having a variable called *strCompany* cannot be confused with the control name.

```
Private Sub Company_AfterUpdate()
    Debug.Print Company
    Dim Company As String
End Sub
```

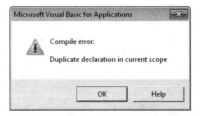

Figure 3-19 The compiler recognizes that the name *Company* would conflict with the control called *Company*.

However, depending on how the code is written this might not be detected. For example, if you change the order of what is written to that shown in Figure 3-20, you end up with code that compiles without detecting the potential error.

```
Private Sub Company_AfterUpdate()
    Dim Company As String
    Debug.Print Company
End Sub
```

Figure 3-20 Re-ordering the code means this code compiles without detecting the error, and the value printed will be an empty string.

Here are some suggestions for naming the built-in data types. The popular approach is to use a three-character prefix:

Data Type	Prefix
String	str
Long	lng
Double	dbl
Boolean	bl or bln or bool

For a more formal approach to naming objects (one that is very popular in the VBA community), we recommend searching online for contributions from Greg Reddick or Stan Leszynski (try starting here: *http://en.wikipedia.org/wiki/Leszynski_naming_convention*). The examples in this book follow a consistent, standard naming convention that is close to the spirit of this convention.

In summary, it is possible to write 100% reliable code without having any convention for naming variables, but you need to be careful when doing this. Using a simple convention to prefix a variable with the variable type can save a lot of problems.

INSIDE OUT   Using *Me* to reference controls in program code

In the example shown in Figure 3-20, because we have not referred to the bound control by name, the compiler cannot spot the problem and thinks the value of *Company* is an empty string. But if we had used *Me.Company* this would show that the control actually has a value that is not an empty string. On forms and reports, controls on the object can be referred to using the "Me" object. This also has the advantage of invoking IntelliSense when typing control names, and thus reducing typing errors.

Indenting Code

Indenting your program code makes it easier to read and maintain. The VBA Editor allows you to highlight a block of code and then use the Tab key to right-indent the block by a tab stop (position) or the Shift+Tab key to indent back a tab stop. Figure 3-21 shows a block of code highlighted and indented one tab stop.

```
Sub modCollections_ListTables()
    ' scanning through the tabledefs
    Dim tdef As TableDef

    Debug.Print CurrentDb.TableDefs.Count

    For Each tdef In CurrentDb.TableDefs
        Debug.Print tdef.Name
    Next
End Sub
```

Figure 3-21 Highlighting code and using the Tab or Shift+Tab keys to indent the code forward or backward by one tab position.

Other Variable Naming Conventions

Historically, there was a convention for ending a variable with a special symbol to indicate the data type. For strings, this symbol was the "$" (dollar) character, so *Customer$* indicated a string variable name; for Integers, the "%" (percent) symbol was used. We would not advise using this as a convention because it does not appear to be very popular. The Locals window in Figure 3-22 shows the resulting inferred data types.

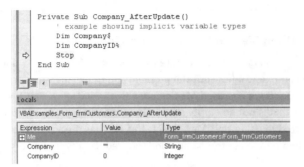

Figure 3-22 The Locals variable window shows how the $ symbol has been implicitly regarded as a string variable.

One of the oldest conventions that you might come across is using the letters I, J, or K for counters in loops. The roots of this convention go back to languages like Fortran, where these variable names were used for integer values in loops.

VBA and Macros

Access has grown up with two different approaches to programming: using macros and using VBA programming code. Macros are designed to be an easy to use programming environment in which people without VBA programming skills can add functionality to an application. Although macros are easy to use, managing macro code, debugging the code, and error handling are more challenging. Although error handling for macros in Access 2010 has been vastly improved, and debugging using local and temporary variables has been added, it is unlikely that these enhancements alone will encourage those using VBA to move away from the standard. Access 2010 has received a significant reworking of the Macro Editor and the macro environment, which includes the addition of Data Macros and support for macro programming in web objects (where VBA is not supported).

Access Basic

Access started out with a language called Access Basic, which evolved from the even more primitive language of BASIC. VBA was a later step that was initially incorporated into Excel and then extended into the other Microsoft Office products.

Because VBA needs to be universal to the entire Office family of products, it cannot incorporate directly all the features of Access into the language. This is why some of the most commonly encountered actions in Access, such as opening a form, do not have an obvious VBA function but use the *DoCmd* object.

Converting Macros to VBA

Macros can be converted to VBA. To do this, locate the macro in the Navigation window, and then on the File tab, in BackStage view, save the object as VBA code, as shown in Figure 3-23.

Figure 3-23 Converting a macro to VBA code.

```
Function MacroToBeConverted()
    DoCmd.OpenForm "frmCustomers", acNormal, "", "", , acNormal
    Beep
    MsgBox "Click close to close this window", vbOKOnly, "Close the window"
    DoCmd.Close acForm, "frmCustomers"
End Function
```

When converting the macro, you are also given options to add error handling and include macro comments.

Error Handling

VBA supports an *On Error* statement to indicate how errors should be handled.

The simplest way to understand how errors can occur is to generate an error and then look at the strategies for handling it. The following code contains an error:

```
Sub modErrorHandler_SimpleError()
' Example of a zero divide error
    Dim lngTotalTurnover As Long
    Dim lngCompanyCount As Long
    Dim lngAverageTurnover As Long

    lngCompanyCount = 0
    lngTotalTurnover = 20
    lngAverageTurnover = lngTotalTurnover / lngCompanyCount
End Sub
```

When you execute the code, it generates the error message illustrated in Figure 3-24.

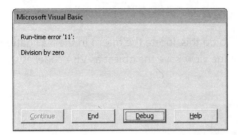

Figure 3-24 The error message displayed as the result of an untrapped error in program code.

This is probably not the kind of interaction that you would like your user to have with your application.

On Error Resume Next

This is a useful, yet possibly dangerous technique—it is dangerous if you fail to very carefully add lines of code to test for when an error has occurred. In the following example, you set this at the beginning of a procedure, which means that after a line executes, any error allows the execution to continue. When this is complete, you need to test the *Err* object to see if an error occurred and to display the message box shown in Figure 3-25:

```
Sub modErrorHandler_SimpleError_Handler2()
' Example of a zero divide error, and how to ignore an error
' but take some action based on the error
    On Error Resume Next
    ' This causes any error to be ignored
    Dim lngTotalTurnover As Long
    Dim lngCompanyCount As Long
    Dim lngAverageTurnover As Long

    lngCompanyCount = 0
    lngTotalTurnover = 20
    lngAverageTurnover = lngTotalTurnover / lngCompanyCount
    If Err <> 0 Then
        MsgBox "Contact support, Err No : " & Err & ", " & Err.Description, _
            vbCritical, "Help"
    End If
    On Error GoTo 0
End Sub
```

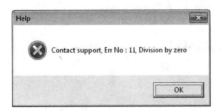

Figure 3-25 Using *On Error Resume Next* to trap an error.

This method can be used to perform special error handling for individual lines, but wherever it is used, you should test to see if the error has occurred and then take appropriate action.

INSIDE OUT   Taking care when using *On Error Resume Next* and *On Error Resume*

The last line of code in the previous example contains an *On Error GoTo 0* statement. This disables any further error handling and suspends the action of the *On Error Resume Next* statement. You can also mix these blocks inside more sophisticated error handlers. So in the following code, we override the main error handler (*On Error GoTo ErrorHandler:*) to perform some specialist error processing (within the *On Error resume Next* area), and then resume the main error handler once we are finished (by restating the *On Error Goto ErrorHandler:*):

```
On Error Goto ErrorHandler:
…….
On Error Resume Next
…… IF Err……

On Error Goto ErrorHandler
```

It is worth emphasizing that just adding *On Error Resume Next* at the top of a procedure is a very dangerous practice, and if you are setting this around a block of code, you should test for any errors, and then use On Error *Goto ErrorHandler:* to either switch back on the main error handler, or *On Error GoTo 0* to switch off error handling.

There is another alternative to using the *On Error Resume Next*, which is *On Error Resume*, which simply means try again. On its own, you are unlikely to use *On Error Resume*, but if you trap the error, you could ask the user if he wants to retry an operation several times (ensuring that they can escape from any program loop you create).

Err Object

When an error occurs, the error object can be used to display the error number and error description. You can also clear the error object by using the *Err.Clear* operation to ensure that subsequent errors are correctly managed, as shown in the following example (see for example in *modErrorHandler_SimpleError_Handler2a*):

```
lngAverageTurnover = lngTotalTurnover / lngCompanyCount
Debug.Print Err.Number, Err.Description
If Err.Number <> 0 Then
    ' take appropriate action
    ' clear the error
    Err.Clear
End If
```

On Error GoTo

This mechanism is the preferred way to handle errors because it allows you to define a unique error handling block of code for every procedure, which can then take a specific action of passing the error to a general purpose piece of code. The following code shows the general structure of this error handling code:

```
Sub modErrorHandler_SimpleError_Handler3()
' Example of a zero divide error

    On Error GoTo ErrorHandler:
    ' This allows better control of the error
    Dim lngTotalTurnover As Long
    Dim lngCompanyCount As Long
    Dim lngAverageTurnover As Long

    lngCompanyCount = 0
    lngTotalTurnover = 20
    lngAverageTurnover = lngTotalTurnover / lngCompanyCount

    Exit Sub

ErrorHandler:
Stop
' We can now take several possible actions
' 1 ignore the error and exit the subroutine or function
' 2 do something and try again using Resume
'Resume
' 3 skip forwards and continue processing
'    using Resume Next
' 4 Activate a custom error handler to log the error
'    alert the user and take some action
' 5 Log the error and get the user to decide on what action to take
End Sub
```

Developing a General Purpose Error Handler

In this section, we outline a general purpose routine for recording the errors and allowing the user to decide what to do after an error occurs. The label *Errorhandler* shown in the code that follows can have the same name in all procedures. To start, you need to decide on what options a user should be presented with:

- Try again

- Skip and Continue

- Exit

```
Sub modErrorHandler_SimpleError_Handler4()

' Example of a zero divide error

    On Error GoTo ErrorHandler:
    Dim lngTotalTurnover As Long
    Dim lngCompanyCount As Long
    Dim lngAverageTurnover As Long

    lngCompanyCount = 0
    lngTotalTurnover = 20
    lngAverageTurnover = lngTotalTurnover / lngCompanyCount

    Exit Sub

ErrorHandler:
    Select Case modErrorHandler_ErrorLogging(Err.Number, _
                                    Err.Description, _
                                    "modErrorHandler_SimpleError_Handler4")

        Case 1: Resume Next
        Case 2: Resume
        Case Else
    End Select
End Sub
```

The error handler in the preceding code calls a library routine, and then depending on the user's interaction with that routine, takes appropriate action.

```
Function modErrorHandler_ErrorLogging(lngErrorNo As Long, _
                                    strErrorText As String, _
                                    strCallingcode As String) As Long
' This is an example of a generic error handler
' It logs the error in a table and then allows the calling procedure
' to decide on the action to take
    Dim db As DAO.Database
    Dim rst As Recordset
    Set db = CurrentDb
    Set rst = db.OpenRecordset("tblErrorLog", dbOpenDynaset)
    With rst
        .AddNew
        !ErrorNo = lngErrorNo
        !ErrorMessage = strErrorText
        !ErrorProc = strCallingcode
        ' Also very useful to log the id of the user generating the error
        !WindowsUserName = modErrorHandler_GetUserName()
        .Update
    End With
```

```
' now allow the user to decide what happens next
    DoCmd.OpenForm "frmError", , , , , acDialog, strErrorText
    ' now as this is a dialog form our code stops here
    ' we will use a global variable to work out
    ' what action the user wants to happen
    modErrorHandler_ErrorLogging = global_lngErrorAction
End Function
```

The code is split into three parts. The first part uses Data Access Objects (DAO) programming to log the error in an error recording table (see Figure 3-26). It also uses a special function called *modErrorHandler_GetUserName()*, which retrieves the users logon name. This uses a Windows API call. Note that this API call will work only in Office 32-bit; it would need to be modified to work in Office 64-bit. This is shown in the sample database and discussed in Chapter 17, "Developing Applications."

```
Declare Function CSM_GetUserName Lib "advapi32.dll" Alias "GetUserNameA" _
(ByVal lpBuffer As String, nsize As Long) As Long

Function modErrorHandler_GetUserName() As String
    Dim USER As String
    USER = Space(255)
    If CSM_GetUserName(USER, Len(USER) + 1) <> 1 Then
        modErrorHandler_GetUserName = ""
    Else
        USER = Trim$(USER)
        USER = Left(USER, Len(USER) - 1)
        modErrorHandler_GetUserName = USER
    End If
End Function
```

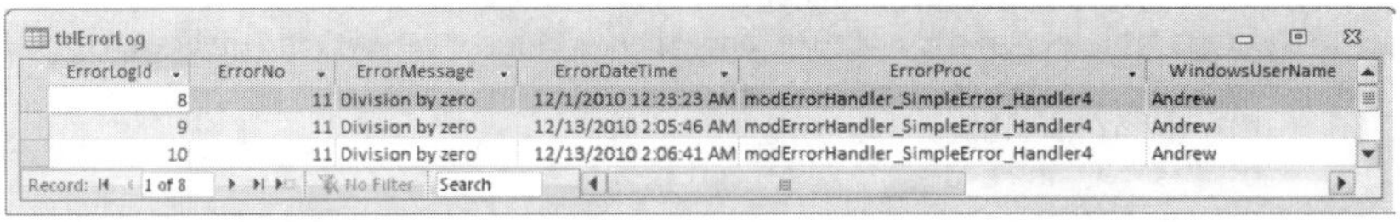

Figure 3-26 A custom error log file.

Figure 3-27 illustrates an example of a form that you can display to log and then take appropriate action when an error occurs (see *modErrorhandler_SimpleError_Handler4* to view the code).

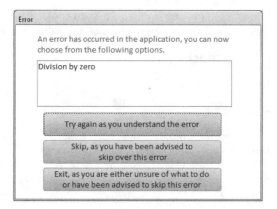

Figure 3-27 A form that provides potential actions for a user to take when an error occurs.

When you open a target form as a dialog form, your program code pauses until the dialog is closed. Yet the dialog form can also still have its own code that executes even when the calling code is paused. This is a very subtle feature.

OpenArgs and Dialog Forms

Chapter 4, "Applying the Access Object Model," shows examples of writing values into the controls of a form after opening the form, and in Chapter 6, "Using Forms and Events," there are examples showing how to call public code on a form after opening the form. But when the form is opened as a dialog form these techniques cannot be used to manipulate the form that you are opening because the code on the calling form will stop execution after opening the dialog form.

For a dialog form, you can make use of the *Open Argument Parameter* (variant) when using the *DoCmd.OpenForm* action (this method is a general technique that can also be used when opening forms other than as a dialog). The following code demonstrates an example of code passing this parameter to a form (in this example, the "|" character separates the parameters):

```
Sub modOpenArgs_MultipleArgs()
' example opening the form frmUsingOpenArgs
    Dim varArgs As Variant
    varArgs = "Text value|1.998|1st january 2011"
    DoCmd.OpenForm "frmUsingOpenArgs", , , , , acDialog, varArgs
    MsgBox "Control returns to calling program"
End Sub
```

The sample form called *frmUsingOpenArgs* (see Figure 3-28) then contains the following code on the open event, which uses the *Split* function to break apart the parameters:

```
Private Sub Form_Open(Cancel As Integer)
    ' reads the OpenArgs
    Dim varArgs As Variant
    Dim lngArgs As Long
    If Not IsNull(Me.OpenArgs) Then
        varArgs = Split(Me.OpenArgs, "|")
        For lngArgs = 0 To UBound(varArgs)
            Me.Controls("txtParameter" & lngArgs) = varArgs(lngArgs)
        Next
    End If
End Sub
```

Figure 3-28 An example form showing the *OpenArgs* being displayed in a set of controls.

Notice that the message box in the calling code is not executed until you close the dialog form.

An alternative method to solving this problem is to load a set of global variables before opening the form, and then read the values of these variables in the form's *Open* event.

Err.Raise

This is a feature of VBA that you are more likely to use if you decide to create your own VBA classes. Classes are complex objects, and as such, they cannot simply return an error code like a function can. An additional problem with classes is that they need have their own internal error handling but still be able to pass an error back to the program code that uses the class. The error code range 513–65535 is available for you to use for raising error numbers, as demonstrated in the code that follows:

```
Sub modErrorHandler_RaiseAnError()
    ' procedure which raises a custom error number
    On Error GoTo Err_handler
    Dim i As Long
    i = 56 / 0
    Exit Sub
```

```
Err_handler:
    Err.Raise 516, "modErrorHandler_RaiseAnError", "Division by zero"
End Sub

Sub modErrorHandler_RaiseAnErrorTest()
    ' test procedure to trap a custom error
    On Error GoTo Err_handler
    modErrorHandler_RaiseAnError
    Exit Sub
Err_handler:
    ' At this point we can manage the custom error
    Debug.Print Err.Number, Err.Description, Err.Source
    Stop
End Sub
```

INSIDE OUT   The *vbObjectError* constant

There is some confusion with respect to a constant called *vbObjectError* (which has the value –2147221504). The Help system and other sources emphasize that you should add this number to your own error number, but this is not normally required.

Chapter 3

Summary

In this chapter, you were introduced to the VBA Programming Language features. The following points summarize key areas with which you should now be familiar:

- The use of built-in function libraries

- How object variables are used in program code

- The benefits of having conventions for naming objects in your application

- The principles of defining error handling in program code

PART 2

Access Object Model and Data Access Objects (DAO)

CHAPTER 4

Applying the Access Object Model 127

CHAPTER 5

Understanding the Data Access Object Model 161

Applying the Access Object Model

The *Application* Object Methods and Properties 128

The *CurrentProject* and *CurrentData* Objects 134

The *DoCmd* Object. 138

Manipulating the *Forms* and *Reports* Collections. 143

Using the *Screen* Object 150

Enhancing the User Interface 152

It helps to think of Microsoft Access as being an object that contains other objects and collections of objects. When you open a form in the application, each control on the form is an object that is contained in a controls collection for that form object. The open form is contained in the *Forms* collection of the *Application* object (until you close the form). The *Forms* and *Reports* collections are very important for programming Access and contain open forms or reports.

If you want to look at all forms in an application (regardless of whether they are open), they reside in the *CurrentProject* object, in a collection called *AllForms*. The *CurrentProject* object is contained in the *Application* object.

Similar objects are held in an object collection, and an object can contain several of these collections. The Access *Application* object has more than 70 methods and over 40 properties, and many of these properties are themselves objects that contain further collections. In this chapter, you look into some of the more important objects and collections that are contained in the Access *Application* object, as shown in Figure 4-1.

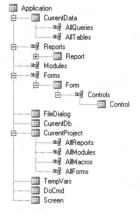

Figure 4-1 A simplified view of part of the Access *Application* object.

After reading this chapter, you will:

- Be able to use the *Forms* and *Reports* collections to manage how different parts of an application can control other objects by using these important collections

- Understand how to use other important parts of the Access *Application* object in your applications

> **Note**
> As you read through this chapter, we encourage you to also use the companion content sample database, AccessObjectModel.accdb, which can be downloaded from the book's catalog page.

The *Application* Object Methods and Properties

In this chapter, there are separate sections to deal with the more complex application objects. To begin though, we look at a variety of the simpler *Application* object's methods and properties.

> **Note**
> When working with these methods and properties, you can omit the "Application" prefix. For example, you can type **Run** rather than **Application.Run**. Using the prefix is useful, however, when you want full assistance from IntelliSense.

The *Run* Method

Using *Application.Run*, you can execute a custom Microsoft VBA procedure. The following example demonstrates how to dynamically execute a procedure and pass parameters to the procedure:

```
Sub modRun_PromptUser(strmsg As String)
    MsgBox strmsg
End Sub
Sub modRun_DynamicRun()
    ' example showing the use of Run to
    ' dynamically execute code and pass parameters
```

```
    Dim strProc As String
    Dim strMessage As String
    strMessage = "Operation Completed"
    strProc = "modRun_PromptUser"
    Run strProc, strMessage
End Sub
```

In the next example, we have copied the subroutine into another Access database. The code then opens the second Access database and runs the *Public* code:

```
Sub modRun_DynamicRunInAnotherAccessDatabase()
    ' example showing the use of Run to
    ' dynamically execute code and pass parameters
    ' to another Access application
    Dim strProc As String
    Dim strMessage As String
    Dim strTarget As String
    strTarget = CurrentProject.Path & "\NewDatabase.accdb"
    strMessage = "Operation Completed"
    strProc = "modRun_PromptUser"
    Dim objAccess As Access.Application
    Set objAccess = GetObject(strTarget, "Access.Application")
    objAccess.Run strProc, strMessage
    Set objAccess = Nothing
End Sub
```

The *RunCommand* Method

The *Application.RunCommand* mimics the actions that a user can perform by using the built-in Access menus. To invoke a specific menu action, you need to have a suitable context; for example, to display a find dialog, you need to have a form that contains controls that can be searched, and to perform an Undo record, the record needs to have been changed.

The sample form *frmRunCommand* includes some button examples, which are illustrated in the following code:

```
Private Sub cmdFind_Click()
    RunCommand acCmdFind
End Sub

Private Sub cmdSave_Click()
    If Me.Dirty Then
        RunCommand acCmdSaveRecord
    End If
End Sub

Private Sub cmdUndo_Click()
    If Me.Dirty Then
        RunCommand acCmdUndo
    End If
End Sub
```

Unfortunately, the built-in Help system does not provide a good description of how and when to use the different commands. But you can pick up the use of the different commands by examining code snippets in this book and by searching online. If you search online for a specific command, such as *acCmdSaveRecord*, you will find sites that are dedicated to explaining the different commands.

Simplifying Filtering by Using *BuildCriteria*

The *BuildCriteria* method of the *Application* object is a tool that is designed to assist you in constructing valid *Where* clause syntax. The method call involves passing the *FieldName*, *FieldType*, and *Criteria*. This method can be combined with *InputBox* commands or dialog forms to build *Where* clauses for code and filters.

The *frmEmployeesList* form contains a button that uses an input box to apply a filter. If you enter an "*" (asterisk) character at the end of the name, the *BuildCriteria* method constructs an appropriate *Where* clause by using the *like* keyword, as demonstrated in the following:

```
Private Sub cmdFilterByLastname_Click()
    Dim strLastname As String
    Dim strFilter As String
    strLastname = InputBox("Enter employees last name", _
                          "Last Name Filter", "")
    If strLastname = "" Then
        Me.FilterOn = False
    Else
        strFilter = BuildCriteria("[Last Name]", dbText, strLastname)
        Me.Filter = strFilter
        Me.FilterOn = True
    End If
End Sub
```

The *ColumnHistory* and *Append Only* Memo Fields

In Table design, if you scroll to the very last property of a memo field, you will find the *Append Only* property, as shown in Figure 4-2.

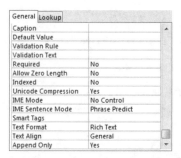

Figure 4-2 The Append Only property of a memo field in Table design, for the field Notes in the table *Customers*.

With Append Only set to *Yes*, each time the field is edited, the previous contents are recorded in the column history. To display the column history information (see Figure 4-3), right-click the memo field in Datasheet or Form view, and then choose Show Column History from the shortcut menu.

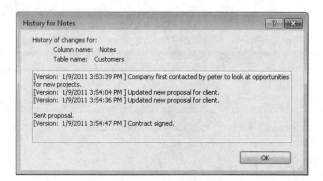

Figure 4-3 Displaying the column history for an *Append Only* memo Field.

There is no feature to trim down or edit the column history information for a table. To clear the history you need to create a new field, update the existing data, remove the old field, and then rename the new field.

To display the column history by using an unbound control on a form or in a query, you can use a custom VBA function, as shown in the following:

```
Function modApp_ColumnHistory(strTableName As String, _
                              strColumnName As String, _
                              strKeyName As String, _
                              strKeyValue As Variant) As String
    ' returns the memo history data
    Dim strQueryString As String
    strQueryString = "[" & strKeyName & "] = "
```

Chapter 4

```
    If Not IsNumeric(strKeyValue) Then
        ' this could be extended for other data types
        strQueryString = strQueryString & "'" & strKeyValue & "'"
    Else
        strQueryString = strQueryString & strKeyValue
    End If
    modApp_ColumnHistory = Application.ColumnHistory(strTableName, _
                                                     strColumnName, _
                                                     strQueryString)

End Function
```

This function can be enhanced to handle different types of primary key values and provide more sophisticated formatting by parsing the string for the appropriate version information tags, as shown in Figure 4-4.

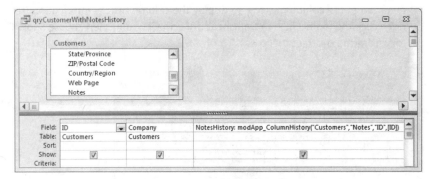

Figure 4-4 Using a custom VBA function to display the column history information.

Examining *TempVars*

Unlike VBA, when programming by using macros, you cannot define variables to hold values of controls and other settings. There are many circumstances in macro programming in which you need to save a temporary value for later re-use. You can use the *TempVars* collection to create these temporary variables. This collection also allows you to share values between macro and VBA code.

Using the following VBA code, you can quickly dump a list of the temporary variables to the Immediate window:

```
Sub modApp_ListTempvars()
    ' Set some example temporary variables
    TempVars!FormName = "frmScreenForm"
    TempVars.Add "Current User", Application.CurrentUser
    ' list all values for temporary variables
    Dim tv As TempVar
    Debug.Print "Listing TempVars" & TempVars.Count
    Debug.Print "_____"
```

```
    For Each tv In TempVars
        Debug.Print tv.Name, tv.Value
    Next
End Sub
```

In VBA and macro programming, when you attempt to use a *TempVar* that has not already been used, it is automatically added to the *TempVars* collection. The collection supports methods to *Add*, *Remove*, and *RemoveAll* items (corresponding to the *SetTempVar*, *RemoveTempVar*, and *RemoveAllTempVars* macro commands).

Invoking the Expression Builder

The Expression Builder is an extremely useful tool to have when writing code that needs to refer to forms and reports. In the VBA Code Editor, there is no button to display the Expression Builder; it can only be displayed when you are in the Design mode of an Access object, such as a form, or in the Query grid.

This means developers often find themselves needing to go into a query or form in Design mode to display the Expression Builder.

It is possible to mimic this action by specifying a function key that will display the Expression Builder with a single keystroke, as demonstrated here:

```
Function modApp_InvokeBuilder()
    ' Create an Autokeys Macro using F6 to activate this code
    DoCmd.OpenForm "frmLaunchExpressionBuilder", acDesign
    ' This command launches the expression builder
    RunCommand acCmdInvokeBuilder
End Function
```

This function opens a form called *frmLaunchExpressionBuilder* in Design mode (see Figure 4-5) and then sends the *acCmdInvokeBuilder* command. This command can only be executed when you have an appropriate object open in Design view.

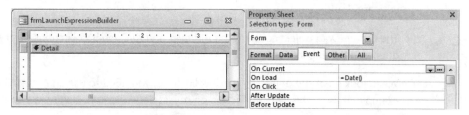

Figure 4-5 A dummy form with no controls can be used to launch Expression Builder.

To prevent a pop-up from appearing that prompts you to choose between displaying the Expression Builder, Macro Builder, or writing code, we have added an expression to the form's default load event.

Chapter 4

We next create an *AutoKeys* macro (see Figure 4-6) that ties the F6 key to executing the VBA code.

Figure 4-6 Using a Submacro name that corresponds to a keycode and saving the macro with the special name *AutoKeys* redefines how function keys and other keys operate.

Now, when you display the Access interface you can launch Expression Builder by pressing the F6 key, as shown in Figure 4-7.

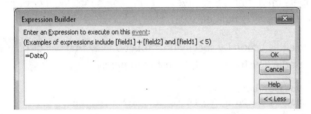

Figure 4-7 A quick technique for launching Expression Builder.

The *CurrentProject* and *CurrentData* Objects

The *CurrentProject* object contains a number of useful properties, such as the *CurrentProject.Path()*, which returns the path to your database. It also contains collections called *AllForms*, *AllReports*, *AllMacros*, and *AllModules*, which hold the Access Objects in your application.

The *CurrentData* object contains the *AllTables* and *AllQueries* collections for the tables and queries in the application.

When looking at the objects in these collections, you need to use an Access Object. For an example of using this, see the section on object dependencies, beginning on page 137.

The *Application* object contains two very important collections called the *Forms* and *Reports* collections. These collections contain the currently open forms or reports in your application and are used extensively in VBA programming.

Retrieving Version Information

The Access *Application* object and associated objects provide product version information, as shown in Figure 4-8. In some cases, you need to look at different parts of the object hierarchy to locate the information you need.

```
Sub modApp_VersionInformation()
    ' displays version information
    Debug.Print "Database Version : " & CurrentDb.Version
    Debug.Print "Database Version : " & DBEngine.Version
    Debug.Print "Application.Version : " & Application.Version
    Debug.Print "Application.Build :" & Application.Build

    Debug.Print "Application.BrokenReference :" & Application.BrokenReference
    Debug.Print "Application.IsCompiled :" & Application.IsCompiled

    Debug.Print "CurrentProject.Path :" & CurrentProject.Path
    Debug.Print "CurrentProject.ProjectType :" & CurrentProject.ProjectType
    Debug.Print "CurrentProject.Connection :" & CurrentProject.Connection
    Debug.Print "CurrentProject.BaseConnectionString :" & CurrentProject.BaseConnectionString
    Debug.Print "CurrentProject.FileFormat :" & CurrentProject.FileFormat
End Sub
```

```
Immediate

modApp_VersionInformation
Database Version : 14.0
Database Version : 14.0
Application.Version : 14.0
Application.Build :4750
Application.BrokenReference :False
Application.IsCompiled :True
CurrentProject.Path :C:\ASC08\AccessInsideOutVBA\CodeExamples\Chapter3
CurrentProject.ProjectType :2
CurrentProject.Connection :Provider=Microsoft.ACE.OLEDB.12.0;User ID=Admin;Data Source=C:\ASC08\Ac
CurrentProject.BaseConnectionString :PROVIDER=Microsoft.ACE.OLEDB.12.0;DATA SOURCE=C:\ASC08\Access
CurrentProject.FileFormat :12
```

Figure 4-8 Displaying popular properties by using different parts of the object hierarchy.

INSIDE OUT   Version numbers and functionality

Notice that when you create a new Access 2010 database, the value of *CurrentDB. Version* is 12.0, and *DBEngine(0)(0).Version* is 14.0.

If you were to create a table with a calculated field—for example, you add a field called *ADate* and then a calculated field *Year([ADate])*—then when you look at *CurrentDB. Version,* it will have changed to become 14.0.

This change means that your database will no longer be compatible with an earlier version of Access because it contains an Access 2010-specific feature.

If you want to revert your database and restore its compatibility, you might find that removing the calculated field is not sufficient. If this is the case, you need to create a new database, and then import the objects from the old database (where you have removed the new feature) to ensure compatibility.

For more information about the *DBEngine* object and *CurrentDb*, see Chapter 5, "Understanding the Data Access Object Model."

Chapter 4

The *CurrentProject* object contains information about your Access project. One of the most useful properties of this object is the *Path* property, which displays the windows folder path where your Access project resides, regardless of how a user launches the application, as presented in the following code:

```
Sub modApp_ListFilesInCurrentDirectory()
    ' list all files in the application directory
    Dim strPath As String
    strPath = CurrentProject.Path
    Dim strFileName As String
    strFileName = Dir(strPath & "\")
    Do While strFileName <> ""
        Debug.Print strFileName
        strFileName = Dir
    Loop
End Sub
```

Changing Form Datasheet View Properties

Sometimes you want to run through all your reports and forms and make a global change to a property. This can be achieved by using some code to open each form, make the change, and then save the changes. The key to achieving this is to use the *OpenForm* or *OpenReport* command with the *acDesign* option.

In the example that follows, you want to change the presentation properties of the Datasheet view. Note that these properties are not available in Design mode and require VBA code to set them:

```
Sub modCreate_ChangeDataSheetProperties()
    ' Uses the AllForms collection to change
    ' datasheet presentation settings for a form
    ' Available settings are
        'DatasheetFontItalic
        'DatasheetFontHeight
        'DatasheetFontName
        'DatasheetFontUnderline
        'DatasheetFontWeight
        'DatasheetForeColor
        'DatasheetBackColor
        'DatasheetGridlinesColor
        'DatasheetGridlinesBehavior
        'DatasheetCellsEffect
    Dim objfrm As Object
    Dim frm As Form
    Dim prop As Property
    Dim strProperty As String
    strProperty = "DatasheetFontName"
'    strProperty = "DatasheetFontItalic"
    Dim varPropertyValue As Variant
    varPropertyValue = "Calibri"
```

```
'   varPropertyValue = True
    For Each objfrm In CurrentProject.AllForms
        ' open the form in design view
        DoCmd.OpenForm objfrm.Name, acDesign
        Set frm = Forms(objfrm.Name)
        Set prop = frm.Properties(strProperty)
        prop.Value = varPropertyValue
        DoCmd.Close acForm, objfrm.Name, acSaveYes
    Next
End Sub
```

Object Dependencies

You can list object dependencies by using the *GetDependencyInfo* function. This function returns an object that contains collections of those objects on which the selected object depends, and those objects that depend on the selected object.

If you want to return dependency information on a table or a query, the Access object is found in the *CurrentData.AllTables* or *CurrentData.AllQueries* collections. If you want to return information on a form or report, use the *CurrentProject.AllForms* or *CurrentProject. AllReports* collections:

```
Sub modDep_DepInfo()
    Dim objDep As AccessObject
    Dim objAccess As AccessObject
    Dim depInfo As DependencyInfo
    Set objAccess = CurrentData.AllTables("Customers")
    ' AllTables, AllQueries
    Set depInfo = objAccess.GetDependencyInfo()
    Debug.Print "Object Dependants for Table Customers"
    Debug.Print "*************************************"
    For Each objDep In depInfo.Dependants
        Debug.Print objDep.Name
    Next
    Set objAccess = CurrentProject.AllForms("Order Details")
    ' AllTables, AllQueries
    Debug.Print "Object Dependencies for Form Order Details"
    Debug.Print "*************************************"
    Set depInfo = objAccess.GetDependencyInfo()
    For Each objDep In depInfo.Dependencies
        Debug.Print objDep.Name
    Next
End Sub
```

Chapter 4

INSIDE OUT   Dependency checking and embedded macros

If you run the example in the sample database, when it analyses the form called *[Order Details]*, you see error messages such as "MISSING: Shipper Details". This indicates that the dependency checker has been able to search through an embedded macro and spot that a *DblClick* event on the *[Shipping Information]* tab on the *[ShippingID]* control references a form called *[Shipper Details]*, which is not present in the database.

The dependency checker can spot problems with macros that refer to objects that do not exist in a database, but because of the flexibility in VBA code, it will not spot missing objects inside VBA code.

The *DoCmd* Object

The *DoCmd* object allows VBA to use the set of 65 macro commands in Access. A number of these commands are not often used because there are equivalent commands or techniques in VBA.

In the *modDoCmd* module, we have listed all the commands and also grouped them into a number of categories. In this section, we will look at the essential commands with which you should become familiar.

Controlling the Environment

There are three macro commands that you can use to great effect to enhance a user's experience when interacting with an application.

- **DoCmd.Echo** When *Echo* is set to *True* (the default), the user sees everything that happens in the interface. Be aware that this setting might entail some performance issues, such as screen flicker when forms open and close and other operations are performed by your code. To preclude this, set the *Echo* to *False*. You need to remember to switch the *Echo* back to *True*. If you become stuck with the *Echo* switched off, press Ctrl+G, and then type **DoCmd.Echo True** into the Immediate window.

- **DoCmd.Hourglass** This command changes the mouse pointer to an hourglass, which is useful for signaling to a user to wait until an operation is complete. As with *DoCmd.Echo*, you need to switch this back to *False* when you have completed the operation (or if an error occurs).

- **DoCmd.SetWarnings**   This is potentially a *very dangerous* command. The main reason that people use this command to turn warnings off is because they use the *OpenQuery* command to execute Action Queries; configuring *SetWarnings* to *False* prevents a user from seeing a message box to confirm making changes to the data when each *OpenQuery* command is executed. It is a better idea to use *CurrentDb. Execute* to run an action query, because then you do not see the warnings being displayed, so you don't need to switch the warnings off. The reason why the *Set-Warnings* command is dangerous is because if your code fails and never switches the warnings back on, the next time you go into a form and make a design change and then click close, Access does not ask you if you want to save your changes. It just closes the form, and you lose any unsaved design changes. Once you have lost some work this way, you will appreciate why when you use this command, you need to be very careful.

The following code demonstrates the *DoCmd.Echo* and *DoCmd.Hourglass* macros:

```
Sub modDoCmd_EchoExample()
    ' example showing how Echo can control
    Dim lngCount As Long
    DoCmd.Hourglass True
    DoCmd.Echo False
    DoCmd.OpenTable "Customers"
    For lngCount = 1 To 5000
        DoEvents
    Next
    DoCmd.Echo True
    DoCmd.Hourglass False
End Sub
```

Controlling Size and Position

The four macro commands described in this section are used to control the size and position of forms and reports on the screen. The macros are:

- **DoCmd.Maximize**   Enlarges a form or report to the full size of the screen.

- **DoCmd.Minimize**   Reduces a form or report to a minimal size on the screen.

- **DoCmd.Restore**   Restores a maximized or minimized window to previous size.

- **DoCmd.MoveSize**   Positions a form or report to an absolute screen position. Positional units are twips (there are 1,440 twips per inch [567 per cm]).

Chapter 4

The following code is from the *frmCustomersBriefDetails* form, which contains examples of these commands:

```
Private Sub cmdMaximize_Click()
    DoCmd.Maximize
End Sub

Private Sub cmdMinimize_Click()
    DoCmd.Minimize
End Sub
Private Sub cmdRestore_Click()
    DoCmd.Restore
End Sub

Private Sub cmdPosition_Click()
    Const lngTwipsPerInch = 1440
    Const lngTwipsPerCm = 567
    Dim lngRight As Long
    Dim lngDown As Long
    Dim lngWidth As Long
    Dim lngHeight As Long

    ' determine position based on metric or imperial measurement
    If modInternational_IsUSSystem() Then
        ' inches
        lngRight = 2 * lngTwipsPerCm
        lngDown = 2 * lngTwipsPerCm
        lngWidth = 12 * lngTwipsPerCm
        lngHeight = 6 * lngTwipsPerCm
    Else
        ' cm
        lngRight = 5 * lngTwipsPerCm
        lngDown = 5 * lngTwipsPerCm
        lngWidth = 30 * lngTwipsPerCm
        lngHeight = 15 * lngTwipsPerCm
    End If

    DoCmd.MoveSize lngRight, lngDown, lngWidth, lngHeight
End Sub
```

Application Navigation

There are several important commands that can be used to build the navigation experience for users when opening and closing forms and reports and other objects. These commands are:

- **DoCmd.OpenForm**   Opens a form and displays filtered data.

- **DoCmd.OpenQuery**   Opens a query or runs an action query.

- **DoCmd.OpenReport**   Opens a report and displays filtered data.

- **DoCmd.OpenTable**   Open a table of data.

- **DoCmd.SelectObject**   Selects an object (often then followed by the *DoCmd.Close* to close the selected object).

- **DoCmd.Close**   Closes an object.

- **DoCmd.Quit**   Quit the application.

The following code is from the *frmNavigation* form, which contains examples of using these commands. Note that when using *OpenReport*, if you do not specify to preview the report; by default it will be printed:

```
Private Sub cmdOpenForm_Click()
    Dim strWhere As String
    strWhere = "[State/Province] = 'CA'"
    DoCmd.OpenForm "frmCustomers", , , strWhere
End Sub
Private Sub cmdOpenQuery_Click()
    DoCmd.OpenQuery "qryCustomersInCA"
End Sub
Private Sub cmdOpenreport_Click()
    Dim strWhere As String
    strWhere = "[State/Province] = 'CA'"
    DoCmd.OpenReport "rptCustomers", acViewPreview, , strWhere
End Sub
Private Sub cmdOpenTable_Click()
    DoCmd.OpenTable "Customers"
End Sub
Private Sub cmdQuit_Click()
    If MsgBox("Do you want to quit the application ?", _
            vbYesNo, "Quit") = vbYes Then
        DoCmd.Quit
    End If
End Sub
Private Sub cmdSelectAndClose_Click()
    DoCmd.OpenForm "frmCustomers"
    If MsgBox("Would you like to close the Customers form ?", _
            vbYesNo, "Select and Close") = vbYes Then
        DoCmd.SelectObject acForm, "frmCustomers"
        DoCmd.Close
    End If
End Sub
```

Chapter 4

Data Exchange

The macro commands described in this section allow data to be imported, exported, printed, and sent as an email. Some of the commands only apply to tables and queries, whereas others can be used with forms, reports, and other objects.

- **DoCmd.TransferDatabase**   Imports and exports database objects in different database formats. This is used often to import and export between Access databases.

- **DoCmd.TransferSharePointList**   Imports or links to data in Microsoft SharePoint (as a linked table).

- **DoCmd.TransferSpreadsheet**   Imports or exports data in spreadsheet formats (from tables or queries).

- **DoCmd.TransferText**   Imports or exports text file formats (from tables or queries).

- **DoCmd.SendObject**   Sends objects and attachments in an email.

- **DoCmd.OutputTo**   Outputs data from database objects in different formats.

- **DoCmd.PrintOut**   Prints output from different database objects.

The following code is from the *frmImportExport* form, which contains examples of these commands:

```
Private Sub cmdSendObject_Click()
' acFormatHTML, acFormatRTF, acFormatSNP, acFormatTXT, acFormatXLS
' acFormatXLSB, acFormatXLSX, acFormatXPS, acFormatPDF
    On Error Resume Next
    DoCmd.SendObject acSendTable, "Customers", acFormatXLS, , , , "Test", _
        "Customers table attached", True
    If Err <> 0 Then
        MsgBox Err.Description, vbInformation, "Data Not Sent"
    End If
End Sub

Private Sub cmdTransferSpreadsheet_Click()
    DoCmd.TransferSpreadsheet acExport, acSpreadsheetTypeExcel5, _
        "qryCustomersInCA", CurrentProject.Path & "\CaCustomers.xls", True
    MsgBox "Data export completed", vbInformation, "Completed"
End Sub

Private Sub cmdTransferText_Click()
    DoCmd.TransferText acExportDelim, , "Customers", _
        CurrentProject.Path & "\Customers.txt", True
    MsgBox "Data export completed", vbInformation, "Completed"
End Sub
```

Manipulating the *Forms* and *Reports* Collections

In this section, you will focus on the *Forms* collection. What you will see described applies equally to the *Reports* collection, but because most programming effort is against forms, this is where we will focus your attention.

The *Forms* collection is one of the most powerful concepts in Access VBA programming. When you start Access and have no forms open, the forms collection is empty, as shown in the following:

```
?Application.Forms.Count
 0
?Forms.Count
 0
```

> **Note**
> In the interest of convenience, we will omit the "Application" prefix and refer to this collection simply as *Forms*.

If you open the *Employee List* form and switch to the Immediate window, you will see that the *Forms* collection contains one entry.

> **Note**
> As with all collections in Access, the collection presented in this example is a zero-based collection.

```
?Forms.Count
 1
?Forms(0).Name
Employee List
?Forms("Employee List").Controls.Count
   9
?Forms![Employee List].RecordSource
Employees
```

You can refer to the form either by its index in the collection as *Forms(0)*, by its name *Forms("Employee List")*, or by using the "!" as *Forms![Employee List]* (you need square brackets in this case, because the name has a space in it).

Chapter 4

Using the Expression Builder

To launch Expression Builder, use either the technique described in the previous section, or create a dummy query, as shown in Figure 4-9.

Figure 4-9 Launching Expression Builder from the Query grid.

Using Expression Builder, you can browse into the list of loaded forms (forms open in the application) and drill down to various properties, controls, and subforms, as shown in Figure 4-10.

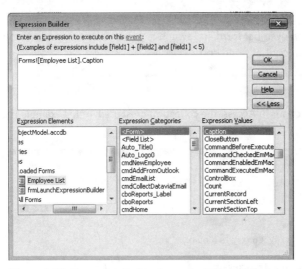

Figure 4-10 Expression Builder is particularly useful when referencing subforms, where the syntax is more complicated.

This ability to link either queries or VBA code to the forms or reports in your Access application is one of the keystones of Access programming. While we have the Employee List form open, type the following in the Immediate window:

```
Forms![Employee List].Caption = "My Employee List"
```

You will then see that the form's *Caption* property has been changed, as shown in Figure 4-11.

Figure 4-11 Form properties, control values, and control properties can be changed by manipulating the objects in the *Forms* collection.

Referencing controls on a main form uses the form's controls collection. The two syntax examples that follow show how the "!" character is used to reference an item in a collection:

```
?Forms![Employee List]![Last Name]
?Forms![Employee List].Controls("[Last Name]")
```

Referencing Controls on a Subform

The syntax to reference controls on the main form is fairly simple, but for complex forms with subforms, the syntax becomes a little more complicated. Even for experienced programmers, remembering just how the syntax changes can be difficult. For circumstances such as this, Expression Builder can guide you through the reference syntax, which you can then copy to the clipboard and add to your code.

To see an example of this, look at the Order Details form depicted in Figure 4-12 to see how you can refer to the Qty field.

Chapter 4

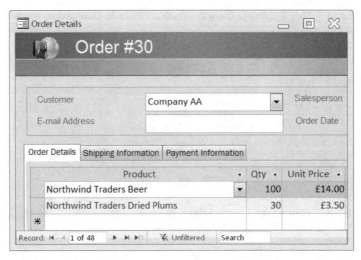

Figure 4-12 The Order Details form with subforms in a tab control.

Using Expression Builder, you browse to the subform, as shown in Figure 4-13.

Figure 4-13 Browsing to the subform to get the correct syntax.

The syntax to refer to the quantity is as follows:

```
Forms![Order Details]![sbfOrderDetails].Form![Quantity]
```

This syntax deserves some explanation: if you have a form called *FormName*; the part *Forms!FormName* references the form; then adding *!Subform* references the control called *Subform*, but because this is control is a form, you need to add the special keyword *Form* to indicate this; then *Form!Field* references the field on the form. This leads to the full syntax: *Forms!FormName!Subform.Form!Field*.

The ! (exclamation) character is used to make a reference to an object in a collection, and the . (period) character refers to a property. Therefore, this reads as: in the Forms collection, find the form called *[Order Details]*, and then in the *Controls* collection (or shorthand form's default property, which is the *Controls* collection) of the form, find the control *sbfOrderDetails*, and because this is a subform, use the special syntax *Form*. Then in the subforms *Controls* collection, find the control called *Quantity*.

Figure 4-14 shows equivalent ways to refer to the control:

```
Immediate
?Forms![Order Details]![sbfOrderDetails].Form![Quantity]
  100
?Forms![Order Details].Controls("sbfOrderDetails").Form![Quantity]
  100
?Forms![Order Details].Controls("sbfOrderDetails").Form.Controls("Quantity")
  100
```

Figure 4-14 Referencing a control on a subform.

INSIDE OUT   Syntax when using a VBA class module

There is yet one additional way to manage the syntax, which is a bit more subtle. It relies on the form having some program code behind it (*HasModule* property set to Yes, Access sets this property automatically when you add code, or you can manually change the property). When this is set, the form gets a class module with which you can then reference the controls.

Now, you can refer to the form by using the syntax in the Immediate window: ?[Form_ Order details].name, rather than ?Forms![Order Details].name. You need to look closely at the syntax here. *Forms!* refers to the forms collection, whereas *Forms_* refers to the class module. If you use the *Forms!* syntax, then the form must already be open, but if you use the *Form_* syntax, it will automatically open the form if it is not already open; the form will not be visible and you require [Form_Order Details]. Visible = True to make the form visible.

When you refer to a subform control, use the following syntax: ?Forms![Order Details]![sbfOrderDetails].Form![Quantity], but if the subform has a code module, you can shorten the syntax and use: ?[Form_Order Subform for Order Details].Quantity.

The advantage of using the *Form_* syntax is improved IntelliSense support, the disadvantage is that if you build using the Expression Builder, it does not construct expressions using this syntax.

Chapter 4

There are some very interesting properties of the *CurrentProject* collections that provide further information on all the forms and reports in your database, as shown in Figure 4-15.

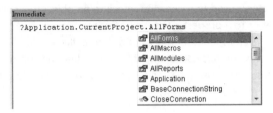

Figure 4-15 The *CurrentProject* collections.

Figure 4-16 shows the *Count* property for the total number of saved forms, and the *IsLoaded* property, which indicates whether a form is open.

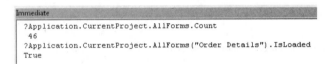

Figure 4-16 Referencing properties in the *CurrentProject* collections.

You know that a form has a *Caption* property, so if you look inside the *AllForms* (just like the Forms) collection, you might be surprised to see that this property is not available, as is revealed by the lack of IntelliSense in Figure 4-17.

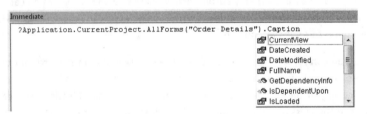

Figure 4-17 The *AllForms* collection does not expose the objects and properties inside individual forms.

This is because the *AllForms* collection acts as a set of documents; you can see what documents you have, but you cannot look inside the documents. However, when you work with the *Forms* collection, the document is open, so you can look inside each document to see what it contains.

Creating Access Objects in Code

The application object supports *CreateForm*, *CreateControl*, *CreateReport*, *CreateReport-Control*, and *CreateGroupLevel* methods, which you can use to create reports and forms by using VBA code, as shown in the following:

```
Sub modCreate_AccessForm()
    Const lngTwipsPerInch = 1440
    Const lngTwipsPerCm = 567

' Create a new Access form
    Dim frmPrompt As Form
    Set frmPrompt = Application.CreateForm
    With frmPrompt
        .Caption = "Prompt for user input"
        ' Name is read-only so can not be changed here
        '.Name = "frmUserPrompt"
    End With
    Dim ctrl As Control
    Set ctrl = Application.CreateControl(frmPrompt.Name, _
            acTextBox, acDetail, , , 2 * lngTwipsPerCm, 2 * lngTwipsPerCm, _
            lngTwipsPerCm * 5, lngTwipsPerCm * 1)
    ctrl.Name = "txtPrompt"
    ' SendKeys for saving the form and press enter key
    ' False ensures no waiting to process the
    ' keystrokes
    SendKeys "frmUserPrompt{Enter}", False
    RunCommand acCmdSave
    ' select and close the object
    RunCommand acCmdClose
End Sub
```

Because the form's *Name* property is read-only, at the end of this procedure, you use the *SendKeys* action to push keystrokes into the keyboard buffer, which will then be processed when the *RunCommand* action saves the form.

As an alternative to using the *Sendkeys*, which is very difficult to debug, you can consider using the following code to replace the last three lines in the subroutine:

```
DoCmd.Save
DoCmd.Close
DoCmd.Rename "frmUserPrompt1", acForm, "Form1"
```

The preceding technique can also be used to generate Reports by using program code. In Chapter 5, we will see how Tables and Queries can be created by using the Data Access Objects (DAO) model.

Using the *Screen* Object

The *Screen* object can be used to change the mouse pointer shape and assist in writing code in a module that responds to the *Active Form* or *Report* and the *Active* Control.

Changing the Mouse Pointer Shape

The *Application.Screen* object represents the active screen; you can use the *MousePointer* property to read or set the mouse cursor, as shown in Figure 4-18.

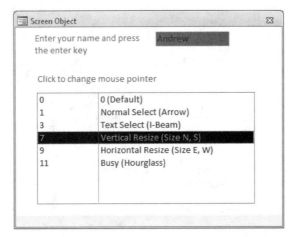

Figure 4-18 Use the *frmScreenObject* form to change the mouse pointer when you click any of the options in the list box.

```
Private Sub lstMousePointer_Click()
    Screen.MousePointer = Me.lstMousePointer.Column(0)
End Sub
```

The *Screen* object represents the currently active form or report in an application (through the *ActiveForm*, *ActiveReport*, and *ActiveControl* properties). You can use it to develop code that can be called for any form or report in an application, and you can identify the name of the form/report and control that is active when the code is called. Notice that with objects in the *Application* object, you do not need to use the "Application" prefix, which means you can shorten *Application.ScreenObject* to just *ScreenObject*.

Note

In older versions of Access, it was very difficult to debug code by using the *Screen* object because at breakpoint, the *Screen* object would no longer refer to the Active Window executing the code. Although in Access 2010 this is no longer a problem, it is still useful in program code to define variables and set the variables to the *Screen* object.

The example database contains a function called *modApp_ScreenObject()* in a module. This is linked to the *AfterUpdate* event of the unbound control shown in Figure 4-19.

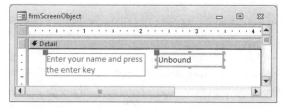

Figure 4-19 An unbound control.

Figure 4-20 illustrates how a reference to the function has been added to the *AfterUpdate* event.

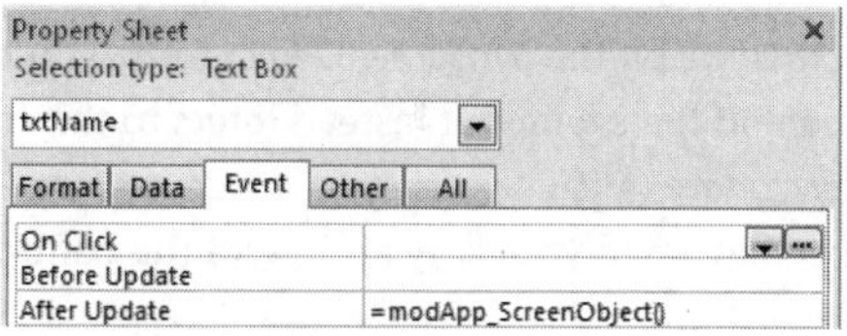

Figure 4-20 The *AfterUpdate* event calls a function without the need to create additional code behind the event for the control.

Working with the *ActiveForm* and *ActiveControl*

You can use the *Screen* object to manipulate both the active form and the active control, as shown in the following:

```
Function modApp_ScreenObject() As Variant
    ' ActiveForm, ActiveControl, ActiveReport, ActiveDatasheet
    ' Demonstrates the use of the Screen object
    Dim ctrl As TextBox
    Dim frm As Form

    Set ctrl = Screen.ActiveControl
    Set frm = Screen.ActiveForm

    Debug.Print "The active form is called " & frm.Name
    Debug.Print "The active control is called " & ctrl.Name

    ctrl.BackColor = vbRed
    Stop

End Function
```

In this example, you want to set the *BackColor* on any text control that has been edited on a form to the color red, so you need to define the active screen control to be a *TextBox* control.

You can use the following definition if you want to call the code from any kind of control:

```
Dim ctrl as Control
```

You could have referred directly to *Screen.ActiveControl*, but because not all controls have a *BackColor* property, IntelliSense would show only common control properties when working with the control object type. By using an explicit *TextBox* object, you get IntelliSense for the required property.

Enhancing the User Interface

This section looks at some of the features of the *Application* object that can be used to enhance the user interface.

Setting and Getting Options

The *Application.SetOption* command can be used to modify the application options, and the *Application.GetOption* command can be used to read option settings.

In the demonstration database, there is a table called *tblOptionTabItems* (containing 98 options) and a routine for reading the current values in the application into this table. This uses a DAO *Recordset* (described in detail in Chapter 5), as presented in the following example:

```
Sub modApp_GetOption()
    ' Updates the table tblOptionTabItems for current
    ' application settings
    Dim db As Database
    Set db = CurrentDb
    Dim rst As Recordset
```

```
        Dim varSetting As Variant
        Set rst = db.OpenRecordset("tblOptionTabItems", dbOpenDynaset)
        Do While Not rst.EOF
            rst.Edit
            rst!CurrentSetting = Nz(Application.GetOption(rst!Option))
            rst.Update
            rst.MoveNext
        Loop
        rst.Close
        Set rst = Nothing
        db.Close
        Set db = Nothing
        MsgBox "Options Read"
End Sub
```

As an example, to read the value for the *Compact On Close* option (on the current database options accessible from the options in Backstage view), you use *GetOption("Auto Compact")*. The *SetOption* command can be used to change the option setting, as shown in the following:

```
Sub modApp_SetOption()
    ' change the auto compact option
    Debug.Print GetOption("Auto Compact")
    SetOption "Auto Compact", -1
    Debug.Print GetOption("Auto Compact")
End Sub
```

It's interesting to note that the *Application* object does not have a properties collection, and the *CurrentProject* object has a *Properties* collection with no defined properties. If you look in the *CurrentDB* object, this contains 48 properties, of which, 10 match the options available through the *Set/Get* option commands (see the query qry*CurrenDBPropertiesMatchedToOptions* for the matched options). The following example includes code that reads the *CurrentDB* properties and writes them to a table called *tblProperties*:

```
Sub modApp_ReadCurrentDatabaseOptions()
    CurrentDb.Execute "DELETE * FROM tblProperties"
    Dim db As Database
    Set db = CurrentDb
    Dim rst As Recordset
    Set rst = db.OpenRecordset("tblProperties", dbOpenDynaset)
    Dim prop As Property
    For Each prop In CurrentDb.Properties
        rst.AddNew
        rst!ObjectName = "CurrentDB"
        rst!PropertyName = prop.Name
        On Error Resume Next
        rst!PropertyValue = prop.Value
        On Error GoTo 0
        rst.Update
        Debug.Print prop.Name
```

```
        Next
        ' note there are no properties in the
        ' following collection
        For Each prop In CurrentProject.Properties
            rst.AddNew
            rst!ObjectName = "CurrentProject"
            rst!PropertyName = prop.Name
            On Error Resume Next
            rst!PropertyValue = prop.Value
            On Error GoTo 0
            rst.Update
            Debug.Print prop.Name
        Next
        rst.Close
        Set rst = Nothing
        db.Close
        Set db = Nothing
        MsgBox "Properties Read"
End Sub
```

Locking Down Access

The *CurrentDB* object contains a number of very important options that can be set to
control what the user is able to do in an application, including displaying the database window. One property that you might want to add to your database is *AllowBypassKey*. This
property prevents a user from pressing the Shift key while opening a database to bypass
any startup code. The following routine is used to set a database property, or create and
append the property if it does not already exist:

```
Function modApp_SetProperty(strPropertyName As String, _
                            blSetting As Boolean) As Boolean
    ' This function sets or clears boolean properties
    ' if the property does not exist it creates the property
    Dim prop As Property
    Dim db As Database
    Set db = CurrentDb
    On Error Resume Next
    Set prop = db.Properties(strPropertyName)
    If Err <> 0 Then
        ' Create the property
        On Error GoTo Err_Handler
        Set prop = db.CreateProperty(strPropertyName, dbBoolean, blSetting)
        db.Properties.Append prop
    Else
        On Error GoTo Err_Handler
        prop.Value = blSetting
    End If
    modApp_SetProperty = True
    Exit Function
Err_Handler:
    modApp_SetProperty = False
End Function
```

You then create a function that can set or clear the desired properties:

```
Function modApp_UnlockApplication(blEnable As Boolean)
    ' Call to unlock or lock down the application
    If Not modApp_SetProperty("StartUpShowDBWindow", blEnable) Then Stop
    If Not modApp_SetProperty("AllowShortcutMenus", blEnable) Then Stop
    If Not modApp_SetProperty("AllowFullMenus", blEnable) Then Stop
    If Not modApp_SetProperty("AllowSpecialKeys", blEnable) Then Stop
    ' Prevents Shift key operation when opening the database
    ' This property will be added to the properties collection
    If Not modApp_SetProperty("AllowBypassKey", blEnable) Then Stop
    If blEnable Then
        MsgBox "Application unlocked, close and re-open the database"
    Else
        MsgBox "Application locked, close and re-open the database"
    End If
End Function
```

It's a good idea to first prepare a routine or a hotkey to unlock everything before you implement a lockdown; otherwise, you can find yourself unable to easily get back into the application. In the demonstration database, we used the F4 key in an *AutoKeys* macro to provide a call to unlock the application.

To lock down the application, call the function, passing the parameter as *False modApp_ UnlockApplication(False)*. After unlocking or locking a database with these options, you need to close and re-open the database to see the effect of the changes.

Monitoring Progress with *SysCmd*

Ths *SysCmd* object can provide a progress meter on the status bar (shown in the example *frmSysCmd* form and in the code that follows). The Access Status bar is displayed when two options are set to *True* in the Access Options in Backstage view. The option in both cases is called Status Bar; the first option is located in Current Database settings, and the second place this occurs is in the Client Settings (both are set *True* by default):

```
Private Sub cmdShowProgress_Click()
    Const lngRange = 10
    Dim varReturn As Variant
    Dim lngStep As Long
    varReturn = SysCmd(acSysCmdInitMeter, "Showing progress", lngRange)
    For lngStep = 0 To lngRange Step 2
        varReturn = SysCmd(acSysCmdUpdateMeter, lngStep)
        MsgBox "Next Step " & lngStep
    Next
    varReturn = SysCmd(acSysCmdSetStatus, "Processing last step")
    MsgBox "Change status on left"

    ' clear status bar text
    varReturn = SysCmd(acSysCmdSetStatus, " ")
End Sub
```

Chapter 4

Figure 4-21 shows the resulting progress bar.

Figure 4-21 Calling *SysCmd* with the *acSysCmdInitMeter* and *acSysCmdUpdateMeter* displays a progress bar in the lower-right corner of the screen.

Figure 4-22 shows the status message being displayed.

Figure 4-22 Calling *SysCmd* with *acSysCmdSetStatus* clears the progress bar and displays a status message instead (this is displayed in the lower-left corner of the screen, not the lower-right).

Custom Progress Bars

You might prefer to create your own pop-up progress bar by using a form. The demonstration database includes an example of this that uses the form called *frmProgress* and a module called *modBars*. The progress bar consists of ten colored rectangles. Figure 4-23 shows the form in Design mode with the set of colored rectangles.

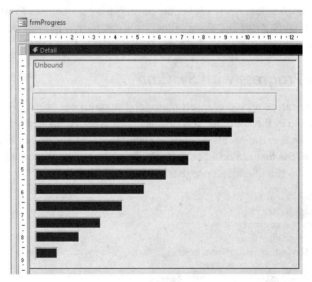

Figure 4-23 The *frmProgress* form contains colored rectangles and an unbound text box for displaying text information.

Figure 4-24 presents the rectangles as stacked on top of each other to create the custom progress bar.

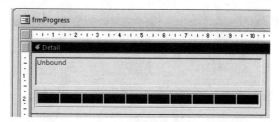

Figure 4-24 For this custom progress bar, the colored rectangles are stacked on top of each other. To create an increasing bar, we control the visibility of the rectangles.

Figure 4-25 shows the progress bar when the sample action is 50% complete.

Figure 4-25 The progress bar displaying 50% completion.

The following is an example of how to implement the custom progress bar:

```
Sub Testing()
    Dim lngItem As Long
    modBars_Open 200, "Processing 200 Items...please wait"
    For lngItem = 1 To 200
        Bars_ShowProgress lngItem, "Processing Item " & lngItem & "...."
        If lngItem = 100 Or lngItem = 200 Then
            Stop
        End If
    Next
    modBars_Close
End Sub
```

Selecting Files with the Office *FileDialog*

Use the *Application.FileDialog* (shown in Figure 4-26, followed by sample code) to present users with a professional pop-up dialog, from which they can select a file.

Chapter 4

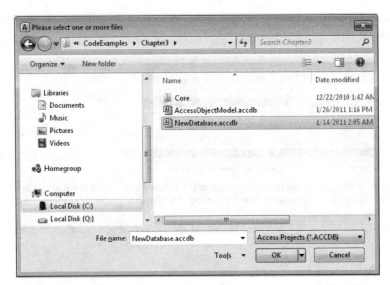

Figure 4-26 You can use *FileDialog* to give user the ability to specify different filters and select multiple files.

```
Sub modApp_FileDialog()
' Requires reference to Microsoft Office 14.0 Object Library.
   Dim fDialog As Office.FileDialog
   Dim varFile As Variant
   ' Set up the File Dialog.
   Set fDialog = Application.FileDialog(msoFileDialogFilePicker)
   With fDialog

      ' Allow user to make multiple selections in dialog box
      .AllowMultiSelect = True
      ' Set the title of the dialog box.
      .Title = "Please select one or more files"
      ' Clear out the current filters, and add our own.
      .Filters.Clear
      .Filters.Add "Access Databases", "*.MDB"
      .Filters.Add "Access Projects", "*.ADP"
      .Filters.Add "Access Projects", "*.ACCDB"
      .Filters.Add "All Files", "*.*"

      ' Show the dialog box. If the .Show method returns True, the
      ' user picked at least one file. If the .Show method returns
      ' False, the user clicked Cancel.
      If .Show = True Then
         'Loop through each file selected and add it to our list box.
         For Each varFile In .SelectedItems
            Debug.Print varFile
         Next
```

```
        Else
            MsgBox "You clicked Cancel in the file dialog box."
        End If
    End With
End Sub
```

Notice in the comments at the top of the preceding code that you need to provide a reference to the Microsoft Office 14.0 Object Library, as shown in Figure 4-27.

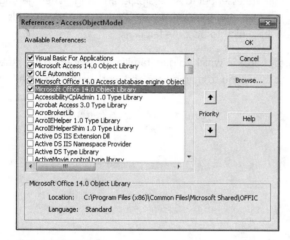

Figure 4-27 Adding a reference into your Access project.

In the VBA Editor, click Tools | References, scroll down the list of references until you find the appropriate reference, and then click the check box to include the reference. The references help Access to understand what value the constant *msoFileDialogFilePicker* has (which is 3), as well as to understand the object *Office.FileDialog* and provide IntelliSense assistance.

You can avoid the need to add a reference by substituting the value 3 for the constant (*msoFileDialogFilePicker*) and defining the *FileDialog* as an object:

```
Dim fDialog As Object
```

Doing this would avoid the need for adding the reference and use a technique called Late Binding (described in Chapter 13, "Integrating Microsoft Office"), which some developers prefer because it avoids the need to add the reference.

Chapter 4

Summary

In this chapter, you learned about the Access *Application* object. But because you do not need to explicitly state, for example, *Application.DoCmd,* and instead can use the shorthand reference, *DoCmd,* it is not always clear that you are using the *Application* object.

You also saw how this object, its methods, properties, and collections support a very wide and rich set of features that are essential to Access programming. When getting started with VBA programming, you will find the *DoCmd* and *RunCommand* methods are among the most useful features with which to become familiar.

The second most important area in which to gain familiarity is working with the *Forms* and *Reports* collections, which allow you to manipulate and work with data on a form or report.

Understanding the Data Access Object Model

The DAO Model 162

Working with Databases 164

Manipulating Data with *Recordsets* 188

Working with Queries in Code 215

Investigating and Documenting Objects 222

Sample Applications 224

I n Chapter 4, "Applying the Access Object Model," you looked at the Microsoft Access Object and learned how you can make forms and reports interact in an application. There are other object models that can be used to construct your application, and in this chapter, you will look in detail at the Data Access Object (DAO) model, with which you can manipulate the database structure and content by using program code. An overview of the DAO structure is presented in Figure 5-1.

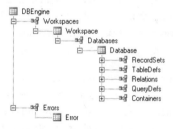

Figure 5-1 The DAO model structure.

Chapter 18, "Using ADO and ADOX," presents an alternative object model called ActiveX Data Objects (ADO). ADO can be regarded as either an alternative or complementary approach to manipulating data. Historically, DAO was the only method for the detailed manipulation of data under program control. Later, ADO became available and was regarded by some people as a better choice because it offered slightly better performance. However, ADO failed to become the dominant choice because DAO was, by then, well established. More recently, emphasis has shifted back to DAO as the Access Database Engine (ACE)—which was previously called Joint Engine Technology (JET)—has gained a new lease on life.

After completing this chapter, you will:

- Be able to understand how the DAO is organized, and how to manipulate the objects it contains.

- Be able to manipulate data by using SQL, queries, and *Recordset*s in program code.

> **Note**
> As you read through this chapter, we encourage you to also use the companion content sample database, DAOExamples.accdb, which can be downloaded from the book's catalog page.

The DAO Model

In Chapter 4, "Applying the Access Object Model," you were introduced to the concept that Access consists of objects, and we emphasized that being able to manipulate the *Forms* and *Reports* collections was a bread and butter programming skill for a Microsoft VBA programmer with Microsoft Access. In this chapter, you are going to focus on a new set of objects called the DAO; this is also a bread and butter programming skill.

The VBA programming environment is a technology into which you can add other technologies by using references. In fact, the DAO fell out of favor a few years ago, and by default, when you created a database with some earlier versions of Access, the libraries didn't get loaded. Time has moved on, and the DAO is again the key technology for an Access Database. If, however, you decide to use an Access Data Project (ADP) (which is discussed in Chapter 15, "Upsizing Access to SQL Server"), you will find that it does not have the DAO technology but uses the ADO technology.

With an Access database file, many of the key objects in the DAO are automatically created for you. It is instructive to look at the references to see where the DAO resides. This is shown in Figure 5-2.

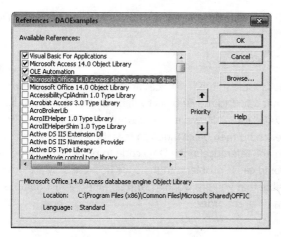

Figure 5-2 DAO references, now called the Access Database Engine Objects.

If you look farther down the list of references, you see older explicit references to the DAO libraries, as shown in Figure 5-3.

Figure 5-3 Previous DAO libraries were called "DAO Object Library."

In the examples in this and following chapters, you will notice that we do not show the code for closing objects and setting the objects to *Nothing*. The reason for this is to save space in the book, although whether you choose to do this in your own code is a matter of preference for programming style (best practice would be to close all objects and set the object variables to *Nothing*; see Chapter 2, "Understanding the VBA Language Structure," and Chapter 3, "Understanding the VBA Language Features," for examples of this).

DAO, ADO, and References

Beginning on page 188, you will be working with an object in the DAO called a *Recordset*, and in Chapter 18, you will work with the ADO object model, which also has an object called a *Recordset*. When a new database is created with Access 2010, the default library loaded in the references is the DAO Library, and you can refer to a *Recordset* in either of the two following ways:

```
Dim rstDAO As DAO.Recordset
Dim rst As Recordset
```

If we added a new ADO library to the references, then we would define an ADO *Recordset* object as follows:

```
Dim rstADO As ADODB.Recordset
```

Because the DAO library is listed in the references as coming before the entry for the ADO library, the DAO code that refers to the *rst* object will be taken from the order of the references as meaning the DAO Library. However, it is possible to take out and then add back in references and the order could then be changed so that the ADO library came before the DAO library. In this case, the reference in the DAO code to *rst* would now be taken to mean the ADO library; this would cause problems in the code because they are not the same kind of object. It is also possible that you are working with an older Access database in which the references occurred in a different order.

INSIDE OUT Correctly referring to an object when both ADO and DAO Libraries are present

You can easily determine which kind of object the *rst* variable represents by typing **rst. Edit** (for a DAO *RecordSet* this method will be displayed by IntelliSense, but not for ADO, which does not have this method for a *Recordset* object).

If you are likely to be working with both ADO and DAO in the same project, then you either need to ensure that the references are always ordered correctly, or use the DAO prefix when referring to DAO objects and the ADODB prefix when referring to ADO objects to prevent you from referring to the wrong object.

Working with Databases

We should probably apologize in advance for presenting this section (which is a bit heavy to read in advance of the rest of this chapter) rather than allowing you to dig in to what is definitely the richest aspect of the Access product. So, if you want to move on to getting your hands dirty with real programming code, feel free to indulge yourself and skip on to the next section "Manipulating Data with *Recordset*s," beginning on page 188.

You could read this section and only take away the benefit of one line in VBA, which is to get a reference to the current database. But if you really want to understand how the DAO architecture fits together and how you can push your understanding of this to an advanced level of DAO programming, then at least skimming through this section will prove to be essential. At some point, you need to dig in deeper to the DAO, and we hope this section will explain some of those deeper aspects.

The *DBEngine* Object

The *DBEngine* is the root of the DAO hierarchy; you never need to create this object as it is always available.

Inside the *DBEngine* object is the *Workspaces* collection. Each workspace is a transactional unit acting as a logon/session, and like the *DBEngine*, which was created for us, we also get a default workspace created that is referred to as *Workspaces(0)*.

Inside each *Workspace* is a *Databases* collection, and in *Workspaces(0)* we have the current database, *Database(0)*.

Whenever you start Access, you log on (even though you are not normally prompted), you get a workspace, and because you are in a database, you also get a database object.

The *DBEngine* object contains the *Workspaces* collection, which in turn contains the *Databases* collection open in each *Workspace*.

This leads to the expression:

```
DBEngine.Workspaces(0).Databases(0)
```

Or, a shorthand for this is:

```
DBEngine(0)(0)
```

Typing this into the Immediate window yields the following result:

```
?DBEngine.Workspaces(0).Name
#Default Workspace#
?DBEngine(0)(0).Name
C:\ASC08\AccessInsideOutVBA\CodeExamples\Chapter4\DAOExamples.accdb
```

Understanding this might look like it is complicated, because we have the idea of a database engine that contains workspaces, each of which can contain open databases. But this is really a preamble to getting down to work, although understanding what comes next in the hierarchy will give you a valuable insight into how Access works. If all you want to do is get on with the most common programming tasks, then you can skip the explanation of *Workspaces* and *Databases* (until you need to use some of these features) and move on to *Recordset*s.

The *Workspace* Object

The last section described how when you start Access, you get a *workspace* for *free*, which is *Workspaces(0)*. The *Workspace* object acts like a user session, with code able to force an additional logon to create a new workspace, if required. The second feature of a workspace will be discussed beginning on page 166, when we look at transactions.

The reasons for creating a new workspace would be either to gain fine control of how transactions behave, or to log on to an Access database as a different user connected to the same security Workgroup (although with .accdb files, WorkGroup security is no longer supported; it is only available in an .mdb file).

To get a reference to the default workspace, which is called *#Default Workspace#*, you can use the following code:

```
Sub modWorkspace_ListWorkspaceInformation()
    Dim wks As Workspace
    Set wks = DBEngine.Workspaces(0)
    ' An alternative syntax is shown below
    ' Set wks = DBEngine(0)
    Debug.Print "Workspace name :" & wks.Name
    ' dbUseODBC for ODBCDirect workspaces are no longer supported
    Debug.Print "Workspace type (2 - JET) : " & wks.Type
    Set wks = Nothing
End Sub
```

Any references to *ODBCDirect* (workspace type *dbUseODBC*) are no longer valid; this is an older technology that is no longer supported.

To create a new workspace, you use the following syntax:

```
Sub modWorkspace_CreateANewWorkspace()
    Dim wks As Workspace
    ' options are dbUseJet or dbUseODBC
    Set wks = DBEngine.CreateWorkspace("Access2", "Admin", "", dbUseJet)
    Debug.Print "Workspace count : " & DBEngine.Workspaces.Count
    DBEngine.Workspaces.Append wks
    Debug.Print "Workspace count : " & DBEngine.Workspaces.Count
    Set wks = Nothing
End Sub
```

Because workspaces are not permanent objects, once the program code finishes execution we are again left with only one workspace (the default workspace). The line of code that appends the newly created workspace to the workspaces collection is to some extent redundant because workspaces are temporary sessions and can be used without adding to the workspaces collection.

Transactions

Transactions serve two purposes in a database. The first purpose is to ensure that changes made to several tables (or several records in a single table) are either all completed or none of the changes are applied (if the transaction fails, then any partially completed work is discarded or rolled back). The second reason for using a transaction is to improve performance.

If you have multiple changes being made to data, and you need to ensure that the changes are consistently applied, then you should consider using a transaction to wrap around the sequence of operations.

An example of where transactions are required is a stock management system that verifies that all the products for a given order are in stock when preparing to dispatch the order and ship the goods. The associated tables and relationships are shown in Figure 5-4.

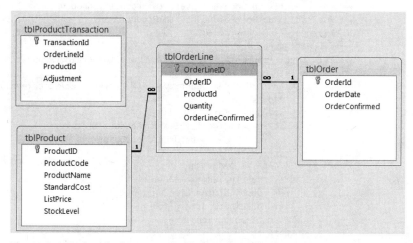

Figure 5-4 Each order has several orderlines for different products.

When you process an order, you want to complete the operation only when all stock is available. The *OrderConfirmed* flag (in *tblOrder*) is set once all the stock is available for an order, and on each line item, you have an *OrderLineConfirmed* flag that you can set to indicate that the orderline is completed. Completing an orderline involves adjusting the stock level and recording the change in a table called *tblProductTransaction*.

The unit for transactions is the workspace. When making a change to several pieces of data, you can *Begin* a transaction, make the changes, and then either *Commit* (complete) or *Rollback* (undo) the transaction. In the following code example, if you are unable to complete any part of the process or an error occurs, then the *RollbackStockAdjustment* is called to undo the transaction. The *ExitProcessing* step is called in all situations to tidy up the object variables:

```
Function modTrans_ProcessAnOrder(lngOrderId As Long) As Boolean
    ' Confirm an order and all orderlines
    ' Adjust stock levels and record in transaction table
    On Error GoTo RollbackStockAdjustment
    Dim db As Database
    Dim wks As Workspace
    Dim rstOrderLine As Recordset
    Dim rstProduct As Recordset
```

```
Dim rstTrans As Recordset
Dim strOrderLines As String
strOrderLines = "SELECT * FROM tblOrderLine " & _
                "WHERE OrderId = " & lngOrderId & _
                " AND OrderLineConfirmed = False"
Set wks = DBEngine(0)
wks.BeginTrans
    Set db = wks.Databases(0)
    Set rstOrderLine = db.OpenRecordset(strOrderLines, dbOpenDynaset)
    Set rstProduct = db.OpenRecordset("tblProduct", dbOpenDynaset)
    Set rstTrans = db.OpenRecordset("tblProductTransaction", dbOpenDynaset)
    Do While Not rstOrderLine.EOF
        ' Update stock item
        rstProduct.FindFirst "ProductId = " & rstOrderLine!ProductId
        If Not rstProduct.NoMatch Then
            If Nz(rstOrderLine!Quantity) <= Nz(rstProduct!Stocklevel) Then
                ' Adjust stock
                rstProduct.Edit
                rstProduct!Stocklevel = rstProduct!Stocklevel - _
                                rstOrderLine!Quantity
                rstProduct.Update
                ' Confirm Orderline
                rstOrderLine.Edit
                rstOrderLine!OrderLineConfirmed = True
                rstOrderLine.Update
                ' Log Transaction
                With rstTrans
                    .AddNew
                    !OrderLineId = rstOrderLine!OrderLineId
                    !ProductId = rstOrderLine!ProductId
                    !Adjustment = rstOrderLine!Quantity
                    .Update
                End With
            Else
                ' problem no stock available
                GoTo RollbackStockAdjustment
            End If
        Else
            ' problem stock item not found
            GoTo RollbackStockAdjustment
        End If
rstOrderLine.MoveNext
    Loop
    ' Confirm the Order
    db.Execute "UPDATE tblOrder SET OrderConfirmed = True " & _
                "WHERE OrderId = " & lngOrderId
wks.CommitTrans dbForceOSFlush
modTrans_ProcessAnOrder = True

ExitProcessing:
    ' Tidy up
    rstOrderLine.Close
    Set rstOrderLine = Nothing
```

```
        rstProduct.Close
        Set rstProduct = Nothing
        db.Close
        Set db = Nothing
        wks.Close
        Set wks = Nothing
        Exit Function

RollbackStockAdjustment:
        wks.Rollback
        modTrans_ProcessAnOrder = False
        GoTo ExitProcessing
End Function
```

If you are going to write transaction-based code, you will need to undertake careful testing to see that your code can handle different scenarios when multiple users engage the activities. In the sample database, the tables and code are in a single database, but to test this, you would need to put the tables in a separate database and link two front-ends to the shared tables. Then you can easily mimic what happens when two users try to make changes at the same time.

Access logs transactions in a temporary file that is located in the windows TEMP profile setting, and when committing a transaction it is advisable to use the *dbForceOSFlush* option to ensure that the changes are written to the database.

If you pause the execution of the code after it has updated a stock item and look in the tables, you will not see the resulting changes (because these are pending inside the transaction). You will find that the record has been row-level locked (which prevents any changes while the transaction is running).

INSIDE OUT   More than one transaction inserting on the same table will fail

Care needs to be taken if you are using Access transactions to perform inserts on a table, because while a transaction is inserting data in a table and a second transaction also attempts to insert into the same table, the second transaction will fail and generates a trappable error that would need to be handled in code.

The second use of transactions is to improve performance. Transactions help an Access application to reduce disk access by buffering updates and then writing to disk. To do this, you need to decide on how big the blocks are and then issue the commands to begin and commit each transaction block. You should also consider the implications on locking when doing this, because data that has been changed inside a transaction will block other users from changing any records on locked pages.

Access allows you to perform a dirty read—that is, you can view data that has been changed by a pending transaction. This is different for Microsoft SQL Server, for example, which prevents dirty reads on uncommitted data (default isolation level).

When you connect Access to SQL Server, transactions can also improve performance, but in a different way. If you run the SQL Server profiler and compare when using and not using transactions, you will see a lot less activity when using transactions. For example, for 91 edits, without transactions there are 829 events; with a transaction, 291 events. This reason for this difference is that when you work without transactions, Access issues additional instructions to *COMMIT* each row as they are individually passed to SQL Server.

INSIDE OUT
Transactions on a continuous form allow multiple edits with an option to roll back the changes

Access transactions lack many of the features found in SQL Server transactions in terms of handling concurrent transactions, but they do offer the scope to perform some very clever user interface operations. The *frmCustomersTransactions* form illustrates a technique on a continuous form that permits a user to edit multiple records and then when closing the form, roll back or commit the changes. This shows that it is possible to bind the transactional model to a form, as shown in the following code:

```
Option Compare Database
Option Explicit
Dim blInTransaction As Boolean
Private Sub Form_Dirty(Cancel As Integer)
    ' user starts an edit, and start a transaction if required
    If Not blInTransaction Then
        ' if not in a transaction then start one
        DBEngine.BeginTrans
    End If
    blInTransaction = True
End Sub

Private Sub Form_Open(Cancel As Integer)
    Dim db As DAO.Database
    Dim rs As DAO.Recordset
    Set db = CurrentDb
    Set rs = db.OpenRecordset("SELECT * FROM Customers", dbOpenDynaset)
    Set Me.Recordset = rs
    blInTransaction = False
End Sub
```

```
Private Sub Form_Unload(Cancel As Integer)
    If blInTransaction Then
        If MsgBox("Do you want to commit all changes?", vbYesNo) = vbYes Then
            DBEngine.CommitTrans dbForceOSFlush
        Else
            DBEngine.Rollback
        End If
    End If
End Sub
```

The *Errors* Collection

In Chapter 3, you learned both how to handle errors in code and how to use the *Err* object to retreive an error number and description. The DAO has its own errors collection, called *Errors*, which can handle multiple error messages. When an error occurs you will normally find that the *Errors* collection contains one error.

Notice that if you generate a code error, such as division by zero using variables, you will get a value in the *Err* object, but nothing in the *Errors* collection. This is because this collection only records the DAO errors. But when you get a DAO error, the last error in the collection is reflected in the *Err* object.

To handle errors, test *Err.Number*, and then look at *Err.Description*. The sample code that follows is an example of working with the *Errors* collection.

If you are only working with Access data, you are unlikely to ever see more than one error in the collection. But as soon as you start working with a product like SQL Server, you are going to see multiple errors.

The following code is working with a Linked SQL Server table called Customers, and the code attempts to generate a duplicate primary key (the code can be found in the in the sample database, SQLServerExamples.accdb, which is provided with Chapter 14, "Using SQL Server"):

```
Sub modErrors_DAOMultipleErrors()
    ' generates a duplicate primary key
    Dim db As Database
    Dim rst As Recordset
    Dim errorDAO As Error
    Set db = CurrentDb
    Set rst = db.OpenRecordset("Customers")
    rst.AddNew
    rst!CustomerID = "ANATR"
'    On Error Resume Next
```

```
        rst.Update
        If Err <> 0 Then
            For Each errorDAO In Errors
                Debug.Print errorDAO.Number, errorDAO.Description, errorDAO.Source
            Next
        End If
        Debug.Print Err.Number, Err.Description, Err.Source
        rst.Close
        Set rst = Nothing
        db.Close
        Set db = Nothing
End Sub
```

When this code generates an error, you see the error message shown in Figure 5-5.

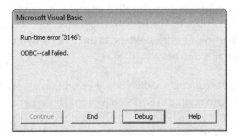

Figure 5-5 The error message displayed by Access is the message from the *Err* object; what you need is the message in *Errors*.

INSIDE OUT   The error message normally displayed when you are working with SQL Server is not the error message that you are interested in

If you look in the *Err* object, you will see the following error number, message, and source:

```
3146        ODBC--call failed.          DAO.Recordset
```

But if you look in the *Errors* collection, you will see three error messages:

```
515         [Microsoft][ODBC SQL Server Driver][SQL Server]Cannot insert the
value NULL into column 'CompanyName', table 'Northwind.dbo.Customers'; column
does not allow nulls. INSERT fails.    ODBC.Recordset
 3621        [Microsoft][ODBC SQL Server Driver][SQL Server]The statement has
been terminated.    ODBC.Recordset
 3146        ODBC--call failed.          DAO.Recordset
```

The error message that you want to record and/or display is always:

```
Errors(0).Number and Errors(0).Description.
```

In the demonstration database for Chapter 14, we have included the following error handling code that logs errors from the *Err* object, except when there is a DAO error, in which case it uses *Errors(0)*, as shown in the following:

```
Function modErrors_ErrorLogging(ByVal lngErrorNo As Long, _
                                ByVal strErrorText As String, _
                                ByVal strCallingcode As String)
' To make this handler allow for multiple error messages
' include the following code
    If Errors.Count > 1 Then
        ' use the first DAO Error
        strErrorText = Errors(0).Description
        lngErrorNo = Errors(0).Number
    End If
' This is an example of a generic error handler
' It logs the error in a table and then allows the calling procedure
' to decide on the action to take
    Dim db As DAO.Database
    Dim rst As Recordset
    Set db = CurrentDb
    Set rst = db.OpenRecordset("tblErrorLog", dbOpenDynaset)
    With rst
        .AddNew
        !ErrorNo = lngErrorNo
        !ErrorMessage = strErrorText
        !ErrorProc = strCallingcode
        ' Also very useful to log the id of the user generating the error
        !WindowsUserName = modErrors_GetUserName()
        .Update
    End With

' now allow the user to decide what happens next
    DoCmd.OpenForm "frmError", , , , , acDialog, strErrorText
        ' now as this is a dialog form our code stops here
        ' we will use a global variable to work out
        ' what action the user wants to happen
    modErrors_ErrorLogging = global_lngErrorAction
End Function
```

The *Database* Object

As with *Workspace(0)*, upon starting Access, the current database is registered as *Databases(0)*.

To obtain a reference to the current database, use the following code:

```
Sub modDatabase_DefaultDatabase()
    Dim db As Database
    Set db = DBEngine.Workspaces(0).Databases(0)
```

```
    ' equivalent syntax is shown below
    'Set db = DBEngine.Workspaces(0)(0)
    'Set db = DBEngine(0)(0)
    Debug.Print db.Name
End Sub
```

To open a link to another Access database, use the following:

```
Sub modDatabase_OpenNewDatabase()
    Dim db As Database
    ' open a path to another access database in the current workspace
    Set db = DBEngine(0).OpenDatabase(CurrentProject.Path & "\DocDAO.accdb")
    'Set db = DBEngine.OpenDatabase(CurrentProject.Path & "\DocDAO.accdb")
    Debug.Print "Databases count : " & DBEngine(0).Databases.Count
    db.Close
    Set db = Nothing
End Sub
```

It is worth noting that we do not append this new database object into the *Workspace(0).Database* collection because it is automatically created here when we open the database object. Like workspaces, these database references are not permanent, and once the code finishes execution, they are removed from the collection.

As an example of what you can do by using a *Database* reference, the following routine lists out the contents of a table in another database:

```
Sub modDatabase_ListInformation()
    Dim db As Database
    Dim rst As Recordset
    ' open a path to another access database in the current workspace
    Set db = DBEngine(0).OpenDatabase(CurrentProject.Path & "\DocDAO.accdb")
    'Set db = DBEngine.OpenDatabase(CurrentProject.Path & "\DocDAO.accdb")
    Debug.Print "Tables in the database : " & db.TableDefs.Count
    Set rst = db.OpenRecordset("tblReport", dbOpenDynaset)
    Do While Not rst.EOF
        Debug.Print rst!ReportID, rst!ReportName
        rst.MoveNext
    Loop
    db.Close
    Set db = Nothing
End Sub
```

In this chapter, you are going to see how the DAO is an extremely powerful tool that you can use to create objects and modify data in the current database. By using the reference to another database that was shown in the preceding example, you can also perform all these operations on other Access databases.

The sample database file DocDAO.accdb uses this technique to read the design of other Access databases into a set of tables; this is a useful tool if you want to have a central data dictionary that records the structure of several Access databases.

CurrentDB, DBEngine, and CodeDB

In the last section, you saw how to get a reference to a database with the *Database* object. In programming the DAO, you will come across a couple of standard programming lines of code that get a reference to the current database. There are two ways to do this:

```
Dim db As Database
Set db = DBEngine(0)(0)
```

Or:

```
Dim db As Database
Set db = CurrentDb
```

When you refer to *DBEngine(0)(0)*, you get a reference back to the *Workspaces(0).Databases(0)* object (you saw how Access creates this for you). When you refer to *CurrentDB*, Access will create an object that is guaranteed to be up to date with any newly created objects.

If you look at *CurrentDB.Version*, you get a value of 12.0, and if you look at *DBEngine(0)(0). Version* you get a value of 14.0, which is enough for you to see that these objects are not identical.

INSIDE OUT   Choosing between using *CurrentDB* and *DBEngine(0)(0)*

Because a *CurrentDB* reference involves creating an object, technically, it is slower than when working with *DBEngine(0)(0)*. However, because this happens extremely quickly and a single reference is made at the beginning of a code block, you will not see any appreciable delay. Some developers argue for creating a global variable to reference the current database; if you're using *CurrentDB*, this can be justified, but less so if you're using *DBEngine(0)(0)* because this does not incur the same performance overhead. In general, you can use whichever method you prefer, although there are circumstances for which it is better to use *CurrentDb*; for example, when designing wizards.

The following code demonstrates that if an object is created by using *CurrentDB*, then that object cannot be seen in *DBEngine(0)(0)* until the database is re-opened or the appropriate collections refreshed. However, an object created in *DBEngine(0)(0)* can be seen immediately in *CurrentDB*. Executing this code displays the message "Using CurrentDb : DBEngineTest", but not the message "Using DBEngine : CurrentDBTest":

```
Sub modDatabase_GetTheCurrentDatabase()
    Dim db1 As Database
    Set db1 = DBEngine(0)(0)
```

Chapter 5

```
      Dim db2 As Database
      Set db2 = CurrentDb

      Debug.Print "DBEngine(0)(0) : " & db1.Name
      Debug.Print "Currentdb : " & db2.Name

      db1.CreateQueryDef "DBEngineTest", "SELECT * from Customers"
      db2.CreateQueryDef "CurrentDBTest", "SELECT * from Customers"

      On Error Resume Next
      Debug.Print "Using CurrentDb : " & db2.QueryDefs("DBEngineTest").Name
      Debug.Print "Using DBEngine : " & db1.QueryDefs("CurrentDBTest").Name
      db1.Close
      Set db1 = DBEngine(0)(0)
      Debug.Print "Using DBEngine(2) : " & db1.QueryDefs("CurrentDBTest").Name

      db2.Close
      Set db1 = Nothing
      Set db2 = Nothing
      Application.RefreshDatabaseWindow
End Sub
```

After running this code, close and then re-open the database. You will see the newly created objects in the Navigation window as a result of having executed the *RefreshDatabaseWindow* command (see Figure 5-6). Both of the new objects will be available when using *CurrentDB*, but not with *DBEngine* until you execute *DBEngine(0)(0).QueryDefs.Refresh*.

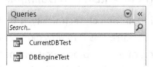

Figure 5-6 Objects created in code are not automatically refreshed in the Navigation window until you execute the *RefreshDatabaseWindow* command.

CodeDB

Building code libraries in VBA it not something that most developers undertake, but it is a very nice little feature that can be exploited across the range of Microsoft Office products (and it is very simple to use). In this next example, you will use a database called Country Library.accdb to look up ISO country codes (this is used in many of the sample applications). The database contains a local table (see Figure 5-7) that maps country names to ISO country codes, and a suitable function for performing a lookup.

INSIDE OUT   Techniques when writing VBA libraries

In addition to *CurrentDB* and *DBEngine*, there is a third way to reference a database when writing DAO code: *CodeDB()*.

The need to use *CodeDB* arises only if you are developing Access libraries or wizards. A library or wizard can contain tables, and, for example, when code in a library executes, it needs to draw a distinction between *CurrentDB* and *DBEngine*, which will refer the database into which the library has been linked, and referring to a local "in the library table," where it needs to use *CodeDB*.

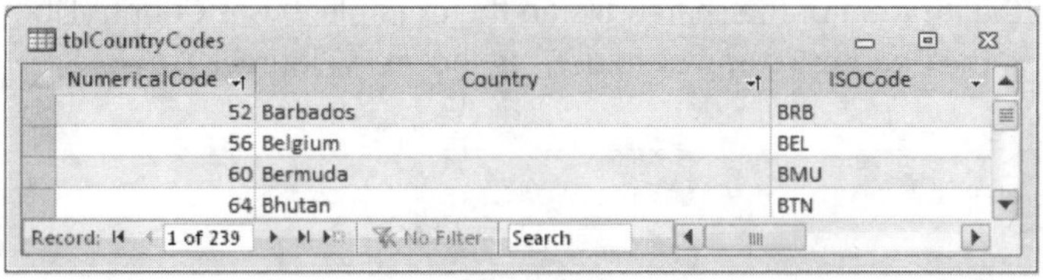

Figure 5-7 A lookup table listing ISO country codes that you will use in a VBA Library

This database contains functions that can look up an ISO code from this table, as demonstrated in the following:

```
Function modCountry_LookupISOCode(strCountryName As String) As String
    ' Test function looking up the ISO Code for a country
    ' Demonstrates difference between CodeDB and CurrentDB
    Dim db As Database
    Dim rst As Recordset
    Dim strSQL As String
    Set db = CodeDb
    MsgBox "The value for CurrentDb is " & CurrentDb.Name & _
            " the value for CodeDB is " & CodeDb.Name, _
            vbInformation, _
            "CodeDB vs. Currentdb"
    strCountryName = Replace(strCountryName, "'", "''")
    strSQL = "SELECT ISOCode FROM [tblCountryCodes] WHERE [Country] = '" & _
            strCountryName & "'"
    Set rst = db.OpenRecordset(strSQL, dbOpenDynaset)
    If Not rst.EOF Then
        modCountry_LookupISOCode = rst!ISOCode
```

```
    Else
        ' indicates not found
        modCountry_LookupISOCode = ""
    End If
    rst.Close
    Set rst = Nothing
    db.Close
    Set db = Nothing
End Function
```

You would probably want to place this database in a folder that is accessible to all of your other Access applications. The companion content contains a sample application called UsesCountryLibrary.accdb that uses this shared library. To create your own version of this, create a new database and call up the references in the VBA Editor, select the Browse option (change the default drop-down for Files Of Type to show *.accdb files), and then browse to the location of the shared file (in the example, this is CountryLibrary.accdb, which is located in the Chapter5 samples folder), as shown in Figure 5-8.

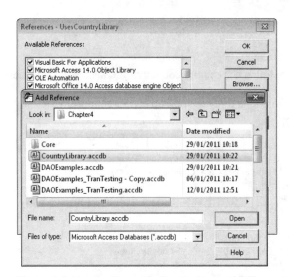

Figure 5-8 Use the Browse button to locate the library to be added, and then change the file type selection.

After adding this into your project, the project window will now look like Figure 5-9.

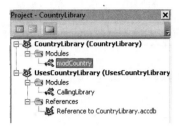

Figure 5-9 The library has now been added to the VBA project.

This shows how a VBA project is actually designed to allow multiple project libraries to be loaded.

Now we can add the following code to our project, which will use the shared routine in the loaded library:

```
Sub TestLibraryCall()
    Debug.Print modCountry_LookupISOCode("Australia")
End Sub
```

Executing this code should not only return the appropriate ISO code, but it should also displays a message box showing the value for *CurrentDB* and *CodeDB* in the executing code.

This illustrates why the library code needs to use *CodeDB* to work with a local table, because *CurrentDB* references the current project and not the code library.

The *TableDefs* Collection and Indexes

The *TableDefs* collection contains Table Definition objects; these are all the physical tables, linked tables, and system tables in the Access database. With this collection, you can create tables (in this or other Access Databases) and manage links to tables in other data sources, including Access, Microsoft SQL Server, Microsoft SharePoint, and so on.

The following code lists all of the tables and linked tables in the database:

```
Sub modTableDef_ListTables()
    Dim db As Database
    Dim tdef As TableDef
    Set db = DBEngine(0)(0)
    For Each tdef In db.TableDefs
        If Left(tdef.Name, 4) <> "MSys" Then
            Debug.Print tdef.Name, tdef.Connect
        End If
    Next
    db.Close
    Set db = Nothing
End Sub
```

Chapter 5

Tables that are held in another data source will have a *Connect* property that reflects the path to the linked data. If the path to the associated data source is changed, you can use the *TableDefs* collection to change this and refresh the link.

The sample database contains linked tables, as shown in Figure 5-10.

Figure 5-10 Linked data sources need to be relinked if the file locations are changed.

These files will not have been installed in the same folder as you have used, so you need to run the following code to relink the tables:

```
Sub modTableDef_RelinkTables()
' This routine expects to find the Northwind 2007.accdb file in
' the current folder

    Dim db As Database
    Dim tdef As TableDef
    Dim strTargetPath As String
    Dim strSourcePath As String

    strTargetPath = CurrentProject.Path
    strSourcePath = "C:\ASC08\AccessInsideOutVBA\CodeExamples\Chapter4"

    'Excel connect : Excel 12.0 Xml;HDR=YES;IMEX=2;ACCDB=YES;DATABASE=...
    'Text file connect : Text;DSN=Customers Link Specification.....
    'Access connect : ;DATABASE=.....

    Set db = DBEngine(0)(0)
    For Each tdef In db.TableDefs
        If Left(tdef.Name, 4) <> "MSys" Then
            If tdef.Connect <> "" Then
                tdef.Connect = Replace(tdef.Connect, _
                    strSourcePath, strTargetPath)
                tdef.RefreshLink
            End If
            Debug.Print tdef.Name, tdef.Connect
        End If
    Next
    db.Close
    Set db = Nothing
End Sub
```

In the next example, you see how to create a table and primary key index by using the *TableDefs* collection. The companion content contains a table called *tblFieldList* that has a list of fields to be created, as shown in Figure 5-11.

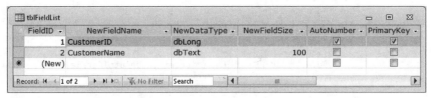

FieldID	NewFieldName	NewDataType	NewFieldSize	AutoNumber	PrimaryKey
1	CustomerID	dbLong		☑	☑
2	CustomerName	dbText	100	☐	☐
(New)				☐	☐

Record: ◄ ◄ 1 of 2 ► ►I ►≡ No Filter Search

Figure 5-11 The list of fields to be created in a table.

The code starts by creating the *TableDef*. Next, it creates each field and appends the fields into the *Fields* collection of *TableDef*. If the table has a primary key, then we create an index for the primary key and create new fields that are appended into the Indexes *Fields* collection. The final step is to append the new index into the *Index* collection of *TableDef*. The objects involved in these steps are shown in Figure 5-12, with the sample code provided thereafter.

```
TableDefs
    TableDef
        Indexes
            Index
                Fields
                    Field
        Fields
            Field
```

Figure 5-12 An overview of the objects that need to be created for the table.

```
Sub modTableDef_CreateATable()
    Dim db As Database
    Set db = CurrentDb
    Dim tdef As TableDef
    Dim fld As Field
    Dim ifld As Field
    Dim idx As Index
    Dim rst As Recordset
    Dim strTableName As String
    strTableName = "Companies"
    Set db = DBEngine(0)(0)
    On Error Resume Next
    Set tdef = db.TableDefs(strTableName)
    If Err = 0 Then
        MsgBox "Table already exists", vbInformation, strTableName
        Exit Sub
    End If
    On Error GoTo 0
    Set rst = db.OpenRecordset("tblFieldList", dbOpenDynaset)
    Set tdef = New TableDef
```

```
        tdef.Name = strTableName
        ' create the fields and save them in the tabledefs
        ' fields collection

        Do While Not rst.EOF
            Set fld = New Field
            fld.Name = rst!NewFieldName
            fld.Type = rst!NewDataType
            If rst!Autonumber Then
                fld.Attributes = fld.Attributes Or dbAutoIncrField
            End If
            If rst!PrimaryKey Then
                Set ifld = New Field
                ifld.Name = rst!NewFieldName
                ifld.Type = rst!NewDataType
                If idx Is Nothing Then
                    Set idx = New Index
                    idx.Primary = True
                    idx.Name = "idx" & strTableName
                End If
                idx.Fields.Append ifld
            End If
            tdef.Fields.Append fld
            rst.MoveNext
        Loop
        If Not idx Is Nothing Then
            tdef.Indexes.Append idx
        End If
        rst.MoveFirst

        ' Now save the table
        db.TableDefs.Append tdef
        Set tdef = Nothing
        Set db = Nothing
        Application.RefreshDatabaseWindow

    End Sub
```

When creating these DAO objects, you will find that this is a two-step process, in which an object like a field is created, and then the object must be appended into a collection. You will also notice in the code that to detect whether the table already exists, you attempt to set a reference to the object. This portion of the code is protected with an *On Error Resume Next* to detect the error, and an *On Error GoTo 0* after testing to ensure any other errors in the code are not ignored.

INSIDE OUT
Missing decimal precision when examining fields properties using the DAO

If you use a *Decimal* data type when you create the field, a precision (total number of digits in the number) and scale (number of decimal places) are specified. When using the DAO *Field2* object, the property, called *Decimal Places*, always gives a value of 255. It is only possible to find the actual precision by using ADOX, which is described in Chapter 18.

The Data Definition Language

Access also supports Data Definition Language (DDL) instructions, which is part of the SQL Standard. These can be used to create and drop tables, indexes, and other DDL objects. Sometimes, you might find it simpler to use DDL than the DAO to manage database objects:

```
Sub modDDL_CreateTable()
    ' BINARY, BIT, TINYINT, COUNTER, MONEY, DATETIME, UNIQUEIDENTIFIED
    ' DECIMAL, REAL, FLOAT, SMALLINT, INTEGER , IMAGE, , TEXT, CHARACTER
    ' Synonyms such as CURRENCY, BOOLEAN, LOGICAL etc.
    ' constraint naming is optional
    Dim db As Database
    Dim qdef As QueryDef
    Dim strSQL As String
    Set db = CurrentDb
    Set qdef = db.CreateQueryDef("")
    strSQL = "CREATE TABLE tblParent( " & _
            "ParentID COUNTER CONSTRAINT pk_tblParent PRIMARY KEY," & _
            "ParentDesc TEXT(20)" & _
            ")"
    qdef.SQL = strSQL
    ' To remove a table we could use the DROP statement
    'strSQL = "DROP TABLE tblParent"
    qdef.Execute

    strSQL = "CREATE TABLE tblChild( " & _
            "ChildID COUNTER PRIMARY KEY," & _
            "ParentId LONG," & _
            "ChildDesc TEXT(20)" & _
            ")"
    qdef.SQL = strSQL
    ' To remove a table we could use the DROP statement
    'strSQL = "DROP TABLE tblParent"
    qdef.Execute
    Application.RefreshDatabaseWindow
End Sub
```

Chapter 5

Managing Datasheet Properties

When you display a table of data in your datasheets, the properties associated with the *RowHeight*, *Fonts*, and *Colors* are defined in each *TableDef*. The sample database includes the *frmTableDefProperties* form (see Figure 5-13), which you can use to open a table, in which you can change the layout of the datasheet and display the properties. On this form, we have added some individual unbound controls that show some example properties as well as a list box that displays all of the table's properties (using a bubble sort to order in alphabetic order).

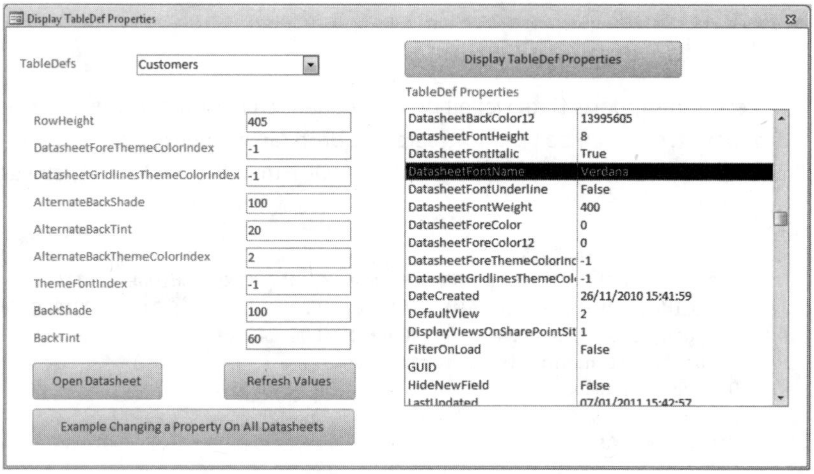

Figure 5-13 After selecting a *TableDef*, open the datasheet and use the ribbon menus to change the colors in the datasheet. Close and save the datasheet, and then refresh the *TableDefs* properties to see which properties have changed.

Behind the Example Changing A Property On All Datasheets button, there is sample code that changes the font on all the datasheets in the database. Because not all the datasheets will have a *DataSheetFontName* property, you might need to create this property and append it into the *Properties* collection of *TableDefs*:

```
Private Sub cmdChangeProperty_Click()
    Dim strTableDefs As String
    Dim db As Database
    Set db = CurrentDb
    Dim tdef As TableDef
    Dim strProp As String
    strProp = "DatasheetFontName"
    Dim strPropvalue As String
```

```
    Dim prop As Property
'     strPropValue = "Calibre"
    strPropvalue = "Verdana"
    For Each tdef In db.TableDefs
        If Left(tdef.Name, 4) <> "MSys" And _
            Left(tdef.Name, 4) <> "USys" Then
            On Error Resume Next
            tdef.Properties(strProp) = strPropvalue
            If Err <> 0 Then
                Set prop = tdef.CreateProperty(strProp, dbText, strPropvalue)
                tdef.Properties.Append prop
            End If
        End If
    Next
    Set tdef = Nothing
    db.Close
    Set db = Nothing
    MsgBox "Changed " & strProp & " to value " & strPropvalue, _
    vbInformation, "Datasheets Changed"
End Sub
```

The form contains an unbound combo box for listing all the *TableDefs*, the *RowSourceType*
has been set to *Value List*, and the following code is used to load the list of *TableDefs* into
the control's *RowSource* when the form loads:

```
Private Sub Form_Load()
    Dim strTableDefs As String
    Dim db As Database
    Set db = CurrentDb
    Dim tdef As TableDef
    Dim strcbo As String
    ' initialise list of tables
    strcbo = ""
    For Each tdef In db.TableDefs
        If Left(tdef.Name, 4) <> "MSys" And _
            Left(tdef.Name, 4) <> "USys" Then
            If strcbo <> "" Then strcbo = strcbo & ";"
            strcbo = strcbo & tdef.Name
        End If
    Next
    Me.cboTableDefs.RowSource = strcbo
    Set tdef = Nothing
    db.Close
    Set db = Nothing
End Sub
```

When assembling the properties in the list box, they are placed into an array, which is then
sorted alphabetically by using a bubble sort in the *modSort* module.

Chapter 5

The bubble sort is a simple method for sorting items by which items "bubble up" a list (the algorithm here is not a very efficient, but it is very simple):

```
Sub modSort_BubleSort(ByRef strArray() As String)
    ' perform a bubble sort on an array
    Dim lngLower As Long
    Dim lngUpper As Long
    Dim lngArrayItem As Long
    Dim strTemp As String
    lngLower = LBound(strArray)
    lngUpper = UBound(strArray)
    Dim blSorted As Boolean
    Do While Not blSorted
        blSorted = True ' assume array sorted
        For lngArrayItem = 0 To lngUpper - 1
            If strArray(lngArrayItem) > strArray(lngArrayItem + 1) Then
                ' swap with next item
                strTemp = strArray(lngArrayItem + 1)
                strArray(lngArrayItem + 1) = strArray(lngArrayItem)
                strArray(lngArrayItem) = strTemp
                blSorted = False
            End If
        Next
    Loop
End Sub
```

Relationships

In addition to creating tables by using DAO code, you might also choose to create relationships in code. The most common problem encountered when doing this is putting the tables in the wrong order when you create the relationship, for example *tblOrder*, *tblOrder-Line* will work, but *tblOrderLine*, *tblOrder* will not work:

```
Sub modTableDef_CreatingARelationship()
    ' create a relationship between tblOrder and tblOrderLine
    ' using the OrderId field
    Dim db As Database
    Dim rel As Relation
    Dim fld As Field
    Set db = CurrentDb
    ' attribute values are logically OR'ed together to turn on
    ' bits in the attribute
    ' create the relation
    On Error Resume Next
    Set rel = db.Relations("reltblOrderLinetblOrder")
    On Error GoTo 0
    If Not rel Is Nothing Then
        Debug.Print "Relationship already exists reltblOrderLinetblOrder"
        Set db = Nothing
        Exit Sub
    End If
```

```
        Set rel = db.CreateRelation("reltblOrderLinetblOrder", _
                      "tblOrder", "tblOrderLine", _
                      dbRelationUpdateCascade Or dbRelationDeleteCascade)
        ' create all fields used in the relation
        Set fld = rel.CreateField("OrderId")
        fld.ForeignName = "OrderId"
        ' save the fields
        rel.Fields.Append fld
        ' save the relation
        db.Relations.Append rel
        Set fld = Nothing
        Set rel = Nothing
        Set db = Nothing
End Sub
```

INSIDE OUT Creating relationships by using DDL

You can create relationships by using DDL; however, there appears to be inconsistent information on the Internet regarding support for *ON UPDATE CASCADE* and *ON UPDATE DELETE*, which are *not* presently supported in DDL. It is also important to create the relationship from the correct table. In the example that follows, the relationship is created from the child table *tblChild*. Attempting to create the relationship from *tblParent* will not work (notice that this is the opposite order in terms of what was chosen when using the *CreateRelation* method call in the previous example):

```
Sub modDDL_CreateRelationship()
    ' creating a relationship
    Dim db As Database
    Dim qdef As QueryDef
    Dim strSQL As String
    Set db = CurrentDb
    Set qdef = db.CreateQueryDef("")
    strSQL = "ALTER TABLE tblChild ADD CONSTRAINT reltblParenttblChild " & _
            "FOREIGN KEY ([ParentId]) REFERENCES tblParent([ParentId]) "
    ' no unique index found for referencing field of the primary table
    'strSQL = "ALTER TABLE tblParent ADD CONSTRAINT reltblParenttblChild " & _
            "FOREIGN KEY ([ParentId]) REFERENCES tblChild ([ParentId])"
    ' to drop the relationship
    '   strSQL = "ALTER TABLE tblChild DROP CONSTRAINT reltblParenttblChild "
    qdef.SQL = strSQL
    qdef.Execute
End Sub
```

Manipulating Data with *Recordsets*

You have already seen examples of *Recordsets* being used in code. In this section and those that follow, you will look at *Recordsets* in greater detail.

A *Recordset* is like looking at a datasheet with your code: you can look across a record at each field (using the *Fields* collection) or move through the *Recordset* looking at different rows of data. *Recordsets* can also be referred to as *Cursors*.

There are three different kinds of *Recordsets*:

- **dbOpenDynaset**   This is the most flexible type of *Recordset*. It can be updated, and once opened, if other users add new records, these records are not seen until you *Requery* the *Recordset* (changes made by other users are visible in the *Recordset*; records deleted by other users are marked as deleted). You can open *dbOpenDynaset* on tables, queries, and SQL statements.

- **dbOpenTable**   This is the fastest kind of *Recordset*. It can be updated, but it is more restrictive because searches must be on indexed fields, and it can only operate on local tables in the database. Note you *cannot* use *dbOpenTable* for linked Access tables.

- **dbOpenSnapShot**   This provides a read-only snapshot of data. If used on large tables, this can take time to prepare because a copy of all records are required. You can open *dbOpenSnapShot* on tables, queries, and SQL statements.

A good policy for deciding on the type of *Recordset* to use is to always choose a *dbOpen-Dynaset*, unless you specifically need a fixed static view of the data.

INSIDE OUT   Choosing between *Recordset* and *Recordset2* Objects

There are two types of *Recordset* objects: one is called *Recordset*, and the other *Recordset2*. Associated with these are the object types *Field* and *Field2*. The *Recordset2* and *Field2* are newer additions to Access and have more features, including support for the *Attachments* data types and multi-value data.

Searching

The following code example shows an example of using a *dbOpenTable Recordset* and searching on both a single index and composite indexes:

```
Sub modRST_TableRecordset()
' Example of a table recordset
    Dim db As Database
    Dim rst As Recordset2
    Set db = DBEngine(0)(0)
    Set rst = db.OpenRecordset("Customers", dbOpenTable)
    ' comparisons allowed are <, <=, =, >=, or >
    ' upto 13 key values can be searched
    With rst
        .Index = "PrimaryKey"
        .Seek "=", 9
        If Not .NoMatch Then
            Debug.Print !ID, !Company
        End If
    End With
    With rst
        .Index = "idxContact"
        .Seek "=", "Thomas", "Axen"
        If Not .NoMatch Then
            Debug.Print !ID, !Company
        End If
    End With
End Sub
```

The following example shows a snapshot *Recordset* in which the *Find* and *FindNext* methods are used to locate records:

```
Sub modRST_SnapshotRecordset()
' Example of a snapshot recordset
    Dim db As Database
    Dim rst As Recordset2
    Set db = DBEngine(0)(0)
    Set rst = db.OpenRecordset("Customers", dbOpenSnapshot)
    With rst
        .FindFirst "[Job Title] like '*Accounting*'"
        Do While Not .NoMatch
            Debug.Print !ID, !Company
            .FindNext "[Job Title] like '*Accounting*'"
        Loop
    End With
End Sub
```

The next example shows a *Dynaset*. With either a snaphot or *Dynaset*, if you know the search criteria, it will be more efficient to open the *Recordset* by using the criteria:

```
Sub modRST_DynasetRecordset()
' Example of a dynamic recordset
    Dim db As Database
    Dim rst As Recordset2
    Set db = DBEngine(0)(0)
```

Chapter 5

```
        Set rst = db.OpenRecordset("SELECT * FROM Customers " & _
                                    "WHERE [Job Title] like '*Accounting*'" _
                                    , dbOpenDynaset)
    With rst
        Do While Not .EOF
            Debug.Print !ID, !Company
            .MoveNext
        Loop
    End With
End Sub
```

You can move through a *Recordset* by using *MoveFirst*, *MoveNext*, *MovePrevious*, *MoveLast*, and *Move* (this is a relative movement from the current cursor position and can be offset from a bookmark). You can also use *AbsolutePosition* and *PercentPosition*, both of which can display the current positional information and move to an absolute position, based on a row number or percentage of total rows.

The *Recordset* also has a *RecordCount* property, but you need to ensure that you perform a *MoveLast* before relying on its value to represent the total number of records in the *Recordset*. This is because the *Recordset* does not normally read to the end of the dataset when it is opened (in order to maintain good performance).

When you open a *Recordset*, if it has no records, then the *BOF* and *EOF* properties are *True*, if the *Recordset* contains data, *BOF* is true only when you *MovePrevious* on the first record, and *EOF* is true only if you *MoveNext* of the last record (you can think of *BOF* and *EOF* as parking spots beyond the beginning and ending records; when the cursor (current position) is on *BOF* or *EOF* you cannot refer to any field values in the *Recordset* row):

```
Sub modRST_Movement()      Dim db As Database
    Dim rst As Recordset2
    Set db = DBEngine(0)(0)
    Set rst = db.OpenRecordset("Customers", dbOpenDynaset)
    Debug.Print "Number of records : " & rst.RecordCount
    rst.MoveLast
    Debug.Print "Number of records : " & rst.RecordCount
    ' Relative movement of the cursor
    rst.MoveFirst
    rst.MoveNext
    rst.MovePrevious
    rst.MoveLast

    Debug.Print "EOF : " & rst.EOF, "BOF : " & rst.BOF
    ' now move off the last records
    rst.MoveNext
    Debug.Print "EOF : " & rst.EOF, "BOF : " & rst.BOF
    rst.MoveFirst
    rst.MovePrevious
    Debug.Print "EOF : " & rst.EOF, "BOF : " & rst.BOF
```

```
    ' Absolute positioning
    rst.MoveFirst
    Debug.Print rst.AbsolutePosition
    rst.AbsolutePosition = 10
    Debug.Print "Company ID is " & rst!ID & " using AbsolutePosition"
    rst.PercentPosition = 50
    Debug.Print "Company ID is " & rst!ID & " using PercentPosition"
    rst.Move 10 ' move forwards 10 rows
    Debug.Print "Company ID is " & rst!ID & " using relative movement"
End Sub
```

Bookmarks

Bookmarks are defined as variables that you can use to mark a position and then later return to that same position. The values are valid only as long as the *Recordset* is held open. They can be held in string or variant variables. There is also a property called *Bookmarkable*, with which you can check whether the *Recordset* supports bookmarks (linked tables to Microsoft Excel, TextFiles, and SQL Server are normally bookmarkable):

```
Sub modRST_Bookmarks()
' examples of recordset movement using bookmarks
    Dim db As Database
    Dim rst As Recordset2
    Set db = DBEngine(0)(0)
    Set rst = db.OpenRecordset("Customers", dbOpenDynaset)
    ' Bookmarks
    Dim bk As String
    rst.FindFirst "[Job Title] like '*Accounting*'"
    Debug.Print "Company ID is " & rst!ID
    bk = rst.Bookmark
    rst.FindFirst "[Job Title] like '*owner*'"
    Debug.Print "Company ID is " & rst!ID
    rst.Bookmark = bk
    Debug.Print "Company ID is " & rst!ID & " using the bookmark"
    rst.Close
    Set rst = db.OpenRecordset("Customers_InTextFile", dbOpenDynaset)
    Debug.Print rst.Bookmarkable & " Bookmarkable for linked text file"
End Sub
```

Field Syntax

In this section, you will see the different forms of syntax that can be used when working with fields in a *Recordset*.

INSIDE OUT   Syntax for referencing a field in a *Recordset*

When referencing a field that includes a space in its name, enclose the name in square brackets [...]. When referencing a field in a *Recordset*, you can use either the "." (period) or "!"(exclamation) character if you are specifying the field by name. For example, the *Company* field in the *Recordset rst* could be referenced by using the following syntax:

- rst!Company

- rst.Company

- rst.Fields(lngFieldNo)

- rst.Fields("Company")

- rst.Fields(strFieldName)

```
Sub modRST_FieldSyntax()
' Example of field syntax
    Dim db As Database
    Dim rst As Recordset2
    Dim strField1 As String
    Dim strField2 As String
    Dim fld As Field
    strField1 = "ID"
    strField2 = "[Company]"
    Set db = DBEngine(0)(0)
    Set rst = db.OpenRecordset("qryCustomersInCA", dbOpenDynaset)
    With rst
        Do While Not .EOF
            Debug.Print !ID, !Company
            Debug.Print ![ID], ![Company]
            Debug.Print .[ID], .[Company]
            Debug.Print .Fields(0), .Fields(1)
            Debug.Print .Fields("[ID]"), .Fields("Company")
            Debug.Print .Fields(strField1), .Fields(strField2)
            .MoveNext
        Loop
    End With
    rst.MoveFirst

    For Each fld In rst.Fields
        If fld.Type <> dbAttachment Then
            Debug.Print fld.Name, fld.Value
        End If
    Next

End Sub
```

In the last part of the code, where you loop through the *Fields* collection of the record, the *Attachment* field data type is excluded because this would be more complex to display.

Filter and *Sort* Properties

The *Filter* and *Sort* properties of a *Recordset* might not be what you imagine them to be. The properties do not change the data in the *Recordset*; instead, they change the properties that will be applied when you open another *Recordset*, based on the current *Recordset* (note that these properties are not applied when you clone a *Recordset*).

In the following example, *rst2* is opened with the *Filter* and *Sort* properties specified on *rst*:

```
Sub modRST_FilterAndSort()
    ' example using Filter and Sort properties
    Dim db As Database
    Dim rst As Recordset2
    Dim rst2 As Recordset2
    Set db = CurrentDb
    Set rst = db.OpenRecordset("Employees", dbOpenDynaset)
    ' Apply a filter and sort
    rst.Filter = "[ReportsTo] = 2"
    rst.Sort = "[Lastname] DESC"
    ' next demonstrating sort and filter properties
    Set rst2 = rst.OpenRecordset
    rst2.MoveFirst
    Do While Not rst2.EOF
        Debug.Print rst2!Lastname
        rst2.MoveNext
    Loop
End Sub
```

Adding, Editing, and Updating Records

When adding a new record, you call the *AddNew* method on the *Recordset*, and then you call the *Update* method to save the new record. A useful additional statement is to set the *Bookmark* for the *Recordset*s to the *LastModified* property; this resynchronizes the cursor to point of the newly added record.

When updating a record, you call the *Edit* method. To save the changes, call the *Update* method.

To delete a record, call the *Delete* method. Note that the cursor will not be pointing at a valid record following this operation; therefore, you might need to use a *Move* command to set the cursor to a valid position:

```
Sub modRST_AddEditDelete()
' examples of Add, Edit and Delete with a Recordset
    Dim db As Database
    Dim rst As Recordset2
```

```
        Set db = DBEngine(0)(0)
        Set rst = db.OpenRecordset("Customers", dbOpenDynaset)
        Stop
        ' Add a new record
        rst.AddNew
        rst!Company = "Company Z"
        rst.Update
        ' reposition the cursor on the newly added record
        rst.Bookmark = rst.LastModified

        ' Update a record
        rst.Edit
        rst![Last Name] = "Bedecs"
        rst.Update
        ' cursor will still be on this record

        ' Delete a record
        rst.Delete
        ' cursor is now in valid
End Sub
```

Multiple-Values Lookup Fields

When you define a lookup field, you have the option to hold multiple values. This is a very clever internal and hidden feature in DAO, whereby a single field appears to be able to pack in more than one value.

In Table Design setting, the Allow Multiple Values for a combo box creates a multi-value field, as shown in Figure 5-14.

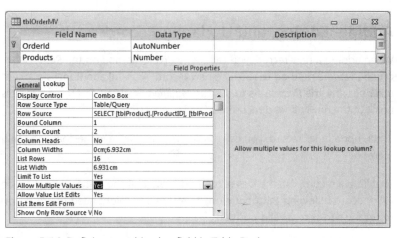

Figure 5-14 Defining a multi-value field in Table Design.

If you have used the Lookup Wizard to create this field, it will have created a relationship for you, and you can edit the relationship to add referential integrity, as shown in Figure 5-15.

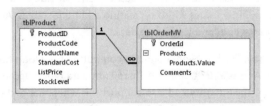

Figure 5-15 After creating a multi-value field, referential integrity can be added.

The fact that you can add referential integrity to a field indicates that this field is actually behaving like a table; in fact, a multi-value field creates a hidden table (which you cannot list in the *TableDefs*).

You will realize that a multi-value field is special because in the relationships diagram, we appear to have two items: the field called *Products*, and something called *Products.Value*.

In VBA code, you cannot directly manipulate the multi-value field, but instead, you need to open a *Recordset* on its *Value* property and treat it as a child *Recordset*, as shown in the following:

```
Sub modMV_ListValues()
    ' displays all the multivalues in a multivalue field
    Dim db As Database
    Dim rst As Recordset2
    Dim rstMV As Recordset2
    Set db = CurrentDb
    Set rst = db.OpenRecordset("tblOrderMV", dbOpenDynaset)
    Do While Not rst.EOF
        Debug.Print "Order Id : " & rst!OrderId
        ' Note you can not do the following
        'Debug.Print rst!products
        Set rstMV = rst!products.Value
        Do While Not rstMV.EOF
            Debug.Print "Product Id : " & rstMV!Value
            rstMV.MoveNext
        Loop
        rst.MoveNext
    Loop
End Sub
```

INSIDE OUT   Using multi-value fields

Multi-value fields can model a many-to-many relationship and provide a quick and easy method for storing multiple values without creating additional tables; Access creates hidden system tables for holding multi-value data.

The concept of multi-value fields has been around in computing for a long time, and these were introduced in Access 2007 to map to SharePoint data types. Because multi-value fields support referential integrity and also support this when mapped to a web database in SharePoint, they can be a shorthand notation for creating a table of lookup values; as such, they are designed to save you time when designing a database.

If you intend to convert your database to SQL Server, remember that SQL Server does not support multi-value fields, and the fields will need to be normalized into real tables before you can do this. Also, any SQL using multi-value fields will not be easy to convert to SQL Server.

Querying against a multi-value field introduces more than one possibility for specifying the SQL syntax and returning appropriate results. Figure 5-16 shows how to return one row per record for the multi-value data, and Figure 5-17 shows the resulting data.

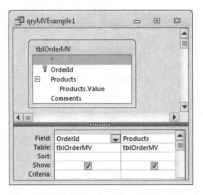

Figure 5-16 Selecting the multi-value field results in one row per record, with the field values packed and separated by commas.

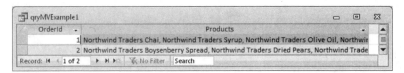

Figure 5-17 The result of selecting the multi-value field displaying two records.

Alternatively, by selecting the value of the multi-value field, as shown in Figure 5-18, you get multiple rows with one row for each multiple value, as shown in Figure 5-19.

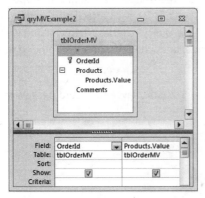

Figure 5-18 Selecting the value field splits the results into one row per value.

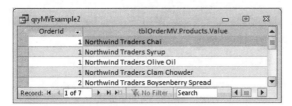

Figure 5-19 Results showing one row per multiple value.

Attachment Fields

Attachment data types were introduced into Access for compatibility with SharePoint. They can be used as an alternative to the older *OLE* data type for storing, images, spreadsheets, databases, and other documents. In addition to their compatibility with SharePoint, *Attachment* data types offer better storage performance because the documents are compressed.

INSIDE OUT   Limitations when using *Attachment* data types

If you are creating an append query, then you must exclude any *Attachment* data types or multi-value fields from the list of fields, which means that having code to copy *Attachment* data types between tables is useful. If you are constructing a *UNION* query, then *Attachment*, *OLE*, *multi-value*, and *Memo* data types are not supported. Data macros have similar limitations when working with *Attachments*.

Attachment data types are not compatible with standard SQL Server data types and normally need converting to *OLE* data types when migrating data directly to SQL Server tables.

Chapter 5

When you look at an Attachment field in query design, you will see that in addition to selecting the Attachment field itself, you can also select the inner components of an Attachment FileData (the attachment data), FileName (the file name), and FileType (the file type). If you select these fields, you will get one record for each attachment. If you query to select specific attachments, use these fields for the query criteria. When working with image data, the attachment normally shows the image, and when working with other data types it displays the appropriate icon.

Selecting an Attachment field (see Figure 5-20) displays one record per row in the original table, as shown in Figure 5-21.

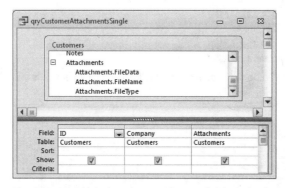

Figure 5-20 Displaying the Attachment field on the Query grid.

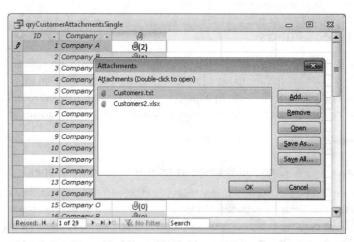

Figure 5-21 Right-click the Attachment field (shown with the paper-clip icon), and then select to manage the attachment from the shortcut menu.

It is also possible to select the inner parts of an attachment (see Figure 5-22), which displays one record for each attachment, as shown in Figure 5-23.

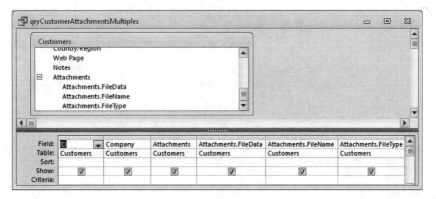

Figure 5-22 If you select the attachment attributes on the Query grid, you generate one row per attachment value.

If you select this, one row for each attachment is displayed. As long as you include the Attachment field, you will also be able to manage the attachments, and you will see the file details for each attached piece of data.

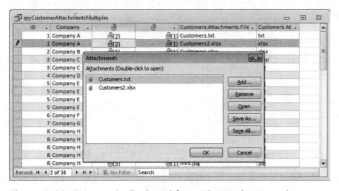

Figure 5-23 One row is displayed for each attachment value.

To get the most out of working with attachments, you will find that DAO code using the *RecordSet2* and *Field2* objects is required. One big advantage of *Attachment* data types when compared against *OLE* data types is support for the *SaveToFile* and *LoadFromFile* methods, which make saving and importing attachments very easy.

The sample application includes two forms, *frmCustomersAttachmentsMultiples* (one record per attachment, multiple records for each customer) and *frmCustomersAttachmentsSingle* (one record per customer displaying multiple attachments), which show how DAO code can be used for managing attachments. Figure 5-24 displays the form *frmCustomersAttachments Single,* which displays the first attachment and provides navigation buttons to display the other attachments, the second form, *frmCustomersAttachmentsMultiples*, is almost identical, except that it displays one record for each attachment. The code described in this section can be found on both the sample forms.

Figure 5-24 Buttons and informational fields can be added to a form to assist in managing the attachments.

Buttons are provided on both the sample forms for moving through and displaying each of the attachments. This code uses the *Forward* and *Back* methods of the *Attachment* control, such as in the following:

```
Private Sub cmdNextAttachment_Click()
    Me.Attachments.Forward
End Sub
```

Displaying Information

On each form's *Current* event, the subroutine *DisplayAttachmentInfo* is executed (contained in the forms module) to populate the list box with details of all attachments on the record:

```
Sub DisplayAttachmentInfo()
    If IsNull(Me.ID) Then
        Exit Sub
    End If
    Dim db As Database
    Dim rst As Recordset2
    Dim rstAttach As Recordset2
    Dim afld As Field2
    Dim strListBox As String
    Me.txtAttachmentCount = Me.Attachments.AttachmentCount
    If Me.Attachments.AttachmentCount > 0 Then
        Set db = CurrentDb
```

```
            Set rst = db.OpenRecordset("SELECT * FROM  Customers" & _
                                " WHERE ID = " & Me.ID)
        Set afld = rst!Attachments
        Set rstAttach = afld.Value
        strListBox = ""
        Do While Not rstAttach.EOF
            If strListBox <> "" Then strListBox = strListBox & ";"
            strListBox = strListBox & """" & rstAttach!FileName & """;"""
            strListBox = strListBox & rstAttach!FileType & """"
            rstAttach.MoveNext
        Loop
        Me.lstAttachmentInfo.RowSource = strListBox
        Me.lstAttachmentInfo.Selected(0) = 1
        Me.lstAttachmentInfo = Me.lstAttachmentInfo.ItemData(0)
        Me.txtAttachmentIndex = 1
        lngAttachment = 1
        Me.cmdExportAttachment.Enabled = True
        Me.cmdDeleteAttachment.Enabled = True
        Me.cmdImportAttachment.Enabled = True
        ' resynchronises after deletes and inserts
        lstAttachmentInfo_AfterUpdate
    Else
        Me.lstAttachmentInfo.RowSource = ""
        Me.txtAttachmentIndex = Null
        lngAttachment = 0
        Me.cmdExportAttachment.Enabled = False
        Me.cmdDeleteAttachment.Enabled = False
        Me.cmdImportAttachment.Enabled = True
    End If
End Sub
```

This following code opens the *Recordset rst* for the current record. Note that the *Field2* variable, *aField*, is set to the attachment field *rst!Attachments*:

```
        Set rst = db.OpenRecordset("SELECT * FROM  Customers" & _
                            " WHERE ID = " & Me.ID)
        Set afld = rst!Attachments
```

Then, a new child *Recordset rstAttach* is opened on the attachment field:

```
        Set rstAttach = afld.Value
```

Because the attachment control does not expose a property that indicates which of the available attachments is being displayed, you have a variable, *lngAttachment*, which is used to work out which attachment to display; clicking any attachment file name in the list box updates the attachment control to display the selected object.

Delete

The following code behind the button that deletes attachments opens the child attachment *Recordset* and deletes the row. This also requeries the form and uses the forms *Recordset-Clone* to ensure that the user's record position in the position in the underlying *Recordset* remains unchanged (so the user is still viewing the same record after the attachment is deleted):

```
Private Sub cmdDeleteAttachment_Click()
    Dim db As Database
    Dim rst As Recordset2
    Dim rstAttach As Recordset2
    Dim afld As Field2
    Dim lnga As Integer
    Dim lngkey As Long
    Set db = CurrentDb
    Set rst = db.OpenRecordset("SELECT * FROM  Customers" & _
                        " WHERE ID = " & Me.ID)
    Set afld = rst!Attachments
    Set rstAttach = afld.Value
    ' now use out index to find the appropriate attachment
    For lnga = 1 To lngAttachment - 1
        rstAttach.MoveNext
    Next
    If MsgBox("Delete " & rstAttach!FileName & "?", vbYesNo, _
        "Delete Attachment") = vbYes Then
        rstAttach.Delete
        ' requery the form and relocate the current record
        lngkey = Me.ID
        Me.Requery
        Me.RecordsetClone.FindFirst "[ID] = " & lngkey
        Me.Bookmark = Me.RecordsetClone.Bookmark
    End If
End Sub
```

SaveToFile

The code for exporting an attachment again opens the child *Recordset* and uses the *Save-ToFile* method. This also uses the *Kill* command to delete the file if it already exists:

```
Private Sub cmdExportAttachment_Click()
    Dim db As Database
    Dim rst As Recordset2
    Dim rstAttach As Recordset2
    Dim afld As Field2
    Dim strSavepath As String
    Dim lnga As Integer
    strSavepath = Application.CurrentProject.Path
    Set db = CurrentDb
```

```
        Set rst = db.OpenRecordset("SELECT * FROM  Customers" & _
                             " WHERE ID = " & Me.ID)
        Set afld = rst!Attachments
        Set rstAttach = afld.Value
        ' now use out index to find the appropriate attachment
        For lnga = 1 To lngAttachment - 1
            rstAttach.MoveNext
        Next
        strSavepath = strSavepath & "\" & rstAttach!FileName
        If MsgBox("Save to " & strSavepath & "?", vbYesNo, _
                  "Save Attachment") = vbYes Then
            On Error Resume Next
Save:
            rstAttach!FileData.SaveToFile strSavepath
            If Err = 3839 Then
                Err.Clear
                If MsgBox("Over-write existing file ?", vbYesNo, _
                      "File Exists") = vbYes Then
                    Kill strSavepath
                    GoTo Save:
                End If
            Else
                MsgBox "Attachment Saved", vbInformation, _
                      "Attachment Saved"
            End If
        End If
End Sub
```

LoadFromFile

The code for importing attachments uses the *LoadFromFile* method and the Windows *FileDialog* for selecting the file. There is one very special point to note: before you issue the *rstAttach.AddNew* command, you must first have the parent *Recordset* in edit mode by using *rst.Edit*:

```
Private Sub cmdImportAttachment_Click()
    Dim db As Database
    Dim rst As Recordset2
    Dim rstAttach As Recordset2
    Dim afld As Field2
    Dim strLoadpath As String
    Dim lnga As Integer
    Dim lngkey As Long
    strLoadpath = Nz(modApp_FileDialog())
    If strLoadpath = "" Then
        Exit Sub
    End If
    Set db = CurrentDb
    Set rst = db.OpenRecordset("SELECT * FROM  Customers" & _
                        " WHERE ID = " & Me.ID)
```

```
    Set afld = rst!Attachments
    Set rstAttach = afld.Value
    ' note we must put the parent recordset into edit mode
    rst.Edit
    rstAttach.AddNew
    On Error Resume Next
    rstAttach!FileData.LoadFromFile strLoadpath
    If Err <> 0 Then
        MsgBox Err.Description, vbInformation, strLoadpath
        Exit Sub
    End If
    rstAttach.Update
    rst.Update
    ' update the attachments
    ' requery the form and relocate the current record
    lngkey = Me.ID
    Me.Requery
    Me.RecordsetClone.FindFirst "[ID] = " & lngkey
    Me.Bookmark = Me.RecordsetClone.Bookmark
End Sub
```

Copying Attachments

Because you cannot include attachments in Append queries, you will find it useful to
have some code that can append attachments. The following code illustrates how to copy
attachments between tables and records. Notice that only two of the available Attachments
fields, *FileData* and *FileName*, are copied. This is because the other fields are read-only:

```
Function modAttach_AppendAttachments(strSourceTable As String, _
                            strSourceKeyName As String, _
                            lngSourceKeyValue As Long, _
                            strSourceAttachmentName As String, _
                            strTargetTable As String, _
                            strTargetKeyName As String, _
                            lngTargetKeyValue As Long, _
                            strTargetAttachmentName As String) As Boolean

    ' copies the attachments between records in the same
    ' or different tables
    ' Note only works for single part primary key
    ' Note assumes primary key is numeric but could be easily extended
    ' to other key value types
    Dim db As Database
    Dim sourcerst As Recordset2
    Dim targetrst As Recordset2
    Dim strSourceSQL As String
    Dim strTargetSQL As String
    Dim fldSource As Field2
    Dim fldTarget As Field2
    Dim childsourcerst As Recordset2
    Dim childtargetrst As Recordset2
```

```
        Set db = CurrentDb
        strSourceSQL = "SELECT [" & strSourceKeyName & "], " & _
                       "[" & strSourceAttachmentName & "]" & _
                       " FROM [" & strSourceTable & "]" & _
                       " WHERE [" & strSourceKeyName & "] = " & _
                       lngSourceKeyValue

        strTargetSQL = "SELECT [" & strTargetKeyName & "], " & _
                       "[" & strTargetAttachmentName & "]" & _
                       " FROM [" & strTargetTable & "]" & _
                       " WHERE [" & strTargetKeyName & "] = " & _
                       lngTargetKeyValue
        Set sourcerst = db.OpenRecordset(strSourceSQL, dbOpenDynaset)
        Set targetrst = db.OpenRecordset(strTargetSQL, dbOpenDynaset)
        If sourcerst.EOF Or targetrst.EOF Then
            ' no rows to copy between
            modAttach_AppendAttachments = False
            Exit Function
        End If
        Set fldSource = sourcerst(strSourceAttachmentName)
        Set fldTarget = targetrst(strTargetAttachmentName)
        Set childsourcerst = fldSource.Value
        Set childtargetrst = fldTarget.Value
        If childsourcerst.EOF Then
            ' nothing to copy
            modAttach_AppendAttachments = False
            Exit Function
        End If
        ' put parent recordset into edit mode
        targetrst.Edit
        Do While Not childsourcerst.EOF
            childtargetrst.AddNew
            childtargetrst!FileData = childsourcerst!FileData
            childtargetrst!FileName = childsourcerst!FileName
            childtargetrst.Update
            childsourcerst.MoveNext
        Loop
        targetrst.Update
        ' should clean up variables before exit
End Function
Sub modAttach_Test()
    Dim blResult As Boolean
    Dim strSourceTable As String
    Dim strSourceKeyName As String
    Dim lngSourceKeyValue As Long
    Dim strSourceAttachmentName As String
    Dim strTargetTable As String
    Dim strTargetKeyName As String
    Dim lngTargetKeyValue As Long
    Dim strTargetAttachmentName As String
    strSourceTable = "Customers"
    strSourceKeyName = "ID"
```

```
lngSourceKeyValue = 1
strSourceAttachmentName = "Attachments"
strTargetTable = "CustomersForAppend"
strTargetKeyName = "ID"
lngTargetKeyValue = 1
strTargetAttachmentName = "Attachments"
blResult = modAttach_AppendAttachments(strSourceTable, _
                                       strSourceKeyName, _
                                       lngSourceKeyValue, _
                                       strSourceAttachmentName, _
                                       strTargetTable, _
                                       strTargetKeyName, _
                                       lngTargetKeyValue, _
                                       strTargetAttachmentName)

    Debug.Print blResult
End Sub
```

The *OLE Object* Data Type

The *OLE Object* data type can be used to store documents (spreadsheets, binary files, images, and so on) in your database tables. When compared with the *Attachment* data type, *OLE Object* data types offer the advantage that the data can be converted to SQL Server *IMAGE* or *VARBINARY(MAX)* data types.

INSIDE OUT   Importing and exporting *OLE Object*s

There are two ways to transfer data into an *OLE Object*. The first (and probably not the most popular choice) is to perform a binary transfer of a file. The disadvantage of this method is that Access cannot launch the *OLE Object* by double-clicking it. The advantage of a binary transfer, however, is that in addition to importing data, the OLE data can also be easily exported. The data is displayed as *Long Binary* data.

The second method is to use the familiar approach of inserting an object, which can then be viewed by double-clicking the object; provided the computer has the appropriate OLE Server installed. One disadvantage of this approach is that although the objects can be loaded under program control, exporting the data back to a file under program control can be very difficult. This is because once the data is imported, it is held with additional header information, which you would need to remove if you want to export the data.

Using Binary Transfer

After performing a binary transfer, when the data is loaded, it is displayed as *Long Binary* data, as shown in Figure 5-25. The advantage with this is that you can export the data to an external file.

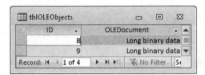

Figure 5-25 When you work with *Long Binary* data types, you cannot double-click to display the information.

When you load a binary file, it is read in blocks into a data buffer. Before reading blocks of data, the buffer is prepared by filling with space characters. A calculation is also performed to read exactly any leftover bytes from the block calculation, as illustrated in the following:

```
Const lngBlockSize = 32768 ' blocksize for copying data

Function modOLEBinary_LoadFromFile(fld As Field, _
                                   strSourceFile As String)
' reads strSourceFile into OLE Field
    On Error GoTo Err_Handler
    Dim lngBlocks As Long
    Dim lngCount As Long
    Dim lngExtraBytes As Long
    Dim lngFileSize As Long
    Dim strBuffer As String
    Dim lngFileId As Long
    On Error GoTo Err_Handler
    ' Open strSourceFile
    lngFileId = FreeFile ' gets next available file id
    Open strSourceFile For Binary Access Read As lngFileId
    lngFileSize = LOF(lngFileId)
    ' Find number of blocks and extra bytes
    lngBlocks = lngFileSize \ lngBlockSize
    lngExtraBytes = lngFileSize Mod lngBlockSize

    ' allocate space in the buffer
    strBuffer = Space(lngBlockSize)
    For lngCount = 1 To lngBlocks
        Get lngFileId, , strBuffer
        fld.AppendChunk (strBuffer)
    Next
    ' resize the buffer for any extra data
```

Chapter 5

```
        If lngExtraBytes <> 0 Then
            strBuffer = Space(lngExtraBytes)
            Get lngFileId, , strBuffer
            fld.AppendChunk (strBuffer)
        End If
        Close lngFileId
        modOLEBinary_LoadFromFile = True
        Exit Function
Err_Handler:
Stop
        modOLEBinary_LoadFromFile = False
        Exit Function
End Function
```

A similar function can be constructed to write the data to a file:

```
Function modOLEBinary_SaveToFile(fld As Field, _
                                      strTargetFile As String) As Boolean
' write to strSourceFile from OLE Field
    On Error GoTo Err_Handler
    Dim lngBlocks As Long
    Dim lngCount As Long
    Dim lngExtraBytes As Long
    Dim lngFileSize As Long
    Dim strBuffer As String
    Dim lngFileId As Long
    On Error GoTo Err_Handler
    ' Open strSourceFile
    lngFileId = FreeFile ' gets next available file id
    Open strTargetFile For Binary Access Write As lngFileId
    lngFileSize = fld.FieldSize()
    ' Find number of blocks and extra bytes
    lngBlocks = lngFileSize \ lngBlockSize
    lngExtraBytes = lngFileSize Mod lngBlockSize

    ' allocate space in the buffer
    strBuffer = Space(lngBlockSize)
    For lngCount = 1 To lngBlocks
        strBuffer = fld.GetChunk((lngCount - 1) * lngBlockSize, _
                            lngBlockSize)
        Put lngFileId, , strBuffer
    Next
    ' resize the buffer for any extra data
    If lngExtraBytes <> 0 Then
        strBuffer = Space(lngExtraBytes)
        strBuffer = fld.GetChunk(lngBlocks * lngBlockSize, lngExtraBytes)
        Put lngFileId, , strBuffer
    End If
    Close lngFileId
    modOLEBinary_SaveToFile = True
    Exit Function
Err_Handler:
```

```
Stop
    modOLEBinary_SaveToFile = False
    Exit Function
End Function
```

The following is a test routine for reading and then writing the data:

```
Sub modOLEBinary_Test()
    ' example reading and then writing a binary file
    Dim strSourceFile As String
    Dim strTargetFile As String
    Dim db As Database
    Dim rst As Recordset
    Set db = CurrentDb
    Set rst = db.OpenRecordset("tblOLEObjects", dbOpenDynaset)
    rst.AddNew
    rst!Comments = "Binary Transfer Test"
    strSourceFile = CurrentProject.Path & "\DocDAO.accdb"
    rst!FileName = strSourceFile
    If modOLEBinary_LoadFromFile(rst!OLEDocument, strSourceFile) Then
        Debug.Print "File written"
    Else
        Debug.Print "File Write Failed"
    End If
    rst.Update
    rst.Bookmark = rst.LastModified

    strTargetFile = CurrentProject.Path & "\DocDAOCopy.accdb"
    ' remove the file if it exists
    If Dir(strTargetFile) <> "" Then
        Kill strTargetFile
    End If

    If modOLEBinary_SaveToFile(rst!OLEDocument, strTargetFile) Then
        Debug.Print "File written"
    Else
        Debug.Print "File Write Failed"
    End If

    rst.Close
    db.Close
End Sub
```

Inserted Documents

To load an OLE document, you create a form with the *OLE Object* as a bound control. *OLE Object*s can then be loaded into the control by using a few lines of VBA code. When *OLE Object*s are loaded in this manner, they are registered and can then be opened by double-clicking the object (assuming the OLE Server is available), which is shown in Figure 5-26 and demonstrated in the code that follows for the *frmOLEObjects* form.

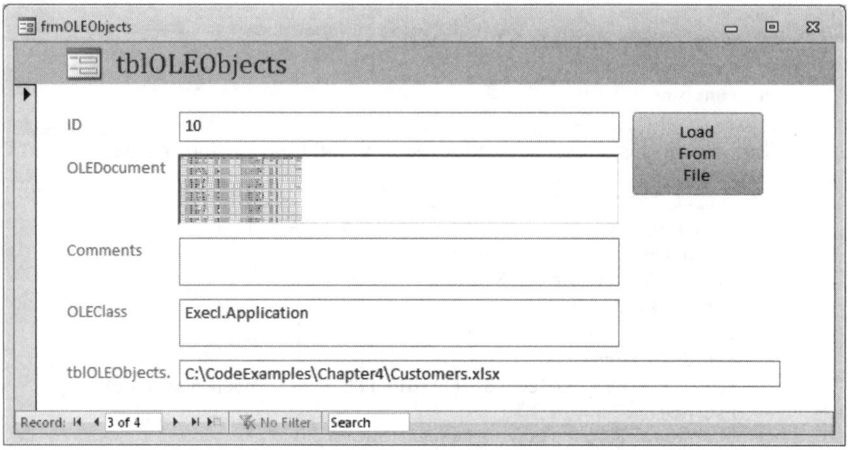

Figure 5-26 When *OLE Object*s are loaded from a file, they are displayed as an icon or graphic and can be double-clicked to display the document.

```
Private Sub cmdLoadFile_Click()
    RunCommand acCmdRecordsGoToNew
    ' code to read an OLE Object From file
    Dim strFileName As String
    strFileName = CurrentProject.Path & "\Customers.xlsx"
    Me.FileName = strFileName
    Me.OLEDocument.Class = "Excel.Application"
    Me.OLEDocument.OLETypeAllowed = acOLEEmbedded
    Me.OLEDocument.SourceDoc = Me.FileName
    Me.OLEDocument.Action = acOLECreateEmbed
    Me.Dirty = False
End Sub
```

To load a document in this way, you need to provide the OLE Class for the object. During the loading process, additional data is added to the object, which then makes exporting the data back to a file a very difficult task. But as long as you intend to keep the data in a database, *OLE Object*s are a great feature to work with.

Calculated Fields

Calculated fields provide a way for simple expressions in a table design to display a calculation based upon other fields in the same table and a limited set of built-in expressions. These fields are deterministic (the values only change if the dependent data changes) in that you cannot use functions such as *Date()* or *Now()* as part of the calculation; therefore, as an example, you cannot create a calculated field to show an employee's age based on holding their date of birth and knowing the current date. Calculated fields cannot be indexed and cannot use custom VBA functions. This field type has been constructed to be compatible with SharePoint calculated fields, and the values are only updated when the dependent field values change, which offers improved performance when filtering and sorting data.

In VBA, a calculated field can be manipulated by using the *Field2* object. The *Field2.Type* property is a standard type, such as *dbText*, and indicates the return type from the *Field2. Expression* property that contains the expression. To create a calculated field in code you provide a value for the *Expression* property.

In a typical example, you can use a calculated field to concatenate an employee's FirstName and LastName by using the expression `Trim([FirstName] & " " & [LastName])`. This saves you from having to enter this calculation in other parts of a system.

For more information on string concatenation and string functions such as *Trim*, see Chapter 3.

In the following example, we use DAO code to add a calculated field to a table that takes a contract number and adds a text prefix and pads additional leading 0's to the contract number (1 becomes CN-000001). This is an example of using a calculated field to save having to add a calculation in several other parts of the system, it also has the advantage of ensuring that if the calculation needs to change, it only needs to be changed at one point in the system:

```
Sub modTableDef_AddACalculatedColumn()
    ' Example adding a calculated field to a table
    Dim db As Database
    Dim tdef As TableDef
    Dim fld As Field2
    Dim strFieldName As String
    Set db = CurrentDb
    strFieldName = "ContractNo"
    Set tdef = db.TableDefs("ContractEmployees")
    On Error Resume Next
    Set fld = tdef.Fields(strFieldName)
    On Error GoTo 0
    If Not fld Is Nothing Then
        Debug.Print "Field already exists " & strFieldName
        Set fld = Nothing
        Set tdef = Nothing
        Exit Sub
    End If
    Set fld = tdef.CreateField(strFieldName, dbText, 200)
    fld.Expression = "'CN-' & String(6-Len([ContractId]),'0') & [ContractId]"
    tdef.Fields.Append fld
    Set fld = Nothing
    Set tdef = Nothing
End Sub
```

Cloning and Copying *Recordsets*

Rather than create a new *Recordset*, it is sometimes more useful to create a clone of an existing *Recordset*. The code example that follows defines a table that contains a list of employees with a ReportsTo field that lookups the manager in the same table (self-joined).

Cloning a *Recordset* is more efficient than creating a second *Recordset* and also has the benefit that *Bookmarks* are shared between the two *Recordsets*.

In the following example, a new record is inserted in the clone, a bookmark is recorded, and the existing *Recordset* is repositioned at the cursor defined inside the clone:

```
Sub modRST_Clone()
    ' example using a recordset clone
    ' and shared bookmarks
    Dim db As Database
    Dim rst As Recordset2
    Dim rst2 As Recordset2
    Dim bk As String
    Set db = CurrentDb
    Set rst = db.OpenRecordset("Employees", dbOpenDynaset)
    'clone the recordset
    Set rst2 = rst.Clone
    rst.FindFirst "[EmployeeId] = 2"
    bk = rst.Bookmark
    Debug.Print rst!EmployeeId
    ' Move the cloned recordset to same position
    rst2.Bookmark = bk
    Debug.Print rst!EmployeeId
    With rst2
        .AddNew
        !ReportsTo = 2
        !FirstName = "Fred"
        !Lastname = "Bloggs"
        .Update
        .Bookmark = .LastModified
        bk = .Bookmark
    End With
    rst.Bookmark = bk
    Debug.Print rst!FirstName
End Sub
```

In some applications, records need to be copied between very similar structures; for example, copying employee details onto a contract where a snapshot of the employee information needs to be preserved for contractual reasons (see Figure 5-27). This would be an alternative method to using append queries; whereas append queries are more efficient for copying a large number of records, this approach reduces the number of queries required in the application.

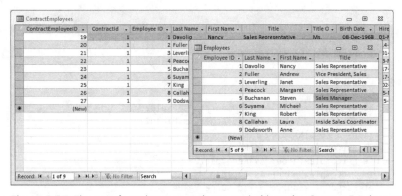

Figure 5-27 The set of employee records are copied into the *ContractEmployees* table with the addition of the *ContractID* field.

If you have complex multi-value fields or attachments, then when copying between *Recordset*s, you need to copy the child records in the multi-value fields, as shown in the following:

```
Sub modRST_CopyRecords(rstSource As Recordset2, _
                       rstTarget As Recordset2, _
                       strNewKeyName As String, _
                       varNewKeyValue As Variant)
    ' Copies each record from sourceRST to targetRST
    ' also we need to add a value for the NewKeyName
    ' in the target recordset
    Dim fldSource As Field2
    Dim fldTarget As Field2
    If rstSource.EOF Then Exit Sub
    Do While Not rstSource.EOF
        ' copy a record
        rstTarget.AddNew
        For Each fldSource In rstSource.Fields
            Select Case fldSource.Type
                Case dbAttachment, dbComplexByte, dbComplexInteger, _
                    dbComplexLong, dbComplexSingle, dbComplexDouble, _
                    dbComplexGUID, dbComplexDecimal, _
                    dbComplexText: modRST_CopyComplexField fldSource, _
                                        rstTarget(fldSource.Name)
                Case Else
                    If fldSource.Expression <> "" Then
                        ' calculated field so skip copy
                    Else
                        ' simple data type
                        rstTarget(fldSource.Name) = fldSource.Value
                    End If
            End Select
```

```
            Next
            rstTarget(strNewKeyName) = varNewKeyValue
            rstTarget.Update
            rstSource.MoveNext
        Loop
    End Sub

    Sub modRST_CopyComplexField(fldSource As Field2, _
                                fldTarget As Field2)
        ' copy a complex type field
        Dim rstComplexSource As Recordset2
        Dim rstComplexTarget As Recordset2
        Dim fldComplexSource As Field2
        Set rstComplexSource = fldSource.Value
        Set rstComplexTarget = fldTarget.Value
        If rstComplexSource.EOF Then
            ' no multiple values
            rstComplexSource.Close
            rstComplexTarget.Close
            Exit Sub
        End If
        Do While Not rstComplexSource.EOF
            rstComplexTarget.AddNew
            For Each fldComplexSource In rstComplexSource.Fields
                If fldSource.Type = dbAttachment Then
                    ' don't copy any readonly fields
                    ' fields to copy are FileData and FileName
                    If fldComplexSource.Name <> "FileFlags" And _
                        fldComplexSource.Name <> "FileURL" And _
                        fldComplexSource.Name <> "FileType" And _
                        fldComplexSource.Name <> "FileTimeStamp" Then
                        rstComplexTarget(fldComplexSource.Name) = fldComplexSource
                    End If
                Else
                    ' other multi-value fields
                    rstComplexTarget(fldComplexSource.Name) = fldComplexSource
                End If

            Next
            rstComplexTarget.Update
            rstComplexSource.MoveNext
        Loop
        rstComplexSource.Close
        rstComplexTarget.Close
    End Sub

    Sub modRST_CopyRecordsTest()
        Dim lngContractId As Long
        lngContractId = 1
        Dim db As Database
        Dim rstEmployee As Recordset2
        Dim rstContractEmployee As Recordset2
```

```
        Set db = CurrentDb
        ' copies all the employee records
        Set rstEmployee = db.OpenRecordset("Employees", dbOpenDynaset)
        Set rstContractEmployee = db.OpenRecordset("ContractEmployees", _
                            dbOpenDynaset)
        modRST_CopyRecords rstEmployee, rstContractEmployee, _
            "ContractID", 1
End Sub
```

In the preceding example, a significant part of the code deals with copying multi-value fields. If you are not copying these field types, the code can be significantly simplified.

Reading Records into an Array

You can use the *GetRows* method of the *Recordset* object to dynamically allocate a two dimension array, where the first dimension is the field, and the second dimension is the row. Multiple rows can then be read into the array with a single command, as demonstrated in the following:

```
Sub modRTS_GetRows()
    Dim db As Database
    Dim varRowArray() As Variant
    Set db = CurrentDb
    Dim rst As Recordset
    Dim strSQL As String
    Dim lngCount As Long
    ' exclude selecting complex types or including Memo and Long Binary fields
    strSQL = "SELECT ID, Company, [Last name] from Customers"
    Set rst = db.OpenRecordset(strSQL, dbOpenDynaset)
    ' this will generate a 2 dimensional array, where
    ' first element is the column and the second element the row
'     ReDim varRowArray(rst.Fields.Count - 1, 1) explicit dimensioning
    varRowArray = rst.GetRows(1) ' array will be dynamically sized
    Debug.Print UBound(varRowArray)
    For lngCount = 0 To rst.Fields.Count - 1
        Debug.Print varRowArray(lngCount, 0)
    Next
    rst.Close
    db.Close
End Sub
```

Working with Queries in Code

Using the DAO, we can create temporary queries, create saved queries, execute queries, change the SQL in saved queries, and open *Recordsets* on queries. We can also manipulate queries with *Parameters*. Working with *QueryDefs* is an area in which you will probably spend a lot of time.

Inside the *Database* object, you will find the *QueryDefs* collection (see Figure 5-28). This collection holds all the queries in your application.

Figure 5-28 The *QueryDefs* and *Parameters* collections.

The following code loops through the entire *QueryDefs* collection and displays basic information about each object:

```
Sub modQueryDefs_ListQueries()
    ' Example listing queries in the current database
    ' Also displays a list of any query parameters
    Dim db As DAO.Database
    Dim qdef As DAO.QueryDef
    Dim param As DAO.Parameter

    Set db = CurrentDb
    For Each qdef In db.QueryDefs
        Debug.Print "*********************************"
        Debug.Print qdef.Name & " : " & qdef.SQL
        If qdef.Parameters.Count > 0 Then
                Debug.Print "---------------------------"
        End If
        For Each param In qdef.Parameters
            Debug.Print vbTab & param.Name, param.Type
        Next
        Debug.Print "*********************************"
    Next
    db.Close
    Set db = Nothing
    Debug.Print "Completed : modQueryDefs_ListQueries"
End Sub
```

Temporary *QueryDefs*

The first type of *QueryDef* to investigate is the temporary *QueryDef.* If you want to execute a block of SQL, there are several techniques that can be used.

INSIDE OUT   Different methods for executing SQL

Access provides a number of different methods for executing SQL. It is possible to use a pre-saved query and execute the query by using either *DoCmd.OpenQuery* "qryname" (which we don't recommend because you need to switch warnings off to prevent messages, and you can easily forget to switch them back on), or you could use *CurrentDB. Execute* "qryname".

As an alternative you can construct the SQL in program code and then execute the code by using either *CurrentDB.Execute strSQL* or *DoCmd.RunSQL strSQL*, as shown in the following:

```
Sub modQueryDefs_ExecuteSQL()
    ' example showing direct execution of SQL
    Dim strSQL As String
    strSQL = "UPDATE Customers SET [ZIP/Postal Code] = Null " & _
            "WHERE [State/Province] = 'MA'"
    CurrentDb.Execute strSQL
    DoCmd.RunSQL strSQL
    Debug.Print "Completed : modQueryDefs_ExecuteSQL"
End Sub
```

QueryDefs provide another method for executing SQL, and they can create temporary and permanent queries. *Recordsets* can also be opened on the *QueryDef* objects.

It is also possible to create a temporary *QueryDef* to perform this operation. The advantage of doing this is that you can then manipulate other more advanced query properties. For example, when working with SQL Server, you can create a temporary pass-through *QueryDef* to execute SQL against SQL Server, a simpler example is shown here:

```
Sub modQueryDefs_TempActionQuery()
    ' example showing how a temporary query can be created and
    ' executed in code
    Dim db As DAO.Database
    Dim qdef As DAO.QueryDef
    Dim strSQL As String

    Set db = CurrentDb
    Set qdef = db.CreateQueryDef("")
    strSQL = "UPDATE Customers SET [ZIP/Postal Code] = Null " & _
            "WHERE [State/Province] = 'MA'"
    qdef.SQL = strSQL
    qdef.Execute
```

```
        qdef.Close
        db.Close
        Set qdef = Nothing
        Set db = Nothing
        Debug.Print "Completed : modQueryDefs_TempActionQuery"
End Sub
```

If you look at the *qdef.Name* property during execution, you will see it has the value *#Temporary QueryDef#*.

QueryDefs and *Recordsets*

It is also possible to create a temporary *QueryDef* by using a SQL statement or saved query, and then open a *Recordset* on the temporary object. This again becomes a very powerful technique when you are working with external sources of data, such as SQL Server:

```
Sub modQueryDefs_TempSelectQuery()
    ' example showing how a temporary query can be created and
    ' a recordset opened on the query
    Dim db As DAO.Database
    Dim qdef As DAO.QueryDef
    Dim strSQL As String
    Dim rst As DAO.Recordset

    Set db = CurrentDb
    Set qdef = db.CreateQueryDef("")
    strSQL = "SELECT * FROM Customers " & _
            "WHERE [State/Province] = 'MA'"
    qdef.SQL = strSQL

    Set rst = qdef.OpenRecordset(dbOpenDynaset)
    Do While Not rst.EOF
        Debug.Print rst!Company
        rst.MoveNext
    Loop

    rst.Close
    qdef.Close
    db.Close
    Set rst = Nothing
    Set qdef = Nothing
    Set db = Nothing

    Debug.Print "Completed : modQueryDefs_TempSelectQuery"
End Sub
```

Creating *QueryDefs*

New *QueryDefs* can be created in program code by using the *CreateQueryDef* method of the database, as illustrated in the following:

```
Sub modQueryDefs_CreateQueryDef()
    ' example creating a querydef in code
    Dim db As DAO.Database
    Dim qdef As DAO.QueryDef
    Dim strSQL As String
    Set db = CurrentDb
    Set qdef = db.CreateQueryDef("qryCreatedInCode")
    qdef.SQL = "SELECT * FROM Customers"
    qdef.Close
    db.Close
    Set qdef = Nothing
    Set db = Nothing
    Application.RefreshDatabaseWindow
    Debug.Print "Completed : modQueryDefs_CreateQueryDef"
End Sub
```

In addition to creating *QueryDefs*, you can also modify the SQL in existing *QueryDefs*, as follows:

```
Sub modQueryDefs_ChangeTheSQL()
    ' Example show that changes you make to the SQL in a query
    ' change the actual SQL stored in the saved query
    ' Notice that we do not need to perform a save as this
    ' happens automatically

    Dim db As DAO.Database
    Dim qdef As DAO.QueryDef
    Set db = CurrentDb
    Set qdef = db.QueryDefs("qryListCustomersChangedInCode")
    qdef.SQL = "SELECT Customers.Company, Customers.[State/Province] " & _
            "FROM Customers " & _
            " WHERE (((Customers.[State/Province])='IL'))"
    Stop
    ' Now open the query in design, look at the sql, then close the query
    qdef.SQL = "SELECT Customers.Company, Customers.[State/Province] " & _
            "FROM Customers " & _
            " WHERE (((Customers.[State/Province])='WA'))"
    Stop
    ' Now open the query in design, look at the sql, then close the query

    ' Now we try and enter some incorrect SQL, this will cause an error
    qdef.SQL = "SELECTxxxx Rubbish"
    Stop
    ' but the following will work even when a table does not exist
    qdef.SQL = "SELECT Rubbish"

    ' Access will syntax check your SQL but not check that the objects exist

    db.Close
    Set db = Nothing

    Debug.Print "Completed : modQueryDefs_ChangeTheSQL"
End Sub
```

INSIDE OUT   Changes to the SQL in a *QueryDef* need to use valid SQL, but not necessarily reference a valid object, and changes are automatically saved

When you change the SQL in a *QueryDef*, you do not need to save your changes, because they are automatically saved for you. In the previous example, you will see that if you try to change the SQL to invalid syntax, it will fail, but if you reference objects that do not exist it will not fail (until you execute or use the query).

QueryDef Parameters

The example that follows shows how you can populate parameter values in an existing parameterized query:

```
Sub modQueryDefs_ActionQuery()
    ' example showing how an existing parameterised query
    ' can be executed by program code
    Dim db As DAO.Database
    Dim qdef As DAO.QueryDef

    Set db = CurrentDb
    Set qdef = db.QueryDefs("qrySetZipForStateToNull")

    ' There are several equivalent ways to set a parameter
    qdef.Parameters!TheStateProvince = "MA"
    qdef.Parameters(0) = "MA"
    qdef.Parameters("TheStateProvince") = "MA"

    qdef.Execute

    qdef.Close
    db.Close
    Set qdef = Nothing
    Set db = Nothing

    Debug.Print "Completed : modQueryDefs_ActionQuery"
End Sub
```

In a similar manner to referencing fields in a *Recordset*, there are several equivalent ways to refer to a parameter in a *QueryDef*.

INSIDE OUT   Creating parameters in a *QueryDef* by using program code

If you want to create parameters in program code, you do this in the SQL and *not* with the *Parameters* collection (which is indicated as read-only in the Help system in so far as you cannot add or remove parameters, but only set the parameter value), as illustrated in the following example:

```
Sub modQueryDefs_ActionQueryParameters()
    ' example showing how create parameters
    ' can be executed by program code
    Dim db As DAO.Database
    Dim qdef As DAO.QueryDef

    Set db = CurrentDb
    Set qdef = db.CreateQueryDef("")
    qdef.SQL = "PARAMETERS TheStateProvince Text ( 255 ); " & _
               " UPDATE Customers SET Customers.[ZIP/Postal Code] = Null" & _
               " WHERE (((Customers.[State/Province])=[TheStateProvince]));"
    ' There are several equivalent ways to set a parameter
    qdef.Parameters!TheStateProvince = "MA"
    qdef.Execute

    qdef.Close
    db.Close
    Set qdef = Nothing
    Set db = Nothing

    Debug.Print "Completed : modQueryDefs_ActionQueryParameters"
End Sub
```

The sample database contains a query called *qryCustomersForCountry*, which has a parameter tied to a control on the *frmCustomersForCountry* form. The following code shows how to programmatically use this query and supply the parameter from the form that is open:

```
Sub modQueryDefs_OpenParameterQuery()
    Dim db As DAO.Database
    Dim qdef As DAO.QueryDef
    Dim rst As DAO.Recordset
    Set db = CurrentDb
    DoCmd.OpenForm "frmCustomersForCountry"
    [Forms]![frmCustomersForCountry]![txtCountry] = "USA"
    Set qdef = db.QueryDefs("qryCustomersForCountry")
    Dim param As DAO.Parameter
    For Each param In qdef.Parameters
        'Debug.Print param.Name, param.Value
        param.Value = Eval(param.Name)
```

```
        Next
        Set rst = qdef.OpenRecordset()
        Do While Not rst.EOF
            Debug.Print rst!Company
            rst.MoveNext
        Loop
    End Sub
```

Investigating and Documenting Objects

In this section, you look at using the DAO to examine the forms, reports, macros, and modules in an application.

INSIDE OUT   The DAO *Containers* collections and *Application* objects

The DAO object hierarchy contains *Containers* collections, and inside each *Container* is a *Documents* collection. Each Document corresponds to the objects inside your database.

This information is also available through an alternative set of collections in *Application.CurrentProject object*. Information about queries and tables can be accessed through either the DAO *QueryDefs* and *TableDefs* collections or through the *Application.CurrentData* object.

Containers and Documents

The *AllForms, AllReports, AllModules,* and *AllMacros* properties of the *CurrentProject* object can provide limited information on your saved design objects, as shown in the following:

```
Sub modDocuments_AllForms()
    ' Note for all of these we must use a generic object
    ' we can not use a Form or Report object
    Dim objfrm As Object
    Dim Prop As Property
    For Each objfrm In CurrentProject.AllForms
        Debug.Print objfrm.Name
    Next
    Dim objrpt As Object
    For Each objrpt In CurrentProject.AllReports
        Debug.Print objrpt.Name
    Next
    Dim objmcr As Object
```

```
        For Each objmcr In CurrentProject.AllMacros
            Debug.Print objmcr.Name
        Next
        Dim objmd As Object
        For Each objmd In CurrentProject.AllModules
            Debug.Print objmd.Name
        Next
    End Sub
```

However, you can extract more information by looking inside the *Containers* collections in the DAO (we have not shown all the available document properties in the sample code):

```
Sub modDocuments_Containers()
    Dim db As DAO.Database
    Dim cont As DAO.Container
    Dim doc As DAO.Document
    Set db = CurrentDb
    For Each cont In db.Containers
        Debug.Print "+++++++++++Container++++++++++"
        Debug.Print cont.Name, cont.Documents.Count
        For Each doc In cont.Documents
            Debug.Print doc.Name, doc.LastUpdated, doc.DateCreated
        Next
        Debug.Print "++++++++++++++++++++++++++++++"
    Next
End Sub
```

The nine containers are described in Table 5-1.

Table 5-1 Summary of Container Usage

Container	Description	Use
Database	MSysDb, SummaryInfo, UserDefined	Internal
Forms	Forms	Documenting an application
Reports	Reports	Documenting an application
Scripts	Macros	Documenting an application
Modules	Modules	Documenting an application
Relationships	Relationships	Better to use the Relationships collection
SysRel		Internal
Tables	Tables, including system tables, Queries, and compiled queries and compiled SQL for forms and reports	Better to use the *TableDefs* and *QueryDefs* collections
DataAccessPages	Old DataAccessPages	No longer used

Chapter 5

If you look in the Tables collection, there are some interesting objects; for example, in the sample database, there is ~sq_ffrmCustomers (and a form called *frmCustomers*). There is also ~sq_rrptCustomers (and a report called *rptCustomers*). These internal queries contain the SQL for the form/report *RecordSource* and the *RowSource* for combo and list boxes, when these objects do not use a pre-saved query, but use SQL or a table reference in the *RecordSource* or *RowSource* property.

Object Properties

In this chapter, you have seen many examples of working with the properties of objects. The properties for an object can be listed, and the properties themselves also have proper-ties (*Value*, *Name*, *Type*, and *Inherited*), as demonstrated in the following:

```
Sub modProp_ListDatabaseProperties()
    ' list the database properties
    Dim prop As Property
    Dim propprop As Property
    Dim db As Database
    Set db = CurrentDb
     On Error Resume Next
    ' printing out some properties in this manner can generate
    ' some errors if printing the property value when it
    ' returns an object
    For Each prop In db.Properties
        Debug.Print prop.Name, prop.Value
    Next
    On Error GoTo 0
    ' a property can also have properties
    Debug.Print "Properties of a Property"
    Debug.Print "************************"
    Set prop = db.Properties("Transactions")
    For Each propprop In prop.Properties
        Debug.Print propprop.Name, propprop.Value
    Next
    Set prop = Nothing
End Sub
```

Sample Applications

We have included two sample applications that can be used as a foundation for construct-ing your own utilities to document and search for information in a database.

Documenting a Database by Using the DAO

This sample database DocDAO.accdb shown in Figure 5-29 is an application that you can use as a starting point in developing your own utility for documenting the contents of an Access database. The application contains a table, *tblDatabaseObject*, which can contain a list of design objects in multiple databases; the table contains fields that can record whether objects have been added or deleted since a database was last analyzed. The techniques used in this application are based around the methods described in this chapter.

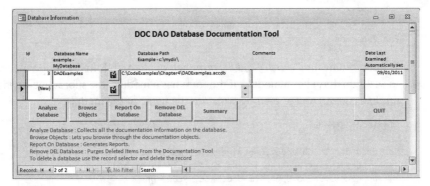

Figure 5-29 The utility for documenting a database structure by using the DAO objects. To run the sample database, use the button represented by the disk icon to browse and change the path to the sample database.

Finding Objects in a Database by Using the DAO

The sample database Find_IT.accdb (see Figure 5-30) can be used to search applications for keywords in controls, forms, program code, and other objects.

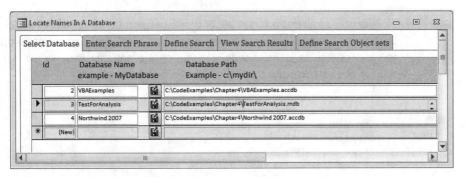

Figure 5-30 *Find_IT* search results when searching objects in an Access database for keywords.

This tool is able to search through module code by using the technique illustrated in the following code examples. Here, a global variable, *dbTarget*, is set to open a connection to a target database. The code examples are located in the database Find_IT.accdb:

```
Function mod_Search_LinkToTargetDatabase(strPath As String) _
        As Boolean
' connect to target database
   On Error Resume Next
```

```
    Set dbTarget = DBEngine.OpenDatabase(strPath)
    If Err <> 0 Then
        MsgBox Err.Description, vbCritical, "Unable To Open Database"
        mod_Search_LinkToTargetDatabase = False
        Exit Function
    End If
    mod_Search_LinkToTargetDatabase = True
End Function
```

The subroutine *modSearch_ModuleForm* then opens each form in Design mode and checks
to see if the form has a module. If the form has a module, the subroutine opens the forms
module code using the prefix "Form_" for the name of the module:

```
Dim tmod As Module
......
For Each doc In dbTarget.Containers("Forms").Documents
    ' need the error trap incase the module is already open
    appAccess.DoCmd.OpenForm doc.Name, acDesign
    ' Continue if it has a module.
    If Not appAccess.Forms(doc.Name).HasModule Then
        ' close the form and move on
        appAccess.DoCmd.SelectObject acForm, doc.Name
        appAccess.DoCmd.Close
        GoTo SkipFormAsNoCode
    End If

    appAccess.DoCmd.OpenModule "Form_" & doc.Name
    Set tmod = appAccess.Modules("Form_" & doc.Name)
```

Module objects have a rich number of properties, and the code that follows shows how we
process the declaration lines of the module. The *CountOfDeclarationLines* properties is used
to cycle through each line of code in the procedure, and the *Lines* method is used to read
the line of each code into a string, which can then be searched:

```
lngCountDecl = tmod.CountOfDeclarationLines
lngCount = tmod.CountOfLines
strProcName = "Declarations"
lngMatchCount = 0
If Not boolOnlyNameMatch Then
    For lngI = 1 To lngCountDecl
        strline = Trim(tmod.Lines(lngI, 1))
        If InStr(1, strline, strPhrase) <> 0 Then
            With rstResults
                .AddNew
                !SearchId = lngSearchId
                !SearchAreaId = lngSearchAreaId
                !ResultInformation1 = doc.Name
                !ResultInformation2 = strProcName
                !ResultInformation3 = strline
                !Exact = False
                .Update
```

```
            End With
            lngMatchCount = lngMatchCount + 1
            If lngMatchCount >= lngMaxModuleMatches Then
                rstResults.Bookmark = rstResults.LastModified
                rstResults.Edit
                rstResults!ResultInformation4 = _
                    "Maximum matches reached for this module " & _
                    lngMaxModuleMatches
                rstResults.Update
                GoTo SkipRestOfModule
            End If
        End If
    Next
End If
```

Summary

In this chapter, you looked into the DAO, which has long been the most popular object library for those programming with Access. The two key features of the DAO that developers use extensively are:

- Working with *Recordsets* to manipulate data in a similar manner as to working with a DataSheet, but by using VBA.

- Writing, executing, and modifying SQL, either by using temporary objects or pre-saved queries.

In addition to working with these objects, the DAO offers a rich hierarchy of objects that handle almost everything you might want to do with the objects in your database.

Chapter 5

PART 3

Working with Forms and Reports

CHAPTER 6
Using Forms and Events **231**

CHAPTER 7
Using Form Controls and Events **273**

CHAPTER 8
Creating Reports and Events **323**

Displaying Records.............................. 233		Interacting with Records on a Form 253	
Filtering by Using Controls........................ 236		Editing and Undo on a Record..................... 262	

A t this point in the book, you should understand the important role of objects, and you have seen examples of how they can be created and interact with each other. In this chapter, we introduce how to work with events.

Events are opportunities to implement an action when a user interacts with an application or an application interacts with other objects and the external environment. Controlling the behavior of your forms involves understanding the events that can occur and writing code in response to these events. Sometimes, when a user performs a single operation, such as attempting to delete a record, a sequence of different events is set into motion.

After reading this chapter, you will:

- Understand that form events occur in specific sequences, and you will know how to program using the event sequences.

- Know how to control the presentation of objects on a form as a user browses through the data.

- Be able to control filtering on forms by using different techniques.

> **Note**
> As you read through this chapter, we encourage you to also use the companion content sample database, FormExamples.accdb, which can be downloaded from the book's catalog page.

The properties for a specific section of the form can be displayed either by using the Selection Type drop-down menu or by clicking in the area of the form for which you want information, as shown in Figure 6-1.

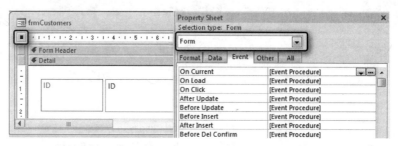

Figure 6-1 You can display form properties by clicking the small square (upper-left part of the form window) or by using the Selection Type drop-down menu.

Most programming is done in the Form section, which offers a rich set of events. The Detail, Form Header, and Form Footer sections offer only *Paint*, *OnClick*, *OnDblClick*, *OnMouse-Down*, *OnMouseUp*, and *OnMouseMove* events; however, it is quite rare to program against these events.

When a user interacts with a form and the objects on a form, her actions trigger a sequence of several events. In the following sections, we describe the most common event sequences and the programming techniques that can be used against events in these sequences.

To demonstrate the event sequences, the *frmCustomers* form has program code written behind each form event (see Figure 6-2). This lets you see the different event sequences as you interact with the form. Open it and try moving through records and updating data to see some of the event sequences. You can revisit the form when reading through a particular event sequence described in the chapter.

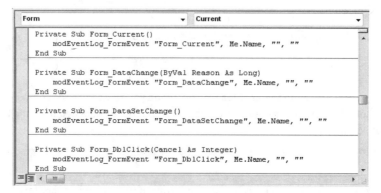

Figure 6-2 The *frmCustomers* form contains code behind the key events that calls a routine to populate a table with details of the events.

This form contains a subform that is updated to show the event sequence as you perform different operations; the results are presented in a table, as shown in Figure 6-3.

Ev ▾	MainObjectN ▾	EventName	▾	ActiveControl ▾
1610	frmCustomers	Form_Open		
1611	frmCustomers	Form_Load		
1612	frmCustomers	Form_Resize		
1613	frmCustomers	Form_Activate		
1614	frmCustomers	Form_Current		
* #####				

Figure 6-3 The embedded subform displays the event sequences as you interact with the form.

Displaying Records

In this section, you look at the key events that are used to control how the form displays data when it is opened and closed. From there, you will look at a number of different techniques that you can use to control how the data on a form is filtered.

Bound and Unbound Forms

Forms have a Record Source property, which can contain the name of a table, query, or an explicit piece of SQL that is used to determine the data to be made available to the form. Figure 6-4 shows the Record Source property bound to a table.

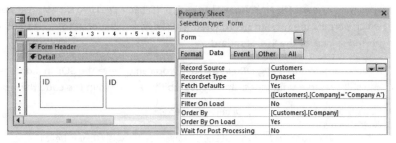

Figure 6-4 An example of a bound form, with the Record Source property bound to a table. Bound controls on the form refer to columns from the Record Source.

Where a Record Source is specified, we describe the form as being bound to the data; forms without a Record Source are described as unbound. Unbound forms are very common. They are used to collect information from users and then take appropriate actions. Sometimes developers choose to create a form that starts life as a bound form. They then unbind the form and set the form's data source on the *Open* event to obtain better control over the data that is displayed in the form.

Controls on a form can be bound or unbound (if the form is bound). Examples of unbound controls include displaying calculations based on other control values. On an unbound form, all controls are unbound. When designing an unbound form, you normally choose to hide the navigation buttons and record selectors, and because these forms are often small, it is common to set the Scroll Bars to *Neither* and Auto Center to *Yes*.

INSIDE OUT
Updateability of a Record Source when using *DISTINCT* and *DISTINCTROW*

When creating a Record Source for a form that is based on multiple tables, *DISTINCTROW* can be used to permit updateability for situations in which *DISTINCT* would limit updateability.

If you use SQL on an [Orders] table to select only the [OrderID] and [Order Date], but you want to join this table to [Order Details] such that we only include [Orders] that have [Order Details], then you would get multiple records (one corresponding to each row in the [Order Details], as shown in the following:

```
SELECT [Orders].[Order ID], [Orders].[Order Date]
FROM Orders INNER JOIN [Order Details]
ON Orders.[Order ID] = [Order Details].[Order ID];
```

If you want to eliminate the duplicates, you can set the query property Unique Values to *Yes*. This adds the keyword *DISTINCT* to the SQL (*SELECT DISTINCT ...*), but the rows will now be read-only.

Microsoft Access has a special query property called Unique Records. This property adds the keyword *DISTINCTROW* to the SQL (*SELECT DISTINCTROW ...*) statement, which permits the rows to be updated. This keyword is special to Access and is not supported as part of the SQL Standard.

As an alternative to using *DISTINCTROW*, you can rewrite the SQL in a different way and still preserve uniqueness and updateability, as shown in the code that follows:

```
SELECT Orders.[Order ID], Orders.[Order Date]
FROM Orders
WHERE Orders.[Order ID] In (SELECT [Order ID] FROM [Order Details]);
```

Modal and Pop-Up Forms

To enable a form to pop up, you set the forms Pop Up property to *Yes*. Pop-up forms can overlap other pop-up forms. To enable overlapping forms, you need to change the default setting in the Backstage view. To do so, in Backstage view, click Current Database | Document Windows Option, and then select the Overlapping Windows option.

Pop-up forms are great for drawing a user's attention to a specific operation, such as entering data in an unbound form that is used to generate a report. Often, you do not want a user to be able to switch away from the pop-up form. To prevent this, set the form's Modal property to *Yes*. When creating a pop-up and/or modal form, a popular choice is to set the form's Border Style to *Dialog,* and possibly the forms Control Box property to *No.*

Open and *Load* **Events**

When a form is opened, it goes through the following event sequence:

Open → *Load* → *Resize* → *Activate* → *Current*

Even if the form is opened for data entry, the *Current* event will fire. This event will also fire on an unbound form.

The *Open* event is called before the user sees the data, but the data will already be prepared and ready for display. The difference between *Open* and *Load* events is that the form can be closed during the *Open* event by setting the *Cancel* argument on the event to *True.* Typical activities to program on these events are setting filters or setting the form's Record Source.

The form *frmCustomersBindOnOpenEvent* is an unbound form that uses the *Open* event to bind the form's Record Source.

When testing the sample forms, notice that swapping a form between Design view and Form view might result in some noticeable flicker because you can see the controls being bound. You can avoid this flicker by opening the form directly. The form's *Open* event sets the *RecordSource*, as shown in the following:

```
Private Sub Form_Open(Cancel As Integer)
    Me.RecordSource = "SELECT * FROM Customers " & _
                    " WHERE [State/Province] = 'WA'"
End Sub
```

Another alternative to this approach is to have a bound form and set the forms *Filter* property on the *Open* event, as demonstrated in the following code for the sample form *frmCustomersFilter:*

```
Private Sub Form_Open(Cancel As Integer)
    Me.Filter = "[State/Province] = 'WA'"
    Me.FilterOn = True
End Sub
```

In Access 2007, two new form properties, *FilterOnLoad* and *OrderByOnLoad*, were added. The *FilterOnLoad* property (default *False*) sets a form to remember the last used filter, which is stored in the form's *Filter* property. This can create a useful effect, improving performance by setting a filter when the form first retrieves the data to be displayed, but it can also cause issues when combined with other filtering techniques. You will find that if you need to clear the *Filter* property, then you can do this in the form's *Open* event, but not in the *Close* event, which can cause problems if the *FilterOnLoad* property is *True*.

Filtering by Using Controls

In this example, you will add a combo box control to the form's header that will allow a user to choose a single value for filtering the data on the form. The demonstration form is called *frmCustomersFilterChoice*.

Start by adding an unbound control to the form header section, selecting the Customers table as the source of data and choosing the State/Province field, as shown in Figure 6-5.

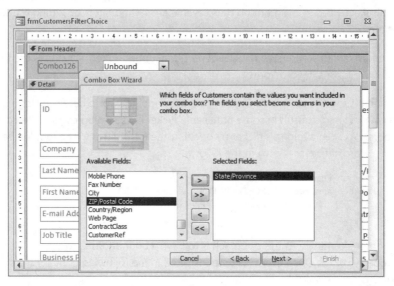

Figure 6-5 Adding a combo box in a form header to display a list of filtering choices.

When you reach the last item in the combo box, select Remember The Value For Later Use (this makes the field an unbound field). Figure 6-6 shows the page in the wizard after you select the required field. Note that in this example, you do not want to select the ID field, but the wizard does not allow this to be removed. You will remove this later.

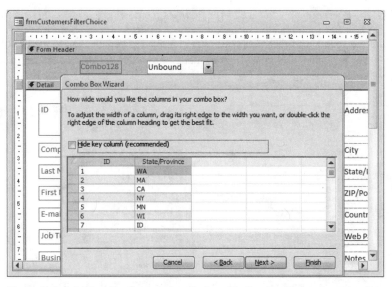

Figure 6-6 Selecting the fields to be displayed in the combo box by using the Combo Box Wizard.

Once you have added the control, give it a meaningful name and save the form. Figure 6-7 shows the new control name, which in this example, includes the prefix "cbo" to indicate that it is a combo box.

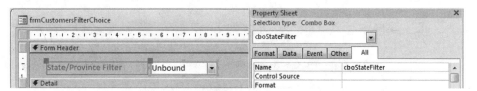

Figure 6-7 After the control has been added, change its name so that it is meaningful.

Note that when you run the form, the new combo box displays the list of states, as expected, but you also see duplicate values (one value for each record in the Customer table). To remove the duplicates, modify the Row Source of the combo boxes by using the Build button (...), as shown in Figure 6-8.

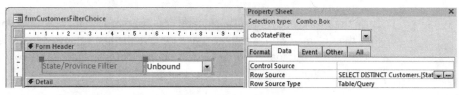

Figure 6-8 By clicking the build button adjacent to Row Source, you can change the SQL in the Query designer.

Chapter 6

Click the Build button adjacent to the Row Source property.

There are several changes that you want to make to the SQL: delete the ID column, add an Is Not Null filter, and finally, in the Queries Properties, set Unique Values to *Yes*. The result should look like Figure 6-9.

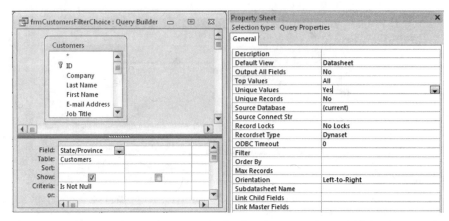

Figure 6-9 Change Unique Values to *Yes* in the Queries Properties to add the *DISTINCT* keyword to the SQL.

At this point, you can also view the results of the SQL by using the ribbon menu and then clicking the Close button. Click Yes to save the changes, as shown in Figure 6-10.

Figure 6-10 The prompt to save your changes when exiting the Query designer.

Now save the form. The SQL behind the combo box is as follows:

```
SELECT DISTINCT Customers.[State/Province] FROM Customers
    WHERE (((Customers.[State/Province]) Is Not Null));
```

Because the wizard added the ID field (and you just removed that), you also need to change the Column Count from 2 to 1 and remove the first column width. The exact width for the column is not that important; what is important is to only have 1 column width to match the 1 column count, as shown in Figure 6-11.

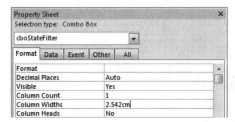

Figure 6-11 Adjusting the column widths to match the column count.

When you display your form, a drop-down menu appears, presenting a choice of states. Press Ctrl+G and switch to the Immediate window so that you can print out the value of the unbound control (`Forms!frmCustomersFilterChoice.cboStateFilter`), as shown in Figure 6-12.

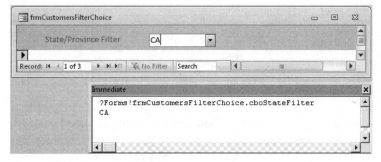

Figure 6-12 The Immediate window next to the form window (this appears in the separate VBA Editor Window).

The next step is to change the form's Record Source so that it uses the *cboStateFilter* control value to filter the data. To do this, click the Build button (Figure 6-13) next to the form's Record Source.

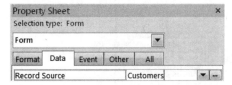

Figure 6-13 Click the Build button adjacent to Record Source to display the result in the Query grid.

Select all the fields by using the '*' on the Query grid, select the State/Province field, and then clear the Show box (it is important not to include the same field to be shown more than once on the Query grid). Right-click the Query grid, and then select the Build option, as shown in Figure 6-14.

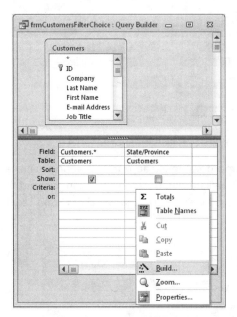

Figure 6-14 To access Expression Builder, right-click the mouse while the cursor is in the criteria field, in the State/Province column.

Use Expression Builder to locate the new, unbound control on the form by clicking FormExamples.accdb | Forms | LoadedForms | frmCustomersFilterChoice. When you locate the cboStateFilter, double-click it, as shown in Figure 6-15.

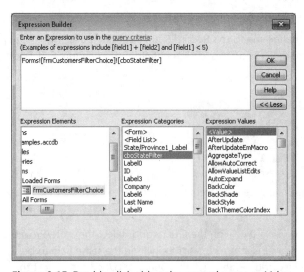

Figure 6-15 Double-click either the control name or Value.

Click OK to select the expression, close and save the changes to the Record Source, and then save the changes to the form. The Record Source then contains the following SQL:

```
SELECT Customers.* FROM Customers WHERE (((Customers.[State/Province])=[Forms]!
    [frmCustomersFilterChoice]![cboStateFilter]));
```

You now need to ensure that when a user makes a selection from the combo box, it forces the data in the form to call *Requery*. The event to use for this is the *AfterUpdate* event on the *cboStateFilter* control.

Locate the *AfterUpdate* event property for the control, as shown in Figures 6-16.

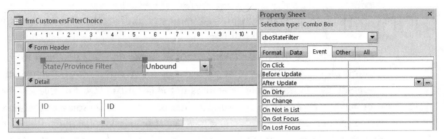

Figure 6-16 Locating the *AfterUpdate* event for the *cboStateFilter* control.

Press the Build button and then choose the Code Builder option from the Choose Builder pop-up, as shown in Figure 6-17.

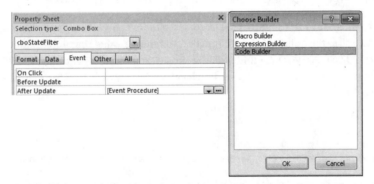

Figure 6-17 Alternatively, you can select [Event Procedure] from the drop-down menu on the event, and then click the Build button.

Add the following code behind the event. This code ensures that after a user updates the filter choice, the form is requeried, and because the form's Record Source is tied to the control, it will filter the data to match the choice made in the combo box.

```
Private Sub cboStateFilter_AfterUpdate()
    Me.Requery
End Sub
```

Chapter 6

With this approach, the form opens with a *NULL* value in the control, which means that no data is displayed. The code that follows could be added to the form's *Open* event to set a default value and requery the data. *ItemData(0)* sets the combo box to display the first available data item, as shown here:

```
Private Sub Form_Open(Cancel As Integer)
    If Me.cboStateFilter.ListCount <> 0 Then
        Me.cboStateFilter = Me.cboStateFilter.ItemData(0)
    End If
    Me.Requery
End Sub
```

INSIDE OUT   Managing *NULL* values when referring to controls in a form's Record Source

One disadvantage to this technique becomes apparent when you start to add multiple controls for filtering. This can be achieved by following the steps that were previously presented to add more field references to the *RecordSet* SQL. But this assumes that the user makes a choice from all available filter controls. If only some of the available filters were selected, other controls could have *NULL* values. We can illustrate this by showing how to change the Record Source SQL so that it will allow a *NULL* value in the filter to show all records, as shown in the following:

```
SELECT Customers.* FROM Customers WHERE (((Customers.[State/Province])=
IIf([Forms]![frmCustomersFilterChoice]![cboStateFilter] Is Null,
[State/Province],[Forms]![frmCustomersFilterChoice]![cboStateFilter])));
```

As an alternative to using the *IIF* statement, a more compact way to write this would be to utilize the ability of the *NZ* function to return a value that you can define when the field value is *NULL* (in this case it returns [State/Province] and the *WHERE* clause becomes [State/Province]= [State/Province], which is always true for a *NULL* values in the control):

```
SELECT Customers.*
FROM Customers
WHERE (((Customers.[State/Province])=
Nz([Forms]![frmCustomersFilterChoice]![cboStateFilter],[State/Province])))
```

If you have several filtering controls, the SQL will start to become unmanageably complex. Another problem with this approach is that the criteria in the forms Record Source is hardwired to refer to the form by name. This means that if you make a copy of the form, these references need to be changed. In the next section, you see a better way to avoid both of these problems.

Filtering by Using the *Filter* Property

The next method uses the natural *Filter* property of the form to provide a more flexible approach to filtering the data. This is shown in the completed sample, *frmCustomersFilter Choice2*. You can create and name your own form to use as a sample as you follow through the technique.

As with the last example, you start by adding a combo box to the form, changing the *RowSource* of the combo box to display unique values for the state. But rather than changing the form's *RowSource* to connect it to a control, you create a filter function.

Add the following function to the forms code module:

```
Function FilterResults()
    Dim strCriteria As String
    strCriteria = ""
    If Nz(Me.cboStateFilter) <> "" Then
        strCriteria = "[State/Province] = '" & _
                Me.cboStateFilter & "'"
    End If
    If strCriteria <> "" Then
        Me.Filter = strCriteria
        Me.FilterOn = True
    Else
        Me.Filter = ""
        Me.FilterOn = False
    End If
End Function
```

Next, change the *AfterUpdate* Event on the *cboStateFilter* control to reference this function, as shown in Figure 6-18.

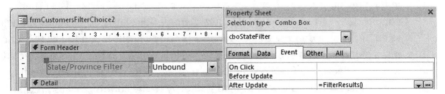

Figure 6-18 Type **=FilterResults()** for the event property. The *cboStateFilter* control now directly calls the code when the event is activated.

INSIDE OUT   Referencing a VBA function from a control's event property

The ability to have a control directly reference any public function from the controls event property normally finds greatest use with command buttons. For example, if you have a Close button on your forms, rather than continually typing the code for *DoCmd. Close()* behind each button, you could create a *Public* function called *modUtils_Form Close()*, and then on the buttons *OnClick* event, type **=modUtils_FormClose()**. Now, whenever you copy and paste the Close button onto a new form, it will already have the code reference copied with it.

You can also pass references to other controls as arguments on a function call in a similar manner to that which would be used when creating the *ControlSource* for a calculated field.

You can also add the following code to the form's *Open* event to set a default value, and then call the filtering function:

```
Private Sub Form_Open(Cancel As Integer)
    On Error Resume Next
    Me.cboStateFilter = Me.cboStateFilter.ItemData(0)
    Dim dummy As Variant
    dummy = FilterResults()
End Sub
```

The code On Error Resume Next has been added to handle the situation in which the control does not contain any value, and the use of *ItemData(0)* gets the first choice available in the combo box. Note that this would be a less elegant alternative to the example in the previous section in which we tested (Me.cboStateFilter.ListCount <> 0) before conditionally setting the control to *ItemData(0)*. To call the *FilterResults()* function, we need to define a dummy variant variable (Access will allow you to call the function without a dummy variable, but we prefer to make it explicit in the code that we are calling a function). Because a function without a specified return type will be variant, we had to use a function to be allowed to bind it directly to the control, as was previously shown in Figure 6-18.

It's simple to extend this technique to use multiple controls for filtering. For example, the demonstration form includes the [Job Title] as an additional filter. After adding the control to the form and hooking up the *AfterUpdate* event for that control to call the routine *Filter Results()*, all that remains is to modify the *FilterResults()* routine to include the new field, as shown in the following code:

```
If Nz(Me.cboJobTitle) <> "" Then
    If strCriteria <> "" Then
        strCriteria = strCriteria & " AND "
    End If
    strCriteria = strCriteria & _
            "[Job Title] = '" & _
            Me.cboJobTitle & "'"
End If
```

This approach is extremely easy to maintain: each time you add a control, set the controls *AfterUpdate* property, and then add some logic to the *FilterResults()* function. As an alternative to filtering whenever a control changes, you can add a command button; rather than calling the *FilterResults()* function on each control, only call it once when the user presses the command button after filtering.

In more advanced programming situations, you might need to take into account whether the user is going to be allowed to use the built-in features in Access to apply other filters. This can be handled by using the *ApplyFilter* event, described on page 247.

Filtering by Using Another Form

Another popular technique is to design a pop-up form that can then open the form showing the main data and apply a filter, as shown in the sample form *frmCustomersFilterPopup*. Start by creating a blank, unbound form. Set the form's properties to match those shown in Figure 6-19.

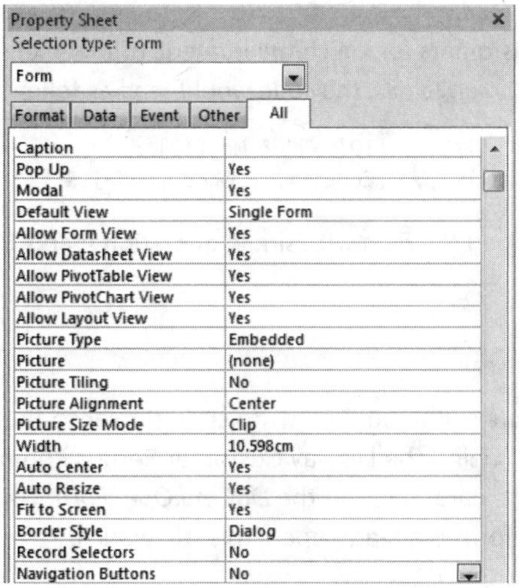

Figure 6-19 Set the properties for a new, unbound form (Pop Up = Yes, Modal = Yes, Auto Center = Yes, Record Selectors = No, Navigation Buttons = No).

Chapter 6

Next, add the controls that you want to use for filtering, as shown in Figure 6-20.

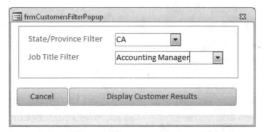

Figure 6-20 The form containing combo boxes for the user to select filter values and command buttons for filtering.

INSIDE OUT   Opening a form by using a *Where* clause

One of the most simple and yet most powerful techniques used in creating applications is to open a form from another form/report but restrict the data by choices that have been made in the first form. This can then be used to open reports or forms to show records, based upon a set of choices made in controls on the driving form.

One of the simplest applications of this technique is when you have a continuous form that lists records. You can add a button to the continuous form, either in the footer or in the detail section next to each record, which when clicked, displays a pop-up that contains the complete details for that particular record.

For example, in a form listing customers for which the numeric primary key is [ID] and the detail form is called *frmCustomerDetails*, the code would read as follows:

```
DoCmd.OpenForm "frmCustomerDetails",,,"[ID] = " & Me.[ID]
DoCmd.OpenForm "frmCustomerDetails",,,"[Code] = '" & Me.[Code] & "'"
```

In the second example, we surround the field with single quotation marks because the primary key is a text field.

You do not program the *AfterUpdate* event, but you write code similar to that which was used in the *FilterResults()* function behind the Display Customer Results command button. This time, however, you use this as a parameter on the *DoCmd.OpenForm* command (it doesn't matter whether the target form is already open; this still works):

```
Private Sub cmdDisplayResults_Click()
    Dim strCriteria As String
    strCriteria = ""
```

```
       If Nz(Me.cboStateFilter) <> "" Then
           strCriteria = "[State/Province] = '" & _
                   Me.cboStateFilter & "'"
       End If

       If Nz(Me.cboJobTitle) <> "" Then
           If strCriteria <> "" Then
               strCriteria = strCriteria & " AND "
           End If
           strCriteria = strCriteria & _
                   "[Job Title] = '" & _
                   Me.cboJobTitle & "'"
       End If
       DoCmd.OpenForm "frmCustomers2", , , strCriteria
       DoCmd.SelectObject acForm, Me.Name
       DoCmd.Close
End Sub
```

You can also add a command button on the *frmCustomers2* form that pops up the unbound filter selection form to allow users to change filter criteria, as shown in the following:

```
Private Sub cmdFilter_Click()
    DoCmd.OpenForm "frmCustomersFilterPopup"
End Sub
```

The *ApplyFilter* Event

When a filter is applied, this then results in the event sequence shown in the following (the *Current* event is called twice):

   ApplyFilter → Current → Current

It is very common for developers to open a form with a filter or a *Where* clause and still allow users to take advantage of the built-in filtering features of Access. However, you might want to ensure that a user cannot remove the filtering that your code has applied (see the *frmCustomersFilterApplyFilter* form). You can do this by setting *Cancel* to *True* when the *ApplyType* is *0*, as shown in the code that follows:

```
Private Sub Form_ApplyFilter(Cancel As Integer, ApplyType As Integer)
    ' 0 -- acShowAllRecords (removes filter)
    ' 1 -- acApplyFilter (applies new filter)
    ' 2 -- acCloseFilterWindow (no filter applied)
    If ApplyType = 0 Then
        ' prevent user removing the filter on this form
        Cancel = True
    End If
    MsgBox "ApplyType : " & ApplyType
End Sub
```

```
Private Sub Form_Open(Cancel As Integer)
    Me.Filter = "[State/Province] = 'WA'"
    Me.FilterOn = True
End Sub
```

Unload and *Close* Events

When you close a form, it goes through the following event sequence:

> *Unload* → *Deactivate* → *Close*

The forms *Unload* event can be used to ensure that users can only close a form after completing appropriate actions, as demonstrated in the following (see the *frmCustomers2* form in the samples database):

```
Private Sub Form_Unload(Cancel As Integer)
    If MsgBox("Close this form ?", vbYesNo, _
            "Confirmation Required") = vbNo Then
        Cancel = True
    End If
End Sub
```

Note that any changes to the record will already have been saved by the time this code executes, so the *Dirty* property will be *False*. If you want to provide validation with respect to data changes, use the form's *BeforeUpdate* event (described on page 262).

Working with the *RecordsetClone*

For many people, their first encounter with the *RecordsetClone* of a form was when they created a combo box (on a bound form) for use in record navigation (see Figure 6-21). In previous versions of Access, the Combo Box Wizard generated *RecordsetClone* VBA code, but in Access 2010, the wizard generates a *SearchForRecord* macro. In this section, we will outline the required VBA to perform this operation.

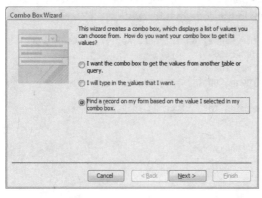

Figure 6-21 The option to locate a record generates macro code in Access 2010.

Rather than use the feature just described, you start by adding a combo box into the header or footer section of a bound form (for an example, look at the demonstration form, *frmRecordsetClone*, which shows the result of this). The combo box has two fields: the ID (hidden) and the CompanyName (visible). You can write the following code to provide navigation in VBA, similar to the *SearchForRecord* macro:

```
Private Sub cboCompany_AfterUpdate()
    Me.RecordsetClone.FindFirst "[ID] = " & Me.cboCompany.Column(0)
    If Not Me.RecordsetClone.NoMatch Then
        Me.Bookmark = Me.RecordsetClone.Bookmark
    End If
End Sub
```

In the previous example, we illustrated a classic technique that involves using a form's *RecordsetClone*, which can be easily extended and applied to different problems. You could have also used the following simpler piece of code:

```
Me.Recordset.FindFirst "[ID] = " & Me.cboCompany
```

INSIDE OUT   Synchronizing bookmarks with the form and the *RecordsetClone* and avoiding write conflicts

The *RecordsetClone* is a property of a form which is a clone of the underlying *Recordset* that supports the form. This means that we can use VBA *Recordset* code and treat this as a proper *Recordset*. *Bookmarks* are shared between the form (which has a special *Bookmark* property) and the *RecordsetClone*. Thus, we search and locate a record in the clone, and then by pointing the form's *Bookmark* to the *Bookmark* of the clone, the form will automatically synchronize and display the desired record.

A common mistake is trying to edit the same data in the clone while simultaneously allowing a user to edit the record through the forms controls. We have provided a sample form called *frmRecordSetCloneEdit* that is designed to show you exactly how to generate this problem; the code on the form will fail with a write conflict, as demonstrated in the following (this is an example of what *not* to do):

```
Private Sub cmdEdit_Click()
    ' First we simulate a user editing the record
    Me.[First Name] = "Andrew"
    ' locate the same records
    Dim rst As Recordset
    Set rst = Me.RecordsetClone
    rst.FindFirst "[ID] = " & Me.ID
```

```
        If Not rst.NoMatch Then
            rst.Edit
            rst![First Name] = "Fred"
            rst.Update
        End If
        ' now try and save the changes to the form
        Me.Dirty = False
End Sub
```

Other than the need to be aware of and avoid write conflicts, the form's *RecordsetClone* is a very powerful tool; for example, one form can open another form and then manipulate data in the clone as well as resynchronize the other form to the clone.

Refresh, *Repaint*, *Recalc*, and *Requery* Commands

Refresh, *Repaint*, *Recalc*, and *Requery* commands can be called when you want information displayed on a screen to be updated. The following is a brief description of each:

- **Recalc**   *Form only.* Forces all calculations to be updated.

- **Refresh**   *Form only.* Updates changes made by other users to records, doesn't show new records or remove deleted records (except in an adp). *Requery* is often a better choice to make when updating the display of records.

- **Repaint**   *Form only.* Forces any pending screen updates to be completed, also forces a *Recalc*.

- **Requery**   *Form and controls (often used with combo and list boxes to refresh displayed lists of data).* Removes any deleted records and adds any new records.

In this book, you will see many examples of how to use *Requery* to update the data in forms and controls. *Recalc* is occasionally used; *Repaint* and *Refresh* are used infrequently.

In the demonstration database, the *frmCalculations* form (Figure 6-22) contains two text boxes into which a user can type a number, and a third text box that displays the result.

The two text boxes are called [txtX] and [txtY], and the calculation is shown in the following code:

```
=CLng(Nz([txtX]))+CLng(Nz([txtY]))
```

Two important features of this calculation are *CLng* and *Nz*. *CLng* prevents numbers in the fields from being treated as text and thus string concatenated; *Nz* prevents an unnecessary error message from being displayed in the result until both the text boxes have valid values.

When you type values into the two unbound controls, the calculated control is automatically updated (without the need for any program code). If you have calculated fields that refer to other controls on the form, Access will update those dependent fields. However, if you were, for example, to create a control that uses a more complex expression such as a domain function linked to other fields on the form, then because the form cannot work out when to update the data, you need to call *Recalc* explicitly in your code. In this case, the form cannot work out when to update the result).

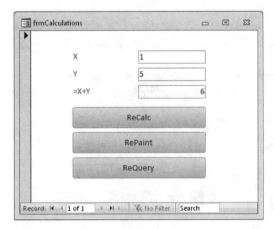

Figure 6-22 The *frmCalculations* form showing the differences between *ReCalc*, *RePaint*, and *ReQuery*.

Calling Procedures Across Forms

In a form, you can define a subroutine or function as *Public*; this means that any other part of the application can call the procedure on the form (while the form is open). A typical example for using this is when you have some special programming on a form that needs to be executed because another form has made changes to the data being displayed on the form.

INSIDE OUT
Calling public code on a form

In addition to calling subroutines and functions, it is also possible to make any standard event handler on a form public, which allows other forms to call these events. The code required to call code on another form involves setting a form object variable to reference the target form, and then execute the code on the form (when doing this, you will not have IntelliSense to assist you). The example that follows shows a code fragment for calling a function called *GetResults()* on the form called *tfrmTarget*:

```
DoCmd.OpenForm "frmTarget"
Set frm = Forms!frmTarget
Dim varResult As Variant
varResult = frm.GetResults()
```

The demonstration database contains the two forms: *frmTarget* and *frmSource*. The target form consists of two controls. Figure 6-23 shows *frmSource* opening *frmTarget*.

Figure 6-23 A form calling code on another form.

We added the following code on the target form:

```
Public Sub UpdateResults()
    Me.txtResultsUpdate = "Result updated on by UpdateResults " & Now
End Sub

Public Function GetResults() As Variant
    Me.txtResultsUpdate = "Result updated on " & Now
End Function

Public Sub txtResults_AfterUpdate()
    Me.txtResultsUpdate = "Result updated on " & Now
End Sub
```

The source form presents buttons that instruct how to open the target form and then call the appropriate code, as previously defined.

```
Private Sub cmdCallEvent_Click()
    Dim frm As Form
    DoCmd.OpenForm "frmTarget"
    Set frm = Forms!frmTarget
    frm.txtResults_AfterUpdate
End Sub

Private Sub cmdCallFunction_Click()
    Dim frm As Form
    DoCmd.OpenForm "frmTarget"
    Set frm = Forms!frmTarget
    Dim varResult As Variant
    varResult = frm.GetResults()
    MsgBox varResult
End Sub

Private Sub cmdCallSubroutine_Click()
    Dim frm As Form
    DoCmd.OpenForm "frmTarget"
    Set frm = Forms!frmTarget
    frm.UpdateResults
End Sub
```

Interacting with Records on a Form

In this section, you start by looking at one of the most important events in form program-ming: the *Current* event. This event is triggered when a user moves to a record, and it is often used to change controls on the form to match details of the record being viewed. You then look at *Deactivate*, *Activate*, *Timer*, and *Mouse* events.

The *Current* Event

As you move between records, for each record that you arrive on (including the new record) the *Current* event will be fired.

Current → Current → Current

The *Current* event is extensively used in the programming of a form; its main purpose is to enable/disable controls on a form that are dependent on the data content of the record.

For example, the Customers table contains a ContractClass field, which we only want to dis-play when a company outside the United States is displayed. Figure 6-24 shows the field in the table design.

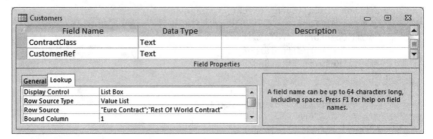

Figure 6-24 The ContractClass field, which we only want to display for certain customer records.

On the *frmCustomersContractClass* form, we have added code to hide/display the *cboContractClass* control. The control is visible in Figure 6-25. The code that follows could have been written directly on the *Current* event for the form, but because we also want to change the visibility if the Country/Region field changes, it is worthwhile writing the code in a separate procedure, which is called from both the *Current* form event and *AfterUpdate* control event.

Figure 6-25 Changing the display to show a customer in the United States causes the *cboContractClass* combo box to be hidden.

```
Sub DisplayHideControls()
    If Nz(Me.Country_Region) <> "USA" Then
        Me.cboContractClass.Visible = True
    Else
        Me.cboContractClass.Visible = False
    End If
End Sub

Private Sub Country_Region_AfterUpdate()
    DisplayHideControls
End Sub

Private Sub Form_Current()
    DisplayHideControls
End Sub
```

INSIDE OUT   Controlling column visibility in a Continuous form

Changing the visibility of controls on a form works well for a form in Single Form View; however, it can produce disturbing effects when used on a Continuous form, where the field suddenly appears for all records or for no records, depending on the value in the current record. Figure 6-26 shows what happens when a user moves from a European customer record to the record of a customer in the United States.

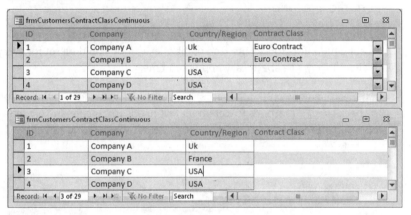

Figure 6-26 The ContractClass field in the *frmCustomersContractClassContinuous* form flickers on and off, depending on the data held in the row.

In this situation, you might consider moving the control into the form's header or footer sections, or making the control locked rather than hiding it.

Deactivate and *Activate* Events

In addition to moving between records, a user can switch between forms; when you click off of a form, the *Deactivate* event fires; when you click a form, the *Activate* event fires. These events are not commonly programmed, and you will find that if you try to manage window focus in these events, you do not always acheive reliable results.

Deactivate → *Activate*

Setting the Timer Interval Property of the *Timer* Event

If you want to exploit timed operations, you need to consider how these will impact user interaction with the data on forms. The Timer Interval property (measured in milliseconds) allows the *Timer* event to be fired at a specified interval. Setting this to a value of 1000, for example, generates a *Timer* event once every second. When the Timer Interval is set, you can write code on the *Timer* event that is triggered at each timed interval. It is a good idea to ensure that the time required for the code to execute is less than that of the Timer Interval setting (it is also possible to stop the timer from running by setting a value of 0 for the Timer Interval).

There are many ways to utilize the Timer Interval. The sections that follow present two suggested applications.

Periodic Execution

By polling a *Timer* event, you can set up an application to run on the desktop and wait for an appointed time to execute. The point of execution could be set for every timer interval, or alternatively, at a specifically appointed time.

In the companion content that accompanies this chapter, the *frmPolling* form is configured to check every 20 seconds to determine if it needs to execute any procedures. The table *tblExecutionEvents* acts as a work list of processes that need to run every day, as shown in Figure 6-27.

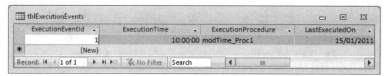

Figure 6-27 A table of events used for polling a timed event.

Events are logged in the table *tblExecutionLog*, as shown in Figure 6-28.

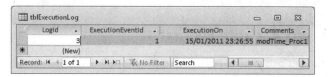

Figure 6-28 Events are logged as they are executed.

The execution procedure is defined as follows:

```
Sub modTime_Proc1(LogId As Long)
    ' example timer event
    ' updates the log record with a comment
    Dim strSQL As String
    strSQL = "UPDATE [tblExecutionLog] " & _
            " SET Comments = 'modTime_Proc1 Executed'" & _
            " WHERE LogId = " & LogId
    CurrentDb.Execute strSQL
End Sub
```

On the *frmPolling* form, we have defined a Timer Interval and written the code that follows to execute on each *Timer* event, as shown in Figure 6-29.

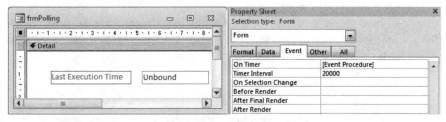

Figure 6-29 A Timer Interval of 20000 milliseconds (20 seconds).

```
Private Sub Form_Timer()
    ' search all the execution events
    ' when not executed today
    ' check for ellaspsed time and execute the event
    Dim db As Database
    Dim rst As Recordset
    Dim rstLog As Recordset
    Set db = CurrentDb
    Dim strSQL As String
    ' all events  not yet executed and scheduled time
    ' has elapsed
    Me.txtExecutionPoint = Time
    strSQL = "SELECT *  FROM tblExecutionEvents " & _
            " WHERE ExecutionTime < Time() AND LastExecutedOn < Date()"
    Set rst = db.OpenRecordset(strSQL, dbOpenDynaset)
    Set rstLog = db.OpenRecordset("tblExecutionLog", dbOpenDynaset)
    Do While Not rst.EOF
        ' update active events
        rst.Edit
        rst!LastExecutedOn = Date
        rst.Update
        ' log the event execution
        rstLog.AddNew
        rstLog!ExecutionEventId = rst!ExecutionEventId
        rstLog!ExecutionOn = Now
        rstLog.Update
        rstLog.Bookmark = rstLog.LastModified
        ' Execute the procedure
        Run rst!ExecutionProcedure, rstLog!LogId
        rst.MoveNext
    Loop
    rst.Close
    rstLog.Close
End Sub
```

Monitoring

In this second example, we have designed a hidden form with a *Timer* event that polls a table and advises users when the system will shut down for maintenance. If the time has elapsed, then the routine will close all the user's forms and reports and quit the application. An administrator can use the table depicted in Figure 6-30 to set a shutdown time and post a user message.

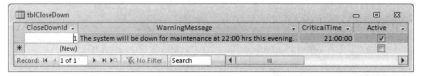

Figure 6-30 The Active flag indicates the event is scheduled for activation.

This application will have a hidden form that is launched upon startup and monitors the table for warning messages. Users are then be given a number of warnings, after which the application will close.

To implement this, you need the following code at startup:

```
Sub modTimer_LaunchMonitor()
    DoCmd.Echo False
    DoCmd.OpenForm "frmSilent"
    Forms("frmSilent").Visible = False
    DoCmd.Echo True
End Sub
```

The form shown in Figure 6-31 and the code that follows it incorporates a Dismiss button that allows the user to ignore the warning until they have completed their work (as long as they don't ignore it for too long).

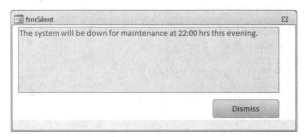

Figure 6-31 The user can press the Dismiss button to hide the window.

```
Option Compare Database
Option Explicit
Dim lngCriticalWarnings As Long ' flags critical warnings to a user
Const lngMaxWarnings = 2
Dim blUnloading As Boolean

Private Sub cmdDismiss_Click()
    ' hide the form
    Me.Visible = False
End Sub
Private Sub Form_Load()
    lngCriticalWarnings = 0
    blUnloading = False
End Sub

Private Sub Form_Timer()
    Dim db As Database
    Dim rst As Recordset
    Dim rstLog As Recordset
    Set db = CurrentDb
    Dim strSQL As String
    ' find any critical shutdown messages that apply
    strSQL = "SELECT *  FROM tblCloseDown " & _
            " WHERE CriticalTime > dateadd('n',-30,time())" & _
            " AND Active = True"

    Set rst = db.OpenRecordset(strSQL, dbOpenDynaset)
    If Not rst.EOF Then
        lngCriticalWarnings = lngCriticalWarnings + 1
        If lngCriticalWarnings > lngMaxWarnings Then
            ShutDown
        Else
            ' warn the user
            Me.Visible = True
            Me.txtWarning = rst!WarningMessage
            ' this stays on the screen until the user clicks dismiss
        End If
    End If
    rst.Close
End Sub

Sub ShutDown()
    ' shut down the application
    ' close any forms
    On Error Resume Next
    Dim lngfrmCount As Long
    Dim lngrptCount As Long
    Dim lngCount As Long
    lngfrmCount = Forms.Count
    lngrptCount = Reports.Count
    ' close all forms
```

```
        For lngCount = 0 To lngfrmCount - 1
            DoCmd.SelectObject acForm, Forms(lngCount).Name
            DoCmd.Close
        Next
        ' close all reports
        For lngCount = 0 To lngrptCount - 1
            DoCmd.SelectObject acReport, Reports(lngCount).Name
            DoCmd.Close
        Next
        blUnloading = True
        DoCmd.Quit
End Sub

Private Sub Form_Unload(Cancel As Integer)
    If Not blUnloading Then
        Me.Visible = False
        Cancel = True
    End If
End Sub
```

If you are using hidden forms, it's worthwhile considering what happens to these forms if a user attempts to leave the application. In the sample menu form *frmFormsMenu*, the following code is added to the *Close* event to tidy up the hidden form:

```
Private Sub Form_Close()
    ' close frmSilent if it is loaded
    If CurrentProject.AllForms("frmSilent").IsLoaded Then
        Forms("frmSilent").ShutDown
    End If
End Sub
```

The *Mouse* Events

Mouse events occur for the form, the different form sections, and the controls on the form that can be used to control how a user interacts with the data in the form. With these events, you can determine the mouse position, whether the Shift key is being held down, and which mouse button is pressed. There is also a *MouseWheel* event on the form.

The *frmMouseEvents* form, which can be found in the companion content that accompanies this chapter, can be used to investigate these events and display the corresponding values in screen controls for the mouse position and state of the buttons, as shown in Figure 6-32.

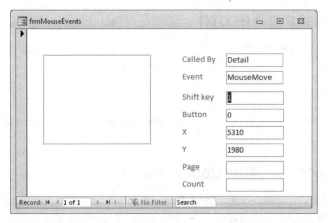

Figure 6-32 The *MouseMove* event tracks the position of the mouse; *MouseUp* and *MouseDown* reacts to button events; *MouseWheel* to wheel movements.

The main events used for programming mouse events on a form are those on the detail section, as demonstrated in the following example:

```
Private Sub Detail_MouseDown(Button As Integer, _
            Shift As Integer, X As Single, Y As Single)
    ShowMouseEvents "Detail", "MouseDown", Button, Shift, X, Y, 0, 0
End Sub
```

INSIDE OUT   Mouse events when a form is in Datasheet view

The form mouse events are also activated when the form is in Datasheet view, as shown in Figure 6-33, but not when it is in Form view (except if you click the forms record selector).

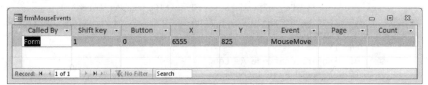

Figure 6-33 Mouse events also occur when a form is in Datasheet view.

Editing and Undo on a Record

As you start to edit a record, the *OnDirty* event is fired. If you press the escape key or otherwise undo the changes you've made, the *OnUndo* event fires.

> *OnDirty* → *OnUndo*

If you save your changes to an existing record, then the *BeforeUpdate* event fires, followed by the *AfterUpdate* event.

BeforeUpdate and *AfterUpdate* Events

You can use the *BeforeUpdate* event to perform validation and accept or reject a user's changes to either a control or record. With the *AfterUpdate* event, you can take action after the validation has been completed.

> *BeforeUpdate* → *AfterUpdate*

The *BeforeUpdate* event on both a form and the controls on a form are used primarily for validation checking before a value is saved. On a control, the control's *Undo* method can be called to undo any attempted change. On a *BeforeUpdate* event, the *Cancel* argument on the procedure call is set to *False* to reject any changes.

In the *frmCustomersBeforeUpdateEvents* form (in the companion content), the *BeforeUpdate* event on the [ZIP/Postal Code] field shows how you can start to build a sophisticated validation routine. This example also shows how the *ctrl.Undo* method can undo the user's changes (only for that control). This code is intended for countries other than the United States to verify that the first character of the postal code is text (A...Z, a...z). If the first character is not text, it cancels the update and undoes the text typed in by the user:

```
Private Sub ZIP_Postal_Code_BeforeUpdate(Cancel As Integer)
    If Nz(Me.Country_Region) = "USA" Then
        Exit Sub
    End If
    Dim lngFirstCharCode As Long
    If Nz(Me.ZIP_Postal_Code) <> "" Then
        lngFirstCharCode = Asc(Left(Me.ZIP_Postal_Code, 1))
        If (lngFirstCharCode >= Asc("A") And _
            lngFirstCharCode <= Asc("Z")) Or _
            (lngFirstCharCode >= Asc("a") And _
            lngFirstCharCode <= Asc("z")) Then
        Else
            Cancel = True
            Me.ZIP_Postal_Code.Undo
            ' Note don't use Me.Undo unless you want to
            ' undo all changes to the record
```

```
            MsgBox "Must start with a letter", vbInformation, _
                    "Change not accepted"
        End If
    End If
End Sub
```

What if a user has not yet entered a value for the Country, but begins to type the code? One solution is to approach this in a similar manner to that of the *ContractClass*, but this time write a statement to only enable the [ZIP/Postal Code] if the user has entered a [Country/Region]:

```
Sub EnableFields()
    If IsNull(Me.Country_Region) Then
        Me.ZIP_Postal_Code.Enabled = False
    Else
        Me.ZIP_Postal_Code.Enabled = True
    End If
End Sub


Private Sub Country_Region_AfterUpdate()
    EnableFields
End Sub


Private Sub Form_Current()
    EnableFields
End Sub
```

What if a user sets the Country to USA, types in a number for the ZIP code, and then changes the country to France? You can get around this by adding further code to the *Country_Region_AfterUpdate* event. An alternative, which would also mean that existing data was validated, is to add code to the form's *BeforeUpdate* event. We have also added a *SetFocus* command to move the cursor into the field that needs to be changed:

```
Private Sub Form_BeforeUpdate(Cancel As Integer)
    If Not IsNull(Me.Country_Region) And _
            Nz(Me.Country_Region) <> "USA" Then
        Dim lngFirstCharCode As Long
        If Nz(Me.ZIP_Postal_Code) <> "" Then
            lngFirstCharCode = Asc(Left(Me.ZIP_Postal_Code, 1))
            If (lngFirstCharCode >= Asc("A") And _
                lngFirstCharCode <= Asc("Z")) Or _
                (lngFirstCharCode >= Asc("a") And _
                lngFirstCharCode <= Asc("z")) Then
            Else
                Cancel = True
                MsgBox "Postal/Zip Code Must start with a letter", _
                    vbInformation, "Change not accepted"
                Me.ZIP_Postal_Code.SetFocus
            End If
        End If
    End If
End Sub
```

The *AfterUpdate* event on a form and the controls on a form are used primarily to carry out special activities following an acceptable change to the data, such as controlling the visibility or values in other controls.

Locking and Unlocking Controls

The next code example is the *frmCustomersAndOrders* form, which illustrates how you can change a form's behavior so that users are forced to either press a function key or a button to unlock the controls for editing. The form contains a call during the *Current* event to lock all controls against editing as well as a button to enable editing of data in all controls.

This example also illustrates how we can exclude certain controls from this process by using the control's *Tag* property. This is a very useful property, and you can decide for yourself how best to use it.

The following code has been added to the form:

```
Private Sub cmdEdit_Click()
    modFormLockUnlock_LockUnlock Me, False
End Sub

Private Sub Form_Current()
    modFormLockUnlock_LockUnlock Me, True
End Sub
```

In a module *modFormLockUnlock*, we have written a general purpose routine for locking and unlocking the controls on the form, as follows:

```
Sub modFormLockUnlock_LockUnlock(frm As Form, blLockSetting As Boolean)
    ' Locks all the controls on a form against editing
    Dim ctrl As Control
    Dim ctrlSubfrom As Control
    For Each ctrl In frm
        ' not every control supports these properties
        On Error Resume Next
        If ctrl.Tag <> "SkipLock" Then
            ctrl.Locked = blLockSetting
            ' if we have a subform then lock
            ' all controls on the subform
            If TypeOf ctrl Is SubForm Then
                For Each ctrlSubfrom In ctrl.Controls
                    On Error Resume Next
                    ctrl.Locked = blLockSetting
                Next
            End If
        End If
    Next
End Sub
```

INSIDE OUT   Using *Me* vs. *Screen.ActiveForm* to pass a reference to a form

When calling the procedure *modFormLockUnlock_LockUnlock* (detailed in the previous section), the calling form passes a reference to itself by using the special *Me* keyword. It is tempting in this module to consider *Screen.ActiveForm* as an alternative method of getting a reference to the active form. However, during the first call to *Current*, when the form opens, the window is not yet active, and so this reference will fail.

BeforeInsert and *AfterInsert* Events

After the first key press on a new record, the *BeforeInsert* event and then the *Dirty* event fire.

> *BeforeInsert* → *Dirty*

If you save your changes to the new record, then the *BeforeUpdate*, *AfterUpdate*, and *AfterInsert* events fire, as illustrated in the following

> *BeforeUpdate* → *AfterUpdate* → *AfterInsert*

As an example of coding for these events, *frmCustomersBeforeInsert* has code added on the *BeforeInsert* event that retrieves a special unique key value from a lookup table and adds this to the record. This can be used as a method for getting unique key values for data, as shown in Figure 6-34.

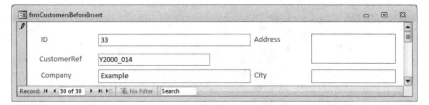

Figure 6-34 When inserting a new record, a key is generated by looking up values in a table that holds the last used keys.

Unique key values are issued from a table of keys, as shown in Figure 6-35.

Figure 6-35 The unique key can have a prefix and pad out the number with extra zeros, which could be used for a number of tables.

Chapter 6

The following example shows the code that added to the *BeforeInsert* event on the form to retrieve a new value for the key:

```
Private Sub Form_BeforeInsert(Cancel As Integer)
    Dim strKey As String
    Dim strField As String
    strKey = modKeys_GetKeyValue("Customers", strField)
    Me(strField) = strKey
End Sub
```

Alternatively, this code can be added to the *AfterInsert* event, depending on exactly when you need the key issued.

In the code that follows, *modKeys_GetKeyValue* looks up the tablename and then obtains the next sequenced key value. It also has some additional features including adding a prefix to the key (for example, Y2000) and padding the number with leading zeros; for example, 1 would become 001. The most important part of the routine is the lock retries to resolve any multi-user conflicts when two or more users try to get the next key at the same time. This process is implemented with a transaction to protect against multiple users requesting keys at the same time; if a transaction fails, it performs a *Rollback* then issues a *DoEvents* to allow some time to elapse before trying the transaction again. We have also set a constant to control the maximum number of times that the transaction can be attempted:

```
Function modKeys_GetKeyValue(strTableName As String, _
                        ByRef strKeyFieldName As String) As String
    On Error GoTo Err_Handler
    Const lngMaxLockRetry = 10
    ' Lookup a unique key value from tblTableKeys
    ' for the specified table strTableName
    Dim db As Database
    Dim wks As Workspace
    Dim rst As Recordset
    Dim strKeyPrefix As String
    Dim lngPadKeyZeros As Long
    Dim lngLastUsedKey As Long
    Dim strSelect As String
    Dim KeyValue As String
    Dim lngPad As Long
    Dim lngTryCount As Long
    Set wks = DBEngine(0)
    Set db = wks.Databases(0)
    lngTryCount = 0
    strSelect = "SELECT * FROM tblTableKeys WHERE [TableName] " & _
                " = '" & strTableName & "'"
```

```
retry:
    wks.BeginTrans
    lngTryCount = lngTryCount + 1
    Set rst = db.OpenRecordset(strSelect, dbOpenDynaset)
    With rst
        .Edit
        strKeyPrefix = Nz(!KeyPrefix)
        lngPadKeyZeros = Nz(!PadKeyZeros)
        lngLastUsedKey = Nz(!LastUsedKey)
        ' update the last used key
        lngLastUsedKey = lngLastUsedKey + 1
        !LastUsedKey = lngLastUsedKey
        strKeyFieldName = !KeyFieldName
        .Update
    End With
    wks.CommitTrans
    ' build the key
    KeyValue = lngLastUsedKey
    If lngPadKeyZeros <> 0 Then
        ' option to add 0's for padding
        Do While lngPadKeyZeros > Len(KeyValue)
            KeyValue = "0" & KeyValue
        Loop
    End If
    ' option to add a prefix
    KeyValue = strKeyPrefix & KeyValue
    modKeys_GetKeyValue = KeyValue
    Exit Function
Err_Handler:
    ' Retry in event of a locking problem
    If lngTryCount < lngMaxLockRetry Then
        wks.Rollback
        DoEvents
        GoTo retry
    Else
        ' special handling of what happens here
        MsgBox "Error maximum lock retries reached", vbInformation, _
            "Error Getting Unique Key Value"
        modKeys_GetKeyValue = 0
    End If
End Function
```

The *Delete* Event

Deleting a record initiates the following event sequence:

Delete → Current → BeforeDelConfirm → AfterDelConfirm

You then have the option of writing code against these events to display your own confirmation messages and suppress the confirmation message that Access displays, such as shown in the following:

```
Private Sub Form_BeforeDelConfirm(Cancel As Integer, Response As Integer)
    If MsgBox("Delete customer " & Me.Company & " ?", vbYesNo, _
                        "Delete Company") = vbYes Then
        Cancel = False
        ' supress the access message box
        Response = acDataErrContinue
    Else
        Cancel = True
    End If
End Sub
```

INSIDE OUT   Using *AfterDelConfirm* to detect actions by a user when deleting records

In the *AfterDelConfirm*, you can detect and act upon the earlier action taken in the *BeforeDelConfirm* event and choices made by the user. To see an example of the following code in action, look at *frmRecordsetClone*, which is available in the companion content for this chapter (note that to see *acDeleteUserCancel* condition you would need to remove the code from the *BeforeDelConfirm* event):

```
Private Sub Form_AfterDelConfirm(Status As Integer)
    Select Case Status
        Case acDeleteOK
            ' delete as expected
        Case acDeleteCancel
            MsgBox "Programmer canceled the deletion."
        Case acDeleteUserCancel
            MsgBox "User canceled the deletion."
    End Select
End Sub
```

KeyPreview and Key Events

You can pass information about what keys the user presses to the form's *KeyPress* event by setting the *KeyPreview* property for a form to *True*. By default this is not set, so when typing into controls, you need to check the keystrokes for each individual control on the form. The *KeyPreview* feature was added to work around this problem and allow keystrokes to be checked at a single point on the form.

KeyDown → *KeyPress* → (*Dirty* if first edit) → *KeyUp*

The *Error* Event

The *Error* event allows you to take control of error message boxes that Access displays when a user edits data through the form, as shown in Figure 6-36.

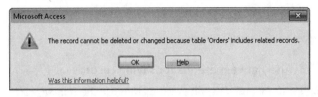

Figure 6-36 A trappable error when a user tries to delete a record, but the record has related records.

The *AccessError* function can be used to lookup the Access Error message. By setting the Response flag, you can control whether the built-in error message is also displayed. See the companion content example form, *frmRecordsetClone*, for this code:

```
Private Sub Form_Error(DataErr As Integer, Response As Integer)
    ' Respone can be acDataErrContinue or acDataErrDisplay
    Dim strErrorMessage As String
    If DataErr = 3200 Then
        strErrorMessage = AccessError(DataErr)
        ' replace the default error message box
        MsgBox "Unable to delete this record " & strErrorMessage, _
                vbInformation, "Operation not Available"
        ' supress Access error message
        Response = acDataErrContinue
    End If
End Sub
```

Figure 6-37 shows the new error message. Note that because we looked up the error message, it does not contain the name of the table that contains the related records that blocked the delete action.

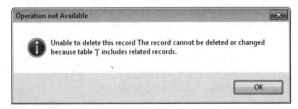

Figure 6-37 The Access error message box replaced with a custom dialog box.

An example of how this is extremely useful is when you are working with SQL Server; in this case Access displays a generic ODBC error message. If you look in the *Errors* collection and display *Errors(0)*, then you can provide a much better description of the error.

Saving Records

As users move to a new record or a subform, Access automatically saves changes to the record, but during interaction with the form, after the program code makes changes to a record, there will be points in time when you want to force a record to be saved. Several different methods exist for saving a record.

INSIDE OUT   Alternative methods for saving records

The first and oldest technique for saving records is to use the *SendKeys* action to simulate the user pressing the Shift+Enter keystroke combination, which forces the currently active record to be saved. The *True* argument indicates that the code should wait until the keystrokes have been processed:

```
SendKey "+{Enter}",True
```

The second method is to use the *RunCommand* action:

```
RunCommand acCmdSaveRecord
```

Note that if you debug code when using either the *RunCommand* or *SendKeys* methods, the application throws error messages indicating that the record cannot be saved (if it is not already being edited). Usually, this means that you need to add an On Error Resume Next before the save actions; the problem with this is in knowing when there has been a genuine error during the save operation.

A third method is to force the record to save by setting the *Dirty* property of the form to *False*, as shown in the following:

```
Me.Dirty = False
```

In some older systems, you might also see the use of the *DoMenuItem* command, which simulates the user making a menu selection to save a record.

Summary

In this chapter, you learned how to program forms by writing code in response to events. Although forms have a large number of events, you will probably find that you spend most of your time programming against a small subset of them. The following presents some of the key events described in this chapter.

- **BeforeUpdate**   Used for validating and rejecting attempts to enter or change data.

- **AfterUpdate**   Used to control enable/disable or hide other controls, based on the recent changes or entry of new data.

- **OnOpen** or **OnLoad**   Used to set up controls when a form is first used.

- **OnCurrent**   Used to make the controls reflect the data when a user moves to a record.

- **Error**   Used to intercept errors and provide alternative messages.

Using Form Controls and Events

Control Events. 274

Combo Boxes 278

List Boxes. 286

The *TreeView* Control. 295

The *Tab* Control 311

I n Chapter 6, "Using Forms and Events," we introduced events by demonstrating various techniques that are used when programming Microsoft Access 2010 forms. In this chapter, we start by discussing the key programming events that apply to most controls. We then move on to systematically examine programming with more sophisticated controls.

The first control to examine is the combo box. In this section, you look at how to synchronize data displayed in multiple controls and see the various features that can be used for dynamically adding data to the available values in the control.

Next, you look at programming list boxes and handling multiple values in code as compared to the techniques for working with multiple list boxes, and demonstrate how list boxes can be used to behave like a subform.

The section on the *TreeView* control demonstrates how to enhance your application with a hierarchical tree view of data. This section also shows you how to implement drag-and-drop and add graphical images.

The final section in this chapter looks at the *Tab* control. Here, you see how to manage refreshing data across pages and look at building tabs that can dynamically load and unload subforms.

After reading this chapter, you will:

- Understand the general principles of programming for events on controls.

- Be able to undertake advanced programming tasks with more complex controls.

> **Note**
> As you read through this chapter, we encourage you to also use the companion content sample databases, Controls.accdb and TreeBuilder.accdb, which can be downloaded from the book's catalog page.

Control Events

You interact with a form through its controls, for example, text boxes, command buttons, list boxes, combo boxes, and so on. Controls can have different types of events, although there are some events that are common to most controls. In this section, we will look at how to write code in response to the most commonly used events. In the Controls.accdb database, the form *frmSimpleEvents* contains the code shown in this section.

Having the Control Wizard active when placing a list box, combo box, or option group on a form is usually helpful, but if you are writing Microsoft VBA code in an application the Control Wizard's assistance with the command button is not so helpful because you do not want the macro code that the wizard generates.

When adding an unbound control to a form, Access automatically gives the control a default name such as txt1, and because the control name is concatenated with the event name—for example, txt1_Click()—and you might also be referring to the control at other points in the code (Me.txt1), it will improve the readability of your code to give the control a more meaningful name, for example, *txtTotalOrderValue*. If you decide to change a control name after you have written the event code, then you need to change all the other references to the control, including the names of any event handlers for the control (this is a very important point, because after renaming a control that has associated event code, the code will no longer operate unless you also rename each associated event to incorporate the changed control name).

All controls have a default event, which is generated when you add code to your control. For example, when you are in Form design and you have selected a control, right-click the control, select Build Event, and then on the shortcut menu, click Code Builder, Access will write the event stub for the default event; this defaults to generate a *Click* Event, which is often not what you want.

When you want to write code behind an event, you can either click the ellipse button adjacent to the event name and select code builder, or you can click the drop-down menu, select [Event Procedure] (see Figure 7-1), and then click the ellipse button, which takes you straight to the code.

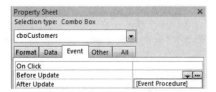

Figure 7-1 Adding code behind a control's event.

Once you have written code behind events on a control, there are additional points to consider when making copies of a control. If you copy and paste a control that has macro code written behind it, the macro is copied with the control; if you copy a control that has VBA written behind its events, the VBA code is not copied. The only exception is if you make a direct reference from the control's event to either a function behind the form or a public function (see Figure 7-2), then when the control is copied, the reference is also copied.

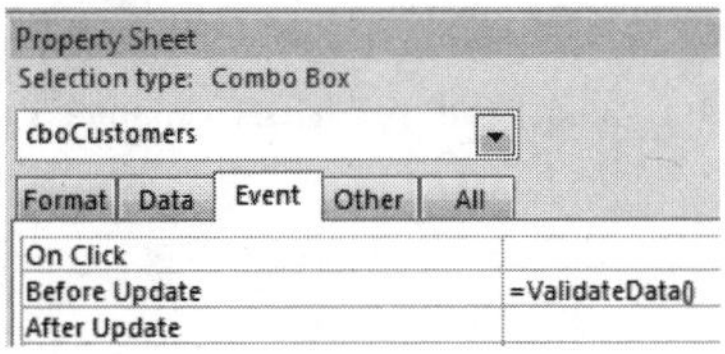

Figure 7-2 Making direct references to a VBA function from a control's event.

A further point to consider when deciding to write code behind events for a control, is that you can instruct a control to call the event code on another control, which saves duplicating units of code:

```
Private Sub cmdCallEvent_Click()
    Me.CurrencyRegion = "Domestic"
    CurrencyRegion_AfterUpdate
End Sub
```

Or calling a validation event:

```
Private Sub cmdCallEvent_Click()
    Me.ExchangeRate = 999
    Dim blCancel As Integer
    ExchangeRate_BeforeUpdate blCancel
End Sub
```

The *Click* and *DblClick* Events

The *Click* and *DblClick* events are commonly used in programming for a variety of actions—particularly when working with a Command button—including creating application navigation to other forms and reports:

```
Private Sub cmdProducts_Click()
    DoCmd.OpenForm "frmProducts"
End Sub
```

DblClick is another popular navigation action to have on controls other than a Command button. For example, you can color certain text boxes a specific color to indicate to the user that a double-click pops up a form that shows more detailed information.

The *BeforeUpdate* Event

You can use *BeforeUpdate* to validate the data that a user has entered and choose to accept or reject the change. In the following code for the form *frmSimpleEvents*, you see a typical example of validation code written on the *BeforeUpdate* event for a *textbox* control:

```
Private Sub ExchangeRate_BeforeUpdate(Cancel As Integer)
    If Nz(Me.ExchangeRate) <= 0 _
        Or Nz(Me.ExchangeRate) > 10 Then
        Cancel = True
        Me.ExchangeRate.Undo
        MsgBox "A value between 0 and 10 is required for the exchange rate", _
            vbInformation, "Missing Information"
    End If
End Sub
```

INSIDE OUT   Controlling behavior during validation

The *BeforeUpdate* event of a control has a single parameter called *Cancel As Integer*. If you set this value to *True*, you are rejecting any new value a user enters. If you issue the *Me.ControlName.Undo* command, any changes that the user typed in the control will be undone, and if you issue the *Me.Undo* command, all changes made to the record since the edit was started will be undone. If the control is unbound—for example, as with the control *txtExchangeRate* in *frmSimpleEvents*—then using the *Undo* methods do not have any effect on the data being displayed (the code *Me.txtExchangeRate. Undo* fails to undo the change to the data).

Other points to note are that while you are within the *BeforeUpdate* event, you are not allowed to either force the record to be saved or shift focus to any other control (the *AfterUpdate* event can be used to save the record or shift focus) . A useful property of the control is *Me.ControlName.OldValue*, which gives the *OldValue* before the user attempted to change the data (the sample code for this is in the *frmSimpleEvents* form in the Controls. accdb database).

The *AfterUpdate* Event

The *AfterUpdate* event is the post update event for the control, for which the most common uses is to hide or show other controls by using the *Visible* property, or enable or disable other controls by using the *Enabled* property (which prevents or allows a shift of focus into a control), or lock or unlock other controls by using the *Locked* property to prevent or allow data to be changed. Because you might want to change these settings for particular controls when each record is displayed, it is a good idea to place the code in a procedure that can be called both from the form's *OnCurrent* event and the *AfterUpdate* event of a control, as demonstrated in the following:

```
Sub DisplayCurrencyRates()
    If IsNull(Me.cboCurrencyRegion) Then
        Me.txtExchangeRate.Visible = False
    Else
        Me.txtExchangeRate.Visible = True
    End If
    If Nz(Me.cboCurrencyRegion) <> "Domestic" Then
        Me.txtExchangeRate.Enabled = True
    Else
        Me.txtExchangeRate.Enabled = False
    End If
End Sub
```

Having a separate subroutine means that you can call this code both after data is changed and when displaying a different record:

```
Private Sub cboCurrencyRegion_AfterUpdate()
    DisplayCurrencyRates
End Sub

Private Sub Form_Current()
    DisplayCurrencyRates
End Sub
```

Notice that with the *cboCurrencyRegion* control in code, you can refer to the bound value either as *Me.cboCurrencyRegion* or *Me.CurrencyRegion*. In the second case, you are referencing the field in the underlying *Recordset*, and in the first case, you are referring to the bound control. This flexibility can often be confusing.

The *GotFocus* and *LostFocus* Events

The focus events can be programmed to create actions when a user clicks into or out of a control. It is also possible to use *SetFocus* to move focus to another control; this is often used within *Click* and *AfterUpdate* events. Another common use of *Focus* events is to apply conditional logic (for example in a continuous form) to prevent a user from clicking into a particular field under certain conditions; in this case, you can use the *SetFocus* events to move a user into another field:

```
Private Sub cmdShiftFocus_Click()
    Me.CurrencyRegion.SetFocus
End Sub
```

Combo Boxes

In this section, you will begin by looking at how two combo box controls can be linked together so that the choice made in one control effects the available data in the second control, this technique can also be used with subforms and other types of controls. You will also look at how the *RowSource* of a combo box can be manipulated, the column properties, and various methods for adding to the data being displayed in the control.

Synchronizing Data in Controls

This example looks at synchronizing controls so that a selection made in one control changes what is available in another control. There are several ways to link the controls together, but the key element in all of the methods is for a selection in the first box to *Requery* the data to be displayed in the second box.

The sample *frmComboSynchronised* form contains two unbound combo boxes: the first is called *cboCategory*, and the second is *cboProduct*, as shown in Figure 7.3.

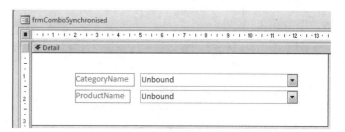

Figure 7-3 Controls can be set up so that they depend on the values in other controls; the data choices are then synchronized.

The *RowSource* in the second combo box has been tied to filter by the control value selected in the first combo box, as shown in Figure 7-4.

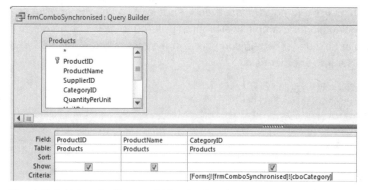

Figure 7-4 Using the Query grid for the *RowSource* to make a data choice in one control filters the available data choices in a second control.

Before changing the *RowSource* in the second combo box, ensure that you name the controls. After changing the *RowSource*, you need to add some code on the *AfterUpdate* for the first combo box, as shown in the following:

```
Private Sub cboCategory_AfterUpdate()
    Me.cboProduct.Requery
    IF Me.cboProduct.ListCount > 0 Then
        Me.cboProduct = Me.cboProduct.ItemData(0)
        Me.cboProduct.SetFocus
        Me.cboProduct.Dropdown
    End If
End Sub
```

The first command, *Requery*, instructs the second controls data source to be updated, and because the value in *cboCategory* has changed and the *RowSource* uses this control as a filter, the results in the second control will be updated.

INSIDE OUT   Setting combo box defaults and displaying the drop-down list

By using the *ItemData* property of a combo box, you can iterate through the values for the bound column from *0* to *ListCount-1*. This can be tested by using the following code:

```
Dim lngItem As Long
Stop
For lngItem = 0 To Me.cboProduct.ListCount - 1
    Debug.Print Me.cboProduct.ItemData(lngItem)
Next
```

In the main example code block, the value *ItemData(0)* forces the control to display the first value (if it has a value available). This must be protected by checking the *ListCount* property. The *SetFocus* command forces the mouse to move into the target combo box, and the *DropDown* method forces the control to display (drop down) a selection of choices.

One disadvantage of this code is that the second combo box *RowSource* explicitly refers to the form by name. Unfortunately, we cannot replace the name of the form in the *RowSource* with the *Me* keyword. The *frmComboSyncronised2* form illustrates a solution to this problem, wherein you use VBA to rewrite the *RowSource* SQL before updating the control, as demonstrated here:

```
Private Sub cboCategory_AfterUpdate()
    Me.cboProduct.RowSource = "SELECT ProductID, ProductName" & _
        " FROM Products WHERE CategoryID = " & Me.cboCategory
    Me.cboProduct.Requery
```

```
        IF Me.cboProduct.ListCount > 0 Then
            Me.cboProduct = Me.cboProduct.ItemData(0)
            Me.cboProduct.SetFocus
            Me.cboProduct.Dropdown
        End If
End Sub
```

This method can equally be used with one text box and a combo box, or other combinations of controls.

Combo Box *RowSource* Type

A combo box can source data from a Table/Query, Value List, or Field List. It is also possible to use program code that utilizes a callback function to gain complete control of how a combo box is populated. (This is discussed in Chapter 17, "Developing Applications.") With the Table/Query, you can refer to a query, table, or specify an explicit SQL string. Using the Value List, you can specify a set of explicit list of data values to display.

In the previous example, you saw combo boxes that displayed data from a table by using SQL. In the following example, you see how a list of explicit values can be displayed in a combo box. Figure 7-5 shows the *frmComboBoxList* form, where we have set the *RowSourceType* to a *Value List* and supplied a string of values for the *RowSource*.

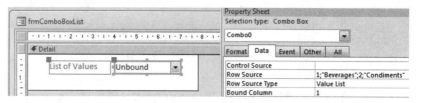

Figure 7-5 Supplying a list of values to a combo box.

The third option of using a Field List is less often used, but it can be useful if you want to develop your own wizard style forms; for example, listing columns from a selected table. The sample *frmComboFieldList* form lists all available forms in the database, and after selecting a form, it displays a list of all the fields in each form's *RecordSource*. Figure 7-6 shows the result of building the list of values dynamically.

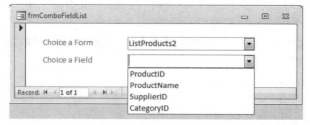

Figure 7-6 The second combo box displays a list of fields; the data for the first combo box is created with program code.

You begin by developing a routine that uses the *CurrentProject* object to gather a list of all the forms; the text names are surrounded by double quotes and delimited by a semicolon. These are then assigned to the *RowSource* of the first combo box, which has a *RowSourceType* of *Value List*:

```
Sub BuildListOfForms()
    Dim strForms As String
    Dim lngForm As Long
    For lngForm = 0 To CurrentProject.AllForms.Count - 1
        If CurrentProject.AllForms(lngForm).Name <> Me.Name Then
            If strForms <> "" Then strForms = strForms & ";"
            strForms = strForms & """" & _
                CurrentProject.AllForms(lngForm).Name & """"
        End If
    Next
    Me.cboForm.RowSource = strForms
End Sub
```

After the user has selected the form, the controls *AfterUpdate* event opens the target form in Design mode to read the SQL in the form's *RecordSource*, which is then set to the *RowSource* of the second combo box. Because the second combo box has a *RowSourceType* of Field List, it automatically displays the list of field names from the SQL, as demonstrated here:

```
Private Sub cboForm_AfterUpdate()
    Dim strSQL As String
    Dim frm As Form
    ' find the recordsource for the target form
    ' we need to open the form in design view to get
    ' this information
    If cboForm <> "" Then
        DoCmd.Echo False
        DoCmd.OpenForm cboForm, acDesign
        Set frm = Forms(cboForm)
        strSQL = frm.RecordSource
        DoCmd.Close acForm, cboForm
        DoCmd.Echo True
        Me.cboField.RowSource = strSQL
        Me.cboField = Null
        Me.cboField.Requery
    End If
End Sub
```

Code is then added to the forms *Open* event to populate the first combo box, as shown in the following:

```
Private Sub Form_Open(Cancel As Integer)
    BuildListOfForms
End Sub
```

If you want to ensure that a user cannot select from the second combo box until a selection is made in the first box, set the *Enabled* property of the second combo box to *False* during the form's *Open* event, and then set it to *True* before shifting focus in the *AfterUpdate* event for the first control.

Combo Box Columns

Combo boxes are often used to hold more columns than they display (setting any column width to 0 hides the column). This means that additional data values can be easily looked up by using the *Columns* property of the combo box (see the form *frmComboBoxColumns*), as shown in Figure 7-7.

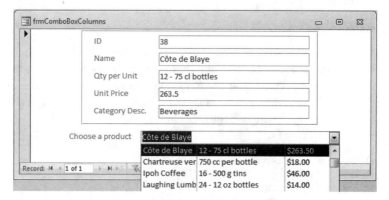

Figure 7-7 If you load additional columns into a combo box, other associated data values can be easily referenced in code.

Additional data values can be read by indexing the *Column()* property that applies to the currently selected row, as illustrated in the following:

```
Private Sub cboProduct_AfterUpdate()
    If Not IsNull(Me.cboProduct) Then
        Me.txtID = Me.cboProduct.Column(0)
        Me.txtProductName = Me.cboProduct.Column(1)
        Me.txtQuantityPerUnit = Me.cboProduct.Column(2)
        Me.txtUnitPrice = Me.cboProduct.Column(3)
        Me.txtCategoryDescription = Me.cboProduct.Column(4)
    End If
End Sub
```

INSIDE OUT
Solving problems when working with a multi-value field connected to a combo box

Combo boxes do not have a *MultiSelect* property; however, if you bind one to a multi-value field, you can make multiple selections (see the sample form *frmComboMulti Valued*). There are restrictions on coding here.

It is only possible to read a value for the *ItemSelected.Count* property with event code written behind an event on the combo box; code on any other control will always display 0. It is possible to iterate over the *ItemSelected* collection for the combo box (note that *For ... Each* is not supported), and the value in *Column(0,row)* represents the check box value that is automatically displayed when bound to a multi-value data field. The following code can be used to display the column values for all the selected choices:

```
For lngCount = 0 To Me.cboCategoryID.ItemsSelected.Count - 1
    varItem = Me.cboCategoryID.ItemsSelected(lngCount)
    Debug.Print Me.cboCategoryID.Column(0, varItem), _
        Me.cboCategoryID.Column(1, varItem), _
        Me.cboCategoryID.Column(2, varItem)
Next
```

To examine the selections from any events when the combo box does not have focus, you should use *Recordset* code, as shown in the following:

```
Private Sub cmdRecordSet_Click()
    ' uses a recordset to get the multiple values
    Dim rst As Recordset2
    Dim rstChild As Recordset2
    Set rst = Me.RecordsetClone
    ' locate the record
    rst.FindFirst "[ProductId] = " & Me.ProductID
    Set rstChild = rst!CategoryID.Value
    Do While Not rstChild.EOF
        Debug.Print rstChild(0)
        rstChild.MoveNext
    Loop
    rstChild.Close
    Set rstChild = Nothing
    rst.Close
    Set rst = Nothing
End Sub
```

The *rstChild.RecordCount* provides the number of selected values.

Value List Editing

In the Property Sheet dialog box, on the Data tab, if your combo box is using the *Value List* setting for the Row Source Type, then by setting Limit To List to *No* and ensuring that the column width of the first column is not 0, users can type in values that are not in the list of choices. If you want to restrict users to entering only the values that are in the list, set Limit To List to *Yes* and set Allow Value List Edits to *No*, as shown in Figure 7-8.

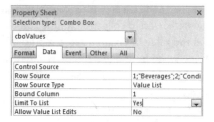

Figure 7-8 Use Limit To List to restrict values to only the available choices.

Another option is to set Limit To List to *Yes*, but allow the user to add to the list by setting Allow Value List Edits to *Yes*. This is equivalent to going into Design mode and editing the *RowSource* for the value List. You will find that this mechanism works best when you do not have any hidden columns and when the combo box displays a single column (see the *frmComboBoxValueListEditing* form for the sample code). Figure 7-9 shows the built-in pop-up box for adding new items to the list.

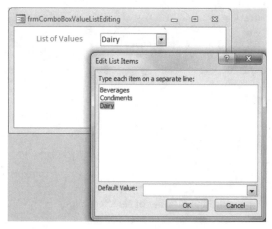

Figure 7-9 After entering values, the combo box is automatically updated with the new choices, but you will need to then select any new values added when editing the list.

Be aware that when a user makes changes this way, he is changing the actual design of the form, so when closing the form, he is prompted to save the design changes, as shown in Figure 7-10.

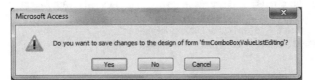

Figure 7-10 Altering the list values changes the design of the form, so the user is asked if he wants to save the changes when closing the form.

Table/Query Editing

If you have a Row Source Type that is of type Table/Query, several techniques are available to enable users to add to the list of choices.

The first method is to specify a List Items Edit Form. With this method, if a user tries to type in a value that is not in the list, a prompt appears asking if she wants to add the value, and then the corresponding form is displayed. After adding a new record and closing the pop-up form, the combo box is automatically refreshed to show any changes to the available items, as shown in Figure 7-11.

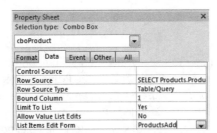

Figure 7-11 Specifying *ProductsAdd* as the form to display when adding values that are not in the list.

After the new value has been added, the user then needs to select the new value.

When viewing a drop-down list in Form view, users can also right-click the control and select Edit List Items, or as shown in Figure 7-12, click the edit icon displayed when the list is displayed (see the *frmComboBoxQueryEditing* form).

Figure 7-12 The user can click the edit icon in the lower-left corner to display the *ProductsAdd* form.

The second technique is to program a solution by using the *NotInList* event (see the *frmComboBoxQueryEditingNotInList* form). The following code illustrates how you can programmatically add a value to the list that was not previously one of available choices:

```
Private Sub cboProduct_NotInList(NewData As String, Response As Integer)
    ' acDataErrDisplay - use built in message box
    ' acDataErrContinue - display a custom message
    ' acDataErrAdded - add new item to the list
    Dim db As Database
    Dim rst As Recordset
    Set db = CurrentDb
    Set rst = db.OpenRecordset("Products", dbOpenDynaset)
    rst.AddNew
    rst!ProductName = NewData
    rst.Update
    Response = acDataErrAdded
End Sub
```

List Boxes

In this section, you look at working with list boxes. You will see how list boxes can be used to allow users to easily make multiple selections and an alternative approach using two synchronized list boxes, in which the second list box contains the selections made in the first list box. The last part of this section explores using list boxes to mimic the role played by subforms.

Multiple Selections

You can configure a list box to allow a user to select either a single item or multiple items (see Figure 7-13). To restrict selection to one list item only, in the Property Sheet dialog box, on the Other tab, set Multi Select to *Simple*; the user can click an individual item to select or deselect that item. If you set Multi Select to Extended, the user can press the Shift key to select multiple, adjacent list items, or press the Ctrl key to select multiple, non-adjacent items.

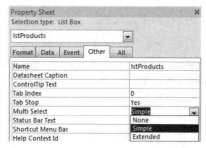

Figure 7-13 Multi Select can be set to *Simple* or *Extended*. When set to *Extended*, the user can press the Shift or Ctrl keys to select multiple list items.

You can add buttons to your form that will assist users when working with multiple selections, as shown in Figure 7-14.

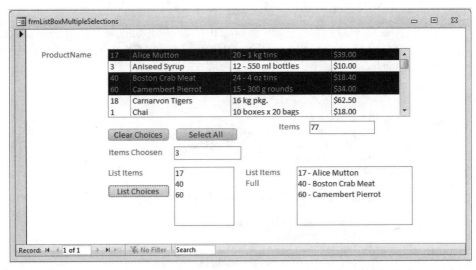

Figure 7-14 You can add buttons to quickly clear choices or select all available choices.

INSIDE OUT   Key properties when working with multiple selections in a list box

Multiple-selection list boxes are more complex to work with than single-selection list boxes for a number of reasons. The following list presents a summary of the key properties of multiple-selection list boxes:

- **ListCount**   Counts the total number of items in the list.

- **Selected()**   *Boolean* collection, one for each row, read/write, indicating whether an item in the list is selected, use either a *For ... Each* with a variant or a long integer to index the array.

- **ItemsSelected.Count**   Number of selected choices.

- **ItemsSelected**   Variant collection of the selected items. Use a variant variable to read values from this collection.

- **ItemData(row)**   Returns the data in the bound column for each list item

- **Column(index,row)**   The values for the column for any item in the list box.

With a multiple-selection list box, the actual control value does not have a simple meaning and cannot be directly manipulated.

Setting the control source on an unbound text box can display the total number of items available for selection, as shown in the following:

```
=[lstProducts].[ListCount]
```

The *Selected* collection can be used to clear or set items as having been selected; there is one entry in this collection for each item in the list. The following code clears all choices in the list:

```
Private Sub cmdClearChoices_Click()
    ' clear any choices
    Dim lngItem As Long
    For lngItem = 0 To Me.lstProducts.ListCount
        Me.lstProducts.Selected(lngItem) = False
    Next
End Sub
```

To select all available choices, use this code:

```
Private Sub cmdSelectAll_Click()
    ' select all choices
    Dim lngItem As Long
    For lngItem = 0 To Me.lstProducts.ListCount
        Me.lstProducts.Selected(lngItem) = True
    Next
End Sub
```

To establish which items have been selected, you have two options: you can scan through the *Selected* collection and extract the identifier for each item, or you can scan through the *ItemsSelected* collection using a variant variable, which can then be used as an index into the control's *Columns* to extract other column values for the selected items. The following code shows both methods being used to build a string that contains the choices that are displayed in a text box; *vbCrLf* is used to split the results over multiple lines:

```
Private Sub cmdListChoices_Click()
    Dim strSelections As String
    ' list choices made
    Dim lngItem As Long
    strSelections = ""
    For lngItem = 0 To Me.lstProducts.ListCount
        If Me.lstProducts.Selected(lngItem) Then
            If strSelections <> "" Then
                strSelections = strSelections & vbCrLf
            End If
            strSelections = strSelections & Me.lstProducts.ItemData(lngItem)
        End If
    Next
    Me.txtListOfChoices = strSelections
    ' more efficent would be to use the ItemSelected collection
    strSelections = ""
```

```
        Dim varItem As Variant
        For Each varItem In Me.lstProducts.ItemsSelected
            If strSelections <> "" Then
                strSelections = strSelections & vbCrLf
            End If
            ' include data in first 2 columns
            strSelections = strSelections & Me.lstProducts.Column(0, varItem) & _
                        " - " & Me.lstProducts.Column(1, varItem)
        Next
        Me.txtListOfChoicesFull = strSelections
    End Sub
```

INSIDE OUT   Making the selected choices in a list box that is bound to a multi-value control appear at the top of the list.

When paging through records containing a list box that is bound to a multi-value field, it is possible to write VBA code that ensures that all the selected items are displayed at the top of the list (see the sample form *frmListBoxMultiValuedNoChanges*).

The technique is to construct a union query that adds together first the selected choices and then the non-selected choices, and then sort the data appropriately.

The following code displays the selected choices and then all other available choices:

```
Sub Build_ListRowSource()
    Dim strSQL As String
    Dim strChoosenSet As String
    Dim varItem As Variant
    strChoosenSet = ""
    ' Build a list of everything Choosen
    For Each varItem In Me.lstCategoryID.ItemsSelected
        If strChoosenSet <> "" Then
            strChoosenSet = strChoosenSet & ","
        End If
        strChoosenSet = strChoosenSet & Me.lstCategoryID.ItemData(varItem)
    Next
    If strChoosenSet <> "" Then
        strChoosenSet = "IN (" & strChoosenSet & ")"
        ' order Choosen items at the begining
        strSQL = "SELECT Categories.CategoryID, Categories.CategoryName, " & _
                " Categories.Description, 0 As [Selected] FROM Categories" & _
                  " WHERE CategoryID " & strChoosenSet & _
                  "  UNION " & _
            "SELECT Categories.CategoryID, Categories.CategoryName, " & _
                " Categories.Description, 1 as [Selected] FROM Categories" & _
                  " WHERE CategoryID NOT " & strChoosenSet & _
                  " ORDER BY  [Selected], CategoryName "
```

```
        Else
            strSQL = "SELECT Categories.CategoryID, Categories.CategoryName, " & _
                    " Categories.Description, 1 as [Selected] FROM Categories " & _
                        " ORDER BY  [Selected], CategoryName "
        End If
        ' Note we require to add our selected Field to the
        ' Categories table, even when we are not using it
        ' Otherwise the Order By things that [Selected]
        ' is a parameter, when the form is first opened
        Me.lstCategoryID.RowSource = strSQL
        Me.lstCategoryID.Requery
End Sub
```

In the preceding example, we created a field called [Selected] for controlling the ordering of the data. To prevent the *ListBox* control with the multi-valued field from prompting for a parameter when first opening the form, we have had to add this as a physical field in the table from which we are selecting.

Multiple Selections with Two List Boxes

As an alternative method for making multiple selections, you can use a list box that is set for simple selection, and then display the values in a second list box, as shown in Figure 7-15.

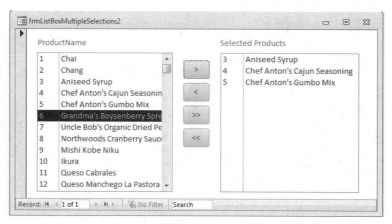

Figure 7-15 By using two list boxes, items that the user has already selected remain visible in the second box as he continues to scroll and select items in the first list box.

For the list box on the left, the *RowSourceType* is set to a *Table/Query*; for the list box on the right, *RowSourceType* is set to *Value List*. To show that data is selected in the second list box involves manipulating the *RowSource* for the control as different choices are being made.

To clear all selected choices, set the *RowSource* to an empty string, as shown here:

```
Private Sub cmdUnpickAll_Click()
    ' clear all choices
    Me.lstProductsSelected.RowSource = ""
End Sub
```

To pick all the available choices, scan through all the available items, and then add them to the *RowSource*, as demonstrated in the following:

```
Private Sub cmdPickAll_Click()
    Dim strItem As String
    Dim lngItem As Long
    Me.lstProductsSelected.RowSource = ""
    For lngItem = 0 To Me.lstProducts.ListCount - 1
        strItem = Me.lstProducts.Column(0, lngItem) & ";""" & _
                    Me.lstProducts.Column(1, lngItem) & """;"
        Me.lstProductsSelected.RowSource = Me.lstProductsSelected.RowSource & _
                                            strItem
    Next
End Sub
```

To select an individual item, add the new item to the *RowSource*. The second part of this code unit advances the highlighted row in the available products to the next available entry, as illustrated in the following:

```
Private Sub cmdPick_Click()
    ' add current item to selected list
    If IsNull(Me.lstProducts) Then MsgBox "No product selected": Exit Sub
    Dim strItem As String
    strItem = Me.lstProducts.Column(0) & ";""" & _
            Me.lstProducts.Column(1) & """;"
    ' only add if not already in the list
    If InStr(1, Me.lstProductsSelected.RowSource, strItem) = 0 Then
        Me.lstProductsSelected.RowSource = Me.lstProductsSelected.RowSource & _
                                            strItem
    End If
    ' move selection down the list
    ' optional step
    ' find next item
    Dim lngItem As Long
    For lngItem = 0 To Me.lstProducts.ListCount - 1
        If CStr(Me.lstProducts) = Me.lstProducts.ItemData(lngItem) Then
            If lngItem = Me.lstProducts.ListCount - 1 Then
                ' back to top of list
                Me.lstProducts = Me.lstProducts.ItemData(0)
                Exit For
            Else
                Me.lstProducts = CLng(Me.lstProducts.ItemData(lngItem + 1))
                Exit For
            End If
        End If
    Next
End Sub
```

To remove a selection, remove the string from the *RowSource* by using the *Replace* string function:

```
Private Sub cmdUnPick_Click()
    ' locate and remove the current choice
    Dim strItem As String
    strItem = Me.lstProductsSelected.Column(0) & ";""" & _
            Me.lstProductsSelected.Column(1) & """;"
    Me.lstProductsSelected.RowSource = _
                Replace(Me.lstProductsSelected.RowSource, strItem, "")
End Sub
```

Using the List Box as a *Subform*

Some developers chose to use list boxes rather than subforms. The main reason for this is to keep the form lightweight. In addition to using a list box, you might decide to only bind the list boxes to display data at certain points when the user is interacting with the form.

One convenient feature of a list box is that when you call a *Requery* on it, the currently selected item remains highlighted. If you want to provide the ability to add or edit records, then you need a pop-up form to display the record's details. For example, you might decide to limit the details that are presented in the list box but use the pop-up to display or edit the record's details in their entirety.

The *frmListBoxAsASubform* form shown in Figure 7-16 contains a list box with some additional code to open a detailed form when required.

Product Name	Unit Price	Units In Stock	Units On Order
Chai	$18.00	39	0
Chang	$19.00	17	40
Aniseed Syrup	$10.00	13	70
Chef Anton's Cajun Seasoning	$22.00	53	0
Chef Anton's Gumbo Mix	$21.35	0	0
Grandma's Boysenberry Spread	$25.00	120	0
Uncle Bob's Organic Dried Pears	$30.00	15	0

| Edit | Add | Delete |

Figure 7-16 A list box configured to function like a subform.

The following code is added behind the delete button:

```
Private Sub cmdDelete_Click()
    ' delete the item and refresh the list
    CurrentDb.Execute "DELETE * FROM Products WHERE " & _
                    "[ProductID] = " & Me.lstProducts
    Me.lstProducts.Requery
End Sub
```

To enable a record for editing, you can write the following code on the *DblClick* event for the list box, behind the Edit button:

```
Const strTargetForm = "frmListBoxAsASubformDetails"
Const strSourceControl = "lstProducts"

Private Sub cmdEdit_Click()
    ' open a detail form for editing
    Dim frm As Form
    Dim strWhere As String
    If IsNull(Me.lstProducts.Column(0)) Then
        Exit Sub
    End If
    strWhere = "[ProductID] = " & Me.lstProducts.Column(0)
    DoCmd.OpenForm strTargetForm, , , strWhere
    Set frm = Forms(strTargetForm)
    frm("txtCallingForm") = Me.Name
    frm("txtCallingControl") = strSourceControl
    Set frm = Nothing
End Sub
```

The code for editing a record needs to open the target editing form and pass values for the calling form and calling control. By using constants for some of the names, you begin to make the code more general purpose and reduce the amount of code that you need to write. There are several ways to pass values to a target form, and this technique of writing values into controls has the added benefit of helping to debug an application (once debugged, you can set the visibility of the controls to *False*). Figure 7-17 shows a pop-up detail form.

Figure 7-17 The controls in the header are unbound and hidden from the user.

Code is then required on the form's *Close* or *Unload* events to refresh the calling form's control:

```
Private Sub Form_Unload(Cancel As Integer)
    ' requery the calling forms control
    Forms(Me.txtCallingForm).Controls(Me.txtCallingControl).Requery
    If Not IsNull(Me.txtAdding) Then
        ' force list box to display new selection
        Forms(Me.txtCallingForm).Controls(Me.txtCallingControl) = Me.ProductID
    End If
End Sub
```

On the calling form, behind the Add button, add the following code:

```
Private Sub cmdAdd_Click()
    ' open form for adding a new product
    Dim frm As Form
    DoCmd.OpenForm strTargetForm, , , , acFormAdd
    Set frm = Forms(strTargetForm)
    frm("txtCallingForm") = Me.Name
    frm("txtCallingControl") = strSourceControl
    frm("txtAdding") = "Adding"
    Set frm = Nothing
End Sub
```

As a bonus to the user, the code in the *Form_Unload* event also passes a value to instruct the target form to highlight the last new record (just one of many enhancements that can be added).

INSIDE OUT   Using a list box as a subform to allow multiple records to be selected for editing

You can extend the idea of using a list box as a subform by setting the Multi Select property to *Simple* to highlight multiple records. Then by adding some VBA code, you can pop up a form that filters to display the multiple records for editing as a group.

The sample form *frmListBoxAsASubform2* shows this interesting extension where Multi Select is set to *Simple*. We have also placed the editing routine in a subroutine called *Edit-Selections* to prevent repeating the code behind the button and on the *DblClick* event:

```
Sub EditSelections()
    ' open a detail form for editing
    ' this version supports multiple selections
    ' of records for editing
    Dim frm As Form
    Dim strWhere As String
```

```
        If IsNull(Me.lstProducts.Column(0)) Then
            Exit Sub
        End If
        ' Build a list of records for editing
        strWhere = ""
        Dim varItem As Variant
        For Each varItem In Me.lstProducts.ItemsSelected
            If strWhere <> "" Then
                strWhere = strWhere & ","
            End If
            strWhere = strWhere & Me.lstProducts.Column(0, varItem)
        Next
        strWhere = "[ProductID] IN(" & strWhere & ")"

        DoCmd.OpenForm strTargetForm, , , strWhere
        Set frm = Forms(strTargetForm)
        frm("txtCallingForm") = Me.Name
        frm("txtCallingControl") = strSourceControl
        Set frm = Nothing
End Sub

Private Sub cmdEdit_Click()
    EditSelections
End Sub

Private Sub lstProducts_DblClick(Cancel As Integer)
    EditSelections
End Sub
```

In this second example, we have also set the *RowSource* of the list box to an empty string, and hidden the associated buttons. We have then provided a button on the form that calls the following routine to make the list box available for use:

```
Sub BindListBox()
    Dim strSQL As String
    strSQL = "SELECT [ProductID], [ProductName], [UnitPrice], " & _
             "[UnitsInStock],[UnitsOnOrder] FROM Products "
    Me.lstProducts.RowSource = strSQL
    Me.lstProducts.Visible = True
    Me.cmdAdd.Visible = True
    Me.cmdDelete.Visible = True
    Me.cmdEdit.Visible = True
End Sub
```

The *TreeView* Control

The sample database TreeBuilder.accdb, contains the form *frmNodeBuilderWithImages*, which present an example of using the *TreeView* control (see Figure 7-18) and demonstrates a number of its features.

> **Note**
>
> The *TreeView* control and other 32-bit ActiveX controls are not supported in Microsoft Office 64 bit.

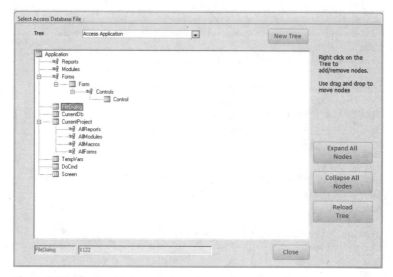

Figure 7-18 The *TreeView* control can be used as an application menu or for manipulating hierarchical data (as shown here).

Adding the *TreeView* Control

Begin with a blank form. On the Design tab, click ActiveX Controls, as shown in Figure 7-19.

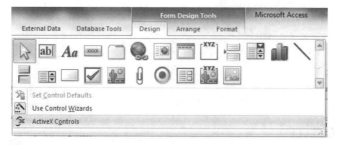

Figure 7-19 The option on the Design tab to add ActiveX controls to a form.

The Insert ActiveX Control dialog box opens (see Figure 7-20), in which you can locate and select the Microsoft TreeView Control (note that your computer might have more than one version of this control).

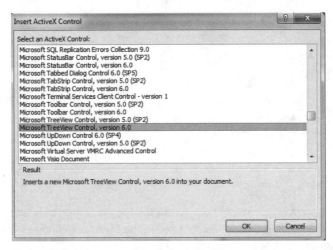

Figure 7-20 Select a version of the ActiveX control to be installed on any computers that will use the application.

Once you have added the control to the form, you can resize it to the required size. Figure 7-21 shows the control added to a form at its default size.

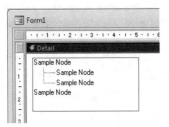

Figure 7-21 The *TreeView* control when it is first added to a form.

After adding the control, in the form's class module, add in the appropriate reference that will be needed as you start programming the control, as shown in Figure 7-22.

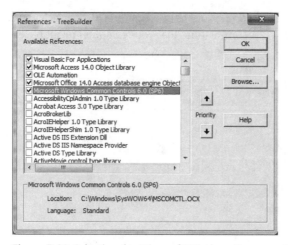

Figure 7-22 Selecting the Microsoft Windows Common Controls in the list of references.

When adding references, you might need to use the Browse button to locate a particular file, but the *TreeView* control, which is contained in the Microsoft Windows Common Controls, should be in the list of available references.

Populating the Tree

The companion content contains a table called *tblTreeNode* that holds the data to be displayed in multiple trees of data. Figure 7-23 shows the *tblTreeNode*, which in this example has been filtered for tree number 2. The nodes have a relative order reading from top to bottom, and each node holds the identifier of its parent node (ParentKey field).

	TreeNodeId	TreeId	NodeText	ParentKey	RelativeOrder
⊞	42	2	Connection		15
⊞	80	2	Command		16
⊞	81	2	Recordset		17
⊞	82	2	Record		18
⊞	83	2	Stream		19
⊞	84	2	Error	85	20
⊞	85	2	Errors	42	21
⊞	88	2	Parameters	80	24
⊞	89	2	Parameter	88	25
⊞	90	2	Fields	81	26
⊞	91	2	Field	90	27

Figure 7-23 Create your own table of data, which will be loaded into the *TreeView* control.

In the form, you add some basic code to construct the nodes in the tree. It is simpler at this point to add all the nodes without specifying the exact parent/child structure, which can be subsequently added. The nodes need to have a text key, so a simple text prefix of "X" is added to the node keys. You begin by defining variables and constants at the top of the module, as shown in the following:

```
Dim tv As TreeView
Dim lngOrder As Long
Dim lngTreeId As Long
Dim db As DAO.Database
Dim rst As DAO.Recordset
Const NodePrefix = "X"
```

Code is the added to the *Open* and *Close* events to initialize and terminate your variables:

```
Private Sub Form_Open(Cancel As Integer)
    lngOrder = 0
    Set tv = Me.TreeView0.Object
    lngTreeId = 2
    Set db = CurrentDb
    LoadTheTree
End Sub

Private Sub Form_Close()
    db.Close
    Set db = Nothing
    Set tv = Nothing
End Sub
```

The *LoadTheTree* routine generates the nodes from the *RecordSet*, as illustrated here:

```
Sub LoadTheTree()
    ' loads a specified Tree
    Dim strParentkey As String
    Dim strNodeKey As String
    Set rst = db.OpenRecordset("SELECT * FROM tblTreeNode  " & _
        "WHERE [TreeId] = " & lngTreeId & _
        " ORDER BY RelativeOrder", dbOpenDynaset)
    tv.Nodes.Clear
    If rst.EOF Then
        Exit Sub
    End If
    Do While Not rst.EOF
        strNodeKey = NodePrefix & rst!TreeNodeId
        tv.Nodes.Add , , strNodeKey, rst!NodeText
        rst.MoveNext
    Loop
End Sub
```

Figure 7-24 shows the tree view after a list of nodes has been added to the control, but the parent/child relationships have not been established.

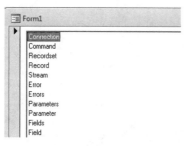

Figure 7-24 Initially you load the tree with all nodes.

INSIDE OUT Quickly loading parent/child-related data into a *TreeView* control

Although it is possible to build a tree of data by positioning each child record correctly as it is added to the tree, this can be difficult, because there is no easy mechanism in Access to produce the data from a single table in a hierarchical form, and you cannot specify a relationship to a node that is not already loaded in the tree. It is simpler to first add all the nodes and then edit each one, specifying the relationship to the parent node; once all the nodes are created, the order in which relationships are constructed is not important.

Use the *Add* method to populate the tree, which creates each node, as demonstrated in Figure 7-25.

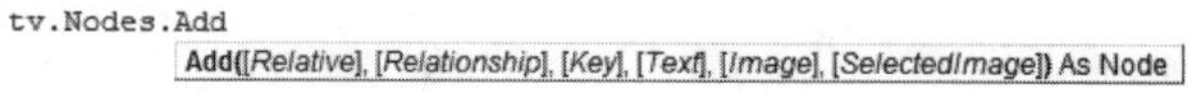

```
tv.Nodes.Add
         Add([Relative], [Relationship], [Key], [Text], [Image], [SelectedImage]) As Node
```

Figure 7-25 Creating nodes by using the *Add* method.

The next step is to modify the *LoadTree* routine by adding the following code, which maps the parent child relationships for the nodes. Keep in mind that you need to ensure that you have already created a node before referencing it as a parent node:

```
rst.MoveFirst
Do While Not rst.EOF
    If Nz(rst!Parentkey) <> 0 Then
        strNodeKey = NodePrefix & rst!TreeNodeId
        strParentkey = NodePrefix & rst!Parentkey
        Set tv.Nodes(strNodeKey).Parent = tv.Nodes(strParentkey)
    End If
    rst.MoveNext
Loop
```

This will then render the tree with the correct structure. Once you have this code working, it is useful to add a *DoCmd.Echo False* at the beginning of the *LoadTree* routine and a *DoCmd. Echo True* at the end of the routine. This prevents screen flicker as the tree is rendered and re-organized, as shown in Figure 7-26.

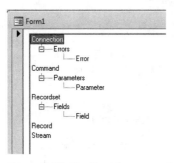

Figure 7-26 The *TreeView* control showing the hierarchical organization of the data.

Adding Graphics

To display images in the *TreeView* control, add an *ImageList* ActiveX control to the form, as shown in Figure 7-27.

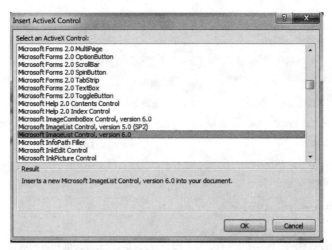

Figure 7-27 Adding the *ImageList* ActiveX control to hold the images that will be used by the tree.

Next, you need to prepare a set of graphical images for each type of node. Each type has two images: one for when the node is selected, and the other for when it is not selected.

In the form's *Open* event, load the images from file into the *ImageList* control, as shown here:

```
Dim imgListObj As ImageList
```

The *Open* event is then changed to the following:

```
Private Sub Form_Open(Cancel As Integer)
    lngOrder = 0
    Set tv = Me.TreeView0.Object
    lngTreeId = 2
    Set db = CurrentDb
    Set imgListObj = Me.ImageList1.Object
    imgListObj.ListImages.Add 1, "Object", _
        LoadPicture(CurrentProject.Path & "\Object.bmp")
    imgListObj.ListImages.Add 2, "ObjectSelected", _
        LoadPicture(CurrentProject.Path & "\ObjectSelected.bmp")
    imgListObj.ListImages.Add 3, "Collection", _
        LoadPicture(CurrentProject.Path & "\Collection.bmp")
    imgListObj.ListImages.Add 4, "CollectionSelected", _
        LoadPicture(CurrentProject.Path & "\CollectionSelected.bmp")    LoadTheTree
End Sub
```

In the *tblTreeNodes* table, three more columns have been added to hold the references to the images to display as well as a flag to indicate whether the node is expanded by default, as shown in Figure 7-28.

tblTreeNode

NodeText	ImageNumber	SelectedImageNumber	Expanded
⊞ Connection	1	2	☑
⊞ DBEngine	1	2	☑
⊞ Workspace	1	2	☑
⊞ Errors	3	4	☐

Figure 7-28 You can create your own fields in your table to record which images to display on any node and whether the nodes are initially displayed as expanded.

You need to make the following change to the loop that loads the nodes in the *LoadTree* processing routine:

```
tv.ImageList = imgListObj
Do While Not rst.EOF
    strNodeKey = NodePrefix & rst!TreeNodeId
    If Nz(rst!ImageNumber) <> 0 And Nz(rst!SelectedImageNumber) <> 0 Then
        ' two images
        tv.Nodes.Add , , strNodeKey, rst!NodeText, _
            CLng(rst!ImageNumber), CLng(rst!SelectedImageNumber)
    Else
        If Nz(rst!ImageNumber) <> 0 Then
            ' one images
            tv.Nodes.Add , , strNodeKey, rst!NodeText, _
                CLng(rst!ImageNumber)
```

```
            Else
                If Nz(rst!SelectedImageNumber) <> 0 Then
                    ' one image
                    tv.Nodes.Add , , strNodeKey, rst!NodeText, , _
                        CLng(rst!SelectedImageNumber)
                Else
                    ' no images
                    tv.Nodes.Add , , strNodeKey, rst!NodeText
                End If
            End If
        End If
        rst.MoveNext
    Loop
```

You should also now change the forms *Close* event, as follows:

```
Private Sub Form_Close()
    On Error Resume Next
    rst.Close
    Set rst = Nothing
    db.Close
    Set db = Nothing
    Do While imgListObj.ListImages.Count > 0
        imgListObj.ListImages.Remove (1)
    Loop
    Set tv.ImageList = Nothing
    Set imgListObj = Nothing
    Set tv = Nothing
End Sub
```

Expanding and Collapsing Nodes

To expand or collapse a node, you set the nodes *Expanded* property. The following code can be used to expand or collapse the entire tree:

```
Sub ExpandAllNodes(State As Boolean)
    Dim nd As Node
    For Each nd In tv.Nodes
        nd.Expanded = State
    Next
End Sub
```

Drag-and-Drop

The *TreeView* control supports drag-and-drop, which you can use to create a *TreeView* and easily re-arrange items on the tree.

To enable drag-and-drop, right-click the *TreeView* control to display the shortcut menu, click the *TreeCtrl* Object, and then click Properties, as shown in Figure 7-29.

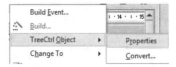

Figure 7-29 The *TreeView* properties need to be changed to support drag-and-drop.

In the TreeCtrl Properties dialog box, verify that OLEDragMode is set to *1 – ccOLEDrag-Automatic*, and OLEDropMode is set to *1 – ccOLEDropManual*, as shown in Figure 7-30.

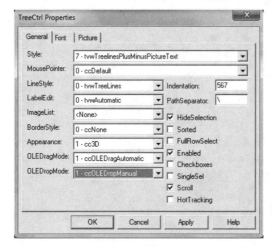

Figure 7-30 The settings in the TreeCtrl Properties window to add drag-and-drop capability to the *TreeView* control.

You then need to add three sections of event processing code. In the example, the *TreeView* control is called *TreeView0*; you might need to change this, check by compiling your code and verifying that all references are appropriately changed.

INSIDE OUT   Referring to methods and properties in an ActiveX Control

What might be a little confusing in the development of this form is that there is an ActiveX object called *TreeView0* on the form. There is also a *TreeView* object variable called *tv* that during the forms *Open* event is set to point at the object *TreeView0*.

The reason for having the *tv* object variable is that it allows you to execute a method like *tv.Add* because you cannot use *Me.TreeView0.Add*, which will not work because the *TreeView0* is a external object. As an added benefit, the *tv* object variable supports IntelliSense for the *TreeView* control.

What might appear equally confusing is when we come to define an event handling procedure (in the sections that follow) called *TreeView0_OLEStartDrag*. The question is why we did not use *tv_OLEStartDrag*?

The answer is that Access can automatically hook up the event handling for the ActiveX object; which is why *TreeView0_OLEStartDrag* works. There is a way to use the reference to *tv_OLEStartDrag*, but to do that, you would have to use a special syntax called *With-Events* (described in Chapter 10, "Using Classes and Events") when you declared the object variable, *Dim WithEvents tv As TreeView*.

The *OLEStartDrag* event clears the selected node, allowing a new node to be selected, as demonstrated in the following:

```
Private Sub TreeView0_OLEStartDrag(Data As Object, _
                             AllowedEffects As Long)
    tv.SelectedItem = Nothing
End Sub
```

The *OLEDragOver* highlights the node as you drag over an area:

```
Private Sub TreeView0_OLEDragOver(Data As Object, _
              Effect As Long, _
              Button As Integer, _
              Shift As Integer, _
              x As Single, _
              y As Single, _
              State As Integer)

    If tv.SelectedItem Is Nothing Then
        Set tv.SelectedItem = tv.HitTest(x, y)
    End If

    'Highlight the node being dragged over as a potential drop target.
    Set tv.DropHighlight = tv.HitTest(x, y)
End Sub
```

The *OLEDragDrop* routine is more complex because it needs to reposition the node in the new tree structure. Note that a *Root* node is indicated by having a null value for the *Parent-Key*, as illustrated here:

```
Private Sub TreeView0_OLEDragDrop(Data As Object, _
                            Effect As Long, _
                            Button As Integer, _
                            Shift As Integer, _
                            x As Single, _
                            y As Single)
```

```
Dim nodDragged As Node
Dim strKey As String
Dim strParentkey As String
Dim lngKey As Long
Dim lngParentKey As Long
Dim strText As String
If tv.SelectedItem Is Nothing Then
Else
    ' Reference the selected node as the one being dragged.
    Set nodDragged = tv.SelectedItem
    ' If the node was dragged to an empty space
    ' table and make a root node, set ParentKey to Null.
    If tv.DropHighlight Is Nothing Then
       strKey = nodDragged.Key
        lngKey = ExtractKey(strKey)
'       strParentkey = nodDragged.Parent
       ' Delete the current node
'       tv.Nodes.Remove nodDragged.Index
       rst.FindFirst "TreeNodeId = " & lngKey
       If Not rst.NoMatch Then
           rst.Edit
           rst!Parentkey = Null
           rst.Update
       End If
       ' regenerate the tree
       LoadTheTree

    ' If you are not dropping the node on itself.
    ElseIf nodDragged.Index <> tv.DropHighlight.Index Then
       ' Set the drop target as the selected node's parent.
       Set nodDragged.Parent = tv.DropHighlight
        ' update the table of data
       strKey = nodDragged.Key
       strParentkey = tv.DropHighlight.Key
       lngKey = ExtractKey(strKey)
       lngParentKey = ExtractKey(strParentkey)
       rst.FindFirst "TreeNodeId = " & lngKey
       If Not rst.NoMatch Then
           rst.Edit
           rst!Parentkey = lngParentKey
           rst.Update
       End If
    End If
End If
```

```
    ' Deselect the node
    Set nodDragged = Nothing
    ' Unhighlight the nodes.
    Set tv.DropHighlight = Nothing

End Sub
Function ExtractKey(Key As String) As Long
    Dim strKey As String
    strKey = Right(Key, Len(Key) - Len(NodePrefix))
    ExtractKey = CLng(strKey)
End Function
```

Deleting a Node with Recursion

When you delete a node, all the child nodes below that node should also be deleted, as follows:

```
Public Sub DeleteNode(Key As String)
    ' delete a node in the tree
    Dim lngDataKey As Long
    ' get numerical part of the key
    lngDataKey = ExtractKey(Key)
    ' delete any child nodes this is a bit more complex
    ' because each child node can also have child nodes
    rst.FindFirst "Parentkey = " & lngDataKey
    Do While Not rst.NoMatch
        ' has child nodes
        ' NOTE THIS CODE IS RECURSIVE
        DeleteNode NodePrefix & rst!TreeNodeId
        rst.FindNext "Parentkey = " & lngDataKey
    Loop
    rst.FindFirst "TreeNodeId = " & lngDataKey
    If Not rst.NoMatch Then
        rst.Delete
    End If
    On Error Resume Next
    tv.Nodes.Remove Key
End Sub
```

This code routine is an example of recursive code, which means that the procedure keeps calling itself from within itself, nesting to the required number of levels, and then as execution at any particular level ends, it backs itself out to resume execution at the previous level.

INSIDE OUT Writing and debugging recursive VBA Code

In the previous example, you see that when you delete a node, you must delete all of the child nodes, and then for each child node, you must delete all child nodes for that child node. You need to repeat this process until all the related nodes in the tree are deleted. The example contains the following objects keys and parent keys:

- Forms: X123 → Parent 116, DeleteNode(X123) – Delete all with Parent 123

- Form: X130 → Parent 123, DeleteNode(X130) – Delete all with Parent 130

- Controls: X131 → Parent 130, DeleteNode(X131) – Delete all with Parent 131

- Control: X132 → Parent 131, DeleteNode(X132) – Delete all with Parent 132

Later in this section, you will see that the Call Stack assists in monitoring the code, which you can use to see the depth of recursive nesting. The main problem with recursive code is in understanding how the logic branches. At first glance, it looks like the logic cannot work because it uses a single *Recordset*. But the key to this code is that after deleting child nodes in the loop, it uses a *FindFirst* to reposition on the parent record.

Recursive code can be quite difficult to debug, but it often provides a very simple solution to an otherwise complex problem. Figure 7-31 shows a sequence of nodes to be deleted.

Figure 7-31 A sequence of nodes that must be deleted.

If you want to further explore how a node is deleted, then place a breakpoint (see Figure 7-32) in the *DeleteNode* subroutine.

```
Public Sub DeleteNode(Key As String)
    ' delete a node in the tree
    Dim lngDataKey As Long
    ' get numerical part of the key
    lngDataKey = ExtractKey(Key)
    ' delete any child nodes this is a bit more complex
    ' because each child node can also have child nodes
    rst.FindFirst "Parentkey = " & lngDataKey
    Do While Not rst.NoMatch
```

Figure 7-32 Insert a breakpoint into the code to trace through a recursive delete operation.

With the form in Form view, right-click the node called *Forms* to display the node operations form (see Figure 7-33). With this form, you can view details of a node and delete nodes. This pop-up form then calls the public code on the main form that has the *TreeView* control.

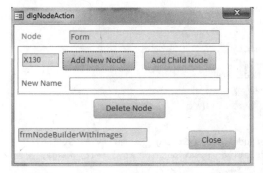

Figure 7-33 Using this pop-up form, you can add and delete nodes.

Next, click the Delete Node button. Tracing through the routine and examining the Call Stack illustrates the recursive nature of this routine, as shown in Figure 7-34.

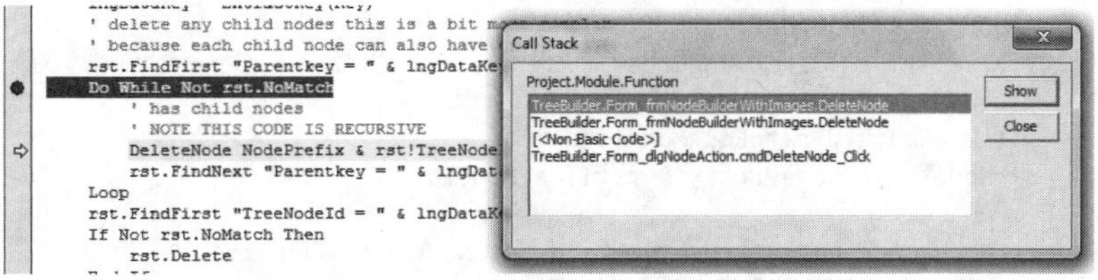

Figure 7-34 The Call Stack helps you to understand how the code works.

Adding Nodes

The code that follows presents the two routines with which you can add nodes. The first adds the node to the bottom of the tree. You then drag the node to a particular position. The second method is to add the node as a child node to the current node. In both cases, the node is added to the data table:

```
Public Sub AddNewNode(NodeName As String)
    'TreeView0.Nodes.Add(relative, relationship, key, text, image,
    ' selectedimage)
    Dim strNodeKey As String
    rst.AddNew
    rst!NodeText = NodeName
    rst!TreeId = lngTreeId
    lngOrder = lngOrder + 1
    rst!RelativeOrder = lngOrder
```

```
        rst.Update
        rst.Bookmark = rst.LastModified
        strNodeKey = NodePrefix & rst!TreeNodeId
        tv.Nodes.Add , , strNodeKey, NodeName
        ' force refresh
        Me.txtNodeKey = strNodeKey
        Me.txtNodeName = NodeName
        Dim frm As Form
        On Error Resume Next
        Set frm = Forms!dlgNodeAction
        If Err.Number = 0 Then
            frm.txtNodeName = NodeName
            frm.txtKey = strNodeKey
        End If
    End Sub

    Public Sub AddNewChildNode(NodeName As String, Parentkey As String)
        'TreeView0.Nodes.Add(relative, relationship, key, text, image,
        ' selectedimage)
        Dim strNodeKey As String
        rst.AddNew
        rst!NodeText = NodeName
        ' Val gets the number from the string skipping the text prefix
        rst!Parentkey = ExtractKey(Parentkey)
        rst!TreeId = lngTreeId
        lngOrder = lngOrder + 1
        rst!RelativeOrder = lngOrder
        rst.Update
        rst.Bookmark = rst.LastModified
        strNodeKey = NodePrefix & rst!TreeNodeId

        tv.Nodes.Add Parentkey, tvwChild, strNodeKey, NodeName
        tv.Nodes(Parentkey).Expanded = True
        ' force refresh
        Me.txtNodeKey = strNodeKey
        Me.txtNodeName = NodeName
        Dim frm As Form
        On Error Resume Next
        Set frm = Forms!dlgNodeAction
        If Err.Number = 0 Then
            frm.txtNodeName = NodeName
            frm.txtKey = strNodeKey
        End If
    End Sub
```

The *Tab* Control

In this section, you look at using a *Tab* control with subforms, and how you can synchronize controls in subforms with controls on other tab pages. You then look at how to dynamically load subforms into *Tab* control pages (this is demonstrated in the sample database controls.accdb)

Refreshing Between Tabs and Controls

In the *frmTabProducts* form, there is a *Tab* control with two tabs, and the form is bound to the *Products* table. The first tab contains some of the fields from the *Products* table, including the product category. The second tab contains a subform that lists the available categories, as shown in Figure 7-35.

To place the subform on the tab page, you drag it from the navigation window of the *frmCategories* onto the second tab page.

Switch to Form view and take a look at this form. You will find that if you click the Product List tab, the Categories tab becomes hidden; clicking the Products tab makes it visible again. This is intentional, and the code for this is described later in this section.

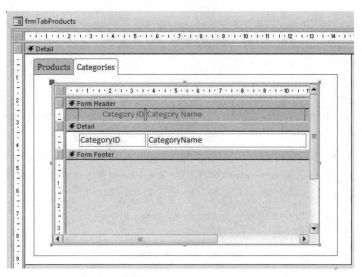

Figure 7-35 Dragging a subform onto a page of the *Tab* control.

When you positioned the subform, the Child/Master linking field properties are automatically set. These choices need to be cleared (see Figure 7-36), because you do not want the subform to display only the category for the displayed product record; you want to use the subform to manage the list of categories.

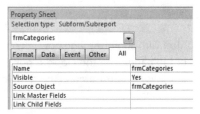

Figure 7-36 After you add a subform, always check the Link Master Fields and Link Child Fields properties to verify that they are set correctly (here, the properties have been cleared).

In this example, after you enter or change a record on the subform on the Categories tab page, you want the combo box (see Figure 7-37) on the Products page to be updated with changes made to the list of categories.

Figure 7-37 The choices made on the Categories tab of this subform are reflected in controls on the Products tab.

To do this, use the code that follows on the categories subform, which refreshes a single control, *CategoryID*. There is also code in these events to refresh another subform called *frmProductsList*, which we will discuss following the code sample:

```
Private Sub Form_AfterDelConfirm(Status As Integer)
    Me.Parent.cboCategoryID.Requery
    Me.Parent.frmProductsList.Form.Requery
End Sub

Private Sub Form_AfterUpdate()
    Me.Parent.cboCategoryID.Requery
    Me.Parent.frmProductsList.Form.Requery
End Sub
```

Figure 7-38 shows an additional tab that lists products. You want to add some code so that whatever product record a user browses in the first Products tab (the main form), the Product List tab is automatically synchronized to display the appropriate record, and similarly, when moving in the Product List tab, the Products tab changes.

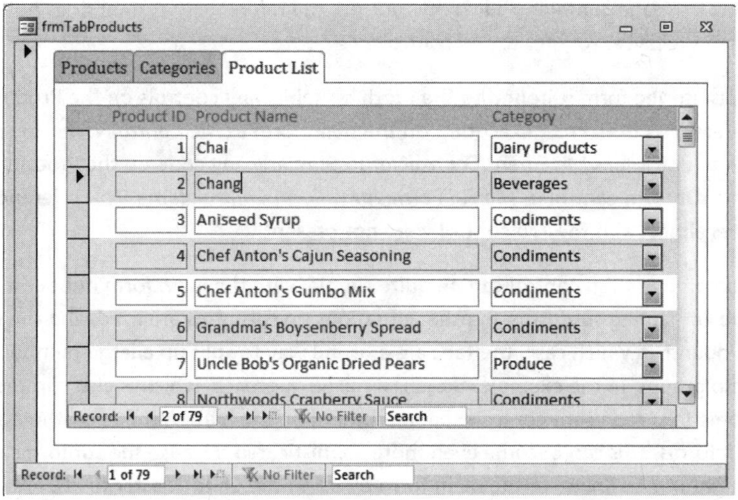

Figure 7-38 As a user pages through product records, the Product List synchronizes to the same record that's displayed in Products tab.

This time you write the code in the *Current* event for the *frmProductList subform*. This will synchronize the main form to the record in the Product List, as follows:

```
Private Sub Form_Current()
    Me.Parent.RecordsetClone.FindFirst "[ProductID] = " & Me.ProductID
    Me.Parent.Bookmark = Me.Parent.RecordsetClone.Bookmark
End Sub
```

Similar code can be written on the main form's *Current* event to keep the details in the *frmProductList* synchronized with the main record, as shown here:

```
Private Sub Form_Current()
    Me.frmProductsList.Form.RecordsetClone.FindFirst "[ProductID] = " _
                                                       & Me.ProductID
    Me.frmProductsList.Form.Bookmark = _
                    Me.frmProductsList.Form.RecordsetClone.Bookmark
End Sub
```

INSIDE OUT   Referring to controls in the *Tab* control

In the previous example, it is important to realize that although graphically the *Tab* control contains pages, and each page in turn contains controls (for example, the Products List page contains a subform control), the referencing system does not use the tab then the pages to refer to the controls.

Because the form is bound to the Products table, any controls on the Products page are referenced from code executing on the main form as *Me.ControlName*, or from code on a subform as *Me.Parent.ControlName*. Similarly any code on the Product page refers to a subform control as *Me.SubFormName.Form.ControlName*. This referencing operates almost as if the *Tab* control were not present.

Sometimes a *Tab* control can be quite simple, with the main form unbound and each tab containing subforms. In other situations no subforms are used, and the main form is bound, in which case, the tabs are a useful way to split up a large number of controls into groups. In the example, there is a mixed approach, which is also common, in which some tabs represent controls that are bound on the main form, and others are separate subforms. This can become even more sophisticated because the subforms might or might not be linked to the main form by using the Child/Master fields.

The *OnChange* Event

The *Tab* control's *OnChange* event is called whenever a tab is changed. As illustrated in the following code, this is a useful event for controlling page visibility (note that the page numbering is 0-based):

```
Private Sub TabCtl0_Change()
' hide pagCategories when you click on pagProductList
    If Me.tabMain.Value = Me.tabMain.Pages("pagProductList").PageIndex Then
        Me.tabMain.Pages("pagCategories").Visible = False
    Else
        Me.tabMain.Pages("pagCategories").Visible = True
    End If
End Sub
```

Dynamically Loading Tabs

The technique described in this section can be used to construct a rich, multi-tabbed form with which a user can dynamically load and unload tabs. The *frmTabsDynamic* form contains the code for this. This could either be used as a specialist form or as a general navigation interface for an application. The *tblTabPages* table shown in Figure 7-39 contains a set of tab pages for the specified form; *TabOrdering* controls the load order, *DefaultVisible* whether the tab will be visible; *CanUnloadPage* determines whether a page can be unloaded.

Each tab page can also have a *RelatedPage*, which means that when you double-click a page name, it will load the related page, if it has one; otherwise, if it is not marked as *CanUnloadPage*, it unloads the page from the tab.

This means that you could have a *Tab* control, pre-designed with five pages, but have many more pages that can by dynamically loaded and unloaded, as required (this technique means that you can exploit the flexibility of the *Tab* control but manage associated performance issues with having too many tabs). There are many ways in which to enhance this design technique, we provide here a basic framework to get you started.

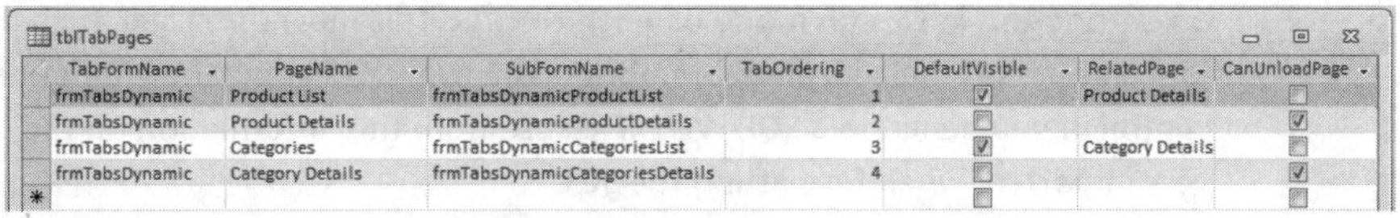

TabFormName	PageName	SubFormName	TabOrdering	DefaultVisible	RelatedPage	CanUnloadPage
frmTabsDynamic	Product List	frmTabsDynamicProductList	1	☑	Product Details	☐
frmTabsDynamic	Product Details	frmTabsDynamicProductDetails	2	☐		☑
frmTabsDynamic	Categories	frmTabsDynamicCategoriesList	3	☑	Category Details	☐
frmTabsDynamic	Category Details	frmTabsDynamicCategoriesDetails	4	☐		☑
				☐		☐

Figure 7-39 A table can be used to contain a list of subforms, which can be dynamically loaded into pages in the *Tab* control.

Each tab page has a subform control that is dynamically bound to the *SubFormName* in the *tblTabPages* table.

The *Tab* control pages and subforms follow a naming convention: the pages are named Page0, Page1..., and the subform control on each page is named Page0SubForm1, Page1SubForm1, and so on.

Loading Pages

At the top of the forms module is an array of types that maps to the columns in *tblTabPages* so that it is effectively dynamically held in memory, as demonstrated in the following:

```
Dim lngArrayPages As Long        ' how many tab pages in the array
Dim lngTabPages As Long          ' how many physical tab pages

Private Type PageInfo
    strPageName As String
    strPageSubForm As String
    strRelatedPage As String
    blCanBeLoaded As Boolean
End Type

Dim AvailablePages() As PageInfo
```

When the form loads, you write all the available pages to the memory array and also load the pages marked as *DefaultVisible* into the physical *Tab* controls pages.

INSIDE OUT   Exploiting the *Tag* property on controls

When you need to develop a generic feature that relates to controls, one of the most valuable assets in Access is the *Tag* property. This is the only built-in property on controls that you can define to be whatever you want. In the example, we use this property to hold an Index in an array, but there are many other uses for this property.

The *Tag* property is particularly useful when you have a form with unbound controls and you need to hold information regarding the type of data that can be entered into the controls; in this situation, you can hold an "s" for a string, a "d" for a date, and so on, setting this in Design mode on each control. This means you can easily write code to scan through the collection of unbound controls and know the type of data in each control. If you generate a SQL *WHERE* clause from this, information on the data types is very important when formatting the SQL

To identify each tab page with a particular array page, you use the *Tag* property of the page to hold an index in the array of all pages. The following routine loads the tab page's subform into the subform control and sets the page caption and tag:

```
Sub LoadThePage(strPageName As String, _
                lngTargetPageNo As Long, _
                lngTargetArrayId As Long)
    ' Load the tab and make it visible
    Me.TabCtl0.Pages(lngTargetPageNo).Visible = True
    Me.TabCtl0.Pages(lngTargetPageNo).Caption = _
                                    AvailablePages(lngTargetArrayId).strPageName
    Me.TabCtl0.Pages(lngTargetPageNo).Tag = lngTargetArrayId
    ' Named PageXSubForm1
    Me.Controls("Page" & lngTargetPageNo & "SubForm1").SourceObject = _
                                    AvailablePages(lngTargetArrayId).strPageSubForm
End Sub
```

When the form opens, it calls the following routine, which populates the array and calls the preceding procedure to dynamically load pages:

```
Sub LoadTabs()
    ' load the dynamic tabs into arrays
    Dim db As Database
    Dim rst As Recordset
    Dim strSQL As String
    Dim lngArray As Long
    Dim lngPageVisibleCount As Long
```

```
Set db = CurrentDb
strSQL = "SELECT * from tblTabPages WHERE TabFormName = '" & _
            Me.Name & "' ORDER BY TabOrdering"
Set rst = db.OpenRecordset(strSQL, dbOpenDynaset)
rst.MoveLast
rst.MoveFirst
lngArrayPages = rst.RecordCount
lngTabPages = Me.TabCtl0.Pages.Count
' allocate working array
ReDim AvailablePages(lngArrayPages - 1)
lngArray = 0
lngPageVisibleCount = 0
Do While Not rst.EOF
    AvailablePages(lngArray).strPageName = rst!PageName
    AvailablePages(lngArray).strPageSubForm = rst!SubFormName
    AvailablePages(lngArray).blCanBeLoaded = rst!CanUnloadPage
    AvailablePages(lngArray).strRelatedPage = Nz(rst!RelatedPage)
    If rst!DefaultVisible And lngPageVisibleCount + 1 < lngTabPages Then
        LoadThePage AvailablePages(lngArray).strPageName, lngPageVisibleCount _
                        , lngArray
        lngPageVisibleCount = lngPageVisibleCount + 1
    End If

    lngArray = lngArray + 1
    rst.MoveNext
Loop
' Hide any remaining unused tabs
' The pages tag property contains the index
' to the active page or is null
Dim lngPage As Long
For lngPage = lngPageVisibleCount To lngTabPages - 1
    Me.TabCtl0.Pages(lngPage).Visible = False
    Me.TabCtl0.Pages(lngPage).Tag = ""
    Me.TabCtl0.Pages(lngPage).Caption = "Page" & lngPage
    Me.Controls("Page" & lngPage & "SubForm1").SourceObject = ""
Next
'    Debuging_ShowTabControl
End Sub
```

This results in the default display shown in Figure 7-40.

Figure 7-40 With the Default Visibility set to *True* for two tab subforms, when you open the form, the first two tabs are loaded and displayed.

Using the Watches window, you can see how the array is loaded into memory, as shown in Figure 7-41.

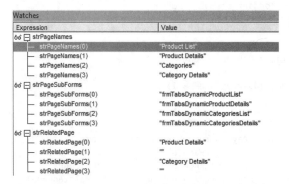

Figure 7-41 Arrays are used to hold the map of subforms that can be potentially loaded into the tab pages.

There is also some debugging code to show the current state of the *Tab* control pages:

```
Sub Debuging_ShowTabControl()

    Dim lngPage As Long
    Stop
    For lngPage = 0 To lngTabPages - 1
        With Me.TabCtl0
            Debug.Print .Pages(lngPage).Name, .Pages(lngPage).Caption, _
                        .Pages(lngPage).Tag, _
                        Me.Controls("Page" & lngPage & "SubForm1").SourceObject
        End With
    Next
End Sub
```

This generates the result displayed in Figure 7-42, which shows the subforms that are currently loaded into each tab page.

```
Immediate
  Page0        Product List  0        frmTabsDynamicProductList
  Page1        Categories    2        frmTabsDynamicCategoriesList
  Page2        Page2
```

Figure 7-42 The two default subforms that are loaded into the first two tab pages.

You can see that Page0 and Page1 have been loaded but Page2 is free to be used.

You can also use the Watches window to display information on the array, which holds information for each page that can be loaded, as shown in Figure 7-43.

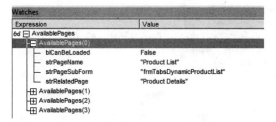

Figure 7-43 The Watches window displays more information on the tab management variables.

Dynamic Loading of a Related Page

Double-clicking certain tabs dynamically loads a related page, if that tab page has been defined to have a related page. The following code checks if the tab page has a related page, checks if you have a free unused tab page, and then dynamically loads the related page:

```
Private Sub TabCtl0_DblClick(Cancel As Integer)
    Dim varNextFreePage As Variant
    ' A double click on a tab means load any related page
    ' indirectly using the Tag property on clicked page
    If AvailablePages(Me.TabCtl0.Pages(Me.TabCtl0).Tag).strRelatedPage _
                                    <> "" Then
        ' we have a related page
        varNextFreePage = GetNextFreeTabPage()
        If Not IsNull(varNextFreePage) Then
            LoadTheRelatedTab AvailablePages( _
                        Me.TabCtl0.Pages(Me.TabCtl0).Tag).strRelatedPage, _
                        CLng(varNextFreePage)
        End If
        Exit Sub
    End If
    ' if this page does not have a related page then the
    ' double click is used to unload then page
    ' if it can be unloaded
    If AvailablePages(Me.TabCtl0.Pages(Me.TabCtl0).Tag).blCanBeLoaded Then
        UnloadTheTab Me.TabCtl0
    End If
End Sub
```

To load the related page, you need to find the page index in your array, and then also check that the page is not already loaded:

```
Sub LoadTheRelatedTab(strPageName As String, lngTargetPageNo As Long)
    ' is the page already loaded ?
    Dim lngPage As Long
    Dim lngArrayId As Long
    lngArrayId = FindArrayId(strPageName)
```

```
            For lngPage = 0 To Me.TabCtl0.Pages.Count - 1
                If Me.TabCtl0.Pages(lngPage).Tag <> "" Then
                    If lngArrayId = CLng(Me.TabCtl0.Pages(lngPage).Tag) Then
                        ' Page is already loaded
                        Exit Sub
                    End If
                End If
            Next
            LoadThePage strPageName, lngTargetPageNo, lngArrayId
        End Sub

        Function FindArrayId(strPageName As String) As Long
            Dim lngArrayPageCount As Long
            For lngArrayPageCount = 0 To lngArrayPages
                If strPageName = AvailablePages(lngArrayPageCount).strPageName Then
                    FindArrayId = lngArrayPageCount
                    Exit Function
                End If
            Next
            Stop
            ' fatal error is you reached this point
        End Function
```

Unloading a Page

The double-click function can also unload a page that is marked as being allowed to be unloaded. This way, non-essential pages can be unloaded to make room for other tab pages:

```
Sub UnloadTheTab(lngPageNo As Long)
    ' unload a tab
    ' first we must shift focus from the active tab
    ' before we can change the visibility
    Dim lngNewTabForFocus As Long
    lngNewTabForFocus = lngPageNo - 1
    If lngNewTabForFocus < 0 Then lngNewTabForFocus = 0
    Me.TabCtl0.Pages(lngNewTabForFocus).SetFocus
    Me.TabCtl0.Pages(lngPageNo).Visible = False
    ' Leave the caption but clear the tag
    Me.TabCtl0.Pages(lngPageNo).Tag = ""
    ' Named PageXSubForm1
    Me.Controls("Page" & lngPageNo & "SubForm1").SourceObject = _
                                                 ""

End Sub
```

Summary

In this chapter, you learned that programming with form controls is an essential part of enhancing a user's experience when interacting with your application. You use key events such as *BeforeUpdate* on a control to perform validation and *AfterUpdate* to take appropriate actions following validation.

You also learned how combo box controls on a form can be tied together so that choices made by a user in one control change the available data choices in other controls.

In addition, you saw how you can make multiple selections in list boxes, either in a single list box, or by using two list boxes, and that a list box can be used to act like a subform.

In the section on the *TreeView* control, you learned how ActiveX controls can significantly extend the power of Access. Chapter 11, "Using Classes and Forms," presents additional examples of this, including the *Slider* control and *Up/Down* button controls.

Finally, you saw the *Tab* control and how it is used to dynamically load pages with different subforms. You also examined the syntax required for synchronizing data presented in different tabs.

CHAPTER 8

Creating Reports and Events

Report Event Sequences 324   Report Layout Control 331

Typically, you spend the majority of your time writing code associated with forms and form controls. By contrast, reports are easily overlooked when it comes to events. This is because the events associated with reports are not the direct result of a user interacting with the page. Reports have a sequence of events associated with the report opening and rendering the pages of data.

In this chapter, you focus on the techniques for programming against events on a report. You also take some time to look at other associated programming techniques that can be used to enhance report output. Microsoft Access 2010 reports can be opened in either Print/Print Preview and also in the more interactive Report view; some techniques are applicable to both views, and other methods apply to only one of the two views.

After reading this chapter, you will:

- Understand the key event sequences when a report is rendered in different views.

- Know a number of techniques that can be used to enhance the presentation of reports.

> **Note**
>
> As you read through this chapter, we encourage you to also use the companion content sample database, Reports.accdb, which can be downloaded from the book's catalog page.

Access 2010 provides a lot of flexibility in how you open a report, but this flexibility can also lead to some confusion. It is not uncommon to find a developer puzzling over why the code on their report is not executing as anticipated, only to find that the reason is the manner by which they opened the report.

The sample reports for this chapter, such as *rptCustomerDrillDownList*, are designed for a user to interact with events on the report—like a *DblClick* event—and so these reports need to be opened in Report view (acViewReport). If you open these reports in the Print

Preview mode (acViewPreview), the click events will not work, because this is a preview for printing. The samples database contains examples using the correct options for opening the examples.

Report Event Sequences

The sample form, *dlgReportEvents*, opens the *rptEvents* report, which demonstrates some of the key event sequences on reports, as shown in Figure 8-1.

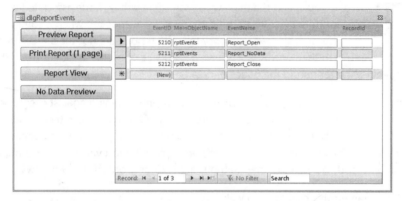

Figure 8-1 The *dlgReportEvents* form, demonstrating event sequences.

Although programming forms is a more common development task than programming reports, reports can be trickier because their event sequences have more variation than those for forms; the sequences change depending on whether you are viewing, previewing or printing the report (we have omitted some of the less important focus and activation events from these sequences).

When printing a report, a typical event sequence is as follows:

Report_Open →

ReportHeader_Format → *ReportHeader_Print* →

PageHeader_Format → *PageHeader_Print* →

Detail_Format → *Detail_Print* →

...

ReportFooter_Format → *ReportFooter_Print* →

PageFooter_Format → *PageFooter_Print* →

Report_Page → *Report_Close*

When printing a report, the *Load* and *Unload* events are not called, and the rendering of the report is controlled from sequences of *Format/Print* events for the different report sections. There might also be *Retreat* events associated with the report Header and Detail sections.

When previewing a report on the screen a typical event sequence as follows:

Report_Open → *Report_Load* →

ReportHeader_Format → *ReportHeader_Print* →

PageHeader_Format → *PageHeader_Print* →

Detail_Format → *Detail_Print* →

...

ReportFooter_Format → *ReportFooter_Print* →

PageFooter_Format → *PageFooter_Print* →

Report_Page → *Report_Unload* → *Report_Close*

The report preview sequences of events are very similar to the report printing, except that there are *Load/Unload* events. As the user pages forward through the report, events fire to render each page; as they page back, no more events are normally required because that part of the report has already been generated.

When displaying a report in Report view on screen, a typical event sequence is as follows:

Report_Open → *Report_Load* →

ReportHeader_Paint →

PageHeader_Paint →

Detail_Paint →

... (can include additional *ReportHeader_Paint*, *PageHeader_Paint* events)

ReportFooter_Paint →

PageFooter_Paint →

Report_Unload → *Report_Close*

Chapter 8

When you have a report in Report view, instead of the *Format/Print* events, you see Paint events. Because the user can interact with the report, you can also get *OnCurrent* events if the user clicks into a field in a record. In Report view, as a user pages back and forth between pages, resizes the screen, or otherwise interacts with the report, sequences of paint events are continuously executed. *ReportHeader_Paint* and *PageHeader_Paint* events are also regularly executed.

When you use *NoData* to close a report, the following sequence is triggered:

   Report_Open → *Report_NoData* → *Report_Close*

From the event sequences, you can see that if you intend to add programming to control the detailed rendering of individual records, then for Print Preview or printing, you program against the *Format/Print* events, but for viewing the report on screen in the Report view, you need to use the *Paint* events.

Creating Drill-Down Reports and Current Event

In Report view, you can manipulate behavior by using events similar to those normally found in forms, such as *Current*, *Click*, and *DblClick*. These events can be used to interactively open other reports or forms to provide more detailed information to the user. In the sample *rptCustomerDrillDownList* report code, there are two events that demonstrate how a user can drill down through a report, opening a second report to display more details on a record. The following code, written for the *Current* event, opens the second report when you click on each record:

```
Private Sub Report_Current()
    DoCmd.OpenReport "rptCustomerDetails", acViewReport, _
            , "[Customer Number] = " & Me.Customer_Number
End Sub
```

The second example places similar code on the *DblClick* event for a specific field:

```
Private Sub Customer_Name_DblClick(Cancel As Integer)
    DoCmd.OpenReport "rptCustomerDetails", acViewReport, _
            , "[Customer Number] = " & Me.Customer_Number
End Sub
```

To see the effect of these events, you must be in Report view.

INSIDE OUT   Side-by-side details using multiple copies of a report

When drilling down into a report, you might want to open the same report more than once and display them side-by-side. This is possible by using a technique for forms that is described in Chapter 11, "Using Classes and Forms." The sample code is shown in the *rptCustomerDrillDownListMultiples* form; a collection of reports has been defined in the code module, and the *DblClick* event opens a new copy of the report. Note that to make this work, the target report, *rptCustomerDetails*, must have a code module, even if the code module does not contain any code (to create an empty code module, you open the report in Design view. Next, on the ribbon, select View Code, and then save the report, or you can set the report's *HasModule* property to *True*):

```
Dim colReports As New Collection

Private Sub Customer_Name_DblClick(Cancel As Integer)
    Dim rpt As Report_rptCustomerDetails
    Set rpt = New Report_rptCustomerDetails
    rpt.Filter = "[Customer Number] = " & Me.Customer_Number
    rpt.FilterOn = True
    colReports.Add rpt, CStr(CLng(Rnd * (2 ^ 31)))
    rpt.Visible = True
End Sub

Private Sub Report_Close()
    Dim rpt As Report_rptCustomerDetails
    For Each rpt In colReports
        Set rpt = Nothing
    Next
End Sub
```

Creating a Boxed Grid with the *Print* Event

In this example, you look at how to program against the *Detail_Print* event to create a report in which fields are boxed in a grid pattern. If you set your text boxes to have a solid border and add a rectangle behind any check boxes, you can create the grid effect, as shown in Figure 8-2.

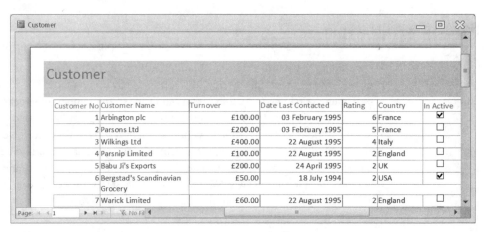

Figure 8-2 Use text boxes and borders to create a grid effect.

The *rptCustomerGrid* shown in Figure 8-2 has a problem with the gridlines because the *CanGrow* property for one of the boxes is set to *True*. One solution to this problem is to add rectangles around all the controls, but set the control borders to transparent.

INSIDE OUT   Report events and drawing graphics

If you are drawing lines or rectangles and other graphics, this can only be performed in the *OnPrint*, *OnFormat*, and *OnPage* events. Using the *OnPrint* event, you can add borders before a page is printed. This means that these drawing operations cannot be performed in Report view, which would require the *OnPaint* event.

To create the effect, you need to perform the processing with the *OnPrint* event, which means that you can only see the effect when in Print Preview or Printing a report. The code has been written in a subroutine, so you can easily experiment to see how this will not work on other events:

```
Sub DrawRectangles()
    Dim dblheight As Double
    dblheight = 0
    Dim ctrl As Control
    Dim txtBox As TextBox
    Dim rect As Rectangle
    ' Find maximum height
```

```
      For Each ctrl In Me.Section(0).Controls
          If TypeOf ctrl Is TextBox Then
              Set txtBox = ctrl
              If txtBox.Height > dblheight Then
                  dblheight = txtBox.Height
              End If
          End If
          If TypeOf ctrl Is Rectangle Then
              Set rect = ctrl
              If rect.Height > dblheight Then
                  dblheight = rect.Height
              End If
          End If
      Next

      Dim lnglineColour As Long
      lnglineColour = RGB(0, 0, 0)
      For Each ctrl In Me.Section(0).Controls
          If TypeOf ctrl Is TextBox Then
              ' is a text box create rectangle
              Set txtBox = ctrl
              Me.Line (txtBox.Left, txtBox.Top)- _
                        Step(txtBox.Width, dblheight), lnglineColour, B
          End If
          If TypeOf ctrl Is Rectangle Then
              ' is a text box create rectangle
              Set rect = ctrl
              Me.Line (rect.Left, rect.Top)- _
                          Step(rect.Width, dblheight), lnglineColour, B
          End If
      Next
  End Sub
```

This procedure is then called from the *OnPrint* event for the detail section, as follows:

```
Private Sub Detail_Print(Cancel As Integer, PrintCount As Integer)
    DrawRectangles
End Sub
```

The resulting report, *rptCustomerGridRectangles*, is shown in Figure 8-3.

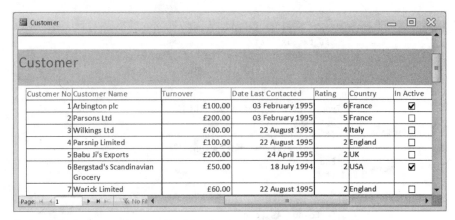

Figure 8-3 The report displayed in Print Preview with the corrected grid.

Layout Control and the *Format* Event

In this example, we will demonstrate how you can achieve a more detailed level of control over printing by using the *Format* event. The sample *rptSkipPrinting* report is designed with a layout for three labels across the page. The program code on the report allows you to specify a number of label positions to be skipped before printing commences.

INSIDE OUT   Layout control during printing

The *MoveLayout* property of a report controls the movement to the next printing location, the *PrintSection* property controls whether the section is printed, and *NextRecord* advances to the next record position.

The code on the report is shown in the following:

```
Dim lngSkipPosition As Integer
Private Sub Detail_Format(Cancel As Integer, FormatCount As Integer)
If lngSkipPosition <> 0 Then
    Me.MoveLayout = True
    Me.NextRecord = False
    Me.PrintSection = False
    lngSkipPosition = lngSkipPosition - 1
End If
End Sub
```

```
Private Sub Report_Open(Cancel As Integer)
    Dim varInput As Variant
    varInput = InputBox("No. Of Used Labels To Skip On First Page ? ", , "0")
    If varInput <> "" Then
        lngSkipPosition = CLng(varInput)
    Else
        lngSkipPosition = 0
    End If
End Sub
```

The resulting report is shown in Figure 8-4, in which two printing positions are skipped.

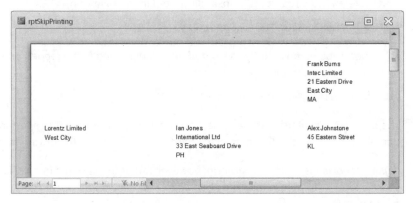

Figure 8-4 The labels report in Print Preview mode, with printing positions skipped.

Report Layout Control

In this section, you look at other examples of how you can apply Microsoft VBA to improve the layout of your reports.

Driving Reports from a Form

When producing a reporting system, you can use a number of different approaches to assemble the combination of forms and reports. The simplest method is to make use of the forms collection to allow a report and its underlying data set to extract values that the user has entered in the form.

The sample *dlgReportDriver* form (see Figure 8-5) contains two controls: the country selection controls the data that is displayed, and the *Title* control is displayed as a title on the report.

Figure 8-5 Using a form as a dialog for users to make selections before generating the report.

In this case, the *rptReportDriver* report has a control for which the control source has been set to reference the reporting form, as illustrated in the following:

```
=Forms!dlgReportDriver![txtReportTitle]
```

The report is based on a query called *qryRptCustomers*, and in the reports query criteria, there is a reference to the reporting form:

```
Like ([Forms]![dlgReportDriver]![txtCountry]) & "*"
```

The disadvantage of using this approach is that if you want to use the report in more than one place in the system, the reference is hard-coded to refer to the driving form.

dlgReportDriver2 is a very similar form; however, rather than using a query that is tied to a specific form, you can use the *WhereCondition* with the *DoCmd.OpenReport* command to filter the data.

The Open The Report button on the form contains the following code:

```
Private Sub cmdOpen_Click()
    glbReportTitle = Me.txtReportTitle
    If Nz(Me.txtCountry) <> "" Then
        ' we use On Error Resume next to
        ' prevent any error if the reports NoData
        ' is activated and closes the report
        On Error Resume Next
        DoCmd.OpenReport "rptReportDriver2", acPreview, , _
            "[Country] = '" & Me.txtCountry & "'"
    Else
        DoCmd.OpenReport "rptReportDriver2", acPreview
    End If
End Sub
```

The report has code written behind two events. The *NoData* event can be used to prevent the report from opening if there is no data to be shown:

```
Private Sub Report_NoData(Cancel As Integer)
    MsgBox "No Data To Display"
    Cancel = True
End Sub
```

The report has an *Open* event that is triggered when the report begins to open; this event provides the opportunity to close a report before it opens. To refer to a control on a report, the code needs to be written on the *Load* event. This code displays the global variable, which holds the report title:

```
Private Sub Report_Load()
    Me.txtTitle = glbReportTitle
End Sub
```

With these changes to the reporting system, you can call a report from different parts of the system, because we have removed any hard-coded references to the form that opens the report.

Reducing Joins with a Combo Box

In the sample database report *rptComboBox* contains a combo box named *cboType*. When rendered, this appears on the report as a text box. The combo box contains two columns, and we can add a second text box control to the report and set the control source for the text box to lookup a related field value by using the bound combo box control:

```
=[cboType].[Column](1)
```

This technique can be used to reduce the number of joins that would otherwise be required in the underlying *RecordSource* used by the report.

Programming a Report Grouping

A report grouping can be based on a field or an expression. It is also possible to base the grouping on a VBA function. The *modRPT* module contains a public function that will accept a value for a company's turnover and return a classification of 1, 2, or 3. The report then groups by this value, as illustrated in the following code:

```
Public Function modRPT_GetTORange(ByVal varTurnover As Variant _
                                 ) As Integer
    ' Group turnover into special Ranges
    If IsNull(varTurnover) Then
        modRPT_GetTORange = 3
        Exit Function
    End If
    Select Case varTurnover
        Case 0 To 110
            modRPT_GetTORange = 1
        Case 111 To 280
            modRPT_GetTORange = 2
        Case Else
            modRPT_GetTORange = 3
    End Select
End Function
```

The *rptGroupBySpecialTurnoverRanges* report contains a group that is based on this VBA function, as shown in Figure 8-6.

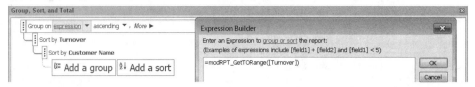

Figure 8-6 Using a custom VBA function for specialist grouping on a report.

Packing Address Information with a *ParamArray*

There are many occasions when you need to pack up information from several fields and generate carriage return linefeeds for each line but skip address lines that are blank.

The method used here is general purpose in that it can be used for any number of parts in an address without changing the main function. The following code for packing the address accepts a *Variant* array of parameters:

```
Function modRPT_PackAddress(ParamArray strAddressLines() As Variant _
                           ) As String
    Dim lngCount As Long
    modRPT_PackAddress = ""
    For lngCount = 0 To UBound(strAddressLines)
        If Not Nz(strAddressLines(lngCount)) = "" Then
            If modRPT_PackAddress <> "" Then
                ' add a CRLF if required
                modRPT_PackAddress = modRPT_PackAddress + vbCrLf
            End If
            modRPT_PackAddress = modRPT_PackAddress & _
                        Trim(strAddressLines(lngCount))
        End If
    Next
End Function
```

To use this function in the example report, *rptPackAddress*, we have added an unbound control called *txtAddress* and set its *CanGrow* property to *True*. The control source is set as follows:

```
=modRPT_PackAddress([Firstname] & " " & [Lastname],[OrganizationName],[Address],
[City],[State])
```

Note that for the first part of the address we are concatenating two fields, which will be treated as a single parameter. Figure 8-7 shows the view of the contents of the *ParamArray*.

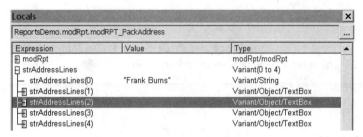

Figure 8-7 The *ParamArray* contains the address fields.

Control of Printers

Access provides considerable control over printers and their settings. The simplest use of this is with the *Application.Printer* object (default printer) and *Application.Printers* collection (available printers).

The following code can be used to examine the available printers and change the default printer:

```
Sub modRpt_ListPrinters()
    Dim prt As Printer
    For Each prt In Application.Printers
        Debug.Print prt.DeviceName, prt.DriverName, _
                prt.PaperSize, prt.Orientation
    Next
    ' details of the default printer
    Debug.Print "Default Printer Information"
    Debug.Print "--------------------------"
    Set prt = Application.Printer
    Debug.Print prt.DeviceName, prt.DriverName, _
                prt.PaperSize, prt.Orientation
    ' to a specific printer as the default printer
    'Application.Printer = Application.Printers(2)
    Application.Printer = prt
End Sub
```

The sample *rptPrinterChoice* report uses the preceding code on a pop-up form so that when a user enters Print Preview, she can select a printer before printing a report. This code can easily be incorporated into a button on a form to make the selection before printing:

```
Private Sub Report_Open(Cancel As Integer)
    ' acCurViewDesign  - Design View
    ' acCurViewPreview  - Print View
    ' acCurViewReportBrowse  - Report View
    ' acCurViewLayout  - Layout View
    If Me.CurrentView = acCurViewPreview  Then
        'Me.UseDefaultPrinter
        DoCmd.OpenForm "dlgChoosePrinter", acDesign, , , , acDialog
    End If
End Sub
```

Chapter 8

> **Note**
>
> There are three other report properties, *PrtDevMode*, *PrtDevNames*, and *PrtMip*, which provide further read/write settings on printer devices.

Summary

In this chapter, you looked at the key event sequences when reports are rendered. You saw that for Print Preview and Printing, the detail section has a sequence of *Format/Print* events. In Report view, this is replaced with the *Paint* event.

You also saw how to enhance your reports by using customized grouping and techniques to pack fields to avoid blank lines. Access also provides a number of features for adjusting and selecting printers.

PART 4

Advanced Programming with VBA Classes

CHAPTER 9
Adding Functionality with Classes 339

CHAPTER 10
Using Classes and Events 359

CHAPTER 11
Using Classes and Forms 381

Adding Functionality with Classes

Improving the Dynamic *Tab* Control. 340   Creating a Hierarchy of Classes 354

You have seen in earlier chapters how Microsoft VBA program code is either contained in a module or held in a form's class module. In this chapter, you look at how VBA also allows you to construct your own class modules.

It is often overlooked that VBA supports Object-Oriented Programming (OOP), so in this chapter, we introduce you to OOP concepts by having you construct your own classes. Many Microsoft Access developers take a look at classes and then give up because they have difficulty seeing the benefit and justification for using classes. It's true that much of what can be achieved with a simple class can also be achieved by using libraries of code, and that to build classes you often need to put in more effort during the initial development, but there are benefits in using classes that will be explored in this chapter as well as in Chapter 10, "Using Classes and Events," and Chapter 11, "Using Classes and Forms."

This chapter focuses on two examples of classes, and uses each example to introduce the techniques for creating your own classes.

The first example involves applying classes to solve a problem of designing a dynamic *Tab* control that saw in Chapter 7, "Using Form Controls and Events." This example will demonstrate how classes can be used to improve the design of a general purpose tool that can be re-used in your applications.

The second example looks at how to build classes to handle data for a specific business problem.

After reading this chapter, you will:

- Understand how to create class modules.

- Know how to use *Let*, *Get*, *Set*, and *New* with classes.

- Be able to create collection classes.

- Be able to create base and derived classes.

- Be able to create a hierarchy of classes.

> **Note**
> As you read through this chapter, we encourage you to also use the companion content sample databases, BuildingClasses.accdb and BuildingClassesAfterExportImport.accdb, which can be downloaded from the book's catalog page.

The object-oriented view to developing software became popular in the 1980s, and in addition to OOP, many terms such as Object-Oriented Design (OOD) and Object-Oriented Analysis (OOA) became increasingly popular.

You have already seen many examples of working with objects in Access. These objects have properties that describe the object, and methods that cause an object to perform an operation. Access maintains collections of like objects; for example, the *Forms* collection, which contains *Form* objects that open on the desktop, and the *TableDefs* collection in the Data Access Object (DAO) model, which contains all the *TableDef* objects. These are examples of working with objects, but not examples of OOP.

OOP Programming (which is supported in VBA) means taking these ideas of working with objects and extending this concept to guide how program code is written.

Classes can be applied in several different ways in Access to:

- Improve the quality of code (OOP can help you develop more maintainable code).

- Extend form/report behavior (OOP allows you to take control of the underlying behavior of Access objects and wrap or extend the behavior).

- Integrate External Components (some external components do not expose all their functionality and OOP features can help with this).

Improving the Dynamic *Tab* Control

In Chapter 7, you saw how to design a dynamic *Tab* control form that can load and unload pages by using an array of Types, where each item in the array corresponds to a form that is loaded into a subform control. The type structure for that is as follows:

```
Private Type PageInfo
    strPageName As String
    strPageSubForm As String
    strRelatedPage As String
    blCanBeLoaded As Boolean
End Type

Dim AvailablePages() As PageInfo
```

As an alternative to using a Type, you will define these pages as objects with properties that correspond to each part of the Type structure, and then you will build a collection to hold these objects, which replaces the array that held the types.

We need the following properties for our object:

- *PageName*

- *SubFormPageName*

- *RelatedPageName*

- *CanBeUnloaded*

You might have noticed that we have renamed the *CanBeLoaded* property in the preceding list to *CanBeUnloaded*. This is because an object-oriented perspective helps you to think in terms of how an object's state can be changed, so this is a more appropriate term to use. With the object's basic properties determined, you can now proceed to create the object class.

Creating a Class Module

To begin, in the Project pane, you create a new class module, as shown in Figure 9-1.

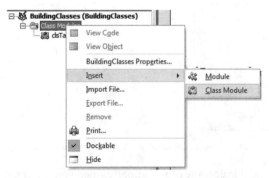

Figure 9-1 Use the Project pane to create a new class module.

With this file created, you then save it using an appropriate class name; for this example, use *clsTabPage*. Because you are now working in a class module, you do not need to explicitly define that you are creating a class (as you would need to do in Microsoft .NET). Next, you define the object's internal variables at the top of the class module code, as illustrated in the following:

```
Option Compare Database
Option Explicit

' These could be declared as either Dim or Private
' as within a class their scope is restricted
Dim p_PageName As String
Dim p_SubFormPageName As String
Dim p_RelatedPageName As String
Dim p_CanBeUnloaded As Boolean
```

Note that these variables include the prefix "p_" to indicate that they are private variables to each class object (other popular prefixes include "m" or "m_"). The next step is to provide the user with a way of reading and writing these variable values.

The *Let* and *Get* Object Properties

After you define the object's internal variables or attributes for your class, you need to create a mechanism to read or write these values. To do this, you define properties. On the Insert menu, click Procedure to open the Add Procedure dialog box, as shown in Figure 9-2.

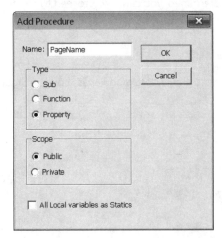

Figure 9-2 Use the Add Procedure dialog box to create a new private or public property.

Ensure that you are not clicked inside any other property when you insert a new property; otherwise, it will fail to add the property correctly to the class. The code that is created needs appropriate data types to be specified for the return type of the property and the parameter type passed to the property.

As shown in the code that follows, you use the *Get* statement to read an object property from the internal private variable, and the *Let* statement to assign a value to the internal private variable. An object can have a number of internal variables, but you might only need to make a few of these available to the user. The idea is to keep the object's external interface very simple, exposing only the minimum number of essential features that a user will need. It is up to you to decide for which properties you want both a *Let* and *Get*, depending on whether the property is to be read-only (*Get* but no *Let*) or write-only (*Let* but no *Get*):

```
Public Property Get PageName() As String
    PageName = p_PageName
End Property
Public Property Let PageName(ByVal PageName As String)
    p_PageName = PageName
End Property
Public Property Get RelatedPageName() As String
    RelatedPageName = p_RelatedPageName
End Property
Public Property Let RelatedPageName(ByVal RelatedPageName As String)
    p_RelatedPageName = RelatedPageName
End Property
Public Property Get CanBeUnloaded() As Boolean
    CanBeUnloaded = p_CanBeUnloaded
End Property
Public Property Let CanBeUnloaded(ByVal CanBeUnloaded As Boolean)
    p_CanBeUnloaded = CanBeUnloaded
End Property
Public Property Get SubFormPageName() As String
    SubFormPageName = p_SubFormPageName
End Property

Public Property Let SubFormPageName(ByVal SubFormPageName As String)
    p_SubFormPageName = SubFormPageName
End Property
```

Creating an Object with *New* and *Set*

To test your new class, you create a module (not a class module) to verify that you can create an object. If you insert a breakpoint and trace through the code execution, you will learn a great deal, as you can trace through the codes execution into the class module code.

You can define the object variable and then later create an object with the *New* keyword, or as is also shown demonstrated in the following code, with the *aTab2* object, you can both define and create the object at the same time. It is largely a matter of personal preference as to which method you choose to use.

Once you have finished with the object, set the object variable to *Nothing*; this destroys the object. The object would be destroyed anyhow when the code stops execution, but explicitly tidying up your objects is good practice and becomes more important when you work with more complex objects:

```
Sub modTabs_TestObject()
    ' test creating an object
    Dim aTab As clsTabPage
    Set aTab = New clsTabPage
    aTab.PageName = "ProductList"
    aTab.RelatedPageName = "Product Details"
    aTab.SubFormPageName = "frmTabsDynamicProductList"
    aTab.CanBeUnloaded = False

    Debug.Print aTab.PageName
    Set aTab = Nothing

    Dim aTab2 As New clsTabPage
    aTab2.PageName = "Product Details"
    Debug.Print aTab2.PageName
    Set aTab2 = Nothing
End Sub
```

INSIDE OUT   *Initialization* and *Termination* Events

When you are in a class module, you can select Class from the upper-left drop-down menu, which normally shows (General). Select Initialize or Terminate from the drop-down list that appears, and then generate the following procedures (in this example the type name *ObjectType* is not a real type but could for example be replaced with a real object type such as a *DAO.RecordSet* object):

```
Private Sub Class_Initialize()
    Set p_Object = New ObjectType
End Sub
Private Sub Class_Terminate()
    Set p_Object = Nothing
End Sub
```

Because class objects can contain other class objects or built-in class objects such as a *Recordset*, you might need to use the *New* keyword in *Initialize* to create an object that is assigned to a private variable, and then set the objects to *Nothing* to close the objects in the *Terminate* procedure. Externally, when your class object is created, the *Initialize* procedure is executed, and when it is set to *Nothing* or the variable goes out of scope, the *Terminate* procedure is executed.

Collection of Objects

A VBA collection is a set of objects that you can use in a similar manner as the built-in collections, such as the *Forms* collection that you worked with in earlier chapters.

The example that follows defines a collection that is used to hold our Tab page objects:

```
Sub modTabs_Collection()
    ' test creating an object
    Dim TabPages As New Collection
    Dim aTab As clsTabPage
    Set aTab = New clsTabPage
    aTab.PageName = "ProductList"
    aTab.RelatedPageName = "Product Details"
    aTab.SubFormPageName = "frmTabsDynamicProductList"
    aTab.CanBeUnloaded = False
    TabPages.Add aTab, aTab.PageName
    Set aTab = Nothing

    Set aTab = New clsTabPage
    aTab.PageName = "Product Details"
    aTab.RelatedPageName = ""
    aTab.SubFormPageName = "frmTabsDynamicProductDetails"
    aTab.CanBeUnloaded = True
    TabPages.Add aTab, aTab.PageName
    Set aTab = Nothing

    For Each aTab In TabPages
        Debug.Print aTab.PageName, aTab.SubFormPageName, _
aTab.RelatedPageName, aTab.CanBeUnloaded
    Next
    Debug.Print TabPages.Count

    Stop
    Set aTab = TabPages("ProductList")
    Debug.Print aTab.PageName
    Debug.Print TabPages("Product Details").PageName
    ' note 1 based collection unlike built in collections
    Debug.Print TabPages(1).PageName
    Set TabPages = Nothing
    Set aTab = Nothing
End Sub
```

Notice how the *aTab* variable is used several times to create objects, and how setting it to *Nothing* does *not* destroy the object. This is because once you have created an object, you add it to the collection, which is then responsible for managing the object (when the collection is set to *Nothing*, it will destroy the objects it contains.

When you add an object to a collection, you must also specify a collection key value (which must be unique). Doing this means that rather than referring to a collection object as

TabPages(1), you can use the key and refer to this as TabPages("Product List"). The *Collection* object's *Add* method also allows you to specify an optional *Before* or *After* argument for positioning an object relative to other objects in the collection. The collections first element is 1 and not 0 (which is what the built-in Access collections use).

Be aware that when you refer to an object by using TabPages(1).PageName, you cannot take advantage of IntelliSense assistance. This is because this type of collection can hold different types of objects, so the environment cannot know exactly which properties would apply to an object.

INSIDE OUT   VBA collection classes

The built-in VBA collection classes that you have been working with are different from an Access collection. The first difference is that the Access collections, such as *TableDefs*, can only hold one type of object; a VBA collection can hold different types of objects (this explains why the IntelliSense is limited). The second difference is that VBA collection classes are 1-based, whereas the Access collections are 0-based.

In the next section, you will be creating your own collection classes that wrap around the VBA collection class. These collections will start to look more like an Access collection.

Once you have added an object to a collection and specified the key value, you will find that you cannot subsequently display the key value—it is hidden. If your procedures need to be able to refer to the key, you might find it useful to add your own property to the object class, which saves and holds the key value in each object. Looking in the class *clsTabPage*, you see the following (it is not essential to do this in the class):

```
Dim p_Key As String
Public Property Get Key() As String
    Key = p_Key
End Property
Public Property Let PageName(ByVal PageName As String)
    p_PageName = PageName
    p_Key = PageName
End Property
```

Creating Collection Classes

A VBA *Collection* object supports a limited number of operations—*Add*, *Count*, and *Remove*. You will likely want to be able to add more operations to your collection. To do that, you need to define your own collection class, called *clsTabPageCollection*.

Defining a collection class follows the same steps as defining a normal class to create the class module. Your collection class will contain a VBA collection, so you define an internal variable called *p_TabPages*. As we previously described, classes can have two specially named methods for initializing and terminating the class. The simple *clsTabPage* didn't need any special operations, but the new class needs to create a VBA collection, and then remove all the objects from the collection when it is terminated, as illustrated in the following code:

```
Private p_TabPages As Collection

Private Sub Class_Initialize()
    Set p_TabPages = New Collection
End Sub

Private Sub Class_Terminate()
    Dim aClassPage As clsTabPage
    For Each aClassPage In p_TabPages
        p_TabPages.Remove CStr(aClassPage.PageName)
    Next
    Set p_TabPages = Nothing
End Sub
```

You also want to have the standard operations for counting, adding, and removing items from the class, so you need to add these methods to our collection (you also add an *Item* method, which is another standard feature of a class):

```
Public Property Get Count() As Long
    Count = p_TabPages.Count
End Property

Public Sub Add(aClassPage As clsTabPage)
    p_TabPages.Add aClassPage, aClassPage.PageName
End Sub

Public Sub Remove(PageName As Variant)
    p_TabPages.Remove CStr(PageName)
End Sub

Public Function Item(PageName As Variant) As clsTabPage
    Set Item = p_TabPages(PageName)
End Function
```

Once you start defining your own collection class, you will find that a number of the expected built-in collection class features no longer work. For example, you cannot use a *For Each* loop, or index the collection by using the friendly key name (you will see how to get around this). The following procedure can be used to test the class; the program lines that are commented out have been included to show what will not work in our collection class:

```
Sub modTabs_clsTabPageCollection()
    ' test creating an object
    Dim TabPages As New clsTabPageCollection
    Dim aTab As clsTabPage
    Dim lngCount As Long
    Set aTab = New clsTabPage
    aTab.PageName = "ProductList"
    aTab.RelatedPageName = "Product Details"
    aTab.SubFormPageName = "frmTabsDynamicProductList"
    aTab.CanBeUnloaded = False
    TabPages.Add aTab
    Set aTab = Nothing

    Set aTab = New clsTabPage
    aTab.PageName = "Product Details"
    aTab.RelatedPageName = ""
    aTab.SubFormPageName = "frmTabsDynamicProductDetails"
    aTab.CanBeUnloaded = True
    TabPages.Add aTab
    Set aTab = Nothing

'   For Each aTab In TabPages
'       Debug.Print aTab.PageName, aTab.SubFormPageName, _
'               aTab.RelatedPageName, aTab.CanBeUnloaded
'   Next
    For lngCount = 1 To TabPages.Count
        Set aTab = TabPages.Item(lngCount)
        Debug.Print aTab.PageName, aTab.SubFormPageName, _
                aTab.RelatedPageName, aTab.CanBeUnloaded
    Next
    Set aTab = Nothing
'   Set aTab = TabPages("ProductList")

    ' following will work
    Set aTab = TabPages.Item(1)
    Debug.Print TabPages.Item(1).PageName
    Debug.Print aTab.PageName
    Set aTab = Nothing
    Set TabPages = Nothing
End Sub
```

There are two techniques available to get around the problem of not being able to refer to the collection class by using the key names. The first technique involves adding an *AllItems* function to the collection class, and the second method involves exporting, editing, and re-importing the class.

INSIDE OUT   Adding *AllItems* to a collection class

When you use the *AllItems* method, you need to add the following property to the class (you can give this property an alternative name):

```
Public Function AllItems() As Collection
    Set AllItems = p_TabPages
End Function
```

In the sample testing file, modTabs_clsTabPageCollection2, you can see how to use this feature. The important code is as follows:

```
' works with allitems
For Each aTab In TabPages.AllItems
    Debug.Print aTab.PageName, aTab.SubFormPageName, _
        aTab.RelatedPageName, aTab.CanBeUnloaded
Next
Set aTab = TabPages.AllItems("ProductList")
Debug.Print aTab.PageName
Debug.Print TabPages.AllItems("ProductList").PageName
```

This is a satisfactory solution as long as you are prepared to insert the *.AllItems* reference when using the collection with the object's key.

Exporting and Re-importing the Class

The reason that you cannot refer to collections by using standard syntax is because VBA classes do not allow special attributes to be set on a class, and these are required to support standard syntax.

If you right-click the collection class module in the project window, export it to a text file, and then open the text file in notepad, you will see the following header information in the class:

```
VERSION 1.0 CLASS
BEGIN
  MultiUse = -1  'True
END
Attribute VB_Name = "clsTabPageCollection"
Attribute VB_GlobalNameSpace = False
Attribute VB_Creatable = False
Attribute VB_PredeclaredId = False
Attribute VB_Exposed = False
Option Compare Database
Option Explicit
' class clsTabPagesCollection
Private p_TabPages As Collection
```

These attributes are not exposed in the VBA environment. There is a special attribute value, which when set to 0, sets the member as the default member for the object. You want the *Item* method to be the default member and you need to change the method adding the following attribute definition (this will enable references such as *TabPages("ProductList")* to work). Also, to support enumeration in a *For ... Each* loop, you need to add the *NewEnum* method, as shown in the following:

```
Public Function Item(ByVal Index As Variant) As clsTabPage
Attribute Item.VB_UserMemId = 0
        Set Item = p_TabPages(Index)
End Function

Public Function NewEnum() As IUnknown
Attribute NewEnum.VB_UserMemId = -4
        Set NewEnum = p_TabPages.[_NewEnum]
End Function
```

After saving these changes, import the class back into your project, as shown in Figure 9-3.

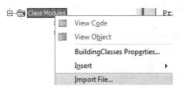

Figure 9-3 Re-importing a class back into Access.

If you look in the VBA Editor, you will not be able to see the new attribute you just added in the *Item* method because it remains hidden.

This then means that the following references will work (note that in the sample database BuildingClassesAfterExportImport.accdb, the following code will work, because we have performed this rather complex operation; in the sample database BuildingClasses.accdb, this code has been commented out because it will not work):

```
For Each aTab In TabPages
    Debug.Print aTab.PageName, aTab.SubFormPageName, _
        aTab.RelatedPageName, aTab.CanBeUnloaded
Next
Set aTab = TabPages("ProductList")
Debug.Print TabPages("ProductList").PageName
Debug.Print aTab.PageName
```

This process needs to be repeated for each collection class in your project.

Using Classes with the Dynamic Tab

You are now able to modify the code in the *frmTabsDynamic* form to make use of your new classes.

At the top of the module, where you had defined an array of types, declare your collection class as shown here:

```
Option Compare Database
Option Explicit
Dim TabPages As clsTabPageCollection
Dim lngTabPages As Long
```

The form's *Open* and *Close* events then create and dispose of the collection, as shown in the following:

```
Private Sub Form_Close()
    Set TabPages = Nothing
End Sub

Private Sub Form_Open(Cancel As Integer)
    Set TabPages = New clsTabPageCollection
    LoadTabs
End Sub
```

In the following code, in the *LoadTabs* procedure, you create and load your class objects into the collection:

```
    Do While Not rst.EOF
        Set aTabPage = New clsTabPage
        aTabPage.PageName = rst!PageName
        aTabPage.SubFormPageName = rst!SubFormName
        aTabPage.CanBeUnloaded = rst!CanUnloadPage
        aTabPage.RelatedPageName = Nz(rst!RelatedPage)
        TabPages.Add aTabPage
        Set aTabPage = Nothing
        If rst!DefaultVisible And lngPageVisibleCount + 1 < lngTabPages Then
            LoadThePage aTabPage, lngPageVisibleCount
            lngPageVisibleCount = lngPageVisibleCount + 1
        End If

        lngArray = lngArray + 1
        rst.MoveNext
    Loop
```

There are some other minor references in the code that used the array of types that now need to be changed to use the new collection and objects.

Simplifying the Application with Classes

In the preceding sections, you have been able to change your dynamic tab to use classes, but it has not as yet resulted in any simplification of the applications code. In fact, you now have more code to maintain than when you started. But you now have a framework in which you can start to work that will lead to simplification and improved maintenance of your code.

In examining the *frmTabsDynamic* form, you can see that it has a general routine *LoadTabs* that involves reading information and placing the information into your collection. This operation could be placed inside the collection. So we can start to enhance our collection (*clsTabPageCollection2*) by adding the data loading function. But the process of loading the information also involves setting values in controls on the form. This means you also want to allow the collection to reference the controls on the form.

To begin, add new private members to the class:

```
' class clsTabPagesCollection
Private p_TabPages As Collection
Private p_TabControl As TabControl
Private p_Controls As Controls
```

You must change the termination routine to clear the new variables and provide properties for setting the new variables, as follows:

```
Private Sub Class_Terminate()
    Dim aClassPage As clsTabPage
    For Each aClassPage In p_TabPages
        p_TabPages.Remove CStr(aClassPage.PageName)
    Next
    Set p_TabPages = Nothing
    Set p_TabControl = Nothing
End Sub
Public Property Let TabControl(ByRef TabCtl As TabControl)
    Set p_TabControl = TabCtl
End Property
Public Property Let Controls(ByRef Ctrls As Controls)
    Set p_Controls = Ctrls
End Property
```

You can then move the appropriate routines programmed into the form into the collection class.

> ## Note
> The full code for this can be seen in the sample file.

The result of this is an impressive reduction in the code on the form, which now shrinks to the following (see *frmTabsDynamic2*):

```
Option Compare Database
Option Explicit
Dim TabPages As clsTabPageCollection2
Private Sub Form_Close()
    Set TabPages = Nothing
End Sub
Private Sub Form_Open(Cancel As Integer)
    Set TabPages = New clsTabPageCollection2
    TabPages.TabControl = Me.TabCtl0
    TabPages.Controls = Me.Controls
    TabPages.LoadFromTable Me.Name, "tblTabPages"
End Sub
Private Sub TabCtl0_DblClick(Cancel As Integer)
    TabPages.TabPageDoubleClick CLng(Me.TabCtl0)
End Sub
```

Although the total amount of code remains unchanged, much of the code has moved out of the form and into the classes. There are a couple of advantages to creating classes to perform these operations:

- The code on the form is significantly simplified; it will be easy to add it to other forms or in other applications.

- The new classes are easy and intuitive to work with, so using them in the future should improve your applications, and you can add more features to these classes.

Some might argue that rather than using classes, which involves constructing a framework, you could more simply have built a re-useable library. This line of argument nearly always holds; thus, the decision to use classes becomes a question of whether it seems more intuitive and natural than using a traditional code module.

INSIDE OUT   Classes and associated terminology

Another term for creating an object is *instantiating* the class object. This means using the *New* keyword to create the class object.

The term *Encapsulation* is often used to convey the idea of tucking away all the functionality inside the class, such that the class only exposes as small a public interface as required to fulfill its purpose. With a class, you are wrapping up all the messy code and placing that inside a box so that you don't need to deal with it on a regular basis.

Chapter 9

Creating a Hierarchy of Classes

In this example, you look at creating a hierarchy of classes, which demonstrates the ability of classes to be used as building blocks for improving the design in managing data objects. The example involves a business problem for which the classes need to perform complex calculations (although you will stick to simple calculations in the example).

Suppose that you have analyzed an insurance company's business, the result of which revealed that the company sells a large number of different insurance products, but you noticed that there are common features in the products. Often, one type of policy only differs from another in a small number of ways. The task is to build an Access application that assists with generating the policy documents and performing appropriate calculations for the different policies.

Creating a Base Class

The first task is to identify common features to all policies as well as the most standard calculations that a policy would require to perform. This involves creating a class, which will serve as the base class. In the following code, this is called *clsPolicy*.

From the project window in the VBA Editor, create a class module, and then save the module with the name *clsPolicy*, as demonstrated in the following code:

```
Option Compare Database
Option Explicit

' clsPolicy is the base class which has common features
' required in other classes

Dim p_MonthlyPremium As Currency

Public Property Get MonthlyPremium() As Currency
    MonthlyPremium = p_MonthlyPremium
End Property

Public Property Let MonthlyPremium(ByVal MonthlyPremium As Currency)
    p_MonthlyPremium = MonthlyPremium
End Property

Public Function CalculateAnnualPolicyValue() As Currency
    CalculateAnnualPolicyValue = p_MonthlyPremium * 12
End Function
```

This class can then be tested by using the following code:

```
Sub modInsurance_Policy()
    ' create a Policy from clsPolicy
    Dim Policy As New clsPolicy
    Policy.MonthlyPremium = 10
    ' Expect 120
    Debug.Print Policy.CalculateAnnualPolicyValue()
    Set Policy = Nothing
End Sub
```

Derived Classes

With the basic insurance policy class created, you can now create several other classes that will all use some of the base class features. This involves creating a class, which will serve as the derived class, and in the following code is called *clsHomePolicy*, being derived from the base class *clsPolicy*. The term derived is used because the class is in some way related or derived from the base class:

```
Option Compare Database
Option Explicit

' clsHomePolicy uses clsPolicy
Dim p_Policy As clsPolicy

Private Sub Class_Initialize()
    Set p_Policy = New clsPolicy
End Sub
Private Sub Class_Terminate()
    Set p_Policy = Nothing
End Sub

Public Property Get MonthlyPremium() As Currency
    MonthlyPremium = p_Policy.MonthlyPremium
End Property

Public Property Let MonthlyPremium(ByVal MonthlyPremium As Currency)
    p_Policy.MonthlyPremium = MonthlyPremium
End Property

Public Function CalculateAnnualPolicyValue() As Currency
    CalculateAnnualPolicyValue = p_Policy.CalculateAnnualPolicyValue() + 50
End Function
```

The first derived class, *clsHomePolicy*, contains a base class object, *clsPolicy*, so you need to have initialization and termination events to create and dispose of the base class object.

The *clsHomePolicy* is only loosely tied to *clsPolicy*, which means that you need to add all the required properties and methods into the new class. But if you look at the *CalculateAnnual PolicyValue* method, you will see how it can take advantage of the calculation in the base class.

Chapter 9

INSIDE OUT   Inheritance and polymorphism in classes

Note that we are using the term *derived* here in a very loose manner. Many OOP languages incorporate the concept of *inheritance*, which means truly deriving classes, and they use the term *polymorphism* for how derived classes can implement variations on methods available through base classes.

VBA does *not* support direct inheritance or explicit polymorphism, but you can use the approach described here to create structures that offer some of these characteristics.

Another OOP term is *multiple inheritance*, which means inheriting from more than one base class; by embedding other classes using this technique, we can also form structures that behave in some respects like those having multiple inheritance. The techniques used here to produce a hierarchy can also be described by the term *wrapper*, where we wrap around one class for the purpose of extending or changing its functionality.

As is illustrated in the code that follows, you can now define two additional classes, one called *clsSpecialHomePolicy*, which is derived from *clsHomePolicy*, and the other, called *clsCarPolicy*, is derived from *clsPolicy* (you can view the code in the sample database):

```
Option Compare Database
Option Explicit

' clsSpecialHomePolicy
Dim p_Policy As clsHomePolicy

Private Sub Class_Initialize()
    Set p_Policy = New clsHomePolicy
End Sub
Private Sub Class_Terminate()
    Set p_Policy = Nothing
End Sub

Public Property Get MonthlyPremium() As Currency
    MonthlyPremium = p_Policy.MonthlyPremium
End Property

Public Property Let MonthlyPremium(ByVal MonthlyPremium As Currency)
    p_Policy.MonthlyPremium = MonthlyPremium
End Property

Public Function CalculateAnnualPolicyValue() As Currency
    CalculateAnnualPolicyValue = p_Policy.CalculateAnnualPolicyValue() + 100
End Function
```

These classes can be tested with the following code:

```
Sub modInsurance_Policy()
    ' create a Policy from clsPolicy
    Dim Policy As New clsPolicy
    Policy.MonthlyPremium = 10
    ' Expect 120
    Debug.Print Policy.CalculateAnnualPolicyValue()
    Set Policy = Nothing

    ' create a HomePolicy
    Dim HomePolicy As New clsHomePolicy
    HomePolicy.MonthlyPremium = 10
    ' Expect 120+50 = 170
    Debug.Print HomePolicy.CalculateAnnualPolicyValue()
    Set HomePolicy = Nothing

    ' create a SpecialHomePolicy
    Dim SpecialHomePolicy As New clsSpecialHomePolicy
    SpecialHomePolicy.MonthlyPremium = 10
    ' Expect 120+50+100 = 270
    Debug.Print SpecialHomePolicy.CalculateAnnualPolicyValue()
    Set SpecialHomePolicy = Nothing

    ' create a CarPolicy
    Dim CarPolicy As New clsCarPolicy
    CarPolicy.MonthlyPremium = 10
    ' Expect 120+80 = 200
    Debug.Print CarPolicy.CalculateAnnualPolicyValue()
    Set CarPolicy = Nothing
End Sub
```

Summary

In this chapter, you learned about classes via two examples. In the first example, you saw how a general purpose framework for working with form *Tab* controls can dynamically load subforms and be re-written using classes. The final result was simplified application code with the complexity hidden within the class.

The second example introduced techniques for building a hierarchy of classes by using a base class and several derived classes. This provides a more structured and maintainable solution when using classes.

Using Classes and Events

WithEvents Processing 360
Friend Methods 378
Abstract and Implementation Classes 370

In this chapter, you begin by looking at a process called *WithEvent* processing (also known as subclassing). You will see how to develop your own event handlers that can act upon Microsoft Access 2010 form or control events. As an example, you will develop your own *OnError* event handler, which can then be hooked into all your application's forms.

You will also learn you how to construct your own asynchronous batch processor for Microsoft SQL Server by using *RaiseEvent* and asynchronous event processing. This will illustrate another general technique of classes producing and consuming events.

Toward the end of the chapter, you will look at using abstract classes and implementation classes to provide frameworks for building classes. The chapter finishes with a look at *Friend* methods for sharing functionality between classes.

After reading this chapter, you will:

- Understand how to create classes for handling form and control events.

- Know how to use *RaiseEvent* to work with classes that produce and consume events.

- Understand abstract and implementing classes.

- Understand how to use *Friend* methods.

> **Note**
>
> As you read through this chapter, we encourage you to also use the companion content sample database, ClassesAndEvents.accdb, which can be downloaded from the book's catalog page.

WithEvents Processing

When you include the *WithEvents* statement in a class, you are indicating that the class can receive notification of events for a particular type of object. In this section, you look at applying this technique to handle events and controls for a form.

Handling Form Events

In a form's class module, you can write code against specific events, but it is also possible to define your own class for handling specific events on a form. In this example, you see how to design an error handling class that can manage the error events on a form.

To begin, create a new class module, and then save this class by using the name *clsError Handler*. At the top of the class, you use the *WithEvents* syntax to indicate that this form can handle events for a form type object, as shown in the following:

```
Option Compare Database
Option Explicit
' class clsErrorHandler designed
' to manage error events for an an Access form
Private WithEvents frm As Access.Form
```

After you have defined this, select the *frm* object inside the class module. You can now write code against any of the standard form events, as shown in Figure 10-1.

Figure 10-1 By selecting the form object *frm*, you can define the standard form events handlers within your class.

In this case, you want to write an error handler in your class that writes errors to a log table, as follows:

```
Private Sub frm_Error(DataErr As Integer, Response As Integer)
    ' Respone can be acDataErrContinue or acDataErrDisplay
    Dim strErrorMessage As String
    strErrorMessage = AccessError(DataErr)
    ' record the error
    Dim db As DAO.Database
    Dim rst As Recordset
    Set db = CurrentDb
```

```
        Set rst = db.OpenRecordset("tblErrorLog", dbOpenDynaset)
        With rst
            .AddNew
            !ErrorNo = DataErr
            !ErrorMessage = strErrorMessage
            !ErrorProc = frm.Name
            ' Also very useful to log the id of the user generating the error
            !WindowsUserName = modErrorHandler_GetUserName()
            .Update
        End With
        rst.Close
        Set rst = Nothing
        db.Close
        Set db = Nothing

        ' take an appropriate action
        If DataErr = 3200 Then
            ' replace the default error message box
            MsgBox "Unable to delete this record " & strErrorMessage, _
                   vbInformation, "Operation not Available"
            ' supress Access error message
            Response = acDataErrContinue
        End If
End Sub
```

You also need to provide a procedure that enables the class to be linked into a form. You can do this by defining a public property in the class:

```
Public Property Set Form(frmCallingForm As Access.Form)
    Set frm = frmCallingForm
End Property
```

The class is used on the sample *frmCategoriesErrorHandling* form. At the top of the form's class module, add the following definition:

```
Option Compare Database
Option Explicit

Dim instErrorHandler As clsErrorHandler
```

On the form's *Open* event, create an object of the new class, set the *Form* property for the new class to point at the current form, and then indicate that there is a processing routine for the *OnError* Event.

```
Private Sub Form_Open(Cancel As Integer)
    Set instErrorHandler = New clsErrorHandler
    Set instErrorHandler.Form = Me
    ' Assign responsibility for handling these events
    Me.OnError = "[Event Procedure]"
End Sub
```

Chapter 10

This form can be tested by clicking the record selector and pressing the Delete key while viewing the form; referential integrity will prevent the delete and trigger the error handler in your class. You will also notice that if you attempt to delete a category record when viewing the tables of data or in a form without error handling that you get a more informative error message informing you that the delete is prevented because of records in the related *Products* table. Unfortunately, when you use your own error handling for errors on a form, the returned error message only displays a "|" (vertical bar) symbol rather than showing the related table's name.

INSIDE OUT   Subclassing form events

It is possible to have additional local error handling code on the form behind the *OnError* event. In this circumstance, the local error handler executes before the code in your class module. This technique of subclassing a form's events can be used to add this error logging to all forms in an application.

Handling Control Events

You can handle events for a particular control on a form in a manner similar to handling events for a form.

You begin by creating a class module called *clsNotification* and indicating that the class will process events for a command button control:

```
Option Compare Database
Option Explicit
' clsNotification designed to handle events for
' certain a command button on a form
Private WithEvents Cmd As Access.CommandButton
```

As in the previous example, the drop-down menu of procedures in the upper-right corner now shows all the events for a command button.

This example contains a routine that logs whenever a button is clicked. You can use this to record when a user invokes specific operations with a form, as illustrated in the following code:

```
Private Sub Cmd_Click()
    Dim db As DAO.Database
    Dim rst As Recordset
    Set db = CurrentDb
    Set rst = db.OpenRecordset("tblActionLog", dbOpenDynaset)
    With rst
```

```
            .AddNew
            !CallingForm = Cmd.Parent.Name
            !Action = "Executing special code in the class for button : " & _
                    Cmd.Name
            ' Also very useful to log the id of the user
            !WindowsUserName = modErrorHandler_GetUserName()
            .Update
        End With
        rst.Close
        Set rst = Nothing
        db.Close
        Set db = Nothing
    End Sub
```

The preceding example uses the *Parent* property of the command button to gain access to properties of the calling form. A new property is required to allow a command button to be hooked in to the new class, as follows:

```
Public Property Set CmdButton(cmdCallingButton As Access.CommandButton)
    Set Cmd = cmdCallingButton
End Property
```

The sample *frmCategoriesCommandButton* form shows how this can be used:

```
Option Compare Database
Option Explicit

Dim instCmdNotify As clsNotificationButton

Private Sub Form_Close()
    Set instCmdNotify = Nothing
End Sub

Private Sub Form_Open(Cancel As Integer)
    Set instCmdNotify = New clsNotificationButton
    Set instCmdNotify.CmdButton = Me.cmdNotify
'    Set instCmdButton
    Me.cmdNotify.OnClick = "[Event Procedure]"
End Sub
```

Asynchronous Event Processing and *RaiseEvent*

This example shows how to use *WithEvent* processing to create a form and associated classes that can be used to asynchronously execute stored procedures in SQL Server by using ActiveX Data Objects (ADO). ADO and SQL Server are discussed further in later chapters.

INSIDE OUT   Producing and consuming events

With classes, a producer task can source (raise) events, and a consumer task can sink (receive) the events. You can take advantage of this by uncoupling tasks within an application and using events as a communication method between the tasks. In practice, these techniques are often used with ActiveX components to trap events raised by the external objects. In the example in this chapter, we use an ADO connection to produce events and a VBA class to consume the events.

A producing class (*clsProduced*) defines the event that it will raise and then raises the event at some point in the code, as follows:

```
Public Event ChangeText()
……
    RaiseEvent ChangeText
```

Then the consumer form or class defines a variable of the producer type, specifying the *WithEvents* option, and then declares a procedure to match that defined by the producer and combines the variable name with the event name:

```
Private WithEvents objProduced As clsProducer
…..
Private Sub objProduced_ChangeText()
…
End Sub
```

Stored Procedures

In an appropriate SQL Server database, create the following two stored procedures (Create-BatchProcedures.sql):

```
USE [AccessInsideOut]
GO

CREATE PROC usp_Proc1 @BatchLogId INT
AS
BEGIN
   -- Wait for a delay to simulate
   -- a batch running
   WAITFOR DELAY '00:00:15';
   SELECT @BatchLogId AS ReturnInfo
END
GO
```

```
CREATE PROC usp_Proc2 @BatchLogId INT
AS
BEGIN
    -- Wait for a delay to simulate
    -- a batch running
    WAITFOR DELAY '00:00:15';
    SELECT @BatchLogId AS ReturnInfo
END
GO
```

You need to created a table in Access that holds a list of the available stored procedures, as shown in Figure 10-2.

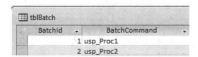

Figure 10-2 This table can be used to schedule a list of stored procedures for execution.

The ADO Asynchronous Execution Class

This example needs to use ADO because we want to be able to start a stored procedure running asynchronously. This will allow multiple stored procedures to be executed, and the user can then continue to work with the application and receive notification when the stored procedures have completed. You begin by adding a reference to the ADO library and then create the class *clsBatchProcessingSQLServer*.

At the top of the module, add the code that follows (entering appropriate information in the connection string for your SQL Server). This enables the class to manage events for an ADO *Connection* object; it also defines a public event called *BatchCompleted*, which is used for raising an event once processing is complete:

```
Option Compare Database
Option Explicit

' clsBatchProcessingSQLServer
' Performs asynchronous batch processing
' Event for notification when completed
Public Event BatchCompleted(ByVal lngBatchId As Long)

Const strConnect = "DRIVER=SQL Server;SERVER=VISTAULTRA64\SQL2008R2;" & _
                "Trusted_Connection=Yes;DATABASE=AccessInsideOut"
Dim WithEvents con As ADODB.Connection
Dim rstCollection As Collection
```

The class is constructed around the connection object but contains a collection of ADO *Recordsets*, each of which can be executing a different stored procedure. You need initialization and termination procedures to manage this internal collection. These are presented in the following code:

```
Private Sub Class_Initialize()
    Set con = New ADODB.Connection
    Set rstCollection = New Collection
    con.CursorLocation = adUseClient
    ' set an infinit timeout period
    con.CommandTimeout = 0
    ' Open the connection.
    con.Open strConnect
End Sub

Private Sub Class_Terminate()
    con.Close
    Set con = Nothing
    Dim rstADO As ADODB.Recordset
    On Error Resume Next
    For Each rstADO In rstCollection
        rstADO.Close
        Set rstADO = Nothing
    Next
    Set rstCollection = Nothing
End Sub
```

In the next step, you create a procedure that generates an ADO *Recordset* object, executes it asynchronously, and then adds it to the *Recordset* collection (this sample also includes some DAO code that writes a log of the executing stored procedures), as follows:

```
Public Sub ExecuteBatch(ByVal lngBatchId As Long, _
                        strCallingForm As String)
    ' read the batch instruction and execute the batch
    Dim db As Database
    Dim rst As Recordset
    Dim strBatchCommand As String
    Set db = CurrentDb
    Set rst = db.OpenRecordset("SELECT * FROM tblBatch " & _
                        " WHERE BatchId = " & lngBatchId, dbOpenDynaset)
    strBatchCommand = rst!BatchCommand
    rst.Close
    Set rst = db.OpenRecordset("tblBatchLog", dbOpenDynaset)
    With rst
        .AddNew
        !BatchDescription = strBatchCommand
        !CallingForm = strCallingForm
        !WindowsUserName = modErrorHandler_GetUserName()
        !BatchStartTime = Now()
```

```
           .Update
           .Bookmark = .LastModified
          strBatchCommand = strBatchCommand & " " & CStr(!BatchLogId)
           .Close
      End With

      ' Execute the batch command asynchronously
      Dim rstADO As ADODB.Recordset
      Set rstADO = New ADODB.Recordset
      rstADO.Open strBatchCommand, _
        con, adOpenKeyset, adLockOptimistic, adAsyncExecute
      rstCollection.Add rstADO, CStr(rstCollection.Count + 1)

End Sub
```

The ADO connection has an *ExecuteComplete* method, which is called when a batch asynchronously completes execution. This method updates the logged event relating to the stored procedure and then raises an event by using *RaiseEvent* to the procedure *BatchCompleted*:

```
Private Sub con_ExecuteComplete(ByVal RecordsAffected As Long, _
                                ByVal pError As ADODB.Error, _
                                adStatus As ADODB.EventStatusEnum, _
                                ByVal pCommand As ADODB.Command, _
                                ByVal pRecordset As ADODB.Recordset, _
                                ByVal pConnection As ADODB.Connection)

' This gets called when the asnychronous ADO recordset
' is completed
    Dim db As Database
    Dim rst As Recordset
    Set db = CurrentDb
    Set rst = db.OpenRecordset("SELECT * FROM tblBatchLog " & _
                     " WHERE BatchLogId = " & pRecordset(0), dbOpenDynaset)
    With rst
        .Edit
        !BatchEndTime = Now
        !BatchFailed = False
        !BatchCompleted = True
        !BatchReturnInformation = pRecordset(0)
        .Update
        .Close
    End With
    ' notify calling form that process is completed
    RaiseEvent BatchCompleted(pRecordset(0))
    Set rst = Nothing
    db.Close
    Set db = Nothing
End Sub
```

Batch Processing Form

Figure 10-3 shows the *frmBatchProcessingSQLServer* form, which is used to perform the batch processing. To execute the batches, select a batch from the drop-down menu, and then click the Execute Asynchronous Batch button. (You need to do this quite quickly because each batch is set to execute for 15 seconds.) Wait until the screen refreshes to see the completed batches.

> **Note**
> You can interact with the form and other parts of Access while batches are processing (you need to keep the form open while the batches are running).

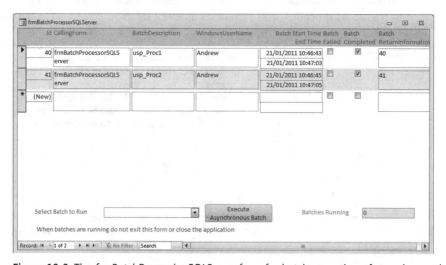

Figure 10-3 The *frmBatchProcessingSQLServer* form for batch execution of stored procedures.

At the top of the form's module, declare a *WithEvents* reference to the batch processing class, as follows:

```
Option Compare Database
Option Explicit
Private WithEvents BatchProcessor As clsBatchProcessingSQLServer
```

In the form's *Open* and *Close* events, you manage the creation and removal of the object:

```
Private Sub Form_Close()
    Set BatchProcessor = Nothing
End Sub
```

```
Private Sub Form_Open(Cancel As Integer)
    Me.txtBatchRunCount = 0
    Set BatchProcessor = New clsBatchProcessingSQLServer
End Sub
```

The code behind the Execute Asynchronous Batch button that executes the batch command is shown in the following:

```
Private Sub cmdExecute_Click()
    If Not IsNull(Me.cboBatch) Then
        ' call a batch processing routine
        Me.txtBatchRunCount = Me.txtBatchRunCount + 1
        BatchProcessor.ExecuteBatch CLng(Me.cboBatch), CStr(Me.Name)
    End If
End Sub
```

The form also has a *BatchProcessing* procedure. This was the procedure name declared in
the class; it is used by the class to raise an event on the target form:

```
Private Sub BatchProcessor_BatchCompleted(ByVal lngBatchId As Long)
    Me.txtBatchRunCount = Me.txtBatchRunCount - 1
    Me.Requery
End Sub
```

To summarize, the execution proceeds as follows (see Figure 10-4):

1. The form opens and creates a batch processing class called *BatchProcessor*; the class
    initializes a collection for the ADO *Recordset*s.

2. The form also declares that it can accept incoming events in its *BatchProcessor_
    BatchCompleted* routine.

3. The user clicks to perform the *ExecuteBatch* command, which creates and executes
    an ADO *Recordset* in the class. This is added to the class's collection of executing
    *Recordset*s.

4. The class listens for any incoming events on the *Connection*, and when it receives an
    event after an ADO *Recordset* is completed through *con_ExecuteComplete*, it notifies
    the form by using the *RaiseEvent* method.

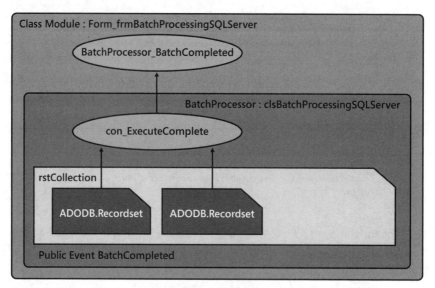

Figure 10-4 The form for batch execution of stored procedures.

Abstract and Implementation Classes

In this section, you look at an example of creating classes by using abstract and implementation classes. The example illustrates how to build classes that assist with data import and export.

Although it costs some time to correctly construct class libraries, the benefit is that once you have them built and tested, you will get a lot of use out of them. The advantage of using abstract classes is that they create a definition that you need to follow when constructing additional classes, which helps you to ensure that you add all the required features when creating new classes.

Abstract Classes

An abstract class is a template for building other classes. It contains placeholders for your subs, functions, and properties.

The functions, subs, and properties do not contain any code, because once they have been defined in the abstract class and you create a real (or concrete) class that implements the abstract class, you are forced to allow for a stub function, sub, or property to match each item in the abstract class. The derived classes then provide the code to implement the place holders defined in the abstract class. When using abstract classes you will also be using the *Implements* keyword to build classes that implement the abstract classes.

INSIDE OUT   Abstract classes and code

Although an abstract class acts to provide a template for other classes to add implementation code, it is possible to place common code inside the abstract class; to make
use of this shared code you need to create an instance of the abstract class inside an
implementation class (discussed on page 372). In general, the term abstract class means
that you do not create instances of the class, but in VBA, because an abstract class
is not a special class in terms of how it is defined, you can create an instance of an
abstract class.

An abstract class file is created in exactly the same way as any other class file.

The samples database contains a class called *clsExportImport*, which will act as an abstract
class, as demonstrated in the following (only part of the class in this and other examples
will be shown):

```
Option Compare Database
Option Explicit

' clsExportImport is an abstract class
Enum enExportType
    TextFile
    ExcelSpreadsheet
End Enum

Public Function ExportData() As Boolean
End Function

Public Function ImportData() As Boolean
End Function

Public Property Get FileName() As String
End Property

Public Property Let FileName(ByVal strNewFilename As String)
End Property
```

Notice that the class does not have any member variables; it only has place holders for the
properties and functions/subs. For the sake of convenience, the sample defines an enumerated type which is placed inside the abstract class. This will be used in the derived classes
that you will be building.

Implementation Classes

The next step is to build specific implementation classes that follow the abstract class template. You do this by using the *Implements* keyword. There are two implementation classes: one called *clsImportExportText* for handling text files, and the other called *clsImportExport-Excel* for handling spread sheets.

At the top of the file, define the member variables, as shown in the following:

```
Option Compare Database
Option Explicit
' Interface class clsImportExportText

Implements clsImportExport
' Applies to all classes
Private p_FileName As String
Private p_ExportType As enExportType
Private p_DataSource As String
Private p_HasFieldNames As Boolean
Private p_ErrorMessage As String
' Specific to this class
Private p_SpecificationName As String
```

If you select the class object as shown in Figure 10-5, you can view or create the two events associated with the class.

Figure 10-5 Adding an initialization for each class.

Because you have entered the *Implements* keyword, you can now select the abstract class name from the drop-down menu (see Figure 10-6). Items for which you already have a stub function are displayed in bold; those for which you need to add a stub function will not be bold.

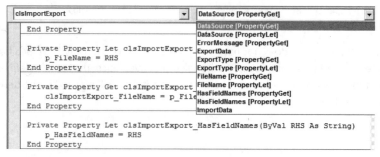

Figure 10-6 Entries must be selected for every *Let/Get* property and every function/subroutine defined in the abstract class.

One particular function in the abstract class—a stub function to *Get* the *Filename*—is defined as follows:

```
Public Property Get FileName() As String
End Property
```

When you add this to the implementing class, the following code results:

```
Private Property Get clsImportExport_FileName() As String
    clsImportExport_FileName = p_FileName
End Property
```

The line of code has been typed in and was not provided when the stub function was generated.

The *Get* property of the class defined previously is not going to be visible as a property in the derived class. This is because it is marked as private. Also, look at the name *clsImport Export_FileName*; if you made it public, it would not look like a desirable name for a property.

This is quite subtle, and it is not until you actually implement the abstract class and trace the code execution path that it becomes clear what is happening. You will also notice in the code where Access has generated stub functions for *Let* statements that the parameter is named *RHS*; this means right-hand-side, which indicates that the *Let* statement will make an assignment using this variable on the right of an expression.

Implementing an Abstract Class

What lies at the heart of implementing an abstract class is the ability to work with an object variable that references the abstract class but that can point to any of the derived classes, but have the code executed in the derived class.

So you can perform the following trick (look very carefully at the first two lines of code where the variable is of type *clsImportExport*, but you create an object with this variable of type *clsImportExportExcel*):

```
Sub modImportExport_Testing()
    Dim ExportProcess As clsImportExport
    Set ExportProcess = New clsImportExportExcel
    ExportProcess.FileName = CurrentProject.Path & "\test.xls"
    ExportProcess.DataSource = "Products"
    If ExportProcess.ExportData() Then
        Debug.Print "Export completed"
    Else
        Debug.Print ExportProcess.ErrorMessage
    End If
    Set ExportProcess = Nothing
```

Figure 10-7 presents the result of tracing through the code execution into the derived classes code and also illustrates the parameter naming *RHS*, for right-hand-side generated by Access.

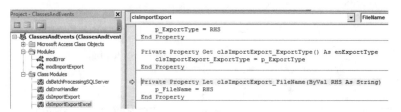

Figure 10-7 When a variable of the abstract class type is set to a derived class object, it executes the code in the derived class.

If you trace the execution in Debug mode, you find that the procedure and methods that are called are in the object type *clsImportExportExcel*; for example, this occurs when assigning the property *ExportProcess.FileName*. When you call a property with the name *FileName* (which is only defined in the abstract class), it actually executes the code in the derived class called *clsImportExport_FileName*. The abstract class exposes the property name but then hooks up the code to execute in the class that implements the abstract interface.

If you want to add a new property to your classes, you have two options. You can add a *Let* and *Get* (or for read-only, just a *Get*) to the *clsImportExport*, but if you do that, it means adding a stub procedure to all the derived classes. The second option is you can just add the new property to the derived class to which it applies.

The question becomes, what happens if you just add something in the derived class? To demonstrate, in your *clsImportExportText* class, add the following *Let* and *Get*:

```
Public Property Let SpecificationName(ByVal strSpecificationName As String)
    p_SpecificationName = strSpecificationName
End Property

Public Property Get SpecificationName() As String
    SpecificationName = p_SpecificationName
End Property
```

Now, in Debug mode, if you look at the *ExportProcess* properties, you will not see this new property. This is because it is not defined in the abstract class, so you need to create a new object variable of type *clsImportExportText* and make it point at the object. You can see an example of this in *modImportExport_Testing*, as shown in Figure 10-8.

```
      Dim EPText As clsImportExportText
      Set ExportProcess = New clsImportExportText
      Set EPText = ExportProcess
      ' EPText.SpecificationName = ""
      ExportProcess.FileName = CurrentProject.Path & "\test.txt"
```

```
mmediate

 ?EPtext.
          SpecificationName
```

Figure 10-8 This breakpoint in the Immediate window shows how you can use the extended property *SpecificationName* in the derived class.

So, you define a variable called *EPText*, which is of type *clsImportExporText*, and make it point to the object by using the following:

```
SET EPText = ExportProcess
```

You can now use the *EPText* object variable to access the extended properties defined in the derived class.

INSIDE OUT Establishing an object type with *TypeOf*

You refer to an object by using an object variable that is defined as a type matching the abstract class. The *TypeOf* statement allows you to establish the type of object being referenced through a variable defined as being of a type corresponding to the abstract class:

```
If TypeOf ExportProcess Is clsImportExportExcel Then
    Debug.Print "Special processing for the object"
End If
```

If you then want to use features specific to that class, you need to use the variable type matching that of the implementing class.

What you have achieved in the sample code thus far is referred to in many programming languages as type casting of pointers; here you have done this through the features of VBA abstract classes.

You now have a property in the implementing class called *clsImportExport_ImportData()*, which is not exposed, and in the abstract class is called *ImportData()*. At first glance, this appears to be a problem, but it is not, because when you call the method with a pointer to an abstract class type (having created an implementing class for this object), it executes the code in the implementing class. This is a clever feature of abstract classes.

Chapter 10

If you need to explicitly expose the properties and methods in the abstract class when working with a variable referencing the implementing class, you can use the following technique to define a *Public Function* in the implementing class:

```
Private Function clsImportExport_ImportData() As Boolean
    On Error Resume Next
    DoCmd.TransferText acImportDelim, p_DataSource, p_FileName, p_HasFieldNames
    If Err = 0 Then
        clsImportExport_ImportData = True
    Else
        p_ErrorMessage = Err.Description
        clsImportExport_ImportData = False
    End If
End Function

Public Function ImportData() As Boolean
    ImportData = clsImportExport_ImportData()
End Function
```

Using the previously described approach, you can hold and execute common code from within an abstract class; this extends the idea of an abstract class acting as a placeholder, to contain executable code.

We wish to be clear about one point: a variable defined of type matching the abstract class type needs to be used when manipulating the properties defined in the abstract class, but a variable matching the type of the implementing class needs to be used when referring to features defined in the implementing class, but not in the abstract class.

Hybrid Abstract and Non-Abstract Classes

Purists will state outright that VBA fails to meet the accepted definitions of polymorphism and inheritance expected of object-oriented languages, and even though that is true, VBA does have some very clever features, such as using *WithEvents*, that go beyond the basic object-oriented definitions.

Although defining member variables and writing code in the abstract class is permitted, it does not appear to be a useful idea, because you cannot use these variables, or any code written in the abstract class (because an abstract class is a template). But you can add to a derived class a reference to an instance of the abstract class by using a form of wrapper around the abstract class. This might be a poor man's version of inheritance, but it does lead to some interesting possibilities.

It is possible to mix and match features from abstract and non-abstract classes when implementing an interface.

To show how this works, we have created a new base class called *clsImportExport2*. In this class, we have added a member variable *p_FileName* and changed the *Let/Get* to use this private member variable. This is now a hybrid class in that it is part concrete and part abstract:

```
Option Compare Database
Option Explicit

' clsImportExport2 is both abstract and non-abstract class

Private p_FileName As String
Public Property Get FileName() As String
    FileName = p_FileName
End Property

Public Property Let FileName(ByVal strNewFilename As String)
    p_FileName = strNewFilename
End Property
```

In the new derived class called *clsImportExportText2*, you need to create an instance of the abstract class (you are both wrapping the class and implementing the class at the same time), as follows:

```
Option Compare Database
Option Explicit

Implements clsImportExport2
' Applies to all classes
Private p_clsImportExport As clsImportExport2
Private p_ExportType As enExportType
Private p_DataSource As String
Private p_HasFieldNames As Boolean
Private p_ErrorMessage As String
' Specific to this class
Private p_SpecificationName As String

Private Sub Class_Initialize()
    p_ExportType = TextFile
    p_clsImportExport = New clsImportExport2
End Sub
Private Sub Class_Terminate()
    Set p_clsImportExport = Nothing
End Sub
```

Because you are implementing this abstract class, you still need the appropriate entries for the *FileName Let/Get*, but you now call the code in the base/abstract class from the derived class:

```
Private Property Let clsImportExport2_FileName(ByVal RHS As String)
    p_clsImportExport.FileName = RHS
End Property

Private Property Get clsImportExport2_FileName() As String
    clsImportExport2_FileName = p_clsImportExport.FileName
End Property
```

Friend Methods

When you develop a class, you invest a lot of time and effort constructing the class. And as you have seen, everything except the very essential elements that you need are private to a class. But if you devise a very useful private internal function in a class and then decide another class that wraps around this class needs to dig into its structure and use the internal function, then there is a method for doing this, and it involves the use of the *Friend* keyword.

Inside the *class clsImportExportText*, there is an internal function called *ExtractFileName*, which extracts the file name from *p_FileName* (which includes the path and file name). If you create a new class called *clsDemoFriend* that wants to use this function, but you don't want to simply expose this as a property of the class, then you define the function by using the *Friend* keyword. The following code iilustrates a modified definition of the function in the class *clsImportExportText*:

```
Friend Function ExtractFileName(FullPathName As String) As String
    ' This private function extracts the filename from
    ' FullPathName which looks like C:\...\...\xxx.txt
    ' returning xxx.txt
    Dim lngpos As Long
    Dim strRev As String
    strRev = StrReverse(FullPathName) ' reverse the string
    lngpos = InStr(1, strRev, "\") ' find last \
    If lngpos <> 0 Then
        ExtractFileName = Left(strRev, lngpos - 1)
    Else
        ExtractFileName = p_FileName
    End If
    ExtractFileName = StrReverse(ExtractFileName)
End Function
```

In the new class *clsDemoFriend*, you can work with *ExtractFileName*, which is the internal part of *clsImportExportText*. To do this, you need to create an instance of the object that contains the *Friend* function in the class, as follows:

```
Option Compare Database
Option Explicit

' example class using a friend function
Dim p_clsImportExportText As clsImportExportText
Private Sub Class_Initialize()
    Set p_clsImportExportText = New clsImportExportText
End Sub
Private Sub Class_Terminate()
    Set p_clsImportExportText = Nothing
End Sub

Public Property Get GetTheFileName(FullPathName As String) As Variant
    GetTheFileName = p_clsImportExportText.ExtractFileName(FullPathName)
End Property
```

This new class is then able to make a reference to the *ExtractFileName()* function, which is contained in *clsImportExportText*. The only reason that you are creating an instance of *clsImportExportText* is so that you can make use of the *Friend* function in that class. This is demonstrated in the procedure *modFriend_Test*.

Summary

In this chapter, you saw how we can use the *WithEvents* keyword to develop your own classes, which can provide general purpose event handling procedures to handle events in forms and for controls on forms, by using a process known as subclassing.

Techniques were also demonstrated for using the *RaiseEvent* keyword to generate events that can then be processed by other classes. In the example, a class generated events that were then processed by a form's class module.

You also saw how to construct an abstract class that acts as a template for creating other classes, which used the *Implements* keyword. In this case, these classes can be called derived classes.

The hybrid nature of classes was then demonstrated where we had a derived class which also wrapped around an instance of the abstract class (in which case, the abstract class then behaves as both a non-abstract class and abstract class).

Finally, you were introduced to the *Friend* keyword, which allows a class to borrow features from another class, where these features are not normally exposed as part of the class.

Chapter 10

Using Classes and Forms

Opening Multiple Instances of a Form 381

ActiveX Controls and Events 386

Classes and Binding Forms 383

T HIS chapter focuses on working with classes and Microsoft Access forms. You also look at using classes to open multiple copies of the same form.

After reading this chapter, you will:

- Be able to open multiple copies of the same form in an application.

- Use classes to manage the *RecordSource* of a form.

- Understand how to work with ActiveX controls and a form.

> **Note**
>
> As you read through this chapter, we encourage you to also use the companion content sample database, ClassesAndForms.accdb, which can be downloaded from the book's catalog page.

Opening Multiple Instances of a Form

You can use programming code and classes to open multiple instances of the same form in the application, as shown in Figure 11-1.

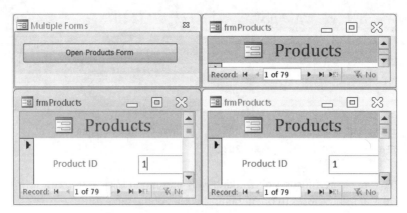

Figure 11-1 Opening multiple copies of the same form by using VBA code.

To open multiple instances of a form, you first need to ensure that the form has a code module. When you first create a form, it does not have a code module associated with it; to generate a code module, you need to view the code behind for the form, or set the form's *HasModule* property to *Yes*.

The sample database contains two forms, *frmProducts*, which has the code module *Form_frmProducts*, and *frmMultipleProducts*, which can open multiple instances of a form. To open an instance of a form, all that is required is a form variable, but to open multiple instances, you need multiple form variables, or alternatively, a collection that can hold the references to the forms, as displayed in the following:

```
Option Compare Database
Option Explicit
Dim colForms As New Collection

Private Sub cmdBrowse_Click()
    Dim frm As Form_frmProducts
    Set frm = New Form_frmProducts
    colForms.Add frm, CStr(CLng(Rnd * (2 ^ 31)))
    frm.Visible = True
End Sub

Private Sub Form_Close()
    Dim frm As Form_frmProducts
    For Each frm In colForms
        Set frm = Nothing
    Next
End Sub
```

Open multiple copies of the form and then look inside the forms collection. In the Immediate window, you see the following:

```
?Forms(0).Name
frmMultipleProducts
?Forms(1).Name
frmProducts
?Forms(2).Name
frmProducts
```

INSIDE OUT   Making references in code to multiple forms

In the preceding example, the syntax *Forms!frmProducts.Requery* is not supported. In this circumstance, you either need to use the numerical index into the forms collection—for example, *Forms(2).Requery*—or use your own form variable.

Classes and Binding Forms

Some developers choose to bind the *Recordset* displayed in a form by using program code. The simplest way to do this is to set the forms *Recordset* property to a *Recordset* that you have created when the form opens.

Binding a Form to a Data Access Object *Recordset*

The first example uses the sample form *frmProductsBoundToAClassDAO* to bind the forms *Recordset* to a Data Access Object (DAO) *Recordset*. You begin by defining the following *clsProductDataDAO* class:

```
Option Compare Database
Option Explicit

' clsProductDataDAO
' a class which will be bound to a form
Dim p_db As Database
Dim p_rst As RecordSet

Private Sub Class_Initialize()
    Set p_db = CurrentDb
    Set p_rst = p_db.OpenRecordset("Products", dbOpenDynaset)
End Sub
```

```
Private Sub Class_Terminate()
    p_rst.Close
    Set p_rst = Nothing
    p_db.Close
    Set p_db = Nothing
End Sub

Public Property Get RecordSet() As RecordSet
    Set RecordSet = p_rst
End Property
```

On the form's *Open* event, you create the new *Recordset*, and then you change the form's *Recordset* property to associate it with the new *Recordset*. On the form's *Close* event, dispose of the *Recordset*. The following code demonstrates how to do this:

```
Option Compare Database
Option Explicit
Dim Productdata As clsProductDataDAO

Private Sub Form_Open(Cancel As Integer)
    Set Productdata = New clsProductDataDAO
    Set Me.RecordSet = Productdata.RecordSet
End Sub
Private Sub Form_Unload(Cancel As Integer)
    Set Productdata = Nothing
End Sub
```

Binding a Form to an Active Data Object *Recordset*

It is also possible to bind a form to an ActiveX Data Objects (ADO) *Recordset*. To do this, you first need to add the appropriate ADO references to your project. This is shown in the sample form *frmProductsBoundToAClassADO*. To begin, you create the *clsProductDataADO* class, as follows:

```
Option Compare Database
Option Explicit

' clsProductDataADO
' a class which will be bound to a form
Dim p_cn As ADODB.Connection
Dim p_rst As ADODB.RecordSet

Private Sub Class_Initialize()
    Set p_cn = CurrentProject.Connection
    Set p_rst = New ADODB.RecordSet
```

```
    With p_rst
        Set .ActiveConnection = p_cn
        .Source = "SELECT * FROM Products"
        .LockType = adLockOptimistic
        .CursorType = adOpenKeyset
        .CursorLocation = adUseClient
        .Open
    End With
End Sub

Private Sub Class_Terminate()
    p_rst.Close
    Set p_rst = Nothing
    p_cn.Close
    Set p_cn = Nothing
End Sub


Public Property Get RecordSet() As ADODB.RecordSet
    Set RecordSet = p_rst
End Property
```

Next, add the following code to the form, which is almost identical to the code you used for the previous example:

```
Option Compare Database
Option Explicit
Dim Productdata As clsProductDataADO

Private Sub Form_Open(Cancel As Integer)
    Set Productdata = New clsProductDataADO
    Set Me.RecordSet = Productdata.RecordSet
End Sub

Private Sub Form_Unload(Cancel As Integer)
    Set Productdata = Nothing
End Sub
```

INSIDE OUT   *Connection* and *ActiveConnection*

In the example, we based our ADO *Recordset* on the *CurrentProject.Connection* (which uses Microsoft.ACE.OLEDB.12.0). If we had used *CurrentProject.AccessConnection* (which uses Microsoft.Access.OLEDB.10.0), then once bound to the form, the form data can no longer be updated. When you work with ADO, if problems occur, it will help your troubleshooting efforts to determine which of these options is being used.

ActiveX Controls and Events

Using ActiveX controls, you can add extra functionality to your application forms and reports. These controls are available from both Microsoft and other companies (note that not all ActiveX controls will work correctly with Access). You should consult any third-party documentation regarding details for using specific controls. In this section, you will see two examples of popular controls.

For an example that demonstrates how to work with the *TreeView* control, see Chapter 7, "Using Form Controls and Events."

INSIDE OUT   ActiveX on 64-bit computers

If you are using the 64-bit version of Microsoft Office, you will not be able to use these 32-bit controls; 64-bit versions of these controls are not available. Both of these points might change in later Service Packs.

Adding a *Slider* Control

With the *Slider* control, a user can move a slider to change a value. To add the control, start with a blank form. In Form design, on the Design tab, click ActiveX Controls, as shown in Figure 11-2.

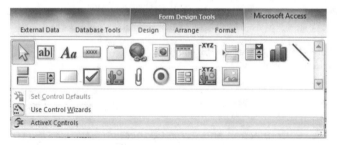

Figure 11-2 Click ActiveX Controls on the Design tab to add an ActiveX control to a form.

In the Insert ActiveX Control window, click the *Slider* control, as shown in Figure 11-3.

Figure 11-3 Adding an ActiveX control to the form.

Figure 11-4 shows the slider control in the sample form *frmSliderControl*.

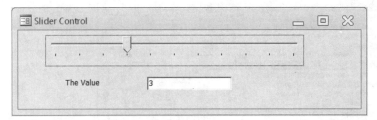

Figure 11-4 A form with a *Slider* control.

To detect where a user has positioned the slider, you need to capture an event from the slider object. If you look in the references, you might see an entry for the Windows Common Controls. If it is present, then select the reference; if you do not see the reference, you will need to browse to locate the file MSCOMCTL.OCX, as shown in Figure 11-5.

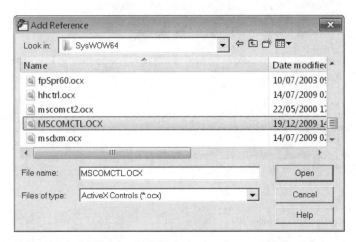

Figure 11-5 Adding the OCX file to create the entry in the references when you do not already have the reference on a 64-bit operating system.

Figure 11-6 shows that for a 64-bit system, the file resides in the SysWOW64 directory.

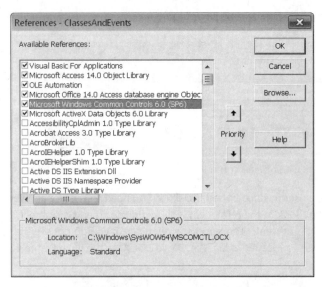

Figure 11-6 Windows Common Controls 6.0 reference.

After adding the reference, you can write the following code on the form to respond to the *Scroll* event for the slider control:

```
Option Compare Database
' Add references to Microsoft Windows Common Controls
Private WithEvents SliderObject As Slider

Private Sub Form_Load()
    Set SliderObject = actSlider.Object
End Sub

Private Sub Form_Unload(Cancel As Integer)
    Set SliderObject = Nothing
End Sub

Private Sub SliderObject_Scroll()
    txtValue = SliderObject.Value
End Sub
```

The *UpDown* or *Spin* Control

The *UpDown* or *Spin* control consists of two buttons that are used to increase or decrease a number. This control is normally used with a text box to display the value. In Form design, on the Design tab, click ActiveX Controls to display the Insert ActiveX Control window, and then choose the control, as shown in Figure 11-7.

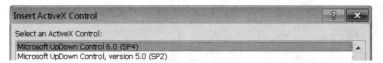

Figure 11-7 Inserting the *UpDown* ActiveX control on the form.

Figure 11-8 shows the *Spin* control in the sample form *frmUpDownButton*.

Figure 11-8 A form demonstrating the *Spin* control; the spin control buttons are next to a text box that displays the value.

You want to trap events generated by the buttons, so you need to add a reference to the Windows Common Controls-2. If you do not have this reference (it should already be added when you place the control on the form), then you need to browse and locate the file mscomct2.ocx, as shown in Figure 11-9.

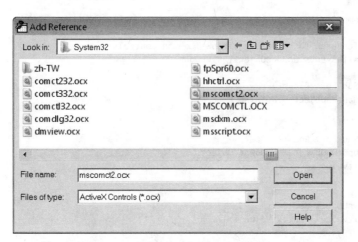

Figure 11-9 Adding the reference to mscomct2.ocx for the spin control.

On a 64-bit system, the file resides in the SysWOW64 directory as illustrated in Figure 11-10.

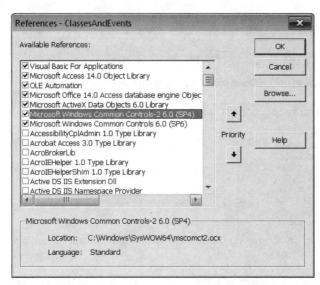

Figure 11-10 Windows Common Controls-2 reference for the spin control.

After adding the reference, you can write the following code on the form to respond to these *UpDown* events when a user clicks one of the spin buttons:

```
Option Compare Database

' Add references to Microsoft Windows Common Controls
Private WithEvents UpDownObject As UpDown

Private Sub Form_Close()
    Set UpDownObject = Nothing
End Sub

Private Sub Form_Load()
    Set UpDownObject = UpDown4.Object
    Me.txtValue = 0
End Sub

Sub UpDownObject_UpClick()
    Me.txtValue = Me.txtValue + 1
End Sub

Sub UpDownObject_DownClick()
    Me.txtValue = Me.txtValue - 1
End Sub
```

Summary

In this chapter, you saw how you can use VBA code to open multiple copies of a form at the same time. You also saw how to enhance your forms by adding the *Slider* and *UpDown* and *Spin* button controls.

PART 5

External Data and Office Integration

CHAPTER 12
Linking Access Tables 395

CHAPTER 13
Integrating Microsoft Office 437

CHAPTER 12

Linking Access Tables

Linking Access to Access 396

Linking to Excel and Text Files 406

Linking to SQL Server 407

Linking to SQL Azure 420

Linking to SharePoint Lists 426

Linking Access Web Databases 430

Microsoft Access 2010 has extensive features for connecting an Access database to different sources of data; this means that you can exploit the productivity with which applications can be constructed by using the product even when the data is not being held inside Access.

In this chapter, you will see how to connect an Access database to different sources of data and how to use Microsoft VBA to relink the database when you need to use an alternative data source. The most compelling reason to automatically relink a database is to undertake development work in a system that is not connected to live data, and then switch a live system over to a new application once the changes have been tested (although Access has the ability to import new and altered design objects, this approach is not always ideal and can involve more testing).

You begin by looking at the Access to Access link, in which one database contains the data and the other database contains the application. Then, you will look at extending this to linking to data in Microsoft Excel and text files. As Microsoft SQL Server is an extremely popular data source, you will be looking at how to link and relink SQL Server tables, and how this is extended to relink views. You will also look at how this approach is modified to handle Microsoft SQL Azure. The final sections deal with relinking to Microsoft SharePoint lists, and Access Web Databases, which use Access Data Services.

As you proceed through the chapter, you will be building a generic relinking utility, which will demonstrate the different requirements when linking to a variety of data sources.

After reading this chapter, you will:

- Understand how and why Access databases are often split into a front and back end.

- Be able to relink Access databases to other sources of data.

> **Note**
>
> As you read through this chapter, we encourage you to also use the companion content sample databases, Sample_fe.accdb, Orders_be.accdb, Employees_be.accdb, NorthwindAzure.accdb, WebDatabase.accdb, instnwnd.sql, and instnwndtesting.sql, which you can download from the book's catalog page.

Linking Access to Access

Access databases can start life as a single database file that contains all the application forms, reports, and so on, together with the tables that hold the data. For a small single user database, this might be all that is required. But once you have a number of users on an application, it is no longer possible to work on the design while others are sharing the database (unless you are working with a web database, where design changes are managed through a synchronization process). For this reason, and also because you will want to test new changes before changing to use a new version of your application, having the database split into a back-end file that holds the data, and a front-end file that holds the application is an important step in supporting your development.

Once you split a database, the front-end contains links to the tables, which now reside in the back-end, and to make design changes in the tables, you need to open the back-end database when it is not in use (you can also write Data Access Object (DAO) code to apply the design changes to the back-end from another front-end, but that is not what most people choose to do).

There are many other good reasons for having a database split. Among them, it can improve management of systems by allowing you to build multiple application files and multiple back-end data files. One restriction with multiple back-end databases is that you cannot implement referential integrity between tables in different database files.

Another reason for splitting the database is that you can consider giving each user a separate copy of the front-end database file. This copy can then be located on each user's local computer to improve network performance, or it can be held on a personal area of the network. Another advantage of giving users separate application files is that it can improve robustness against corruption; if one user's application becomes corrupt, it does not stop others from using the system. The only disadvantage to doing this is that you will need a mechanism for distributing a new copy of the application to each user whenever it changes or upgrades occur. This can be achieved by using either a simple batch file to copy the files, or possibly using more ingenious ideas such as having local and shared tables that contain version numbers, which can be checked when the application starts (there are also third-party products for assisting in distributing front-end files to users).

One final reason for using multiple front-end copies of the application is that the application can more easily contain local tables for each user. This overcomes the limitation in Access to holding distinct temporary results tables for each user. For example, imported data can be held temporarily in a table called *tblTEMP*, if more than one user attempted this operation at the same time, then you would need to distinguish each user's dataset; to do that, you could add a *UserName* column to the table, and then use a function like *Environ("USERNAME")* to populate this column and thus separate each user's data. If you are regularly allowing users to import large amounts of data into local temporary tables, you can also suffer from the bloating effect by which the Access front-end continues to grow in size over a period of time; giving each user a separate front-end simplifies overcoming this problem for a user.

INSIDE OUT   Temporary tables and SQL Server

A useful feature in SQL Server is the ability to hold results in temporary tables that can have the same name for all users, for example *#TempResults*. These tables are then unique in each database connection. This means that SQL Server has an easily used capability to work around a very common problem suffered when working solely in Access.

Using the Database Splitter

Many developers start with two databases, but if you are starting with only one database and you want to split it into data files and an application file, Access has a built-in tool for doing this. The database splitter is available by going to Database Tools | Move Data | Access Database, as shown in Figure 12-1.

Figure 12-1 Splitting a database into separate application (front-end) and data (back-end) files. For example, a database called *Orders* becomes *Orders_be* and *Orders_fe*.

Linked Table Manager

Once you have split a database, the database name and file path is hardcoded into the linked tables. This can cause problems if you decide to rename the back-end database or move the file to a different path. To help you to resolve problems like this, Access has a tool called the Linked Table Manager, with which you can redirect the linked tables to a new database name and location.

To access the Linked Table Manager, go to External Data | Import & Link | Linked Table Manager. A menu appears from which you can select and refresh any combination of links (see Figure 12-2). If you have moved the table, you are prompted to browse to the new location. You can also select the Always Prompt For New Location check box to force the selection of the new file location (this is very useful when you need to redirect to a test system, but the live system is still available on the network).

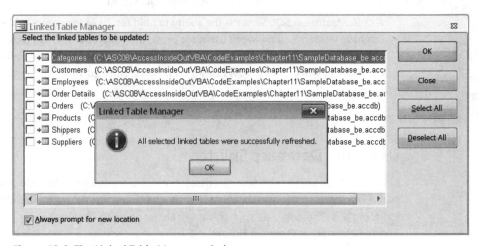

Figure 12-2 The Linked Table Manager window.

If you have, for example, 100 links pointing at several different data sources, you would soon find that the Linked Table Manager can be difficult to use for refreshing the links; this can be overcome with some VBA programming for automatically relinking tables.

Automating Relinking

It is worth taking the time to construct a general purpose relinker, which you can then use throughout your applications to perform relinking tasks. The sample database *Sample_fe.accdb* contains an example of a relinker. A description of this is provided in the following section.

The relinker uses three tables; each table name is prefixed with the letter z to distinguish them from the application tables, group them together, and sort them at the end of the list of tables. The first table, *ztblLinkedDataSources*, records the different data sources you will use. If you link to four other Access databases, you would have four data sources. There are three important columns in this table which relate to the target environment called ProductionPath, TestPath, and DevPath, as shown in Figure 12-3. These allow the application to be quickly switched between different environments.

DataSourceId	ProductionPath	TestPath	DevPath	ObjectName	SourceType
9	C:\ASC08\AccessInsideOutVBA\	C:\ASC08\Acces	C:\ASC08\Acces	Orders_be.accdb	Access
10	C:\ASC08\AccessInsideOutVBA\	C:\ASC08\Acces	C:\ASC08\Acces	Customers.xlsx	Excel
11	C:\ASC08\AccessInsideOutVBA\	C:\ASC08\Acces	C:\ASC08\Acces	Customers.txt	Text
12	C:\ASC08\AccessInsideOutVBA\	C:\ASC08\Acces	C:\ASC08\Acces	Employees_be.accdb	Access

Record: 1 of 4   No Filter   Search

Figure 12-3 Planning for production, test, and development environments by recording different paths for each data source.

The second table is *ztblLinkedSystem*, which contains only one row that records to which environment the system is currently linked, as shown in Figure 12-4.

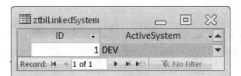

ID	ActiveSystem
1	DEV

Record: 1 of 1   No Filter

Figure 12-4 A table recording the currently linked environment.

The third table, shown in Figure 12-5, is the *ztblLinkedTables*. This table has a number of fields for recording when new links are added, deleted, or refreshed, which is useful for determining if links fail to refresh; for example, if a table no longer exists, or cannot be relinked for some other reason.

LinkId	LinkedTableName	LinkedSourceTableName	LinkFailed	LinkDeleted	LinkAdded	LinkRefreshec
36	Categories	Categories				✓
37	Customers	Customers				✓
38	Customers_Excel	Customers$				✓
39	Customers_LinkCopy	Customers				✓
40	Customers_Txt	Customers.txt				✓
41	Employees	Employees				✓

Record: 1 of 11   No Filter   Search

Figure 12-5 This example shows that several tables links were recently refreshed.

INSIDE OUT
Essential details for relinking a table

The idea behind relinking a table is quite simple: each *TableDef* has a *Connect* property that is either an empty string for a local table or contains a connection string that varies for different data sources. The following code is a very simple example of relinking a single set of linked tables:

```
Sub modLinks_VerySimpleRelink()
    ' Lists the connection strings for all linked tables.
    ' ;DATABASE=C:\....\Orders_be.accdb
    Dim tdef As TableDef
    Dim strNew As String
    strNew = ";DATABASE=C:\path\Orders_be.accdb"
    For Each tdef In CurrentDb.TableDefs
        If Left(tdef.Connect, Len(";DATABASE=")) = ";DATABASE=" Then
            If InStr(tdef.Connect, "Orders_be.accdb") Then
                Debug.Print tdef.Name, tdef.Connect
                tdef.Connect = strNew
                tdef.RefreshLink
            End If
        End If
    Next
End Sub
```

To relink a table, you assign the new *Connect* property to the new connection string and execute the *Refresh* method on the *TableDef* object.

As discussed previously, a relinker can be very simple; all you need to do is run through the *TableDefs* collection and change the *Connect* property. However, if things go wrong and relinking fails, then it is useful to have planned to record failures, show any new objects that were added, and flag objects that have been deleted since the relinker was last run.

The *ztblLinkedTableReLinker* form operates the relinker. The first time that you use this in an application, press the Clear Data button to delete all the data in the tables used for managing the relinking. Then press the Relink To DEV System, Relink To TEST System, or Relink To PRODUCTION System buttons to automatically populate the data sources and linked tables, as shown in Figure 12-6.

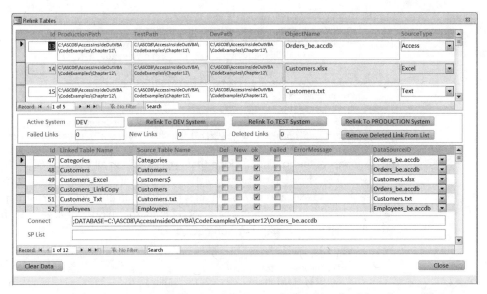

Figure 12-6 After first use, the Production/Test/Dev paths can be edited to point to different environments and the appropriate relinking button used to relink the application.

As mentioned earlier, the relinker consists of three tables, one form and two subforms. In addition, it also has a module called *modLinks*. This set of objects can then be imported into any application to add relinking functionality.

The key function responsible for the relinking is *modLinks_Tables*. The module *modLinks* starts by defining an enumerated type that has the values of *dev*, *test* and *production*; the use of an enumerated type is a convenient choice of programming style to make in this situation, as demonstrated in the following:

```
Enum SystemType
    dev
    test
    Production
End Enum
```

The first part of the function prepares a *RecordSet rst* for managing the links, and a *RecordSet rstds* for managing the data sources, and then clears the flags indicating the status of each link, as shown here:

```
Function modLinks_Tables(System As SystemType) As Boolean
    Dim lngDataSourceId As Long
    Dim db As Database
    Dim tdef As TableDef
    Dim rst As Recordset
    Dim rstds As Recordset
    Dim strTableName As String
```

```
Dim blSourceMatched As Boolean
' Flag any existing links as possibly deleted
CurrentDb.Execute "UPDATE ztblLinkedTables SET " & _
                  "LinkDeleted = True, ErrorMessage = Null, " & _
                  "LinkRefreshed = False, LinkAdded = False, LinkFailed = False"
' search through the tabledefs collection
' updating the links
Set db = CurrentDb
Set rst = db.OpenRecordset("ztblLinkedTables", dbOpenDynaset)
Set rstds = db.OpenRecordset("ztblLinkedDataSources", dbOpenDynaset)
```

The main part of the routine is a loop that cycles through all the *TableDefs*. This loop excludes any *MSys* or *USys* system tables, any temporary internal tables (*~TMP*), the *ztbl* tables, and it also excludes any local tables that have an empty *Connect* string (although the internal *ztbl* tables are, in this case, local tables, this might not always be the case, as you will see later when relinking web databases):

```
For Each tdef In db.TableDefs
    strTableName = tdef.Name
    If Left(strTableName, 4) = "~TMP" Then
        ' skip system tables
        GoTo SkipTable
    End If
    If tdef.Connect = "" Then
        ' skip local tables including MSys, USys tables
        ' Except USysApplicationLog and MSysASO if relinking
        ' a web database
        GoTo SkipTable
    End If
    ' Special requirement for re-linking web database
    If Left(strTableName, 4) = "ztbl" Then
        ' skip the relinker tables
        GoTo SkipTable
    End If
```

The following section of the code creates or locates the linked table in our list of linked tables:

```
' Extract the object information
rst.FindFirst "[LinkedTableName] = '" & strTableName & "'"
If rst.NoMatch Then
    rst.AddNew
    rst!LinkedTableName = tdef.Name
    rst!LinkedSourceTableName = tdef.SourceTableName
    rst!LinkAdded = True
    rst!LinkDeleted = False
    rst.Update
    rst.Bookmark = rst.LastModified
```

```
        Else
            rst.Edit
            rst!LinkDeleted = False
            rst.Update
        End If
```

In the sample that follows, you can see that the next part of the processing depends on the type of link that you are attempting relink. In this example, there are a set of functions for each link type, which will be explained as we continue through the chapter:

```
        ' Now change details in the link and refresh
        If Left(tdef.Connect, Len(";DATABASE=")) = ";DATABASE=" Then
            If Not modLinks_Access(System, rst, rstds, tdef) Then
                modLinks_Tables = False
                Exit Function
            End If
            blSourceMatched = True
        End If
        If Left(tdef.Connect, Len("Excel")) = "Excel" Then
            If Not modLinks_Excel(System, rst, rstds, tdef) Then
                modLinks_Tables = False
                Exit Function
            End If
            blSourceMatched = True
        End If
        If Left(tdef.Connect, Len("Text")) = "Text" Then
            If Not modLinks_Text(System, rst, rstds, tdef) Then
                modLinks_Tables = False
                Exit Function
            End If
            blSourceMatched = True
        End If
        If Left(tdef.Connect, Len("ODBC")) = "ODBC" Then
            If Not modLinks_ODBC(System, rst, rstds, tdef) Then
                modLinks_Tables = False
                Exit Function
            End If
            blSourceMatched = True
        End If
        If Left(tdef.Connect, Len("ACEWSS")) = "ACEWSS" Then
            If Not modLinks_SharePoint(System, rst, rstds, tdef) Then
                modLinks_Tables = False
                Exit Function
            End If
            blSourceMatched = True
        End If
        If Not blSourceMatched Then
            ' unknown data source
            Stop
        End If
SkipTable:
    Next
```

The final part of the processing routine updates your record of the currently active system, as illustrated here:

```
' update the active system
Select Case System
    Case dev: CurrentDb.Execute "UPDATE ztblLinkedSystem " & _
                              "SET ActiveSystem = 'DEV'"
    Case test:  CurrentDb.Execute "UPDATE ztblLinkedSystem " & _
                              "SET ActiveSystem = 'Test'"
    Case Production:  CurrentDb.Execute "UPDATE ztblLinkedSystem " & _
                              "SET ActiveSystem = 'Production'"
End Select
modLinks_Tables = True
End Function
```

The connection string for a linked Access table looks similar to the following example:

```
;DATABASE=C:\......\Chapter12\Orders_be.accdb
```

Let's take a moment to explain the logic for the relinking of an Access table; the other routines all have a very similar form. The processing routine illustrated in the following code starts by taking the existing *Connect* connection string and extracts the name of the database *strObjectName* and the path *strObjectPath*:

```
Function modLinks_Access(System As SystemType, _
                      rst As Recordset, _
                      rstds As Recordset, _
                      tdef As TableDef) As Boolean
    Dim strObjectName As String
    Dim strObjectPath As String
    Dim strOldConnect As String
    Dim strPrefix As String
    Dim strConnect As String
    Dim lngPos As Long
    Dim lngDataSourceId As Long
    ' Access datasource
    ' Assumes DATABASE={Drive:\...\...\Database.accdb or .mdb
    strConnect = tdef.Connect
    strOldConnect = strConnect
    lngPos = InStr(1, strConnect, ";DATABASE=") + Len(";DATABASE=")
    strPrefix = Left(strConnect, lngPos - 1)
    strConnect = StrReverse(Mid(strConnect, lngPos, 255))
    lngPos = InStr(1, strConnect, "\")
    strObjectName = StrReverse(Left(strConnect, lngPos - 1))
    strObjectPath = StrReverse(Mid(strConnect, lngPos, 255))
```

The next part of the processing searches to see if you already have the data source with this name; this is where the code is able to detect and create the list of data sources. If it already has the data source name, it will extract the appropriate Dev\Test\Production path and build the new connection string, as shown in the following:

```
rstds.FindFirst "[ObjectName] = '" & strObjectName & "'"
If rstds.NoMatch Then
    ' Create a new datasource
    rstds.AddNew
    rstds!SourceType = "Access"
    rstds!ObjectName = strObjectName
    rstds!devpath = strObjectPath
    rstds!Testpath = strObjectPath
    ' best set manually
    rstds!ProductionPath = strObjectPath
    rstds.Update
    rstds.Bookmark = rstds.LastModified
End If
lngDataSourceId = rstds!DataSourceID
strConnect = strPrefix
Select Case System
    Case dev: strConnect = strConnect & rstds!devpath & _
                            rstds!ObjectName
    Case test: strConnect = strConnect & rstds!Testpath & _
                            rstds!ObjectName
    Case Production: strConnect = strConnect & rstds!ProductionPath & _
                            rstds!ObjectName
End Select
```

The final processing steps involve refreshing the link for the new path and logging any errors that have occurred as a result of the operations:

```
' refresh the link
On Error Resume Next
tdef.Connect = strConnect
tdef.RefreshLink
If Err <> 0 Then
    ' log the error
    rst.Edit
    rst!Linkfailed = True
    rst!DataSourceID = lngDataSourceId
    rst!Connect = strOldConnect
    rst!ErrorMessage = Err.Description & " : " & strConnect
    rst.Update
    If MsgBox("An Error Occured " & Err.Description & ".Stop ?", _
                vbYesNo, "Error Relinking") = vbYes Then
        modLinks_Access = False
        Exit Function
    End If
Else
    rst.Edit
    rst!LinkRefreshed = True
    rst!DataSourceID = lngDataSourceId
    rst!Connect = tdef.Connect
    rst.Update
End If
On Error GoTo 0
modLinks_Access = True
End Function
```

In our demonstration system, we set the Production, Dev, and Test paths to the same location. You should try creating a subfolder, copy the files into that folder, and then editing, for example, the Dev path to point to that folder. Run the relinker, and then you can hover over the linked tables to see that the paths have been changed.

INSIDE OUT   Linked table names and *SourceTableName*

In the sample database, there are two links with the names *Customers* and *Customers_ LinkCopy* (*TableName* property), both of which link to the same table called *Customers* (*SourceTableName* property). Access supports multiple links to the same table as long as the *TableName* property is different.

You will also see other examples in which the *TableName* does not match the *Source- TableName*; a text file called Customers.txt would be linked as *Customers_txt*, and a SQL Server table called *dbo.Customers* would become either *dbo_Customers* or be renamed to *Customers* (the period following dbo is not allowed in a linked table name; therefore, it is converted to the underscore character).

Linking to Excel and Text Files

In this section, you will look at linking and refreshing links when working with either Excel or text files.

Linking to Excel

Use the Excel menu (External Data | Import & Export | Excel) to generate a dynamic, read-only link from Access to an Excel spreadsheet. The following code shows an example of the connection string:

```
Excel 12.0 Xml;HDR=YES;IMEX=2;ACCDB=YES;DATABASE=C:\path...\Customers.xlsx
```

To repoint this link at the spreadsheet when moved to a different location, you need to construct a new connection string with the path replaced by a new, alternative path. The companion content contains a routine, *modLinks_Excel*, that performs this with our relinker.

Linking to Text Files

Use the Text File menu (The External Data | Import & Export | Text File) to generate a dynamic, read-only link from Access to a text file. The following code shows an example of the connection string (shown in the following split over two lines):

```
Text;DSN=Customers Link Specification;
FMT=Delimited;HDR=NO;IMEX=2;CharacterSet=1252;ACCDB=YES;DATABASE=C:\...\Chapter12
```

The interesting point to note with this connection string is the reference using the DSN= to the Customer Link Specification. If you link to a fixed width text file, you would get the following string (shown in the following split over two lines):

```
Text;DSN=Customers2 Link Specification
;FMT=Fixed;HDR=NO;IMEX=2;CharacterSet=1252;ACCDB=YES;DATABASE=C:\.... \Chapter12
```

Using the navigation options to unhide the system objects and looking in the system table *MSysIMEXSpecs*, you will find the import and export specifications; the table *MSysIMEX Columns* contains the column definitions for the specifications.

The routine *modLinks_Text* is used in the relinker to repoint the path for text files.

Linking to SQL Server

In this section, you look at how SQL Server links can be refreshed. This section assumes that you have successfully installed SQL Server or SQL Server Express, and you want to get started using the product when linked to Access.

The best way to get started with SQL Server is to look at a sample database, that includes a script file for creating one of the standard SQL Server sample database, *Northwind*. We have included two scripts, the first, instnwnd.sql, creates the *Northwind* database, and the second, instnwndtesting.sql, creates a similar database called *NorthWindTesting*. With this configuration, you can create links to the databases and investigate relinking an Access application to different databases or servers.

Setting up the Sample Database

After you start the SQL Server Management Studio, you are prompted to connect to the Server. You should already see the name of your SQL Server database displayed for you, and you should be able to select Windows Authentication to connect to the server, as shown in Figure 12-7.

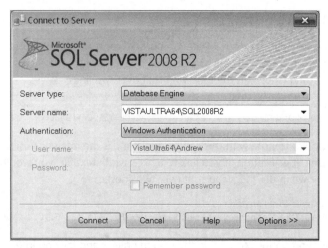

Figure 12-7 Connecting to the SQL Server.

Your server name might only be your computer name, for example, MYPC rather than MYPC\SQLServer, or it could be simply SQLExpress. This information is displayed during the SQL Server installation. If you are having problems, try entering **(local)** in the Server Name field.

INSIDE OUT   SQL Server instances

When you install SQL Server on a computer, during the installation you are presented with the option to use the default instance or create a new instance of SQL Server. SQL Server allows you to install multiple copies of the same or different versions of the product on the same computer; the most general naming for this is {Computer name}\{Instance name}, where each installed copy is called an Instance. There is also a short-hand notation called (local), which refers to the default instance. In what follows, we will specify the instance name that we are using.

Management Studio allows you to connect to multiple SQL Server databases at the same time, local, network, remote, and SQL Azure.

To begin, go to File | Open | File. Next, locate and open the file instnwnd.sql. Your screen should appear similar to that shown in Figure 12-8.

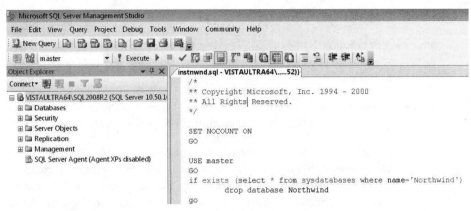

Figure 12-8 A script opened in Management Studio. This script creates the sample database.

Press the Execute button on the Toolbar to run the script and create your database. Next, right-click the Database folder, and then select refresh from the drop-down menu to see the resulting database, as shown in Figure 12-9.

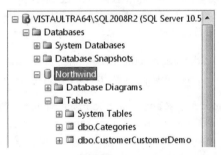

Figure 12-9 Executing the script file creates the sample database. You should also open and run the second script, instnwndtesting.sql.

INSIDE OUT   Script Files

You can work with SQL Server either by using the GUI, which is very intuitive as all you need to do is just right-click objects and folders to create and manage them. But as you learn more about SQL Server, you will begin to find that Script Files offer a fantastic way to work with the product. Using Management Studio, you can create Query windows (click the New Query icon on the Toolbar to see this). These windows can be used to either load Script Files or act as a scratch pad window, into which you can type SQL and commands and execute them. Then you can save your work by saving what you typed in the Query window.

Creating a DSN

A Data Source Name or DSN defines a source of the data. There are two types of data sources that you can choose when connecting in this way to SQL Server: a *File DSN*, or a *Machine DSN*.

A File DSN is probably the simplest to use, because all the information to connect to SQL Server is saved in the *Connect* property of each linked table, in the *TableDef* objects.

A Machine DSN holds only the name of the Machine DSN in the *Connect* property for each *TableDef*. When using a Machine DSN, if you go to a different computer, you need to ensure that the Machine DSN is created on that computer or that the details are copied onto it. In Windows 7, System DSN information is held in the Windows Registry (HKEY_CURRENT_USER\Software\ODBC\odbc.ini\) and File DSNs are located in the user's C:\Users\Username\Documents folder.

Machine DSNs have the advantage that changes can be made to the connection information with minimum impact on the application. If, for example, a server name is changed when using a File DSN, then because the server name is held in *Connect* property of each *TableDef*, the links need to be changed and refreshed. Machine DSNs have the advantage that links to tables do not need to be changed.

Each method has advantages and disadvantages. For the beginner, a File DSN is often simpler to work with, and in the following, we describe how to work with a File DSN.

Use the ODBC Database menu in your Access application to make a link to SQL Server. Go to External Data | Import & Link | ODBC Database, and then select the option to Link To SQL Server. The Select Data Source dialog box opens, as shown in Figure 12-10.

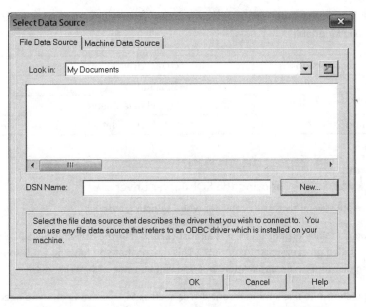

Figure 12-10 Creating a new data source to connect to SQL Server.

Select the File Data Source tab, and then click the New button.

The Create New Data Source dialog box opens, in which you can select an ODBC driver, as shown in Figure 12-11.

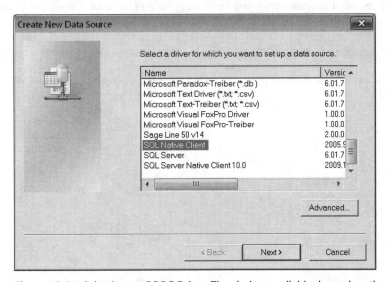

Figure 12-11 Selecting an ODBC Driver. The choices available depend on the version of SQL Server on your computer.

Your choice of SQL Server ODBC driver depends upon your version of SQL Server, as shown in the following table:

SQL Server version	ODBC driver name
All Versions	SQL Server
2005	SQL Native Client
2008 and 2008 R2	SQL Server Native Client 10.0

INSIDE OUT Choosing the SQL Server driver

There are several factors to consider when selecting a driver.

If you go to any organization, it is almost certain that the driver called SQL Server will be installed on every client computer. This means that you have no work to perform when distributing an application, but you will be using older technology.

If you choose to use a more recent driver, such as SQL Native Client, you need to download and install the drivers on each desktop. However, you get the benefits of working with a better driver that has more features and might be faster to use. Be aware, though, that there are problems when using memo fields with the SQL Native Client drivers. For more information about this, go to *http://msdn.microsoft.com/en-us/data/aa937733.aspx*.

If you want to work with a new technology such as SQL Azure, you need to use the recommended driver for Azure (SQL Server Native Client 10.0 or later).

You are then prompted to provide a name for your data source, as shown in Figure 12-12.

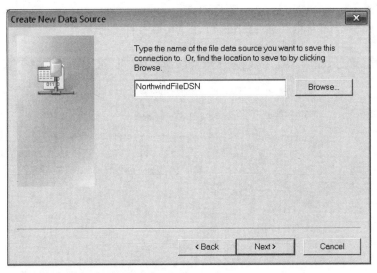

Figure 12-12 Providing a name for the data source.

After you name your data source, you are presented with a sequence of screens, depending on the specific database driver you select. For example, if you are connecting to Oracle or DB2, you can expect to see different screens. The first screen for SQL server is shown in Figure 12-13.

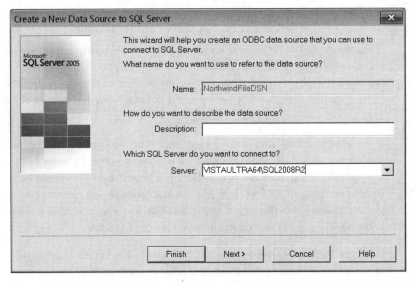

Figure 12-13 Enter the SQL Server Instance name that you used earlier in this section, and then add an optional description, if you want.

The next dialog requests that you either use Windows authentication or enter a specific SQL Server authentication, as shown in Figure 12-14.

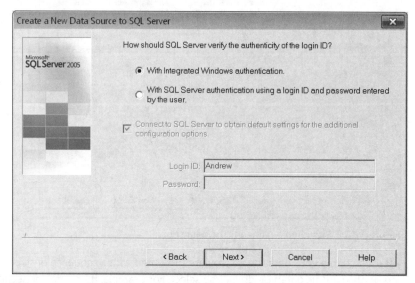

Figure 12-14 Using Windows authentication is the simplest choice when getting started with SQL Server.

INSIDE OUT   Windows vs. SQL Server authentication

If you are deploying an application within your own company or to client sites where you are able to be involved in managing the Windows Security, then Windows authentication is the better choice. This can be quite painless because Windows Groups can be easily authenticated in SQL Server, and it will also allow you to track details on individual users working with your system.

If you want to avoid using Windows authentication, you can use SQL Server security; this is often appealing when you want to set up a one-off activity for configuring security without getting involved in maintaining different users (you could have all users logging on to the SQL Server with a single SQL login, or you can also have multiple logon accounts). It is also worth noting that SQL Azure requires that you use SQL Server authentication, as Windows authentication is not supported.

One topic to consider when using a SQL Server login is handling the password and user name. You have three options here: you have an application where users are in some way prompted for the password and/or login; you embed the credentials in the linked tables; or you use some startup code to make the connection where the credentials are protected in the source code.

After providing the server name and authentication, a connection can be made to the server. The next screen provides a drop-down list of available databases, as shown in Figure 12-15.

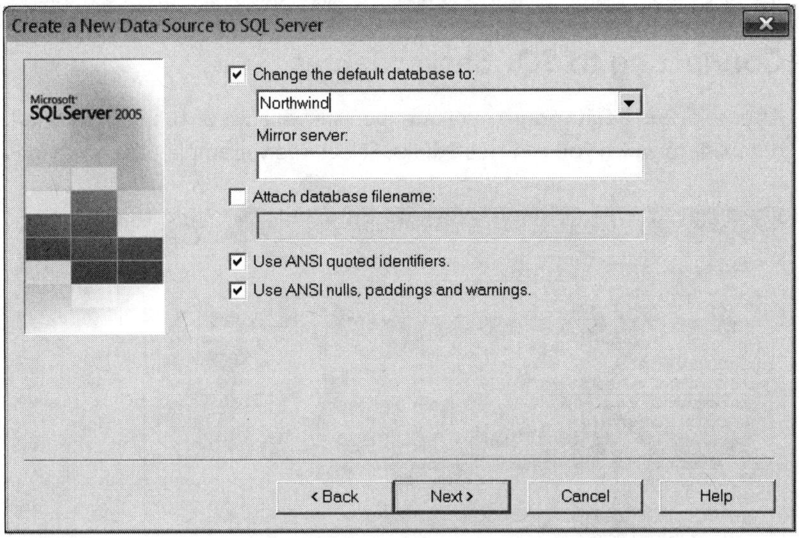

Figure 12-15 Selecting the target database on the server.

In the next screen, you can test the database connection, and then you will be returned to the selection data source screen, with your newly created DSN highlighted (see Figure 12-16). Press OK to complete the setup.

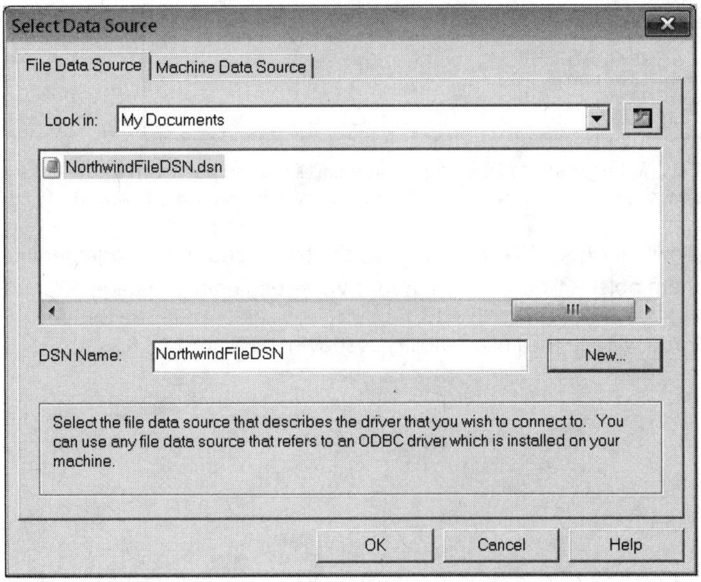

Figure 12-16 Selecting the new data source.

Once this setup is complete and the details for both Machine and File DSNs are saved on your development computer, you can select the DSN for future projects without repeating the operation of creating it through all the subsequent configuration questions.

Connecting to SQL Server Tables

After selecting a Data Source, you are then shown a list of all the objects in the SQL server database to which you can create links. Select a few examples, as shown in Figure 12-17.

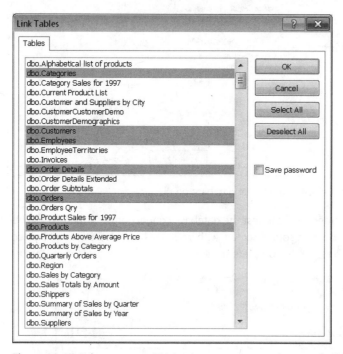

Figure 12-17 When you use SQL Logins, you can save the password in the links by selecting the Save Password check box (this does not apply to Windows authentication).

The list shown in Figure 12-17 includes all the tables and Views, together with a large number of system objects. You will learn about Views beginning on page 505.

Press OK. You will see the linked tables, as shown in Figure 12-18.

Figure 12-18 Linked tables in Access. All tables created in SQL Server are prefixed by dbo_. Here, the *Products* table has been renamed to remove this.

INSIDE OUT   Renaming linked tables to remove the dbo_ prefix

When you create tables in SQL Server, they are created in a Schema. Schemas offer the ability to have multiple tables with the same name, as long as they are placed on different Schemas (object groupings). The default Schema is dbo, so when Access links, for example, to the table *dbo.Products,* the linked name becomes *dbo_Products*. You will learn about using Schemas in Chapter 15, "Upsizing Access to SQL Server."

Later, if you write queries in Access, you might want to copy the SQL into SQL Server and this would mean changing a reference like *dbo_Products* to *dbo.Products*. You might find that it is easier at an early point in development to remove the dbo_ prefix from the name of any linked table.

Refreshing SQL Server Linked Tables

Examples of ODBC connection strings for the different SQL Server drivers are shown in the following:

```
ODBC;DRIVER=SQL Server;Data Source=VISTAULTRA64\VISTAULTRA64_08;
Database=Nothwind; Trusted_Connection=Yes;
ODBC;DRIVER=SQL Native Client;Data Source=VISTAULTRA64\VISTAULTRA64_08;
Database=Nothwind; Trusted_Connection=Yes;
ODBC;DRIVER=SQL Server Native Client 10.0;Data Source=VISTAULTRA64\VISTAULTRA64_08;
Database=Nothwind; Trusted_Connection=Yes;
```

When you are developing with SQL Server, your test and development systems can be on different servers, in which case, for relinking you need to use a different server name. Or you can use several databases on the same server; in which case, the database name needs to be changed. For example, if connecting to a different database on the same server we could use the following:

```
ODBC;DRIVER=SQL Native Client;SERVER=VISTAULTRA64\SQL2008R2;Trusted_
Connection=Yes;APP=Microsoft Office 2010;DATABASE=NorthwindTesting;
```

In our sample relinker, to use an alternative server or database name, you can edit the appropriate part of the connection string in the TestPath, DevPath, ProductionPath fields, changing the database name and/or server names; we have added additional code in the procedure *modLinks_ODBC* to handle this. This procedure records the change to a database object name in the field *ChangedObjectName*, and then after relinking, it runs an update to the *ObjectName* in the relinker.

Connecting to a View in SQL Server

In SQL Server, the equivalent to a Select Query is a View. Executing the following SQL in Management Studio will create a View in SQL Server (the *WITH CHECK OPTION* means that you can only insert or change data in the view that can be reflected back through the view. In this example, it ensures that the *Country* field is *France*:

```
CREATE VIEW vw_FranceCustomers AS
SELECT * FROM Customers
WHERE Country = 'France'
WITH CHECK OPTION
```

We have used the convention to name all of our views with the prefix vw_. You can now use the DSN to create a linked table to the View. Once you select to link to the View, the pop-up dialog shown in Figure 12-19 opens.

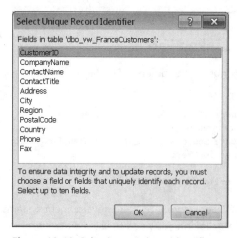

Figure 12-19 Selecting a unique identifier to make the View updateable.

This creates a link to the View called *dbo_vw_FranceCustomers*, which you can rename to *vw_FranceCustomers*. If you selected a unique record identifier, Access makes the View updateable. You should ensure that you do select a combination of fields that are unique; otherwise, you will get unpredictable results when working with the View (if a View returns unpredictable results, check the unique record selector).

INSIDE OUT   Updateability and Views

Access supports the updateable Views by creating an index called *_uniqueindex* in the *TableDef* for the View. This can be checked by using the following commands in the Immediate window:

```
?currentdb.TableDefs("vw_FranceCustomers").Indexes(0).Name
__uniqueindex
?currentdb.TableDefs("vw_FranceCustomers").Indexes(0).fields.count
 1
?currentdb.TableDefs("vw_FranceCustomers").Indexes(0).Fields(0).Name
CustomerID
```

There are limitations on View updateability. One limitation is that if you have a View with multiple base tables, any update can only affect data in one of the base tables.

If you execute the following in the Immediate window, you will see that there is a potential problem with refreshing Views:

```
currentdb.TableDefs("vw_FranceCustomers").RefreshLink
?currentdb.TableDefs("vw_FranceCustomers").Indexes.count
 0
```

If you *Refresh* a View, it can destroy the Index and you then lose updateability. In the next section, you will look at methods to solve this.

Refreshing SQL Server Views

In the previous section, you saw that when you refresh a linked View, it can lose updateability because the index is destroyed. If this happens, you can execute the following SQL DDL command, which recreates the index and restores updateability (note that this is shown split over two lines in our code:

```
CurrentDB.Execute "CREATE UNIQUE INDEX __uniqueindex ON
vw_FranceCustomers(CustomerID)"
```

Chapter 12

In *modLinks_ODBC*, the lines of code that refresh the link are modified to save the index information and then execute the DDL following the refresh operation, as shown in the following:

```
' refresh the link
strIndexSQL = ""
If tdef.Indexes.Count = 1 Then
    If tdef.Indexes(0).Name = "__uniqueindex" Then
        ' we have a view
        strIndexSQL = "CREATE UNIQUE INDEX __uniqueIndex " & _
                      " ON [" & tdef.Name & "](" 
        strFieldSQL = ""
        For Each fld In tdef.Indexes(0).Fields
            If strFieldSQL <> "" Then
                strFieldSQL = strFieldSQL & ","
            End If
            strFieldSQL = strFieldSQL & "[" & fld.Name & "]"
        Next
        strIndexSQL = strIndexSQL & strFieldSQL & ")"
    End If
End If
On Error Resume Next
tdef.Connect = strConnect
tdef.RefreshLink
If Err = 0 Then
    CurrentDb.Execute strIndexSQL
End If
```

Linking to SQL Azure

Before reading this section, you might want to read Chapter 16, "Using SQL Azure," for a detailed explanation of how to create a SQL Azure database. This section assumes that you have created SQL Azure databases and that you need to understand more about how to link to an Azure database and change your links between a development and test or production system.

SQL Azure DSN

When using SQL Azure, you don't want to use your main Azure account information in the application, so the first step is to use Management Studio to create a test account.

The companion content includes two SQL Azure databases, *Northwind* and *Northwind-Testing*, as shown in Figure 12-20. If you select the Logins folder (see Figure 12-20) and then press the New Query button on the toolbar, you can create a new query window for executing T-SQL in the Master database.

Figure 12-20 The SQL Azure server showing the *Northwind* and *NorthwindTesting* databases.

You can then execute the following Script in *Master* to create a new SQL Server login account:

```
-- Create a test login account in Master
CREATE LOGIN TestUser WITH PASSWORD = 'TestAzureAccount444333222'
GO
```

For each of the test databases, you register the login by creating a user account and assigning the user a database role (normally, you would create an appropriate role, but to get started you will assign the user the *db_owner* role). The easiest method for doing this is to click the Database in Object Explorer, and then click New Query and execute the following script (verify that you are executing this in the test database and not in *Master*):

```
-- Create a user account
CREATE USER TestUser FROM LOGIN TestUser

-- Assign user to a database role
EXEC sp_addrolemember 'db_owner', 'TestUser'
```

INSIDE OUT   SQL Azure supports security stored procedures

SQL Azure supports the stored procedures *sp_addrolemember*, *sp_droprolemember*, and *sp_helprole* for managing security.

When you create new user accounts, these accounts will not be able to directly connect to the Master database. This means that when you set up DSN connections by using the ODBC Manager, you need to use your primary login account.

At this point, it is useful to close and re-open Management Studio by connecting with the logon details for the newly created user account (notice that the new account can connect to *Northwind* and *NorthwindTesting*, but not to *Master*).

You can then follow a similar set of steps to those described in the SQL Server section of this chapter, using the sample database *NorthwindAzure.accdb*. In this section, we will only show the important steps. Go to External Data | Import & Link | ODBC Database to create a new file DSN. In the Create A New Data Source dialog box, select the ODBC Driver shown in Figure 12-21.

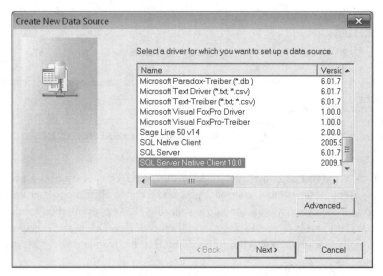

Figure 12-21 Select the latest ODBC drivers for use with SQL Azure.

When entering the server name, enter your Azure server details in the format shown in the following line of code and in Figure 12-22:

```
ServerName.database.windows.net
```

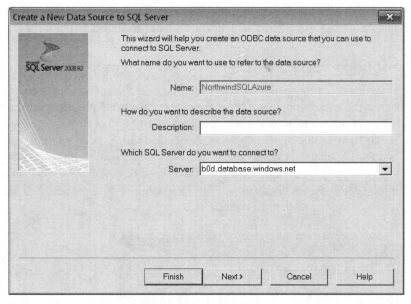

Figure 12-22 Enter your server name for SQL Azure.

When entering the SQL Server Login, use the format shown in the following line of code and in Figure 12-23:

```
MainAccountName@ServerName
```

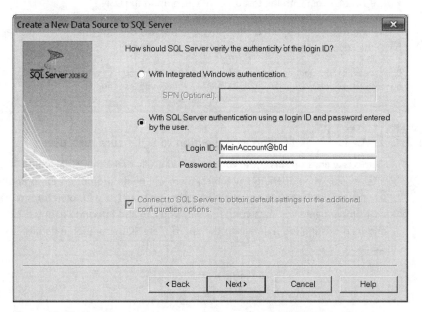

Figure 12-23 Use your main account when creating the DSN connection.

After completing these details, follow through the subsequent screens to enter the appropriate database name (*Northwind* or *NorthwindTesting*), and then test the connection.

Connecting to SQL Azure

When making a connection to SQL Azure, you have the option to save password information in the links, if you do not select the option, then when you open the first table, you will be prompted to enter the SQL Azure login name and password. However, it is very simple to make this initial connection in code and supply a user name and password, and even when the table links do not contain this information, this will no longer involve any prompting, because the connection will already be established. Go to External Data | Import & Link | ODBC Database and link to SQL Azure using the DSN. You are prompted to log in, as shown in Figure 12-24.

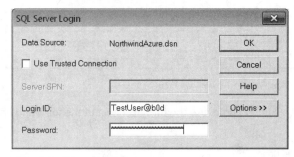

Figure 12-24 Login with the test account when using the DSN.

Then, link to the tables, but do not save the password in the links, the *TableDefs* will then have the following *Connect* property:

```
ODBC;DRIVER=SQL Server Native Client 10.0;SERVER=b0d.database.windows.
net;APP=Microsoft Office 2010;DATABASE=NorthwindTesting;
```

INSIDE OUT   Making a connection to SQL Azure for a user

With a few lines of VBA code, you can dynamically make the initial link to SQL Azure, after which, when opening any tables, there will be no prompting for login details. To use this method when the application starts, you can use your own form to capture the user's login name and password; this way you can also integrate to any existing security and map existing login details to the appropriate SQL Azure login details.

In SQL Azure you can use the *SUSER_SNAME()* function, which will return the SQL Server Login user name. This can be very useful for identifying which user made changes to data, or in providing tables that only show specific rows of data for a specific user.

To modify the connection string you need to insert `;UID=TestUser@b0d;PWD=TestAzure Account444333222;` before the `;DATABASE=` part of the connection string.

The following code shows an example of adding the user's credentials to the connection string and making the link:

```
Sub modAzure_Login()
    Const strLogin = "TestUser@b0d"
    Const strPassword = "TestAzureAccount444333222"
    Dim strConnect As String
    Dim strCredentials As String
    On Error Resume Next
    Dim db As Database
    Dim qdef As QueryDef
    Set db = CurrentDb
    ' extract the connection string from an existing TableDef
    strConnect = db.TableDefs("Customers").Connect
    Set qdef = db.CreateQueryDef("")
    strCredentials = ";UID=" & strLogin & ";PWD=" & strPassword
    strConnect = Replace(strConnect, ";DATABASE=", strCredentials & ";DATABASE=")
    strConnect = strConnect & "Encrypt=yes;"
    qdef.Connect = strConnect
    ' qdef.SQL = "select @@version" ' useful alternative check
    qdef.SQL = "SELECT SUSER_SNAME()"
    qdef.ReturnsRecords = True
    Dim rst As Recordset
    Set rst = qdef.OpenRecordset()
    If Err <> 0 Then
        MsgBox strConnect, vbCritical, "Connection Failed"
    Else
        MsgBox strConnect, vbInformation, "Connection OK"
    End If
    Debug.Print rst(0)
    rst.Close
    qdef.Close
    db.Close
End Sub
```

Chapter 12

The relinker incorporates a few minor modifications to allow it to relink to a SQL Azure database. The procedure for using the relinker is identical to that described in the earlier sections of this chapter. The changes required to refresh these links involve ensuring that you have logged into SQL Azure, as described in this section. The procedure *modLinks_Tables* contains the following additional check (a similar test has been added to *modLinks_ODBC* to log in to the new target server when changing the links):

```
If InStr(tdef.Connect, ".database.windows.net") <> 0 Then
    If Not blSQLAzureLoggedIn Then
        blSQLAzureLoggedIn = modAzure_TestLogin(tdef.Connect)
        If Not blSQLAzureLoggedIn Then
            Stop
        End If
    End If
End If
```

Linking to SharePoint Lists

In this section, you will look at linking Access to SharePoint. For example and testing purposes, use the demonstration database *WebDatabase.accdb*, which is a Web Legal Access Web Database that can be published to Access Data Services. If you want to try this yourself and you don't have the facilities to publish Access Web Database, you can follow along using a version of SharePoint, which has some lists of data to which you can link.

In this example, you have a standard Access .accdb file, and you want to link this database to SharePoint Lists. In the example, these SharePoint Lists are actually an Access Web Database which has been published.

Using a new Access database (not a web database) which contains only our linker software components, go to External Data | Import & Link | More | SharePoint List. In the dialog box that opens, choose the option to Link to data by using a URL similar, for example, to the following: **http://xxx.accesshosting.com/NorthWind**, and then log on. You are then presented with a list of available SharePoint Lists, as shown in Figure 12-25.

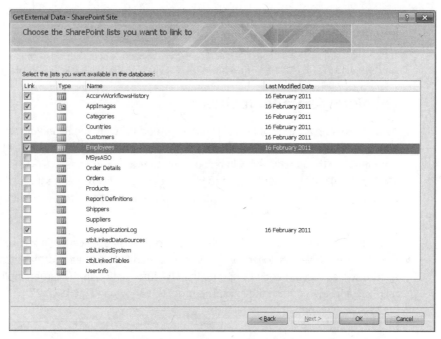

Figure 12-25 The Available SharePoint Lists on the site.

This then provides updateable lists of the data on the SharePoint site, as shown in Figure 12-26.

Figure 12-26 Updateable links to the lists in SharePoint.

Looking at the *Connect* property of the *TableDefs*, you see a connection string similar to the following example:

```
ACEWSS;HDR=NO;IMEX=2;ACCDB=YES;DATABASE=http://xxxx.accesshosting.com/
NorthWind;LIST={857C11A0-CE1D-420E-A774-018D03571D1E};VIEW=;RetrieveIds=Yes
```

Relinking SharePoint Lists

As with other application links, you need a method to relink the SharePoint Lists if you switch between a development and test or production environment. The key to understanding how this is achieved is in recognizing that the long code LIST={857C11A0-CE1D-420E-A774-018D03571D1E} needs to be changed. If you can change these, then you can relink to the alternative site. You might also notice that the Linked Table Manager is not available for relinking these links.

You will need an application linked to *Site1*, and then an application linked to *Site2*. If you then scan the *TableDefs* collection for an application linked to each of the sites, all you need is some program code to update the *LIST* information in the target application to be relinked, and then refresh the links. The process is shown in Figure 12-27.

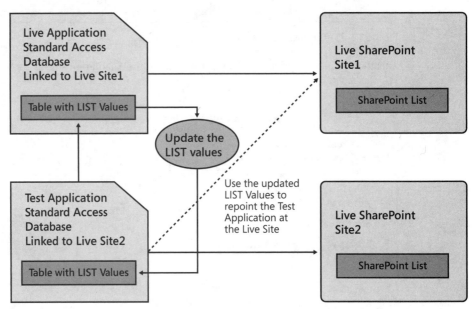

Figure 12-27 The *Site2* application uses the table in *Site1* to update the *LIST* values. It then repoints the application at the new SharePoint Site.

In the previous example, we published our sample web database to *Site1* and linked a new standard Access database to the SharePoint Lists in *Site1*. To follow along here, you need to publish a second copy of the web database to *Site2*, and link a new standard Access database to it, as well. The following refers to the two standard Access databases, now linked to *Site1* and *Site2*.

Because our relinker will get this information, we run the relinker in two applications that populates the local table *ztblLinkedTable*. Figure 12-28 demonstrates in *Site2*, that you have also linked to the table *ztblLinkedTable* in *Site1* (*ztblLinkedTable1*).

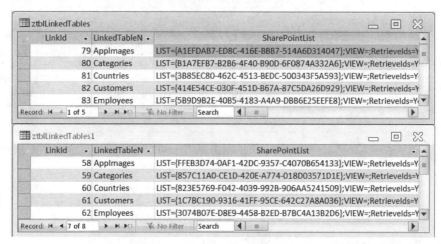

Figure 12-28 Showing the *LIST* settings in the current site and the values you need to change to connect to the second site.

You then run the following SQL, which updates the relinker table in the active site to have the correct values for the second site:

```
Sub modSharePointPatch_UpdateLists()
    ' table ztblLinkedTables contains SharePointList LIST values
    ' for this database
    ' table ztblLinkedTables_1 contains SharePointList LIST values
    ' for the production database
    ' We need to copy the new List Values
    Dim strSQL As String
    strSQL = "UPDATE ztblLinkedTables " & _
            "INNER JOIN ztblLinkedTables1 " & _
            "    ON ztblLinkedTables.LinkedTableName = " & _
                "ztblLinkedTables1.LinkedTableName " & _
            " SET ztblLinkedTables.SharePointList = " & _
            " [ztblLinkedTables1].[SharePointList] " & _
            " WHERE Left([ztblLinkedTables.LinkedTableName],4) <> 'ztbl'"

    CurrentDb.Execute strSQL
End Sub
```

Chapter 12

Figure 12-29 illustrates how the relinker table is now updated.

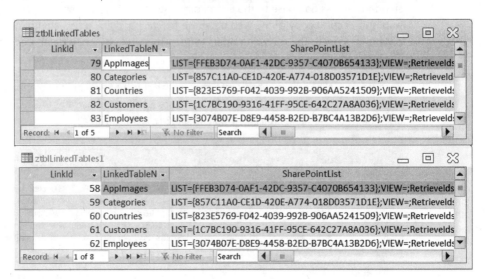

Figure 12-29 Showing the *LIST* settings in the current site and the values that need to change to connect to the second site.

The last remaining step is to edit the information shown in Figure 12-30 for the Production-Path so that it refers to *Northwind*, rather than *Northwind2*, which is the test system.

Figure 12-30 Changing the production path in preparation to relink the tables.

Then you simply run the relinker and press the button to relink the application to the pro-duction system.

Linking Access Web Databases

The process of linking to tables in a Published Access Web Database (linking to the Share-Point Site) was described in the previous section. With an Access Web Database, the process of linking to SharePoint is replaced with the idea of publishing the database. When success-fully completed, this publishes the tables to SharePoint. In this section, you will look at the links themselves and the need to change the linked tables when you move between devel-opment and production systems.

For example and testing purposes, use the demonstration database *WebDatabase.accdb*. Make two copies of this database, one called *WebDatabaseNorthwind.accdb*, and the other, *WebDatabaseNorthwind2.accdb*. Publish the first copy to a SharePoint site called Northwind (Live Site), and then publish the second copy to a site called Northwind2 (Test Site).

Before you begin, here are some general comments on importing and linking data with a Web Database. If you try to subsequently import external Access Tables into a Web Database (which has been published), they will be converted into a SharePoint List, which will be published when you next synchronize the database.

A Web Database is allowed to link to external data sources, although you cannot design browser components that use these linked objects; the use of these links is restricted to your client objects. Figure 12-31 depicts an example of a Web Database that has been published but also contains links to local external data files.

Figure 12-31 A published Access Web Database with additional links to local external data.

INSIDE OUT   Linking an Access database to an Access Web Database

If you have an Access Web Database that you have published to SharePoint, the question arises as to what happens if you then create an ordinary Access database and attempt to link to the Access Web Database?

If you go to External Data | Import & Link | Access and choose the link option, you are presented with any empty list of tables to which to link. However, if you choose the Import option, after you have logged in, you will see a list of available tables, and if you choose a table, it will create a linked table to the SharePoint List.

The answer is that you cannot link to an Access Web Database, but by using the Import option, you can quickly create SharePoint List links to the underlying site.

Relinking to an Access Web Database

Now, let's look at the situation in which you want to replace the live web application with the test web application. To do this, you use a similar technique that you applied in the last section, which is shown schematically in Figure 12-32.

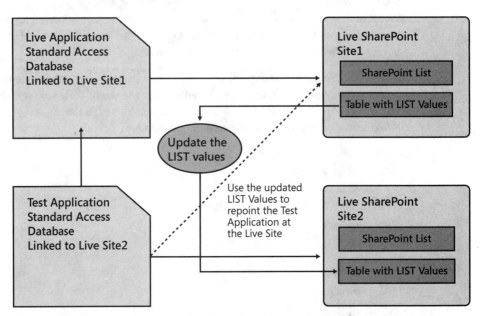

Figure 12-32 Swapping the test application web database to replace the live web database application.

You begin with two web databases called *Live* and *Test*. The objective is to replace *Live* web database with the *Test* web database. Working with each of the two published databases, open the relinker form called *ztblLinkedTableReLinker* and click the Relink To Dev System button. This populates the table *ztblLinkedTables* with the link information (do this for each system). Ensure that you re-synchronize both systems after running the relinker.

Close the *Live* system web database, and then in *Test*, import the table *ztblLinkedTables* from the *Live* web database, which creates the linked table, as shown in Figure 12-33.

Tables
Search...
ztblLinkedTables1
ztblLinkedTables
ztblLinkedSystem
ztblLinkedDataSources
Suppliers
Shippers
Products

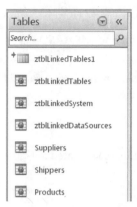

Figure 12-33 The Test system linked to the table *ztblLinkedTables* in the *Live* site, which is called *ztblLinkedTables1*.

Execute the procedure *modSharePointPatch_UpdateLists()* described in the previous section; this will update the SharePoint fields in *ztblLinkedTables* to the values from *ztblLinkedTables_1*.

Next, open the relinker form. Figure 12-34 shows the existing *Connect* information and the new SharePoint list reference for an example table.

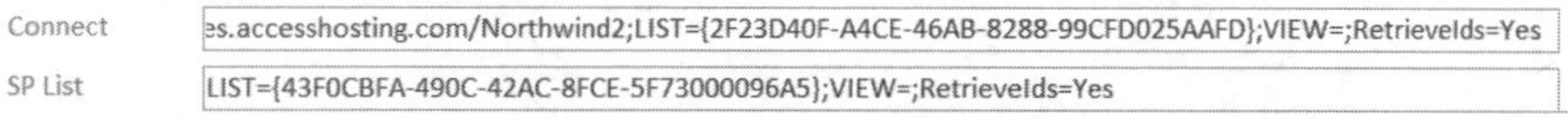

Connect
es.accesshosting.com/Northwind2;LIST={2F23D40F-A4CE-46AB-8288-99CFD025AAFD};VIEW=;RetrieveIds=Yes
SP List
LIST={43F0CBFA-490C-42AC-8FCE-5F73000096A5};VIEW=;RetrieveIds=Yes

Figure 12-34 The relinker, ready to repoint the SharePoint links.

Before running the relinker, edit the ProductionPath as shown in Figure 12-35.

Relink Tables
Id ProductionPath
1
http://xxx.accesshosting.com/Northwind

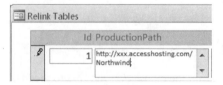

Figure 12-35 Change the site name from *Northwind2* to *Northwind*.

Next, click the Relink To Production System button. After running, you will see that for each table, the connection strings have now been changed, as shown in Figure 12-36.

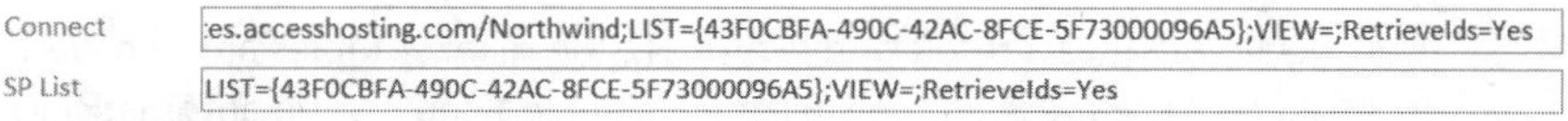

Connect
es.accesshosting.com/Northwind;LIST={43F0CBFA-490C-42AC-8FCE-5F73000096A5};VIEW=;RetrieveIds=Yes
SP List
LIST={43F0CBFA-490C-42AC-8FCE-5F73000096A5};VIEW=;RetrieveIds=Yes

Figure 12-36 Connection details on all the tables have been changed, the site has changed and the *LIST* has changed.

INSIDE OUT   Relinking *USysApplicationLog* and *MSysASO*

If you are writing your own routine to perform the relinking, it is critical that you relink the system tables *MSysASO* and *USysApplicationLog*. These tables are used by Access to establish the URL of the site against which to publish.

After you relink the list of tables, the database appears as illustrated in Figure 12-37. You should delete the bottom four linker utility tables.

Figure 12-37 After relinking, you can hover the mouse over the links to see that they have been repointed. You can delete the bottom four linker tables.

The final step is to perform a compact and repair. When this finishes, you are prompted to log on to the *Live* site. If you now synchronize to the *Live* site, the new application design is uploaded to replace the old application design.

You will find that as a result of this process, the relinker tables are removed from the *Live* site, but because these are only used for relinking and can be automatically repopulated, they can easily be imported back into the site.

Summary

In this chapter, you learned that splitting an Access database application into a front-end and back-end database provides a more flexible approach to building applications. You also saw the importance of being able to relink the application when moving from test to live systems.

In more sophisticated applications, you might need to link to a wide variety of external sources of data; thus, you saw how taking a general approach to relinking to different data sources means that you can develop an approach to relinking that can be reused in different applications.

Integrating Microsoft Office

Working with Objects and Object Models 438

Connecting Access to Word 443

Connecting Access to Excel. 451

Connecting Access to Outlook. 471

I f you are building applications that will be deployed in an environment containing other Microsoft Office products, you can pick and choose from the strengths of each Office product and produce a more integrated solution. Because Microsoft VBA is a universal language for the Office family, you have flexibility to program in the different products.

For example, in a project management system built in Microsoft Access 2010, you can integrate with Microsoft Outlook to produce and log outgoing emails together with any incoming emails in the database. You can also synchronize contact details between the database and Outlook. For producing quotes, these can be generated from the database in Microsoft Word by using a placeholder document, or template (this is not related to Office or Word templates), but would still allow staff to accomodate special projects by editing the generated documents. Microsoft Excel can be used to perform financial analysis based on both the data held in the database and other separate financial spreadsheets. An integrated approach to the design means that staff can blend their own expertise in using Office products with the labor saving benefits of an automated system.

After reading this chapter, you will:

- Be able to generate Word documents to create boiler-plate specifications and merge data to generate quotations.

- Be able to structure Excel spreadsheets that are dynamically updated from the database, allowing financial users flexibility in reporting.

- Be able to transfer information between Access and Outlook.

> **Note**
>
> As you read through this chapter, we encourage you to also use the companion content sample databases, OfficeApplications.accdb, ExcelAnalysis.accdb, WordQuote.accdb and OutlookContacts.accdb, which you can download from the book's catalog page.

Working with Objects and Object Models

Each of the Office products has an object model that provides a roadmap of how the product can be programmatically manipulated. In Chapter 4, "Applying the Access Object Model," you saw how Access has an object model, and in Chapter 5, "Understanding the Data Access Object Model," you were introduced to the Data Access Objects (DAO) model, which is the most natural extension to the Access objects. If you are programming in Excel, you can use these models to develop an Excel application that drives an Access application. Similarly, to drive an Excel application from Access, you need to understand the Excel object model.

In this section, you will look at the general rules for constructing objects that enable one Office application to refer to objects in another Office application. Use the file OfficeApplications.accdb for this section.

Early vs. Late Binding and *CreateObject* vs. *New*

To explain early binding and late binding, we are going to introduce the *CreateObject* syntax, which creates an instance of an object; the objects in this case are the Office applications. If you want to follow along with this code, close any copies you have of Excel or Word and step through the execution of the code, looking to see how at each step an application is opened. We have intentionally excluded Outlook for the moment because there are some special considerations here that are described in the Outlook section of this chapter.

The following code will launch each of the Office applications and then close them:

```
Sub modObject_OpenAnApplication()
    Dim objApplication As Object
    ' Start Excel
    Set objApplication = CreateObject("Excel.Application")
    objApplication.Visible = True
    Stop
    objApplication.Quit
    Set objApplication = Nothing
    ' Start Word
    Set objApplication = CreateObject("Word.Application")
    objApplication.Visible = True
End Sub
```

The preceding code uses the general purpose *Object* data type. When you do this, it is called *late binding*. This is because Access cannot check in advance whether a property such as *Visible* is valid for the object. Because you do not have IntelliSense to guide you in configuring these objects, programming can be very difficult.

Both Excel and Word have a *Visible* property, which you can use to make the application visible, and both have a *Quit* method to exit the application. You knew the names to use, *Word.Application* and *Excel.Application*, because these are the names of the root objects for these products.

You will see later on that you can start by creating other objects for each of these applications, but the syntax is then specific to each product; for example, you can create a *Word. Document* object but not an *Excel.Workbook* object (to do this you need to follow other steps in Adding a *WorkBook* object to the application object).

Early binding is a technique whereby you use the references to allow specific objects for each application to be created. Early binding provides IntelliSense support.

In the References – Office Applications dialog box, add three references to Excel, Outlook, and Word, as shown in Figure 13-1.

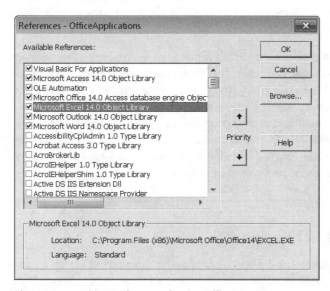

Figure 13-1 Adding references for the Office products.

With the references added, you can now explicitly define objects of each particular type, as shown in the following code. The code now also has IntelliSense. In this example, rather than use *CreateObject*, which returns a generic *Object* type, you use the *New* keyword to create an object of a specific type:

```
Sub modObject_OpenAnApplicationWithObjectTypes()
    Dim objExcel As Excel.Application
    ' Start Excel
    Set objExcel = New Excel.Application
    objExcel.Visible = True
```

Chapter 13

```
        Stop
        objExcel.Quit
        Set objExcel = Nothing
        Dim objWord As Word.Application
        ' Start Word
        Set objWord = New Word.Application
        objWord.Visible = True
        Stop
        objWord.Quit
        Set objWord = Nothing
End Sub
```

INSIDE OUT   Converting early to late binding

Some developers choose to use early binding while developing code and use *New* rather than *CreateObject*. Then before distributing an application they would change to using late binding, changing all object variables to use the generic *Object* data type rather than a specific Object.

One reason for choosing to do this is that you can avoid any issues relating to different references on target computers that are running older versions of Office. If you had early binding code that referred to a property that did not exist in an earlier version of an Office product, and then placed the application on a computer that used the earlier version, this could lead to problems with compiling the code. Early binding offers a slight performance gain over late binding. You might want to consider using conditional compilation statements to allow you to take advantage of both early and late binding, as appropriate to different activities.

The *GetObject* Keyword

You have seen that there are two forms of syntax that you can use for creating an instance of an Office application. When using the *CreateObject* or *New* methods, they create an additional instance of the Office product running on the desktop. This has the advantage of isolating the operations so that they do not interfere with any existing work open in a copy of the product.

In some circumstances, you might prefer to get a reference to an open copy of the application. In this case, you use the *GetObject* keyword, as demonstrated here:

```
Sub modObject_GetObject()
    Dim objExcel As Excel.Application
    ' Use open copy of Excel
    On Error Resume Next
    Set objExcel = GetObject(, "Excel.Application")
```

```
    If Err <> 0 Then
        Debug.Print Err.Number, Err.Description
        Err.Clear
    End If
    Set objExcel = Nothing
    Dim objWord As Word.Application
    ' Use open copy of word
    Set objWord = GetObject(, "Word.Application")
    If Err <> 0 Then
        Debug.Print Err.Number, Err.Description
        Err.Clear
    End If
    Set objWord = Nothing
End Sub
```

If there is not an open copy of the product, the application throws the exception *error 429 — ActiveX component can't create object*.

You can combine *GetObject* and *New* to produce code that will either use any open version of a product or open a new version if the product is not already running, as shown in the following:

```
Sub modObject_LaunchApplication()
    Dim objExcel As Excel.Application
    ' Use open copy of Excel
    On Error Resume Next
    Set objExcel = GetObject(, "Excel.Application")
    If Err <> 0 Then
        Err.Clear
        ' create  a new copy of execl
        Set objExcel = New Excel.Application
        If Err <> 0 Then
            Debug.Print Err.Number, Err.Description
        Else
            objExcel.Visible = True
        End If
        Err.Clear
    End If
    Set objExcel = Nothing
    Dim objWord As Word.Application
    ' Use open copy of word
    Set objWord = GetObject(, "Word.Application")
    If Err <> 0 Then
        Err.Clear
        ' create a new copy of word
        Set objWord = New Word.Application
        If Err <> 0 Then
            Debug.Print Err.Number, Err.Description
```

```
            Else
                objWord.Visible = True
            End If
            Err.Clear
        End If
        Set objWord = Nothing
End Sub
```

Opening Existing Files

In the previous examples, you used *GetObject, New*, and *CreateObject* to work with the
application object. You can open existing files by using two methods: you can create an
application object and then use *Open* commands to open a file, or you can directly open
the file by using *GetObject*. It is also useful to have different object variables; for example,
you can open a *Word.Document* object called *objDocument*, and to refer to the application
object, you can use *objDocument.Application*, but it can be clearer in your code to define
a separate object variable and set that to the application object. The following code shows
examples of this:

```
Sub modObject_OpenAnApplicationOtherObjects()
    Dim objExcel As Excel.Application
    Dim objWorkbook As Excel.Workbook
    Dim strFile As String
    strFile = CurrentProject.Path & "\SpecificationToRead.xlsx"
    ' opens an existing file
    Set objWorkbook = GetObject(strFile)
    Set objExcel = objWorkbook.Application
    objExcel.Visible = True
    objExcel.Windows(1).Visible = True
    Stop
    Set objWorkbook = Nothing
    Set objExcel = Nothing
    Dim objWord As Word.Application
    Dim objDocument As Word.Document
    ' open an existing file
    strFile = CurrentProject.Path & "\Quote.docx"
    Set objDocument = GetObject(strFile)
    Set objWord = objDocument.Application
    objWord.Visible = True
    Stop
    objWord.Quit
    Set objWord = Nothing
End Sub
```

Connecting Access to Word

In this section, you will look at connecting Access to Word by using VBA programming. Typical applications of these techniques are to generate documents, filling in details at pre-defined points via a placeholder document with bookmarks, and boiler plating a document by merging in sections from other documents.

Figure 13-2 shows the Word object model. The use of bookmarks and ranges have a number of overlapping features in the object model; this supports the different ways to manipulate areas of text.

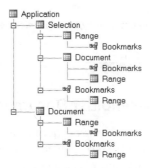

Figure 13-2 The Word object model.

The key objects in the Word object model are:

- **Application**   This is used to control the Word environment.

- **Document**   A document.

- **Selection**   A selection of one or more blocks of areas of text; for example, selecting text to then apply formatting. This represents the currently selected areas of text.

- **Range**   An area of text. A document can support multiple ranges.

- **Bookmark**   A named area of text that can be visible or hidden.

As described earlier in this chapter, you need to add a reference to the Word Object Library before developing the code described in this section. The sample database file to use in this section is WordQuote.accdb.

INSIDE OUT   Pasting links to queries from Access into Word

If you select a query in Access from the navigation window and copy it to the clipboard, you can paste the link into Word by clicking Home | Paste | Paste Special Paste | Paste Link. This gives you a dynamic link from Word to the query.

If you then use the shortcut menu and select Edit Field, you will see that the link looks like the following:

```
- DDEAUTO MSAccess "C:\\ASC08\\ACCESS~1\\CODEEX~1\\CHAPTE~4\\WORDQU~1.
ACC;Query qryToPasteIntoWord" All \r
```

This is further explained in the knowledge base article *http://support.microsoft.com/ kb/100931*.

Generating Documents from a Placeholder Document

The example in this section shows how to construct a placeholder document, into which data from tables in the database can be merged; this is a technique that can be used to generate quotations, specifications, and other documents. You begin by setting up tables in the database that are used to manage multiple placeholder documents. Figure 13-3 shows a table that you can use to manage your documents.

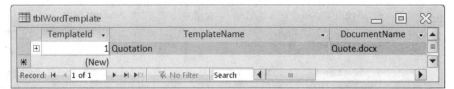

Figure 13-3 Creating a table to hold a list of placeholder documents, referred to as templates. This could hold related information on document paths, document versions, and so on.

We have also created a table that will hold a list of the database fields to be processed for each document, together with bookmark names, which you will create in the Word placeholder document. So that you can make this a general purpose feature for your applications, there are fields indicating the access query that will be used to source the data, a flag to indicate whether the data will be merged into a table in word, and a processing order field to control the order in which the merging is processed. This is illustrated in Figure 13-4.

Chapter 13

TemplateId	BookmarkName	DatabaseFieldName	DataSource	ProcessingOrder	TableToProcess
Quotation	bkCompanyName	Company	qryQuotationHeader	1	☐
Quotation	bkLastName	Last Name	qryQuotationHeader	2	☐
Quotation	bkAddress	Address	qryQuotationHeader	3	☐
Quotation	bkOrderDate	Order Date	qryQuotationHeader	4	☐
Quotation	bkShippingDate	Shipped Date	qryQuotationHeader	5	☐
Quotation	bkItemTable	Product Name	qryQuotationDetails	6	✓
Quotation	bkItemTable	Quantity	qryQuotationDetails	7	✓
Quotation	bkItemTable	Unit Price	qryQuotationDetails	8	✓

tblWordTemplateBookMark

Record: ◄ ◄ 1 of 8 ► ►► No Filter   Search

Figure 13-4 Creating a table to hold a list of the bookmarks and show how they map to each database field.

To create a placeholder document in Word, start a new document, and then from the options menu, select Advanced | Show Document Content | Show Bookmarks. This will help you when laying out the document. On the ribbon, on the Insert tab, click Links | Bookmark to manage the bookmarks in the document, as shown in Figure 13-5.

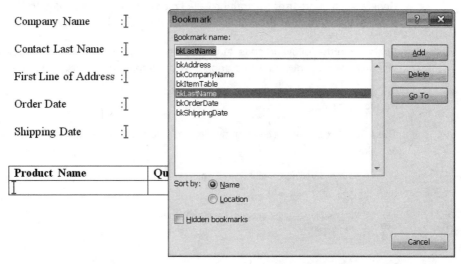

Figure 13-5 To populate a table of data, create a table with one row after your header, and then insert a bookmark in the first cell.

The sample database includes a form (see Figure 13-6) containing a button that you can use to generate a quote. Place a breakpoint behind this button and trace through the execution of the code.

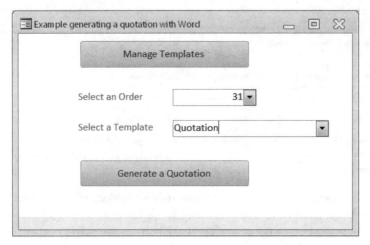

Figure 13-6 Selecting a quotation placeholder template for generating a document.

Opening a Placeholder Document

Generating a quote uses the routine called *modTesting_WriteAQuotation*. We will describe the key operations that this routine performs when creating a document.

As shown in the following code, at the top of the module, two object variables are declared; The first one manages the Word application, and the other refers to the specific document:

```
Dim appWord As Word.Application
Dim docQuote As Word.Document
```

The first two steps of processing involve opening Word, and then opening the document, as follows:

```
    If Not modWord_OpenWord(True) Then
        Exit Sub
    End If
    If Not modWord_OpenDocument(strDoc) Then
        Exit Sub
    End If
```

The function for opening Word either uses an existing copy of Word or starts a new copy:

```
Function modWord_OpenWord(UseExisting As Boolean) As Boolean
' open a copy of Word, if UseExisting is true try and use any existing open copy
' otherwise create a new instance of Word
    If UseExisting Then
        On Error Resume Next
        Set appWord = GetObject(, "Word.Application")
        Err.Clear
    End If
```

```
    If appWord Is Nothing Then
        Set appWord = CreateObject("Word.Application")
        appWord.Visible = True
    End If
    If Err <> 0 Then
        MsgBox "An error occured trying to start MS Word : " & _
            Err.Description, vbCritical, "Unable To Start MS Word"
        modWord_OpenWord = False
    Else
        modWord_OpenWord = True
    End If
End Function
```

The second function uses the *Open* method of the *Documents* collection to open the place-holder document, as demonstrated in the following:

```
Function modWord_OpenDocument(strFileName As String) As Boolean
' Open an existing word document
    On Error Resume Next
    Set docQuote = appWord.Documents.Open(strFileName)
    If Err <> 0 Then
            MsgBox "An error occured trying to start open the file : " & _
            strFileName & ": " & _
            Err.Description, vbCritical, "Unable To Open Document"
            modWord_OpenDocument = False
    Else
            modWord_OpenDocument = False
    End If
End Function
```

Merging Data with Bookmarks

The next steps are to systematically read through the data in the database, locate each bookmark in Word, and then merge in the data.

As shown in the following code example, you start by defining variables for performing the merge and reading through the *Recordset*:

```
    Dim db As DAO.Database
    Set db = CurrentDb
    Dim rstBookmark As DAO.Recordset
    Dim rstData As DAO.Recordset
    Dim strDataSource As String
    Dim strData As String
    Dim strBookMark As String
    Dim boolProcessingATable As Boolean
    Dim bkTableProcessing As String           ' variable for recording a bookmark

    Set rstBookmark = db.OpenRecordset("SELECT * FROM tblWordTemplateBookMark " & _
                    " WHERE TemplateId = " & lngTemplateId _
                    & " ORDER BY ProcessingOrder", dbOpenDynaset)
    strDataSource = ""
    boolProcessingATable = False
```

The next section of code commences a loop through all the bookmarks defined in the database. It also dynamically opens and closes the required Access *Recordsets*, depending on the required source of data; different queries could be used for different parts of the document.

```
Do While Not rstBookmark.EOF
    If strDataSource <> rstBookmark!DataSource Then
        ' Need to change the datasource
        Set rstData = db.OpenRecordset("SELECT * FROM [" _
                & rstBookmark!DataSource & "] WHERE [Order Id] = " & _
                lngOrderId, dbOpenDynaset)
        strDataSource = rstBookmark!DataSource
    End If
```

The next step is to read the data from the database field by using the line of code including Nz(rstData(rstBookmark!DatabaseFieldName)). Here, you use the field name, which is contained in rstBookmark!DatabaseFieldName, to index the field in the *Recordset rstData*, as shown in the following:

```
AnotherRow:
    On Error Resume Next
    strData = Nz(rstData(rstBookmark!DatabaseFieldName))
    If Err <> 0 Then
        MsgBox "Unable to find field " & rstBookmark!DatabaseFieldName & _
                " in data source " & strDataSource, _
        vbCritical, "Unable To Get Data"
        Exit Sub
    End If
    strBookMark = rstBookmark!BookmarkName
```

If we are then simply inserting a value at a bookmark then we use the following code:

```
        boolProcessingATable = False
        ' simple merge of data to a bookmark
        If Not modWord_InsertAtBookMark(strData, strBookMark) Then
            Exit Sub
        End If
```

This calls the routine *modWord_InsertAtBookMark*, which uses the line docQuote. Bookmarks(strBookMark).Select to select the point at the bookmark where data will be inserted, and then docQuote.Application.Selection.InsertAfter strData to merge the data:

```
Function modWord_InsertAtBookMark(strData As String, strBookMark As String) _
        As Boolean
' Inserts the data at a specific bookmark
On Error Resume Next
    docQuote.Bookmarks(strBookMark).Select
```

```
    If Err <> 0 Then
        MsgBox "Failed to locate bookmark : " & strBookMark, _
            vbCritical, "Failed To Find Bookmark"
        modWord_InsertAtBookMark = False
        Exit Function
    End If
    docQuote.Application.Selection.InsertAfter strData
    If Err <> 0 Then
        MsgBox "Failed to insert data: " & strData & " at " & _
            strBookMark, vbCritical, "Failed Merge Data"
        modWord_InsertAtBookMark = False
    Else
        modWord_InsertAtBookMark = True
    End If
End Function
```

The outer processing routine is also designed to write data into a Word table. To do this, when processing the first line, you locate the bookmark. Then, for all subsequent lines, you use the *MoveRight* method, which causes the cursor in the table to move beyond the current cell to the next line and insert a new row. This uses the following code:

```
If Not boolProcessingATable Then
    ' find the bookmark to start processing from
    bkTableProcessing = rstBookmark.Bookmark

    If Not modWord_FindBookMark(strBookMark) Then
        Exit Sub
    End If
    ' insert the data
    If Not modWord_InsertData(strData) Then
        Exit Sub
    End If
    boolProcessingATable = True
Else
    ' move right and enter data
    If Not modWord_MoveRight() Then
        Exit Sub
    End If
    If Not modWord_InsertData(strData) Then
        Exit Sub
    End If
End If
```

This results in the completed document, as shown in Figure 13-7.

Quotation to Be Filled In By Access

Company Name   : Company D

Contact Last Name   : Lee

First Line of Address : 123 4th Street

Order Date   : 01/20/2006

Shipping Date   : 01/20/2006

Product Name	Quantity	Unit Cost
Northwind Traders Dried Pears	10	30
Northwind Traders Dried Apples	10	53
Northwind Traders Dried Plums	10	3.5

Figure 13-7 A completed document generated in Word.

The final code sections call a routine to save the document and then a tidy up routine, which could be configured to leave the documents open in Word, or close Word after producing the document, as presented in the following:

```
Function modWord_SaveAs(strNewDocName As String) As Boolean
    docQuote.SaveAs2 strNewDocName
    If Err <> 0 Then
        modWord_SaveAs = False
    Else
        modWord_SaveAs = True
    End If
End Function
Function modWord_CleanUp(boolCloseDocument As Boolean, boolCloseWord As Boolean) As _

        Boolean
    If boolCloseDocument Then
        docQuote.Close
    End If
    If boolCloseWord Then
        appWord.Quit
    End If
    Set appWord = Nothing
    Set docQuote = Nothing
    If Err <> 0 Then
        modWord_CleanUp = False
    Else
        modWord_CleanUp = True
    End If
End Function
```

INSIDE OUT   Mail merge

In addition to adding links to data in the database and writing data under program control into a document, you can also use the mail merge features in Word to produce documents by using data from the database. A wizard is available to assist you in setting up your mail merge. To access it, on the ribbon, click Mailings | Start Mail Merge | Step By Step Mail Merge Wizard. Using the wizard, you can select a data source and merge the results of a table or query into a document.

Connecting Access to Excel

In this section, you will be looking at working with some of the key objects in Excel. Figure 13-8 shows a simplified object model of Excel.

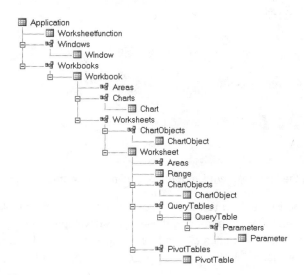

Figure 13-8 A simplified Excel object model.

Excel supports a large number of different object types, some of the key object types are as follows:

- **Application**   Used to manipulate the Excel environment

- **Workbook**   A file that contains multiple Worksheets

- **Worksheet**   A spreadsheet

- **Range** A region within Excel
- **Cell** A cell
- **PivotTable** A pivot table with a possible connection to external data such as Access tables/queries

As described earlier in this chapter, you need to add a reference to the Excel Object Library before developing the code described in this section. The sample database file to use in this section is ExcelAnalysis.accdb.

Writing Data to a Spreadsheet

In this section, you will look at situations in which you need to either directly read or write information into a spreadsheet. This is particularly useful when receiving or providing information to other people in or outside your organization who will not have any access to your database. The demonstration form *frmExcelOperations* shown in Figure 13-9 is used to read and write data to Excel.

Figure 13-9 Opening the *frmExcelOperations* form for reading and writing data to Excel.

The first example demonstrates how to transfer information from database tables to a placeholder spreadsheet. To facilitate re-using the methods developed here and in other parts of an application, we have created a table for holding a list of placeholder template documents, as shown in Figure 13-10.

tblExcelTemplate

TemplateId	TemplateName	DocumentName	DocumentPath	WriteData
1	Product Specification	ProductSpecification.xlsx		☑
2	Product Specification To Read	SpecificationToRead.xlsx		☐
(New)				☐

Record: 1 of 2 No Filter Search

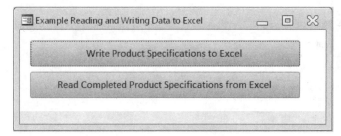

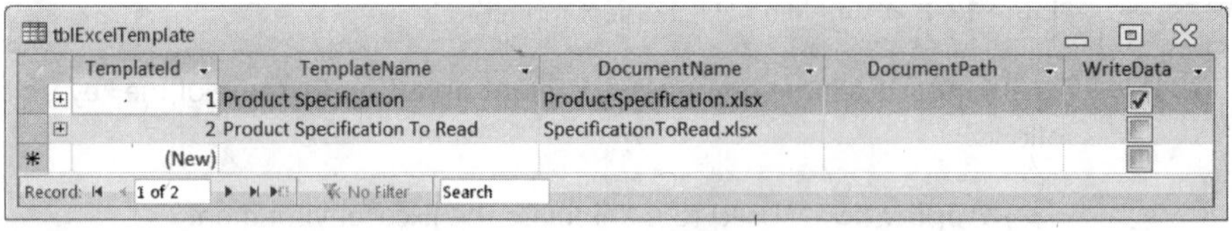

Figure 13-10 A table designed to support reading and writing of data from different spreadsheets. Each placeholder spreadsheet is referred to a template in the code.

Notice that each placeholder template has entries in a related table (see Figure 13-11), which is used to tie up the reference in a cell to a field in the database (this technique can be easily extended to handle multiple spreadsheets in a workbook).

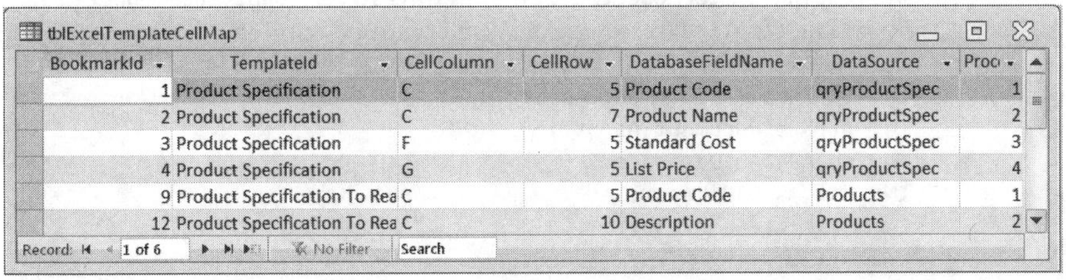

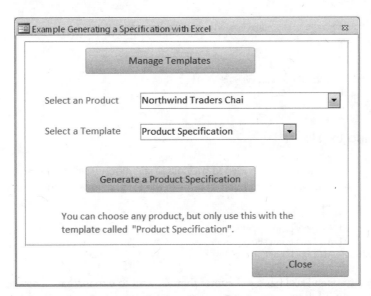

Figure 13-11 Each spreadsheet uses a table of instructions for reading and writing data. This links the database field names to the cell positions in Excel.

Referring back to Figure 13-9, use the Write Product Specifications To Excel button to display a form, from which you select the specification template and database products, as shown in Figure 13-12.

Figure 13-12 Use the sample form *frmExcelProductSpecWrite* to select a product and specification document template, and then generate a document in Excel.

The code behind the Generate A Product Specification button calls a routine in a library to generate the specification, passing the identifiers for the product and the specification, as shown in the following:

```
modTesting_WriteProductSpec Me.cboTemplateId, Me.cboProductId
```

As demonstrated in the following code sample, the first part of the processing routine looks up some key information based on the document and product identifiers, and then prepares to open the spreadsheet in Excel:

```
Sub modTesting_WriteProductSpec(lngTemplateId As Long, lngProductId As Long)
    ' uses a template to write a product specification

    Dim strTemplateDocument As String
    Dim strSpecDocument As String
    Dim db As DAO.Database
    Dim rst As DAO.Recordset
    Dim crst As Recordset

    strSpecDocument = DLookup("[Product Code]", "Products", "[ID] = " _
                              & lngProductId)
    strTemplateDocument = DLookup("[DocumentName]", "tblExcelTemplate", _
            "[TemplateId] = " & lngTemplateId)
    strSpecDocument = CurrentProject.Path & "\" & strSpecDocument & ".xlsx"
    strTemplateDocument = CurrentProject.Path & "\" & strTemplateDocument
    If Not modExcel_OpenExcel(True) Then
        Stop
    End If
    If Not modExcel_OpenWorkBook(strTemplateDocument) Then
        Stop
    End If

    If Not modExcel_OpenActiveWorkSheet() Then
        Stop
    End If
```

Opening Excel

All the Excel operations are contained within a single module called *modExcel*, at the top of the module, variables are defined to refer to the Excel objects, as shown in the code that follows:

```
Dim appExcel As Excel.Application
Dim wkbExcel As Excel.Workbook
Dim wksExcel As Excel.Worksheet
```

The code to open Excel has a parameter that allows it to either create a new Excel application or use an existing instance of Excel. If the parameter is set to use an existing instance of Excel and one does not exist, it will create a new instance, as shown here:

```
Function modExcel_OpenExcel(UseExisting As Boolean) As Boolean
' open a copy of Excel
    If UseExisting Then
        On Error Resume Next
```

```
        Set appExcel = GetObject(, "Excel.Application")
        appExcel.Visible = True
        Err.Clear


    End If
    If appExcel Is Nothing Then
        Set appExcel = CreateObject("Excel.Application")
        appExcel.Visible = True
    End If
    If Err <> 0 Then
        MsgBox "An error occured trying to start MS Word : " & _
                Err.Description, vbCritical, "Unable To Start MS Excel"
        modExcel_OpenExcel = False
    Else
        modExcel_OpenExcel = True
    End If
End Function
```

The second routine loads the Excel Workbook:

```
Function modExcel_OpenWorkBook(strFileName As String) As Boolean
' Open an existing Excel document
    On Error Resume Next
    Set wkbExcel = appExcel.Workbooks.Open(strFileName)
    If Err <> 0 Then
        MsgBox "An error occured trying to start open the file : " & _
                strFileName & " : " & Err.Description, vbCritical, _
                "Unable To Open Workbook"
        modExcel_OpenWorkBook = False
    Else
        modExcel_OpenWorkBook = True
    End If
End Function
```

The third routine gets a reference to the active worksheet. You can modify this routine to get a reference to a specifically-named worksheet (an example of which is shown in *modExcel_SyntaxForWorkSheets*):

```
Function modExcel_OpenActiveWorkSheet() As Boolean
' Open an existing word document
    On Error Resume Next
    Set wksExcel = wkbExcel.ActiveSheet
    If Err <> 0 Then
        MsgBox "An error occured trying to choose active sheet in workbook :" _
                & Err.Description, vbCritical, "Unable To Select ActiveSheet"
        modExcel_OpenActiveWorkSheet = False
```

```
        Else
            modExcel_OpenActiveWorkSheet = True
        End If
End Function

Sub modExcel_SyntaxtForWorkSheets(strExpectedName As String)
    'Set wksExcel = wkbExcel.Sheets(i)
    Dim sheetExcel As Excel.Worksheet
    ' use code like the following to locate a specific worksheet
    For Each sheetExcel In wkbExcel.Worksheets
        If sheetExcel.Name = strExpectedName Then
            Set wksExcel = sheetExcel
        End If
    Next
End Sub
```

Writing the Data

Returning now to your main outer code loop, you can examine the additional *Do While Not crst.EOF* loop that writes all the data entries into the worksheet, as shown here:

```
' Now process the data
Set db = CurrentDb
Set rst = db.OpenRecordset("SELECT * FROM qryProductSpec WHERE [ID] = " _
                            & lngProductId, dbOpenDynaset)
Set crst = db.OpenRecordset("SELECT * FROM tblExcelTemplateCellMap " & _
                            " WHERE [TemplateId] = " _
                            & lngTemplateId, dbOpenDynaset)
Do While Not crst.EOF
    If Not modExcel_WriteCell(crst!CellColumn, crst!CellRow, _
                        CStr(rst(crst!databaseFieldName))) Then
        Stop
    End If
    crst.MoveNext
Loop
```

This code uses the *Recordset crst* to find the name of the database field, and then uses the expression CStr(rst(crst!databaseFieldName)) to extract the value from the *Recordset*.

You can set a breakpoint in the code to display the key values in the variables and expressions in the Watches window, as shown in Figure 13-13.

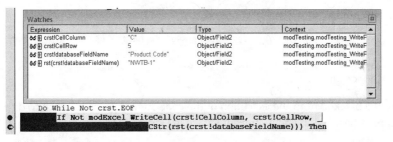

Figure 13-13 Using the Watches window to examine the key variables used to write data to the spreadsheet.

Figure 13-13 shows that the cell reference is C5 and the database field name of Product Code extracts the value NWTB-1.

The *WriteCell* procedure is as follows:

```
Function modExcel_WriteCell(strCol As String, lngRow As Long, _
                            strCellvalue As String) As Boolean
' Write to a cell
    On Error Resume Next
    wksExcel.Cells(lngRow, modExcel_MapLetterToColumn(strCol)) = strCellvalue
    If Err <> 0 Then
        MsgBox "An error occured trying to write to excel : " & Err.Description, _
            vbCritical, "Unable To Write Data"
        modExcel_WriteCell = False
    Else
        modExcel_WriteCell = True
    End If
End Function
```

Because you are referencing the cell by using a column number and not a column letter, we have added a function to map the column letter to a numeric value, as shown in the following:

```
Function modExcel_MapLetterToColumn(strCol As String) As Long
    ' map excel columns to a number
    ' A......Z AA.....ZZ
    Dim lngCol As Long
    Dim strChar As String
    If Len(strCol) = 0 Or Len(strCol) > 2 Then
        modExcel_MapLetterToColumn = 0
        Exit Function
    End If
    strChar = UCase(Left(strCol, 1))
    lngCol = Asc(strChar) - 64
```

```
        If Len(strCol) > 1 Then
            strChar = UCase(Mid(strCol, 1, 1))
            lngCol = (lngCol + 1) * 25 + (Asc(strChar) - 64)
        End If
        modExcel_MapLetterToColumn = lngCol
End Function
```

Add a breakpoint to the execution of the code so that you can switch to display the Excel spreadsheet cells being written, as shown in Figure 13-14.

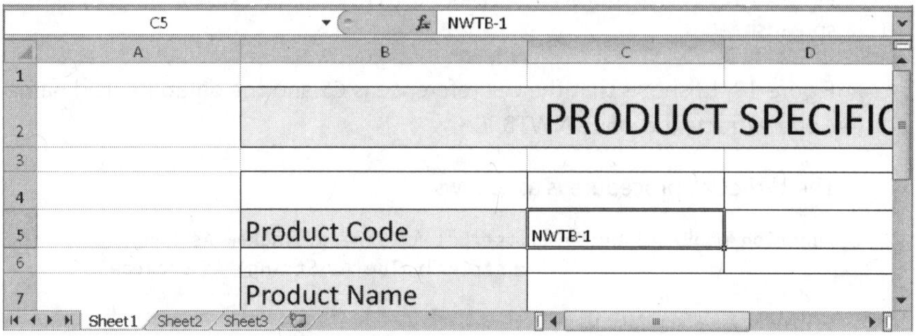

Figure 13-14 Monitoring activity in Excel as data is written to the spreadsheet.

The last portion of your code calls a routine to save the spreadsheet:

```
    If Not modExcel_SaveAs(strSpecDocument) Then
        Stop
    End If

Function modExcel_SaveAs(strNewDocName As String) As Boolean
    wkbExcel.SaveAs strNewDocName
    If Err <> 0 Then
        modExcel_SaveAs = False
    Else
        modExcel_SaveAs = True
    End If
End Function
```

INSIDE OUT   Using Excel to drive an Access application

In the sample spreadsheet ExcelOpeningAccess.xlsm, we have written sample code that allows Excel to directly manipulate objects in an Access application by using the following VBA code:

```
Sub StartAccess_Click()
    Dim appAccess As Access.Application
    Dim db As DAO.Database
```

```
        Dim rst As DAO.Recordset
        Dim strDatabase As String
        strDatabase = ActiveWorkbook.Path & "\ExcelAnalysis.accdb"
        Set appAccess = GetObject(strDatabase)
        Set db = appAccess.CurrentDb
        Set rst = db.OpenRecordset("Employees", dbOpenDynaset)
        Do While Not rst.EOF
            Debug.Print rst![Last Name]
            rst.MoveNext
        Loop
        Stop
        appAccess.Quit
End Sub
```

References have been added to the Microsoft Access 14.0 Object Library and Microsoft Office 14.0 Access database engine Object Library. This then allows all the types of code that you have been looking at in this book to be executed from inside Excel.

Reading Data from a Spreadsheet

The process of reading data from an Excel spreadsheet is very similar to the previously described operations for writing data. In the sample code that follows, we have shown part of the code from the module *modTesting_ReadProductSpec*, which performs the read operation.

Rather than read the data directly into the table, we have created a temporary table into which you will read the data. You can then use this to update the main tables in the database:

```
' now empty the temporary table
CurrentDb.Execute "DELETE * FROM tblTEMP_Products"

' Now process the data
Set db = CurrentDb
Set rst = db.OpenRecordset("SELECT * FROM tblTEMP_Products", dbOpenDynaset)
Set crst = db.OpenRecordset("SELECT * FROM tblExcelTemplateCellMap  " & _
                            " WHERE [TemplateId] = " & _
                            lngTemplateId, dbOpenDynaset)
rst.AddNew
Do While Not crst.EOF
    strReadValue = ""
    If Not modExcel_ReadCell(crst!CellColumn, _
                            crst!CellRow, strReadValue) Then
        Stop
    End If
    ' save the results
    rst(crst!databaseFieldName) = strReadValue
    crst.MoveNext
```

```
    Loop
    rst.Update

    ' now we could have appropriate validation
    ' and then execute the update
    CurrentDb.Execute "qryUpdateProductsFromExcel"

    If Not modExcel_CleanUp(True, True) Then
        Stop
    End If
```

The following code illustrates the *ReadCell* processing routine is the reverse of the *WriteCell* operation:

```
Function modExcel_ReadCell(strCol As String, lngRow As Long, _
                           ByRef strCellvalue As String) As Boolean
' Read from a cell
' Note we are ensuring that by using an Explicit ByVal that this routine can modify
the value
    On Error Resume Next
    strCellvalue = wksExcel.Cells(lngRow, modExcel_MapLetterToColumn(strCol))
    If Err <> 0 Then
        MsgBox "An error occured trying to read from excel : " _
                & Err.Description, vbCritical, "Unable To Read Data"
        modExcel_ReadCell = False
    Else
        modExcel_ReadCell = True
    End If
End Function
```

Reporting with Excel Linked to Access

In this example, you will look at a very simple and effective way to use Excel for management reporting. There are two compelling reasons for using Excel in this manner (in particular when working with financials). First, the people consuming the data might prefer to use Excel for reporting because it also enables them to tie in their own data from other Excel applications. Second, Excel has many wonderful reporting features that can be difficult to reproduce in Access.

When you link Excel to queries in Access, there are restrictions regarding the use of Access-specific functions, such as the *Nz* function or custom VBA functions in a query; you need to avoid these. You also cannot use any queries that contain references to controls on Access forms.

To get around this restriction of having an Access query that directly references controls on a form, one simple approach to reporting is to create a local table that contains a user's reporting selections and include this table to filter data in any queries. This can then be linked directly to Excel. To use this approach, the simplest solution is to give each user a copy of an Access front-end application with a local table containing these choices for reporting (or if the application were shared, only one user at a time could use this reporting feature).

If you decide that rather than creating this for yourself that you prefer to use our example Excel spreadsheet, ExcelReporting.xlsx, you will need to edit the existing connections in the spreadsheet if your database is on a different path to the one we have used. On the ribbon, on the Data tab, click the Connections group, and then click the Connections icon. You will see four items; for the two items, ExcelAnalysis(1), go to Properties | Connection String, and then edit the path to ExcelAnalysis.accdb. For the two items, Query from ExcelAnalysisDatabase(1), make the same change, but notice that you make the change twice in each connection string.

You start by creating a table that will have only one row that is set to the user's reporting choices, as shown in Figure 13-15. Note that this is a single-user solution.

Figure 13-15 The table holding parameter choices for a user. The first field is the primary key, although this table only ever holds one record.

Use the form called *frmExcelReporting* (see Figure 13-16), which contains a combo box that you use to select a reporting period. The combo box is bound to the ReportingMonth column in *tblReportingParameters*.

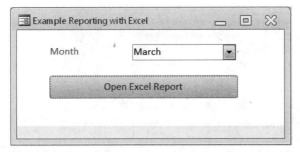

Figure 13-16 The sample form *frmExcelReporting* for opening Excel and refreshing links to Access.

You start by constructing a query in Access that will use the user's reporting choices to restrict the data. This uses a cross-join or Cartesian product to restrict the records to the user's choice of parameters, the query *qryProductSales* is shown in Figure 13-17.

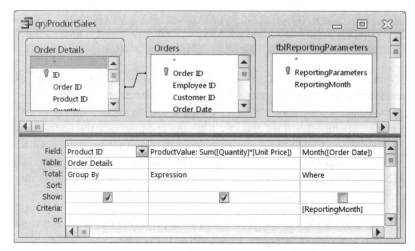

Figure 13-17 A query displaying product sales for a selected month.

The actual products sold each month can change and you want to produce a query that includes all the products. To do this, you create another query that brings the main product and sales information together. This query is called *qryProductSalesAllProducts* (see Figure 13-18), and it uses an outer join to bring together all the product records.

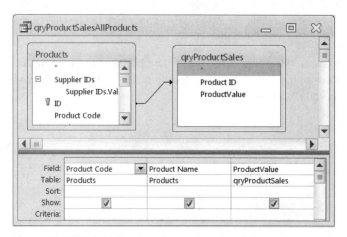

Figure 13-18 Combining the sales and product information together.

There is one more piece of information that you want to include: the reporting month. To do this, you create a top-level query that uses a Cartesian product to project the month information. This uses the *qryProductSalesForExcel* query, as shown in Figure 13-19.

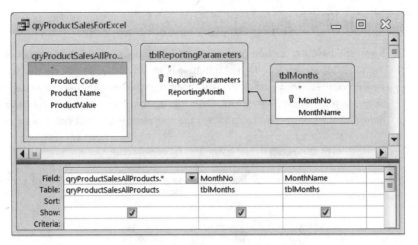

Figure 13-19 A Top-level query displaying month information.

With all the queries saved and closed, you can now open Excel and create a link to the query with the resulting data.

In a new spreadsheet, on the ribbon, on the Data tab, click the Access icon to create the link, as shown in Figure 13-20.

Figure 13-20 Getting external data from Access.

Then, browse until you locate the ExcelAnalysis.accdb database, as shown in Figure 13-21.

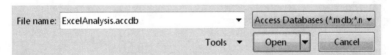

Figure 13-21 Use the file dialog to browse and locate your Access database file.

INSIDE OUT   Setting Data Link advanced properties

If you still have Access open and click the Test Connection on the Connection tab, a message displays indicating that database is already open. To resolve this, in the Data Link Properties window, click the Advanced tab. You will see that the Access Permissions are set to Share Deny Write. Clear this option, and then select the Read check box. Return to the Connection tab and test the connection; the test will now succeed.

Figure 13-22 shows the Data Link connection and the Access Permissions for the connection.

Figure 13-22 Click the Advanced tab on the Data Link Properties dialog box to set the Access Permissions properties.

After you successfully test the connection (on the Connection tab) and click the OK button, Excel displays a list of tables and queries in Access (see Figure 13-23). Notice that this list does not show queries that Excel cannot understand; for example, any query using a custom VBA function. The query *qryProductSalesAllProductsUsingIIF* is displayed, but the query *qryProductSalesAllProductsUsingNZ* is not displayed because it contains the *Nz* function in an expression.

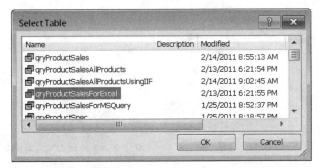

Figure 13-23 Selecting from available tables and queries. Not all queries will be shown, depending on their content.

The Import Data dialog box opens and prompts you to select whether you want the data displayed in a Table, PivotTable Report, or a PivotChart And PivotTable Report, as shown in Figure 13-24.

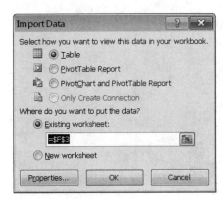

Figure 13-24 Although this is the Import Data dialog box, you are constructing a dynamic link to the query in the Access Database.

After pressing OK to create the linked table of data, place your cursor inside the area of the table, right-click to display the shortcut menu, and then click the Refresh option, which refreshes the data in the table if any changes were made to the data in Access.

Figure 13-25 shows the shortcut menu option to manage the external data for the table.

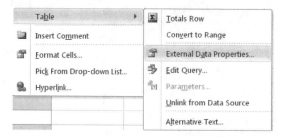

Figure 13-25 The External Data Properties can be used to manage settings for the table.

Figure 13-26 presents the External Data Properties dialog box. Click the button adjacent to the Connection Name text box to manage the connection details and make changes to the name of the query, table, or SQL used for the external data.

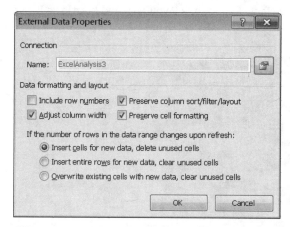

Figure 13-26 Click the button next to the Connection Name box to open a window, in which you can change connection properties.

INSIDE OUT   Planning for linking to external data

A useful approach to managing external data links is to allocate one spreadsheet page (for example, called *RawData*) and place all of your linked tables on this single page. Other spreadsheet pages can then link to this data page.

Depending on how you construct your queries, it can be useful to have a database field to control the ordering of the data being linked from Excel so that when new data rows are added, they do not disrupt any dependencies on row ordering that you build into the spreadsheet formulae. It can also be useful to change the options shown in Figure 13-26 and select the option Overwrite Existing Cells With New Data, Clear Unused Cells so that additional data does not move other linked tables of data. Planning your layouts to allow for growth in tables of data is important, and placing multiple tables to the right of each other and not below each other can help with allowing for the growth of data.

After selecting the query, you are offered a number of options for adding the data as a linked table or pivot table. For this example, choose to display the data as a table.

On the Data tab, click the Connections group, and then click the Connections button to display the Workbook Connections dialog box. Here, you can manage all the connections for the Workbook, as shown in Figure 13-27.

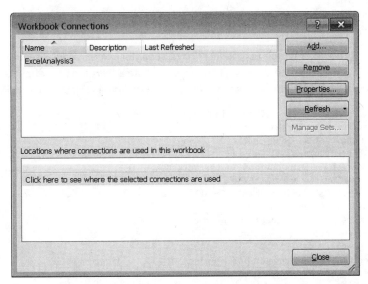

Figure 13-27 Use the Workbook Connections dialog box to manage all the connections in the Workbook.

Save and close the spreadsheet, return to the Access application where you will construct some VBA code to allow the user to make selections, and then open and refresh the Excel spreadsheet.

The code behind the button that refreshes the Excel spreadsheet is as follows:

```
Private Sub cmdReportInExcel_Click()
    ' save any changes made by the user
    Me.Dirty = False
    Dim strExcelWorkBook As String
    strExcelWorkBook = CurrentProject.Path & "\" & "ExcelReporting.xlsx"
    If Not modExcel_OpenExcel(True) Then
        Stop
    End If
    If Not modExcel_OpenWorkBook(strExcelWorkBook) Then
        Stop
    End If

    If Not modExcel_OpenActiveWorkSheet() Then
        Stop
    End If
    If Not modExcel_RefreshConnections () Then
        Stop
    End If
End Sub
```

The details behind the open procedures have been discussed in earlier sections. The procedure that refreshes the Excel workbook can execute a *RefreshAll* to refresh all items, or it
can selectively refresh the connections (and associated data tables) and any pivots:

```
Function modExcel_RefreshConnections() As Boolean
    On Error GoTo Err_Handler
    Dim lngCount As Long
'    wkbExcel.RefreshAll
    ' refresh all connections in the workbook
    For lngCount = 1 To wkbExcel.Connections.Count
        wkbExcel.Connections(lngCount).Refresh
    Next
    modExcel_RefreshConnections = True
    Exit Function
Err_Handler:
    modExcel_RefreshConnections = False
    Exit Function
End Function
```

Using MS Query and Data Sources

In the previous section, you linked Excel to Access by using connections; this is not the only
method that can be used when connecting Excel to Access. If you are working with older
linked spreadsheets, they are likely to use the second technique, which is described in this
section.

On the Data tab, click the Get External Data group, and then click From Other Sources | From
Microsoft Query. This displays the Choose Data Source dialog box shown in Figure 13-28.

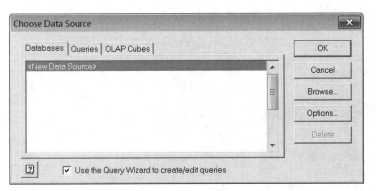

Figure 13-28 Select the Use The Query Wizard To Create/Edit Queries check box if you want the wizard to provide assistance while setting up or editing queries.

If you do not already have a data source, select <New Data Source>, and then click OK. The Create New Data Source dialog box opens, as shown in Figure 13-29.

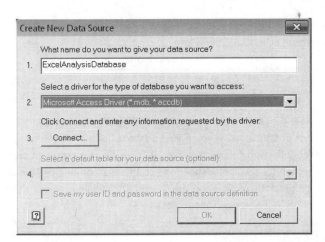

Figure 13-29 Enter a name for your data source, and then select the Microsoft Access Driver.

Use the Connect button to browse and select your Access Database. (You might find that you need to close the Access Database to avoid messages indicating that the database is already in use.) You can then select your new database connection, which will be displayed in the Choose Data Source dialog.

You might notice that unlike the connection wizard described in the previous section, the Query Wizard will display queries that you are not allowed to use, and if you try to connect to an illegal query, such as *qryProductSalesAllProductsusingNZ*, you will see the error message displayed in Figure 13-30.

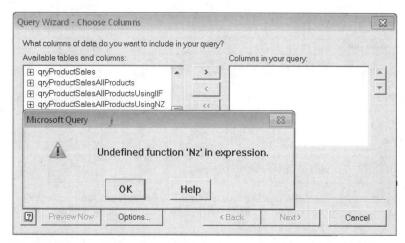

Figure 13-30 The error message that pops up if you attempt to use a query that contains an unsupported function.

In the sample spreadsheet called ExcelReporting.xlsx, we have added both a *Table* and *Pivot Table* to the spreadsheet called *MSQueryData*.

INSIDE OUT   *QueryTables* and *ListObjects*

The Excel worksheet contains two collections called *PivotTables* and *QueryTables*. With older versions of Office, when you linked a table of data, this created an entry in the *QueryTables* collection, but with Office 2010, it does not create an entry in the *QueryTables* collection for the spreadsheet object. Instead, connections are created as described in the previous section and the *QueryTable* can be accessed through the *ListObjects* collection in the *SpreadSheet* object

In the spreadsheet ExcelReporting.xlsm, we have included some example module code for listing *Connection* and *QueryTable* information, as shown below:

```
Sub modCon_Connections()
    Dim lngCount As Long
    Dim ODBCCon As ODBCConnection
    Dim OLEDBCon As OLEDBConnection
    For lngCount = 1 To ActiveWorkbook.Connections.Count
        With ActiveWorkbook.Connections(lngCount)
            Debug.Print .Type
            If .Type = xlConnectionTypeODBC Then
                Set ODBCCon = ActiveWorkbook.Connections(lngCount).ODBCConnection
                Debug.Print "ODBC " & .Name
                Debug.Print ODBCCon.CommandText
            End If
```

```
            If .Type = xlConnectionTypeOLEDB Then
                Set OLEDBCon = ActiveWorkbook.Connections(lngCount).OLEDBConnection
                Debug.Print "OLEDB" & .Name
                Debug.Print OLEDBCon.CommandText
            End If
        End With
    Next
    Dim qtable As QueryTable
    Dim lstObject As ListObject
    For Each lstObject In ActiveWorkbook.Worksheets("MSQueryData").ListObjects
        Debug.Print lstObject.Name
        Set qtable = lstObject.QueryTable
        Debug.Print qtable.CommandText
        Debug.Print qtable.Connection
    Next
End Sub
```

Connecting Access to Outlook

Figure 13-31 shows a simplified view of the Outlook object model. At the heart of the Outlook object model is the *Namespace*, the only supported namespace is MAPI, so very much like when working with DAO, wherein you need a reference to the database object, in Outlook, you need a reference to the namespace before you can undertake a lot of programming.

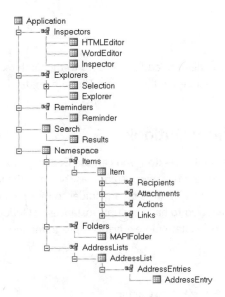

Figure 13-31 A simplified Outlook object model.

A very clever feature of the object model is that the *Application* object supports *CreateItem* syntax without the need to traverse the hierarchy to create an object of a specific type.

The *Items* collections in Outlook can hold different types of objects (note that *Item* contained in the collection is, in fact, an object data type); this is a very flexible mechanism as it allows for a folder to hold both email items and subsequent folders. But this also means that when traversing a collection, you will need to define a generic object type, and then test the class of object type before subsequently assigning the object to a particular known type of object (to get IntelliSense in your code).

The key objects with which to get started in the Outlook object model are as follows:

- **Application**   Used to control the outlook environment

- **Explorer**   User interface windows that display content

- **Inspector**   Window displaying a single item such as an email message

- **MAPIFolder**   Folder containing email messages, tasks and appointments, and so on

- **MailItem**   Email message

- **AppointmentItem**   An appointment

- **TaskItem**   A task

- **ContactItem**   A contact

As described earlier in this chapter, you need to add a reference to the Outlook Object Library before developing the code described in this section. The sample database file to use is OutlookContacts.accdb.

Extracting Information from Outlook

If you already have Outlook running on the desktop, you can use *GetObject* to get a reference to it; if it is not running, you can create a new instance, as shown in the following code, note that you need to call the *Display* method on any folder to make Outlook visible (if required). Also note that you are allowed to have multiple instances of Outlook. There are also *Logon* and *LogOff* methods to facilitate more advanced programming:

```
Sub modOutlook_OpenOutlook()
    ' Initialize outlook objects
    On Error Resume Next
    Set appOutlook = GetObject(, "Outlook.Application")
    If Err <> 0 Then
        ' attempt to start outlook
        ' Note that this code can be used to start a second instance of outlook
```

```
        Set appOutlook = New Outlook.Application
        Set namespaceOutlook = appOutlook.GetNamespace("MAPI")
        Dim folderOutlook As Folder
        Set folderOutlook = namespaceOutlook.GetDefaultFolder(olFolderInbox)
        ' make outlook visible on the desktop
        folderOutlook.Display
    Else
        Set namespaceOutlook = appOutlook.GetNamespace("MAPI")
    End If
End Sub
```

Following good coding practice, you need a tidy up operation, which could also incorporate the *Quit* method on the application object if you were creating a new instance, as
shown in the following:

```
Sub modOutlook_TidyUp()
    ' tidy up objects
    Set namespaceOutlook = Nothing
    Set appOutlook = Nothing
End Sub
```

The first example of extracting data from Outlook lists the available accounts; with all these
examples, you can easily write data through to database tables:

```
Sub modOutLook_ListAccounts()
    ' list outlook accounts
    modOutlook_OpenOutlook
    Dim accOutlook As Outlook.Account
    For Each accOutlook In namespaceOutlook.Accounts
        Debug.Print accOutlook.DisplayName
    Next
    modOutlook_TidyUp
End Sub
```

The next example iterates through the folders and subfolders:

```
Sub modOutlook_ListFolders()
    ' List outlook folders and subfolders
    modOutlook_OpenOutlook
    Dim fldOutlook As Outlook.Folder
    Dim fld2Outlook As Outlook.Folder
    For Each fldOutlook In namespaceOutlook.Folders
        ' Archive Folders and Personal Folders
        Debug.Print fldOutlook.Name, fldOutlook.Description
        For Each fld2Outlook In fldOutlook.Folders
            ' cycle through the folders
            Debug.Print fld2Outlook.Name, fld2Outlook.Description
        Next
    Next
    modOutlook_TidyUp
End Sub
```

You can also choose a specific folder and iterate through the documents in the folder, as demonstrated here:

```
Sub modOutlook_ListSpecificFolder()
    ' List notes in a specific folder
    modOutlook_OpenOutlook
    Dim fldOutlook As Outlook.Folder
    Dim noteOutlook As Outlook.NoteItem
    Dim lngItem As Long
    Set fldOutlook = namespaceOutlook.GetDefaultFolder(olFolderNotes)
    For lngItem = 1 To fldOutlook.Items.Count - 1
        ' cycle through the folders
        If fldOutlook.Items(lngItem).Class = olNote Then
            Set noteOutlook = fldOutlook.Items(lngItem)
            Debug.Print noteOutlook.Body
        End If
    Next
    modOutlook_TidyUp
End Sub
```

Note that the previous example iterates by using an index (the variable *lngItem*) as an index into the collection to count through the objects. You can also use a *For … Each* loop with a generic object variable.

INSIDE OUT   Restrict and Find operations

Outlook supports a number of Find operations when searching for data, but probably the most powerful function is *Restrict*, with which you can specify criteria and then iterate through the resulting collection. The problem with *Restrict* is that when you need to wildcard the search to match a pattern using the SQL keyword *like*, it is not obvious that this syntax will not work. For example, to search the subject, strCriteria = "[Subject] = 'Fred'" will work, but strCriteria = "[Subject] like '%Fred%'" will not work. The following code resolves this problem:

```
Sub modOutlook_RestrictItems()
    ' Filter Items for a subset of items
    modOutlook_OpenOutlook
    Dim fldOutlook As Outlook.Folder
    Dim mailOutlook As Outlook.MailItem
    Dim restrictedItems As Outlook.Items
    Dim anItem As Object
    Dim strCriteria As String
    Set fldOutlook = namespaceOutlook.GetDefaultFolder(olFolderInbox)
'    strCriteria = "@SQL=" & Chr(34) & "urn:schemas:httpmail:subject" & _
```

```
'        Chr(34) & " like '%SAFARI%'"
        strCriteria = "@SQL=" & Chr(34) & _
                    "urn:schemas:httpmail:textdescription" & _
                    Chr(34) & " like '%SAFARI%'"
        ' urn:schemas:httpmail:sender
'        strCriteria = "[Subject] = 'Fred'"
        strCriteria = "@SQL=" & Chr(34) & "urn:schemas:httpmail:sender" & _
                        Chr(34) & " like '%Karl%'"
        Set restrictedItems = fldOutlook.Items.Restrict(strCriteria)
        For Each anItem In restrictedItems
            ' cycle through the folders
            If anItem.Class = olMail Then
                Set mailOutlook = anItem
                Debug.Print mailOutlook.Subject, mailOutlook.Sender, _
                    mailOutlook.SenderEmailAddress
            End If
        Next
        modOutlook_TidyUp
End Sub
```

This is not a completely intuitive syntax to follow, but the key is urn:schemas:httpmail followed by the property that will be searched. Notice also how this code checks the object class and then only assigns the object of the correct class when the object is matched.

Creating Objects in Outlook

In this section, you will look at sample code for creating emails, adding contacts, adding an appointment to the diary, and creating tasks.

The first example creates an email with an attachment. The *Display* option displays the email and the *Send* action transmits the email:

```
Sub modOutlook_SendMail()
    ' example sending an email with outlook
    modOutlook_OpenOutlook
    Dim mailOutlook As Outlook.MailItem
    Dim strDoc As String
    strDoc = CurrentProject.Path & "\quote.docx"
    Set mailOutlook = appOutlook.CreateItem(olMailItem)
    With mailOutlook
        .Subject = "Sample email sent by OutlookContacts.accdb"
        .To = "andy@ascassociates.biz"
        .Body = "Attached to this document is our proposal."
        .Attachments.Add strDoc
        ' display the email
        .Display
```

```
                         ' send the email
                         ' .Send
                     End With
                     Set mailOutlook = Nothing
                     modOutlook_TidyUp
                 End Sub
```

The next example demonstrates adding an entry to the diary:

```
Sub modOutlook_AddToDiary()
    ' example adding to the diary outlook
    modOutlook_OpenOutlook
    Dim diaryOutlook As Outlook.AppointmentItem
    Set diaryOutlook = appOutlook.CreateItem(olAppointmentItem)
    With diaryOutlook
        .Start = Now
        .End = DateAdd("h", 1, Now)
        .Subject = "Appointment for next hour"
        .Body = "Appointment generated by OutlookContacts.accdb"
        .Save
    End With
    Set diaryOutlook = Nothing
    modOutlook_TidyUp
End Sub
```

In this example, we show how to add a new task:

```
Sub modOutlook_AddToTasks()
    ' example adding to the task list outlook
    modOutlook_OpenOutlook
    Dim taskOutlook As Outlook.TaskItem
    Set taskOutlook = appOutlook.CreateItem(olTaskItem)
    With taskOutlook
        .Subject = "Microsoft Outlook Operations"
        .Body = "Complete Chapter 13"
        .DueDate = Now()
        .Save
    End With
    Set taskOutlook = Nothing
    modOutlook_TidyUp
End Sub
```

The final example in this section is adding a new contact. This example first searches to establish if the record already exists. Because we are performing an exact pattern match, the *strCriteria* can have a very simple form:

```
Sub modOutlook_AddToContacts()
    ' example adding a contact
    ' check to see if contact already exists
    modOutlook_OpenOutlook
```

```
    Dim contOutlook As Outlook.ContactItem
    Dim fldOutlook As Outlook.Folder
    Dim restrictedItems As Outlook.Items
    Dim strCriteria As String
    Dim strFirstName As String
    Dim strLastName As String
    strFirstName = "A"
    strLastName = "Couch"
    strCriteria = "[FirstName] = '" & strFirstName & _
                  "' and [Lastname] = '" & strLastName & "'"
    Set fldOutlook = namespaceOutlook.GetDefaultFolder(olFolderContacts)
    Set restrictedItems = fldOutlook.Items.Restrict(strCriteria)
    If restrictedItems.Count > 0 Then
        ' exit as name already exists
        Exit Sub
    End If
    Set contOutlook = appOutlook.CreateItem(olContactItem)
    With contOutlook
        .FirstName = strFirstName
        .LastName = strLastName
        .Save
    End With
    Set contOutlook = Nothing
    modOutlook_TidyUp
End Sub
```

Writing to Access from Outlook

In this section, you will look at developing some VBA code that can be added to Outlook for recording an incoming and outgoing email in an Access database. You start by creating the table shown in Figure 13-32 for recording the email activity.

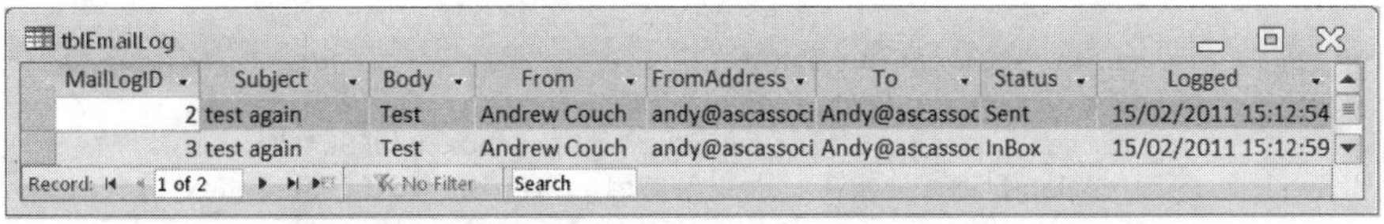

MailLogID	Subject	Body	From	FromAddress	To	Status	Logged
2	test again	Test	Andrew Couch	andy@ascassoci	Andy@ascassoc	Sent	15/02/2011 15:12:54
3	test again	Test	Andrew Couch	andy@ascassoci	Andy@ascassoc	InBox	15/02/2011 15:12:59

Record: ◄ ◄ 1 of 2 ► ►I ►* ✕ No Filter   Search

Figure 13-32 An Access table for recording incoming and outgoing email.

In Outlook, you then use the Developer-Visual Basic option to write VBA code in the *ThisOutlookSession* module, as shown in Figure 13-33.

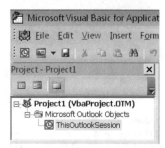

Figure 13-33 Select the *ThisOutlookSession* module to write startup code for Outlook.

Use the references to add the Microsoft Office 14.0 Access database engine Object Library.

You begin by defining *WithEvents* objects, which intercept emails from the *InBox* and *SentMail* folders, and appropriate variables for using the database:

```
Option Explicit
' Event handling
Private WithEvents InboxItems As Outlook.Items
Private WithEvents SentItems As Outlook.Items
' Global varaibles
Dim nsOutlook As Outlook.NameSpace
Dim db As Database
Dim rst As Recordset
' constants
Const strdbPath = "C:\......\CodeExamples\Chapter12\"
Const strdbName = "OutlookContacts.accdb"
Const strTableName = "tblEmailLog"
```

You then write the application startup code, which hooks in your *WithEvent* processing to the Outlook folders and sets the database variables, as shown in the following:

```
Private Sub Application_Startup()
    Set nsOutlook = GetNamespace("MAPI")
    ' attach our event processing to the InBox and SentMail
    Set InboxItems = nsOutlook.GetDefaultFolder(olFolderInbox).Items
    Set SentItems = nsOutlook.GetDefaultFolder(olFolderSentMail).Items
    ' setup database logging
    Set db = OpenDatabase(strdbPath & strdbName)
    Set rst = db.OpenRecordset(strTableName, dbOpenDynaset)
End Sub
```

You then write a tidy up routine for when the application closes:

```
Private Sub Application_Quit()
    ' tidy up variables
    On Error Resume Next
    rst.Close
    db.Close
    Set nsOutlook = Nothing
End Sub
```

The final procedures to be added are the routines for writing to the database:

```
Private Sub InboxItems_ItemAdd(ByVal Item As Object)
    ' process inbox emails
    Dim mailOutlook As MailItem
    Dim rec As Recipient
    If Item.Class = olMail Then
        Set mailOutlook = Item
        With mailOutlook
            rst.AddNew
            rst!Subject = Left(.Subject, 255)
            rst!Body = .Body
            rst!From = .Sender
            rst!FromAddress = .SenderEmailAddress
            rst!Status = "InBox"
            rst!Logged = .ReceivedTime
            For Each rec In .Recipients
                rst!To = rst!To & rec.Name & " : " & rec.Address & ";"
            Next
            rst.Update
        End With
    End If
End Sub

Private Sub SentItems_ItemAdd(ByVal Item As Object)
    ' process outgoing emails
    Dim mailOutlook As MailItem
    Dim rec As Recipient
    If Item.Class = olMail Then
        Set mailOutlook = Item
        With mailOutlook
            rst.AddNew
            rst!Subject = Left(.Subject, 255)
            rst!Body = .Body
            rst!From = .Sender
            rst!FromAddress = .SenderEmailAddress
            rst!Status = "Sent"
            rst!Logged = .SentOn
            For Each rec In .Recipients
                rst!To = rst!To & rec.Name & " : " & rec.Address & ";"
            Next
            rst.Update
        End With
    End If
End Sub
```

To save typing, we have included this code in the file Outlook.txt, which is located in the sample databases.

In the Trust Center, click Macro Settings and adjust the macro security (see Figure 13-34). Close and re-open Outlook for the email logging to start.

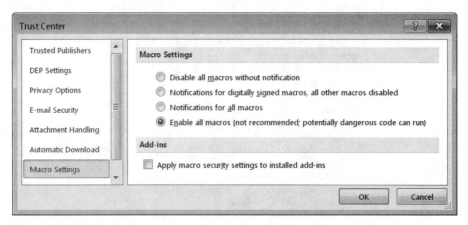

Figure 13-34 Adjusting the macro security to allow the VBA code to execute.

Summary

The degree of integration available in the Office products is awesome, and the freedom that VBA gives you to copy and paste code and easily work with code in the different products means that your VBA skills are transferable among the Office suite—once you can program one product, you can program them all. The key to your productivity is in understanding the individual object models, and also in understanding any special requirements for interconnecting the products.

- When working with Excel, the most important concept to embrace is the change in focus from *TableQuery* to the *Connection* object, which is a significant shift from earlier versions of Office.

- When working with Outlook, the most important concept is the generic nature of the object model and the *Items* collection. The ability to create objects in a generic manner from the *Application* objects by using one method should not be overlooked.

- Word has always been left trailing behind the other Office products from the perspective of having a more complex object model. However, the comparable simplicity of this object model is also its strength by keeping it very simple to automatically drive Word.

PART 6

SQL Server and SQL Azure

CHAPTER 14
Using SQL Server 483

CHAPTER 15
Upsizing Access to SQL Server 543

CHAPTER 16
Using SQL Azure 589

Using SQL Server

Introducing SQL Server 484

Getting Started with the SQL Server
Management Studio 495

Creating Tables and Relationships 496

Working with Views 505

Introducing T-SQL 517

Working with Stored Procedures 511

Working with Triggers 526

Working with Transactions 530

User-Defined Functions 534

Getting Started with SQL Server Security 536

A lthough Microsoft Access 2010 is the world's best small-scale database, the product does have limitations; as you add more data or more users to an application, it will eventually run out of steam. It is truly amazing just how far you can push an Access database, but eventually you will begin to have issues with either performance or the stability of the database. The cutoff point will vary, but if we said 200 MB, or more than 20 concurrent users, that would not be an unreasonable measure of when you want to start looking at storing the data in Microsoft SQL Server.

This is the first of three chapters in which we discuss Access working with SQL Server as a means of extending the power of your Access databases. Before you can begin to effectively work with SQL Server, you need an understanding of both what SQL Server is and how to use the tools that come with it.

In this chapter, you will gain an overview of the essential topics to understand when working with SQL Server. Key concepts that you will master include:

- Gaining an overview of key SQL Server product features and the Transact SQL (T-SQL) programming language.

- Understanding how to create tables and relationships.

- Seeing how Views and stored procedures can provide equivalent features to Access queries but with improved performance.

- Gaining an overview of how to use triggers and transactions to enhance your applications.

> **Note**
>
> As you read through this chapter, we encourage you to also use the companion content sample database, SQLServerExamples.accdb and the associated script files, which you can download from the book's catalog page.

Introducing SQL Server

In our experience, it is difficult to find an Access developer who hasn't taken like a duck to water when working with SQL Server. Access and VBA are beautifully crafted products to work with and likewise, so is SQL Server. Although, if this is your first time working with SQL Server, just remember how long it takes to truly master Access, and don't be surprised that it will take some effort to master SQL Server.

SQL Server offers you a familiar and easy to use GUI for undertaking design work, but it has one very significant advantage over Access: it also allows you to ignore the GUI and do everything with script files by using T-SQL. The SQL Server Management Studio has a clever feature, with which you can point at design objects in the GUI and with a quick right-click, you can get the tool to write the T-SQL script for you. Finding the balance between using the GUI and gradually using more T-SQL is how you more fully exploit the product's power at your own pace.

This first section of the chapter discusses a number of important topics relating to SQL Server, but if this is your first time using it, you might want to quickly skim read this section and then return to this once you have had a chance to work with the product, in which case the section, "Getting Started with the SQL Server Management Studio," beginning on page 495, is a great point to get under way.

Programs vs. Services

Access is a program that can be run on your computer. The Access program is loaded into memory and then when the program needs to manipulate data that is on, for example, a shared directory, the data is loaded into your computer memory, as and when it is required, possibly passing over the network. Then it is filtered, manipulated, and displayed. This filtering of data can often mean that large parts of the database need to be transferred over the network to your computer memory. Access then uses a shared locking file to manage the updating of this shared data.

In as much as file–server-based databases such as Access are exceptionally good, as more users are added to the system and the amount of data in a system increases, performance can be reduced, and corruption can be more likely. One reason for this is that as you increase the demand on the data, you increase the network traffic, and you can have more copies of parts of the dataset in different computer's memories. The question arises, what happens when a computer is inadvertently switched off when it is part way through an operation? The answer is that in most cases, it is the indexing that can become inconsistent, and you might need to compact and repair the database.

SQL Server is a *client-server* database. The database resides on a server. The server is dedicated to handling incoming requests for data, and then returning parts of the dataset to the client computers. If the client computers fail, the server can still guarantee the integrity of the data. Although you can think of SQL Server as a program, it is installed as a set of *Windows Services*, which are running in the server memory, listening for commands and taking appropriate actions. This client-server design has advantages when it comes to scaling up as more users and larger volumes of data are present. It also offers better security; because the server is normally not directly accessible, your database can't be easily compromised.

Client-Server Performance

When you run Access linked to SQL Server, you still have the Access program in memory, but Access no longer uses the shared file for managing updates to the data, and it is now forced to communicate through a special interface (normally ODBC or ADO, which you'll read more about, shortly). This makes for a much better architecture on larger systems. But, there can still be problems with performance, and these problems relate to the volumes of data being sent from the server to the client.

INSIDE OUT   Minimizing the amount of data requested to be displayed in a form

Access encourages developers to build forms bound to tables that can have thousands of rows and allow, for example, users to perform a Find operation to search for records. This approach works well for native Access Databases but is not a good idea in client-server; if you run a performance analyzing tool such as the SQL Server Profiler (discussed in Chapter 15, "Upsizing Access to SQL Server"), you will soon see how it generates very inefficient operations.

In a well designed client-server system, you attempt to minimize the amount of data that you ask for. If your application uses filters and prompts users to make choices before then displaying more limited data volumes, you will significantly improve performance.

The second big part of an Access application is queries. Normally after switching to work with SQL Server, at least some of the queries will be slow to execute; developers tend to build very complex hierarchies of queries, many of which include very complex VBA or Access-specific functions.

Access can communicate with SQL Server by using linked tables from a standard Access database; these linked tables communicate via a technology called *Open Database Connectivity* (ODBC). This acts to translate requests from Access to a form that SQL Server can understand. This means that when you write an Access query, that query has to be passed through ODBC to SQL Server. But if that query uses specific Access features for which there is no easy translation through ODBC, then ODBC needs to request a lot more of the data and have Access perform local processing to use all those special features. This is why some of your queries might be running slowly. The good news is, with a little effort, they can normally be made to run a lot faster than they did in Access.

To improve performance, what we need to do is to convert the slow Access queries into a set of Views and stored procedures in SQL Server. This means that when converting the SQL, you might need to find equivalents to special Access and VBA operations by using T-SQL. Once converted, because everything executes in the server, you minimize the amount of data being sent to Access, and so resolve the performance issues.

There are several other alternatives that can also help with improving performance, but the best solution is to move the complex query logic on to the server. One alternative that we will consider later in this book is to use a technology called ActiveX Data Objects (ADO), rather than Data Access Objects (DAO) model; this technology forces you to use SQL Server syntax in operations that avoids translation and can offer improved performance. Another alternative is to use Pass-Through queries, which will be described in Chapter 15. The third alternative is to build your application by using an Access Data Project (ADP). ADP brings you much closer to working with SQL Server and avoids using ODBC and instead uses ADO.

SQL Server Versions

The most recent versions of SQL Server are 2005, 2008, and 2008 R2 (and the corresponding SQLExpress versions). You can take backups from an earlier version and restore them into a database in a newer version, and you can alternatively detach an older version and attach it to a newer version and the databases will be upgraded. You cannot take a newer version and attach that to an older version of SQL Server. It is worth noting that SQL Server 2008 R2 is a newer version than SQL Server 2008, and you cannot attach a SQL Server 2008 R2 database to a SQL Server 2008, so if you detach a 2008 database, and then attach it to a 2008 R2 system, you cannot detach that and then re-attach it back to 2008, because it will have been automatically upgraded.

SQL Express and SQL Server Products

The SQL Server product range extends from the free SQL Express version to a truly enterprise-wide product. If you're getting started, then SQL Express is an ideal starting point. You will also find that as a developer, for minimum expense you can purchase a Developer Edition, with which you can more fully appreciate the different product features. You can then still use a SQL Express target because the databases are interchangeable between the different editions for a given product version.

At the time of this writing, the SQL Express download packages very much reflect the options that are available when performing a full product installation. You have the choice of downloading either the 32 or 64-bit versions of the product. If you have a 64-bit version of Windows, you can install either version, but the 64-bit version provides better performance.

You can download and install any one of the following:

- **Database Only**   This installs only the database without any management tools, an unlikely choice for a developer computer, and a possible choice for a live environment.

- **Management Tools (Only)**   This installs only the management tools, such as the SQL Server Management Studio; this is likely to appeal to you if you are working in an environment in which you have a server set up and you just want the tools on a workstation.

- **Database with Management Tools**   The best choices to get started as you get the database and tools on your developer computer.

- **Database with Advanced Services**   If you want to experiment with Report Server, this would be the choice to get everything that is available with SQL Express.

SQL Express is one of the greatest giveaways of the century. You get a fully functional SQL Server database, which allows databases up to 10 GB in size (with 2008 R2; 4 GB with older versions) and you get all the core features. Everything is also compatible if later on you migrate to a full product version.

Now considering things from the perspective of deploying the application to your client you might ask the following questions: what don't you get and does it matter? Could SQL Express run a small business?

SQL Express is also limited to using one gigabyte of operating system memory and one CPU, which for many applications is not an issue. Apart from some of the more esoteric features, the one feature that you don't get is the SQL Server Agent. The Agent is a powerful feature with which you can schedule maintenance plans, backups, and other operations.

So if you are using Express, you either need to find a way to run backups, or have some backup software that can back up a live running SQL Server.

Just like Access needs a Compact and Repair, to maintain a SQL Server database in good condition, you need to run Maintenance Plans. The Maintenance Plans can perform integrity checking and backups, but more important, they rebuild indexing and create space for growth in the indexes. If you ignore this requirement then you can expect eventually to see a performance penalty.

> **Note**
>
> SQL Express does not include the Maintenance Plans feature.

A general rule of thumb to apply is that if you are operating on a shoestring budget and building smaller applications, SQL Express will meet your needs. But if you have clients with the appropriate budget, then encourage them to purchase the full product version, which will better suite a larger business and reduce your need to find a workaround to common problems.

INSIDE OUT   The essence of a Maintenance Plan

We have included a sample script file called ExpressRebuild.SQL to help you with creating your own Maintenance Plan for SQL Express, this file uses more sophisticated techniques, which we will not cover in the book, but we believe it is useful to the more advanced programmer. In VBA, you can program with *Recordsets*, where you sequentially move through the records performing an operation. SQL Server has an equivalent mechanism called a *cursor*. Cursor programming is more difficult than working with a VBA *Recordset* because it is rather primitive and you need to take control of all the fields that you want to use. Having issued that disclaimer, cursors are very powerful, but sadly outside of the scope of this book. In the following code example, we have inserted a section of this code to give you a flavor of what is possible.

What follows is a nice example of cursor programming. It's a more complex example of T-SQL programming, so feel free to skip this until you have read the rest of this chapter:

```
-- find all the tables in the database
-- and rebuild all the indexes on each table
-- also run the database consistency checker on each table
DECLARE @TargetDatabase AS VARCHAR(50)
DECLARE @FillFactor AS INT
```

```
DECLARE @TableSchema as Sysname
DECLARE @TableName AS sysname
DECLARE @Command AS VARCHAR(200)
-- Set the table fill factor
SET @FillFactor = 80
PRINT 'REBUILDING ALL INDEXES AND RUNNING CHECK ON TABLES'
PRINT '-------------------------------------------------------------------------'
DECLARE reb_cursor  CURSOR
FOR
SELECT TABLE_SCHEMA,TABLE_NAME FROM
    INFORMATION_SCHEMA.TABLES WHERE TABLE_TYPE = 'BASE TABLE'
OPEN reb_cursor
FETCH NEXT FROM reb_cursor INTO @TableSchema, @TableName
WHILE @@FETCH_STATUS <> -1
BEGIN
    IF @@FETCH_STATUS <> -2
    BEGIN
        PRINT @TableSchema + ' - ' + @TableName
        SET @Command = 'ALTER INDEX ALL ON [' + @TableSchema +
            '].[' + @TableName +
            '] REBUILD WITH (FILLFACTOR =' +
            CAST(@Fillfactor AS VARCHAR(10)) + ');'
        EXEC (@Command);
        SET @Command = 'DBCC CHECKTABLE ("[' + @TableSchema +
            '].[' + @TableName + ']")'
        EXEC (@Command);
    END
    FETCH NEXT FROM reb_cursor INTO @TableSchema, @TableName
END
CLOSE reb_cursor
DEALLOCATE reb_cursor
```

Database File Locations

Once SQL Server is installed, by default, new databases are created in a specific folder. The folder name varies according to the main product version and whether it is a 32-bit or 64-bit version. It's an easy process to change the folder path in the Database Files property when creating a new database, as shown in Figure 14-1. When you enter the Database Name, this creates two logical file names <DatabaseName> and <DatabaseName>_Log. If you choose your own folders, then the only issue to watch out for is any required permissions that SQL Server needs on the folders.

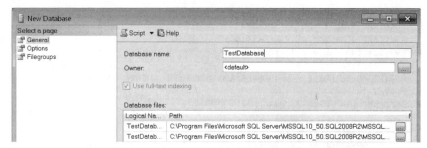

Figure 14-1 The available pages and properties when creating a new database are different from those shown in Figure 14-2, once a database has been created.

In this case, the two files TestDatabase.mdf and TestDatabase_Log.ldf are located on the path C:\Program Files\Microsoft SQL Server\MSSQL10_50.SQL2008R2\MSSQL\DATA.

Log Files and Recovery Models

After you create a database, right-click the database name in Object Explorer to display the properties. Configure the different settings for each database, as needed. Figure 14-2 shows the Recovery Model set to *Full*.

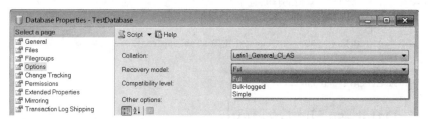

Figure 14-2 If you are using a SQLExpress version, the Recovery Model defaults to Simple; when using the full SQL Server version, the default is Full.

An explanation of the differences in the Recovery Model relates to the Log files. In the previous section, you saw that when a database is created, you specify two physical files, one is the database file, and the other is the Log file.

When changes are made to the data in a database, these changes are recorded in the Log file. SQL Server uses the Log file for a number of purposes. First, it can roll back transactional work by using the Log file. It can also provide special views called INSERTED and DELETED, based around the data in the Log file (this will be described beginning on page 526, when we discuss writing trigger code). The Log files can also be shipped to other servers on a periodic basis by using a process called Log Shipping, in which they can be replayed to provide for backup Servers. SQL Server also supports mirror servers, including a hot-standby mode for server switching.

If you have a very large database, you can decide to back up the full database weekly, and only backup these Log files, recording the changes on a more regular basis. Once backed up, the Log file is then cleared out for re-use.

If you use a Full Recovery Model, the Log files continue to grow until you perform a backup on either the database or the Log files. In practice, over time the Log files can become very large if you are not regularly backing up the databases; they can even exceed the size of your database, swallowing up a lot of storage on your development computers.

On a development computer, you probably want to choose the Simple Recovery Model. Using this setting, the Log files are continuously shortened, which keeps them under control. This still allows you to be taking periodic backups of your database; it just means that you cannot use the more sophisticated features such as Log Shipping, which is found on production servers.

In production environments, you might find that other people have responsibility for configuring the backup policy. If you are planning this, you could still adopt a Simple Recovery Model and rely on RAID and other technologies to secure your backups (these topics are beyond the scope of this book).

Next, go to Database Properties | Options. Here, you will find two other options that you might wish to consider setting. First, set the Auto Close property to *False* (this is the default on SQL Server, but *True* on SQL Express), and set the Auto Shrink property to *True* (default is *False*).

If you end up with a large Log file and you cannot make it smaller, then investigate the *DBCC SHRINKDATABASE* command for help with this problem.

Instances

As part of the SQL Server installation process you have the choice to install your copy of SQL Server in either the default instance or use a named instance. Instances allow for multiple copies of SQL Server to be installed on the same computer; often these will be different versions of the product to support development for different versions, but it is also possible to install multiple versions of the same product. This could occur if you first install SQL Express and then later install a full version of the product. The name of your instance is by default your <computer_name> when installing the full product, and <computer_name>\SQLExpress> when installing the express version of the product.

When you are defining connections to SQL Server, you specify the name of your instance as part of the connection information.

Management Studio can be used to work with multiple local, network, and remote connections to different SQL Servers at the same time, and it will also work with earlier versions of SQL Server. Figure 14-3 shows Management Studio connected to a local instance of SQL

Server 2008 R2 and SQL Server 2008. By right-clicking a server name, you can disconnect or connect to additional database servers. You can also click the Connect button (in the upper-left corner of the window) to display a drop-down menu, from which you can add other connections.

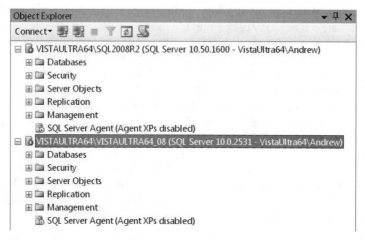

Figure 14-3 Use Object Explorer to connect to multiple database servers.

Windows Services

After you have installed SQL Server, go to Control Panel | Administrative Tools | Services. Here, you can configure a set of services for each SQL Server Instance, as shown in Figure 14-4.

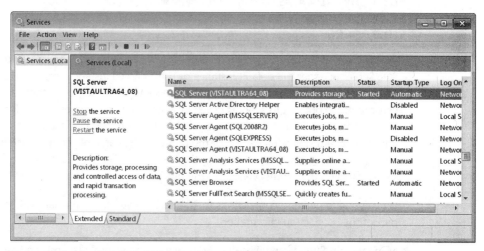

Figure 14-4 After installing SQL Server, you can go to the Services panel to make changes to some of the Windows Services.

Most of the time, you won't need to make changes to these services, and the services that are available depends on whether you installed the full or express version, and whether you chose to also install some of the additional services.

On a developer computer, as a bare minimum, you want to have the main SQL Server and Browser services set to *Automatic*. You might choose to set some of the other services, such as the Agent, to *Manual*, and then switch them on if and when required; this saves your computer's resources. If you have several SQL Server instances, you might decide to stop some instances that are only rarely required and perform a manual start from the Services panel (or by using Management Studio) if you need to run them.

System Databases

Like Access, SQL Server installs some system tables. But it takes this experience further, because in addition to system tables, SQL Server has system databases, as shown in Figure 14-5.

Figure 14-5 The system databases; *master* and *tempdb* are the most important.

Within your backup strategy, you might want to include the *master* database because it holds your server configuration. The following is a brief description of these databases:

- **master**   This is the metadatabase. It records all the information on your databases and is key to running the SQL Server. Back it up as part of your regular backup routine.

- **model**   This is an interesting but seldom-used concept, by which you put commonly used objects in *model*, and then whenever you create a new database, SQL Server clones the objects from *model*.

- **msdb**   This is used for distributed transactions. *msdb* is a good example of a more sophisticated system database (but unfortunately, beyond the scope of this book).

- **tempdb**   This is the working scratchpad for SQL Server. When SQL Server needs to create temporary objects, or when you need to create temporary objects, they go into *tempdb*; you don't need to back up this database.

System Tables

Unless you are diving deep into SQL Server, you can probably live your life without delving into the system tables; the same can be said for Access. Some developers find it essential to work with the *MSys* tables, and others ignore the whole topic. SQL Server has a similar scenario, except that it offers three approaches to this problem.

First, if you want, for example, to get a list of the tables in your database, you can use the following:

```
SELECT * FROM sys.tables
Go
```

But be aware that as with Access, if Microsoft decides to redesign these system tables, you are using what is effectively an unsupported feature. To insulate yourself from the system tables, you could use a built-in system stored procedure, as follows:

```
exec sp_tables
go
```

For a useful and instructive view into both how Microsoft writes T-SQL and how the system tables can be used, in the *master* database, go to Programmability | Stored Procedures | System Stored Procedures, right-click sys.sp_tables, and then select modify. You can see the Microsoft source code for the system stored procedure.

INSIDE OUT   *INFORMATION_SCHEMA* Views

As an alternative to relying on SQL Server system objects or system stored procedures, if you look in your database (Views | System Views), you will see a set of ANSI-compliant Views, these are on the *INFORMATION_SCHEMA* schema. So, you can also use the following:

```
SELECT *
FROM INFORMATION_SCHEMA.TABLES
go
```

Suppose that you want to produce a documentation tool that can find a list of your tables. The best choice is the ANSI-compliant views because Microsoft needs to adhere to this; the second choice is the system stored procedures because Microsoft has maintained this level of insight for developers and is less likely to change these; and third comes the system tables, which do change. Although they give you maximum flexibility, you are likely in the future to have to make alterations if these system tables are significantly changed.

Getting Started with the SQL Server Management Studio

When you install the Client-Tools for SQL Server, you also install a number of essential tools to help with your development. The most important tool to first gain experience with is the SQL Server Management Studio. This tool allows you to create databases, tables, views, stored procedures, and manage all the other essential components of your database. Management Studio can be used to manage local, network, and remote SQL Servers, such as SQL Azure (this is discussed in detail in Chapter 16, "Using SQL Azure").

In the following sections, you will see how to perform certain operations with the GUI and how to repeat these operations using T-SQL in a *script file*. In SQL Server, when you open a Query window, you are in a free-format window, into which you can type and execute portions of SQL. This can then be saved as a script file that you can subsequently execute (in part or in full).

You should understand from the outset that this ability to both work with a GUI interface and with these script files lies at the heart of how to effectively develop with the product. You can balance your choice of interface according to how comfortable you are with working in the GUI versus working with pure SQL.

Running the Demo Database Script

To begin, you will need a sample database. There are three popular database: *pubs* (an older sample database that is often quoted in older documents), *Northwind* (popular with Access developers) and *AdvertureWorks* (shows off all the more advanced features in SQL Server). The best place to get these databases is the CodePlex website at *http://sqlserversamples.codeplex.com*.

To get you started, we have included with the samples the Script File instnwnd.sql. To run this file in Management Studio, proceed as follows.

1. Click File | Open | File, and then open the file instnwnd.sql.

   The file opens in a new query window.

2. On the Toolbar, click the Execute button.

   This creates the *Northwind* database, which contains a full set of tables and data.

3. In Object Explorer, right-click the Databases folder, and then select Refresh.

   You can now explore the sample *Northwind* database.

Chapter 14

Creating a New Database

You also want to create a new empty database, which we have called *NorthwindTesting*. In this empty database, you can experiment with creating new tables and relationships. Proceed as follows:

1. Right-click the Databases folder, and then select New Database.

2. Enter a name for the database, and then click Add.

Creating Tables and Relationships

Tables and relationships can be created either by using the GUI interface or by using T-SQL script. You will quickly pick up the syntax for creating tables; the syntax for creating relationships is a little trickier, but you can use the SQL Server GUI to help you write the correct syntax by generating a script for existing foreign keys.

Database Diagrams

If you click the Database Diagram folder, and you do not already have any diagrams, you are prompted to allow supporting objects to be added to the database, as shown in Figure 14-6. If you have attached a database supplied from another source and you get a warning regarding ownership, go to Database | Properties | Files | Owner, and then verify that this property is correctly assigned.

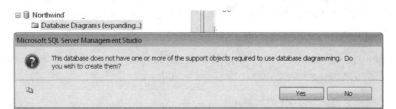

Figure 14-6 Adding support for database diagramming when attempting to create your first diagram.

When you use the shortcut menu to create a new diagram, a list appears that displays any existing tables to add to the diagram. After closing this list, you can right-click in any empty part of the diagram to open the shortcut menu shown in Figure 14-7. From this menu, you can add new tables or choose from the same list of existing tables.

Figure 14-7 Use the diagram shortcut menu and tool bars to add and create tables on a diagram.

When adding a table, as you start to enter the fields, you might find that you want to customize the view of the table, as shown in Figure 14-8.

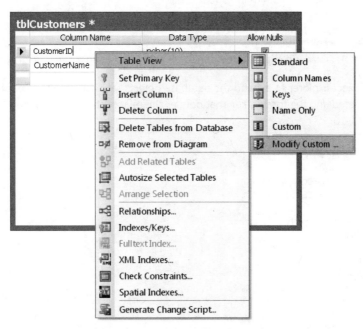

Figure 14-8 In addition to a number of built-in views, you can also customize table views. This is particularly useful when you want to display defaults and the *Identity* property for fields.

Figure 14-9 shows a customized view of two tables. To make any field the primary key, click the field and use the shortcut menu to select the option Set Primary Key. You can select multiple, adjacent fields by holding the Shift key while you click your selections; for non-adjacent selections hold the Ctrl key while clicking your selections.. The final step is to drag the *CustomerID* in *tblCustomers* onto the corresponding *CustomerId* in *tblContacts* to create a relationship. Objects are not changed or created until you save changes to a diagram, so it is important to regularly save the diagram as you work on the design.

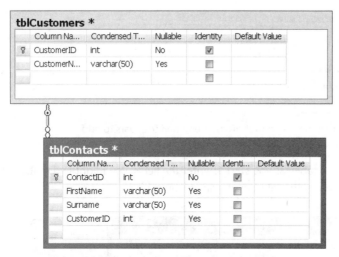

Figure 14-9 Tables and relationships are easily constructed using a database diagram.

Using Object Explorer to expand the database objects, you can see the two tables that have been created and the foreign key that defines the relationship between them, as shown in Figure 14-10.

Figure 14-10 The keys folder contains the primary and foreign keys. You can right-click to generate the T-SQL script for creating the relationships on foreign keys.

As an alternative approach to creating these tables, you can choose the New Table shortcut from the Tables folder, and then create and save each table. Then you can add the tables to a new diagram, dragging them as necessary to create the relationships.

Tables, Relationships, and Script Files

Right-click both tables to open the shortcut menu, and then select Script Table As | Create To | New Query Window, This generates the T-SQL script commands, which looks similar to the following (to reduce the size of this sample, we have removed some of the additional optional statements from the script):

```
USE [NorthwindTesting]
GO

CREATE TABLE [dbo].[tblCustomers](
    [CustomerID] [int] IDENTITY(1,1) NOT NULL,
    [CustomerName] [varchar](50) NULL,
 CONSTRAINT [PK_tblCustomers] PRIMARY KEY CLUSTERED
([CustomerID] ASC)
)
GO
CREATE TABLE [dbo].[tblContacts](
    [ContactID] [int] IDENTITY(1,1) NOT NULL,
    [FirstName] [varchar](50) NULL,
    [Surname] [varchar](50) NULL,
    [CustomerID] [int] NULL,
 CONSTRAINT [PK_tblContacts] PRIMARY KEY CLUSTERED
([ContactID] ASC)
)
GO

ALTER TABLE [dbo].[tblContacts]  WITH CHECK ADD
CONSTRAINT [FK_tblContacts_tblCustomers]
FOREIGN KEY([CustomerID])
REFERENCES [dbo].[tblCustomers] ([CustomerID])
GO
```

INSIDE OUT   Script files and batches of T-SQL commands

A script file is the name of a file that contains T-SQL statements, and a *batch* is a sequence of T-SQL commands that terminate with the *GO* keyword. When you execute a script file, it checks that each batch is syntactically correct as it progresses through the script. If a batch has errors, it is skipped and the process continues on to any remaining batches.

Each T-SQL statement is an implicit transaction that either fully completes or rolls back any changes; if you execute an *UPDATE* statement, you do not need to worry that if the statement failed only part of the available data set would be changed.

If a batch fails during execution, the execution halts and processing moves on to any remaining batches. batches are not transactions, and if you need to protect against a partially completed set of statements in a batch, you will need to add transaction processing.

There are some T-SQL commands that need to be executed as the only command in a batch, and in general, a T-SQL script file often contains more *GO* keywords than the minimum that would be required; once you start programming with variables, batches become more important, because user variables only have scope within a single batch.

Changing the Design of a Table

There are two different ways to make changes to the design of a table. The first method uses the GUI, and the second method uses T-SQL commands.

INSIDE OUT   Changing a table design with the GUI

It is very important to note that when you use the GUI to change the design of tables (for example, when changing a data type), this results in both the table and associated relationships being re-created. If you attempt to do this on a system that is in use, you might find that you are unable to make the change. The alternative is to apply the changes with a script file.

Because this is quite a radical action on the table, the default setting in the Tool in newer SQL Server product versions is to prevent you from doing this. If you want to enable these features, click Tools | Options | Designers | Table And Database Designers, and then clear the Prevent Saving Changes That Require Table Re-Creation option, as shown in Figure 14-11.

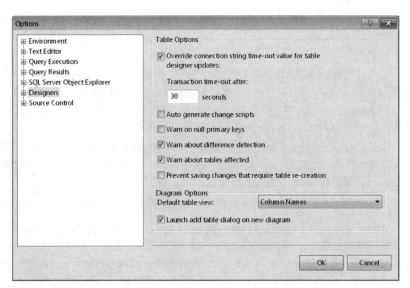

Figure 14-11 Changing the option to allow table designs to be changed by using the GUI interface.

By using the GUI, you can click a table name (see Figure 14-12) to rename the table.

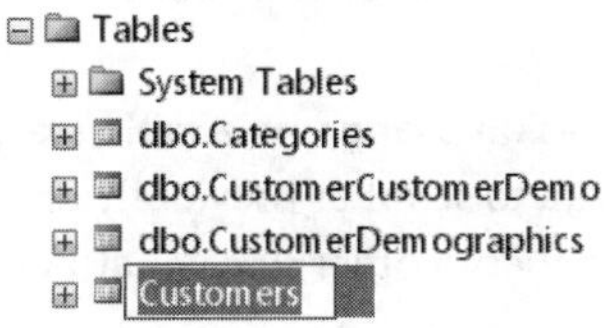

🗀 Tables
  ⊞ 🗀 System Tables
  ⊞ 🗖 dbo.Categories
  ⊞ 🗖 dbo.CustomerCustomerDemo
  ⊞ 🗖 dbo.CustomerDemographics
  ⊞ 🗖 Customers

Figure 14-12 Renaming a table by clicking it and typing a new name.

To make changes to a table, including adding columns, changing the column names and data types, or deleting columns, right-click the table, select Design from the shortcut menu that appears, make the desired changes, and then click the save icon on the Toolbar, as shown in Figure 14-13.

Figure 14-13 Click the Save icon on the top Toolbar to save your design changes.

There is a second option to saving the design changes. You can use the Generate Change Script icon that is shown at the start of the second Toolbar, below New Query (see Figure 14-13). This option can be used to save your changes in a Script File. The file will contain T-SQL script commands to make the change. There are times when this can very helpful, for example, when changing a field name, you will find that the script generated is very useful; in other circumstances, such as changing a data type, the change can result in the table being re-created (this is not always necessary and alternative T-SQL commands are discussed here). This can be a useful tool to learn how to sharpen up your T-SQL skills.

INSIDE OUT   Reasons for using T-SQL script files to record and apply changes

The disadvantages in using the GUI to make design changes in a table are that you don't have a record (unless you save the change to script as previously described) of the change, and you can't easily apply the changes in other systems after testing.

Most developers find it easier to master some simple T-SQL commands for making changes, possibly using the Generate Change Script icon to learn the syntax, and save a set of the changes to a Script File, to which you can keep adding code when recording your design work.

You can then use this file as part of your change procedures for version control, and run the scripts against test systems, and later, production systems.

One final advantage of using scripts is that you can give the objects more meaningful names, which will improve future maintenance. For example, when adding a default to a field, SQL Server automatically names the default; you might prefer to give the default a more informative *constraint* name.

The following sections present examples of the T-SQL syntax for some common changes to column and table information.

Changing a Table Name

```
EXEC sp_rename 'Customers', 'CustomersNew'
GO
```

Changing a Column Name

```
EXEC sp_rename 'Customers.Address', 'Address2', 'COLUMN'
GO
```

Changing a Column Data Type

```
ALTER TABLE [Customers] ALTER COLUMN [Address] nvarchar(80)
GO
```

Adding a Column

```
ALTER TABLE [Customers] ADD [Address2] nvarchar(80)
GO
```

Deleting a Column

```
ALTER TABLE [Customers] DROP COLUMN [Address2]
GO
```

Adding a Column with a Default

```
ALTER TABLE [Customers] ADD [Rating] INT
CONSTRAINT defCustomersRating DEFAULT 0
GO
```

Figure 14-14 demonstrates the difference between naming your own constraints and allowing SQL Server to automatically name them for you.

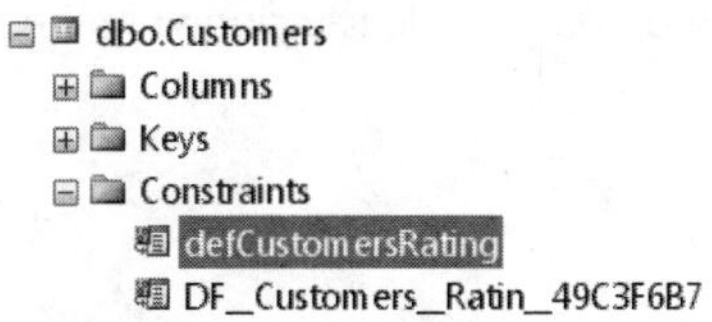

Figure 14-14 The first constraint was named explicitly. The second constraint was named automatically.

The constraint names must be unique for the database. It's a good idea to adopt a convention when naming a default constraint name; for example, use def<table name><column Name>.

Individual constraints can be removed by using the following *DROP* syntax:

```
ALTER TABLE [Customers]
DROP CONSTRAINT defCustomersRating
GO
```

Using the *Identity* **Property**

Access has Autonumber columns, which are Long Integer columns that automatically issue a sequenced number. Four features of AutoNumber columns are as follows:

- If you delete records from a table with an Autonumber column, you will have gaps in the number sequence.

- You can append data directly into the Autonumber column by using an append query.

- You are allowed only one Autonumber column per table.

- If you compact and repair the database, the next Autonumber value will be reset to follow sequentially after the last Autonumber value in the table.

The equivalent feature in SQL Server is the *IDENTITY* property, which can be defined with start number, and an increment. This means that *IDENTITY(1,1)* is equivalent to the Access Autonumber.

One difference in SQL Server is that in order to directly append a value into an *IDENTITY* column, you need to set a system flag. This flag can only be set to act for one table at a time in any given connection, and it is good practice to reset the flag once you have completed the operation, if you intend to keep the connection (Query window) in use. The following example creates a table with an *IDENTITY* column and performs a direct inserts into the column. If you try to run the code without using the *SET* operation, you receive an error warning you to use the *SET* operation. The following code is included in the file Identity Insert.sql:

```
CREATE TABLE DataList(
AnID        INT IDENTITY(1,1) PRIMARY KEY,
Comments nvarchar(255)
)
GO
SET IDENTITY_INSERT DataList ON
GO
-- Insert into the autonumber field
INSERT INTO DataList(AnID,Comments)
```

```
VALUES(999,'Sample record')
GO
SELECT * FROM DataList
GO
SET IDENTITY_INSERT DataList OFF
GO
```

Working with Views

Access offers several different types of queries. The *SELECT* queries correspond to Views in SQL Server. If you have Action Queries that will use *INSERT*, *UPDATE*, or *DELETE* statements, these cannot be written in the equivalent View; instead, they can either be directly executed as SQL statements, or when saved in SQL Server, they are placed inside a stored procedure.

Graphical Interface

With Access, you can either write a query in SQL or use the graphical Query grid to design a query. Similarly, with SQL Server, you can create Views either graphically or by using T-SQL.

The shortcut menu for the Views folder offers an improved version of the Query grid, with which you can create a new View, or edit an existing one. In SQL Server, the window is split into four panes; in the Diagram pane, you can graphically manipulate objects; you can directly edit the SQL in the SQL pane; in the Criteria pane, you can enter criteria; and in the Results pane, you can execute the SQL. All of this is presented in Figure 14-15.

Figure 14-15 The View design interface is split into Diagram, Criteria, SQL, and Results panes.

INSIDE OUT   View updateability in Access

In the previous example, you might have noticed that because we have selected data from more than one table, the cells are read-only (see the bottom of Figure 14-15).

A fantastic feature in Access is that if you link to this View, you can make edits to data in the View, as long as you only edit columns in one table and then save the changes. An edit to different fields in multiple base tables in a single update is not allowed (in this case, you need to use program code to force any changes made to data in each table to be saved before you can edit the columns in a different base table).

A useful convention when saving your views is to prefix the names with vw_, in a similar manner to prefixing the Access queries with qry.

Access developers often build hierarchies of queries that depend on other queries. In SQL Server, you can follow the same approach to building Views. However, there is one very significant difference: if you are explicitly selecting all columns from a table, for example using *SELECT Customers.**, and you add a new field to the *Customers* table, it will not be shown in the View. In this respect, a View acts like a snapshot of the columns in the underlying table when the View was created.

Views and Script Files

Before we look at how to resolve this problem of the static nature of a View, it is useful to indicate how to step through executing different commands in a script file. This example will demonstrate a number of other features of the Query window in SQL Server.

Figure 14-16 illustrates that by clicking the New Query icon twice, you create two new Query windows. In this example, Management Studio was just started, so the database within which you are working is *master*. This is an internal system database and does not contain your data; it is important to always check the database name in which the Query window is executing.

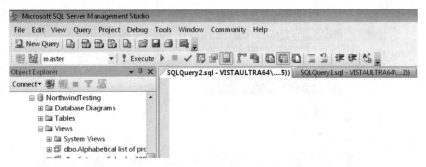

Figure 14-16 Opening two new Query windows. In this example, the active database is *master* as is indicated above the Object Explorer pane, on the Toolbar (this is also indicated at the lower-right of the screen).

If you click an object in your database in Object Explorer and then click New Query, the query window automatically targets your database. If you need to change the active database, you can select it from the drop-down list located just above the Object Explorer pane. Figure 14-17 shows that the active database is now *NorthwindTesting*.

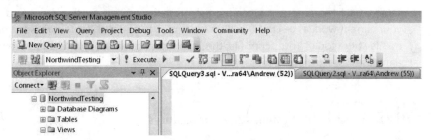

Figure 14-17 You can change the active database for the Query window by using the drop-down list above the Object Explorer pane, or clicking an object in your database in Object Explorer and then clicking New Query.

If while executing a script, objects cannot be found, verify that the Query window is referencing the correct database. This context is set for each individual query window. When you first start working with Query windows, it's common to inadvertently be in the wrong database context (usually, this is *master*).

The Query window works like a scratchpad (this is a super version of the Immediate window). Figure 14-18 illustrates an example of select SQL Commands; the commands do not need to be run in sequence. And by highlighting a command and clicking the Execute button (or pressing Alt+X or F5), you can display the results.

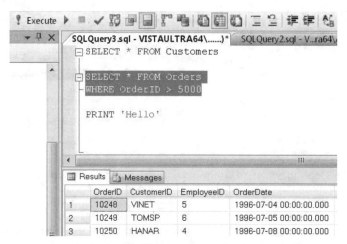

Figure 14-18 The Query window can also show multiple result sets if you were to execute the two blocks of SQL.

Once familiar with the environment, you can work with several of these windows at the same time. For example, you can use the File menu to load existing script files and save your current work as a script file. It's a good idea to add the *Use [databasename] GO* statements at the top of your script file; this means that it will always switch to use the correct database when the script runs.

INSIDE OUT   System stored procedures

Inside the database are a large number of built-in system stored procedures, all prefixed by sp_ or xp_ (linking to resources outside SQL Server). As you need to perform special operations, you will gain familiarity with these stored procedures and will find them extremely useful. SQL Server has an exceptionally good help system, which can guide you through the detailed syntax for each procedure.

In the following example, there are two system stored procedures: *sp_refreshview*, which refreshes a view for underlying changes on dependent objects, and *sp_depends* which lists object dependencies.

The following example (ViewsAndRefreshView.sql) demonstrates how Views are not dynamically updated for changes made in dependent objects. It also shows how to refresh the View using *sp_refreshview*, which updates the View to take into account changes made to the underlying objects used in the View. When you execute this script, use the mouse to highlight all the lines in each batch (the *GO* keyword indicates the end of a batch), and then click the Execute button on the Toolbar to show the results. Highlight the next batch and proceed one batch at a time, as you work through the script:

```
USE NorthwindTesting
GO
-- Create a view
CREATE VIEW vw_Customers
AS
SELECT * FROM Customers
GO
-- Display the results
SELECT * FROM vw_Customers
GO
-- Add a new field
ALTER TABLE Customers
ADD NewComments NVARCHAR(100)
GO
-- The new field will NOT be shown
SELECT * FROM vw_Customers
GO
-- Refresh the view
sp_refreshview vw_Customers
GO
-- The new field will be shown
SELECT * FROM vw_Customers
GO
-- List objects dependent on this view
-- and objects this view depends upon
sp_depends vw_Customers
GO
-- List objects dependent on the table
sp_depends Customers
GO
```

In the preceding example, you can see how a view can also be created in T-SQL by using the *CREATE VIEW* syntax. If you try to run that batch more than once, it informs you that the object already exists, and if you right-click and refresh the Views folder, you can see that the View has indeed already been created. A View can be altered by using the following syntax (you can right-click to the shortcut menu on any View object to create an *ALTER* syntax script):

```
ALTER VIEW vw_Customers
AS
SELECT CustomerID,CompanyName FROM Customers
GO
```

CROSSTAB Queries

CROSSTAB queries can be written in a View, but you need to use the SQL Server *PIVOT* syntax for this. Interestingly, SQL Server also has an *UNPIVOT* syntax for reversing these

Chapter 14

presentations. *PIVOT* syntax can be a little tricky, and the main difference when compared to a *CROSSTAB* is that a *CROSSTAB* can dynamically generate the column headings, but in a *PIVOT* query, these need to be predefined. The following example shows the Access syntax for a *CROSSTAB* query:

```
TRANSFORM Sum(CCur([Order Details].UnitPrice*[Quantity]*(1-[Discount])/100)*100) AS
ProductAmount
SELECT Products.ProductName, Orders.CustomerID, Year([OrderDate]) AS OrderYear
FROM Products INNER JOIN (Orders INNER JOIN [Order Details] ON Orders.OrderID =
[Order Details].OrderID) ON Products.ProductID = [Order Details].ProductID
WHERE (((Orders.OrderDate) Between #1/1/1997# And #12/31/1997#))
GROUP BY Products.ProductName, Orders.CustomerID, Year([OrderDate])
PIVOT "Qtr " & DatePart("q",[OrderDate],1,0) In ("Qtr 1","Qtr 2","Qtr 3","Qtr 4");
```

The following code shows the equivalent *PIVOT* syntax in SQL Server:

```
CREATE VIEW [dbo].[Quarterly Orders by Product]
AS
SELECT
    [ProductName],
    [CustomerID],
    [OrderYear],
    [Qtr 1],
    [Qtr 2],
    [Qtr 3],
    [Qtr 4]
FROM
 ( SELECT Sum(CONVERT(MONEY,[Order Details].[UnitPrice]*[Quantity]*
      (1-[Discount])/100)*100) AS [ProductAmount],
  'Qtr ' + CONVERT(VARCHAR,DATEPART(q,[OrderDate]))
) AS [PIVOT_ITEM],
[Products].[ProductName],
[Orders].[CustomerID],
Year([OrderDate]) AS [OrderYear]
FROM [Products]
    INNER JOIN (Orders
    INNER JOIN [Order Details]
      ON [Orders].[OrderID]=[Order Details].[OrderID])
      ON [Products].[ProductID]=[Order Details].[ProductID]
WHERE (((Orders.[OrderDate]) Between '1/1/1997' And '12/31/1997'))
GROUP BY 'Qtr ' + CONVERT(VARCHAR,DATEPART(q,[OrderDate])),
[Products].[ProductName],Orders.[CustomerID],Year([OrderDate])
) AS p
PIVOT(
Sum([ProductAmount])
    FOR [PIVOT_ITEM]
 IN ([Qtr 1],[Qtr 2],[Qtr 3],[Qtr 4])) AS pvt
GO
```

You can find code online for creating dynamic column headings for *PIVOT* queries in SQL Server. The trick to building dynamic pivots it to create a SQL string and execute it; you need some initial code to work out what the potential column names will be and concatenate this into the string.

Working with Stored Procedures

At the beginning of the last section, we introduced Views and described how a View can return data like a *SELECT* query, and we described how the dataset returned may be updateable. The equivalent to an *INSERT*, *UPDATE* or *DELETE* query in SQL Server is a stored procedure. Stored procedures are in fact more flexible than a simple query that performs one step; for example, updating data in a single table. They are mini programs that can range from a few lines to several pages of code.

In Access, when you need to write a program, you use VBA, in SQL Server, you use T-SQL, which allows for program logic and variables. T-SQL is a specific language for SQL Server; other popular databases have their own variations on SQL to assist with programming; for example, Oracle uses PSQL.

Programing in T-SQL is different to writing VBA. The first difference you will spot is that even though the language has a number of features, it is not as rich and varied as VBA. On the plus side, this means that the language features can be learned quickly. Another big difference is that T-SQL mixes program logic with SQL in a very elegant manner; effectively, the SQL becomes embedded in the code, which means that when you need to mix a variable into a piece of SQL, rather than building up a string to be executed, you can often directly mix the reference to the variable into the flow of the SQL. This is a more elegant code structure.

Before you take a look in depth at the T-SQL language features, you will look at how to create some simple stored procedures. Unlike Views, which can be edited in a GUI in addition to the Query window, stored procedures do not have a graphical editor. The stored procedures are saved in the Programmability | Stored Procedures folder, as shown in Figure 14-19.

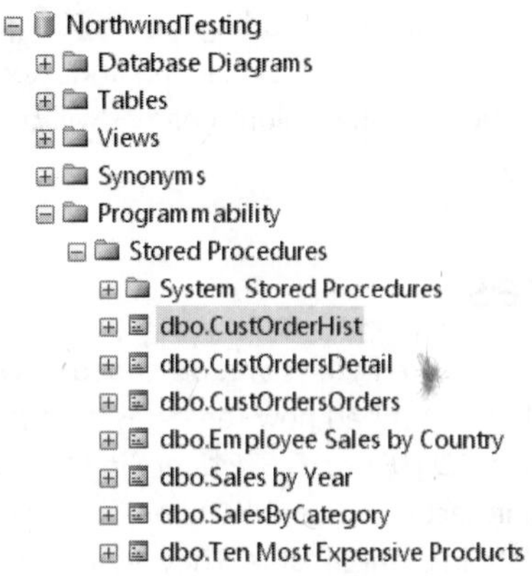

```
⊟ 🗊 NorthwindTesting
   ⊞ 🗀 Database Diagrams
   ⊞ 🗀 Tables
   ⊞ 🗀 Views
   ⊞ 🗀 Synonyms
   ⊟ 🗀 Programmability
      ⊟ 🗀 Stored Procedures
         ⊞ 🗀 System Stored Procedures
         ⊞ 🔲 dbo.CustOrderHist
         ⊞ 🔲 dbo.CustOrdersDetail
         ⊞ 🔲 dbo.CustOrdersOrders
         ⊞ 🔲 dbo.Employee Sales by Country
         ⊞ 🔲 dbo.Sales by Year
         ⊞ 🔲 dbo.SalesByCategory
         ⊞ 🔲 dbo.Ten Most Expensive Products
```

Figure 14-19 The Stored Procedure folder in Object Explorer.

The following example (StoredProcedure.sql) illustrates how to create, execute, change, and remove a stored procedure:

```
USE [Northwind]
GO
-- Create a stored procedure
CREATE PROC usp_UpdateCustomersRating
AS
UPDATE Customers
SET Rating = 1
GO
-- Execute the stored procedure
usp_UpdateCustomersRating
GO
-- Alternative syntax for executing the stored procedure
EXEC usp_UpdateCustomersRating
GO
-- Changing the stored procedure
ALTER PROC usp_UpdateCustomersRating
AS
UPDATE Customers
SET Rating = 5
GO
-- Delete the stored procedure
DROP PROC usp_UpdateCustomersRating
GO
```

One area of possible confusion is in thinking that the preceding example is like a VBA module—it is not. When you execute the T-SQL command to create the stored procedure, the actual code is saved inside the database as a stored procedure object. After executing the lines of code to create the stored procedure and refreshing the folder containing the stored procedures, you will see that the stored procedure has been saved inside the database. To see and modify the stored procedure, you can use the shortcut menu, as shown in Figure 14-20.

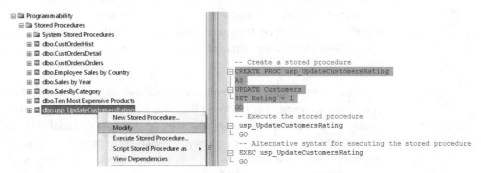

Figure 14-20 After the code has been executed and the stored procedures folder has been refreshed, you can get back to the code by right-clicking the stored procedures and either selecting Modify or Script Stored Procedure from the shortcut menu.

You will find that the syntax for writing queries to *INSERT*, *UPDATE*, and *DELETE* data in SQL Server is similar to that used in Access, but it is not exactly the same.

The *DELETE* Query

In Access, an example of a *DELETE* query would have the following SQL (notice that Access often adds additional brackets in a *WHERE* clause):

```
DELETE Customers.*, Customers.Rating
FROM Customers
WHERE (((Customers.Rating)=99));
```

In SQL Server, you don't have the list of fields following the keyword *DELETE*. The SQL Server syntax shown in the following code would also work in Access. In this situation the additional information for specifying the fields was added by the Access Query designer:

```
DELETE
FROM Customers
WHERE (((Customers.Rating)=99));
```

INSIDE OUT Truncating tables

When you perform any operation to change data in SQL Server, the changes to the data are normally recorded in the LOG file (there are some exceptions to this with respect to Binary and some other data type columns, which due to their size are not recorded in the LOG file). This means that if you try to delete a large amount of data, there will be a lot of data written to the LOG file to record the change, which will take time to execute.

If for example you have a table containing data imports, you might not be interested in having the operation of emptying the table recorded in the LOG file. As long as this import table does not have any relationships, you can use a special *TRUNCATE TABLE <tablename>* syntax to provide a very significant boost to performance. This command is not recorded in the LOG file, which means that it cannot be undone inside a transaction, and if a backup using LOG files were restored, or you are using log shipping or a mirror database, then the change would not be reproduced. But in this situation, you probably don't care about this minor effect.

The *UPDATE* Query

It is only when you come to design an *UPDATE* query that depends on more than one table that you will find the syntax for this command changes. In the following Access SQL, you are updating only customers who have an order in the system:

```
UPDATE Customers INNER JOIN Orders
ON Customers.CustomerID = Orders.CustomerID
SET Customers.Rating = 1
WHERE (((Customers.Rating)=99));
```

This SQL needs to be rewritten as follows:

```
UPDATE Customers
SET Customers.Rating = 1
FROM Customers INNER JOIN Orders
ON Customers.CustomerID = Orders.CustomerID
WHERE (((Customers.Rating)=99));
```

After the keyword *UPDATE*, you need to state only the name of the table that will be updated, and then you need an additional *FROM* clause that restates the main table name and expresses any joins. This involves a cut and paste operation on the first few lines of the SQL.

The *INSERT* and *INSERT INTO* Queries

There are four different forms for *INSERT* operations.

In you want to insert one or more values of data into a table, in Access, you can use the following syntax:

```
INSERT INTO Customers ( CustomerID, CompanyName )
SELECT "XXX" AS Expr1, "Test Company" AS Expr2;
```

Change the double quotes to single quotes, and the same code will run in SQL Server, as shown here:

```
INSERT INTO Customers ( CustomerID, CompanyName )
SELECT 'XXX' AS Expr1, 'Test Company' AS Expr2;
```

But you would not normally write this expression in SQL Server, because SQL Server supports a *VALUES* syntax, which has the added benefit of being able to insert multiple rows with a single statement, as shown in the following:

```
INSERT INTO Customers ( CustomerID, CompanyName )
VALUES('XXX', 'Test Company');
```

This can then be extended for up to 1000 rows:

```
INSERT INTO Customers ( CustomerID, CompanyName )
VALUES('XXX1', 'Test Company 1'),
('XXX2', 'Test Company 2'),
('XXX3', 'Test Company 3')
```

The second form of an insert statement is equivalent to an Access *Make Table* query; in Access you have the following:

```
SELECT Customers.* INTO Customers2
FROM Customers
WHERE (((Customers.Country)="USA"));
```

Apart from changing the double quotes to single quotes, the same SQL executes in SQL Server:

```
SELECT Customers.* INTO Customers2
FROM Customers
WHERE (((Customers.Country)='USA'));
```

The third form of an *INSERT* query is where you want to add values to an existing table. In Access, you create the following *Append* query:

```
INSERT INTO Customers2
SELECT Customers.*
FROM Customers
WHERE (((Customers.Country) Like "*USA*"));
```

In SQL Server, apart from changing the double quotes to single quotes and the wildcard matching character * to a %, the SQL is unchanged:

```
INSERT INTO Customers2
SELECT Customers.*
FROM Customers
WHERE (((Customers.Country) Like '%usa%'));
```

It is interesting to note that the wildcard syntax in SQL Server is also supported in Access, which you will see if you paste the code in the previous example back into Access.

INSIDE OUT   Temporary tables

In Access, you can't easily create a temporary user-specific table, and yet in solving many complex problems, it is essential to stage data into a holding table for further processing. SQL Server allows user-specific temporary tables to be created; this is an extremely powerful feature, and it can be incorporated into your stored procedures. But if you create temporary tables, you need to ensure that your code allows for the fact that the temporary results table might already exist, as illustrated in the following:

```
IF EXISTS(SELECT *FROM tempdb.dbo.sysobjects
WHERE ID = OBJECT_ID(N'tempdb..#Temp'))
BEGIN
    DROP TABLE #Temp
END
SELECT * into #Temp
FROM Customers
GO
```

There are two key points to observe when doing this: first, temporary tables are created inside the Temporary Tables folder in tempdb; this means that you can go into this system database and look at the temporary tables. (If you close the Query window that was used to create the temporary table, the temporary table will be removed from *tempdb*. If you try this, remember to use the shortcut menu and select Refresh to see the folder updated after you have closed the Query window.) Second, these temporary tables exist for as long as the connection exists, which means in Access you could execute a call that creates the temporary table, and then subsequently refer back to the temporary table, because Access will hold the connection open for you.

Introducing T-SQL

Using T-SQL, you can create mini-programs in SQL Server. These programs can then either be executed as a Script File, or saved in the body of triggers, stored procedures and functions. Depending on how familiar you are with writing SQL statements, you might struggle with some of the SQL Syntax, although the T-SQL programming features are quite simple to master.

Defining Variables

In T-SQL, you must prefix any variable name with the "@" (at) symbol and specify an appropriate data type. When declaring your variables, you can use the keyword *As*, but this is not required. To assign a value to a variable, you can either use the *SET* or *SELECT* command. Also notice that when using the *SET* command with a SQL statement, you need to surround the expression with parentheses, and the alternative syntax for assignment when using a *SELECT* statement (which is assumed to return 1 row, and that value for the first row would be assigned to any variable even when multiple rows were returned). The following examples are supplied in the file UsingVariables.sql:

```
DECLARE @CustomerCount INT
DECLARE @EmployeeCount As INT
-- Setting an explicit value for a variable
SET @CustomerCount = 99
-- Using the SET command with SQL to load a variable
-- note the brackets are required
SET @EmployeeCount = (SELECT COUNT(*) FROM Employees)
-- Using the SELECT command with SQL to load a variable
SELECT @EmployeeCount = COUNT(*) FROM Employees
-- Printing out a value
PRINT @CustomerCount
-- Printing out a message
PRINT 'Employee count is ' + CONVERT(NVARCHAR,@EmployeeCount)
GO
```

In the previous example, the *PRINT* command can be used to display additional information. If you connect Access to T-SQL that contains *PRINT* statements, you will not see the results of these statements. The *PRINT* command does not allow you to concatenate different data types without the explicit use of the *CONVERT* or *CAST* statement, which were used in the preceding example to change an integer into a string. Additional examples of this are presented in the next section.

Variables defined in a script file have a scope defined by the batch in which they execute, so after a *GO* keyword, the variables can no longer be referenced.

One very powerful feature of variables is that they can be directly referenced from within a *WHERE* or *HAVING* clause, as demonstrated here:

```
DECLARE @Country As NVARCHAR(30)
SET @Country = 'USA'
SELECT * FROM Customers
WHERE Country = @Country
GO
DECLARE @MinCount As INT
SET @MinCount = 10
SELECT Country,COUNT(*)
FROM Customers
GROUP BY Country
HAVING Count(*) > @MinCount
GO
```

INSIDE OUT Executing SQL statements on the fly

Suppose that you want to create a procedural block of code that allows for a variable in place of a table or column name. In this situation, you are not allowed to directly reference a variable in the embedded SQL as we have been doing with the *HAVING* and *WHERE* clauses. To do this, you approach the problem in a similar manner as you would in VBA, by constructing a string for the SQL:

```
-- Example executing an SQL String
DECLARE @Cmd As NVARCHAR(255)
DECLARE @TableName As NVARCHAR(100)
SET @TableName = 'Customers'
SET @Cmd = 'SELECT * FROM ' + @TableName
PRINT @Cmd
EXEC (@Cmd)
GO
```

Using syntax such as `SELECT @FieldName FROM @TableName` is not allowed in embedded SQL, instead we need to *EXECUTE* or *EXEC* an SQL string.

Using *CAST* and *CONVERT*

Access supports implicit type conversion. This means that, for example, if you use the "&" (ampersand) character to concatenate an integer to a string variable, it automatically converts the integer to a text type. SQL Server demands that you use explicit type conversion between types, both in your SQL and when manipulating variables, as shown in the following code (open the file CastAndConvert.sql):

```
SELECT CompanyName + ' : '
              + CAST(COUNT(*) AS nvarchar(10)) as Orders
FROM Customers c
   INNER JOIN Orders o
      ON c.CustomerID = o.CustomerID
GROUP BY CompanyName
GO
SELECT CompanyName + ' : '
              + CONVERT(nvarchar(10),COUNT(*)) as Orders
FROM Customers c
   INNER JOIN Orders o
      ON c.CustomerID = o.CustomerID
GROUP BY CompanyName
GO
DECLARE @Total Int
SELECT @Total = COUNT(*) FROM Customers
PRINT 'Total Customers ' + CONVERT(nvarchar(10),@Total)
GO
```

In the preceding example, you can also see the use of the *PRINT* statement, which outputs messages to the Messages tab in the results window. This statement is useful for simple debugging in stored procedures, and it does not affect any results being returned to an Access application.

Built-In Functions

T-SQL has a large number of built-in functions for manipulating dates, strings, and other operations. Sometimes, you will find an exact match between an Access function, for example, the *Left* string function, and in other instances the functions have a different name or different order of parameters. We have included a few simple examples (open the file BuiltInFunctions.sql) in the following code, but you will find that the help system is full of examples (search for "functions [SQL Server]"):

```
DECLARE @SampleString NVARCHAR(250)
SET @SampleString = ' Charlotte forgot her lunch box again '
PRINT LTRIM(RTRIM(@SampleString)) -- remove blanks
PRINT LEN(@SampleString) -- length
PRINT LOWER(@SampleString) -- lower case
PRINT UPPER(@SampleString) -- upper case
PRINT CHARINDEX(@SampleString,'CHARLOTTE',2)  -- substring position
PRINT SUBSTRING(@SampleString,2,9) -- substring
DECLARE @TheDate DATETIME
SET @TheDate = '4 December 2005'
PRINT DATEADD(d,10,@TheDate)  -- add to a date
select DATEDIFF(year,@TheDate,GETDATE()) -- difference
```

Chapter 14

Other basic functions that are often used in T-SQL include:

- **COALESCE** Returns the first non-null value from a list of choices.

- **NULLIF** Returns a NULL if two expressions are equal.

- **ISNULL** Returns a replacement value when an expression is null.

- **CASE** Case statements can provide sophisticated logical testing.

System Variables

SQL Server has around 33 built-in system variables (this number can vary a bit, depending on such variables as Service Pack, and so on). These variables all start with the @@ symbols, and you can use them in your program code. In the following (and in UsingSystem Variables.sql), we have listed two of the more commonly used system variables.

@@Version

This variable will return SQL Server version information, which is a useful function for checking the version of SQL Server:

```
CREATE PROC usp_GetSQLServerVersion
AS
SELECT @@VERSION as 'SQLServerVersion'
GO
EXEC usp_GetSQLServerVersion
GO
```

@@IDENTITY, SCOPE_IDENTITY() and IDENT_CURRENT

The following example illustrates the use of three alternative methods to find the last value for the IDENTITY column in a table; these methods are useful after inserting a row when you need to determine the value in a column that issues an automatic number:

```
CREATE TABLE InsertTest(
AnID INT IDENTITY(1,1),
Comment nvarchar(30)
)
GO
INSERT INTO InsertTest(Comment)
VALUES ('Test Record')
GO
SELECT @@IDENTITY
GO
SELECT SCOPE_IDENTITY()
GO
SELECT IDENT_CURRENT('InsertTest')
GO
```

In general, if you are writing a complex procedure in T-SQL, and you need to find the IDENTITY of the last inserted row, you should use *SCOPE_IDENTITY()* rather than *@@IDENTITY*. The reason for this is that if the table into which you insert has a trigger that inserts into a subsequent table that also has an IDENTITY column, *@@IDENTITY* returns the IDENTITY value for the table that the trigger inserted into. SCOPE_IDENTITY() returns the IDENTITY value within the scope of the current code, which is what you want.

In an Access application that performed an insert, you can execute a pass-through query to return the current IDENTITY value for a table.

Alternatively you could create a stored procedure, into which you pass the name of the table and use the *IDENT_CURRENT* function, which returns the current IDENTITY value for a specified table, as shown in the following code:

```
CREATE PROC usp_LastIdentity @TableName VARCHAR(255)
AS
EXEC ('SELECT IDENT_CURRENT(''' + @TableName + ''')')
GO
EXEC usp_LastIdentity 'InsertTest'
GO
```

In summary, if you are writing code in SQL Server, you should use *SCOPE_IDENTITY()* or *IDENT_CURRENT*; if you are writing pass-through SQL in Access, the safest option is to use *IDENT_CURRENT*.

Controlling Program Flow

T-SQL does not have as many language control structures as VBA (for example, it does not have any *FOR* or *FOR … EACH* constructs). However, because of the way in which SQL can be embedded in the code, it doesn't always follow that you get the same kind of structural layout as you expect to see in VBA. With T-SQL, you can program with a layout style similar to VBA, if you prefer a VBA-style layout.

The first structure to examine is the *IF* statement. This takes the form IF *<Boolean Expression> <sql statement or statement block>* ELSE *<sql statement or statement block>*. Note that T-SQL does not include a *Then* keyword. Statement blocks use paired *BEGIN … END* statements to indicate the start and end of the block. The following are examples of using the *IF* statement (open the file ProgramFlow.sql):

```
DECLARE @Country As NVARCHAR(50)
SET @Country = 'usa'
IF EXISTS(SELECT CustomerID FROM Customers
        WHERE Country = @Country)
```

```
BEGIN
    PRINT 'We have ' + @Country + ' customers'
    SELECT * FROM Customers WHERE Country = @Country
END
ELSE
BEGIN
    PRINT 'We do not have any customers for ' + @Country
END
GO

DECLARE @Country As NVARCHAR(50)
DECLARE @CustCount As INT
SET @Country = 'usa'
SET @CustCount = (SELECT Count('*') FROM Customers
                    WHERE Country = @Country)
IF @CustCount > 0
    SELECT * FROM Customers WHERE Country = @Country
ELSE
    PRINT 'We do not have any customers for ' + @Country
GO
```

The second programing structure is the *WHILE* loop, which supports the use of the *Break* statement to exit the loop, and the *CONTINUE* statement to skip subsequent statements and return to the test at the top of the loop. This structure can have the *WHILE* test working like an *IF* statement would work testing an explicit value, or use a SQL expression:

```
CREATE TABLE MessagesToProcess(
MsgId           INT IDENTITY(1,1) PRIMARY KEY,
Country         NVARCHAR(100)
)
GO
INSERT INTO MessagesToProcess(Country)
VALUES ('USA'),('UK')
GO
DECLARE @Country As NVARCHAR(100)
DECLARE @MsgId INT
WHILE EXISTS(SELECT MsgId FROM MessagesToProcess)
BEGIN
    SELECT @MsgId = MsgID, @Country = Country
    FROM MessagesToProcess
    -- Process the message
    SELECT * FROM Customers WHERE Country = @Country
    -- The break statement is useful during testing
    --BREAK
    DELETE FROM MessagesToProcess WHERE MsgId = @MsgId
END
GO
-- Alternative code
DECLARE @Country As NVARCHAR(100)
DECLARE @MsgId INT
DECLARE @RowsToProcess As Int
SET @RowsToProcess = (SELECT COUNT(*) FROM MessagesToProcess)
```

```
WHILE (@RowsToProcess > 0)
BEGIN
   SELECT @MsgId = MsgID, @Country = Country
   FROM MessagesToProcess
   -- Process the message
   SELECT * FROM Customers WHERE Country = @Country
   -- The break statement is useful during testing
   --BREAK
   DELETE FROM MessagesToProcess WHERE MsgId = @MsgId
   SET @RowsToProcess = (SELECT COUNT(*) FROM MessagesToProcess)
END
GO
```

INSIDE OUT   T-SQL statements that control program flow

T-SQL also supports the following statements for control of program flow. Of particular note is the *GOTO* statement which is very useful for structuring complex blocks of code:

RETURN   Used in a stored procedure to return an integer expression and terminate the execution of the procedure.

GOTO <label>   Similar to VBA, you define a label, for example *ResumeCodeHere*, and you can then branch the code to continue execution from the label.

WAITFOR   Pauses the code for a timed delay or until a specified time is reached.

Error Handling

In most cases, your application will be performing error handling, but you might also want to add error handling to your T-SQL code and communicate error information from T-SQL to the application.

In the first example (ErrorHandling.sql), you create a procedure that generates an error. This routine indicates how the *@@ERROR* variable could be used inside the stored procedure to execute statements after the error has occurred:

```
CREATE PROC usp_NumericalError
AS
DECLARE @TotalValue As DECIMAL(10,2)
SET @TotalValue = 6 /0
-- Execution will now continue
IF @@ERROR <> 0
   PRINT 'Error processing logic'
GO
Exec usp_NumericalError
GO
```

In Access, you can use the following code to manage the error. Note that the error (*Errors(1)*) in errors collection (which will contain two errors) contains the generic

ODBC—call failed error message (this is the same message as is shown by *Err.Description*), and you need to look at *Errors(0)* to see the actual SQL Server error text, as demonstrated in the following:

```
Sub modSQLErrors_DivideByZero()
    Dim db As DAO.Database
    Dim qdef As DAO.QueryDef
    Dim rst As DAO.Recordset
    Set db = CurrentDb
    Set qdef = db.CreateQueryDef("")
    ' pick up a connection string
    qdef.Connect = CurrentDb.TableDefs("Customers").Connect
    qdef.SQL = "usp_NumericalError"
    qdef.ReturnsRecords = False
    On Error Resume Next
    qdef.Execute
    Debug.Print Err.Number, Err.Description
    Debug.Print Errors(0).Number, Errors(0).Description
End Sub
```

You are also able to create your own error messages in the *master* database by using the *sp_addmessage* stored procedure. These should be numbered starting at 50,001, as shown in the following:

```
USE master
GO
EXEC sp_addmessage 50001, 16, 'TestErrorMessage'
GO
```

You can then use the *RAISEERROR* command to raise the error. Use a Severity of 16 to allow Access to receive the custom error message:

```
CREATE PROC usp_RaiseCustomError @TotalValue As DECIMAL(10,2)
AS
DECLARE @ProcName AS nvarchar(126)
DECLARE @ParamValue As nvarchar(50)
IF @TotalValue < 100
BEGIN
    SET @ProcName = ERROR_PROCEDURE()
    SET @ParamValue = CONVERT(NVARCHAR,@TotalValue)
    RAISERROR (50001,
        16,                          -- Severity.
        1,                           -- State.
        @ProcName,                   -- First argument
        @ParamValue);                -- Second argument.
END
GO
Exec usp_RaiseCustomError 10.5
GO
```

The following code can then be used in Access to display the error message:

```
Sub modSQLErrors_RaiseError()
    Dim db As DAO.Database
    Dim qdef As DAO.QueryDef
    Dim rst As DAO.Recordset
    Set db = CurrentDb
    Set qdef = db.CreateQueryDef("")
    ' pick up a connection string
    qdef.Connect = CurrentDb.TableDefs("Customers").Connect
    qdef.SQL = "usp_RaiseCustomError 10.5"
    qdef.ReturnsRecords = False
    On Error Resume Next
    qdef.Execute
    Debug.Print Errors(0).Number, Errors(0).Description
End Sub
```

Often a cleaner method for handling errors is to use a *TRY ... CATCH* structure to trap errors. This example returns a *Recordset* with a single record containing a full description of the error. If no error is generated, the routine returns a *Recordset* with columns to match what would be expected when an error occurs, but it uses a 0 to indicate that no error has occurred, as illustrated in the following:

```
CREATE PROC usp_MainRoutine
AS
BEGIN TRY
    -- Execute our stored procedure
    EXECUTE usp_NumericalError
    SELECT 0,0,0,'','',0
END TRY
BEGIN CATCH
    SELECT
        ERROR_NUMBER() AS ErrorNumber,
        ERROR_SEVERITY() AS ErrorSeverity,
        ERROR_STATE() AS ErrorState,
        ERROR_PROCEDURE() AS ErrorProcedure,
        ERROR_MESSAGE() AS ErrorMessage,
        ERROR_LINE() AS ErrorLine;
END CATCH
GO

Exec usp_MainRoutine
GO
```

The advantage of this method for returning error information is that you can get a detailed description. The pass-through query has *ReturnsRecords* set to *True* to allow the return of the Error code information:

```
Sub modSQLErrors_TryCatch()
    Dim db As DAO.Database
```

```
        Dim qdef As DAO.QueryDef
        Dim rst As DAO.Recordset
        Set db = CurrentDb
        Set qdef = db.CreateQueryDef("")
        ' pick up a connection string
        qdef.Connect = CurrentDb.TableDefs("Customers").Connect
        qdef.SQL = "usp_MainRoutine"
        qdef.ReturnsRecords = True
        Set rst = qdef.OpenRecordset()
        If rst(0) <> 0 Then
            Debug.Print rst(0), rst(1), rst(2), rst(3), rst(4), rst(5)
        End If
    End Sub
```

Working with Triggers

SQL Server triggers are another very clever feature that allows for some very powerful pro-graming. Access has *data macros*, which are similar to triggers, but they do not support a transactional model, which is an inbuilt feature of SQL Server triggers.

The idea of both triggers and data macros is to write code that is guaranteed to execute in association with a table, regardless of which form, view, or other technique is used to attempt to modify the data. SQL Server actually supports several different types of triggers, but you will be looking at the classic *After* triggers.

When you work with these triggers, the code executes after the data has been changed. There is a very good reason for this as it allows you to examine the changes during the execution of the trigger code, and if you don't want to accept the changes, you can undo them. SQL Server supports transactions, which are sequences of operations that can be either fully committed or undone in a *ROLLBACK*. Triggers are rather special in that they are an implicit transaction, so you don't need to commit the changes (this is what we mean by implicit), but you do have the option to undo them.

Because these triggers occur after the data has been changed, when you are writing trigger code, you have two special virtual tables with which you can work.

The first virtual table is called *DELETED*, and it shows you the image of the data before the change was applied. The *DELETED* virtual table will contain either any rows that have been deleted or the before image of any rows that have been updated, containing the old val-ues, but not new rows that have been inserted.

The second virtual table is called *INSERTED*. This table shows you the after image of the data, so this contains the updated rows with new values and any newly inserted rows.

A subtle feature of this programming technique is that both *INSERTED* and *DELETED* tables cannot be edited; they act as a guide to what has been changed. A key feature of trigger programing is in understanding that you can still change the real data, and you can use a join to *INSERTED* or *DELETED* to limit how that change is applied.

In this first example (Triggers.sql), you add two new columns to the *Customers* table to record when a new record is entered and the user who entered the record, as follows:

```
ALTER TABLE Customers
ADD LastUpdatedOn DATETIME
CONSTRAINT DefCustomersLastUpdatedOn DEFAULT GetDate()
GO
ALTER TABLE Customers
ADD LastUpdatedBy NVARCHAR(120)
CONSTRAINT DefCustomersLastUpdatedBy DEFAULT SUSER_SNAME()
GO
```

You now need to create a trigger so that when a user edits a record, the previously added new fields are updated. A trigger can be defined for any combination of the three events *UPDATE*, *INSERT*, and *DELETE*, but because you have defaults set for an *INSERT*, you only need to write the trigger for the *UPDATE* event. The trigger in the following example uses the *DELETED* virtual table to ensure that you only change those records that the user edited:

```
CREATE TRIGGER Tr_CustomerAudit_Update
ON Customers
FOR UPDATE
AS
UPDATE Customers
   SET LastUpdatedOn = GETDATE(),
   LastUpdatedBy = SUSER_NAME()
FROM Customers
   INNER JOIN DELETED
      ON Customers.CustomerID = DELETED.CustomerID
GO
```

In the next example, you want to record the old customer record when a user updates the record or deletes the record. You start by creating the audit table, and then adding a new field to record the data operation, as demonstrated here:

```
SELECT * INTO audit_Customers
FROM Customers
WHERE CustomerID IS NULL
GO

-- Add a field to indicate the auditing operation
-- U for Update and D for Delete
ALTER TABLE audit_Customers
ADD Operation NVARCHAR(1)
GO
```

You then need to create two triggers: one for *UPDATE*, and the other for *DELETE*. But because you already have an *UPDATE* trigger, you will modify the existing one:

```
-- Record the old image of the data
CREATE Trigger TR_CustomerRowAudit_Delete
ON Customers
FOR DELETE
AS
INSERT INTO audit_Customers
SELECT *,'D' FROM DELETED
GO
ALTER Trigger TR_CustomerRowAudit_Update
ON Customers
FOR UPDATE
AS
UPDATE Customers
    SET LastUpdatedOn = GETDATE(),
    LastUpdatedBy = SUSER_NAME()
FROM Customers
    INNER JOIN DELETED
        ON Customers.CustomerID = DELETED.CustomerID
INSERT INTO audit_Customers
SELECT *,'U' FROM DELETED
GO
```

If you want to test this from the Access database linked to the *Customers* table, because new fields have been added in the SQL Server table, you should use the Linked Table Manager in Access to refresh the linked table.

Figure 14-21 illustrates that the *Customers* table has two triggers.

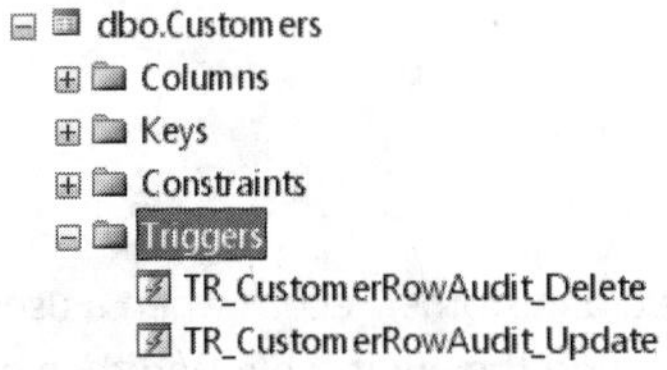

Figure 14-21 The *Customers* table with auditing triggers.

INSIDE OUT   Advanced features of triggers

Triggers are a big subject in and of themselves, and we have only touched on a few features in this section. The following list presents a number of more advanced points relating to designing triggers.

- When you have multiple triggers for the same event, you can control the order in which the triggers fire by specifying whether a trigger will fire first or last in the sequence. You specify this by using the stored procedure *sp_settriggerorder*.

- By default, triggers on one table that change the data in other tables that also have triggers will cause the triggers on the other tables to fire; nesting of triggers to 32 levels is supported. This is a server-level setting, and it can be disabled.

- Triggers can potentially be recursively called, and there is a database-level option to *Recursive Triggers Enabled*, which can control this feature (see the Help system for a discussion of Direct and Indirect recursion).

- *INSTEAD OF* triggers can be defined on Views to improve updateability.

- Triggers can be enabled and disabled; this is a very useful feature when bulk loading data into a system.

- The triggers we have described are DML triggers. SQL Server also support DDL triggers for recording changes made to data structures in response to *CREATE*, *ALTER* and *DROP* statements.

As an example of using *ROLLBACK* in a trigger, you can create a trigger to prevent any insertions or deletions on a table, as follows:

```
CREATE Trigger Tr_Categories_INSERTDELETE
ON Categories
FOR INSERT,DELETE
AS
    ROLLBACK TRAN
GO
```

The next example shows how you can use the *UPDATE* function to detect whether a particular column has been modified. In the following example, this will prevent the changes by using a *ROLLBACK* operation (there is also a more sophisticated *COLUMNS_UPDATED* function to test for changes on multiple columns with a single function):

```
CREATE Trigger Tr_Products_ProductName
ON Products
FOR UPDATE
AS
IF UPDATE([ProductName])
    ROLLBACK TRAN
GO
```

Chapter 14

Working with Transactions

A transaction is a unit of work that is protected so that either all the steps within the transaction are completed or none of the steps are completed. This means that within a transaction, you can have a number of SQL statements updating data in different tables, and you are guaranteed that if any step fails, any partially completed work is undone.

Transactions are valuable when you need to perform updates that cannot be completed with a single SQL statement. For example, in a stock control system, you might need to update quantities for sold items on a customer order, and at the same time decrease inventory stock levels of these sold items. If your program failed after it increased the quantity on a customer order in one step, but before it could decrease the corresponding stock level in the next step, you would have an inconsistency in the system. To prevent this, you can place the two operations inside a single transaction; if the system fails before completing the transaction, then the first step is undone, or rolled back, to leave the data in a consistent state.

There are three statements that control transaction processing:

- **BEGIN TRANSACTION (TRAN)**   Starts a transaction

- **COMMIT TRANSACTION (TRAN)**   Finishes the transaction

- **ROLLBACK TRANSACTION (TRAN)**   Undoes the transaction

You start this example (Transactions.sql) by creating a data table for testing, based on the *Customers* table, and then follow through the script, executing the statements one at a time and monitoring the @@*TRANCOUNT* (which indicates how many open transactions are active):

```
USE Northwind
GO
-- Examples of working with transactions

-- Start by creating a data table to work with
SELECT * INTO tblCompanies FROM Customers
GO
PRINT @@TRANCOUNT
-- Expect 0 for 0 open transactions
BEGIN TRAN
PRINT @@TRANCOUNT
-- Expect 1 for 1 open transaction
UPDATE tblCompanies SET ContactName = 'Test'
SELECT * FROM tblCompanies
COMMIT TRAN
SELECT * FROM tblCompanies
PRINT @@TRANCOUNT
-- Expect 0 for 0 open transaction
```

In the next example, continue through executing the script one line at a time to see the effect of the *ROLLBACK* action:

```
BEGIN TRAN
PRINT @@TRANCOUNT
-- Expect 1 for 1 open transaction
UPDATE tblCompanies SET ContactName = 'Test Rollback'
SELECT * FROM tblCompanies
ROLLBACK TRAN
SELECT * FROM tblCompanies
PRINT @@TRANCOUNT
-- Expect 0 for 0 open transaction
```

INSIDE OUT   Simulating multiuser interaction with a transaction

One very important question to ask is what happens if another user attempts to view data that has been changed but not yet committed or rolled back? Allowing a user to read *dirty data* is not the default setting in SQL Server. The default behavior is to prevent a *dirty read* and leave the other user paused and waiting for the transaction that is locking the data to either commit or rollback. Each Query window that you open in Management Studio behaves as a different connection or user, so it is easy to simulate the multiuser interaction.

If you repeat the execution of the last section of code, and only execute the script up to the line that has updated the data (so that you have not committed the transaction), then open a new Query window and execute SELECT * FROM tblCompanies, you will see that the second window is effectively blocked from execution. Figure 14-22 shows how to display the Activity Monitor (on the top Toolbar, last icon) and Figure 14-23 shows the results in the Activity Monitor.

Once you switch to the first window and execute either a *ROLLBACK* or *COMMIT*, and then return to the second window, you will see that the *SELECT* statement has been completed. This interplay of transactions and processes being temporarily suspended happens in milliseconds and is a natural feature of concurrent users interacting with the database, in this example we can slow down time and examine the logic behind our processing to ensure that the system is operating as anticipated.

Figure 14-22 The Activity Monitor is a useful tool when you're investigating a locking or blocking issue.

In Figure 14-23, you can investigate details of the suspended process.

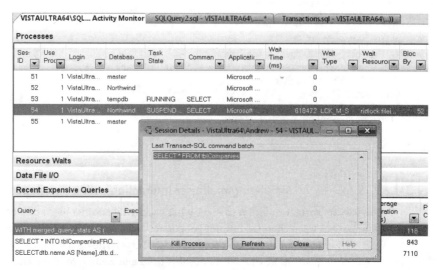

Figure 14-23 In Process 54, you can examine the suspended or blocked SQL; you can see on the right that it is being blocked by Process 52. You can also examine that last executed command by Process 52.

If you find in your application that blocking is causing a problem (which is an uncommon feature of an application), sit and watch the activity monitor while you get users to perform specific tasks. This will help you to track down the problem. Look for parts of your application that, for example, open and hold open a large *Recordset*, or a very complex processing routine that locks areas of the database used by other users.

Transaction Isolation Levels

In the previous section, you learned how the default behavior of SQL Server is to prevent a dirty read. The formal name for this setting is *READ COMMITED*. However, if you want to allow a dirty read, you could use *READ UNCOMMITTED*. SQL Server allows you to change the isolation level in a connection if you want to achieve a different behavior; you will need to set this inside a transaction. The following example illustrates the isolation options:

```
SET TRANSACTION ISOLATION LEVEL
      { READ UNCOMMITTED
      | READ COMMITTED
      | REPEATABLE READ
      | SNAPSHOT
      | SERIALIZABLE}
```

Nesting Transactions

You might decide to have transactions within transactions, or you might have structured your code such that a transaction causes other sections of code to be executed that themselves contain transactions. When working with these nested transactions there are several points to be considered.

The first question is recording the nested depth you have reached; the system variable *@@TRANCOUNT* gives a count of the number of open transactions. Each time a new transaction starts, the count increments by 1, and each time a transaction is committed, the count decreases by 1.

The second question is what happens when at each level in the nested transactions you have a *COMMIT* or *ROLLBACK* action. It is only when the outermost transaction is committed that all the work completed inside the inner nested transactions is finally applied in the database. This means that if you begin three nested transactions, then you required three *COMMIT*s to complete the work. If at any point inside any transaction you have a *ROLLBACK* action, then all the work at all levels will be undone. In the following code, you can see how to use the *@@TRANCOUNT* to test for a *ROLLBACK* in the inner transaction:

```
-- Handling a Rollback from a nested transaction
CREATE PROC usp_ForceRollback
AS
BEGIN
    -- Transcation started
    BEGIN TRAN
    -- The following action would be conditional
    ROLLBACK TRAN
END
GO

-- Transaction test
    BEGIN TRAN
    PRINT @@TRANCOUNT
    EXEC usp_ForceRollback
    IF @@TRANCOUNT > 0
        COMMIT TRAN
```

The third question is, when a transaction encounters a *ROLLBACK* action, how does this affect the execution of the program code? There are two situations in which a *ROLLBACK* can be encountered. The first situation is when your transactional code decides to explicitly call a *ROLLBACK*. In this situation, your code continues to execute, and you are responsible for using *@@TRANCOUNT* to detect that this has occurred and take appropriate action. The second situation is when your code causes a trigger to fire, and the trigger performs a *ROLLBACK* action. In this situation, your code stops execution, as shown in the following example:

```
-- Handling a Rollback generated from a trigger
CREATE TRIGGER Tr_TestRollBack ON tblCompanies
FOR DELETE
AS
BEGIN
    -- prevent any deletes
    ROLLBACK TRAN
END
GO

-- Test processing
-- Execute this as  a block of code
PRINT 'Program Running'
DELETE FROM tblCompanies
PRINT 'Code is still running'
GO
```

One last point to make on transactions is that you can also perform a localized rollback. To use this feature, you define a save point for the transaction, and then when specifying a *ROLLBACK*, you do so to the named save point.

User-Defined Functions

User-Defined Functions (UDFs) are very similar to VBA functions in that you can incorporate them both within queries (or Views) and inside program code (or stored procedures).

When adding them to Views, the same rules apply as in VBA: if you write a vast number of lines of code and execute blocks of SQL, don't be surprised when you add it to generate a column that it is very slow.

Consider the following SQL example (FunctionExample.sql).

> **Note**
> This calculation would work in Access.

```
USE Northwind
GO
SELECT [UnitPrice], [Quantity],
     LineTotal= [UnitPrice]*[Quantity],
     SalesTax = [LineTotal] * 0.20,
     Total = [SalesTax] + [LineTotal]
FROM [Order Details]
GO
```

This will not execute in SQL Server because you are not allowed to refer to a calculated expression in another expression (this might come as a big surprise). So, to make this work, you require the following:

```
SELECT [UnitPrice], [Quantity],
     LineTotal= [UnitPrice]*[Quantity],
     SalesTax = [UnitPrice]*[Quantity] * 0.20,
     Total = [UnitPrice]*[Quantity]* 1.2
FROM [Order Details]
GO
```

One solution to restating the sales tax calculation would be to create the following function and modify the SQL as shown in the example that follows, notice that you need to call the function with the dbo prefix (this is because functions need to be prefixed by the schema that owns the function):

```
CREATE FUNCTION ufn_SalesTax(@LineValue DECIMAL(10,2))
   RETURNS DECIMAL(10,2)
AS
BEGIN
   RETURN(@LineValue * 0.2)
END
GO
SELECT [UnitPrice], [Quantity],
     LineTotal= [UnitPrice]*[Quantity],
     SalesTax = dbo.ufn_SalesTax([UnitPrice]*[Quantity]),
     Total = [UnitPrice]*[Quantity] + dbo.ufn_SalesTax([UnitPrice]*[Quantity])
FROM [Order Details]
GO
```

INSIDE OUT   Table-valued functions

In addition to having functions called *scalar-valued functions* that return a single piece of data, functions returning a table of data in a similar manner as a stored procedure are allowed. These are called *table-valued functions*. These functions also have an advantage over a stored procedure in that they can be inserted in a *FROM* clause. There is also a subset of these functions known as *inline user-defined functions*, which can act like a View that accepts parameters, as shown in the following code (TableValued Functions.sql):

```
CREATE FUNCTION ufn_CustomersInACity
                ( @City nvarchar(15) )
RETURNS table
AS
RETURN (
        SELECT * FROM Customers
        WHERE City = @City
      )
GO

SELECT * FROM ufn_CustomersInACity('London')
GO
```

Getting Started with SQL Server Security

In this section, we provide enough of an overview of SQL Server Security to get you up and running with your development.

Surface Area Configuration

SQL Server installs with a minimum of its *surface area* exposed (to protect the security integrity of the server), which means that once you move from your local development environment to working with SQL Server on a network, you should verify that the surface area is suitably configured to enable you to communicate with the database server.

One of the simplest initial tests to run from the command line is the *ping* program, using the name of your server. This will help you establish that you can see the server on the network (or you could browse the network, or use some other technique to check that the server is available). If you cannot connect to the server, you should check that this is not a network authentication issue.

Once you know that the server is available, the next item to check is that the SQL Server is open for business (check this on the server). The default settings do not make the SQL Server open for communications. Start the SQL Server Configuration Manager by clicking Start | All Programs | Microsoft SQL Server 2008 R2 | Configuration Tools | SQL Server Configuration Manager. This should look similar to Figure 14-24, and you need to enable the appropriate protocols.

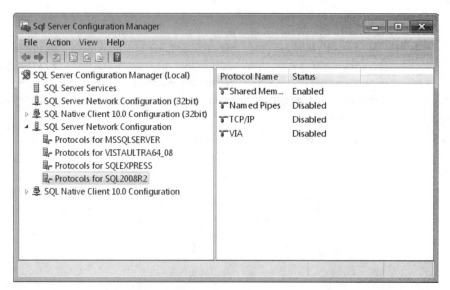

Figure 14-24 Using the SQL Server Configuration Manager. You will most likely want to enable both TCP/IP and Named Pipes for a SQL Server on the network.

The final step is to use a copy of Management Studio (the quickest method), or create or use an ODBC connection to test that you can connect to the server. If you are working with a database administrator (DBA), you might want to consult with him for specific connection details. In some extremely secure environments, DBAs might switch off the SQL Browsing task and change the default ports that the SQL Server will be listening on (but this is not that common).

The error message shown in Figure 14-25 is an indication that you are not able to connect to the SQL Server.

Figure 14-25 This error might be the result of an incorrectly specified server name, or the server is not visible on the network, or the surface area is not open.

The error shown in Figure 14-26 indicates that you are able to connect to the SQL Server, but there is a security problem with the Login, which is described in the next section.

Figure 14-26 This error tells you that you need to look into the login names or passwords or choice of authentication.

Windows authentication is the simpler choice for most security environments, but if you have problems with that, then using a SQL Server Logon is an excellent tool for identifying if a security issue lies with the SQL Server being able to see (authenticate) the required Windows accounts.

SQL Server Authentication

When SQL Server is installed, it can be configured to support either only Windows authentication or both Windows authentication and SQL Server Logons. To change this setting, right-click the server object, and then select properties from the shortcut menu. The Server Properties dialog box opens, as shown in Figure 14-27.

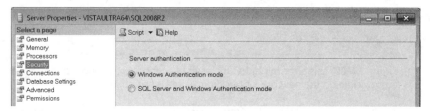

Figure 14-27 Supported authentication is configured by right-clicking the server in Management Studio, and then selecting properties.

When you are working with your own local SQL Server, as part of the installation, you had the option to add your logon account to act as an administrator of the SQL Server. But once you are working with a SQL Server on a network, life can become a bit more complicated. If you have remote login access as an administrator to the target server, you should be able to alter the security to support your choice of security model, if you cannot remotely start Management Studio on the server and connect to the SQL Server, you might need assistance and advice from whoever configured the SQL Server.

Security in SQL Server is defined primarily at the *server level*, and then further fine tuning of the security occurs inside each database. In the following sections, you will create or register accounts at the server level, and then through part of this process, you will create the necessary accounts inside each database. But notice that part of the process of managing the logons at the server level will create the necessary *user level* security in the databases.

To begin, in Object Explorer, click the Security folder, and then right-click the Login folder to open the shortcut menu. Click New Login, as shown in Figure 14-28.

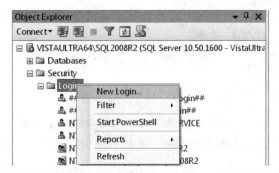

Figure 14-28 Creating a new SQL Server Login.

Next, enter an appropriate login name and select the SQL Server Authentication check box (see Figure 14-29). You might find it useful to disable the Enforce Password Policy (clear the check box), to make things easier when getting started. Farther down this screen, you can also specify a default database for the account.

Figure 14-29 Configuring the password and password policy for a SQL Server Login.

Move to the User Mapping page, select the Map for each database a user needs to use, and then assign the user to the db_owner database role, as shown in Figure 14-30. Later you can create and control your own database roles, which are ideal for managing security; db_owner is a powerful level of access to have in a database.

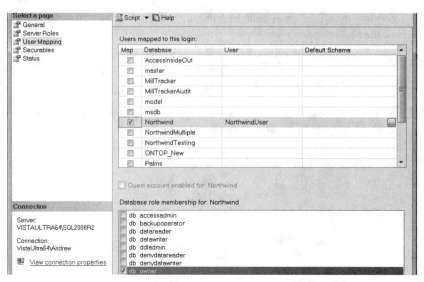

Figure 14-30 Map the user into all databases that they need to use and assign a database role.

Click OK to complete the setup. If you take a look inside the *Northwind* database, you can see that this is where the User Map is maintained (see Figure 14-31). If you later wish to delete a login, you also need to delete the user from this area in each database that they are using. Deleting a Login does not automatically delete the user from each database.

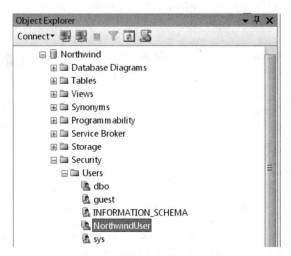

Figure 14-31 As a result of mapping a Login to a database, a corresponding entry is made in the folder called Users, inside each database to which the Login was mapped.

Windows Authentication

To configure Windows authentication, you follow similar steps to those described in the last section, but when creating the Logon, you are adding either an existing Windows User or a Windows Group into the SQL Server. SQL Server checks to see that this is valid selection; you can use the Search button to help you with this, as shown in Figure 14-32.

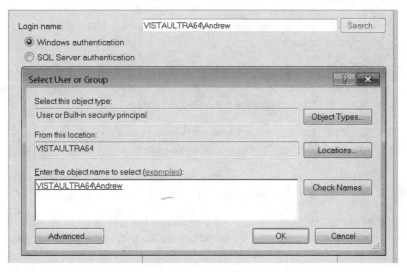

Figure 14-32 Searching to select a Windows User or Group.

After you have added the group name, refer back to the previous section, if necessary, to see how to set the user mapping and database role.

The easiest approach to managing Windows authentication is to have one or two Windows Groups created for the application. These can then be registered in the SQL Server, after which you only need to get the users added to the Windows Group, without the need for any further changes in SQL Server.

Summary

In this chapter, you have gained a good working knowledge of how SQL Server can be used to replace a back-end Access database, and how to use VBA programming in your Access application to utilize some of the features in SQL Server.

The key points that you should have noticed include:

- How SQL Server is architecturally different from Access and offers improved performance and scalability.

- How your Access application might need to be changed to make the most of SQL Server, including converting some of your queries and ensuring that you minimize the data volumes that are presented in forms.

- How to create tables, relationships, Views, stored procedures, and functions, and how an Access application can link to these objects.

- Trigger programming is very flexible and with it, you can implement elegant and sophisticated features in your application.

- How to effectively use the more advanced features in T-SQL. (You might need to brush up on your SQL, or at least allow time to feel more comfortable when writing SQL.)

You should by now appreciate that SQL Server is a big product, and although we have provided an overview of the features that you need to master, we have not covered every feature in the product.

In the next chapter, you look at the issue of taking an Access database and migrating or upsizing the data into SQL Server.

Upsizing Access to SQL Server

Planning for Upsizing 543

The Upsizing Wizard and the SQL Server
Migration Assistant 558

Developing with Access and SQL Server. 574

I n this chapter, you start by looking at the need for planning before you convert an existing Microsoft Access 2010 back-end database to Microsoft SQL Server. You will then
look at two popular Microsoft tools for upsizing a database; the Upsizing Wizard (part
of Access) and SQL Server Migration Assistant, which you can download free of charge. The
final part of the chapter looks at various issues and techniques that you can use to develop
or enhance your converted application.

After reading this chapter, you will be able to:

- Effectively plan how to upsize your databases and avoid common pitfalls.

- Understand how to use the Upsizing Wizard or SSMA to convert an application.

- Understand design techniques that can be used to further develop your application
  after it is upsized.

> **Note**
>
> As you read through this chapter, we encourage you to also use the companion con-
> tent sample databases, Northwind_ProblemsAndFixes.accdb, SQLServerCodeExamples.
> accdb, and the additional script files, which you can download from the book's catalog
> page.

Planning for Upsizing

In this section, you will look at how to plan for upsizing an Access database to SQL Server.
This includes looking at how the available data types in SQL Server can be matched with
those in Access, and the steps that you need to take to verify that your Access database can
be correctly converted. This verification will save you a lot of time, regardless of what tool
you choose to perform the conversion.

Text Data Types and UNICODE

The ASCII character encoding scheme has been in use for a long time, but is has an inherent restriction because it supports only 255 different characters in its code set. UNICODE, however, supports over 65,000 characters. The SQL Server data types for character data are *CHAR*, *VARCHAR*, and an older *TEXT* data type, which is equivalent to the Access *Memo* data type. *CHAR* is a fixed size and *VARCHAR* is varying size, so the Access *Text* data type matches the SQL Server *VARCHAR* data type.

The SQL Server UNICODE data types can be identified by the "N" prefix, such as *NCHAR*, *NVARCHAR* and *NTEXT*. If you choose to use UNICODE, this will double the required storage, which could have an impact on performance, but you gain a greater flexibility and support for international deployment of your application.

SQL Server has an 8 K page—the maximum column size is 8,000 bytes, and the maximum row size is 8,060 bytes (1 row per page). But SQL Server 2008 R2 does allow the combined length of character and certain other data types to exceed this maximum row size.

When dealing with a *Memo* data type, you have the option of mapping this to an older *TEXT* or *NTEXT* data type, or, beginning with SQL Server 2005, you can use *VARCHAR(MAX)* or *NVARCHAR(MAX)* data type, which is a better choice. The *VARCHAR(MAX)* data type can hold up to two gigabytes of data, and is stored in-row, when possible, to improve performance.

Date and Time Data

The Access *Date* data type can hold dates from 1 January, 100 to 31 December, 9999. When no date is given and time-only data is provided, it uses the date 30 December, 1899 to indicate time-only data and hides the date information.

The corresponding data type in SQL Server is the *DATETIME* data type. This can hold dates from 1 January, 1753 to 31 December, 9999. When no date is provided, it defaults the date to 1 January, 1900 (which you might have spotted is different in Access). SQL Server also has a *SMALLDATETIME* data type.

Beginning with SQL Server 2008, there are some new date and time data types, they are: *DATE*, *TIME*, *DATETIME2* and *DATETIMEOFFSET*. When you link Access to these data types, the *DATE* data type will appear as an Access *Date* data type, and can store dates in the range 1 January, 0000 to 31 December, 9999.

The most common choice of mapping is to map the Access *Date* data type to the *DATETIME* data type, but if you only had date data you could consider using the newer *DATE* data type.

If you use a map to the *DATETIME* data type, then because it is possible for your Access tables to contain badly entered dates—for example in the year 100—before you convert your database, you should verify that your date data is no earlier than 1 January, 1753 (this is one of the most common problems that applications can have and can cause data conversions to fail). If you find bad dates, and if the field is not a required field, you can set the value to *NULL*. If it is a required date, set the field to a safe value. The following VBA code in the Northwind_ProblemsAndFixes.accdb can be used to search through all the dates in your database, looking for bad dates and making corrections:

```
Sub modUpsizeTests_CheckDatesAndFix()
' Search through all tables with date fields
' Check that there are not tables containing dates
' which will not be accepted in SQL Server
' set illegal dates to NULL or a SafeDate
    Const strMinDate = "1 January 1753"
    Const strSafeDate = "1 January 1900"
    Dim db As DAO.Database
    Dim rst As DAO.Recordset
    Dim tdef As DAO.TableDef
    Dim fld As DAO.Field
    Dim strSQL As String
    Dim strCriteria As String
    Set db = CurrentDb
    For Each tdef In db.TableDefs
        If Left(tdef.Name, 4) <> "MSys" And _
            Left(tdef.Name, 4) <> "USys" And _
            Left(tdef.Name, 4) <> "~TMP" Then
            For Each fld In tdef.Fields
                If fld.Type = dbDate Then
                    strCriteria = "WHERE " & _
                            "[" & fld.Name & "] < #" & _
                            strMinDate & "#"
                    strSQL = "SELECT Count(*) FROM " & _
                            "[" & tdef.Name & "] " & strCriteria
                Set rst = db.OpenRecordset(strSQL, dbOpenDynaset)
                If rst(0) <> 0 Then
                    Debug.Print tdef.Name, fld.Name
                    If Not fld.Required Then
                        strSQL = "UPDATE [" & tdef.Name & "]" & _
                                " SET [" & fld.Name & "] = NULL " & _
                                strCriteria
                    Else
                        strSQL = "UPDATE [" & tdef.Name & "]" & _
                                " SET [" & fld.Name & "] = #" & _
                                strSafeDate & "# " & strCriteria
                    End If
                    CurrentDb.Execute strSQL
```

```
                    End If
                    rst.Close
                End If
            Next
        End If
    Next
End Sub
```

With *TIME*-only data, you need to be aware that as long as Access is used to continue entering this date, the default 30 December 1899 will be applied. But if you decide to write T-SQL in SQL Server, then ensure that you explicitly supply this date, because the default in SQL Server is 1 January 1900.

Boolean Data

An Access *Yes/No* data type corresponds to the SQL Server *BIT* data type. In Access *TRUE* is −1 and *FALSE* is 0; in SQL Server, *TRUE* is 1 and *FALSE* is 0.

In Access, if you don't provide a default value for a *Yes/No* field, it will be always be displayed as *FALSE*. In SQL Server, if you don't specify a default, the default value is *NULL*. This means that unlike Access, a SQL Server *BIT* (*Yes/No*) field can be *NULL*, *TRUE* or *FALSE*.

Access, when linked to this data type, displays *NULL* as *FALSE*. The best advice is to check all your *Yes/No* fields to verify that they have a default value so that once converted to SQL Server, they have defaults when new data is entered. And in future, when creating new *BIT* fields in SQL Server, always give them a default value. The reason that this is very important is because SQL Server does not treat *NULL* as *FALSE*; it treats *NULL* as *NULL*, and testing for *FALSE* does not identify any rows containing *NULL* values. If you ignore this point, then at some point when you convert an Access query to a SQL Server View, if that query tests for *FALSE*, you will find that it no longer works as expected (during conversion you need to watch that *FALSE* becomes 0 and that −1 or *TRUE* becomes 1 or <>0). The following code sample could be used to add missing defaults to *Yes/No* fields prior to converting your database:

```
Sub modUpsizeTests_CheckBooleansForMissingDefaults()
' Search through all tables with Yes/No fields
' Add any missing defaults

    Dim db As DAO.Database
    Dim tdef As DAO.TableDef
    Dim fld As DAO.Field
    Set db = CurrentDb
    For Each tdef In db.TableDefs
        If Left(tdef.Name, 4) <> "MSys" And _
            Left(tdef.Name, 4) <> "USys" And _
            Left(tdef.Name, 4) <> "~TMP" Then
            For Each fld In tdef.Fields
```

```
            If fld.Type = dbBoolean Then
                If fld.DefaultValue = "" Then
                    Debug.Print tdef.Name, fld.Name
                    ' Set default to false
                    fld.DefaultValue = "0"
                End If
            End If
        Next
    End If
    Next
End Sub
```

Integer Numbers

SQL Server integers range as follows (the Access equivalent types are shown in parentheses): *TINYINT* (*Byte*), *SMALLINT* (*Integer*), *INT* (*Long Integer*), *BIGINT* (no equivalent). If you define a *BIGINT* in SQL Server and use a linked table to Access, the field appears as a *Text* field.

Real Numbers, Decimals, and Floating-Point Numbers

SQL Server can hold very large or very small numbers by using the *FLOAT* data type. The type *REAL* (Access equivalent, *Single*) is equivalent to a *FLOAT(24)*, 24-byte floating-point number. The default *FLOAT* is a *FLOAT(53)*, which is equivalent to an Access *Double*. SQL Server also supports the *DECIMAL* data type, which aligns with the Access *Decimal* data type.

Hyperlinks

SQL Server has no equivalent to the Access *Hyperlink* data type, which you would translate to a *VARCHAR* or *NVARCHAR* data type. You would then require some code in Access to make it behave as a hyperlink, using an unbound hyperlink control. Access stores the hyperlink in a memo type column with the Address, Text, and ScreenTip information.

IMAGE, *VARBINARY(Max)*, and *OLE Data*

SQL Server supports two data types into which you can transfer Access *OLE Data*. These data types are, *IMAGE* (an older data type) and *VARBINARY(MAX)*. The recommended choice is *VARBINARY(MAX)*, but if you encounter any problems when migrating or working with the translated *OLE Data*, then it is worth trying the alternative data type mapping using the *IMAGE* data type.

Memo Data

SQL Server supports two data types into which *Memo* data can be transferred: *TEXT*, (which is the older of the two) and *VARCHAR(MAX)* (and their UNICODE equivalents).

In many respects the better choice is *VARCHAR(MAX)*; if you intend to bind .NET controls such as a *DetailsView* control, then updates with *TEXT* are not supported, but this will work with the *VARCHAR(MAX)* data type.

INSIDE OUT   Driver limitations with *VARCHAR(MAX)*

You should be aware that there is a serious problem when working with *VARCHAR(MAX)* and either the Native Client Driver or Native Client 10.0 Driver. If you try pasting in a large amount of text, you get the error *[Microsoft][SQL Native Client] String Data, right truncation (#0)*. In this case, you either need to stick with the older SQL Server Driver or revert to using the *TEXT* data type, which works with all three drivers. The choice of different drivers is discussed in Chapter 12, "Linking Access Tables."

Currency

SQL Server supports two currency types, *MONEY* and *SMALLMONEY*. The *MONEY* data type maps to the Access *Currency* data type.

Attachments and Multi-Value Data

Unlike Access and Microsoft SharePoint, SQL Server does *not* support multi-value fields (Access and SharePoint provide full support for these), This means that you need to normalize your data by creating a new table to hold the multi-value or *Attachment* field data.

For example, if you have a table called *tblCustomer* with a primary key *CustomerID* and an *Attachment* field called *Documents*, you need to create a new table called *tblCustomer Documents* with an *AutoNumber* primary key, a foreign key to *CustomerID*, and an *OLE Data* field called *Documents*. You then need to create new records in the new table to hold the documents for a customer. Unfortunately, there is no easy way to transfer *Attachment* data to an *OLE Data* field.

One strategy to convert your *Attachment* data is to first use the *SaveToFile* VBA method of an *Attachment* object to scan through your attachments and save them as files to a folder (this was described in Chapter 5, "Understanding the Data Access Object Model"). The next step is to create a form bound to your new *OLEData* Type, and then using the following VBA code for a control called for example *TheOLEObject*, you can load the file into the bound control and save the record:

```
Me.TheOLEObject.SourceDoc = MyPath
Me.TheOLEObject.Action = acOLECreateEmbed
RunCommand acCmdSaveRecord
```

Required Fields

In Access, an existing field can be changed to a *Required* field, but you can skip checking existing data. These fields are created in SQL Server with a *NOT NULL* attribute; during the process of migrating data, this can cause problems. The following code can be used to check if you have *NULL* values in any required field. To fix this problem, you can either go through the data, adding a safe default value for the field, or set the *Required* field attribute to *FALSE*, as shown in the following:

```
Sub modUpsizeTests_CheckRequiredFieldsMissingValues()
' Search through all Required fields
' List any containing NULL values in the data
    Dim db As DAO.Database
    Dim tdef As DAO.TableDef
    Dim rst As DAO.Recordset
    Dim fld As DAO.Field
    Dim strSQL As String
    Set db = CurrentDb
    For Each tdef In db.TableDefs
        If Left(tdef.Name, 4) <> "MSys" And _
            Left(tdef.Name, 4) <> "USys" And _
            Left(tdef.Name, 4) <> "~TMP" Then
            For Each fld In tdef.Fields
                If fld.Required Then
                    strSQL = "SELECT Count(*) FROM " & _
                            "[" & tdef.Name & "] WHERE " & _
                            "[" & fld.Name & "] IS NULL"
                    Set rst = db.OpenRecordset(strSQL, dbOpenDynaset)
                    If rst(0) <> 0 Then
                        ' List where missing values
                        Debug.Print tdef.Name, fld.Name
                    End If
                End If
            Next
        End If
    Next
End Sub
```

Cycles and Multiple Cascade Paths

It is possible to create relationships in Access that cannot be converted into relationships in SQL Server, although this rarely happens. If it does happen, you get an error message similar to the following:

```
may cause cycles or multiple cascade paths. Specify ON DELETE NO ACTION or ON UPDATE
NO ACTION, or modify other FOREIGN KEY constraints.
```

The problem is that your relationship includes cascade update or cascade delete actions, which appear to SQL Server to be causing a feedback loop that can lead to problems. The solution is to remove one or more of the cascade actions. If you still need to implement the cascade operation, you can either write a trigger or create a stored procedure to replace it.

INSIDE OUT Partially-completed foreign keys

In Access, if you have a multi-part foreign key, if you start to enter values for one part of the key, you can only save the record once you have valid values in all parts of the key.

In SQL Server, when you have a multi-part foreign key, you can save the record even if not all parts of the key are complete (some fields in the key can contain *NULL* values). In fact, you can even have illegal values in parts of the key, because it is only when the key is complete that the values are checked.

This is not a common problem, but it's worthy of a note. The SQL Standards show a *MATCH* option that applies to defining relationships (or references); Access uses the *FULL* match option, and SQL Server uses the *SIMPLE* match option.

Mismatched Fields in Relationships

With Access, you can construct relationships between columns of different data types and sizes; for example, in a *Customer* table, you can have a foreign key field to a *Country* table that is *Text(20)*, and in the *Country* table, the corresponding field could be a *Text(30)*.

SQL Server does not allow this, and you need to modify your design to ensure that both fields are the same size and of the same data type. For the previous example, you can set the foreign key to a *Text(30)* field.

You could use code based on the following example to detect and possibly autocorrect these problems:

```
Sub modUpsizeTests_CheckFieldTypesAndSizesInRelationships()
' Check that the fields used in relationships
' are on the same type and size
    Dim db As DAO.Database
    Dim rel As DAO.Relation
    Dim fldInRel As DAO.Field
    Dim fld As DAO.Field
    Dim fld2 As DAO.Field
    Dim tdef As DAO.TableDef
    Dim tdef2 As DAO.TableDef
    Set db = CurrentDb
    For Each rel In db.Relations
```

```
        For Each fldInRel In rel.Fields
            Set tdef = db.TableDefs(rel.Table)
            Set tdef2 = db.TableDefs(rel.ForeignTable)
            Set fld = tdef.Fields(fldInRel.Name)
            Set fld2 = tdef2.Fields(fldInRel.ForeignName)
            If (fld.Type <> fld2.Type) Or (fld.Size <> fld2.Size) Then
                ' need to alter one of the fields
                Debug.Print rel.Name & " has a problem with the fields"
            Else
                Debug.Print rel.Name, tdef.Name, tdef2.Name
            End If
        Next
    Next
End Sub
```

Replicated Databases and Random Autonumbers

If your database was at one time replicated, then the tables will have picked up a number of special replication fields such as *s_Generation*, *s_Lineage*, *s_GUID*, or *s_ColLineage*. It is a good idea to remove these now unwanted fields prior to upsizing, and possibly convert any *ReplicationID* fields, if used as a primary key, to standard autonumbers.

A general feature of Access that is associated with replication is the option to have a random Autonumber sometimes used as a primary key. If, for example, in an Access database you have a table called *Customer2* with a field *NewId* that was a random Autonumber, then if you look in *CurrentDB.TableDefs("Customers2").Fields("NewId").DefaultValue*, you can spot a function called *GenUniqueID()*; this is the internal function that Access uses to generate the random Autonumbers. One nice feature of the Upsizing Wizard is that it will automatically write the following trigger code (usp_GenUniqueID.sql) to generate the random Autonumber in SQL Server, and sets a default of 0 for the field *NewId*, which is the primary key:

```
CREATE TRIGGER [dbo].[T_Customers2_ITrig] ON [dbo].[Customers2]
FOR INSERT AS
    SET NOCOUNT ON
    DECLARE @randc int, @newc int      /* FOR AUTONUMBER-EMULATION CODE */
    /* * RANDOM AUTONUMBER EMULATION CODE FOR FIELD 'NewId' */
    SELECT @randc = (SELECT convert(int, rand() * power(2, 30)))
    SELECT @newc = (SELECT NewId FROM inserted)
    UPDATE Customers2 SET NewId = @randc WHERE NewId = @newc
GO
```

The preceding approach, however, has a logical flaw: if an insert is from data in another table with multiple rows or using multiple values, then, as demonstrated in the code that follows, it generates duplicate primary key values of 0 and fails (remember the trigger fires after the insert). The good news is that this is very easily fixed, and the trigger code gives you all the information to write a SQL Server function to resolve this. This code is interesting because you want to create a generic function that uses the *RAND* function, but it turns out that you are not allowed to use the *RAND* system function inside a user-defined function. So, you must employ a cunning trick and wrap the *RAND* function inside a View, and then you are allowed to do this.

After allowing the Upsizing Wizard to convert the sample table *Customer2*, you can cause the previously described trigger to fail by using the following code:

```
INSERT INTO Customers2(CompanyName)
VALUES('Test'), ('Test2')
GO
```

Next, to resolve this problem, you create a View and then a function to use the View. In the following, notice that the first definition of the function will not work; however, the code starting from creating the View will work:

```
-- This will not work
CREATE FUNCTION usp_GenUniqueID()
RETURNS int
AS
BEGIN
    DECLARE @randc INT
    SELECT @randc = (SELECT convert(int, rand() * power(2, 30)))
    RETURN (@randc)
END
GO
-- Create the view
CREATE VIEW vw_Rand
AS
    SELECT convert(int, rand() * power(2, 30)) As RandomSeed
GO
-- This will work
CREATE FUNCTION usp_GenUniqueID()
RETURNS int
AS
BEGIN
    RETURN (SELECT * FROM vw_Rand)
END
GO
```

To complete this, you need to drop the existing trigger (by using *DROP*), drop the existing default, and then add your new default:

```
-- Drop the trigger
DROP Trigger T_Customers2_ITrig
GO
-- drop the default, your default name would be different to this example
ALTER TABLE [dbo].[Customers2]
DROP CONSTRAINT [DF__Customers__NewId__2C3393D0]
GO
ALTER TABLE [dbo].[Customers2] ADD
```

```
CONSTRAINT def_Customers2_NewID
DEFAULT dbo.usp_GenUniqueID() FOR [NewId]
GO
```

In the preceding code, we have exchanged using a trigger for using a function. The subtle difference is that the function is called once for each individual row that is changed, but the trigger would be called once to process changes to multiple rows.

INSIDE OUT   Allowing for changes to multiple rows in trigger code

The previous example demonstrates how trigger code should always be written to allow for multiple rows to be inserted, updated, or deleted; otherwise, you run the risk that at some point you perform an operation involving multiple rows and the application then generates errors. In some situations (although not in this case), if you cannot write the trigger for multiple rows, then you can consider using the following T-SQL to temporarily disable and then enable a trigger after completing the operation; this would only be recommended for use in maintenance and not while users are interacting with the system:

```
DISABLE TRIGGER T_Customers2_ITrig ON Customers2
GO
ENABLE Trigger T_Customers2_ITrig ON Customers2
GO
```

This example also shows the benefit in having constraints with easily managed names for triggers and other objects in the database.

Unique Index and Ignore Nulls

Access allows you to create a Unique Index that ignores *NULL* values; we have added an example to the Employees EmploymentCode column in the sample database to demonstrate this problem.

In SQL Server, *NULL* is a unique value, and you cannot create a unique index to ignore *NULL* values. You can add a non-unique index and then write the following trigger code to prevent duplicates but allow multiple *NULL* values. After you have converted the sample database to SQL Server, you can take a look at how the code (UniqueIndexIgnoreNull.sql) that follows can be used to resolve this problem in the converted SQL Server database:

```
CREATE INDEX idxEmployee ON Employees(EmploymentCode)
GO
CREATE TRIGGER TR_Employees_EmploymentCode
ON Employees
```

```
FOR INSERT,UPDATE
AS
IF EXISTS( SELECT COUNT(*),EmploymentCode FROM Employees
          WHERE EmploymentCode is NOT NULL
          GROUP BY EmploymentCode
          HAVING COUNT(*) > 1)
          ROLLBACK TRAN


GO

-- Test this
UPDATE Employees
SET EmploymentCode = 'N1123'
WHERE EmploymentCode ='N1156'
```

It's also worthwhile to consider using the following code to identify potential issues with these indexes prior to converting your database:

```
Sub modUpsizeTests_UniqueIndexIgnoreNulls()
    ' Example code to search for any unqiue indexes
    ' which ignore null values
    Dim db As DAO.Database
    Dim tdef As DAO.TableDef
    Dim idx As DAO.Index
    Set db = CurrentDb
    For Each tdef In db.TableDefs
        If Left(tdef.Name, 4) <> "MSys" And _
            Left(tdef.Name, 4) <> "USys" And _
            Left(tdef.Name, 4) <> "~TMP" Then
            For Each idx In tdef.Indexes
                If idx.IgnoreNulls = True Then
                    Debug.Print tdef.Name, idx.Name
                End If
            Next
        End If
    Next
End Sub
```

Timestamps and Row Versioning

When you use a software tool to convert an Access database to SQL Server, you are normally provided with an option to add a TIMESTAMP column to your tables (it cannot be over-emphasized how important this option is when working with Access linked to SQL Server), and when you create new tables in SQL Server, you should remember to add a TIMESTAMP column to each table. Most of the current documentation from Microsoft no longer talks about a *TIMESTAMP* data type but instead discusses a *ROWVERSION* data type. However, Management Studio only displays a *TIMESTAMP* data type and not a *ROW VERSION* data type; you can regard both as meaning the same thing.

When you edit data over a linked table to SQL Server, Access maintains in memory a "Before" image of your data, and once you are ready to save the record, it needs to write the data back to SQL Server by using the Before image to detect any conflict in the data caused by another user simultaneously editing and saving changes to the same record. This standard product feature opens a write-conflict dialog box when a conflict is detected.

Access can use one of two strategies for detecting a conflict during the write-back. If you ignore *TIMESTAMP*s, Access checks that the values in the Before image for every field matches the current data held in the row in SQL Server. It does this by using a *WHERE* clause on the *Update* command, as shown in the following:

```
WHERE fld1 = fld1 (old value) and fld2 = fld2 (old value)
```

The following example illustrates how you can see the trace output from the SQL Server Profiler (discussed beginning on page 586) when you perform an update on the *Customers* table linked to *Northwind*:

```
exec sp_executesql N'UPDATE "dbo"."Customers" SET "ContactTitle"=@P1  WHERE "Cus-
tomerID" = @P2 AND "CompanyName" = @P3 AND "ContactName" = @P4 AND "Contact-
Title" = @P5 AND "Address" = @P6 AND "City" = @P7 AND "Region" IS NULL AND
"PostalCode" = @P8 AND "Country" = @P9 AND "Phone" = @P10 AND "Fax" = @P11',N'@
P1 nvarchar(30),@P2 nchar(5),@P3 nvarchar(40),@P4 nvarchar(30),@P5 nvarchar(30),@
P6 nvarchar(60),@P7 nvarchar(15),@P8 nvarchar(10),@P9 nvarchar(15),@P10 nvar-
char(24),@P11 nvarchar(24)',N'Sales Agent',N'ANATR',N'Ana Trujillo Empareda-
dos y helados',N'Ana Trujillo',N'Owner',N'Avda. de la Constitución 2222',N'México
D.F.',N'05021',N'Mexico',N'(5) 555-4729',N'(5) 555-3745'
```

The problem with this strategy is that if you have 100 fields, then the *WHERE* clause includes 100 comparisons, so this update involves a lot of comparisons. The other danger is when working with floating-point numbers; for example, if there were any difference in the precision with which the numbers were held in the two products, then the update could fail to locate the target record, causing the update to incorrectly register a conflict.

The second strategy is to use a *TIMESTAMP* as soon as you add this column to a table, and then ensure that the linked table is refreshed. Access switches automatically to this second strategy, which involves verifying that the primary key is matched and the *TIMESTAMP* column is unchanged, as shown here:

```
WHERE pkey1 = pkey1 (old value) and TS = TS (old value).
```

If you now add a TIMESTAMP column called TSCustomers to the *Customers* table, and then refresh the linked table and repeat the update, you obtain the following output in the Profiler:

```
exec sp_executesql N'UPDATE "dbo"."Customers" SET "ContactTitle"=@P1  WHERE
"CustomerID" = @P2 AND "TSCustomers" = @P3',N'@P1 nvarchar(30),@P2 nchar(5),@P3
binary(8)',N'Owner',N'ANATR',0x0000000000000FA2
```

Chapter 15

This second method has the advantage of fewer comparisons and no dependencies on the form of internal storage of data in the products (with the exception of the primary key). The TIMESTAMP column data is automatically generated by SQL Server and changed whenever a record is changed. If you want to see this in greater detail, you can use the SQL Server Profiler to monitor what happens under the hood.

Schemas and Synonyms

After you create a SQL Server database, click Security | Schemas. There you will find a list of existing schemas. The *dbo* schema is typically the one that contains all your design objects, and it is where new objects that you create are stored, unless your login has been altered to use a different default schema for the database.

In earlier versions of SQL Server, objects were owned by users, so you could have a table owned by User1.Customers and User2.Customers. However, this caused problems if you wanted to remove User1 from the system but keep an object such as User1.Customers. As a result, in SQL Server 2005 a new interpretation of schemas was introduced that was independent of users.

If you have a large Access database (for example, 200 tables), you can use schemas to split up the tables, Views, and so on, into logical groupings to better manage the database design. You can also use schemas to flexibly and easily configure security; for example, restricting a group of users to having only read permissions on a particular set of tables.

The following example (UsingSchemas.sql) illustrates how to create a *Schema*, create a table in the *Schema*, and then create a *Synonym* to refer to the table without specifying the full *Schema* prefix:

```
-- Example Schema
CREATE SCHEMA [Companies] AUTHORIZATION [dbo]
GO
-- Example Creating a table on a Schema
CREATE Table [Companies].[Company](
CompanyID   INT IDENTITY(1,1),
CompanyName NVARCHAR(100)
)
GO
SELECT * FROM [Companies].[Company]
GO
CREATE SYNONYM [dbo].[Company]
FOR [Companies].[Company]
GO
SELECT * FROM [Company]
GO
```

The *Synonym* is very important, because if you already had a table on the *dbo* schema and moved it to the *Companies* Schema, any SQL that referred to the table would no longer work, but once you add the *Synonym*, that problem is resolved. If you don't specify an explicit schema when creating objects, they will be placed on your default schema, which, as previously mentioned, is normally *dbo*.

The following example shows an object being moved into a *Schema* and creating an appropriate *Synonym* for the object:

```
-- Example moving an object onto a Schema
ALTER SCHEMA Companies TRANSFER dbo.Customers
GO
CREATE SYNONYM [dbo].[Customers]
FOR [Companies].[Customers]
GO
```

If you want to try the previous code and then move the *Customers* table back to the *dbo Schema*, you need to drop the synonym before you do this by using *DROP SYNONYM Customers*. You could then use the following line to move the table back to the *dbo* schema:

```
ALTER SCHEMA dbo TRANSFER Companies.Customers
```

After you have converted your database to SQL Server, you can consider making a list of all your tables, and then create a script to move all your tables into appropriate schemas and simultaneously create appropriate synonyms. You can use *sp_tables* to get a list of all your existing tables and the *TABLE_OWNER* property, which is the schema.

Chapter 15

INSIDE OUT   Using schemas and database roles to manage security

Often in an application you will want to provide users with different permissions on groups of objects in the system. SQL Server has a sophisticated security system with which you can establish fine control of security. One of the simplest approaches to security is to create database roles, and when mapping users, windows groups, or SQL Server logins into your system, assign them an appropriate database role, as demonstrated in the following:

```
CREATE ROLE [ReadOnlyUsers]
GO
CREATE ROLE [Administrators]
GO
GRANT Select, Execute on Schema::Companies TO [ReadOnlyUsers]
GO
GRANT Select, Insert,
Update, Delete, Execute on Schema::Companies TO [Administrators]
GO
```

The *Execute* and *Select* permissions will allow the *ReadOnlyUsers* to both view data and execute procedures on the *Schema*.

The Upsizing Wizard and the SQL Server Migration Assistant

In the following two sections, you look at migrating an Access databases to SQL Server by using the Upsizing Wizard and the SQL Server Migration Assistant (SSMA). To stretch both tools, we have used the sample database Northwind_ProblemsAndFixes.accdb, which contains known problems when migrating data. If you want to use this database, you can see how the tools handle the problems, or you can fix the problems as described earlier in this chapter, on page 543, by running the appropriate tests to look for illegal dates, and so on.

The Upsizing Wizard

Open your database. On the Database Tools tab on the ribbon, under the Move Data group, click the SQL Server icon, The Upsizing Wizard opens. On the first page, you have the option to either create a new database or use an existing SQL Server database.

On the second page, you can choose to use either the (local), which is the default instance of SQL Server, or specify the instance name (which you can determine when you start the SQL Server Management Studio). You also have the option to use either Windows authentication or a SQL Server Logon, as shown in Figure 15-1.

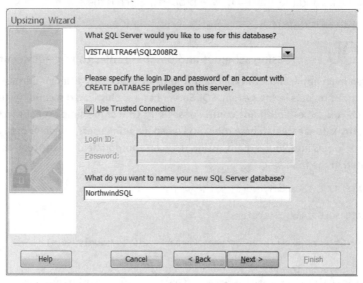

Figure 15-1 Enter your server details and the name for the new SQL Server database in the Upsizing Wizard.

On the next page, you select the tables that you want to upsize. On page four of the wizard (see Figure 15-2), you are presented with a number of optional choices. You can leave these at the default settings. Ensure that the Add Timestamp Fields To Tables? option is set to *Yes, Always*.

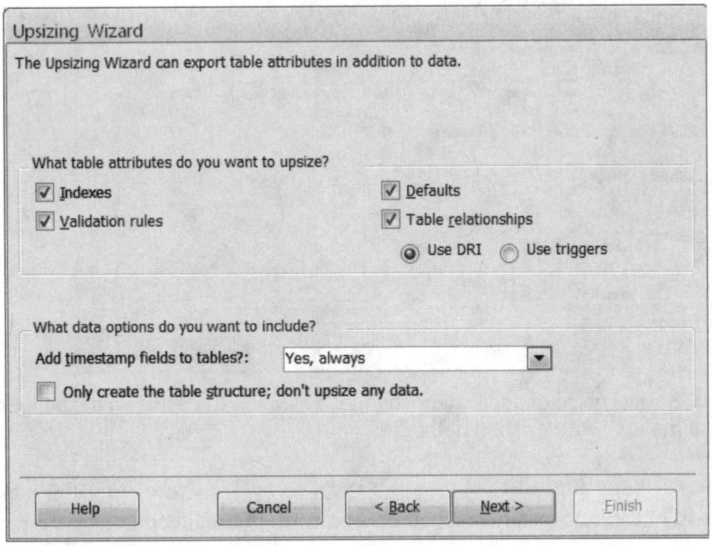

Figure 15-2 Additional choices can be made, including to upsize only the structure and not include the data.

Select the Use DRI option to upsize your relationships. The other option, Use Triggers, is not recommended because it is less efficient than using DRI and it is a throw-back to older databases when referential integrity (RI) was not always supported.

On the last wizard page, you need to complete details, as shown in Figure 15-3. There are three options on this page: leave your database unaltered, replace your tables with links to SQL Server, or create a new Access client/server application (ADP). You will now look first at the option for adding links to the SQL Server tables.

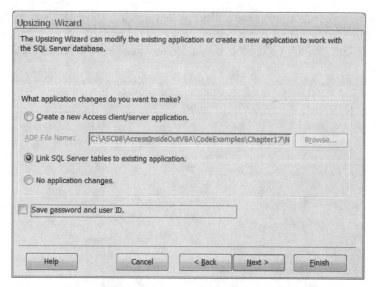

Figure 15-3 The choice of application changes allow you to decide what changes should be made to your existing database.

The Save Password And User ID option is only applicable if you are using a SQL Server Logon and not Windows authentication. And even in that circumstance, if you plan on using multiple SQL Login accounts for different users, embedding the password and user ID in the links is both unsecure and probably not what you want to happen, so leave this option cleared.

After you are finished with the wizard, you are given a report of the setup, along with any error messages.

If you performed the upsize with the illegal dates, you get an error indicating that the relationship was not created. The problem here is that the illegal dates prevent the data from being migrated, and no data in the *Orders* table prevents the relationship with *Order Details* from being switched on. If you look in SQL Server, you can see that the *Orders* table is empty. If you fix the dates and then repeat the upsize, the table converts correctly. The report also contains a warning that a Unique Index could not be created on the Employees, *EmploymentCode* field; this is because you have a *Unique Index Which Ignores Nulls* on that column (as described earlier in this chapter). You could then add your own non-unique index and a trigger to satisfy this requirement (also described earlier in this chapter).

Figure 15-4 shows that the process has renamed the original tables and created new linked tables to SQL Server.

Figure 15-4 The *Order Details* table has been converted, but the *Orders* table has not been fully migrated (and the link is missing) because of illegal dates in that table.

INSIDE OUT   Upsizing Wizard strengths and weaknesses

The least attractive feature of the Upsizing Wizard is that is does not upsize *Required* fields; it should set the attribute *NOT NULL* on any Access column which is a *Required* Field. Even though you can work around this by writing trigger code to perform a *ROLLBACK* if it detected a *NULL* in certain fields, it would be both tedious and inefficient.

The wizard does handle *UNIQUE IGNORE NULL* indexes by skipping over them. It also pleasingly adds a *DEFAULT* of *(0)* to any *Yes/No* field (*Bit* field), to which it also adds the *NOT NULL* attribute. You also need to deal with any multi-value fields and attachments, as described earlier, on page 548.

The Upsizing Wizard does not have any features for controlling alternative mappings on data types, so you are restricted to having *UNICODE* data types and accepting its data type mapping.

Because the Upsizing Wizard cannot be repeated to just convert the data, when you come to go live with a system, you need to repeat the upsizing process. So during development, you should maintain all your design changes in script files, which you can then easily re-run when making the system live and repeating the upsizing process.

Upsizing to Use an Access Data Project

In this section, you take a look at Access Data Projects (ADPs). Referring back to Figure 15-3, you can use the option, Create A New Access Client/Server Application to generate a new ADP. If you choose this option, you not only create a new database, but the Upsizing Wizard performs a lot of additional processing, as shown in Figure 15-5. Constructing an ADP means that you will no longer have any queries left in Access; these queries will need translation into SQL Server Objects (a process with which the wizard can assist you).

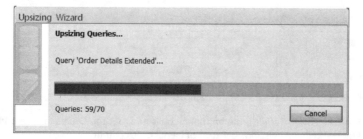

Figure 15-5 The Upsizing Wizard converts queries to SQL Server Objects.

An ADP is a radical departure for Access in some respects because you do not use the ACE database engine. This means that you can no longer have local tables or queries or utilize the Data Access Objects (DAO) model. Instead of DAO, you use an alternative light-weight technology called ActiveX Data Objects (ADO), which we discuss in Chapter 18 "Using ADO and ADOX." The database window becomes a window into SQL Server (it's a bit like a "lite" version of the SQL Server Management Studio inside Access).

Once you have converted to produce an ADP, go into a query in Design for a View, as shown in Figure 15-6.

Figure 15-6 This query is a SQL Server View. The interface looks similar to the Access Query grid and Management Studio; of course, you have the flexibility to use Management Studio to edit this.

You will also notice that you have three kinds of queries, as shown in Figure 15-7.

Figure 15-7 The top two queries are Views, the next is a stored procedure, and the third and fourth are Table-valued functions.

It is interesting to note that the wizard chose to build a function for *Current Product List*. This is because the SQL contained an *ORDER BY* clause, which is only allowed in a View when you use a special *TOP* syntax (you will see more about this when we look at SSMA). This illustrates an interesting strategic difference between SSMA and the Upsizing Wizard. What is even more interesting is that if you open a function, such as *Current Product List*, you will find that it is updateable. This is quite radical, because in an Access database (an .accdb or .mdb), you cannot link to a function, and in Management Studio, you cannot open a function and edit the data; in the background there are some very clever things going on inside an ADP.

Query Conversion

Because you can use Access to write SQL in an infinitely-varied number of forms with a subtle interplay of VBA code, it is unlikely that you will ever get a 100% conversion, but it will have made a good attempt at translating your SQL. Sometimes you will find a query like *Product Sales For 1997*, which at first glance appears to have been converted, in fact has not been effectively converted, because it fails when you try to open the query. In this case, the problem can be fixed very easily because the syntax `'Qtr ' + datepart(q,ShippedDate)` will fail, you would need `'Qtr ' + CONVERT(VARCHAR, datepart(q,ShippedDate))` to make this work; sometimes you need a lot more reworking on the SQL. Also note that the translation of SQL in crosstab queries is not supported (the equivalent in T-SQL is the *PIVOT* statement).

An ADP also provides integration for developing SQL Server-specific objects, as shown in Figure 15-8.

Chapter 15

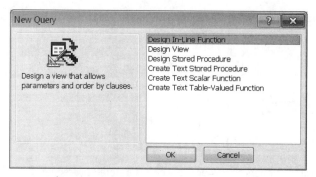

Figure 15-8 With an ADP, you have tighter integration to SQL Server features.

INSIDE OUT ADP strengths and weaknesses

In general, ADPs are not the most common choice when converting a database, but they have a following, and if Microsoft continues to enhance ADP, maybe it will become the preferred path. An ADP can offer better performance, because it ensures that you create your equivalent queries in SQL Server. This can also be a weakness because in any conversion you are forced to spend time possibly fixing a large number of queries, but with a standard Access database, you can focus on only converting those queries with poor performance. You also need to judge the impact on your productivity as a result of losing the ability to have local tables and local queries in any existing application.

SSMA

SSMA is a more generic tool than the Upsizing Wizard and is designed to migrate data from various databases into SQL Server. SSMA is free and can be downloaded from the Microsoft sites.

> **Note**
>
> The version of SSMA described here is 5.0 for Access, upsizing to either SQL Server or SQL Azure.

After you download and install SSMA on a 64-bit version of Windows, you will find two program shortcuts, one for 32-bit Access and the other for 64-bit Access. If you try to run the wrong version, you will see a message warning that you are running the incorrect version of SSMA for the available Access libraries. If there is a problem with any libraries, or you install SSMA on a computer without Access 2010, then links are provided to download the Access 2010 runtime libraries required by SSMA. For a 32-bit Access installation, run the 32-bit version of SSMA.

The Migration Wizard

When you start SSMA, by default, the Migration Wizard is active and ready to guide you through the migration process. Figure 15-9 shows the first page of the wizard, in which you name your project and specify either a SQL Server or SQL Azure migration.

![Migration Wizard - Create New Project]

Migration Wizard

Create New Project

Enter the name and location for the new project.

Name:	TestNorthwindMigration
Location:	C:\Users\Andrew\Documents\SSMAProjects
Migration To:	SQL Server

SQL Server
SQL Azure

Figure 15-9 Naming your migration project.

On the next page, you can add your multiple Access databases to the project, after which the following list appears (see Figure 15-10) from which you the select individual tables and queries in each database to be migrated.

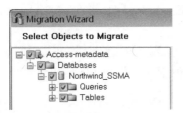

Migration Wizard

Select Objects to Migrate

- ☑ Access-metadata
  - ☑ Databases
    - ☑ Northwind_SSMA
      - ☑ Queries
      - ☑ Tables

Figure 15-10 SSMA acts independent of whether you use an Access database or an ADP project, and allows the selection of both tables and queries.

Following the previous selections, you are able to specify the SQL Server and either select an existing database or type in a new database name. On the next page in the Migration Wizard, you can select the Link Tables check box (the default is not-selected), which replaces your tables with links to SQL Server. You will most likely want to select this option. The next page is the synchronization page (see Figure 15-11), which provides a detailed roadmap of how the migration will proceed; you can leave all the options on this page unchanged when performing this for the first time.

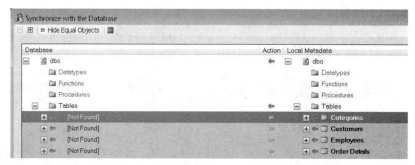

Figure 15-11 This wizard page controls of the data transfer for each table.

After the conversion is run, a summary page opens (see Figure 15-12). This page contains links to lists describing any problems that occurred during the migration.

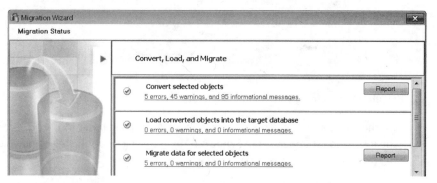

Figure 15-12 Reports provide detailed information on problems that might have occurred during the migration.

One very nice feature in SSMA is a graphical view, with which you can easily see all the objects in your database and identify and investigate those objects that were not converted, as shown in Figure 15-13.

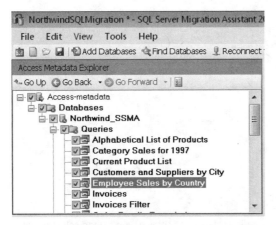

Figure 15-13 The metadata on your Access database means that you can drill down to find information on objects for which there have been conversion problems.

Mapping Data Types

SSMA has a mapping system for converting Access to SQL Server databases, which means that you can fully customize your data type mappings (see Figure 15-14). You display this by clicking the Tables folder in the Access Metadata Explorer.

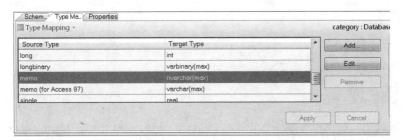

Figure 15-14 Click the Edit button to change the Target Type for each data type mapping.

Using Schemas

SSMA does not offer an option to simply assign combinations of your tables onto different schemas, but it is still possible to make use of schemas with SSMA. In this example, you want to consider a more sophisticated conversion, for this type of conversion you will not want to use the wizard, but perform the conversion with a series of your own steps.

You start by creating a new project, and then adding your Access database, as shown in Figure 15-15.

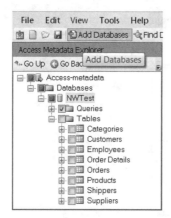

Figure 15-15 A database has been added, but tables haven't been selected yet.

Highlight the database, and then edit the data type mapping to use non-Unicode data types, as shown in Figure 15-16.

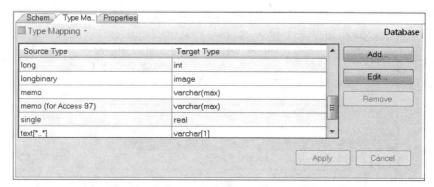

Figure 15-16 The mapping for memo fields after it has been changed from *nvarchar(max)* to *varchar(max)* and text fields from *nvarchar* to *varchar*.

Because this version of SSMA doesn't seem to easily refresh the schema list, once you have registered your database it is a good idea to create a blank database and define some schemas, as shown in Figure 15-17.

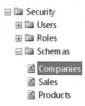

Figure 15-17 New schemas for partitioning your tables.

Returning to SSMA, click Connect To SQL Server, and then select the SQL Server database, as shown in Figure 15-18. Note the new schemas.

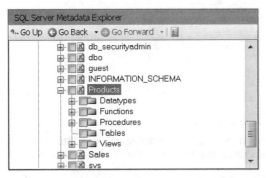

Figure 15-18 In each schema you can see a folder into which you will migrate your tables.

After you click to highlight the Tables folder in the Access Metadata Explorer, you can select the Schema tab, and then change the Schema from dbo to Companies, as shown in Figure 15-19.

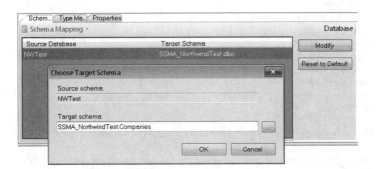

Figure 15-19 Changing the active target schema.

Select the tables that you want to migrate into the active schema, as shown in Figure 15-20.

Figure 15-20 Select the tables to migrate into the active schema. Note in this illustration that Queries is also selected; these should also be cleared after the first migration.

Next, click the Convert, Load And Migrate icon to migrate these tables. Clear these table selections and repeat the procedure to migrate the other tables to their appropriate schemas until you have migrated the set of tables as shown in Figure 15-21.

Figure 15-21 *Northwind* tables migrated onto separate schemas.

After performing this migration, you most likely want to create a set of synonyms for each table, as described earlier, on page 556.

The only restriction on this approach is that because you are effectively performing multiple migrations, SSMA cannot implement all your relationships across the schemas; you can use the database diagram in SQL Server to add back any missing relationships.

Comparing Table Conversion in the Upsizing Wizard and SSMA

SSMA and the Upsizing Wizard use different strategies when performing a conversion.

In our sample databases, we have intentionally inserted known problems so that you can compare how each tool handles these issues. SSMA can convert the *Employees* table, but it doesn't populate any of the data. This is because our table contains a *UNIQUE INDEX* with *IGNORE NULLS*. Unfortunately, this version of SSMA simply adds a *UNIQUE INDEX* to the table; a better strategy would be to ignore any indexing of this type.

SSMA, like the Upsizing Wizard, adds a default of 0 to any *Yes/No* field, which avoids the problems described earlier of *Bit* fields without defaults.

Unlike the Upsizing Wizard, which cannot handle *Required* fields, SSMA correctly maps these to *NOT NULL* in the database structure. SSMA can also partly handle *NULL* values in a *Required* field or illegal dates in the data. The strategy here is to attempt to migrate data that does not have problems. In the sample data, you can see the order number 10257, which contained an illegal date, 01-Jan-100. This then resulted in the order header record not being migrated, but the order detail records are migrated; this can mean that your data is inconsistent with the RI. However, you might feel that it is better to have some data rather than no data. There is no substitute for running the tests described earlier in this chapter, on page 543, for checking dates and missing values in required fields before migrating your data. SSMA produces output advising you of where data has been partially migrated, as shown here:

```
Preparing table Northwind_Problems_ForSSMA.[Orders]...
Migrating data for the table Orders from the database Northwind_Problems_ForSSMA...
The following error occurred during migration of the current batch:
SqlDateTime overflow. Must be between 1/1/1753 12:00:00 AM and 12/31/9999 11:59:59 PM.
……..
See the log for the detailed information.
Data migration complete: 818 rows of 830 migrated.
Data migration operation has finished.
   6 table(s) successfully migrated.
   2 table(s) partially migrated.
   0 table(s) failed to migrate.
```

SSMA provides a split window to compare the data in Access against the migrated data in SQL Server, as shown in Figure 15-22.

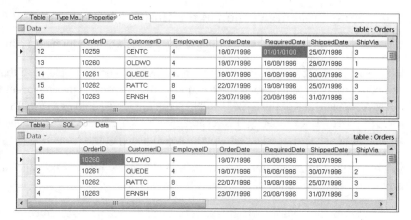

Figure 15-22 The Split data view shows the top 200 rows in Access and SQL Server. The illegal date in the record with `OrderID` 10259 is not migrated.

At one time in the distant past, the behavior of Access changed so that when you added a new text field, it always set the *AllowZeroLength* property to *No*. This was then promptly changed back to default *AllowZeroLength* to *Yes*; this setting tended to make data imports and other activities more difficult in Access. If you have an older database that has this set on all your text fields, then when converting by using the Upsizing Wizard, it ignores this attribute. In the past, SSMA generated a *Check* constraint to do this (which is probably not what you wanted). The new version of SSMA generates a dummy *Check* constraint, which does not actually perform any checking, an example of which is shown in the following code:

```
ALTER TABLE [dbo].[Customers]
CHECK CONSTRAINT
[SSMA_CC$Customers$Address$disallow_zero_length]
GO
```

This strategy is a compromise between not adding the *Checks*, and providing placeholders for them. If you want to avoid this, you can write some code to scan through the fields in each Access table, changing the *AllowZeroLength* to *Yes* before migrating the database.

Comparing Query Conversion in the Upsizing Wizard and SSMA

In SQL Server, you are not allowed to have the SQL *ORDER BY* in a View (which conforms with the SQL standard), and for that reason, the Upsizing Wizard creates a function to return a result, as shown in the following:

```
CREATE FUNCTION [dbo].[Current Product List] ()
RETURNS TABLE
AS RETURN (SELECT TOP 100 PERCENT "Product List".ProductID,
"Product List".ProductName
FROM Products AS "Product List"
```

```
WHERE ((("Product List".Discontinued)=0))
ORDER BY "Product List".ProductName)
GO
EXEC sys.sp_addextendedproperty @name=N'MS_AlternateBackThemeColorIndex',
@value=-1 , @level0type=N'SCHEMA',@level0name=N'dbo',
@level1type=N'FUNCTION',@level1name=N'Current Product List'
GO
```

The Upsizing Wizard also makes extensive use of creating extended properties, which are used to record display settings when displaying the function on a Query grid.

There is a way to put an *ORDER BY* inside a View, and SSMA will create a View for this query by using this strategy, which involves including the *TOP... WITH TIES* statement, as shown here:

```
CREATE VIEW [dbo].[Current Product List]
AS
    SELECT TOP 9223372036854775807 WITH
    TIES [Product List].ProductID,
    [Product List].ProductName
    FROM Products  AS [Product List]
    WHERE (((Product List].Discontinued) = 0))
    ORDER BY [Product List].ProductName
GO
```

The very large number, 9223372036854775807, is used to avoid the need to say TOP 100%, for reasons of internal efficiency.

If you are using an ADP, then the previously mentioned approach with functions can return updateable data, but if you want to use an Access database, you can only utilize a function by using a pass-through query (which is read-only); you cannot link an Access database directly to a function.

Another nice feature of the Upsizing Wizard is that when it converts a query that contains a reference to an Access parameter, it generates a parameterized function, as shown below:

```
CREATE FUNCTION [dbo].[Invoices Filter]
(@Forms___Orders___OrderID1 varchar (255)
)
RETURNS TABLE
AS RETURN (SELECT Invoices.*
FROM Invoices
WHERE (((Invoices.OrderID)=@Forms___Orders___OrderID1)))
GO
```

The original SQL used in the Access query was as follows:

```
SELECT Invoices.*
FROM Invoices
WHERE (((Invoices.OrderID)=[Forms]![Orders]![OrderID]));
```

SSMA is not able to handle this kind of query with references to screen parameters and does not convert the query.

In summary, if you are planning to use an ADP, then the Upsizing Wizard offers a large number of advantages over SSMA when converting queries; but if you are planning to use an Access database (.accdb or .mdb) linked to SQL Server, then you will find that SSMA produces more favorable results when converting your SQL; you can, of course, run a conversion through both tools and copy and paste the preferred results between the systems.

INSIDE OUT   SSMA strengths and weaknesses

If you want better control of the Data Type mappings, and you want to ensure that *Required* fields are correctly translated to *NOT NULL* column attributes, SSMA offers a better choice than the Upsizing Wizard. The support for migration onto Schemas is also a very attractive feature of the product, but it would benefit from a more structured approach that permits a single migration to split multiple tables over schemas and thus preserve the relationships during the migration process.

The only weakness we came across in SSMA was in attempting to translate a *UNIQUE INDEX which ignores Nulls*. That can be easily avoided by checking for this in your database prior to conversion.

Developing with Access and SQL Server

In this section, you will look at some of the changes and design techniques that you might consider using once you have converted your data to SQL Server and relinked your Access database front-end application.

The *dbSeeChanges* Constant

When you have code that opens a *Recordset* on data that includes a column with the *IDENTITY* property (equivalent to an *AutoNumber*), you will find that you need to add an additional constant called *dbSeeChanges* as an option on the *OpenRecordSet* command; otherwise, you get the error shown in Figure 15-23.

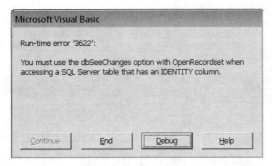

Figure 15-23 An Error message indicating the need to add *dbSeeChanges*.

```
Sub modSQL_dbSeeChanges()
' Examples illustrating how code needs to be altered
' Adding dbSeeChanges
    Dim db As DAO.Database
    Dim rst As DAO.Recordset
    Set db = CurrentDb
    Set rst = db.OpenRecordset("dbo_Products", dbOpenDynaset)
' Corrected code below
'    Set rst = db.OpenRecordset("dbo_Products", dbOpenDynaset, dbSeeChanges)
    rst.Close
    db.Close
End Sub
```

Pass-Through Queries

With pass-through queries, you can create a query that by-passes the checking that Access normally performs when writing SQL. These queries can be used either to execute an operation (when they don't return data) or return a data set. If returning data, then the *Recordset* is always read-only. The SQL written in the query does not support the Query grid because it is written in T-SQL. One of the many uses for pass-through queries is to execute both your own as well as built in stored procedures. These queries can be created by using either DAO code or the query design tool.

To interactively create a pass-through query, start by creating a normal query, but don't select any tables. Next, on the Design tab, click the Pass-Through icon, shown on Figure 15-24.

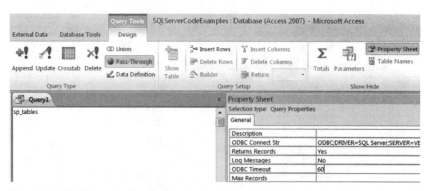

Figure 15-24 When creating a pass-through query, you should also display the property sheet, because you will need to set the ODBC Connection String.

The following list summarizes some of the key properties:

- **ODBC Connect Str**   Use the builder when you have clicked into this property to pick your connection string or paste in a valid string.

- **Returns Records**   Set this according to whether the query returns a *Recordset*.

- **Log Messages**   Stores messages returned from SQL Server in a user-specific table.

- **ODBC Timeout**   You might choose to change this to 0 and avoid early timeouts caused by delays in network traffic.

- **Max Records**   Limits the maximum number of records being returned.

In the example shown in Figure 15-24, you call the built-in stored procedure *sp_tables* to return a list of tables in the database. You could use the alternative syntax including the exec keyword as *exec sp_tables* (but this is not essential). You are allowed to have comments using -- or /*..*/ added to the body of the SQL, but you can only have one T-SQL command block executed in the pass-through query. If you need to execute a sequence of operations, you need to place them in your own stored procedure.

In the following example, you start by creating a stored procedure in SQL Server that accepts a single input parameter; you can either run this in Management Studio or you can execute the SQL in a pass-through query to create the stored procedure from Access, in which case, you omit the *GO* keyword and set *Returns Records* to *No*, as shown here:

```
CREATE PROC uspListCustomersForCountry @Country NVARCHAR(20)
AS
BEGIN
    SELECT * FROM Customers
    WHERE Country = @Country
END
```

To execute this from Access, you create a pass-through query that contains the following single line of SQL:

```
uspListCustomersForCountry 'UK'
```

You could also get away with using *uspListCustomersForCountry UK*, but this is a bad idea. To see why, insert a space in the text, as shown in the following line (which will then fail):

```
uspListCustomersForCountry U K
```

The next parameter to give some attention to is dates; SQL is an ANSI standard and as such, it adopts the convention in the United States for date formats. You need to be very careful about passing a date parameter to a database if you live outside the United States. And if you live in the United States and plan to have your application used in other countries, then you also need to be careful about date formats. There is a very simple shortcut to solving this problem, and that is to format your dates to avoid the issue of mm/dd/yyyy or dd/mm/yyyy, and format your date in an unambiguous way as a text string, such as the following:

```
dd mmmm yyyy.
```

To format a date such as in the preceding code line, in VBA, you use the following syntax:

```
Format(date,"dd mmmm yyyy")
```

In the following example (StoredProceduresAndParameters.sql), a stored procedure illustrates this point:

```
CREATE PROC usp_OrdersByDate @Thedate DATETIME
AS
BEGIN
    SELECT * FROM Orders
    WHERE RequiredDate = @Thedate
END
GO

exec usp_OrdersByDate '1996-08-16'
GO
exec usp_OrdersByDate '16 August 1996'
GO
```

Looking at this problem from the Access perspective, you can write a pass-through query to do this, as shown previously, or this can be written in code.

Creating an on-the-fly pass-through query in code is very simple; the only real issue to consider is how you get the database connection string. You can get this from a global variable, or a function; but in the following code you will get this from a table that is already linked in your database (if using your sample database, you will need to relink the linked tables to your SQL Server database), as shown in the following example:

```
Sub modSQL_PassingDatesInPassthrough()
    ' example of passing a date which
    ' avoids ANSI formating
    Dim db As DAO.Database
    Dim qdef As DAO.QueryDef
    Set db = CurrentDb
    Dim dt As Date
    dt = #8/16/1996#
    Set qdef = db.CreateQueryDef("")
    qdef.ReturnsRecords = True
    ' The following line comes before assigning the SQL property
    ' as the Access will not check the SQL after the connect property
    ' is assigned
    qdef.Connect = db.TableDefs("Orders").Connect
    qdef.SQL = "usp_OrdersByDate '" & Format(dt, "dd mmmm yyyy") & "'"
    Dim rst As Recordset
    Set rst = qdef.OpenRecordset()
    Do While Not rst.EOF
        Debug.Print rst(0)
        rst.MoveNext
    Loop
End Sub
```

INSIDE OUT Using advanced features in stored procedures from Access

In general, linking Access to a stored procedure is very easy, as you saw in the last example on pass-through queries, which is the only technique available for linking to a stored procedure. The more complex question is whether you want to simply utilize the capability of a stored procedure to return a result, or whether you want to utilize some of the more advanced features of stored procedures, such as passing input and output parameters. If you want to dig deeper into stored procedures and utilize more advanced features, you need to take a look at ADO, which is covered in Chapter 18.

Stored Procedures and Temporary Tables

In Access, when you need to perform a sequence of complex operations to deliver a dataset for users to interact with on a form, you might need to create temporary results table, which you then clear down before populating with data with a sequence of queries. For example, in an order processing system, you might want to show past orders, payments, and future orders all in a single list. This involves consolidating data from many parts of the system.

When linking to SQL Server, you have a number of different design strategies from which to choose: you can keep using the existing local temporary tables, or you could put the temporary table in SQL Server and add a column to distinguish between data belonging to different users by using the *SUSER_SNAME()* function.

One elegant solution to this problem is to utilize SQL Server temporary tables inside a stored procedure; for example, you can create the following stored procedure (Stored ProcedureAndTemporaryTable.sql):

```
CREATE PROC usp_Products
AS
BEGIN
-- Drop temporary tables if they exists
IF object_id('tempdb..#TempProducts') is not null
    DROP TABLE #TempProducts

-- create the temporary results set
   SELECT * INTO #TempProducts
   FROM Products
-- return the temporary result set
   SELECT * from #TempProducts
END
GO
-- Testing
exec usp_Products
GO
```

Handling Complex Queries

Converting queries that have complex calculations (we are going to show a simple calculation to explain this feature) can be a big issue when moving to SQL Server. Consider the following Access query:

```
SELECT
   [Order Details].OrderID,
   [Order Details].ProductID,
   [UnitPrice]*[Quantity] AS LinePrice,
   [LinePrice]*0.2 AS LineItemTax,
   [LinePrice]+[LineItemTax] AS FullPrice
FROM [Order Details]
```

This technique of referring to calculated columns inside other expressions is a very common technique in Access. Unfortunately, SQL Server does not support this, and most migration tools are unable to perform a successful conversion of the SQL.

You have several options when converting this SQL. The simplest option is to restate the calculations in full for each calculated field. The second option is to create SQL Server functions for parts of the calculation, and then modify the calculation to use these functions.

The third option is to create a nested query; you then order the calculations so that they are only referenced by an out level of the nesting. The following code demonstrates the three solutions (ComplexCalculation.sql):

```sql
-- Restating the calculations
SELECT
    [Order Details].OrderID,
    [Order Details].ProductID,
    [UnitPrice]*[Quantity] AS LinePrice,
    ([UnitPrice]*[Quantity])*0.2 AS LineItemTax,
    [UnitPrice]*[Quantity]+
    ([UnitPrice]*[Quantity])*0.2 AS FullPrice
FROM [Order Details]
GO
-- using functions
CREATE FUNCTION fn_CalculateLinePrice(@Quantity INT,
                                      @Price MONEY)
RETURNS
    DECIMAL(16,4)
AS
BEGIN
    RETURN(@Quantity * @Price)
END
GO
CREATE FUNCTION fn_CalculateTax(@Quantity INT,
                                @Price MONEY)
RETURNS
    DECIMAL(16,4)
AS
BEGIN
    RETURN(@Quantity * @Price *0.2)
END
GO
SELECT
    [Order Details].OrderID,
    [Order Details].ProductID,
    dbo.fn_CalculateLinePrice([Quantity],[UnitPrice]) AS LinePrice,
    dbo.fn_CalculateTax([Quantity],[UnitPrice]) AS LineItemTax,
    dbo.fn_CalculateTax([Quantity],[UnitPrice]) +
    dbo.fn_CalculateLinePrice([Quantity],[UnitPrice]) AS FullPrice
FROM [Order Details]
GO
-- using a nested query
SELECT
    LinePrice,
    LineItemTax,
    LinePrice + LinePrice AS FullPrice
    FROM
        (SELECT LinePrice, LinePrice* 0.2 AS LineItemTax
```

```
FROM
    (SELECT
    [UnitPrice]*[Quantity] AS LinePrice
    FROM [Order Details]
    ) As Nested1
    ) As Nested2
GO
```

INSIDE OUT   Case statements

At this point, you should appreciate that T-SQL takes writing SQL in Access to a more sophisticated level, and one feature that you don't want to miss is the *CASE* statement (often used to replace *IIF* structures). There are two forms for this, *SIMPLE* and *SEARCHED*. To illustrate this, the following code creates a very simple table that lists the months in a year, demonstrating the two forms of this statement (CASE.sql):

```
CREATE TABLE Months(
MonthID               INT PRIMARY KEY,
TheMonthName          NVARCHAR(15)
)
GO
INSERT INTO Months(MonthID,TheMonthName)
VALUES(1,'January'),(2,'February'),(3,'March'),(4,'April'),
(5,'May'),(6,'June'),(7,'July'),(8,'August'),
(9,'September'),(10,'October'),(11,'November'),
(12,'December')
GO
-- Simple Case
SELECT MonthID , TheMonthName,
    Simplecase =
    CASE MonthID
        WHEN 1   THEN 'January'
        WHEN 2   THEN 'February'
        WHEN 3   THEN 'March'
        WHEN 4   THEN 'April'
        WHEN 5   THEN 'May'
        WHEN 6   THEN 'June'
        WHEN 7   THEN 'July'
        WHEN 8   THEN 'August'
        WHEN 9   THEN 'September'
        WHEN 10  THEN 'October'
        WHEN 11  THEN 'November'
        WHEN 12  THEN 'December'
    Else 'Unknown'
    END
FROM Months
GO
```

```
-- Searched Case
SELECT MonthID , TheMonthName,
    SearchedCase =
    CASE
        WHEN MonthID IN(1,2,3) THEN 'First Quarter'
        WHEN  MonthID IN(4,5,6) THEN 'Second Quarter'
        WHEN  MonthID IN(7,8,9)  THEN 'Third Quarter'
        WHEN  MonthID IN(10,11,12) THEN ' Fourth Quarter'
    Else 'Unknown'
    END
FROM Months
GO
```

Performance and Execution Plans

Access is a bit like a black box in that you can extract some information on what it is doing behind the scenes, (but unfortunately, not a lot of information). By comparison, SQL Server is a much more open environment, and one way to investigate and resolve performance problems is the use of execution plans.

To begin, you should appreciate that not all of the information that you see in the plans is easily understood, simply because it is very comprehensive. But within this complex environment is some very valuable information that can help you to solve serious performance issues. In this section, you will construct examples to show how you dig into the strategies used by SQL Server when processing your SQL.

You start by creating a copy of some existing data in *NorthWind*, as shown in the following script (Indexing.sql):

```
-- Create a test table
SELECT * INTO TestOrders
FROM Orders
GO
-- display any indexing on the table
sp_helpIndex [TestOrders]
GO
-- This should confirm that we have no indexes
```

Figure 15-25 presents part of the Toolbar in Management Studio when working with a query window. This has several options for obtaining more information on the execution of the SQL.

Figure 15-25 The Include Actual Execution Plan option for obtaining information. You can also include an estimated execution plan and client statistics.

Click the Include Actual Execution Plan icon. You can then execute a piece of SQL and view the plan output, as shown in Figure 15-26.

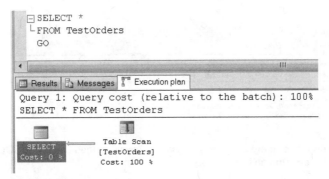

Figure 15-26 This table has no indexing, so SQL Server reads through all of the data by using a *Table Scan*.

Executing the following T-SQL creates a *CLUSTERED INDEX* on the table; all tables should have a clustering key as this is used by other indexes, which are called *NONCLUSTERED* indexes. The clustered index controls the physical ordering of the data; this can impact the speed of retrieval on searches by the key. When you create a table and add a primary key, SQL Server makes that the clustered index (unless you already have another clustered index on the table). The SQL is shown in the following code, with the results shown in Figure 15-27:

```
-- Next create a clustered index
CREATE CLUSTERED INDEX idxTestOrdersClustered
ON TestOrders(OrderID)
GO
```

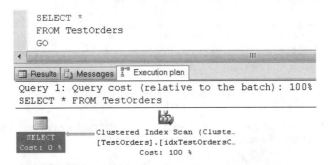

Figure 15-27 SQL Server uses the clustering key to perform an Index Scan.

In the next example, you will be more selective about the rows to retrieve. The result is shown in Figure 15-28.

```
SELECT *
FROM TestOrders
WHERE OrderID between 10252 and 10254
GO
```

Results | Messages | Execution plan

```
Query 1: Query cost (relative to the batch): 100%
SELECT * FROM [TestOrders] WHERE [OrderID]>=@1 AND [OrderID]<=@2
```

SELECT
Cost: 0 %

Clustered Index Seek (Cluste...
[TestOrders].[idxTestOrdersC...
Cost: 100 %

Figure 15-28 This is a lot more efficient because you have specified criteria, so SQL Server searches the index by using an Index Seek.

Next, you create an index on the *OrderDate* field, which is used for searching. The SQL is shown in the following code, with the results shown in Figure 15-29:

```
CREATE INDEX idx_TestOrders_OrderDate
ON TestOrders(OrderDate)
GO
```

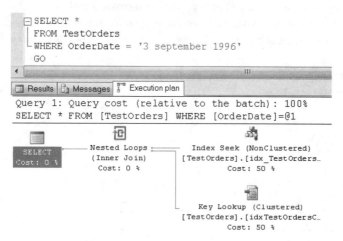

```
SELECT *
FROM TestOrders
WHERE OrderDate = '3 september 1996'
GO
```

Results | Messages | Execution plan

```
Query 1: Query cost (relative to the batch): 100%
SELECT * FROM [TestOrders] WHERE [OrderDate]=@1
```

SELECT
Cost: 0 %

Nested Loops
(Inner Join)
Cost: 0 %

Index Seek (NonClustered)
[TestOrders].[idx_TestOrders...
Cost: 50 %

Key Lookup (Clustered)
[TestOrders].[idxTestOrdersC...
Cost: 50 %

Figure 15-29 SQL Server can use the new index to look up the cluster keys, and then use the clustered index to retrieve the record. This is called a *Key Lookup*.

We mentioned that the clustering key is stored in the *NON-CLUSTERED* indexes, and it is only the *CLUSTERED* index that references the actual physical data. This strategy means that often a search requires a *Key Lookup* to locate the data. The big advantage of this strategy is that if the physical data needs to be moved by SQL Server, for example, to store more data in the record, then only the *CLUSTERED* index needs to be altered to record where the data row has been moved; there is no impact on all the other indexes. As updates are very common in databases, this strategy minimizes the impact of updates.

In the following example, rather that retrieve all the columns, you only want to retrieve the *OrderId*. This is shown in Figure 15-30.

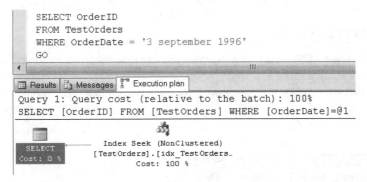

```
SELECT OrderID
FROM TestOrders
WHERE OrderDate = '3 september 1996'
GO
```

| Results | Messages | Execution plan |

```
Query 1: Query cost (relative to the batch): 100%
SELECT [OrderID] FROM [TestOrders] WHERE [OrderDate]=@1
```

```
                        Index Seek (NonClustered)
SELECT                  [TestOrders].[idx_TestOrders...
Cost: 0 %                     Cost: 100 %
```

Figure 15-30 In this example, because all the columns selected and searched are contained in the index, SQL Server does not need to retrieve the actual rows of data. The index covers all the required fields and this search will be very efficient.

Chapter 15

INSIDE OUT   Tips on efficient SQL

Writing your SQL efficiently and giving some thought to what you want to index will improve your applications performance. Here are some tips for how to do that:

- Add indexing to Foreign Keys (Access does this automatically; SQL Server does not). This improves join performance.

- Select only the required fields in your SQL and avoid using * to select all fields.

- Make your *WHERE* clauses as specific as possible.

- Don't over-index the database; indexes have a cost as SQL Server needs to maintain the data in the indexes.

- Choose to index columns that are often searched and contain many different values (they are selective). If your index is not selective, SQL Server might avoid using the index.

- Run maintenance plans to rebuild indexes with space for new growth.

The ability in SQL Server to analyze specific queries and look for where indexing is not being used can help you plan your indexes. It is a good idea to start with very few indexes and then gradually add them to improve performance. SQL Server uses a cost-based optimizer that maintains statistics on the indexes, which can then be used to decide on a minimum I/O cost based strategy for returning your data.

SQL Server Profiler

The SQL Server Profiler is a tool with which you can monitor the communications between your applications and the SQL Server database. Earlier in this chapter, on page 554, we looked at the TIMESTAMP columns and showed the resulting communications between Access and SQL Server when data is updated. When you start the Profiler, it will display the window shown in Figure 15-31.

Figure 15-31 Click the New Trace icon (the first one), and then connect to your SQL Server.

When you create a new trace, a Run button appears at the lower-left of the window that you use to start the trace. The trace window can result in displaying a large amount of information, and you can stop and then restart the trace by using the Toolbar icons, as shown in Figure 15-32.

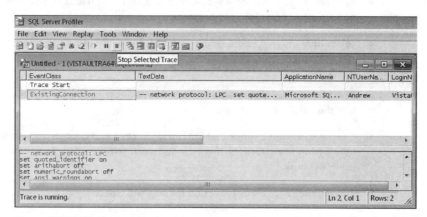

Figure 15-32 Start a trace only when you are ready to perform a specific action that you want to monitor.

With the trace, you can then open various parts of your application and monitor performance; if you take a form bound to a large number of records and perform a search for data (Ctrl+F), you will see the large amount of activity that this causes in the Profiler window. Remember to discontinue the trace once you are finished.

The *MSysConf* Table

After opening your Access application, when Access starts to communicate with SQL Server—for example, if you click on a linked table—you see the following action in the trace window:

```
SELECT Config, nValue FROM MSysConf
```

Access looks to see if it can find a table called *MSysConf* in your database. If you create a table with this name in your database, you can enter values to control how Access interacts with SQL Server. If you create this table, it's important to correctly set any values in the table. The following script (MSysConf.sql) creates this table and includes examples of setting values in the table:

```
CREATE TABLE MSysConf(
Config      SMALLINT      NOT NULL,
chValue     VARCHAR(255)  NULL,
nValue      INTEGER       NULL,
Comments    VARCHAR(255)  NULL
)
GO
INSERT INTO MSysConf(Config,nValue,Comments)
VALUES(101,0,
'Prevent storage of the logon ID and password in linked tables.')
GO
--VALUES(103, 50,
--'number of rows retrieved.')
--VALUES(101,1,
--'Allow storage of the logon ID and password in linked tables.')
--VALUES(102,1,
--'delay in seconds between each retrieval.')
--Note Setting a higher delay time decreases network traffic,
-- but increases the amount of time that read-locks are left on data
-- (if the server uses read-locks).
```

Having set the previous option to prevent saving passwords in linked tables, when connecting to SQL Server the check box option to allow saving user names and passwords is no longer displayed (remember to close and then re-open your database if testing this).

It is also worth pointing out that when we have tested option 103 (which controls the number of rows that should be retrieved), we have not been able to see any easily observable changes when monitoring traffic by using the Profiler.

Chapter 15

Summary

In the first part of this chapter, you looked at the need to plan for upsizing your database, which included the following key points:

- Deciding on whether to use *UNICODE* data types.

- Checking your data for invalid dates.

- Ensuring that your *Yes/No* fields have default values.

- Ensuring that required fields are not *NULL*.

- Deciding how to map *OLE Data* and *Memo* fields.

- Deciding on which version of the SQL Server Drivers to use.

- Normalizing any multi-value data fields into new tables.

- Normalizing and converting any *Attachment* data to *OLE* data.

- Planning for using *Schemas* and *Synonyms*.

Converting large databases from Access to SQL Server is not something that you should expect to get right the first time you attempt to do it. It is also important use a script file to record any changes that you make in the SQL Server database so that these can be re-applied if you need to repeat the upsizing process. In addition to the Upsizing Wizard and SSMA, you can find other companies that offer products to assist with migrating Access databases to SQL Server.

Introducing SQL Azure 590

Migrating SQL Databases 596

The Data Sync Feature 604

Planning and Managing Security 615

Building Multi-Tenanted Applications 617

SQL Server Migration Assistant and Access to Azure . . 624

M ICROSOFT SQL Azure offers an opportunity for developers who are using Microsoft Office for either reporting management information or developing full applications linked to SQL Server to extend the reach of their applications by placing the Microsoft SQL Server database in the Cloud with SQL Azure. As a result, you can continue to use the existing desktop Office applications after they are relinked directly to SQL Azure. Furthermore, you can consider using Azure and .NET to provide a browser-based interface to your applications later.

There are numerous applications of this technology. One example is to provide remote users with an opportunity to test out an application or product without the need to install the SQL backend. Another example is to build a full, multi-tenanted product in the Cloud. This technology also provides a cloud-based SQL Server that is synchronized to your on-premise applications, using the newest version of Data Sync.

In this chapter, we begin by showing you how to get started with SQL Azure. Next, we discuss the structural requirements for the SQL Server database and the migration process. We then move on to discuss the developer tools for working with SQL Azure and address the issue of planning and implementing security.

After reading this chapter, you will:

- Understand how to get started and develop with SQL Azure.

- Understand how to migrate an on-premise SQL Server database to SQL Azure.

- Be able to construct multi-tenanted solutions.

- Understand how to utilize the Data Sync Service.

- Plan and implement a security model in SQL Azure.

- Experience how Microsoft SQL Server Migration Assistant can migrate directly from Microsoft Access to SQL Azure.

> **Note**
> As you read through this chapter, we encourage you to also use the companion content sample script files, which can be downloaded from the book's catalog page.

Introducing SQL Azure

It is possible to have your own SQL Server on the Internet and connect to it directly from your desktop Microsoft Access application. If you have an ISP that provides this service, this is one option for extending the reach of an application. If you try to do this yourself on your own dedicated server, you might find that it's quite challenging and realize that you need to read up about a wide range of technologies, such as configuring firewalls.

One advantage of SQL Azure is that you can have this functionality without the associated difficulty of configuring this for yourself and be up and running very quickly. SQL Azure is *not* SQL Server running on a server on the Internet; it is a service provided by Microsoft to give SQL Server functionality within the context of cloud computing.

Gradually, SQL Azure is supporting more of the functionality associated with an on-premise SQL Server, and the ease and simplicity of using Azure is continuously improving as Microsoft adds support for an ever increasing subset of SQL Server functionality. You will find that the basic database technology is now well established in SQL Azure. New, additional services include a Data Sync, which can synchronize on-premise databases to cloud databases, and support for Report Services.

Creating Databases

Once you have set up your SQL Azure account, you can use the browser-based management interface for managing your account and databases, as is shown in Figure 16-1.

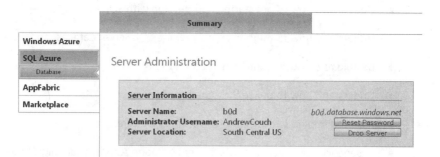

Figure 16-1 Viewed in a browser, the summary page provides the details that you need for connecting to the databases on your server (*https://sql.azure.com/ProjectViewer.aspx*).

On the Databases tab, click the Create Database button (in the lower-right part of the screen), to set up a new database called **Northwind**. Figure 16-2 shows the result of creating two databases in Azure (the master system database is part of the SQL Azure environment).

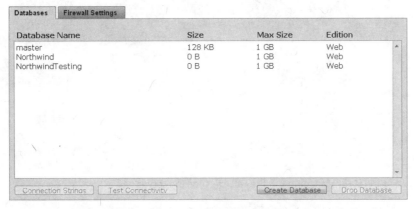

Figure 16-2 You can manage your SQL Azure databases on the Databases tab.

Click the *Northwind* database you just created, and then click the Connection Strings button to display the corresponding connection strings. This displays the following connection string for use with ADO.NET:

```
Server=tcp:b0d.database.windows.net;Database=Northwind;
User ID=AndrewCouch@b0d;Password=myPassword;Trusted_Connection=False;Encrypt=True;
```

The connection string for ODBC will be similar to the following:

```
Driver={SQL Server Native Client 10.0};Server=tcp:b0d.database.windows.net;Database=N
orthwind;Uid=AndrewCouch@b0d;Pwd=myPassword;Encrypt=yes;
```

In the ODBC connection string, the SQL Server Native Client 10.0 driver is used; earlier versions of the ODBC drivers will not work when connecting to SQL Azure. You will find details of how to download these drivers on the Microsoft sites. If you have performed a local installation of SQL Server 2008 R2, the drivers were automatically installed at that time. If you are planning to allow other users to work with the database, then you will need to download and install these drivers on each desktop computer.

Firewall Settings

When working with SQL Azure, there are two basic levels of security: the first is a SQL Server Login (as of this writing, SQL Azure does not support Windows authentication); the second level of security is the firewall, which will only allow access from a remote location with an IP address that falls within ranges defined in the firewall rules. Figure 16-3 shows an example of firewall rules.

Figure 16-3 Managing the firewall rules for the server.

In this example, we have opened up the firewall to allow access from any IP address (0.0.0.0 – 255.255.255.255). The danger in doing this is that you effectively lose the protection of the firewall and must rely solely on the security provided by the SQL Server Login and password. The advantage in setting a wide IP address range is that if you have a dynamic IP address, you will always be able to connect to the server. For example, if you have a database that is used for product demonstrations, then losing this additional security might be acceptable. If you have fixed IP addresses, then you would only enter the appropriate address ranges.

Using Management Studio

To work from your local computer with Microsoft SQL Server Management Studio, you will need to configure the SQL Server 2008 R2 Management Tools; you can download and install the free Express version of SQL Server 2008 R2 to ensure that you have the required tools.

After starting Management Studio, you are prompted to connect to a SQL Server, Figure 16-4 shows the details that you need to enter for your SQL Azure server. Notice that the Options button has been clicked to display the expanded set of tabs for the connection dialog.

Your server has a code; in our example the code is b0d, which means that the server name to be entered is **b0d.database.windows.net**. The authentication needs to be set for SQL Server Authentication, and then enter your user name as *Username@b0d*.

Figure 16-4 Entering the details for connecting to the server.

Before clicking the Connect button, click the Connection Properties tab, as shown in Figure 16-5.

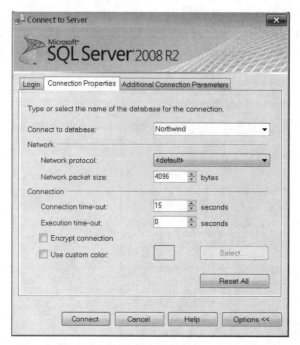

Figure 16-5 Enter the name of the database to which to connect in the Connect To Database field.

Type in the name of the database to connect to (the drop-down menu will not be populated). In Figure 16-5, the selected database is *Northwind*, but you might decide to connect to *Master*. If you choose to connect to *Master*, you will also be able to see and manage all the other databases on the server, as shown in Figure 16-6.

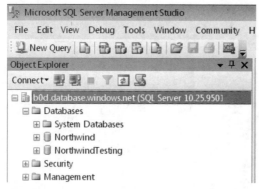

Figure 16-6 Connecting to *Master* allows you to manage all the databases on the server.

INSIDE OUT   SQL Azure and the graphical interface

When you are working with Management Studio and SQL Azure, you might notice that not all of the graphical support is available. For example, typically, when you expand a database in the Object Explorer and locate the Tables folder, if you right-click New Table, you will see a graphical interface for designing a table. With Azure, however, you will see a template script for creating a table that is displayed in the Query window. If you right-click an existing table, you will not have the option to use the graphical interface to change the design of the table, or view or edit the data (you need to type in the SQL in the query window to do this).

For many of the actions for which you have previously used the GUI interface, the only option with Management Studio is to write T-SQL to execute these tasks. If you find that this is difficult to do, then you will want to look at using a new online graphical tool that Microsoft is developing, which as of this writing is called Houston (this is described in the following section).

Developing with the Browser Interface

SQL Azure is an evolving technology and Microsoft has been adding an increasing number of features to the services. Of particular note is the way in which Management Studio has been able to offer an ever increasing amount of support for the management and design tasks required to develop SQL Azure databases.

A separate area for which Microsoft has provided an additional tool is in the browser-based management of the database structure. As of this writing, you can go to *https://www.sqlazurelabs.com/houston.aspx* to launch this new feature. After selecting your data center, enter the credentials, as shown in Figure 16-7.

Chapter 16

Figure 16-7 The Houston Database Manager window.

Figure 16-8 presents an example of the browser interface being used to change the design of a table.

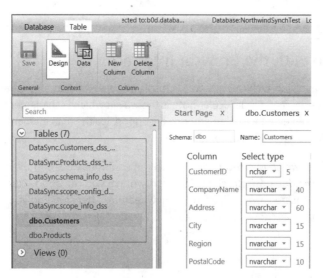

Figure 16-8 Houston offers an interface that complements those features normally found in Management Studio when working with an on-premise database that are not available when connected to SQL Azure.

Migrating SQL Databases

In this section, you will learn how to copy an existing on-premise database to SQL Azure. Using the methods described here, there will be no synchronization or connection between the local database and the database in Azure. (Synchronizing the databases is discussed in the next section.)

To copy the database into Azure, you use the following sequence of steps:

1. Generate a script file to be run in Azure that will create the empty tables.

2. Modify the script file to be compliant with Azure requirements.

3. Generate the empty tables.

4. Use the SQL Server Import And Export Wizard to copy the data into Azure.

Once again, the sample files for this chapter include the instnwnd.sql script to create the *Northwind* sample database in your local SQL Server, ready for use in moving to SQL Azure.

Creating a Set of Tables

The first step is to use Management Studio with your on-premise database to generate a script for creating your database tables, as shown in Figure 16-9.

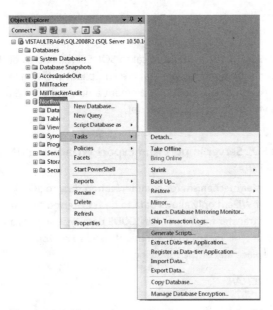

Figure 16-9 Generating a script for creating the tables.

Figure 16-10 shows the process of selecting your tables. Proceed through the various windows to generate a script in the query window.

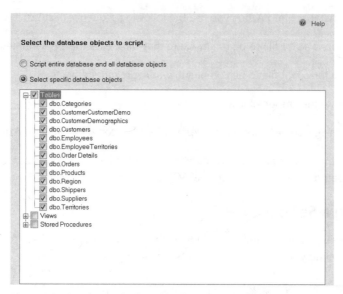

Figure 16-10 Select only the tables.

As previously pointed out, SQL Azure is not identical to SQL Server, and as of this writing, Management Studio does not generate scripts that are compliant with the requirements of SQL Azure. This means that you will need to implement a number of find and replace operations to ensure that you have a compliant script.

INSIDE OUT
The SQL Server Import And Export Wizard and UNICODE data types

When used with the transfer mechanism for communicating data to SQL Azure, the SQL Server Import And Export Wizard only allows data to be transferred to UNICODE data types. It will allow you to transfer from a non-UNICODE data type such as a *VARCHAR* to a UNICODE *NVARCHAR*. This means that you might need to perform a global find in your own script file to replace any of the following:

- *VARCHAR* to *NVARCHAR*

- *CHAR* to *NCHAR*

- *TEXT* to *NVARCHAR(MAX)*

Note that this is only required because in the method outlined in this section, when using the wizard to transfer the data to Azure, SQL Azure does support these data types.

As part of the create table syntax, your script file will contain syntax similar to the following:

```
)WITH (PAD_INDEX  = OFF, STATISTICS_NORECOMPUTE  = OFF, IGNORE_DUP_KEY = OFF,
ALLOW_ROW_LOCKS  = ON, ALLOW_PAGE_LOCKS  = ON) ON [PRIMARY]
) ON [PRIMARY]
```

You will need to change these to read as follows:

```
)WITH ( STATISTICS_NORECOMPUTE  = OFF, IGNORE_DUP_KEY = OFF)
)
```

The easiest way to make this change is with a succession of find and replace operations to replace portions of the script; for example, replacing PAD_INDEX = OFF with an empty string. You will find it helpful to make copies of the script file before trying out the changes. This way, you can take one example of the create table syntax and practice making the replacements in a dummy database so that you can ensure that the script will execute. We have included NorthwindInitialScript.SQL and NorthwindFixedScript.SQL in the sample databases.

Once your script file is prepared and tested, you can use Management Studio to execute the script in your database, taking care to execute it in the correct database.

Create a new database in SQL Azure and call it **NorthwindAzure**; you can do this either by using the browser tools or by using Management Studio and executing the following T-SQL while you are connected to the *Master* database in SQL Azure:

```
CREATE DATABASE [NorthwindAzure]
GO
```

Now execute the script NorthwindFixedScript.SQL in the database *NorthwindAzure* to create a set of empty tables, relationships, and other database objects

Transferring Data with the SQL Server Import and Export Wizard

Now that you have created your empty database structures in SQL Azure, use Management Studio to access your local on-premise database. Right-click the database and select the Export Data option from the Tasks shortcut menu, as shown in Figure 16-11.

Figure 16-11 Exporting data from the on-premise database.

Follow the steps in the SQL Server Import And Export Wizard until you reach the page shown in Figure 16-12.

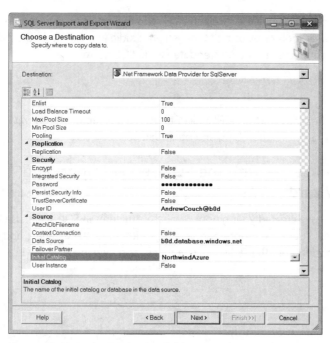

Figure 16-12 In the Destination field toward the top of the wizard page, Select the .Net Framework Data Provider For SqlServer option.

After selecting the correct data provider for your SQL Azure database, you need to enter the Password, User ID, Data Source, and Initial Catalog (Figure 16-12).

On the next page, select the Copy Data From One Or More Tables Or Views option. Choose the tables that you want to copy (do not select the Views; it is also possible to use Views to transfer the data, but we do not require this), as shown in Figure 16-13.

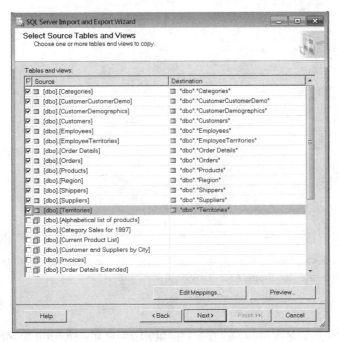

Figure 16-13 Selecting the tables to transfer automatically completes the destination when the names are matched.

On the next page, select Run Immediately. If everything has worked properly, the wizard will look similar to Figure 16-14. If there are errors, the wizard usually provides a good description of the nature of the problem.

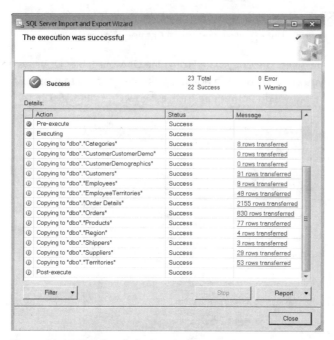

Figure 16-14 Details are displayed after completing the transfer, including any error messages.

For a detailed description of how to link your Access database application to the new SQL Azure database, refer to Chapter 12, "Linking Access Tables."

INSIDE OUT   SQL Import/Export features when transferring to SQL Azure

Normally, when you are transferring data by using the SQL Server Import\Export between two SQL Server databases, you need to consider the following (using the Edit Mappings shown in Figure 16-13):

- For any tables with Identity properties, select the Enable Identity Insert option.

- For any tables with TIMESTAMPS, click the Field Data Type, and then select Ignore.

If you were to use the profiler to monitor how the SQL Server Import And Export Wizard performs the data transfer, you would see insert bulk statements with a CHECK_ CONSTRAINTS option. This means that referential integrity can still prevent data from being transferred, so a great deal of care can be required.

A fantastic feature of SQL Azure is that when you use Import/Export to transfer data to SQL Azure, you do not need to explicitly set these options, and the data transfer avoids any problems associated with referential integrity and the order in which tables are populated with data.

Backing up and Copying a Database

Within SQL Azure, you can copy a database, both within a single server and between SQL Azure servers; this can be used to either provide copies for development or to provide a snapshot backup of the database. The following code shows how to create a backup copy of the *Northwind* database in SQL Azure. It includes commands that can be used to monitor the progress of the operation:

```
-- execute on the master database
CREATE DATABASE NorthwindBackup
    AS COPY OF Northwind
GO
-- retrieve state of the new database
select name, state, state_desc from sys.databases
where name = 'NorthwindBackup'

-- retrieve copying details
select * from sys.dm_database_copies
where database_id = DB_ID('NorthwindBackup')
GO
```

INSIDE OUT   Importing data from SQL Azure

If you want to transfer a SQL Azure database to a new, local on-premise database, you can do this by using Import.

You perform an Import in Management Studio while connected to your local on-premise database, and *not* from the Azure database (if you right-click the Azure database, you will not see any Import/Export tasks). It is best to perform this operation into an empty local SQL Server database; this process will then create unkeyed and unrelated tables of all the data.

If you try to reverse the process that was used to push the data into SQL Azure by first creating tables and constraints in the empty on-premise SQL Database, you will run into the problems described earlier when using the SQL Server Import And Export Wizard to migrate between two local SQL Server databases. The process of exporting to SQL Azure and importing from SQL Azure are not identical.

The Data Sync Feature

In the previous section, you saw how to copy a database to SQL Azure. You can also synchronize your on-premise database with your Azure database by using the Data Sync feature. Data Sync uses the Microsoft Sync Framework and supports complex configurations for synchronizing databases in the Cloud and between the Cloud and your local servers.

As of this writing, not all of the synchronization services are fully available; CTP1 (Community Technical Preview) is available and CTP2 will be available shortly. The following is a brief description of some of the synchronization services:

- **Cloud to Cloud (CTP1)**   Permits synchronization between SQL Azure databases in several different data centers.

- **On-premise to Cloud (CTP2)**   Permits a local SQL Database to be synchronized to an SQL Azure database.

- **Retail & Remote Offices (CTP2)**   Permits combinations of multiple remote SQL Servers—for example, in retail stores—to be synchronized.

- **Offline Devices (CTP2)**   Permits devices such as mobile phones to be synchronized to the SQL Azure databases.

Synchronizing databases for the purpose of extending the reach of an application has always been an ambitious technical step, not least because in any environment, you face the difficult questions of how to resolve data conflicts and transmit changes to the database schema.

SQL Azure is an ambitious technology, and as of this writing, the Data Sync technology is still at the CTP level and will no doubt evolve. But we feel that this is such an exciting technology, and one that has reached a sufficient point of maturity, that it warranted inclusion in this book.

In this section, you start from the assumption that you have an on-premise SQL Server Database, and you want to synchronize this to a mirror of the database in the Cloud.

Beginning with the existing local database, you create a new empty database in SQL Azure by using Management Studio connected to the SQL Azure master database, as shown in Figure 16-15.

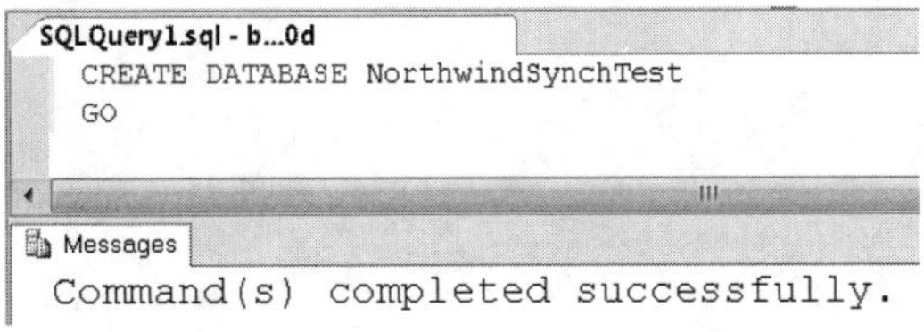

Figure 16-15 Creating a new, empty database in SQL Azure that will be synchronized to the local on-premise database.

Figure 16-16 shows the CTP2 interface to the Data Sync service.

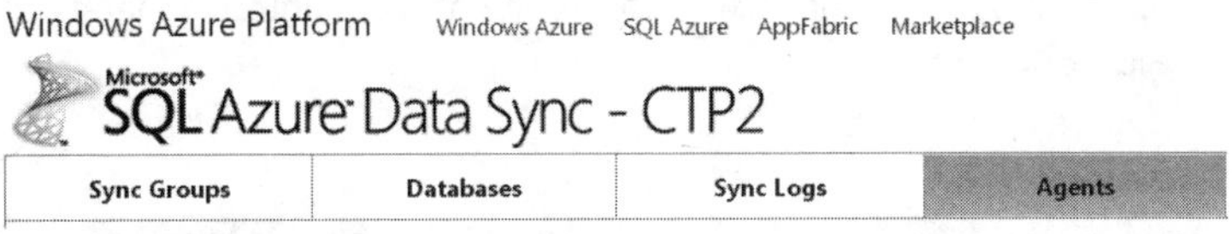

Figure 16-16 The browser interface for managing Data Sync.

The Data Sync Agent

To avoid problems with firewalls and other security issues, the Data Sync service involves the local installation of an *Agent*, which is then responsible for making outbound requests.

The first step is to download and install the Agent; this is available from the Agents tab (download AgentServiceSetup.msi). During the installation process, you will need to provide details of your domain and an appropriate logon password, this information will be saved when a new Windows service is created (if you do not have a domain but your Windows ID is, for example, Andrew, then enter this as **.\Andrew** [with a period before the backslash]). The final window after running the installation appears, as shown in Figure 16-17.

Chapter 16

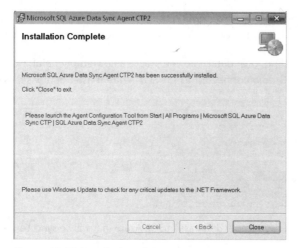

Figure 16-17 Installation of the Data Sync Agent is complete.

After completing the install, use the Agent tab in the browser window to create an Agent with an appropriate name, and then with the Agent highlighted, generate the Agent Key, as shown in Figure 16-18.

Local Agents

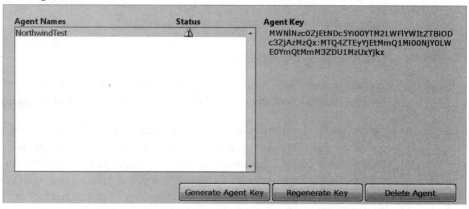

Figure 16-18 Generate the Agent Key in the browser window; the key is shown on the right.

After generating the key, return to the desktop and start the SQL Azure Data Sync Agent application (Figure 16-19). Select the Encrypt Password option, and then click Edit Agent Key. Paste the key generated in the browser into this box (ensure that you have no leading or trailing spaces).

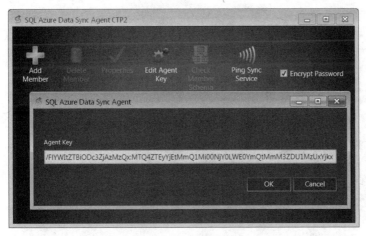

Figure 16-19 Register the Agent Key generated in the browser with the desktop application.

After saving the result, click the Ping Sync Service icon to test that you have correctly edited the key, as shown in Figure 16-20.

Figure 16-20 Use the Ping Sync Service to verify that the key has been correctly entered.

Next, click the Add Member icon to register your local SQL Server database as a member with the Agent. A dialog box opens, in which you can add the database by using either SQL or Windows authentication, as shown in Figure 16-21.

Chapter 16

Figure 16-21 Adding your local SQL Server database as a member, here shown using Windows authentication.

Once this has been completed and you have saved the result, the local SQL Server database appears, as shown in Figure 16-22.

Figure 16-22 The local SQL Server database registered with the Agent.

Looking in the Windows Services (Control Panel | Administrative Tools | Services), you can see that the new Windows service is set to start automatically with the logon credentials you specified during the installation (see Figure 16-23). Right-click to start the service.

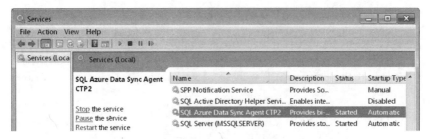

Figure 16-23 SQL Azure Data Sync Agent runs as a Windows service.

When you return to the browser window and display the Databases, you should now see your local database on this list. Click the Add button to register your SQL Azure database, as shown in Figure 16-24.

Figure 16-24 Use the browser to register the SQL Azure database.

A list similar to Figure 16-25 appears which includes both your local SQL Server database and your SQL Azure database.

Database Management

Database Name
VISTAULTRA64\SQL2008R2\Northwind
NorthwindSynchTest - b0d.database.windows.net

Figure 16-25 The database list displays both the local and SQL Azure databases.

At this point, you have completed the configuration of the Agent and registered your databases with the Sync Service. The next step is to set up the synchronization.

Sync Groups and Sync Logs

On the Sync Group tab in the browser window, you can now configure the details of how data will be synchronized between your databases. First, create a new Sync Group and register both the local and SQL Azure databases in the Sync Group, as shown in Figure 16-26.

New Sync Group

Sync Group Name: NorthwindLocalToCloud

Member List

Sync Group Hub: **NorthwindSynchTest - b0d.database.windows.net**

VISTAULTRA64\SQL2008R2\Northwind
NorthwindSynchTest - b0d.database.windows.net

Registered Databases

Database: Select a database to add...

Figure 16-26 Add both your local and SQL Azure databases to a new Sync Group.

Using the lower part of the screen shown in Figure 16-27, select the tables to be synchronized and specify the synchronization schedule.

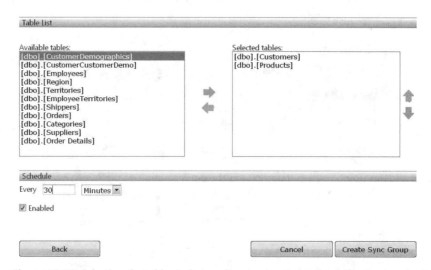

Table List

Available tables:
[dbo].[CustomerDemographics]
[dbo].[CustomerCustomerDemo]
[dbo].[Employees]
[dbo].[Region]
[dbo].[Territories]
[dbo].[EmployeeTerritories]
[dbo].[Shippers]
[dbo].[Orders]
[dbo].[Categories]
[dbo].[Suppliers]
[dbo].[Order Details]

Selected tables:
[dbo].[Customers]
[dbo].[Products]

Schedule
Every 30   Minutes
☑ Enabled

Back   Cancel   Create Sync Group

Figure 16-27 Selecting the tables to be synchronized and specifying the synchronization period. Click the Create Sync Group button when you have completed this information.

After creating your Sync Group, select the group, and then click the Sync Now button to start the synchronization. You are then be moved on to the Sync Logs tab where you can monitor the progress of the synchronization process, as shown in Figure 16-28.

Sync Logs

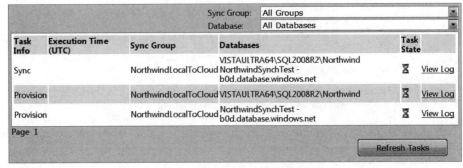

Figure 16-28 Use the Sync Logs tab to monitor the execution of your synchronization tasks.

Return to Management Studio and view the local *Northwind* database (see Figure 16-29). You can see that additional tables have been added to the database to manage the synchronization process.

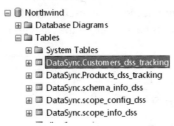

Figure 16-29 The local *Northwind* database contains some additional tables for tracking information on the synchronization.

Moving to display the SQL Azure database (see Figure 16-30), you can see how the synchronization management tables have also been created in the SQL Azure database, and the new synchronized tables are also present.

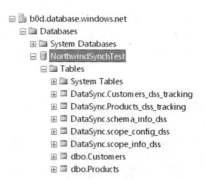

Figure 16-30 The SQL Azure database now contains the management tables and the synchronized versions of the local tables.

Now that you have configured the synchronization between the two databases, the next area to investigate is what happens when changes are made to the data.

Changing Data and Database Structure

The top half of Figure 16-31 shows the result of having first performed an edit on the first record in the local SQL Server and then having waited to refresh the data after an edit has been performed on the second record in SQL Azure. The lower part of the figure shows how we have performed a similar update but on the second record in SQL Azure, and again, waited to refresh the data after synchronization. The result is that the synchronization has correctly executed and both databases have received the changes to data made in the other database.

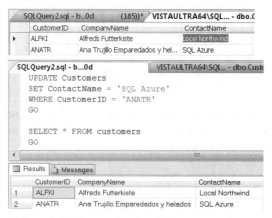

Figure 16-31 The results of making separate changes in the local and SQL Server databases, after a synchronization.

INSIDE OUT   Database synchronization and triggers

For each table that is included in the synchronization, a tracking table is created; thus for the Customers table, we have *DataSync.Customers_dss_tracking* on the DataSync schema. In addition, there are three new triggers added to the table: *Customers_dss_delete_trigger*, *Customers_dss_insert_trigger*, and *Customers_dss_update_trigger*. Each of these triggers changes attributes for the appropriate row in the tracking table; the tracking table has one row for each row in the physical table. These tables are then used by the Sync Framework to synchronize the data.

The next scenario addresses what happens if two users change the same record within the same synchronization period. You need to understand how the conflict is indicated and how to resolve it.

Conflict Resolution in Data

Because the synchronization process is effectively passive to your application, when a conflict occurs, the synchronization process needs to make a decision about which change takes priority. In the CTP, the rules are defined as "the hub wins," with other changes being overwritten. This means that SQL Azure, which by default is the hub, wins all synchronization conflicts.

As of this writing, this is in CTP, and it is likely in the future that mechanisms will be provided for better control of conflict resolution.

Changes to Table Structure

The next question to ask is what happens to the synchronization if the table structures in either the local or SQL Azure databases are changed. The following are three such scenarios:

- If you add new fields to either of the databases, the synchronization continues to operate, but the newly created column is not synchronized.

- If you delete a column, you have created an inconsistency and the synchronization will fail (see Figure 16-32). However, if you then correct the structures so that they are consistent, the synchronization will recover, but the recovered field will contain *NULL* values.

- If you alter the size of a field, synchronization will continue to operate as long as the data being synchronized does not violate your structural changes.

Sync Logs

Task Info	Execution Time (UTC)	Sync Group	Databases		Task State	
			Sync Group:	All Groups		
			Database:	All Databases		
Sync	3/20/2011 9:44:07 PM	NorthwindLocalToCloud	VISTAULTRA64\SQL2008R2\Northwind NorthwindSynchTest - b0d.database.windows.net		✓	View Log
Sync	3/20/2011 9:38:23 PM	NorthwindLocalToCloud	VISTAULTRA64\SQL2008R2\Northwind NorthwindSynchTest - b0d.database.windows.net		✗	View Log

Figure 16-32 The result of causing a synchronization failure by deleting a field, and then recovering the synchronization by adding the field back. Although the synch is recovered, other records will show a *NULL* value in the recovered field.

If you look at editing your Sync Group, you will find that there is no option to refresh individual table structures. There is, however, an option to change the nature of the synchronization from the perspective of creating a central hub to distribute data, as shown in Figure 16-33.

Edit Sync Group - NorthwindLocalToCloud

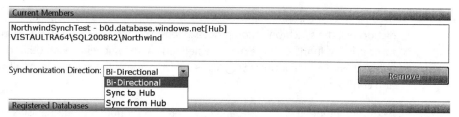

Current Members

NorthwindSynchTest - b0d.database.windows.net[Hub]
VISTAULTRA64\SQL2008R2\Northwind

Synchronization Direction: Bi-Directional
Bi-Directional
Sync to Hub
Sync from Hub

Registered Databases   Remove

Figure 16-33 When you edit a Sync group, you can control the distribution mechanism, but not alter the tables in the synchronization set.

As of this writing, Data Sync is still in CTP, but this is a technology that holds great promise and will allow developers to come up with imaginative methods for distributing data to multiple locations.

Key features of this technology include the following:

- It is a scalable technology that can be extended to handle complex configurations.

- The technology uses a no-code approach to synchronization.

- Conflict resolution is considered within the framework.

- Logging and monitoring features are provided.

- The elastic nature of the service reaches out to data being distributed to different platforms.

Planning and Managing Security

SQL Server offers two security models: Windows authentication, in which a user's Windows logon is integrated to the SQL Server, and SQL Logins, in which you set up specific accounts with passwords. As of this writing, Azure only supports the use of a SQL Login.

One of the most useful functions in SQL Server is *SUSER_SNAME()*. This function will pick up the identity of either the Windows authenticated user or the name of the SQL Login. Because this function is supported in SQL Azure, you have the option to record information on the individual users accessing your database.

Security can be viewed from either the perspective of preventing unauthorized access to a system or in recording the activities of authorized access. The first aspect of security, which we described earlier in this chapter, was in setting the firewall rules for IP address access to the SQL Azure database. Recall that you can either open up a wide range of IP addresses to allow for access from dynamic IP addresses, or you could use fixed IP address ranges for situations in which you have a range of static IP addresses.

As an Access developer, you might already have a security scheme in your application; thus, the issue we discuss here is how to integrate this security scheme with SQL Azure.

You have several alternatives for managing security, including:

- Prompt the user to log on with the Azure logon name and password.

- Hide the Azure logon name but force the user to enter the Azure password.

- Hide both the Azure logon and password and map everything through to your own local table of logons and passwords.

- Hide everything and use a single sign-on for all users.

- Embed the passwords and user names in the linked tables and forget about security.

Assuming that you have not chosen to simply embed a password and user name in your linked tables, the first time a linked table is opened (interactively or in code), you will be prompted to provide logon credentials. These credentials will remain in force while accessing all the other linked tables to that data source.

To avoid the problem of a pop-up box appearing that requests the user to log on, you need to use some program code to open a connection with SQL Azure.

Chapter 16

Start with your tables linked to SQL Azure. Note that we have not saved any credentials in the connection string. In this example, you have the following connection string:

```
ODBC;DRIVER=SQL Server Native Client 10.0;SERVER=b0d.database.windows.
net;APP=Microsoft Office 2010;DATABASE=NorthwindAzure;
```

In the master SQL Azure database, run the following T-SQL to create an account for testing (CreateUser.sql). The *CREATE LOGIN* command must be run in the master database, and the command to *CREATE USER* and assign security should be executed in the *NorthwindAzure* database:

```
-- Create a test login account in Master
CREATE LOGIN TestUser WITH PASSWORD = 'TestAzureAccount444333222'
GO
-- Create a user account in NorthwindAzure
CREATE USER TestUser FROM LOGIN TestUser
GO
-- Assign user to a database role in NorthwindAzure
EXEC sp_addrolemember 'db_owner', 'TestUser'
GO
Now use the following code to make the connection:

Sub modAzure_MakeConnection()
    ' Illustrates making the connection to SQL Azure in code
    Dim strUsername As String
    Dim strPassword As String
    ' You could then prompt the user for appropriate information
    strUsername = "TestUser@b0d "
    strPassword = "TestAzureAccount444333222"
    Dim db As DAO.Database
    Set db = CurrentDb
    Dim qdef As DAO.QueryDef
    Dim rst As DAO.Recordset
    Dim strConnect As String
    ' Get the connection string
    strConnect = db.TableDefs("Products").Connect
    strConnect = strConnect & "UID=" & strUsername & _
                "PWD=" & strPassword
    Set qdef = db.CreateQueryDef("")
    qdef.Connect = strConnect
    qdef.SQL = "SELECT @@version As SQLAzureVersion"
    Set rst = qdef.OpenRecordset()
    Debug.Print rst!SQLAzureVersion
End Sub
```

This constructs the following connection string:

```
ODBC;DRIVER=SQL Server Native Client 10.0;SERVER=b0d.database.windows.
net;APP=Microsoft Office 2010;DATABASE=NorthwindAzure;UID=TestUser@b0d;
PWD=TestAzureAccount444333222;
```

The previous code can then be easily adapted to integrate with your existing user security model.

Building Multi-Tenanted Applications

Whether you are creating a demonstration of your product or building a product that can work for multiple companies, cloud computing makes us all think more carefully about the potential savings from starting to design our database to supporting multiple organizations. The popular terminology for building these applications is to make them *multi-tenanted*—that is, each tenant is a customer.

Most Access developers are used to using the table as the key method for users interacting with data and then layering queries on top of the table to deliver up data that is filtered or organized to meet a particular need. To move to a multi-tenanted architecture, you need to insert another layer on top of your tables that isolates each tenant's information.

The SQL Server terminology for a query is the View. You start with an architecture in which users do not have permissions on the underlying tables but will use a View, and this View will be filtered to only show the tenant data for that user.

User Tables and Views

Because we are going to end up with an increased number of objects to manage in our SQL Server database, we will use schemas to partition the design and manage security. A *schema* is a mechanism for grouping together a set of objects.

Begin by constructing a schema to hold information about your users; use a separate schema for this because you might want to assign read/write permissions for users who could only have read permissions in other parts of the system. On this schema, you will create a filter table that will hold one record for each user in the system (MultiTenanted.sql):

```
-- Tables Schema for holding user specific information
CREATE SCHEMA [Filtering_T]
GO
-- Table holding User specific choices
CREATE TABLE [Filtering_T].[Filter](
    [UserId] INT IDENTITY(1,1) PRIMARY KEY,
    [UserName] nvarchar(255) NOT NULL
    DEFAULT SUSER_SNAME(),
    [TenantID] INT NOT NULL,
    -- List other useful user specific fields here
    [CustomerID] nvarchar(5)
    )
GO
```

Users do not have any permissions on the [Filtering_T] schema. This prevents them from seeing data that belongs to other tenants.

The second step is to create another schema on which users will be granted read/write permissions. On this schema, you create a view through which users can edit data:

```
-- Schema for using user specific information
CREATE SCHEMA [Filtering]
GO
-- User specific view returning 1 row
CREATE VIEW [Filtering].[Filter_VW]
AS
-- User only gets to see other user specific choices
SELECT [CustomerID] FROM [Filtering_T].Filter
WHERE [UserName] = SUSER_SNAME()
WITH CHECK OPTION
GO
```

The use of the *SUSER_SNAME()* function restricts a user to seeing only their own record in the underlying table. To make it simpler for users to refer to the view without the need to specify schema information, you create a synonym, which provides a shortcut name for referring to the view:

```
-- Synonym to ref to users choices
CREATE SYNONYM [Filter] FOR [Filtering].Filter_VW
GO
-- Create an example record for current user
INSERT INTO Filtering_T.Filter(TenantID)
VALUES(1)
GO
SELECT * FROM Filter
GO
SELECT * FROM Filtering_T.Filter
GO
```

These steps create the table and view shown in Figure 16-34.

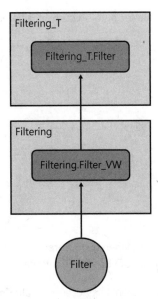

Figure 16-34 Adding new users to the system requires either an administrator to enter data directly in the physical table or some other special processing that can directly access the table.

The final step is to construct a function that can be used in other parts of the system to return the tenant identifier, as demonstrated in the following:

```
-- Create a function to filter by the Tenant
CREATE FUNCTION dbo.fn_GetTenant()
RETURNS INT
AS
BEGIN
    RETURN (SELECT [TenantID] FROM [Filtering_T].Filter
                   WHERE [UserName] = SUSER_SNAME())
END
GO
```

Application Tables and Views

When constructing the application, you should decide on a set of useful schemas to further split up the application. This step is not essential, but it is useful for improving the maintainability of the application. Each schema has an underscore and the letter T appended to the name; all of these schemas will contain the base tables on which no users will have any permissions.

Chapter 16

In the following example, you will construct a table for holding customer details for each tenant:

```
-- Tables schema for information on companies
CREATE SCHEMA [Companies_T]
GO
-- Table holding customer information
CREATE TABLE [Companies_T].[Customers](
    [TenantID] INT NOT NULL DEFAULT dbo.fn_GetTenant(),
    [CustomerID] [nchar](5) NOT NULL,
    [CompanyName] [nvarchar](40) NOT NULL,
    [ContactName] [nvarchar](30) NULL
    CONSTRAINT pk_Customers
    PRIMARY KEY ([TenantID],[CustomerID])
    )
GO
```

By adding the function as a default on the *TenantID*, when users enter new records, they are tagged appropriately. We have also added the *TenantID* to the primary key.

It is also useful to add a trigger to this table that prevents any user from altering the *TenantID* to a value other than that which is allowed for their business:

```
-- Trigger to ensure data correctly marked for the Tenant
CREATE TRIGGER TR_Customers_TenantCheck
ON [Companies_T].[Customers]
FOR UPDATE,INSERT
AS
-- Prevent any manual changes to TenantID
IF EXISTS(SELECT TenantID FROM INSERTED
WHERE TenantID <> dbo.fn_GetTenant())
    ROLLBACK TRANSACTION
GO
```

When you construct a multi-tenanted design, all the primary keys must be composite and include the *TenantID*. This also means that all your foreign keys will be composite. In the following example, you will create a related table, Projects, which has the composite primary key ([TenantID,ProjectID]), and then add the foreign key relationship to the Customers table; the foreign key needs to be composite on ([TenantID],[CustomerID]):

```
-- Adding a related table
-- Table holding project information
CREATE TABLE [Companies_T].[Projects](
    [TenantID] INT NOT NULL DEFAULT dbo.fn_GetTenant(),
    [ProjectID] INT IDENTITY(1,1) NOT NULL,
    [ProjectName] [nvarchar](40) NOT NULL,
    [CustomerID] [nchar](5) NOT NULL
    CONSTRAINT pk_Projects
    PRIMARY KEY ([TenantID],[ProjectID])
    )
```

```
GO
-- Adding the Foreign Key Constraint
ALTER TABLE [Companies_T].[Projects]
WITH CHECK ADD
CONSTRAINT [FK_Projects_Customers]
FOREIGN KEY([TenantID], [CustomerID])
REFERENCES [Companies_T].[Customers] ([TenantID], [CustomerID])
GO
```

The final step is to create a schema on which users will have permissions, and provide a view for managing the data:

```
-- Schema for using company information
CREATE SCHEMA [Companies]
GO
-- Restricted view showing only the users companies
CREATE VIEW [Companies].[Customers_VW]
AS
SELECT * FROM [Companies_T].[Customers]
WHERE [TenantID] = dbo.fn_GetTenant()
WITH CHECK OPTION
GO
--Synonym to refer to Customers
CREATE SYNONYM [Customers] FOR [Companies].[Customers_VW]
GO
-- Test data for an insert
INSERT INTO Customers(CustomerID,CompanyName)
VALUES('TT','Test Company')
GO
SELECT * FROM Customers
GO
-- Attempt an illegal insert, this should fail
INSERT INTO Customers(CustomerID,CompanyName,TenantID)
VALUES('TT2','Test Company2',2)
GO
```

The preceding tables and views and their interaction with the user specific tables are shown in Figure 16-35.

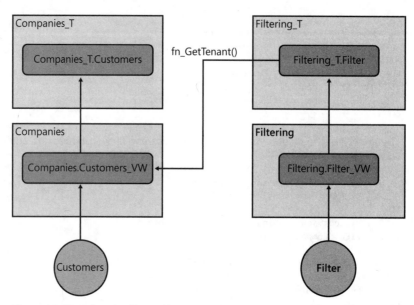

Figure 16-35 Using the filter table so that each user can work only with the data associated with their *TenantID*.

This technique can be extended easily, allowing users to make filtering choices that can then be applied in the system, as shown in the following:

```
-- Example adding user specific choices
UPDATE Filter
SET CustomerID = 'TT'
GO

-- Example filtering by the users choices
SELECT *
FROM Customers
WHERE CustomerID = (SELECT CustomerID FROM Filter)
GO
-- Example using a cross join, useful for multiple filters
SELECT c.*
FROM Customers c
   CROSS JOIN Filter f
WHERE c.CustomerID = f.CustomerID
GO
```

INSIDE OUT
Creating optional parameters by using the *COALESCE* function

In the previous example, when filtering by using the statement `c.CustomerID = f.CustomerID`, you would have a problem when no filter has been set and *f.CustomerID* was *NULL*. One solution to this problem is to use the *COALESCE* function, which returns the first non-null value from a list of choices. If instead you use `WHERE c.CustomerID = COALESCE(f.CustomerID,c.CustomerID)`, then when a *NULL* is supplied for *f.CustomerID*, it will compare *c.CustomerID* to *f.CustomerID*, which is always true (unless *c.CustomerID* is *NULL* because the test `NULL = NULL` would return false; this you might find a surprising fact).

To extend this method to handle a *NULL* in the column *c.CustomerID*, you could use the test `WHERE COALESCE (c.CustomerID, '') = COALESCE(f.CustomerID, c.CustomerID, '')`. This means that if *C.CustomerID* and *f.CustomerID* are both *NULL*, you are comparing two empty strings, which will be true. If you had to perform the comparison on a numeric, you would change the empty string to compare 0 to 0. And if comparing a date, you could use any fixed date; for example, `'1 january 2000' = '1 january 2000'`.

Managing Security

Having organized all your tables into schemas, you can now look at granting security permissions on the schemas. To further simplify managing the security, you will create three database roles and assign permissions on the schemas to the database roles:

```
-- Managing Security
CREATE ROLE ReadOnlyUser
GO
GRANT SELECT
ON SCHEMA::Companies TO ReadOnlyUser
GO
GRANT SELECT,INSERT,UPDATE
ON SCHEMA::Filtering TO ReadOnlyUser
GO
----------------------------------------
CREATE ROLE StandardUser
GO
GRANT SELECT,INSERT,UPDATE,DELETE
ON SCHEMA::Companies TO StandardUser
GO
GRANT SELECT,INSERT,UPDATE
ON SCHEMA::Filtering TO StandardUser
GO
```

Chapter 16

```
----------------------------------------
CREATE ROLE Administrator
GO
GRANT SELECT,INSERT,UPDATE,DELETE
ON SCHEMA::Companies TO Administrator
GO
GRANT SELECT,INSERT,UPDATE,DELETE
ON SCHEMA::Companies_T TO Administrator
GO
GRANT SELECT,INSERT,UPDATE, DELETE
ON SCHEMA::Filtering TO Administrator
GO
GRANT SELECT,INSERT,UPDATE,DELETE
ON SCHEMA::Filtering_T TO Administrator
GO
----------------------------------------
sp_addrolemember 'ReadOnlyUser', 'TestLogin'
GO
```

In the previous example, only the Administrator role is granted permissions on the schemas that contain the actual tables. The system stored procedure *sp_addrolemember* can be used to assign membership for a single user account or Windows group.

SQL Server Migration Assistant and Access to Azure

If rather than moving an on-premise SQL Server database into the Cloud, you are starting with an Access database and wish to directly migrate it to the Cloud, then SQL Server Migration Assistant (SSMA) is well worth examining (remember to run either the 32-bit or 64-bit version of SSMA to match your version of Microsoft Office). This section uses the sample database Northwind_ForAzure.accdb and shows how we can migrate this directly into the cloud. For more information about SSMA, read Chapter 15, "Upsizing Access to SQL Server."

Using the same technique as described earlier, connect to your SQL Azure database with Management Studio, and then execute the following T-SQL to create a new database:

```
CREATE DATABASE SSMA_Northwind
GO
```

Next, start SSMA. Note that for this example we show the steps when running the wizard. When creating your project, choose the SQL Azure option, as shown in Figure 16-36.

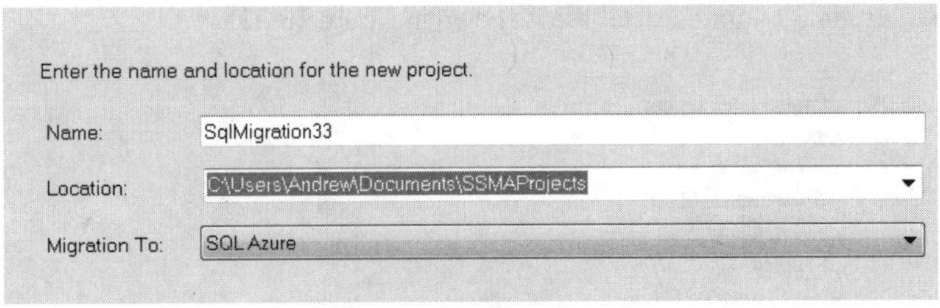

Enter the name and location for the new project.

Name: SqlMigration33

Location: C:\Users\Andrew\Documents\SSMAProjects

Migration To: SQL Azure

Figure 16-36 Choosing to migrate to SQL Azure.

After you select the Access database to be added to the project, you are prompted for your SQL Azure logon to the newly created database, as shown in Figure 16-37.

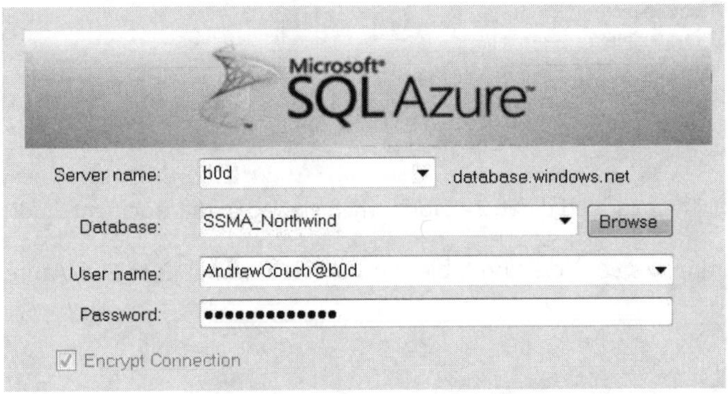

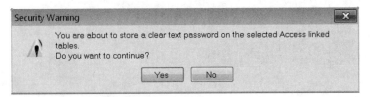

Server name: b0d   .database.windows.net

Database: SSMA_Northwind   Browse

User name: AndrewCouch@b0d

Password: ••••••••••••

☑ Encrypt Connection

Figure 16-37 Connecting to the new SQL Azure database.

In the next window, select the Link Tables option, and then follow the remaining steps to perform the migration. If you select the Link Tables To SQL Azure option, you will see a second prompt toward the end of the migration to provide logon details to SQL Azure as the links are created. At this point, you will also receive a security warning indicating that your ID and password will be saved in the table links (see Figure 16-38). We will discuss this later.

Security Warning

You are about to store a clear text password on the selected Access linked tables.
Do you want to continue?

Yes   No

Figure 16-38 SSMA does not provide any option to create the links without embedding the user name and password.

The resulting migrated database is shown in Figure 16-39.

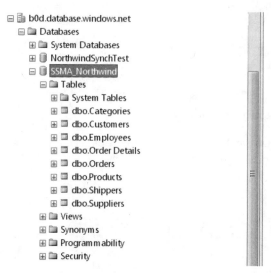

Figure 16-39 The migrated database tables when viewed in Management Studio.

SSMA then renames your existing tables and provide new links to SQL Azure, as shown in Figure 16-40.

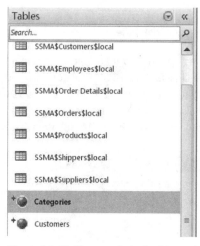

Figure 16-40 The new linked table to the database in SQL Azure.

INSIDE OUT   SSMA, SQL Azure, and changing the Data Type Mapping

Although SSMA allows you to change your Data Type Mapping, you should avoid changing to a NON-UNICODE mapping; for example, changing *NVARCHAR* to *VARCHAR*. If you change this mapping, the data migration will fail.

Figure 16-38 showed that SSMA will embed user name and password information in the linked tables. The following code shows an example of the connection property for one of the tables:

```
ODBC;DRIVER=SQL Server Native Client 10.0;SERVER=b0d.database.windows.
net;UID=AndrewCouch@b0d;PWD=XXXXXXX;APP=SSMA;DATABASE=SSMA_Northwind;
```

Earlier in this chapter, you learned how to create links to SQL Azure that avoid the necessity to embed this information in the links. Therefore, choosing the Link Tables option in the wizard is a good way to get started, but you will probably want to re-create your own links without this embedded information, as described earlier.

If you select a table in the Access Metadata such as the categories table shown in Figure 16-41, you can examine the T-SQL that SSMA uses to create your table by selecting the SQL tab for the table in SQL Azure, which is located in the lower part of the screen.

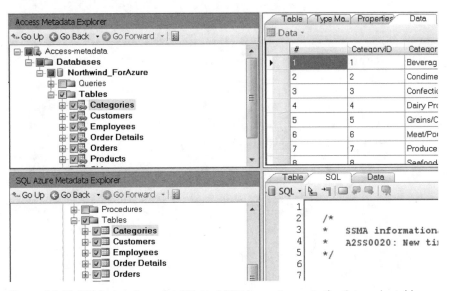

Figure 16-41 Displaying the script SQL that SSMA uses to create the Categories table.

SSMA performs an excellent job of migrating your Access databases directly into SQL Azure. One point you might wish to consider is that because there is no simple method to extract the database from SQL Azure back to an on-premise SQL Server, whether you would prefer to first migrate to an on-premise SQL Server and then migrate that into SQL Azure, or use the Data Sync to maintain a copy both on-premise and in the Cloud.

Summary

In this chapter, you learned how to extend the reach of your database applications by using SQL Azure to take an existing SQL Server database that is linked to Access and moving the SQL database into the Cloud. By using this approach, you can easily reconnect your existing client Access database application directly into SQL Azure.

You also saw that SSMA has tools that can bypass the need for a local SQL Server and perform a direct migration of the Access data into the Cloud.

As of this writing, the latest Data Sync technology is still in CTP2. Once this is available, you will be able to easily extend parts of an existing on-premise database into the Cloud by using a variety of configurations that combine different databases at different locations, using a hub database in SQL Azure to coordinate synchronization of data.

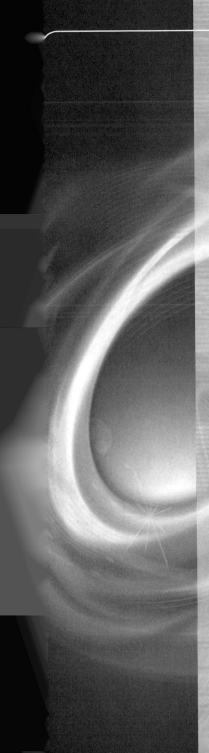

PART 7
Application Design

CHAPTER 17
Building Applications 631

CHAPTER 18
Using ADO and ADOX 659

Building Applications

Developing Applications. 631

Deploying Applications. 655

Completing an Application. 653

I n this chapter, you look at how to develop, complete, and deploy Microsoft Access 2010 applications. You will also be bringing together a number of references to coding techniques that you learned in earlier chapters as you create your applications.

After reading this chapter, you will:

- Be able to decide on how to structure the user interface.

- Know different techniques that can be used to complete an application.

- Understand the implication of design decisions on deploying and subsequently maintaining your applications.

> ## Note
> As you read through this chapter, we encourage you to also use the companion content sample databases, ApplicationDevelopment.accdb, ApplicationDevelopment64Bit.accdb, or ApplicationDevelopment_2007.accdb, which you can download from the book's catalog page.

Developing Applications

In this section, we will demonstrate different approaches that you can take when developing a user interface for your Access applications.

Application Navigation

When you create an application, key decisions to make on the interface design include the following:

- How will you open forms? For example, forms can be maximized to fill the entire screen area, fixed at an absolute positioning on the screen, or displayed in another controlling form.

- Will users be allowed to simultaneously interact with multiple windows?

- When switching between forms, do you preserve, refresh, or synchronize the user's record position on related data records?

- How will you handle different screen resolutions, and how could this impact the appearance of your application?

The first decision you need to make is on a general technique that you want to use for navigating users through your application. What should the look and feel of the interface be? In this section, you will see a number of common approaches to building an application interface.

Push Buttons on a Form

This is one of the simplest and most popular approaches to designing interfaces, and it involves adding command buttons to forms that then open other forms, which either pop up, open maximized, or open at a particular size and position on the screen. Figure 17-1 shows the sample form *frmNavigation_PushButton* as your new interface gets underway.

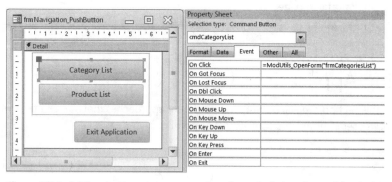

Figure 17-1 Adding buttons to your user interface. Code is written either behind each button, or as shown here, calling a utility function to open a specific form.

In the example, we have chosen a form that is not maximized, but it can work equally well when maximized to the screen area. The main advantage of this approach is that it is very simple. It is also possible to add some Microsoft VBA code to control button visibility, and you could create several of these menus forms and link them together by using code behind the command buttons.

The Switchboard Manager Manager

The Switchboard Manager is a feature in Access with which you can create a table-driven menu system. The resulting design components can be easily tailored to create your own look and feel to the interface.

In Access 2010, this feature is not included on the standard ribbons, but you can either add it to a standard ribbon or the Quick Access Toolbar. To add the Switchboard Manager to your Quick Access Toolbar, do the following:

1. Right-click the Quick Access Toolbar, and then select Customize Quick Access Toolbar from the shortcut,

    A drop-down menu opens.

2. From the drop-down menu, choose Commands, and then choose Commands Not In The Ribbon.

3. Locate and select the Switchboard Manager to add it to your Quick Access Toolbar.

The Switchboard Manager can be activated repeatedly to change the menu system. It has a fixed set of simple commands to create a set of menu pages with buttons for individual menu choice, as shown in Figure 17-2. Behind the scenes, the manager writes data into a table called *Switchboard Items*, which is used to drive the menu system.

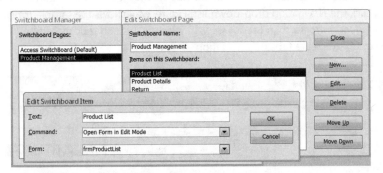

Figure 17-2 Use the Edit Switchboard Page dialog box to maintain the list of switchboard pages; each page can be edited and appropriate commands added to open forms and reports.

Figure 17-3 shows the sample navigation form *frmNavigation_Switchboard* in Design view with an example of the macro code that the switchboard uses to control the menus.

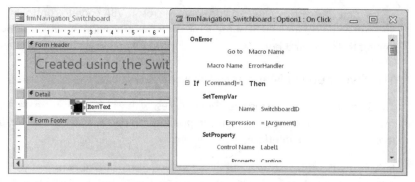

Figure 17-3 The macro code generated by the Switchboard Manager can be converted to VBA to provide an increased level of flexibility in the menu system.

This table-driven approach to generating menus is easily adapted to provide user-specific menus, and the navigation command data in the table can be directly edited. Your navigation design work can be accomplished with a single navigation form (an advantage over the previous technique of using push buttons on a form), and it is particularly productive if you need to add new menus or move commands to different menu areas.

The Navigation Control

As an alternative to the Switchboard Manager, an additional feature introduced in Access 2010 is the Navigation Control. The Navigation Control provides a more browser-based style of interface and is used for navigation in the browser when using Access Web Databases, but it can equally be used in standard databases.

To access the Navigation Control, on the ribbon, on the Create tab, in the Forms group, and then click the Navigation drop-down list. Figure 17-4 shows the sample *frmNavigation_NavigationControl* form in Layout view, in which forms and reports can be dragged onto the control to create tabs for navigation.

Figure 17-4 In Layout view, forms and reports can be easily added to the tab area of the Navigation Control.

The Navigation Control is fairly sophisticated and has macros that support swapping in and out forms to display information. This is a good choice of interface if you believe that you will eventually be using a web database. Because VBA is not supported in published Access web databases when viewed in a browser, if you intend to go down this route, then writing your navigation system by using only macros will save future redesign work.

The *TreeView* Control

The *TreeView* control can be used to create a number of powerful interfaces, including creating an interface that feels like Microsoft Outlook. The sample form *frmNavigation_Tree View* includes a *TreeView* control that is driven from the Switchboard Items table. The form is shown in Figure 17-5. The code behind the *Click* event on the *TreeView* control rebinds the unbound control to display an appropriate form.

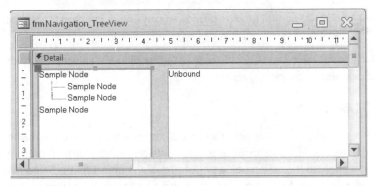

Figure 17-5 On the left is the *TreeView* control, and on the right, an unbound *Subform* control for dynamically displaying forms.

In Chapter 7, "Using Form Controls and Events," you looked in great detail at the programming behind the *TreeView* control, The approach we have taken in the samples database is to drive the menu system from the same table that was used in the previous section with the Switchboard Manager. As a user selects nodes in the tree, the appropriate form is switched into the unbound control shown in Figure 17-5.

If you plan to load forms into another form for display, then you need to take care with how you reference objects on the form. For example, if you open the form *frmCategoriesList*, you can refer to a control on the form as *Forms!frmCategoriesList!CategoryId*. However, if you open this inside your navigation form, the reference becomes *Forms!frmNavigation_TreeView!frmTarget.Form!CategoryId*. As we described in Chapter 4, "Applying the Access Object Model," if the form has a module, you can use the following reference to the control *Form_frmcategoriesList!CategoryId*, which works both when the form is opened independently on the desktop, and when it is opened inside another form by using a *SubForm* control.

The *Tab* Control

Tab controls can provide users with a convenient way to switch between two or more forms or different parts of an application. Figure 17-6 shows the dynamic tab interface described in Chapter 7.

Figure 17-6 The *Tab* control can also provide an easy-to-use interface for navigating through parts of an application.

The *Tab* control can effectively reduce the number of menu choices in a system by condensing groups of operations onto sets of tabs.

The Ribbon

The ribbon can be viewed as either a context-sensitive feature, such that when as a user loads different objects like forms or reports, different ribbons display, presenting operations that apply to the action being performed or the object that is being manipulated (for example, a Sort icon for sorting data displayed on a forms ribbon), or you can use a custom ribbon to provide a sophisticated Icon-driven navigation interface for the entire application. Figure 17-7 shows a system-wide ribbon that we constructed for the sample database to navigate to other forms. The forms in this case are the other navigation systems. We discuss the ribbon in greater detail beginning on page 639. The sample ribbon has additional code associated with it that grays out the currently selected item, which make it easier for users to see when they have clicked on an item in the ribbon.

Figure 17-7 The sample database ribbon is used to display the other navigation interfaces described in this chapter.

INSIDE OUT   Customizing an interface for each user

You might need to either customize the data that a user sees or customize the available menus in an application.

Customizing menus can be achieved by creating for a table of users and assigning each user a particular role, or using *Yes/No* flags to restrict access to administration or other menus (*the Environ$("Username")* function can be used to establish the user's Windows logon name). Then you can change your navigation technique to filter the available choices for each user, depending on the user's permissions. As an alternative, to using the *Environ$* function, you can also use the Windows API to establish the user's identity; this technique was described in Chapter 3, "Understanding the VBA Language Features."

Customizing data, for example, to restrict departments to viewing only their own data can be implemented by classifying your users by department, and then adding a department field to all appropriate tables. Then, by using a filter based on a user's department, you can limit access to only the appropriate data.

Opening Multiple Copies of a Form

Another useful interface design technique is to allow users to open multiple copies of a form, each capable of showing different views of the data. Implementing this involves a bit of object-oriented scripting. Some developers are put off by this part of VBA programming, but as was shown in Chapter 11, "Using Classes and Forms," opening multiple copies of a form is very easy and only takes a few lines of program code to richly enhance the interface.

Navigating with Combo and List Boxes

A very popular approach to reporting is to construct a master form for all reports that contains a combo or list box that displays a set of reports, and to display the reports from either a table of reports or by using program code to search for available reports.

Rather than show a simple example by using a table (which you can find in the Help system) we have included an example *frmCallBackListBox* that shows how to use a *CallBack* function on a list box to populate the *listbox* from program code. This example has an unbound *listbox* for which the *RowSourceType* is set to *ListReports*, the *RowSource* is left blank, and the following function is added to the form:

```
Function ListReports(fld As Control, id As Variant, _
    row As Variant, col As Variant, code As Variant) _
    As Variant
    Dim rpt As AccessObject
    Static strReports() As String ' Array to hold File Names
    Static lngCount As Integer
    Select Case code
        Case acLBInitialize:       ' Initialization
                ListReports = True
        Case acLBOpen:             ' Get the data
                ' Generate unique ID for control
                ListReports = Timer   ' This is very important
                ReDim strReports(CurrentProject.AllReports.Count - 1)
                lngCount = 0
                For Each rpt In CurrentProject.AllReports
                    If rpt.Name <> Me.Name Then
                        strReports(lngCount) = rpt.Name
                        lngCount = lngCount + 1
                    End If
                Next
        Case acLBGetRowCount:      ' return the row count
                ListReports = lngCount
        Case acLBGetColumnCount:   ' return the number of columns
                ListReports = 1       ' Match the property
        Case acLBGetColumnWidth:   ' specify column widths
                ListReports = -1      ' Match default
        Case acLBGetFormat:        ' Get format
                ListReports = -1      ' Return default
        Case acLBGetValue:         ' Return each row, column of data
                ListReports = strReports(row)
        Case acLBEnd:              ' Termination
    End Select
End Function
Private Sub lstReports_DblClick(Cancel As Integer)
    DoCmd.OpenReport lstReports.Value, acViewPreview
End Sub
```

The line of code during the *acLBOpen* processing that reads `ListReports = Timer` is particularly noteworthy; during initialization you need to provide a unique ID for the control and use the *Timer* function to do this. Without this line of code the *listbox* will fail to show any data.

The *Maximize, Popup, Modal,* and *MoveSize* Properties

Another general interface question to ask is this: do you want a Single Document Interface (SDI), in which a user can only interact with one form or report at a time, or do you want a Multiple Document Interface (MDI), in which users can switch between different parts of the system and work in multiple areas at the same time? Access is an MDI tool, but it can easily be made to work like an SDI, or like a wizard that takes a user through a sequence of operations. A related question is, do you want the interface objects maximized (filling the screen), or would you prefer sized windows? Maximizing forms leads you more toward an SDI.

If you want an MDI, then there are two other techniques with which you might want to become familiar. With the first technique, you can use the *DoCmd.MoveSize* command to provide absolute positioning and sizing of objects. The second technique is to switch off the *AutoResize* property on a form, which means it will remember the exact size that you last saved the form when in Design view and display the form using these settings.

Next you might want to think about the *Modal* and *PopUp* properties. Windows that have their *PopUp* property set to *True* respect the order of activation for each window and pop up on top of other pop-up windows. When the *Modal* property of a window is set to *True*, users are prevented from moving away from the window, usually until some required action on the window has been carried out. An associated question is whether you want to allow users to minimize or maximize a window, and if you allow this, what effect would it have on other windows that are not maximized; a normal window that is not maximized will become maximized if you open another form that is maximized. This can be stopped by either making the window a pop-up or by setting the *BorderStyle* to *Dialog* or *Thin*.

One further question to consider is screen resolution. In this case, you can either research the resolutions that your users typically use and make an appropriate decision regarding your form layouts, or look for a third-party tool to dynamically resize screens.

We have also seen techniques for synchronizing data both on forms with multiple subforms and between separate forms; the more you move toward an MDI, the more you need to consider the impact of users changing data in one form and how that will affect the data in other forms and take appropriate actions to refresh related data. You don't want a related form displaying *#Deleted*; this can occur if one form deletes the same data that is being displayed in a second form without a *Requery* operation being performed on the second form.

Ribbon Design

In this section, we will guide you through the process of creating custom ribbons. You might also find it useful to search the Internet for ribbon editors, which can greatly assist with building custom ribbons by checking that your ribbon XML is well formed (Access will not display your ribbon if it is not well formed, and it will not give any assistance in establishing why that has happened). The most common problems are failing to give items a unique identifier (which can be lessened by using a naming convention that we will describe shortly) and incorrectly spelling the names of graphical icons on the ribbon. Before developing your custom ribbons, you might want to go to File | Access Options | Client Settings and select the Show Add-In User Interface Errors check box. This instructs Access to display ribbon XML errors. The ribbon is a big subject, and in this section, we want to focus on general principles when developing a ribbon, and not on providing an exhaustive reference to each kind of control and their specific features.

The *USysRibbons* Table

Before you can begin working with the ribbon, you need to create a special system table. To do this, right-click the database Navigation window, select Navigation Options, and then select the Show System Objects check box, as shown in Figure 17-8. With this setting enabled, when viewing tables, you will see *MSys*-prefixed table names, and later, *USys*-prefixed table names, as well. These are the Access system tables.

Figure 17-8 Setting the Display Options to Show System Objects.

Next, you create the table shown in Figure 17-9, which contains two fields: the first is a text field to name the ribbon, and the second field is a memo that will hold the XML used to define the ribbon. Save this table with the special name **USysRibbons**.

Field Name	Data Type	Description
RibbonName	Text	
RibbonXML	Memo	

Figure 17-9 Creating the special system table, in which you can configure your custom ribbons.

You can create several different ribbons in the *USysRibbons* table. All of the ribbons that you place in this table are loaded and made available for you to use in your application (so after adding or changing a ribbon, you need to re-open the database). This means that you can define a system-wide ribbon for the application, and then override this default when displaying a particular form or a report; you can use these objects in the *Open* event to determine which ribbon to display, or specify the name of the ribbon with the *RibbonName* property.

The ribbons are written in XML, for which, unfortunately, the Microsoft Office family does not provide a built-in editor for constructing the XML or validating that the XML is "well formed." This can be quite painful, because if you get anything wrong in the XML, the ribbon either will not load without giving you error messages, or it will fail to function as anticipated. The most important factor in avoiding problems with ribbons is that each ribbon item has an identifier, and these identifiers need to be unique. We would recommend that you use a simple naming convention for the tags, our convention is to name each tag with the tab *tx*, group *gx*, and button *bx*, which means that button 2 in group 3 on tab 2 would be *t2g3b2*.

In the first line, xmlns is a reference to the schema for the ribbon, and the line *startFromScratch* means that we are defining a new ribbon which does not use any built-in features of the standard ribbons. The following code illustrates a very simple one-button ribbon:

```
<customUI xmlns="http://schemas.microsoft.com/office/2009/07/customui"
 onLoad="modR_OnRibbonLoad">
  <ribbon startFromScratch="true">
   <tabs>
   <tab id = "t1" label = "Menu Systems">
      <group id="t1g1" label = "PushButton"  >
         <button id="t1g1b1"
            label="PushButton Menu"
            imageMso="GroupListViewToolbar" size="large"
            getEnabled="modR_CallbackGetEnabled"
            onAction="modR_HandleOnAction"
            tag="frmNavigation_PushButton"/>
      </group>
   </tab>
    </tabs>
  </ribbon>
</customUI>
```

INSIDE OUT   The elements of a ribbon

The ribbon consist of a number of elements, including:

- **customUI**   Represents the custom ribbon. The *OnLoad* event enables you to get a reference in code to the ribbon.

- **ribbon**   Defines the ribbon.

- **tabs**   Represents the tabs on the ribbon.

- **tab**   Defines a tab. Each tab has an ID and label.

- **group**   Defines a group of controls in a tab. Each group has an ID and a label.

- **controls**   The individual items on the ribbon, such as buttons, combo boxes, and other controls.

The ribbon elements have events that reference procedures in your VBA code which are called *callbacks*; these are the points where you link in to take an action in response to the user interacting with the ribbon or the ribbon loading. The ribbon makes a callback into your VBA code.

Chapter 17

The *OnLoad* Callback

The *OnLoad* callback allows your VBA code to get set a variable to reference the ribbon. To begin, you need to add a reference to the Microsoft Office 14.0 Object Library and define a global variable to reference the ribbon. Then, you write the callback to assign this variable to the active ribbon when it is loaded:

```
Option Compare Database
Option Explicit
Global UIRibbon As IRibbonUI
Public Sub modR_OnRibbonLoad(ribbon As IRibbonUI)
' This gets called when the ribbon loads
    Set UIRibbon = ribbon
End Sub
```

If you look back to the XML you previously used to define the ribbon, you will spot the call to onLoad="modR_OnRibbonLoad".

The *OnAction* Callback

Use the *OnAction* callback to respond when a user clicks the ribbon icon control. The following code uses the convention that a tag that opens a form should have the prefix *frm* in the tag name; by using a convention for specifying the tag, you can write flexible and general purpose code in response to this event:

```
Public Sub modR_HandleOnAction(Control As IRibbonControl)
' Handles selections by the user
    If Left(Control.Tag, 3) = "frm" Then
        DoCmd.OpenForm Control.Tag
    End If
End Sub
```

If you look back to the XML that you previously used to define the ribbon, you will spot the call to onAction="modR_HandleOnAction" on the t1g1b1 button.

The *GetEnabled* Callback

One problem with the ribbon is that when a user clicks an item, there is no indication of what he selected. To assist the user, you can use a technique of graying out the last clicked ribbon element. To do this, you need a variable to store the last selected item, so at the top of the module you add the variable *Global strActiveTag As String* (there is another variable called *blEnableTheTag* that determines whether to enable or disable the active tag). Now, write the following callback to gray out the appropriate control:

```
Sub modR_CallbackGetEnabled(Control As IRibbonControl, _
                    ByRef enabled)
' Can be used to grey out the currently active tag
    If Control.id = strActiveTag Then
```

```
        If blEnableTheTag Then
            ' enable previously selected tag
            enabled = True
        Else
            ' user has selected the tag
            enabled = False
        End If
    Else
        ' any tag other than the active tag gets enabled
        enabled = True
    End If

End Sub
```

If you look back to the XML we previously used to define the ribbon, you will spot the call to getEnabled="modR_CallbackGetEnabled" on the t1g1b1 button.

The next piece of code is a little more complicated because you need to invalidate the control to trigger the callback to activate the code in *modR_CallbackGetEnabled*, which will enable the property to gray out the button. So you need to change the *OnAction* handler, as follows:

```
Public Sub modR_HandleOnAction(Control As IRibbonControl)
    If Nz(strActiveTag) <> "" Then
    ' causes the previously select tag to be unselected
        If Not UIRibbon Is Nothing Then
            blEnableTheTag = True
            UIRibbon.InvalidateControl strActiveTag
            DoEvents
        Else
            MsgBox "UIRibbon is invalid, close and re-open the database"
            Exit Sub
        End If    End If
    strActiveTag = Control.id
    ' causes the currently active tag to be greyed out as selected
    If Not UIRibbon Is Nothing Then
        ' Exclude Reports as they display their own ribbon
        If Left(Control.Tag, 3) <> "rpt" Then
            blEnableTheTag = False
            UIRibbon.InvalidateControl strActiveTag
            DoEvents
        End If
    Else
        MsgBox "UIRibbon is invalid, close and re-open the database"
        Exit Sub
    End If
End Sub
```

The key method in the previous code is the *InvalidateControl* method, which causes the control to be re-initialized and the enabled callback to fire. You will also see that we have added *DoEvents*. This is useful for debugging because it allows any asynchronous event processing to be completed before you code stops at an appropriate breakpoint (otherwise, you might get error messages displayed).

Setting a Default Ribbon for the Application

After you add new ribbons to *USysRibbons* (or make changes to it), you need to close and re-open the database to make the new ribbons available for selection. You can select the ribbon that will be displayed when the database is opened. To do this, in Backstage View, click Options, and then click Current Database. In the Ribbon And Toolbar Options section, choose the ribbon from the Ribbon Name drop-down list, as shown in Figure 17-10.

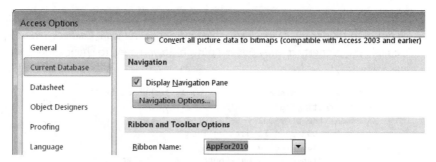

Figure 17-10 Setting the default ribbon to display when a database opens.

If you do not set this system-wide ribbon, you can still use custom ribbons for specific forms and reports, as will be discussed later.

Whether you are using the built-in ribbon or a custom one, you can turn off the system-wide ribbon (note this is a very useful command in applications when you do not want to show any ribbons) by using the following command:

```
DoCmd.ShowToolbar "Ribbon", acToolbarNo
```

To turn it back on, replace acToolbarNo with acToolbarYes. Also note that opening a database while holding down the Shift key stops the custom ribbon from being displayed.

Images

The property imageMso="GroupListViewToolbar" in the XML code provides the ribbon item icon. You can either use one of more than 700 images built into Office for this, or you can define and load your own images. To make it easier to find the right icon, you can download the *Office 2010 Addin Icon Gallery* (available at *http://www.microsoft.com/ download/en/details.aspx?id=21103*), which is a Microsoft Word document containing all these images. Alternatively, Figure 17-11 shows the mouse hovering over built-in ribbon options when customizing the built-in ribbon (right-click a ribbon and select Customize The Ribbon). Use this to quickly get the *imageMSO* for built-in ribbon icons in Access (note that XML is case-sensitive, so you need to ensure that the image names are referenced exactly as they are shown).

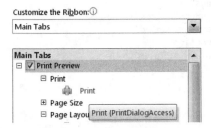

Figure 17-11 Finding the image references for built-in ribbon icons.

Your image options are not limited to the Office gallery; you can also load your own images for use in the ribbon. To do this, add a callback reference in the XML as follows:

```
<customUI xmlns="http://schemas.microsoft.com/office/2009/07/customui"
 onLoad="modR_OnRibbonLoad" loadImage="modR_GetImage">
```

You then add your reference to the image file in the XML:

```
        <group id="t1g7" label = "About"  >
            <button id="t1g6b7"
                label="About"
                image="Book.jpg" size="large"
                getEnabled="modR_CallbackGetEnabled"
                onAction="modR_HandleOnAction"
                tag="frmAbout"/>
        </group>
```

Finally, write the callback function, which will automatically be called to load any images:

```
Public Sub modR_GetImage(imageID As String, _
                    ByRef image As Variant)
    ' Call back will automatically load any images
    Set image = LoadPicture(CurrentProject.Path & "\" & imageID)
End Sub
```

Dynamically Changing Tab Visibility and Focus

You might want to alter the tabs available on the ribbon dynamically, based on the type of user who is working with the application. You can accomplish this by setting the visibility of a tab. To illustrate this, you will create a second administration tab. To begin, you add the following XML to the first tab on your ribbon:

```
<group id="t1g6" label = "Change Ribbon"  >
    <button id="t1g6b1"
        label="Toggle Admin Menus"
        imageMso="AdministrationHome" size="large"
        getEnabled="modR_CallbackGetEnabled"
        onAction="modR_HandleOnAction"
        tag="cmd_Admin"/>
    </group>
</tab>
```

Here is the second tab:

```
<tab id = "t2" label = "Administration" getVisible="modR_GetVisibleCallback">
    <group id="t2g1" label = "Ribbon"  >
        <button id="t2g1b1"
            label="USysRibbons"
            imageMso="RibbonGiveFeedback" size="large"
            getEnabled="modR_CallbackGetEnabled"
            onAction="modR_HandleOnAction"
            tag="frmUSysRibbons"/>
    </group>
</tab>
```

In the event that handles user actions, add the following code (this code also defines a global variable called *blAdministrator* to flag whether a user is an administrator):

```
If Control.Tag = "cmd_Admin" Then
    ' display the admin menus
    blAdministrator = Not blAdministrator
    strActiveTag = ""
    UIRibbon.Invalidate
End If
```

Notice in the definition of the XML for *t2* that there is another callback named *getVisible*. Using this, you can write the following code in response to this event:

```
Public Sub modR_GetVisibleCallback(Control As IRibbonControl, _
                            ByRef visible As Variant)
' called by each tab when the ribbon loads
' used to control which tabs users can see
    If Not blAdministrator Then
        Select Case Control.Id
        Case "t2": visible = False
        Case Else:
            visible = True
        End Select
```

```
        Else
            visible = True
            If Control.Id = "t2" Then
                ' changes focus to the administration ribbon
                UIRibbon.ActivateTab "t2"
            End If
        End If
End Sub
```

The previous code also makes a call to *ActivateTab* which sets the focus to the newly added administrator tab.

INSIDE OUT   Office 2007 and the File menu

If you are creating a ribbon for Office 2007, you can customize the Office menu by using the following XML fragment (which enables only the compact and repair option for the database):

```xml
<customUI xmlns="http://schemas.microsoft.com/office/2006/01/customui">
  <ribbon startFromScratch="true">
  <officeMenu>
   <button idMso="FileCompactAndRepairDatabase" insertBeforeMso
="FileCloseDatabase" />
   <button idMso="FileOpenDatabase" visible="false"/>
   <button idMso="FileNewDatabase" visible="false"/>
   <splitButton idMso="FileSaveAsMenuAccess" visible="false" />
  </officeMenu>
```

You will also notice that the schema reference for 2007 is different than that of 2010.

The Backstage View

There are probably two actions that you will want to undertake with the Backstage view: the first is to disable built-in features, and the second is to add your own specialized features. The following code limits Backstage view to only show a minimum number of options (this code is in the ribbon *AppFor2010_BackStage* and added before the </customUI> tag at the end of the XML):

```xml
<backstage>
   <tab idMso="TabInfo" visible="true"/>
   <button idMso="FileSave" visible="false"/>
   <button idMso="SaveObjectAs" visible="false"/>
   <button idMso="FileSaveAsCurrentFileFormat" visible="false"/>
   <button idMso="FileOpen" visible="false"/>
```

Chapter 17

```
    <button idMso="FileCloseDatabase" visible="false"/>
    <tab idMso="TabRecent" visible="false"/>
    <tab idMso="TabNew" visible="false"/>
    <tab idMso="TabPrint" visible="true"/>
    <tab idMso="TabShare" visible="false"/>
    <tab idMso="TabHelp" visible="false"/>
    <button idMso="ApplicationOptionsDialog" visible="false"/>
    <button idMso="FileExit" visible="true"/>
</backstage>
```

Ribbons for Forms and Reports

You can either design one single ribbon for your application, and then when performing an operation such as print preview use the appropriate part of the main ribbon, or you can design a special ribbon for only previewing a report. In the sample database, we have created a ribbon called *PrintRibbon*; the following code shows the XML definition for one of the icons on this ribbon:

```
<group id="t1g1" label = "Print"  >
   <button id="tpg1b1"
      label="Print"
      imageMso="PrintDialogAccess" size="large"
      getEnabled="modR_CallbackGetEnabled"
      onAction="modR_HandleOnActionReports"
      tag="cmd_Print"/>
</group>
```

In the example report *rptCategories*, on the *Open* event, we have associated this ribbon with the report:

```
Private Sub Report_Open(Cancel As Integer)
    Me.RibbonName = "PrintRibbon"
    strReportBeingPreviewed = Me.Name
End Sub
```

The ribbon has two commands associated with the icons, *cmd_Print* and *cmd_ClosePrint-Preview*, and you can modify the callback event handler to take appropriate actions by adding the following code to the routine *modR_HandleOnActionReports*:

```
' Report Actions
If Control.Tag = "cmd_ClosePrintPreview" Then
    ' Close the report
    strActiveTag = ""
    UIRibbon.Invalidate
    DoCmd.SelectObject acReport, strReportBeingPreviewed
    DoCmd.Close
End If
```

```
If Control.Tag = "cmd_Print" Then
    ' Close the report
    strActiveTag = ""
    UIRibbon.Invalidate
    DoCmd.OpenReport strReportBeingPreviewed, acViewNormal
    DoCmd.Close
End If
```

Figure 17-12 depicts the custom ribbon being displayed for the report.

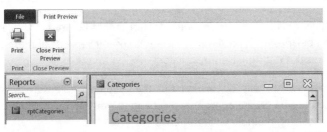

Figure 17-12 The custom ribbon for previewing a report. The XML for this ribbon could be added to the main ribbon if you want a single ribbon for all operations in the application.

INSIDE OUT   Loading a custom ribbon

You have seen how an application can have a custom ribbon, and that additionally, you can specify individual ribbons for forms and reports. These are all made available from the ribbons defined in the *USysRibbons* table.

You have also seen how to dynamically alter the available system-wide ribbon. Although the system-wide ribbon cannot be dynamically replaced, you can dynamically load additional new ribbons by using the following:

```
Application.LoadCustomUI(CustomUIName, CustomUIXML)
```

You can either construct this in code or read it from a table of data. The *CustomUIName* must be different from any ribbons defined in *USysRibbons* or previously loaded. These ribbons can then be used when displaying forms or reports, for example, when changing the available options depends on the type of use.

32-Bit and 64-Bit Environments

Office 2010 introduced VBA7, which is available in both 32-bit and 64-bit installations (for the 64-bit installation, you must be running a 64-bit version of Windows). You can only install either the 32-bit or 64-bit versions of VBA on a single computer; as of this writing, the default installation is the 32-bit version on both 32-bit and 64-bit platforms.

Existing 32-bit Office applications work unchanged on a 64-bit or 32-bit platform. However, if you are planning to use the 64-bit version of Office, your 32-bit applications might need some modification.

Later, when we discuss ACCDE files, you will find that you need an appropriate file created either with the 32-bit or 64-bit version of Office to be used by other Office installations.

32-bit ActiveX controls such as the *TreeView* control cannot be used in Office 64-bit (it cannot load 32-bit binaries), and presently there are no 64-bit versions of these controls; for many developers this is a significant restriction.

If you have Windows API calls (discussed later), then you need to ensure that the API procedures using Office 64-bit are appropriately changed, you can use appropriate compiler directives if supporting multiple environments.

In Chapter 2, "Understanding the VBA Language Structure," we discussed conditional compilation; there are special compiler constants that you can use to isolate code, depending on whether the target computer has the 32-bit or 64-bit versions of Office (note that you do not need to define these as they are built into the VBA environment). The general form for detecting different versions is shown in the following code:

```
#if Vba7 then
' Code is running in the new VBA7 editor
    #if Win64 then
    ' Code is running in 64-bit version of Microsoft Office
    #else
    ' Code is running in 32-bit version of Microsoft Office
    #end if
#else
' Code is running in VBA version 6 or earlier
#end if
```

You can see an example of this in ApplicationDevelopment64Bit.accdb, which is designed to use either the 32-bit or 64-bit VBA API.

Working with the Windows Registry

The Windows Registry is a useful place in which to store configuration information for an application. VBA supports the following procedures for reading and writing registry keys to the hive HKEY_CURRENT_USER\Software\VB and VBA Program Settings. If you need to read/write to other parts of the registry, you need to use Windows API calls:

```
Sub modReg_RegistryFunctions()
    ' Demonstrates registry functions
    Stop
    ' saving key information this creates the section
    SaveSetting strAppName, "General", "Version", "V1.0" ' save a version number
    SaveSetting strAppName, "General", "Country", "USA" ' save country info
    ' reading a single key
    Dim strKey As String
    strKey = GetSetting(strAppName, "General", "Version")
    Debug.Print strKey
    ' reading all keys into an array
    Dim varKeys As Variant
    Dim lngCount As Long
    varKeys = GetAllSettings(strAppName, "General")
    If Not IsEmpty(varKeys) Then
        For lngCount = 0 To UBound(varKeys)
            Debug.Print varKeys(lngCount, 0) & " : " & varKeys(lngCount, 1)
        Next
    End If
    ' delete the entire section of keys
    DeleteSetting strAppName, "General"
End Sub
```

You should consider that in some companies, the registry is locked down and a user might not have privileges on their computer to write information into the registry.

Using the Windows API

You can use API calls to link in to features that are not available in Access, but are available either in a part of the Windows environment, or supplied by a third-party as a DLL. Although this is a popular technique with developers, you should realize that you are building into your application dependencies on these components subsequently being available as the Windows platforms evolve. With Access 2010, if you are planning to support both 32-bit and 64-bit versions, you need to allow for making changes in these API calls, depending on which version is being used; the compiler directives discussed earlier in this chapter can be used to detect the appropriate system version.

Access Developers do not tend to excessively use Windows API calls, but there are situations in which you desperately need to perform an operation that is not supported by the VBA programming environment and not available through any suitable ActiveX control. If you intend to use an API, search online for some code, because if you have to work out the appropriate mechanism for calling an API from scratch, it can be quite difficult. For example, you can download a file called win32api.txt that contains a list of API calls and associated structures. You can download this file from *http://support.microsoft.com/kb/178020*. The file contains 32-bit information on the Windows API, which you could convert to 64-bit. In Chapter 3, we constructed a function called *modErrorHandler_GetUserName()* that illustrates how to retrieve a user's name by using the API.

Using API calls mean that you are likely to need to share data between Access and the external program; this means that an area of memory needs to be allocated for this shared communication. Because both Access and the external program could be reading and writing to memory, it is up to you to ensure that variables are correctly defined; otherwise, the communications can break down. This is also the reason for ensuring that calls are correctly defined for 32-bit and 64-bit communications.

As an example of using an API call, you can look in win32.api.txt, where there is a function for flashing a window that has the following declaration:

```
Declare Function FlashWindow Lib "user32" _
                        (ByVal hwnd As Long, _
                        ByVal bInvert As Long) As Long
```

Declare statements also allow the use of an Alias, with which you can use an API call when the name could conflict with some other procedure or built-in function name. In the following declaration, you can see how to use the Alias:

```
Declare Function API_FlashWindow Lib "user32" _
                        Alias "FlashWindow" _
                        (ByVal hwnd As Long, _
                        ByVal bInvert As Long) As Long
```

This is an interesting function, because to flash the window, you need to know the window's handle *hwnd*; an Access form has this property. You can then write a procedure that uses the Windows API call to flash the window:

```
Sub modAPI_FlashMe(hwnd As Long)
    Const lngMaxPos As Long = 40
    Dim lngCount As Long
    Dim lngRet As Long
    Dim lngState As Long
    Dim lngPause As Long
    lngState = 1
    For lngCount = 1 To 50
        lngRet = modAPI_Flash(hwnd, lngState)
        ' Toggle the state between 1 and 0
        lngState = lngState + 1 Mod 2
        For lngPause = 1 To lngMaxPos
            DoEvents
        Next
    Next
End Sub
```

In the form *frmAbout*, we have added a command button to flash the window. This code could be modified to continue flashing a window when a given condition holds by using a timer event:

```
Private Sub cmdFlash_Click()
    modAPI_FlashMe Me.hwnd
End Sub
```

If you need to write your API call for 64-bit Office, you should download the article from *http://msdn.microsoft.com/en-us/library/ee691831.aspx*, which will help you make the conversion.

The equivalent declaration for our *FlashWindow* function in the 64-bit form is as follows:

```
Declare PtrSafe Function API_Flash Lib "user32" _
                          Alias "FlashWindow" _
                          (ByVal hwnd As LongLong, _
                          ByVal bInvert As LongLong) As LongLong
```

In the sample database, we have added the compiler directives to use the appropriate 32-bit or 64-bit calls and application code. We have also provided a copy of the sample database called ApplicationDevelopment64Bit.accdb, which has all references to the 32-bit ActiveX controls removed.

Completing an Application

In this section, you will look at a number of techniques that can be used to complete your application.

Splash Screens

If you place a .bmp file in the same directory as your application, and the file has the same name as your application, Access will display your custom splash screen as the application loads.

Progress Bars

In Chapter 4, "Applying the Access Object Model," we discussed how to use the built-in progress meter by using the *SysCmd* function, and how to create your own custom progress form. We also discussed using the *DoCmd.Echo* and *DoCmd.Hourglass* actions when you need greater control of what a user sees when your application is performing a large amount of processing.

INSIDE OUT
Exploiting IntelliSense in a standard module

Because the VBA environment provides IntelliSense to code defined in a standard module, you can perform a trick that makes it look like you have created a clever object model inside Access, without in fact creating any objects or doing any complex programming. This is particularly useful when you need to combine a sequence of useful functions into a single operation. As an example, create a standard module, add the following code, and then save the module using the name **Hourglass**:

```
Public Sub TurnOn()
    DoCmd.Hourglass True
    DoCmd.Echo False
End Sub

Public Sub TurnOff()
    DoCmd.Hourglass False
    DoCmd.Echo True
End Sub
```

Then, in your code you can just type **Hourglass.TurnOff**, and as you type, IntelliSense shows you the option to TurnOn or TurnOff.

Error Handling

Adding error handling (described in Chapter 3) becomes increasingly important as you work toward a more completed application. In particular, if you are creating ACCDE files, then as there is no source code recording where an error occurred, this becomes very important. Also, in Access Runtime it becomes essential as untrapped errors will cause your application to terminate.

Locking Down an Application

In Chapter 4, you learned how to lock down your application and prevent users from attempting to bypass startup code and display the database window. Making an ACCDE or delivering in Runtime are also very popular methods for preventing users from stepping outside your application. After you have locked down an application, it is not easy to prevent someone from using another copy of Access to extract data or other design objects or link to data in your application. The only option in this case would be to password-protect the database, or to protect your data, put the data in SQL Server.

Deploying Applications

In this section, you will look at issues relating to deploying Access applications.

Protecting Your Design with ACCDE Files

To make an ACCDE file, your code must all be compiled and not contain any errors. This file can then be distributed to users, and you can feel comfortable in the knowledge that your application code will be protected, and users will not be able to make any design changes to the forms and other objects in the database. An ACCDE file constructed with a specific version of Access will not run on a computer with any other version of Access, this also applies to an ACCDE constructed with 32-bit or 64-bit versions (note that this also applies to having the same Service Packs applied to the environment).

Runtime Deployment

Using Access Runtime (which is free), you can redistribute your application to users who do not have Access. In the Runtime environment, there is no built-in ribbon, no database window and no ability to make design changes. The Runtime tools include a packaging feature with which you can create an installation set, which will both install Runtime and your application. This can be obtained from the Microsoft Download Center (or search the web for the Access 2010 Runtime Download). It is essential to have good error handling, as untrapped errors in program code will cause the application to terminate.

Single and Multiple Application Files

Chapter 12, "Linking Access Tables," points out that it is common to split an Access data-base into two files. The data file can be shared, but you have the option to either have all users share the same application file, or give each user a separate copy of the application.

The advantages in giving each user a separate copy to install on their local computer include:

- Improved performance.

- Reduced bloat.

- Less risk if the application becomes corrupt.

- Easier to manage the need for local user-specific results tables, and changes to queries made in code.

- Avoids problems with getting users out of the shared application file.

The disadvantage is that you must allow for updating files to each users location if the application is updated (there are third-party tools that can assist with this).

DSNs and Relinking Applications

If you are linking to other data sources such as SQL Server, and you choose to use one of the more recent ODBC or OLEDB drivers, then you need to ensure that these are installed on the user's computer. If you're using a Machine DSN, this will need configuring on the individual computers, and if you're using a File DSN, then you will need appropriate code for relinking your application. These topics are discussed in Chapter 12.

Depending on References

If you have added references to your application, for example, to program the *TreeView* control or for other custom controls, you should allow for the need to identify if a computer has a missing or broken reference (this was discussed in Chapter 2).

Custom controls need to be available on each user's computer; a control such as the *TreeView* can normally be anticipated as being already on a user's computer, but third-party controls will need to be installed on a computer. Also remember that 32-bit controls are not supported on Office 64-bit.

Updating Applications

Getting users out of an Access application has always been difficult; placing your data in SQL Server can resolve some but not all issues. Below are some suggested tactics for handling this problem:

- Create a message table into which you can add a message indicating when a system is going down for maintenance, and add a *KickOut* flag to indicate when you want to immediately force people out. Examples of code for this are provided in Chapter 6, "Using Forms and Events."

- When a user starts the application, if within a fixed time period of the maintenance point, then display a warning to the user. If the *KickOut* flag is set, then immediately exit them from the application.

- Add a hidden form or attach to the switchboard a timer event that periodically checks the *KickOut* flag and exits the user if the flag is set or a maintenance time has been reached.

- Send emails to users.

- Use network administration features to close open files. This runs the risk of corruption.

Summary

In this chapter, you looked at different techniques for creating a user interface that integrates your forms and other design objects into an application. You also explored several topics relating to completing an application and issues surrounding the deployment of an application.

Using ADO and ADOX

ActiveX Data Objects 660

Working with SQL Server 663

ADOX 672

A number of years ago, there was a great controversy regarding the future of the Data Access Objects (DAO) model, which was the way to manipulate data in the Joint Engine Technology (JET) that underpins Microsoft Access, and whether Microsoft would continue to support the technology. At the same time, a new technology called ActiveX Data Objects (ADO) was emerging. However, with the advent of Access 2010, the JET Engine technology, has been rebranded as Access Connectivity Engine (ACE) and became the inheritor of the DAO technology—which has given DAO a new lease on life. In the intervening period, ADO has progressed to ADO.NET and has enjoyed a great degree of success, becoming a very well-established technology.

Most Microsoft VBA developers use DAO in preference to ADO. ADO is less integrated with Access than DAO; the advantage of ADO is that it is a lightweight technology giving improved performance, and it has a wider support for different data sources, offering a number of more sophisticated features when working with other types of data sources.

ADO is a complementary technology to DAO, so if you are like most Access programmers, who have a large amount of time and money invested in DAO, you look to ADO only when you need to take advantage of specific features. If you are going down the Access Data Project (ADP) route with SQL Server, then ADO is the natural choice because an ADP does not include the DAO programming model.

In this chapter, you see how ADO can enhance the VBA programming experience. The final part of the chapter looks at ADOX, which is another library that complements and extends ADO to be able to look at the structures inside the database. ADOX can be regarded as a technology that fills in the bits that ADO can't see, as compared to DAO; DAO is similar to ADO plus ADOX in this respect, but the advantage of ADOX is that it works with other data sources such as SQL Server.

After reading this chapter, you will

- Understand how to use ADO to add value to your Access applications beyond what can be achieved with DAO.

- See how ADOX can be used to extract design information from a data source.

> **Note**
>
> As you read through this chapter, we encourage you to also use the companion content sample databases, ADOExamples.accdb, DocADOX.accdb, and other script files, which can be downloaded from the book's catalog page.

ActiveX Data Objects

If you are working with an ADP, then your VBA project will already have the required references for ADO objects. For a standard Access database or MDB database, the references need to be added to the project (see Figure 18-1). To add the relevant references for this section, you need the Microsoft ActiveX Data Objects 6.0 Library (ADO), and later you will require the Microsoft ADO Ext. 6.0 for DDL and Security (ADOX).

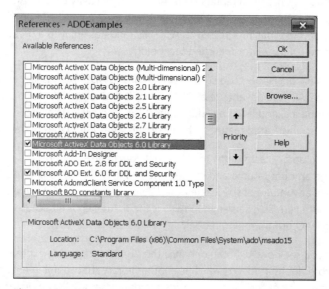

Figure 18-1 When you're working with an Access database or MDB database, use the References dialog box to add the required references.

Figure 18-2 presents a simplified ADO model. Compare this to the DAO model discussed in Chapter 5, "Understanding the Data Access Object Model," and you will see that the ADO model contains far fewer objects. The key object in ADO is the connection. Within a connection, you can either execute a command or open a *Recordset*.

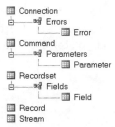

Figure 18-2 The ADO Model.

You will find that ADO programming is very similar to DAO programming. One of the most obvious differences is when you want to edit a record. In DAO, you need to start with an *rst. Edit* command; in ADO, you don't need this command:

```
Sub modADO_EditData()
' Example of editing a record
    Dim rst As New ADODB.Recordset
    rst.Open "Customers", CurrentProject.Connection, adOpenDynamic, adLockOptimistic
    Do While Not rst.EOF
        Debug.Print rst!Id
        rst![E-Mail Address] = "any@ascassociates.biz "
        rst.Update
        rst.MoveNext
    Loop
    rst.Close
    Set rst = Nothing
End Sub
```

ADO leads you to think more carefully about what happens when you try a simple operation like interacting with data because you will find that you need to specify the correct parameters to make an operation work.

Cursors

A *cursor* is another term for a *Recordset*. You can either manipulate the *Recordset* data in your own computer's memory, or you can manipulate it in the memory of the server. If you are working with a pure Access database, there is no server involved, but once connected to SQL Server, there is, of course, a server, so you need to think about what this means.

The DAO is very clever: it copies your data into your computer's memory, and then writes back the changes to the database (Access or SQL Server). What DAO effectively achieves is to disconnect the data from the server while you edit it, and then write back the changes. The technical term for this is a client-side cursor.

Chapter 18

With ADO, you are not restricted in this way, because you have two options. First, you can have a client-side cursor, but not just edit one record. You can edit several records and then perform a batch update of all the changed records. Second, you can choose a server-side cursor.

INSIDE OUT   Cursor location, type, and lock type

ADO makes you think more carefully about how a *Recordset* will operate. Here are three key points to note:

- **CursorLocation** Controls whether the *Recordset* is in the server's memory or your computer's memory. The default setting is *adUseServer*, and the alternative setting is *adUseClient*.

- **CursorType** Controls the updateability of the *Recordset* and can have an impact on performance. The default setting is *adOpenForwardOnly*, and the alternative settings are *adOpenDynamic*, *adOpenKeyset*, or *adOpenStatic*.

- **LockType** Controls the locking and can have an impact on both performance and conflict resolution. The default setting is *adLockReadOnly*, and the alternative settings are *adLockBatchOptimistic*, *adLockOptimistic*, or *adLockPessimistic*.

Not all these options are applicable with Access, but with other data sources such as SQL Server, more of them do apply.

Asynchronous Operations

In Chapter 10, "Using Classes and Events," you saw how by using an ADO *Recordset* and *WithEvents*, you can construct batch processing, during which the client application fires an asynchronous server-side process that allows the Access application to continue execution, and then receive notification of the completed operation from the *ExecuteComplete* method. There is no equivalent feature in DAO to this asynchronous operation.

Forms and ADO *Recordsets*

In Chapter 11, "Using Classes and Forms," we provided code for binding a form to an ADO *Recordset* by using a VBA class. As an alternative, you can avoid using classes and directly embed the code in the form, as demonstrated in the sample database form *frmADOProducts* (shown in the following code example) To construct this form, you start with a bound DAO form, and then empty the *RecordSet* property and add the appropriate code, as shown in the following:

```
Option Compare Database
Option Explicit

Dim p_cn As ADODB.Connection
Dim p_rst As ADODB.Recordset

Private Sub Form_Close()
    p_rst.Close
    Set p_rst = Nothing
    p_cn.Close
    Set p_cn = Nothing
End Sub

Private Sub Form_Load()
   Set p_cn = CurrentProject.Connection
   Set p_rst = New ADODB.Recordset
   With p_rst
      Set .ActiveConnection = p_cn
      .Source = "SELECT * FROM Products"
      .LockType = adLockOptimistic
      .CursorType = adOpenKeyset
      .CursorLocation = adUseClient
      .Open
   End With
   Set Me.Recordset = p_rst
End Sub
```

Working with SQL Server

In this section, you will look at using ADO with SQL Server. You will see demonstrations of how this supports operations that are either not available when working with the DAO or offer improved functionality over using DAO.

Connection Strings

When using DAO to connect to SQL Server, it is possible to use different versions of the ODBC drivers. The ODBC drivers also have corresponding OLEDB providers that can be used with ADO. If you need to use newer features associated with a particular version of SQL Server, then you need to use one of the appropriate providers (see Table 18-1). The computer that has SQL Server components installed will already have the correct providers; on other computers, you need to download and install the drivers. The drivers and further information can be obtained from *http://msdn.microsoft.com/en-us/data/aa937733.aspx*.

Table 18-1 **OLEDB Providers**

SQL Server version	Provider	ODBC driver name
All Versions	SQLOLEDB	SQL Server
2005	SQLNCLI	SQL Native Client
2008 and 2008 R2	SQLNCLI10	SQL Server Native Client 10.0

Examples of the connection strings for each provider are shown in the following code example. These examples use integrated Windows authentication connecting to the database master on a SQL Server called VISTAULTRA64\VISTAULTRA64_08:

```
Provider=SQLOLEDB;Data Source=VISTAULTRA64\VISTAULTRA64_08;Initial
Catalog=master;Integrated Security=SSPI;
Provider=SQLNCLI;Data Source=VISTAULTRA64\VISTAULTRA64_08;Initial
Catalog=master;Integrated Security=SSPI;
Provider=SQLNCLI10;Data Source=VISTAULTRA64\VISTAULTRA64_08;Initial
Catalog=master;Integrated Security=SSPI;
```

Connecting to SQL Server

In some situations, you might find that an ADO connection test can respond faster than an ODBC connection test. The code that follows illustrates how to test a connection by using both ADO and DAO. The timeout settings need to be set long enough to allow for delays in the network. If you only have one instance of SQL Server installed on your computer, you could consider using *(local)* to replace your server name in these examples:

```
Sub modSQL_ADOConnectionTest()
' Example of testing an ODBC Connection
' with the timeout set to 10 seconds
    Dim conn As New ADODB.Connection
    Dim txtConnectionString As String
    txtConnectionString = "Provider=SQLOLEDB;" & _
                          "SERVER=VISTAULTRA64\SQL2008R2;" & _
                          "Initial Catalog=Northwind;" & _
                          "Integrated Security=SSPI"
    conn.ConnectionString = txtConnectionString
    conn.ConnectionTimeout = 10
    On Error Resume Next
    conn.Open
    If Err <> 0 Then
        Stop
        Exit Sub
    End If
    Dim rst As New ADODB.Recordset
    rst.ActiveConnection = conn
    rst.Open ("SELECT @@VERSION")
    Dim ver As String
    ver = Nz(rst(0))
```

```
        MsgBox ver, vbInformation, "Server Version"
        rst.Close
        conn.Close
        Set rst = Nothing
        Set conn = Nothing
    End Sub
```

The test with DAO is as follows:

```
Sub modSQL_DAOConnectionTest()
' Example of testing an ODBC Connection
' with the timeout set to 10 seconds
    Dim db As DAO.Database
    Dim rst As DAO.Recordset
    Dim qdef As DAO.QueryDef
    Dim txtConnectionString As String
    txtConnectionString = "ODBC;DRIVER=SQL Server;" & _
                          "SERVER=VISTAULTRA64\SQL2008R2;" & _
                          "DATABASE=Northwind;" & _
                          "Trusted_Connection=Yes"
    Set db = CurrentDb
    Set qdef = db.CreateQueryDef("")
    qdef.Connect = txtConnectionString
    qdef.ReturnsRecords = True
    qdef.ODBCTimeout = 10
    qdef.SQL = "SELECT @@VERSION"
    On Error Resume Next
    Set rst = qdef.OpenRecordset()
    If Err <> 0 Then
        Stop
        Exit Sub
    End If
    Dim ver As String
    ver = Nz(rst(0))
    MsgBox ver, vbInformation, "Server Version"
    rst.Close
    qdef.Close
    db.Close
End Sub
```

INSIDE OUT   Connection time

In the sample database for the connection code using ADO and DAO, there are timing variables that measure the time for completing the operation. ADO can be very useful for more quickly establishing whether a connection to a server has been successful, and this can be a useful technique if the ODBC connections are timing out due to incorrect information in the connection string (note that you will probably only see differences here when operating over networks).

Command Object

With ADO, you can use the command object to parameterize a block of SQL by using the ? (question mark) character to indicate a parameter in the SQL (this is an example of an implicit parameter and we have not specified the parameter type) as follows:

```
Sub modSQL_CommandObject()
    ' Example of a command object using a parameter
    Dim conn As New ADODB.Connection
    Dim cmd As New ADODB.Command
    Dim rst As New ADODB.Recordset
    Dim param As ADODB.Parameter
    Dim txtConnectionString As String
    txtConnectionString = "Provider=SQLOLEDB;" & _
                          "SERVER=VISTAULTRA64\SQL2008R2;" & _
                          "Initial Catalog=Northwind;" & _
                          "Integrated Security=SSPI"
    conn.ConnectionString = txtConnectionString
    cmd.CommandText = "SELECT * FROM Customers WHERE City = ?"
    cmd.CommandType = adCmdText
    cmd.ActiveConnection = conn.ConnectionString
    cmd.Parameters(0) = "London"
    For Each param In cmd.Parameters
        Debug.Print param.Name, param.Value
    Next
    Set rst = cmd.Execute()
    Do While Not rst.EOF
        Debug.Print rst!CompanyName
        rst.MoveNext
    Loop
    rst.Close
    Set rst = Nothing
    Set cmd = Nothing
    Set conn = Nothing
End Sub
```

This flexibility is not something that you can produce using DAO, because a *QueryDef* does not allow you create parameters in code.

Stored Procedures

In addition to accepting an input parameter on a stored procedure, stored procedures can also return output parameters back to the calling application. You can also use the *Return* statement, which is useful for passing back an integer flag to indicate success or failure with the procedure. In the following example, a stored procedure accepts one input parameter, one output parameter, and uses the return code (usp_CountOrdersByDate2.sql):

```
CREATE PROC usp_CountOrdersByDate2 @Thedate DATETIME,
                                    @OrderCount INT OUTPUT
AS
BEGIN
    SET @OrderCount = (SELECT COUNT(*) FROM Orders
    WHERE RequiredDate = @Thedate)
    RETURN(-1)
END
GO
-- Testing
DECLARE @OC INT
DECLARE @RV INT
exec @RV = usp_CountOrdersByDate2 '16 August 1996', @OC OUTPUT
-- Alternative without the return value
-- exec usp_CountOrdersByDate2 '16 August 1996', @OC OUTPUT
Print @oc
Print @RV
GO
```

The following code illustrates how to pass the parameter into, and receive the parameter
back from the procedure. Note that if you are using the return value, it must be defined as
the first parameter:

```
Sub modSQL_CommandObjectAndStoredProcedure()
    ' Example of a command object using input and output parameters
    Dim conn As New ADODB.Connection
    Dim cmd As New ADODB.Command
    Dim param As ADODB.Parameter
    Dim txtConnectionString As String
    txtConnectionString = "Provider=SQLOLEDB;" & _
                          "SERVER=VISTAULTRA64\SQL2008R2;" & _
                          "Initial Catalog=Northwind;" & _
                          "Integrated Security=SSPI"
    conn.ConnectionString = txtConnectionString
    cmd.CommandText = "usp_CountOrdersByDate2"
    ' Note the above gets changed to { call usp_CountOrdersByDate2 }
    cmd.CommandType = adCmdStoredProc
    cmd.ActiveConnection = conn.ConnectionString
    Set param = cmd.CreateParameter("ReturnValue", adInteger, adParamReturnValue)
    cmd.Parameters.Append param
    Set param = cmd.CreateParameter("Thedate", adDBDate, adParamInput, _
                , "16 August 1996")    cmd.Parameters.Append param
    Set param = cmd.CreateParameter("OrderCount", adInteger, adParamOutput)
    cmd.Parameters.Append param
    For Each param In cmd.Parameters
        Debug.Print param.Name, param.Value
    Next
    cmd.Execute
    Debug.Print cmd.Parameters("OrderCount")
    Debug.Print cmd.Parameters("ReturnValue")
    Set cmd = Nothing
    Set conn = Nothing
End Sub
```

Multiple Active Result Sets and Performance

If you use the SQL Server Native Client provider with an ADO *Recordset*, you can take advantage of the Multiple Active Result Sets (MARS). These *Recordset*s are read-only and forward scrolling. This feature allows you to open a *Recordset* on multiple SQL statements or call a procedure that returns multiple result sets, and move through each *Recordset* in turn.

The following stored procedure returns multiple *Recordset*s:

```
CREATE PROC usp_MarsFeature @Thedate DATETIME
AS
BEGIN
    SELECT * FROM Orders WHERE RequiredDate = @Thedate

    SELECT * FROM [Order Details]
    INNER JOIN Orders
        ON [Order Details].OrderID = orders.OrderID
    WHERE RequiredDate = @Thedate
END
GO
exec usp_MarsFeature '16 August 1996'
go
```

In the ADO code that calls this stored procedure, notice that you need the line of code Set rst = rst.NextRecordset to move through the *Recordset*s:

```
Sub modSQL_Mars()
    ' Example using Mars
    Dim conn As New ADODB.Connection
    Dim cmd As New ADODB.Command
    Dim rst As New ADODB.Recordset
    Dim param As ADODB.Parameter
    Dim txtConnectionString As String
    ' use  SQLNCLI or SQLNCLI10
    txtConnectionString = "Provider=SQLNCLI10;" & _
                          "SERVER=VISTAULTRA64\SQL2008R2;" & _
                          "Initial Catalog=Northwind;" & _
                          "Integrated Security=SSPI;" & _
                          "MARS Connection=True;"
    conn.ConnectionString = txtConnectionString
    cmd.CommandType = adCmdStoredProc
    cmd.ActiveConnection = conn.ConnectionString
    Set param = cmd.CreateParameter("Thedate", adDBDate, adParamInput, _
                , "16 August 1996")
    cmd.Parameters.Append param
    Set rst = cmd.Execute()
    ' Note MovePrevious is not allowed
    Do While Not rst.EOF
        Debug.Print rst!CustomerID
        rst.MoveNext
```

```
        Loop
        Debug.Print rst.RecordCount
        ' This line is very important
        Set rst = rst.NextRecordset
        Do While Not rst.EOF
            Debug.Print rst!ProductID
            rst.MoveNext
        Loop
        Debug.Print rst.RecordCount
        rst.Close
        Set rst = Nothing
        Set cmd = Nothing
        Set conn = Nothing
End Sub
```

By default a connection string using the native client has MARS activated, but in this example, there is an explicit statement to the connection string to ensure that the feature is active.

The example allows only one *Recordset* at a time to be open; the *NextRecordset* operation closes the first *Recordset*.

One advantage of this approach is that both *Recordset*s are obtained with a single trip to the server, which yields improved performance; the stored procedure is called only once.

MARS and Connections

In the second example of working with MARS, there are two alternative connections, the first uses the older *SQLOLEDB* (shown commented out), and the second example uses *SQLNCLI* (activating MARS). The following sample code tests these two alternatives:

```
Sub modSQL_MarsTwoRecordsets()
    ' Example using Mars
    Dim conn As New ADODB.Connection
    Dim rst As New ADODB.Recordset
    Dim rst2 As New ADODB.Recordset
    Dim txtConnectionString As String
    'txtConnectionString = "Provider=SQLOLEDB;" & _
                        "SERVER=VISTAULTRA64\SQL2008R2;" & _
                        "Initial Catalog=Northwind;" & _
                        "Integrated Security=SSPI;"
    ' use  SQLNCLI or SQLNCLI10
    txtConnectionString = "Provider=SQLNCLI10;" & _
                        "SERVER=VISTAULTRA64\SQL2008R2;" & _
                        "Initial Catalog=Northwind;" & _
                        "Integrated Security=SSPI;" & _
                        "MARS Connection=True;"
    conn.ConnectionString = txtConnectionString
    conn.Open
    Set rst = conn.Execute("SELECT * FROM Orders", , adCmdText)
```

```
        Set rst2 = conn.Execute("SELECT * FROM [Order Details]", , adCmdText)
        rst2.Close
        rst.Close
        Set rst2 = Nothing
        Set rst = Nothing
        Set conn = Nothing
End Sub
```

If you execute this code first using *SQLOLEDB* and then using *SQLNCLI* (or *SQLNCLI10*), if you monitor the resulting actions by using the Profiler, you will see an output for *SQLOLEDB* similar to that shown in Figure 18-3.

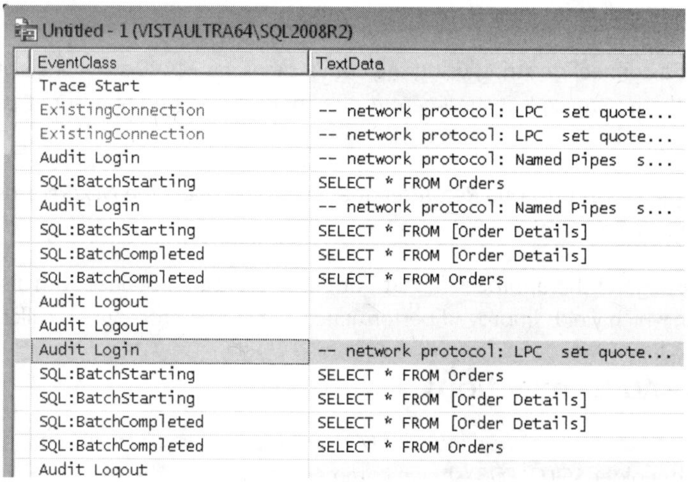

EventClass	TextData
Trace Start	
ExistingConnection	-- network protocol: LPC set quote...
ExistingConnection	-- network protocol: LPC set quote...
Audit Login	-- network protocol: Named Pipes s...
SQL:BatchStarting	SELECT * FROM Orders
Audit Login	-- network protocol: Named Pipes s...
SQL:BatchStarting	SELECT * FROM [Order Details]
SQL:BatchCompleted	SELECT * FROM [Order Details]
SQL:BatchCompleted	SELECT * FROM Orders
Audit Logout	
Audit Logout	
Audit Login	-- network protocol: LPC set quote...
SQL:BatchStarting	SELECT * FROM Orders
SQL:BatchStarting	SELECT * FROM [Order Details]
SQL:BatchCompleted	SELECT * FROM [Order Details]
SQL:BatchCompleted	SELECT * FROM Orders
Audit Logout	

Untitled - 1 (VISTAULTRA64\SQL2008R2)

Figure 18-3 This example creates two connections (two Login/Logout) operations. If you do this with MARS, it would share a single connection.

When multiple *Recordset*s are used with MARS, the *Recordset*s share the same connection. This means that you could hold two *Recordset*s open at the same time on a single connection. The default behavior of ADO when a second *Recordset* is opened is to open a second implicit connection. This can have implications if you are working with transactions and you need both *Recordset*s to operate within the context of a single connection. MARS allows you to manipulate both *Recordset*s within a single transaction. This is illustrated by the second trace shown in Figure 18-4.

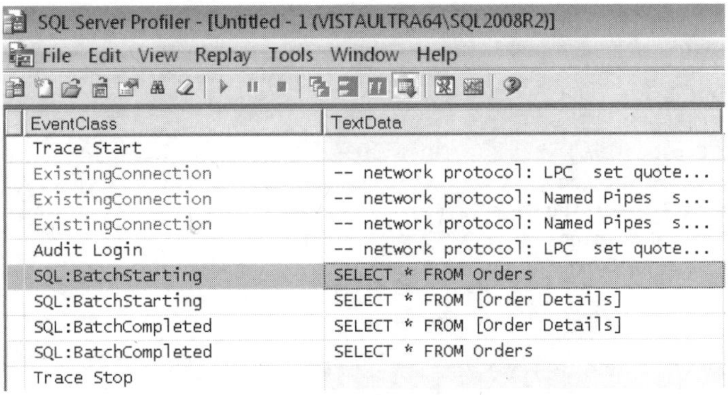

Figure 18-4 This example illustrates the processing within a single MARS connection.

INSIDE OUT   How DAO manages connections

If you run the profiler and open linked tables, or run pass-through queries, or open a *Recordset*, everything takes place within a single connection. If you run the code *modSQL_DAOTwoRecordsets()*, which opens two *Recordset*s, then you see an additional login generating a second connection for the second *Recordset*; this is similar to ADO except that in DAO the first *Recordset* runs in the same connection as any desktop interaction (a useful feature).

The procedure *modSQL_DAOTwoRecordsetsInATransaction()* performs operations within a transaction. This provides a similar environment to MARS for DAO programming, and it will generate a new connection within which to process the multiple *Recordset* operations (this has to happen because it is running in a transaction).

The following code is for *modSQL_DAOTwoRecordsetsInATransaction*; the code for *modSQL_DAOTwoRecordsets* is almost identical but does not have the transaction processing:

```
Sub modSQL_DAOTwoRecordsetsInATransaction()
    Dim db As Database
    Dim rst As DAO.Recordset
    Dim rst2 As DAO.Recordset
    Set db = CurrentDb
    Dim wks As Workspace
    Set wks = DBEngine(0)
    wks.BeginTrans
    Set rst = db.OpenRecordset("SELECT * FROM Orders", dbOpenDynaset, dbSeeChanges)
    Set rst2 = db.OpenRecordset("SELECT * FROM [Order Details]", dbOpenDynaset)
```

```
        rst.MoveLast
        rst2.MoveLast
        wks.CommitTrans
        rst2.Close
        rst.Close
        wks.Close
        Set wks = Nothing
        Set rst2 = Nothing
        Set rst = Nothing
        Set db = Nothing
    End Sub
```

ADOX

ADOX offers an opportunity to develop an approach to structural analysis that is not locked into the DAO model. The object model is shown in Figure 18-5.

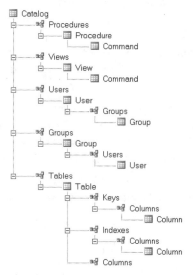

Figure 18-5 The ADOX object model.

The sample database DocADOX.accdb illustrates how you can use ADOX to retrieve information from different data sources. The following sample code for ADOExamples.accdb illustrates how this works:

```
Sub modADOX_ListTables()
    Dim cat As ADOX.Catalog
    Dim strConnectionString As String
    ' create the catalog
    Set cat = New ADOX.Catalog
    strConnectionString = "Provider=SQLNCLI;" & _
                          "SERVER=VISTAULTRA64\SQL2008R2;" & _
                          "Initial Catalog=Northwind;" & _
                          "Integrated Security=SSPI;"

    cat.ActiveConnection = strConnectionString
    Dim tbl As ADOX.Table
    For Each tbl In cat.Tables
        If tbl.Type = "SYSTEM TABLE" Or tbl.Type = "SYSTEM VIEW" Then
            GoTo SkipSystemTables
        Else
            Debug.Print tbl.Name, tbl.Columns.Count, tbl.Type
        End If
SkipSystemTables:
    Next
End Sub
```

Summary

In this chapter, you saw how ADO can be used to extend the functionality of an Access application beyond DAO, and how ADOX can provide a more generic approach to extracting information on the structure of a database.

Index

Symbols

"&" (ampersand) character, using, 86, 92

/Decompile command line switch, 45

@@IDENTITY, SCOPE_IDENTITY() and IDENT_CURRENT in T-SQL, 520

"*" (star) character, 97

"_" (underbar) character, using, 86

A

abstract and implementation classes
- abstract classes, 370
- hybrid abstract and non-abstract classes, 376–378
- implementing an abstract class, 373–376
- implements classes, 372
- libraries, benefits of constructing, 370
- object types, establishing with TypeOf, 375

ACCDE files, protecting designs with, 655

Access 2010
- Access Basic, 114
- Access Connectivity Engine (ACE), 659
- earlier versions of, 38
- locking down, 154

Access collections vs. VBA collection classes, 346

Access Web Databases, linking
- Access database to an Access Web Database, 431
- process of, 430
- relinking, 432–434

Activate and Deactivate events, 255

ActiveForm and ActiveControl, working with, 151

ActiveX controls
- Slider control, adding, 386–388
- TreeView control, 295–300
- UpDown or Spin control, 388–390

ActiveX Data Objects. *See* ADO (ActiveX Data Objects)

address information, packing, 334

ADO (ActiveX Data Objects)
- ADO asynchronous execution class, 365–367
- ADOX, understanding, 672
- Asynchronous operations, 662
- client-server performance, 485
- connections
  - Connection and ActiveConnection, 385
  - DAO management of, 671
  - as the key object in ADO, 660
- cursors (Recordsets)
  - differences with DAO, 661
  - forms, binding to, 384–386
- vs. Data Access Object (DAO) model, 161, 659
- forms and ADO Recordsets, 662
- libraries to add, 660
- program vs. services, 484
- references and, 163
- sample databases, 660
- SQL Server, working with. *See also* SQL Server
  - command objects, 666
  - connecting to, 664
  - connection strings, 663
  - connection time, 665
  - MARS and connections, 669–671
  - MARS and performance, 668
  - stored procedures, 666

ADOX, understanding, 672

ADP (Access Data Project)
- ADO and, 659
- query conversion, 563
- strengths and weaknesses, 564
- understanding, 561–563

AfterDelConfirm event, 268

AfterInsert and BeforeInsert events, 265–267

AfterUpdate event, 276

AllItems method, 349

"&" (ampersand) character, using, 86

Append Only memo fields, 130–132

application development

  application navigation

    combo and list boxes, 637

    custom interfaces for users, 637

    DoCmd object, 140

    forms, opening multiple copies of, 637

    interface design decisions, 632

    locking down an application, 654

    Maximize, Popup, Modal, and MoveSize Properties, 638

    the Navigation Control, 634

    push buttons on a form, 632

    the ribbon, 636

    Switchboard Manager, 633

    Tab controls, 636

    the TreeView control, 635

  completing an application

    error handling, 654

    IntelliSense, using in a standard module, 654

    locking down Access, 154

    progress bars, 653

    splash screens, 653

  deploying applications

    ACCDE files, protecting your design with, 655

    DSNs and relinking applications, 656

    references, depending on, 656

    Runtime deployment, 655

    single and multiple application files, 655

  ribbon design

    Backstage view, 647

    custom ribbon, loading, 649

    default ribbon, setting, 644

    elements of a ribbon, 641

    for forms and reports, 648

    the GetEnabled callback, 642

    images for, 644

    Office 2007 and the file menu, 647

    the OnAction callback, 642

    the OnLoad callback, 642

    tab visibility and focus, dynamically changing, 646–648

    tips, 639

    the USysRibbons table, 640

  sample databases, 631

  32-bit and 64-bit environments, 649

  updating applications, 656

  Windows API, using, 651–653

  Windows Registry, working with, 650

ApplyFilter event, 247

arrays

  determining the dimensions of, 64

  dynamic arrays, 61

  multi-dimensional arrays, 62–64

  option base, 65

  reading records into, 215

  type structures, 65

  working with, 59–61

ASC function, 93, 94

asynchronous event processing and RaiseEvent

  ADO asynchronous execution class, 365–367

  BatchProcessing SQL Server form, 368–370

  stored procedures, 364

  WithEvent processing, 363

asynchronous operations in ADO, 662

attachments

  copying between tables and records, 204–206

  data types, limitations, 197

  fields in Recordsets, 197–200

  importing, using LoadFromFile method, 203

  planning for upsizing to SQL Server, 548

authentication. *See* **security**

Azure. *See* **SQL Azure**

B

backing up SQL Azure databases, 603

Backstage view, in application development, 647

base class, creating, 354

BatchProcessing SQL Server form, 368–370

BeforeDelConfirm event, 268

BeforeInsert and AfterInsert events, 265–267

BeforeUpdate event, 262, 276

binary transfer, using with OLE data, 207–209

bookmarks

  merging data with, 447–451

  in Recordsets, 191

  synchronizing, 249

Boolean data, planning for upsizing to SQL Server, 546

bound forms, 233, 243

boxed grids, creating with the Print event, 327–329

breakpointing code

  breakpoint Step and Run commands, 26–29

  changing code on-the-fly, 34

  conditional Watch Expressions, adding, 32

  Immediate window, working with, 33

  methods for, 23–25

  procedures, tracing with Call Stack, 30

  Set Next command, 25

  variables, displaying in the locals window, 29

  Watching variables and expressions, 31

broken references, 48

BuildCriteria, using to simplify filtering, 130

BuildingClasses.accdb, sample database, 340

BuildingClassesAfterExportImport.accdb, sample database, 340

built-in functions

  ASC function, 94

  date and time functions, 90–92

  format function, 94

  Mid string function, 95

  string functions, 92

ByRef and ByValue parameters, defining, 70–72

C

calculated fields in Recordsets, 210

callbacks

  GetEnabled callback, 642

  OnAction Callback, 642

  OnLoad callback, 642

calling procedures across forms, 251–253

Call Stack

  displaying module linking with, 21

  tracing procedures with, 30

camel notation, 109

Case statements in SQL Server, 581

CAST and CONVERT, using in T-SQL, 518

Choose statements, 79

Chr function, 93

ClassAndForms.accdb sample database, 381

classes

  abstract and implementation classes

    abstract classes, 370

    hybrid abstract and non-abstract classes, 376–378

    implementing an abstract class, 373–376

    implements classes, 372

    libraries, benefits of constructing, 370

    object types, establishing with TypeOf, 375

  advantages of, 339, 340

  asynchronous event processing and RaiseEvent

    ADO asynchronous execution class, 365–367

    BatchProcessing SQL Server form, 368–370

    stored procedures, 364

    WithEvent processing, 363

  binding forms and

    binding to an Active Data Object Recordset, 384

    binding to a Data Access Object Recordset, 383

  class modules

    creating, 341

    locating form or report code in, 7

  Err.Raise and, 122

  friend methods, 378

  hierarchy of, creating

    base class, creating, 354

    derived classes, 355

    inheritance and polymorphism in classes, 356

  producing and consuming events, 364

  sample database, 359

  tabs, dynamically loading

    class module, creating, 341

    collection of objects, 345

    improving, 340

    Initialization and Termination events, 344

classes *(cont.)*

tabs, dynamically loading *(cont.)*

Let and Get object properties, 342

New and Set, creating an object with, 343

simplifying the application code with classes, 352

terminology of, 353

VBA collection classes

vs. Access collections, 346

adding AllItems to, 349

creating, 346–348

exporting and re-importing the class, 349

using with the Dynamic Tab, 351

WithEvents processing

control events, handling, 362

form events, handling, 360–362

Click and DblClick events, 275

client-side cursors, 661

cloning and copying Recordsets, 212–215

Close events, 248

cloud computing. *See* **SQL Azure**

Cloud to Cloud (CTP1) synchronization service, 604

COALESCE function, 623

code. *See also* **debugging**

calling directly from a control's event, 152

calling public code on a form, 252

changing on-the-fly, 33

compiling in VBA, 44

control events, writing code behind, 274

line continuation in VBA, 86

quality of, improving with constants, 49–51

simplifying with classes, 352

CodeDB, 175, 176–179

code, maintainable

Access document objects, naming, 108

database fields, naming, 109

indenting code, 113

naming conventions, 113

unbound controls, naming, 110

using the Me object to reference controls, 113

variables in code, naming, 110–112

CodePlex website, 495

collections

Containers collections, 222

Errors collection, 171–173

objects and, 104, 345

TableDefs collection and indexes, 179–182

columns

adding, in T-SQL, 503

adding, with a default in T-SQL, 503

column data type, changing in T-SQL, 503

ColumnHistory memo fields, 130–132

column name, changing in T-SQL, 503

column visibility, controlling, 255

combo box columns, 282

combo boxes

combo box columns, 282

data, synchronizing in controls, 278–280

defaults and the drop-down list, 279

and list boxes, in application development, 637

multi-value fields, 283

reducing joins with, 333

RowSource Type, 280–282

Table/Query editing, 285

Value List editing, 284

comments, adding in VBA, 40

compiler directives

conditional compilation, 45

early and late binding, 438–440

32-bit or 64-bit, 650

conditional statements and program flow

Choose statements, 79

Do While and Do Until loops, 82–84

Exit statements, 84

For and ForEach loops, 81

GoTo and GoSub statements, 86

If...Then...Else... statements, 77

IIF statements, 78

line continuation, 86

Select Case statements, 80

TypeOf statements, 80

the With statement, 85

conditional Watch Expressions, adding, 32

conflict resolution, in SQL Azure data, 613

constants and variables. *See also* **variables**

  arrays

    determining the dimensions of, 64

    dynamic arrays, 61

    multi-dimensional arrays, 62–64

    option base, 65

    type structures, 65

    working with, 59–61

  code quality, improving with constants, 49–51

  Enum keyword, 51

  global variables, 56

  NULL values, IsNull and Nz, 53–55

  scope rules, 58

  static variables, 55

  type structures, 65

  variables and database field types, 52

  variable scope and lifetime, 57–59

consuming events, 364

contacts in Outlook, adding, 476

Containers and Documents

  Container usage, table of, 223

  investigating and documenting in DAO, 222–224

controls

  ActiveX controls

    dialog box, 297

    referring to methods and properties in, 304

    slider control, adding, 386–388

    UpDown or Spin control, 388–390

  combo boxes

    combo box columns, 282

    data, synchronizing in controls, 278–280

    defaults and the drop-down list, 279

    multi-value fields, 283

    RowSource Type, 280–282

    Table/Query editing, 285

    Value List editing, 284

  control events

    AfterUpdate event, 276

    BeforeUpdate event, 276

    bound or unbound, 233

    calling code directly from, 152

    Click and DblClick events, 275

    GotFocus and LostFocus events, 277

    handling, 362

    writing code behind, 274

  Control Wizard, 274

  defaults for, 274

  dynamically loading tabs, improving, 340

  list boxes

    multiple selections, 286–290

    two list boxes, multiple selections with, 290–292

    using as a subform, 292–295

  sample databases, 273

  tab controls

    dynamically loading tabs, 314–320, 340–355

    OnChange event, 314

    referring to controls in, 314

    refreshing between tabs and controls, 311–313

  Tag property, 316

  TreeView control

    ActiveX controls, 304

    adding, 296–298

    in application development, 635

    drag and drop, 303–307

    graphics, adding, 301–304

    nodes, adding, 309

    nodes, expanding and collapsing, 303

    nodes with recursion, deleting, 307–309

    parent/child-related data, loading, 300

    populating the tree, 298–301

    recursive VBA code, writing and debugging, 308

    sample database example, 295

  using for filtering, 236–242

CONVERT, using in T-SQL, 518

copying SQL Azure databases, 603

CountryLibrary.accdb database, 176

CreateObject vs. New, 438–440

CROSSTAB queries in SQL Server, 509–511

CTP1 synchronization service, 604

CTP2 synchronization service, 604

currency, in upsizing to SQL Server, 548

CurrentDB, 175

Current event, 326

CurrentProject and CurrentData objects

dependency checking and embedded macros, 138

Form Datasheet View properties, changing, 136

object dependencies, 137

version information, retrieving, 135

cursors. *See also* **Recordsets**

DAO, differences with, 661

location, type, and lock type, 662

custom interfaces for users, in application development, 637

custom ribbon, loading, 649

cycles and multiple cascade paths, converting for SQL Server, 549

D

DAO (Data Access Object) model

vs. ActiveX Data Objects (ADO), 161, 659

connections, management of, 671

databases, working with

CodeDB, 176–179

CurrentDB, DBEngine, and CodeDB, 175

DAO and ADO libraries and, 164

Database Object, 173

Data Definition Language (DDL), 183

datasheet properties, managing, 184–186

DBEngine Object, 165

Errors collection, 171–173

relationships, creating, 186

TableDefs collection and indexes, 179–182

transactions, 166–170

Workspace Object, 165

objects, investigating and documenting

Containers and Documents, 222–224

object properties, 224

queries

QueryDef parameters, 220–222

QueryDefs and Recordsets, 218

QueryDefs, creating, 218–220

temporary QueryDefs, 216–218

working with, 215

Recordsets

adding, editing, and updating records, 193

Attachment fields, 197–200

attachments, copying, 204–206

Bookmarks, 191

calculated fields, 210

cloning and copying, 212–215

Delete, 202

field syntax, 191

Filter and Sort properties, 193

forms, binding to, 383

information, displaying, 200

LoadFromFile method, 203

Multiple-Values lookup fields, 194–197

OLE Object data type, 206–209

reading records into an array, 215

SaveToFile method, 202

searching, 188

types of, 188

references and, 163

sample databases

DAOExamples.accdb, 162

DocDAO.accdb, 224

Find_IT.accdb, 225–227

understanding, 162

VBA libraries, techniques when writing, 177

data

data exchange, using DoCmd object, 142

data files, single and multiple application, 655

data types

converting for SQL Server, 547

mapping in SSMA, 567

naming conventions for, 112

text data types and UNICODE, 544

external, linking to, 430–434

extracting from Outlook, 472–475

merging with bookmarks, 447–451

minimizing, for display in forms, 485

multi-value data, planning for upsizing to SQL Server, 548

parent/child-related data, loading, 300

synchronizing in controls, 278–280

Data Access Object model. *See* **DAO (Data Access Object) model**

databases. *See also* **sample databases; upsizing databases**

Access Web Databases, linking

    Access database to an Access Web Database, 431

    process of, 430

    relinking, 432–434

changing structure of, in SQL Azure, 612

database splitting, 396, 397

database systems, moving data between, 91

DFirst and DLast functions in, 100

fields, naming conventions for, 109

in SQL Server. *See also* SQL Server

    database diagrams, 496–498

    demo database script, running, 493

    file locations, 488

    system databases, 493

SQL Azure databases. *See also* SQL Azure

    backing up and copying, 603

    creating, 590

SQL databases, migrating using SQL Azure

    sequence of steps, 596

    set of tables, creating, 597–599

    SQL Import/Export features when transferring to SQL Azure, 602

    SQL Server Import and Export Wizard and UNICODE data types, 598

    SSMA (SQL Server Migration Assistant), 598

    transferring data with the SQL Server Import and Export Wizard, 599–603

variables and database field types, 52

working with in DAO

    CodeDB, 176–179

    CurrentDB, DBEngine, and CodeDB, 175

    DAO and ADO libraries and, 164

    Database Object, 173

    Data Definition Language (DDL), 183

    datasheet properties, managing, 184–186

    DBEngine Object, 165

    Errors collection, 171–173

    relationships, creating, 186

    sample databases, 223–226

    TableDefs collection and indexes, 179–182

    transactions, 166–170

    Workspace Object, 165

Data Definition Language (DDL), 183

Data Link, setting advanced properties, 464

datasheet properties, managing, 184–186

Datasheet view, 261

Data Source Name (DSN). *See* **DSN**

Data Sources, using, 468–471

Data Sync Agent in SQL Azure

    conflict resolution in data, 613

    data and database structure, changing, 612

    database synchronization and triggers, 613

    loading and installing, 605–609

    Sync Groups and Sync Logs, 610–612

    synchronization services, 604

    table structure, changes to, 613

Data Type Mapping, changing in SQL Azure, 627

dates

    Date and Time data, converting for SQL Server, 544–546

    date and time functions, 90–92

    date values, rules for in Where clauses, 97

    default, in data storage systems, 91

DBEngine object, 165, 175

DblClick event, 275

dbo prefixes, renaming, 417

dbSeeChanges constant in SQL Server, 574

DDL, creating relationships with, 187

Deactivate and Activate events, interacting with, 255

debugging

    breakpointing code

        breakpoint Step and Run commands, 26–29

        changing code on-the-fly, 34

        conditional Watch Expressions, adding, 32

        Immediate window, working with, 33

        methods for, 23–25

        procedures, tracing with Call Stack, 30

        Set Next command, 25

        variables, displaying in the locals window, 29

        watching variables and expressions, 31

    Debug Assert command, 23

debugging *(cont.)*

forms

application and VBA code windows, 6–8

database sample, 4

VBA editor, entering, 5

modal forms, 38

modules and procedures

debug commands, 23

debugging code in modules, demonstration of, 20–22

editing environment, accessing, 8–10

functions, executing, 15

modules, creating, 10

procedures, creating, 11

searching code, 19

split window, 17–19

subroutines, executing, 13–15

viewing and searching code, 16

Object Browser and Help system

Help system, configuring, 35

Object Browser, working with, 36

VBA code, recursive, 308

decimals

converting for SQL Server, 547

precision of, in DAO, 183

default ribbon, setting, 644

deleting

Delete events, 267

DELETE query in SQL Server, 513

Recordsets, 202

demo database script, running, 495

dependency checking, and embedded macros, 138

deploying applications

ACCDE files, protecting your design with, 655

DSNs and relinking applications, 656

references, depending on, 656

Runtime deployment, 655

single and multiple application files, 655

derived classes, 355

developing applications. *See* **application development**

developing with SQL Server

Case statements, 581

complex queries, handling, 579–582

dbSeeChanges constant, 574

efficient SQL, tips for, 585

the MSysConf table, 587

Pass-Through queries, 575–578

performance and execution plans, 582–585

SQL Server Profiler, 586

stored procedures and temporary tables, 578

stored procedures, using advanced features in, 578

DFirst and DLast functions, 100

Dialog forms, OpenArgs and, 121

diary entries, adding, 476

DisplayAttachmentInfo subroutine, 200

displaying records

bound and unbound forms, 233

modal and pop-up forms, 234

opening and loading forms, 235

Refresh, Repaint, Recalc, and Requery commands, 250

DISTINCT and DISTINCTROW, 234

DocADOX.accdb sample database, 660

DocDAO.accdb sample database, 224

DoCmd object

in application development, 140

application navigation, 140

data exchange, 142

environment, controlling, 138

size and position, controlling, 139

DoCmd.OpenForm command, 6

DoEvents command, 103

domain functions

description of, 95

Where clauses, constructing, 97

Do While and Do Until loops, 82–84

drag and drop in TreeView control, 303–307

drill-down reports, creating, 326

driver limitations with VARCHAR(MAX), 548

DSN (Data Source Name)

creating, 410–413

Machine DSNs, 410

and relinking applications, 656

in SQL Azure, 420–423

dynamic arrays, 61

Dynamic Tab, and using classes, 351

Dynaset, 189

E

Early Binding vs. Late Binding, 438–440

Editing and Undo on records

   BeforeInsert and AfterInsert events, 265–267

   BeforeUpdate and AfterUpdate events, 262

   Delete events, 267

   Error event, 269

   KeyPreview and Key events, 268

   Locking and Unlocking controls, 264

   in Recordsets, 193

   saving records, 270

edits, multiple using transactions, 170

ellipse button, 274

email

   creating, in Outlook, 475

   writing to Access, from Outlook, 477–479

embedded macros, dependency checking and, 138

embedded quotes, SQL and, 98–101

Employees_be.accdb sample database, 396

Encapsulation, 353

Enum keyword, 51

Err object, 117, 172

Error event, 269

error handling

   in application development, 654

   in T-SQL, 523–525

   in VBA

      Err object, 117

      Err.Raise, 122

      general purpose error handler, developing, 118–121

      how errors occur, 115

      On Error GoTo, 118

      On Error Resume Next, 116

      OpenArgs and Dialog forms, 121

      subclassing form events, 362

error messages, 172

Errors collection in DAO, 171–173

Err.Raise, 122

Eval function, 102

events

   AfterDelConfirm event, 268

   ApplyFilter event, 247

   BeforeDelConfirm event, 268

   BeforeInsert and AfterInsert events, 265–267

   BeforeUpdate and AfterUpdate events, 262

   Close events, 248

   control events

      AfterUpdate event, 276

      BeforeUpdate event, 276

      bound or unbound, 233

      calling code directly from, 152

      Click and DblClick events, 275

      GotFocus and LostFocus events, 277

      writing code behind, 274

   Current event, 251

   Deactivate and Activate events, 255

   Delete events, 267

   Error events, 269

   Initialization and Termination events, 344

   KeyPreview and Key events, 268

   Mouse events, 260

   OnChange event, 314

   Open event, 235

   producing and consuming events, 364

   report event sequences

      boxed grids, creating with the Print event, 327–329

      drawing graphics and, 328

      drill-down reports and current events, creating, 326

      typical, 324–326

   Timer event, 255–260

   Unload and Close events, 248

ExcelAnalysis.accdb sample database, 437

Excel, Microsoft

   connecting Access to

      Data Link advanced properties, setting, 464

      key objects in, 451

      linking to external data, planning for, 466

      MS Query and Data Sources, using, 468–471

      QueryTables and ListObjects, 470

      reporting with, 460–468

      spreadsheets, reading data from, 459

      spreadsheets, writing data to, 452–459

   files, linking to, 406

Exit statements, 84

exporting
  migrating SQL databases, 598, 602
  VBA collection classes, 349
expressions
  conditional Watch Expressions, adding, 32
  Expression Builder
    invoking, 133
    locating, 38
    working with, 144
  Watches window, 31
external data, linking to, 430–434
extracting information from Outlook, 472–475

F

fields
  calculated fields in Recordsets, 210
  field syntax in Recordsets, 191, 192
  mismatched, converting for SQL Server, 550
  Multiple-Values lookup fields, 194–197
  multi-value fields connected to a combo box, 283
  naming conventions for, 109
  required fields, converting for SQL Server, 549
files, opening, 442
filtering
  forms
    ApplyFilter event, 247
    calling procedures across forms, 251–253
    RecordsetClone, 248
    Unload and Close events, 248
    using another form, 245–247
    using controls, 245–251
    using filter property, 243–245
  simplifying by using BuildCriteria, 130
  using controls, 236–242
FilterOnLoad property, 235
Filter property, 193, 243–245
Find and FindNext methods, 189
Find operations, 474
firewall settings in SQL Azure, 591
floating point numbers, converting for SQL Server, 547
flow, program. *See* conditional statements and program
    flow

focus events, 277
For and ForEach loops, 81
foreign keys, partially completed, 550
Format event, layout control and, 330
Format function, 94
Format string function, 93
Form Datasheet View properties, changing, 136
forms
  and ADO Recordsets, 662
  BatchProcessing form, 368–370
  binding forms and
    binding to an Active Data Object Recordset, 384
    binding to a Data Access Object Recordset, 383
  bound or unbound, 233
  calling public code on, 252
  closing, 248
  Continuous forms, controlling column visibility in, 255
  control events and
    AfterUpdate event, 276
    BeforeUpdate event, 276
    Click and DblClick events, 275
    GotFocus and LostFocus events, 277
    writing code behind, 274
  debugging code
    application and code windows, 6–8
    the class module, locating code in, 7
    database sample, 4
    modal forms, 38
    VBA editor, entering, 5
  Dialog forms, OpenArgs and, 121
  driving reports from, 331–333
  Editing and Undo on records
    BeforeInsert and AfterInsert events, 265–267
    BeforeUpdate and AfterUpdate events, 262
    Delete events, 267
    Error event, 269
    KeyPreview and Key events, 268
    Locking and Unlocking controls, 264
    saving records, 270
  filtering
    ApplyFilter event, 247
    calling procedures across forms, 251–253

RecordsetClone, 248
Unload and Close events, 248
using another form, 245–247
using controls, 236–242
using filter property, 243–245
form events
  handling, 360–362
  subclassing, 362
frmCustomers form, 232
linking code to, in modules, 22
minimizing data display in, 485
opening
  multiple copies of, 637
  multiple instances of a form, 381–383
  using DoCmd.OpenForm command, 6
  using a Where clause, 246
properties and
  FilterOnLoad, 235
  OrderByOnLoad, 235
push buttons, in application development, 632
records, displaying
  bound and unbound forms, 233
  modal and pop-up forms, 234
  opening and loading forms, 235
  Refresh, Repaint, Recalc, and Requery commands, 250
records on forms, interacting with
  Current event, 251
  Deactivate and Activate events, 255
  Mouse events, 260
  Timer Interval property of the Timer event, setting, 255–260
ribbon design for, 648
sample databases, 231
size and position, controlling
  DoCmd object, 139
tabs, dynamically loading
  class module, creating, 341
  collection of objects, 345
  Initialization and Termination events, 344
  Let and Get object properties, 342
  New and Set, creating an object with, 343
  options for, 314

pages, loading, 315–318
pages, unloading, 320
related pages, dynamically loading, 319
simplifying the application code with classes, 352
Forms and Reports collections
Access Objects, creating in code, 149
controls on a Subform, referencing, 145–148
Expression Builder, working with, 144
VBA class module, syntax for, 147
working with, 143
friend methods, 378
Full Recovery Model, in SQL Server, 491
functions
built-in functions
  ASC function, 94
  date and time functions, 90–92
  format function, 94
  Mid string function, 95
  string functions, 92
  in T-SQL, 519
changing to subroutines, and vice versa, 14
COALESCE function, 623
DFirst and DLast functions, 100
domain functions
  description of, 95
  Where clauses, constructing, 97
the Eval function, 102
executing, 15
Left, Right, Mid string functions, 93
Len string function, 93
MsgBox function, 14
and procedures
  ByRef and ByValue parameters, defining, 70–72
  calling, variations on standard rules for, 66
  modules and class modules, organizing code in, 76
  ParamArray qualifier, 75
  parameters, Optional and Named, 73
  procedures, private and public, 72
  subroutines and functions, default referencing of parameters in, 71
  subroutines, managing code with, 67–70
  in VBA, 13

functions *(cont.)*
   returning variant or string data, 93
   Shell and Sendkeys, 102
   table-valued functions, 535
   User-Defined Functions (UDFs) in SQL Server, 534–536
   VBA, using in Queries, 101

G

GetEnabled callback, 642
GetObject keyword, 440–442
Get object properties, 342
global variables, 56
GotFocus and LostFocus events, 277
GoTo and GoSub statements, 86
graphical interface
   of SQL Azure, 595
   of SQL Server, 505
graphics
   adding to TreeView control, 301–304
   drawing, and report event sequences, 328
grids, creating with the Print event, 327–329
GUI (graphical user interface), changing table designs
      with, 500–502

H

Help system, configuring, 35
hybrid abstract and non-abstract classes, 376–378
hyperlinks, converting for SQL Server, 547

I

@@IDENTITY, SCOPE_IDENTITY() and IDENT_CURRENT in
      T-SQL, 520
Identity property, using in SQL Server tables, 504
If...Then...Else... statements, 77
Ignore NULLs, in SQL Server, 553
IIF statements, 78
images for ribbon design, 644
IMAGE, VARBINARY (Max), and OLE Data, converting for
      SQL Server, 547
Immediate window, working with, 33
implementation classes, 372. *See also* abstract and
      implementation classes
importing
   data from SQL Azure, 603

   migrating SQL databases, 598, 602
   VBA collection classes, 349
indenting code, 113
indexes, TableDefs collection and, 179–182
INFORMATION_SCHEMA views, in SQL Server, 494
inheritance in classes, 356
Initialization event, 344
INSERT and INSERT INTO queries in SQL Server, 515–517
inserted OLE documents, 209
installing SSMA, 564
instances in SQL Server, 491
Instnwnd.sql sample database, 396
Instnwndtesting.sql sample database, 396
InStr, InStrReverse string functions, 93
integer numbers, converting for SQL Server, 547
interfaces for users, in application development, 632, 637,
      638
IsBroken, references, 48
IsNothing, IsEmpty, and IsObject, 106
isolation levels of transactions, in SQL Server, 532

J

JET (Joint Engine Technology), 659
Join string function, 93

K

KeyPreview and Key events, 268
keys, partially completed foreign, 550

L

language settings in VBA
   comments, adding, 40
   compiling code, 44
   conditional compilation, 45
   /Decompile command line switch, 45
   Option Compare, selecting, 43
   options, setting explicitly, 41
   references, 46–49
   Visual Basic for Applications Extensibility, 48
Late Binding vs. Early Binding, 438–440
layout control
   report grouping, programming, 333
   using the Format event, 330

layout control of reports
   driving reports from a form, 331–333
   during printing, 330
   joins, reducing with a combo box, 333
   ParamArray, packing address information with, 334
   printers, control of, 335
Left, Right, Mid string functions, 93
Len string function, 93
Let object properties, 342
libraries
   ADO libraries to add, 660
   benefits of constructing, 370
   DAO and ADO libraries and, 164
   VBA libraries, techniques when writing, 177
Linked Table Manager, 398
linked TableName, 406
linking
   Access to Access
      database splitter, using, 397
      Linked Table Manager, 398
      linked table name and SourceTableName, 406
      relinking, automating, 398–406
      relinking tables, essential details for, 400
      splitting databases, 396
      temporary tables and SQL Server, 397
   Access Web Databases
      Access database to an Access Web Database, 431
      process of, 430
      relinking, 432–434
   to Excel files
      Data Link advanced properties, setting, 464
      key objects in, 451
      linking to external data, planning for, 466
      MS Query and Data Sources, using, 468–471
      QueryTables and ListObjects, 470
      reporting with, 460–468
      spreadsheets, reading data from, 459
      spreadsheets, writing data to, 452–459
      and text files, 406
   external data links, planning for, 466

   to SharePoint lists
      getting started, 426–428
      relinking SharePoint lists, 428
   to SQL Azure
      connecting to SQL Azure, 424–426
      DSN, 420–423
      security stored procedures, support for, 421
   to SQL Server
      DSN (Data Source Name), creating, 410–415
      getting started, 407
      sample database, setting up, 407–409
      script files, 409
      Server driver, choosing, 412
      Server instances, 408
      Windows vs. SQL Server authentication, 414
   to SQL Server tables
      getting started, 416
      linked tables, refreshing, 417
      linked tables, renaming to remove the dbo_prefix, 417
      updateability and Views, 419
      views in SQL Server, connecting to, 418
      views in SQL Server, refreshing, 419
   to Text Files, 407
list boxes
   in application development, 637
   key properties when working with multiple selections in, 287
   multiple selections, 286–290
   selected choices, working with, 289
   two list boxes, multiple selections with, 290–292
   using as a subform, 292–295
ListObjects, 470
lists
   drop-down list, displaying, 279
   SharePoint lists, 426–428
loading
   LoadFromFile method, 203
   and opening forms, 235
Locals window, displaying variables in, 29
Locking and Unlocking controls, 264
locking down an application, 654

Log files in SQL Server, 490

loops

Do While and Do Until loops, 82–84

For and ForEach loops, 81

LostFocus event, 277

M

Machine DSNs, 410

macros

and VBA, evolution of, 114

converting to VBA, 115

embedded, dependency checking and, 138

Mail Merge, 451

Maintenance Plan, for SQL Express, 488

Management Studio, using, 592–594

MARS (Multiple Active Result Sets)

and connections in SQL Server, 669–671

and performance, 668

master database, in SQL Server, 493

Maximize property, 638

MDI. *See* **Multiple Document Interface (MDI)**

Memo data, converting for SQL Server, 547

Me object, to reference controls, 113

Microsoft Excel. *See* **Excel, Microsoft**

Microsoft Outlook. *See* **Outlook, Microsoft**

Microsoft SQL Azure. *See* **SQL Azure**

Microsoft Word. *See* **Word, Microsoft**

Mid string function, 95

migrating SQL databases using SQL Azure

sequence of steps, 596

set of tables, creating, 597–599

SQL Import/Export features when transferring to SQL Azure, 602

SQL Server Import and Export Wizard and UNICODE data types, 598

SSMA (SQL Server Migration Assistant), 598

transferring data with the SQL Server Import and Export Wizard, 599–603

Migration Wizard, 565–567

missing references, 48

modal forms

debugging, 38

and pop-up forms, 234

Modal property, 638

model database, in SQL Server, 493

modules

class module, creating, 341

naming conventions for, 109

standard modules, using Intellisense in, 654

modules and procedures

the class module, locating code in, 7

code types for, 76

debug commands, 23

debugging code

debug commands, 23

debugging code in modules, demonstration of, 20–22

editing environment, accessing, 8–10

functions, executing, 15

in modules, 10, 20–22

procedures, creating, 11

searching code, 19

split window, 17–19

subroutines, executing, 13–15

viewing and searching code, 16

editing environment, accessing, 8–10

functions, executing, 15

modules and class modules, organizing code in, 76

modules, creating

how to, 10

linking code to forms and reports, 22

naming conventions, 21

scope rules and, 58

searching code, 19

split window, 17–19

subroutines, executing, 13–15

viewing and searching code, 16

Mouse events, interacting with, 260

MousePointer shape, changing, 150

msdb database, in SQL Server, 493

MsgBox function, 14

MS Query, 468–471

MSysASO system table, relinking, 434

MSysConf table in SQL Server, 587

multi-dimensional arrays, 62–64

Multiple Active Result Sets. *See* MARS (Multiple Active Result Sets)

multiple cascade paths, converting for SQL Server, 549

Multiple Document Interface (MDI), 638

Multiple-Values lookup fields, 194–197

multi-tenanted applications in SQL

    application tables and views, 619–622

    optional parameters, creating, 623

    overview, 617

    security, managing, 623

    user tables and views, 617–619

multi-user interaction, simulating with transactions, 531

Multi-value data, and upsizing to SQL Server, 548

N

Named and Optional parameters, 73

naming conventions

    Access document objects, 108

    database fields, 109

    the Me object to reference controls, 113

    for procedures in modules, 21

    unbound controls, 110

    variables in code, 110–112

navigation experience of users, 140

navigation, in application development

    combo and list boxes, 637

    custom interfaces for users, 637

    DoCmd object, 140

    forms, opening multiple copies of, 637

    interface design decisions, 632

    locking down an application, 654

    the Navigation Control, 634

    push buttons on a form, 632

    the ribbon, 636

    Switchboard Manager, 633

    Tab controls, 636

    the TreeView control, 635

nesting transactions in SQL Server, 533

New keyword, 105, 343

nodes

    adding to trees, 309

    expanding and collapsing, 303

    with recursion, deleting, 307–309

non-abstract classes, hybrid, 376–378

NorthwindAzure.accdb sample database, 396

NULL values

    and IsNull and Nz, 53–55

    managing, with multiple controls for filtering, 242

    in SQL Server, 553

    string expressions and, 92

numbers

    converting integers for SQL Server, 547

    real numbers, decimals, and floating point numbers, converting for SQL Server, 547

O

Object Browser, working with, 36, 38

objects

    the class object, instantiating, 353

    command objects in ADO, 666

    creating

        in Outlook, 475–477

        using New and Set keywords, 343

    Database Object in DAO, 173

    DBEngine object, 165

    Excel, key objects in, 451

    investigating and documenting in DAO

        Containers and Documents, 222–224

        object properties, 224

    Let and Get object properties, 342

    object models and

        Early vs. Late Binding and CreateObject vs. New, 438–440

        existing files, opening, 442

        GetObject keyword, 440–442

    object types, establishing with TypeOf, 375

    Recordsets vs. Recordset2 objects, 188

    Word object model, key objects in, 443

    Workspace object, 165

objects and collections

    CurrentProject and CurrentData objects

        dependency checking and embedded macros, 138

        Form Datasheet View properties, changing, 136

        object dependencies, 137

        properties and collections of, 134

        version information, retrieving, 135

objects and collections *(cont.)*

description of, 103

the DoCmd object

application navigation, 140

data exchange, 142

the environment, controlling, 138

size and position, controlling, 139

Forms and Reports collections

Access Objects, creating in code, 149

controls on a Subform, referencing, 145–148

Expression Builder, working with, 144

VBA class module, syntax for, 147

working with, 143

IsNothing, IsEmpty, and IsObject, 106

object methods and properties

ColumnHistory and Append Only memo fields, 130–132

the Expression Builder, invoking, 133

filtering, simplifying by using BuildCriteria, 130

the Run method, 128

the RunCommand Method, 129

TempVars, examining, 132

object variables, 105

Screen Object

ActiveForm and ActiveControl, working with, 151

control's events, calling code directly from, 152

MousePointer shape, changing, 150

user interface, enhancing

locking down Access, 154

Office FileDialog, selecting files with, 157–159

progress bars, custom, 156

Setting and Getting options, 152–154

SysCmd, monitoring progress with, 155

ODBC drivers, 663

OfficeApplications.accdb sample database, 437

Office FileDialog, selecting files with, 157–159

Office, Microsoft. *See also* **specific Office applications**

code to launch Office applications, 438

Office 2007 and the file menu, 647

Offline Devices (CTP2) synchronization service, 604

OLE Data, converting for SQL Server, 547

OLEDB providers, 663

OLE Object data type

advantages of, 206

binary transfer, using, 207–209

documents, inserted, 209

importing and exporting OLE objects, 206

OnAction Callback, 642

OnChange event, 314

On Error GoTo mechanism, 118

On Error Resume Next technique, 116

OnLoad callback, 642

On-premise to Cloud (CTP2) synchronization service, 604

OOP (Object-Oriented Programming)

objects, working with, 340

supported in VBA, 339

Open Args, and dialog forms, 112

opening

Excel, 454–456

existing files, 442

and loading forms, 235

Open event, 235

placeholder documents, 446

Optional and Named parameters, 73

Option Compare, selecting, 43

Option Explicit, selecting, 41

OrderByOnLoad property, 235

Orders_be.accdb sample database, 396

OutlookContacts.accdb sample database, 437

Outlook, Microsoft

connecting Access to

creating objects in, 475–477

extracting information from, 472–475

Outlook object model, 471

Restrict and Find operations, 474

writing to Access from Outlook, 477–479

P

ParamArray

packing address information with, 334

qualifier, 75

parameters

creating, in a QueryDef, 221

creating optional, using the COALESCE function, 623

default values for optional parameters, specifying, 75

Optional and Named, 73

parent/child-related data, 300

Pass-Through queries in SQL Server, 575–578

performance, Multiple Active Result Sets and, 668

periodic execution of a Timer event, 256

placeholder documents

generating documents from, 444–446

opening, 446

polymorphism in classes, 356

popup and modal forms, 234

Popup property, 638

Print event, creating boxed grids with, 327–329

printing

printer controls and settings, 335

reports, layout control during, 330

private and public procedures, 72

procedures

calling, across forms, 251–253

calling, variations on standard rules for, 66

changing types, 14

creating, 11

debug commands, 23

editing environment, accessing, 8–10

functions, executing, 15

in modules, naming conventions, 21

modules and class modules, organizing code in, 76

scope rules, 58

stored procedures

in ADO, 666

in SQL Server, 364, 578

subroutines, executing, 13–15

tracing, with Call Stack, 30

viewing and searching code, 16

producing and consuming events, 364

program flow. *See* **conditional statements and program flow**

progress bars

custom, creating, 156

in application development, 653

properties

Filter and Sort, 193

Identity property, in SQL Server, 504

Let and Get object properties, 342

Managing Datasheet properties, 184–186

Maximize, Popup, Modal, and MoveSize Properties, 638

for multiple-selection list boxes, 287

Tag property, 316

push buttons on a form, 632

Q

queries

complex queries, handling in SQL Server, 579–582

CROSSTAB queries in SQL Server, 509–511

DELETE query in SQL Server, 513

MS Query, using, 468–471

naming conventions for, 109

Pass-Through queries in SQL Server, 575–578

pasting links to, from Access into Word, 444

query conversion, 572–574

QueryDefs

creating, 218–220

parameters, 220–222

and Recordsets, 218

temporary, 216–218

QueryTables, 470

in SQL Server

DELETE query, 513

INSERT and INSERT INTO queries, 515–517

UPDATE query, 514

using VBA functions in, 100

working with, 215

quotation marks, embedded, 98–101

R

RaiseEvent, 363–368

random autonumbers, converting for SQL Server, 551–553

real numbers, decimals, and floating point numbers, converting for SQL Server, 547

Recalc, Requery, Refresh, and Repaint commands, 250

records, displaying

bound and unbound forms, 233

modal and pop-up forms, 234

opening and loading forms, 235

Refresh, Repaint, Recalc, and Requery commands, 250

records, editing and undoing

BeforeInsert and AfterInsert events, 265–267

BeforeUpdate and AfterUpdate events, 262

controls, locking and unlocking, 264

deleting events, 267

multiple records, selecting for editing, 294

saving records, 270

RecordsetClone

synchronizing bookmarks with, 249

working with, 248

Recordsets. *See also* **cursors**

adding, editing, and updating records, 193

ADO, forms and, 662

Attachment fields, 197–200

attachments, copying, 204–206

Bookmarks, 191

calculated fields, 210

cloning and copying, 212–215

Delete, 202

field syntax, 191

Filter and Sort properties, 193

information, displaying, 200

LoadFromFile method, 203

Multiple-Values lookup fields, 194–197

OLE Object data type, 206–209

reading records into an array, 215

vs. Recordset2 objects, 188

SaveToFile method, 202

searching, 188

types of, 188

records on forms, interacting with

Current event, 251

Deactivate and Activate events, 255

Mouse events, 260

Timer Interval property of the Timer event,
      setting, 255–260

Record Source, updateability of, 234

Recovery Models in SQL Server, 490

recursion

deleting and node with, 307–309

in VBA code, writing and debugging, 308

references

in application development, 656

core libraries and, 46–49

refreshing between tabs and controls, 311–313

Refresh, Repaint, Recalc, and Requery commands, 250

relationships

creating, in DAO, 186

creating, using DDL, 187

relinking applications, DSNs and, 656

relinking databases

Access to Access, automating, 398–406

USysApplicationLog and MSysASO, 434

Web Databases, 432–434

Repaint, Recalc, Requery and Refresh commands, 250

Replace string function, 93

**replicated databases and random autonumbers,
      converting for SQL Server, 551–553**

reports

with Excel linked to Access, 460–468

layout control

driving reports from a form, 331–333

during printing, 330

joins, reducing with a combo box, 333

ParamArray, packing address information with, 334

printers, control of, 335

report grouping, programming, 333

using the Format event, 330

linking code to, in modules, 22

opening, 323

report event sequences

boxed grids, creating with the Print event, 327–329

drawing graphics and, 328

drill-down reports and current events, creating, 326

typical, 324–326

Reports.accdb, sample database, 323

ribbon design, in application development, 648

sample reports, 323

side-by-side details, using multiple copies, 327

size and position, controlling, 139

Reports collections

Access Objects, creating in code, 149

controls on a Subform, referencing, 145–148

Expression Builder, working with, 144

VBA class module, syntax for, 147

working with, 143

Requery, Refresh, Repaint, and Recalc commands, 250

Restrict operations, 474

**Retail & Remote Offices (CTP2) synchronization
service, 604**

ribbon design

in application development, Backstage view, 647

custom ribbon, loading, 649

default ribbon, setting, 644

elements of a ribbon, 641

for forms and reports, 648

the GetEnabled callback, 642

images for, 644

Office 2007 and the File menu, 647

the OnAction callback, 642

the OnLoad callback, 642

tab visibility and focus, dynamically changing, 646–648

tips, 639

the USysRibbons table, 640

RowSource Type combo box, 280–282

Row Versioning in SQL Server, 554–556

rules, scope, 58

RunCommand Method, 129

Run method, 128

Runtime deployment, 655

S

sample databases

AccessObjectModel.accdb, 128

ADOExamples.accdb, 660

for application development, 631

BuildingClasses.accdb, 340

BuildingClassesAfterExportImport.accdb, 340

ClassAndForms.accdb, 381

ClassesAndEvents.accdb, 359

Controls.accdb, 273

DAOExamples.accdb, 162

demo database script, 495

DocADOX.accdb, 660

DocDAO.accdb, 224

Employees_be.accdb, 396

FormExamples.accdb, 231

for Microsoft Office applications, 437

Instnwnd.sql, 396

Instnwndtesting.sql, 396

NorthwindAzure.accdb, 396

opening, 4

Orders_be.accdb, 396

Reports.accdb, 323

Sample_fe.accdb, 396

setting up in SQL Server, 407–409

for SQL Azure, 420

for SQL Server, 495

SQLServerExamples.accdb, 484

for upsizing databases from Access to SQL Server, 543

VBAEnvironment.accdb, 4

VBAExamples.accdb, 40

VBAFeaturesExamples.accdb, 89

WebDatabase.accdb, 396

sample reports, 323

SaveToFile method, 202

saving

records, 270

Save button, 7

Schemas

in SQL Server tables, 417

and synonyms in SQL Server, 556

using in SSMA, 567–570

scope

constants and, 51

scope rules, 58

SCOPE_IDENTITY() in T-SQL, 520

Screen Object

ActiveForm and ActiveControl, working with, 151

control's events, calling code directly from, 152

MousePointer shape, changing, 150

script files

in SQL Server, 506–509

in SQL Server tables, 499

SDI. *See* **Single Document Interface (SDI)**

searching
code
for debugging modules and procedures, 16
in modules and procedures, 19
Recordsets, 188

security
planning and managing
firewall settings, working with SQL Azure, 591
in multi-tenanted applications, 623
security models in SQL Server, 615–617
in SQL Server
authentication, 538–540
surface area configuration, 536–538
Windows authentication, 541
Windows vs. SQL Server, 414
in SQL Azure, support for security stored procedures, 421
using Schemas and database roles to manage, 557

Select Case statements, 80

selections, multiple
key properties, 287
list boxes and, 286–290
with two list boxes, 290–292

SendKeys action, 102, 270

Set keyword, 343

Set Next command, 25

Setting and Getting options, 152–154

SharePoint lists, linking to, 426–428

Shell command, 102

Single Document Interface (SDI), 638

64-bit environments
ActiveX on, 386
in application development, 649
using the Windows API, 651–653

Slider control, adding, 386–388

Sort property, 193

SourceTableName, 406

Space and String string functions, 93

Spin control, 388–390

splash screens, in application development, 653

Split string function, 93

splitting databases
Database Splitter, using, 397
reasons for, 396

split window view, 17–19

spreadsheets
reading data from, 459
writing data to
opening Excel, 454–456
when to use, 452–454
writing the data, 456–458

SQL. *See also* **queries**
Data Definition Language (DDL), 183
executing, different methods for, 217
splitting over multiple lines in VBA, 86

SQL Azure
browser interface, developing with, 595
connecting to, 424–426
databases
backing up and copying, 603
creating, 590
sample databases, 420
Data Sync Agent
conflict resolution in data, 613
data and database structure, changing, 612
database synchronization and triggers, 613
loading and installing, 605–609
Sync Groups and Sync Logs, 610–612
table structure, changes to, 613
Data Type Mapping, changing, 627
DSN, 420–423
firewall settings, 591
graphical interface, 595
importing data from, 603
introduction to, 589, 590
Management Studio, using, 420, 592–594
migrating SQL databases
sequence of steps, 596
set of tables, creating, 597–599
SQL Import/Export features when transferring to SQL Azure, 602
SQL Server Import and Export Wizard and UNICODE data types, 598
SSMA (SQL Server Migration Assistant), 624
transferring data with the SQL Server Import and Export Wizard, 599–603

multi-tenanted applications, building
   application tables and views, 619–622
   optional parameters, creating, 623
   overview, 617
   security, managing, 623
   user tables and views, 617–619
security, planning and managing
   firewall settings, 591
   for multi-tenanted applications, 623
   security models, 615–617
security stored procedures, support for, 421
SQL Server Migration Assistant and Access to
   Azure, 624–627
SQL Express and SQL Server products, 487–489
SQL Server. *See also* **upsizing databases**
   ADO, working with
      command objects, 666
      connecting to SQL Server, 664
      connection strings, 663
      connection time, 665
      MARS and connections, 669–671
      MARS and performance, 668
      stored procedures, 666
   BatchProcessing SQL Server form, 368–370
   database file locations, 489
   description of, 485
   developing with
      Case statements, 581
      complex queries, handling, 579–582
      dbSeeChanges constant, 574
      efficient SQL, tips for, 585
      the MSysConf table, 587
      Pass-Through queries, 575–578
      performance and execution plans, 582–585
      SQL Server Profiler, 586
      stored procedures and temporary tables, 578
      stored procedures, using advanced features in, 578
   getting started with
      demo database script, running, 495
      new database, creating, 496
      understanding components of, 495
   INFORMATION_SCHEMA views, 494

instances, 491
introduction to, 484
limitations of, 483
linking to
   DSN (Data Source Name), creating, 410–415
   getting started, 407
   sample database, setting up, 407–409
   script files, 409
   Server driver, choosing, 412
   Server instances, 408
   Windows vs. SQL Server authentication, 414
Log files and Recovery Models, 490
performance, improving, 486
sample database, 484
security
   authentication, 538–540
   surface area configuration, 536–538
   Windows authentication, 541
SQL Express and SQL Server products, 487–489
SQL Server 2008 R2 Management Tools, 592
SQL Server Management Studio, using, 592–594
SQL Server Migration Assistant (SSMA), 624
statements, executing on the fly, 518
stored procedures
   DELETE query, 513
   INSERT and INSERT INTO queries, 515–517
   system stored procedures, 508
   UPDATE query, 514
   working with, 511–513
system databases, 493
system tables, 494
tables and relationships, creating
   database diagrams, 496–498
   Identity property, using, 504
   script files and batches of T-SQL commands, 499
   table design, changing, 500–504
   tables, relationships, and script files, 499
   T-SQL script files, using to record and apply changes, 502
tables, linking to
   getting started, 416
   linked tables, refreshing, 417

SQL server *(cont.)*

  tables, linking to *(cont.)*

    linked tables, renaming to remove the dbo_prefix, 417

    updateability and Views, 419

    views in SQL Server, connecting to, 418

    views in SQL Server, refreshing, 419

  tables, Schemas in, 417

  temporary tables and, 397

  transactions

    nesting transactions, 533

    transaction isolation levels, 532

    working with, 530–533

  triggers, working with, 526–529

  T-SQL (Transact SQL)

    CAST and CONVERT, using, 518

    error handling, 523–525

    functions, built-in, 519

    @@IDENTITY, SCOPE_IDENTITY() and IDENT_CURRENT, 520

    program flow, controlling, 521–523

    system variables, 520

    variables, defining, 517

  User-Defined Functions (UDFs), 534–536

  versions of, 486

  views, working with

    CROSSTAB queries, 509–511

    graphical interface, 505

    INFORMATION_SCHEMA views, 494

    and script files, 506–509

    updateability of, in Access, 506

  Windows services, 492

SQL Server Profiler, 586

SSMA (SQL Server Migration Assistant)

  Access to Azure, 624

  installing, 564

  mapping data types, 567

  Migration Wizard, 565–567

  Schemas, using, 567–570

  strengths and weaknesses, 574

standard modules, 654

"*" (star) character, 97

statements

  in SQL Server, executing on the fly, 518

  in T-SQL, controlling program flow, 523

static variables, 55

Step and Run commands, breakpoint, 25–28

stored procedures

  asynchronous event processing and, 364

  in SQL Server

    DELETE query, 513

    INSERT and INSERT INTO query, 515–517

    system stored procedures, 508

    and temporary tables, 578

    UPDATE query, 514

  using advanced features from Access, 578

StrComp string function, 93

string functions, 92

subclassing. *See* **WithEvents Processing**

subforms

  placing on the tab page, 311

  referencing controls on, 145–148

  using the list box as, 292–295

subroutines

  changing to functions, and vice versa, 14

  DisplayAttachmentInfo, 200

  executing, debugging modules and procedures, 13–15

  and functions, default referencing of parameters in, 71

  managing code with, 67–70

surface area configuration in SQL Server, 536–538

Switchboard Manager, 633

Sync Groups and Sync Logs in Data Sync Agent in SQL, 610–612

synchronization services in SQL Azure. *See* **Data Sync Agent in SQL Azure**

synonyms in SQL Server, 556

SysCmd, monitoring progress with, 155

system databases in SQL Server, 493

system stored procedures in SQL Server, 508

system tables in SQL Server, 494

T

tab controls

  dynamically loading tabs

    class module, creating, 341

    collection of objects, 345

    improving, 340

    Initialization and Termination events, 344

    Let and Get object properties, 342

    New and Set, creating an object with, 343

    options for, 314

    pages, loading, 315–318

    pages, unloading, 320

    related pages, dynamically loading, 319

    simplifying the application code with classes, 352

  OnChange event, 314

  referring to controls in, 314

  refreshing between tabs and controls, 311–313

TableDefs collection, 179–182

Table/Query editing, 285

tables

  DISTINCT and DISTINCTROW, using, 234

  Linked Table Manager, 398

  linked table name and SourceTableName, 406

  MSysConf table in SQL Server, 587

  naming conventions for, 109

  relinking tables, essential details for, 400

  SQL Server tables

    database diagrams, 496–498

    Identity property, using, 504

    linked tables, refreshing, 417

    linked tables, renaming to remove the dbo_prefix, 417

    script files and batches of T-SQL commands, 499

    system tables, 494

    table design, changing using the GUI, 500–504

    tables, relationships, and script files, 499

    temporary tables, 516

    T-SQL script files, using to record and apply changes, 502

  table conversion, comparing methods for, 571

  table name, changing in T-SQL, 503

  table structure, changes to, 613

  temporary tables, in SQL Server, 397, 578

  transactions, using to perform inserts, 169

  truncating, 514

  user tables, in SQL Server databases, 617

  the USysRibbons table, 640

table-valued functions, 535

tabs

  Agents tab, 605

  Dynamic Tab, VBA collection classes and, 351

  Tab controls, 636

  tab visibility and focus, dynamically changing, 646–648

Tag property, 316

tasks in Outlook, adding, 476

tempdb database, in SQL Server, 493

temporary tables, 397

temporary tables, in SQL Server, 516, 578

TempVars, examining, 132

Termination event, 344

Text Files, linking to, 407

32-bit and 64-bit environments, in application development, 649

time and date functions, 90–92

Time data, converting for SQL Server, 544–546

Timer Interval property

  considerations in using, 255

  monitoring, 258–260

  periodic execution, 256

Timestamps and Row Versioning, 554–556

transactions

  multiple edits and, 170

  simulating multi-user interaction with, 531

  in SQL Server

    nesting transactions, 533

    transaction isolation levels, 532

    working with, 530–533

  working with in DAO, 166–170

TreeBuilders.accdb sample database, 273

TreeView control

  ActiveX controls, 304

  adding, 296–298

  in application development, 635

TreeView control *(cont.)*

  drag and drop, 303–307

  graphics, adding, 301–304

  nodes, adding, 309

  nodes, expanding and collapsing, 303

  nodes with recursion, deleting, 307–309

  parent/child-related data, loading, 300

  populating the tree, 298–301

  recursive VBA code, writing and debugging, 308

  sample database example, 295

triggers

  multiple rows in trigger code, allowing for changes in, 553

  in SQL Server, 526–529

Trim, LTrim, and RTrim string functions, 93

T-SQL (Transact SQL)

  CAST and CONVERT, using, 518

  error handling, 523–525

  functions, built-in, 519

  @@IDENTITY, SCOPE_IDENTITY() and IDENT_CURRENT, 520

  script files and batches of commands, 499

  script files, using to record and apply changes, 502

  statements, controlling program flow with, 523

  system variables, 520

  understanding, 511–513

  variables, defining, 517

TypeOf statements, 80, 375

Type structures, for working with arrays, 65, 340

U

UCase and UCase$ functions, 93

unbound controls, naming conventions for, 110

unbound forms, 233, 243

"_" (underbar) character, using, 86

UNICODE data types

  SQL Server Import and Export Wizard and, 598

  text data types and, 544

Unique Index and Ignore NULLs, in SQL Server, 553

Unload and Close events, 248

updateability

  of a Record Source, 234

  support for, 419

  of views, in SQL Server, 506

UPDATE query in SQL Server, 514

updating applications, in development, 656

UpDown or Spin control, 388–390

Upper, Lower, StrConv string functions, 93

upsizing databases

  planning for

    attachments and Multi-Value data, 548

    Boolean data, 546

    currency, 548

    cycles and multiple cascade paths, 549

    Date and Time data, 544–546

    hyperlinks, 547

    IMAGE, VARBINARY (Max), and OLE Data, 547

    integer numbers, 547

    Memo data, 547

    mismatched fields in relationships, 550

    multiple rows in trigger code, allowing for changes in, 553

    partially completed foreign keys, 550

    real numbers, decimals, and floating point numbers, 547

    replicated databases and random autonumbers, 551–553

    Required fields, 549

    Schemas and synonyms, 556

    security, using Schemas and database roles to manage, 557

    text data types and UNICODE, 544

    Timestamps and Row Versioning, 554–556

    Unique Index and Ignore NULLs, 553

  query conversion, comparing in the Upsizing Wizard and SSMA, 572–574

  SSMA

    installing, 564

    mapping data types, 567

    Migration Wizard, 565–567

    Schemas, using, 567–570

    strengths and weaknesses, 574

table conversion, comparing in the Upsizing Wizard and SSMA, 571

Upsizing Wizard
    strengths and weaknesses of, 561
    using, 558–561
    to use an Access Data Project (ADP)
        ADP strengths and weaknesses, 564
        query conversion, 563
        understanding, 561–563

Upsizing Wizard
    strengths and weaknesses of, 561
    using, 558–561

User-Defined Functions (UDFs) in SQL Server, 534–536

user interface
    in application development, 632, 638
    custom, in application development, 637
    enhancing
        locking down Access, 154
        Office FileDialog, selecting files with, 157–159
        progress bars, custom, 156
        Setting and Getting options, 152–154
        SQL Azure, making a connection to, 424
        SysCmd, monitoring progress with, 155
    single and multiple application files, 655

USysApplicationLog and MSysASO system tables, relinking, 434

USysRibbons table, 640

V

validation, controlling behavior during, 276

Value List editing, 284

VARBINARY (Max) Data, converting for SQL Server, 547

variables. *See also* **constants and variables**
    Bookmarks, 191
    complex variables, investigating values in, 31
    displaying in the locals window, 29
    Global variables, using, 56
    naming conventions for, 110–112, 113
    object variables, 105
    scope and lifetime, 57–59
    static variables, using, 55
    system variables in T-SQL, 520
    variables, defining in T-SQL, 517

Watches window, 31

VBA class module
    Object-Oriented Programming (OOP), support for, 339
    syntax when using, 147

VBA collection classes
    vs. Access collections, 346
    adding AllItems to, 349
    creating, 346–348
    exporting and re-importing the class, 349
    using with the Dynamic Tab, 351

VBA editor
    entering, 6
    features of, 37
    Project pane, 9
    Properties pane, 9
    sample database, 4
    windows, opening and closing, 9

VBA language structure
    constants and variables, working with
        arrays, 59–65
        code quality, improving with constants, 49–51
        Enum keyword, 51
        global variables, 56
        NULL values, IsNull and Nz, 53–55
        scope rules, 58
        static variables, 55
        type structures, 65
        variables and database field types, 52
        variable scope and lifetime, 57–59
    control statements and program flow
        Choose statements, 79
        Do While and Do Until loops, 82–84
        Exit statements, 84
        For and ForEach loops, 81
        GoTo and GoSub statements, 86
        If...Then...Else... statements, 77
        IIF statements, 78
        line continuation, 86
        Select Case statements, 80
        SQL, splitting over multiple lines, 86
        TypeOf statements, 80
        the With statement, 85

VBA language structure *(cont.)*

functions and procedures

ByRef and ByValue parameters, defining, 70–72

calling, variations on standard rules for, 66

modules and class modules, organizing code in, 76

ParamArray qualifier, 75

parameters, Optional and Named, 73

procedures, private and public, 72

referencing from a control's event property, 244

subroutines and functions, default referencing of parameters in, 71

subroutines, managing code with, 67–70

understanding in VBA code, 66

language settings

comments, adding, 40

compiling code, 44

conditional compilation, 45

\Decompile command line switch, 45

Option Compare, selecting, 43

Option Explicit, setting, 41

references, 46–49

Visual Basic for Applications Extensibility, 48

sample database, 40, 89

VBA code, recursive, 308

VBA libraries, 177

vbCR, vbCRLF, vbLF, vbTab string functions, 93

vbObjectError constant, 123

version information

retrieving, 135

for SQL Server, 486

views, in SQL Server

connecting to, 418

CROSSTAB queries, 509–511

databases, 617

graphical interface, 505

INFORMATION_SCHEMA views, 494

refreshing, 419

and script files, 506–509

updateability of, in Access, 506

updateable Views, 419

Visual Basic for Applications Extensibility, 48

W

Watches window, 32

WebDatabase.accdb sample database, 396

Web Databases, linking

Access database to an Access Web Database, 431

process of, 430

relinking, 432–434

Where clauses

constructing, 97

opening forms with, 246

windows

application and VBA code windows, 6–8

Immediate window, working with, 33

Locals window, displaying variables in, 29

split window, debugging modules and procedures in, 17–19

Watches window, 32

Windows API, using in application development, 651–653

Windows, Microsoft

authentication, 414

authentication in SQL Server, 541

SQL Server services, 492

Windows Registry, working with, 650

WithEvents statements

control events, handling, 362

form events, handling, 360–362

processing, 363

With statements, 85

Word, Microsoft

connecting Access to

data, merging with bookmarks, 447–451

documents, generating from a placeholder document, 444–446

Mail Merge, 451

placeholder documents, opening, 446

Word object model, key objects in, 443

WordQuote.accdb sample database, 437

Workspace object, working with in DAO, 165

About the Author

Andrew Couch has been working with Microsoft Access since 1992, developing, training, and consulting on Client-Server design projects. With his wealth of experience in Access and SQL products, he has been able to mentor software houses, blue chip companies, and independent developers. Alongside running his own consultancy, Andrew has been heavily involved in the developer community and jointly founded the UK Access User Group more than 13 years ago. He has also earned Access MVP status for the last 5 years.

Andrew's passion lies with VBA programming and extending the reach of VBA programmers into cloud computing and the .NET environment. He hopes that this book serves as an example of his dedication to this exceptional piece of technology and its application.

In addition to consulting and regularly speaking at community events, Andrew has developed the Migration Upsizing SQL Tool (MUST), which is a tool that allows users to easily convert Access Databases to SQL Server by using an Access-based application. Due to the success of MUST, which is used by over 150 companies, SQL Translation capabilities and WebForm code generators for .NET were added to the product range. More recently the MUST technologies have been extended further to deliver automated services for converting Access database to a web legal format for publishing to SharePoint.

How To Download Your eBook

To download your eBook, go to
http://go.microsoft.com/FWLink/?Linkid=224345
and follow the instructions.

Please note: You will be asked to create a free online account and enter the access code below.

Your access code:

TJWLPNM

Microsoft® Access® 2010 VBA Programming
Inside Out

Your PDF eBook allows you to:

- Search the full text
- Print
- Copy and paste

Best yet, you will be notified about free updates to your eBook.

If you ever lose your eBook file, you can download it again just by logging in to your account.

Need help? Please contact:
mspinput@microsoft.com

Choose the Right Book for You

Plain & Simple

- Easy visual approach shows the simplest ways to get things done
- Full color! with easy-to-follow steps and screenshots
- Just the basics—with no jargon

Step by Step

- Build exactly the skills you want
- Take just the lessons you need, or work from cover to cover
- Get ready-made practice files and a complete eBook

Inside Out

- The ultimate, in-depth reference for intermediate to advanced users
- Features hundreds of timesaving solutions, troubleshooting tips, and workarounds
- Includes eBook and custom resources

Resources from Microsoft Press

Plain & Simple

Windows® 7
Plain & Simple
978-0-7356-2666-9

Microsoft® Office 2010
Plain & Simple
978-0-7356-2697-3

Microsoft Access® 2010
Plain & Simple
978-0-7356-2730-7

Microsoft Excel® 2010
Plain & Simple
978-0-7356-2727-7

Microsoft Outlook® 2010
Plain & Simple
978-0-7356-2734-5

Microsoft PowerPoint® 2010
Plain & Simple
978-0-7356-2728-4

Microsoft Word 2010
Plain & Simple
978-0-7356-2731-4

Microsoft SharePoint® 2010
Plain & Simple
978-0-7356-4228-7

Step by Step

Windows 7
Step by Step
978-0-7356-2667-6

Microsoft Office
Professional 2010
Step by Step
978-0-7356-2696-6

Microsoft Access 2010
Step by Step
978-0-7356-2692-8

Microsoft Excel 2010
Step by Step
978-0-7356-2694-2

Microsoft Office Home
and Student 2010
Step by Step
978-0-7356-2721-5

Microsoft Outlook 2010
Step by Step
978-0-7356-2690-4

Microsoft PowerPoint 2010
Step by Step
978-0-7356-2691-1

Microsoft Project 2010
Step by Step
978-0-7356-2695-9

Microsoft SharePoint
Designer 2010
Step by Step
978-0-7356-2733-8

Microsoft Word 2010
Step by Step
978-0-7356-2693-5

Inside Out

Windows 7 *Inside Out*
978-0-7356-2665-2

Microsoft Office 2010
Inside Out
978-0-7356-2689-8

Microsoft Access 2010
Inside Out
978-0-7356-2685-0

Microsoft Excel 2010
Inside Out
978-0-7356-2688-1

Microsoft Outlook 2010
Inside Out
978-0-7356-2686-7

Microsoft Project 2010
Inside Out
978-0-7356-2687-4

Microsoft Word 2010
Inside Out
978-0-7356-2729-1

Other Titles

Windows 7: The Best of
the Official Magazine
978-0-7356-2664-5

Beyond Bullet Points:
Using Microsoft Office
PowerPoint 2007 to Create
Presentations That Inform,
Motivate, and Inspire
978-0-7356-2387-3

Take Back Your Life! Using
Microsoft Office Outlook 2007
to Get Organized and Stay
Organized
978-0-7356-2343-9

Microsoft Office Excel 2007:
Data Analysis and Business
Modeling
978-0-7356-2396-5

Coming Soon!

Microsoft PowerPivot for
Excel 2010: Give Your
Data Meaning
978-0-7356-4058-0

What do you think of this book?

We want to hear from you!
To participate in a brief online survey, please visit:

microsoft.com/learning/booksurvey

Tell us how well this book meets your needs—what works effectively, and what we can do better. Your feedback will help us continually improve our books and learning resources for you.

Thank you in advance for your input!